QUALITY PLANNING AND ANALYSIS

QUALITY PLANNING AND ANALYSIS
From Product Development through Use

Second Edition

J. M. Juran
Author, Consultant, and International Lecturer

Frank M. Gryna, Jr.
Professor of Industrial Engineering
Bradley University

McGraw-Hill Book Company

New York St. Louis San Francisco Auckland Bogotá Hamburg
Johannesburg London Madrid Mexico Montreal New Delhi
Panama Paris São Paulo Singapore Sydney Tokyo Toronto

This book was set in Times Roman by A Graphic Method Inc.
The editors were Julienne V. Brown and Service to Publishers, Inc.;
the production supervisor was Richard A. Ausburn.

QUALITY PLANNING AND ANALYSIS
From Product Development through Use

8910 HDHD 8987654

Library of Congress Cataloging in Publications Data

Juran, Joseph M   date
    Quality planning and analysis.

    Includes index.
    1. Quality control. 2. Quality assurance.
I. Gryna, Frank M., joint author. II. Title.
TS156.J86 1980   658.5'62   79-24082
ISBN 0-07-033178-2

ABOUT THE AUTHORS

J. M. JURAN has since 1924 pursued a varied career in management as engineer, industrial executive, government administrator, university professor, impartial labor arbitrator, corporate director, and management consultant. This career has been marked by a search for the underlying principles which are common to all managerial activity. Applied to the specialty of management of quality control, this search has produced the leading international reference literature and the leading international training courses. His *Quality Control Handbook* (3rd edition, 1974), his *Quality Planning and Analysis* (with Dr. F. M. Gryna, Jr.), and his training book *Management of Quality Control* (3rd edition, 1974) have collectively been translated into 12 languages: French, German, Hungarian, Italian, Japanese, Korean, Polish, Portuguese, Romanian, Russian, Serbo-Croation, and Spanish. He has conducted the course "Management of Quality Control" over 200 times in over 30 countries on all continents, providing a training input to over 15,000 managers and specialists.

In the field of general management, Dr. Juran's book *Managerial Breakthrough* generalizes the principles of creating beneficial change (breakthrough) and of preventing adverse change (control). His book *The Corporate Director* (with J. K. Louden) generalizes the work of the Board of Directors. He has also written *Lectures in General Management, Lectures in Quality Control, Case Studies in Industrial Management* (with N. N. Barish), *Management of Inspection and Quality Control,* and *Bureaucracy: A Challenge to Better Management.* Beyond his 10 published books, he has authored hundreds of unpublished papers.

A holder of degrees in engineering and law, Dr. Juran maintains an active schedule as author and international lecturer while serving various industrial companies, governmental angencies, and other institutions as a consultant. His honors include over 30 medals, fellowships, honorary memberships, etc., awarded by professional and honor societies in 12 countries.

Dr. FRANK M. GRYNA, JR., is Professor of Industrial Engineering at Bradley University, Peoria, Illinois. He is also a consultant in the managerial and statistical aspects of quality and reliability programs, from initial design through field usage. His degrees (all in industrial engineering) are from New York University and the University of Iowa.

Previously, Dr. Gryna served with the U.S. Army Signal Corps Engineering Labs and the Esso Research and Engineering Co. At the Space Systems Division of the Martin Co. he was Manager of Reliability and Quality Assurance.

He was Associate Editor of the second and third editions of the *Quality Control Handbook*, associate editor of the *Reliability Training Text*, and co-editor of *Applying Industrial Engineering to Management Problems*.

He is a Fellow of the American Society for Quality Control, a Certified Reliability Engineer, and a Professional Engineer (Quality Engineering). He has been the recipient of various awards, including the E. L. Grant Award of ASQC, Engineer of the Year Award of the Peoria Engineering Council, and the Award of Excellence of the Quality Control and Reliability Engineering Division of the American Institute of Industrial Engineers.

CONTENTS

PREFACE

This is a textbook about quality—the quality of products and services needed by society.

To a remarkable degree, our lives are increasingly dependent on the quality of products and services. Quality failures can and do result in serious human inconvenience, economic waste, and sometimes loss of life.

To meet the quality needs of society requires an active role by all the major activities of an organization. Market research must discover the quality needs of the users; product development must create designs responsive to these needs; manufacturing planning must devise processes capable of executing the product designs; production must regulate these processes to achieve the desired qualities; purchasing must obtain adequate materials; inspection and test must prove the adequacy of the product through simulated use; marketing must sell the product for the proper application; customer service must observe the usage, remedy failures, and report on opportunities for improvement.

The quality subactivities present in each of these major activities are themselves collectively a major activity which has become known as the "quality function." It may be defined as that collection of activities, no matter where performed, through which the company achieves fitness for use. The outlines of this quality function have been emerging clearly. It has now become evident that, in common with other major company functions, successful conduct of the quality function demands much specialized knowledge and many specialized tools, as well as trained specialists to use these tools and apply this knowledge. The book rejects the concept that the control of quality is primarily a matter of statistical techniques. Instead, it develops the viewpoint that product and service quality requires managerial, technological, and statistical concepts throughout all the major functions in an organization.

The industrial world calls this quality function by many names: quality control, quality assurance, reliability, product integrity, and more. The material in this book encompasses all of these.

This second edition includes a complete updating of all material with additional coverage in motivation, safety and liability, quality costs, information systems for quality, and quality assurance.

In presenting material on a broad subject such as product quality, the topics can be presented in several sequences. The sequence selected for this book takes the viewpoint that the practitioner is often faced with the urgent task of solving the quality problem of current products. An equally important task is the proper planning for quality of future products. This latter task must sometimes wait until the urgent problems are resolved. The foregoing priorities have guided the sequence of topics in the book.

Chapter 2 shows how to evaluate the size of the current quality problem in monetary terms. This evaluation is useful in justifying the resources needed for an improvement program. Chapters 3 and 4 present basic statistical concepts. Chapters 5 and 6 discuss a structured approach for improving the present quality level. The remainder of the book presents the elements of a broad program covering the collection of activities through which we achieve fitness for use. The activities can be viewed as the plans and controls needed to *prevent* the growth of quality problems on future products.

Throughout the book, chapters on statistical concepts have been included, as needed, to supplement the managerial concepts. However, the only mathematical background assumed for the book is college algebra, and there is no attempt to provide a state of advanced knowledge in statistical methodology. There are many excellent books that cover the statistical aspects in greater depth.

Students and practitioners may wish to rearrange the sequence of chapters to meet their specific needs.

All chapters include problems. These problems are so structured as to reflect the "real" world "outside" rather than the more limited world of the classroom. Such problems require the student to face the realities which confront the managers, designers, engineers, marketers, inspectors, users, and others involved in the quality function. Students must make assumptions, estimate the economics, reach conclusions from incomplete facts, and otherwise adapt themselves to the imperfect world of the practitioner.

Many chapters contain sample questions from former ASQC Quality Engineer and Reliability Engineer certification examinations. These questions and the associated answers have been reprinted with permission from *Quality Progress,* February 1976, pp. 22–31, and August 1978, pp. 17–26.

We also draw attention to the relationship of *Quality Planning and Analysis* to *Quality Control Handbook,* 3rd edition (J. M. Juran, editor, McGraw-Hill Book Company, New York, 1974). The handbook is a reference compendium which, through broad sale in the English language plus translation into other languages, has become the standard international reference work on the subject. In preparation of *Quality Planning and Analysis,* we have introduced frequent references to the handbook (as well as to other sources) where space limitations placed restriction on detail.

We are grateful to the Literary Executor of the late Sir Ronald A. Fisher, F.R.S., to Dr. Frank Yates, F.R.S., and to Longman Group Ltd., London, for permission to reprint Table III from their book *Statistical Tables for Biological, Agricultural and Medical Research* (6th edition, 1974). We also appreciate the cooperation of the Ford Motor Company in enabling us to use some material from their Reliability Methods Modules.

Authors have a cliché: a book represents the efforts of many people. But it's true. F.M.G. had a small army. His colleagues at Bradley University were extremely helpful. These included Joseph Emanuel, Antone Alber, Thomas Stewart, Robert Thompson, Herbert Morris, and Rita Newton. There were many others from both the industrial and academic worlds: David Leaman, Lennart Sandholm, Grant Ireson, Douglas Ekings, Austin Bonis, Fred Mc-Norton, Sidney Phillips, Kenneth Stephens, Steve Maple, Daniel Orzel, Thomas Gregorich, Jeff Liu, Albert Bishop, Lawrence Aft, Clyde Coombs, Sherrill Daily, Al Endres, David Gordon, David Harrigan, Glenn Hayes, Jack Henry, Gayle McElrath, Fred Orkin, Jay Perry, Cecil Peterson, Leonard Rado, Ed Reynolds, Nancy Jaster, Susan Raffety, Susan Wiedenmann, and Alfred Anthony.

Leonard A. Seder deserves special mention for his contribution of a case problem on quality costs. In addition, his many contributions to quality control methodology have been reflected in this book.

Where would authors be without secretaries? For F.M.G., the principal secretarial burden was carried by Mrs. Willie Luscher with the help of Janet Ulivi.

Finally, there must be recognition of the families behind this book. Typing and proofreading are now almost family affairs. F.M.G. is forever amazed at the patience and support of his wife Dee, and also Wendy, Derek, and Gary. One must be an author to appreciate the role of the family in writing a book.

J.M.J.'s army has also been extensive. Some of its members are among those already mentioned. Many others attended courses where they shared with J.M.J. their experiences in using the first edition, whether as students or as instructors.

For Mrs. Juran it has involved preparation of typescripts for numerous chapters of yet another book—probably the sixteenth book, if we count revised editions. This active collaboration passed its golden anniversary in the year 1976.

J. M. Juran
Frank M. Gryna, Jr.

QUALITY PLANNING AND ANALYSIS

BASIC CONCEPTS

1-1 FITNESS FOR USE; QUALITY CHARACTERISTIC; PARAMETERS OF FITNESS FOR USE

All human societies make use of natural and artificial materials and forces to provide *products* which consist of:

Goods: e.g., milk, clothes, houses, vehicles.
Services: e.g., electrical energy, bus rides, health care, education.

An essential requirement of these products is that they meet the needs of those members of society who will actually use them. This concept of *fitness for use* is a universal. It applies to all goods and services, without exception. The popular term for fitness for use is *quality,* and our basic definition becomes: *quality means fitness for use.*

The term "fitness for use" applies to a variety of users. A purchaser of a product may be a manufacturer who will perform additional processing operations. To such a manufacturer, fitness for use means the ability to do the processing with high productivity, low waste, minimal downtime, etc. In addition, the resulting products should be fit for use by the manufacturer's clients. Another purchaser may be a merchant who will break bulk and resell the product. To the merchant, fitness for use includes correct labeling and identity, protection from damage during shipment and storage, ease of handling and

1

display, etc. A third purchaser may be a maintenance shop which will use the product as a spare part, with needs for ease of installation, interchangeability, etc. Finally, the purchaser may be the ultimate user of the product.

This wide variety of uses means that products must possess multiple elements of fitness for use. Each of these elements is a *quality characteristic* which is the fundamental building block out of which quality is constructed. The quality characteristic is also the means by which we translate the term "fitness for use" into the language of the technologist.

Quality characteristics can be grouped into various species such as:

Structural: e.g., length, frequency, viscosity.
Sensory: e.g., taste, beauty.
Time-oriented: e.g., reliability, maintainability.
Commercial: e.g., warranty.
Ethical: e.g., courtesy, honesty.

Quality characteristics may also be classified into categories known as *parameters* of fitness for use. Parameters correspond roughly to the broad groupings of responsibility involved in attaining fitness for use. Two of the major parameters are quality of design and quality of conformance. (In later chapters we will discuss other parameters: the "abilities," product safety, field service, etc.)

As a human society acquires affluence, there emerges a spectrum of purchasing power—some members are wealthy, others are poor. In response to this variation in purchasing power, the producers of goods and services evolve variations in quality of those goods and services. These variations are popularly known as *grades*. The more technical name is quality of design, since the differences in grades are intentional. For example, all automobiles provide the user with the service of transportation. However, the various models differ as to size, comfort, appearance, performance, economy, status conferred, etc. These differences are in turn the result of intended or designed differences in the size, styling, materials, tolerances, test programs, etc.

In contrast, quality of conformance is the extent to which the goods and services conform to the intent of the design. This extent of conformance is determined by such variables as:

Choice of processes: i.e., are they able to hold the tolerances?
Training of the supervision and the work force.
Degree of adherence to the program of inspection, test, audit, etc.
Motivation for quality.

A good deal of confusion arises when the word "quality" is used without making clear whether the speaker is referring to quality of design or quality of conformance. Generally speaking, higher quality of design can be attained only at an increase in costs,[1] whereas higher quality of conformance can often be attained with an accompanying reduction in costs.

Note: At the beginning of this chapter we distinguished between goods and services. In the remainder of this book we will frequently use the word "products" as a short generic term to designate both goods and services.

1-2 CONTROL AND QUALITY CONTROL

Control as used in this book refers to the process we employ in order to meet standards. This process consists of observing our actual performance, comparing this performance with some standard, and then taking action if the observed performance is significantly different from the standard.

The control process is in the nature of a *feedback loop* and involves a universal sequence of steps as follows:

1. Choosing the control subject: i.e., choosing what we intend to regulate.
2. Choosing a unit of measure.
3. Setting a standard or goal for the control subject.
4. Choosing a sensing device which can measure the control subject in terms of the unit of measure.
5. Measuring actual performance.
6. Interpreting the difference between actual and standard.
7. Taking action (if any) on the difference.[2]

The foregoing sequence of steps is universal and applies to control of anything, e.g., cost control, inventory control, quality control, etc. "If you know how to control, you can control anything." We can define *quality control* as *the process through which we measure actual quality performance, compare it with standard, and act on the difference.*

In matters of quality, this control process is applied to a variety of control subjects: materials, processes, products, tests, plans, decisions, etc. We will look at these specialized applications in various chapters.

Much activity is also devoted to preventing quality problems from happening. This is done in two major ways:

1. *Quality improvement:* i.e., finding ways to do better than the standard. This is discussed in Chapter 5.
2. *Quality planning:* i.e., launching new products, processes, etc., in ways

---

[1] The activity known as "value analysis" (or "value engineering") is sometimes able to attain higher quality of design at lower cost.

[2] For an extensive discussion of this universal process, see J. M. Juran, *Managerial Breakthrough*, McGraw-Hill Book Company, New York, 1964, chaps. 12 through 20.

which will result in minimal need for subsequent quality improvement. Quality planning is discussed in various chapters.

1-3 QUALITY TASKS; THE QUALITY FUNCTION

Attainment of quality requires the performance of a wide variety of identifiable activities or quality *tasks*. Obvious examples are the study of customers' quality needs, design review, product tests, and field complaint analysis. In tiny enterprises these tasks (sometimes called *work elements*) may all be performed by only one or a few persons. However, as the enterprise grows, specific tasks may become so time-consuming that we must create specialized departments to perform them. In some large modern enterprises it is common to find individual quality tasks which command the full time of numerous employees. We will examine many of these tasks in detail in later chapters. However, it is useful beforehand to look briefly at the historical evolution of these identifiable tasks and at the resulting problem of coordination.

Primitive people were gatherers and users of natural materials. Among their various problems of survival, they faced quality problems, e.g., which plants were edible and which were poisonous. With evolution of early technology, they undertook the growing and processing of natural materials. At first these processes were carried out by the users themselves, i.e., *usufacture*. Under this arrangement, all quality tasks were performed by one person, i.e., the producer-user.

The subsequent emergence of division of work and the associated growth of commerce gave rise to specialized occupations, e.g., farmer, carpenter, mason, shoemaker. In turn, such specialties created a separation—the producer and the user were no longer the same individual. This separation created new quality problems for both producer and user, who now also became seller and buyer in the village market.

In the village marketplace the rule was *caveat emptor*—let the buyer beware. Hence it was up to the buyer to "assure" that the product was fit for use. Generally, the buyer was able to perform this task. The goods were uncomplicated—most quality characteristics could be evaluated by the unaided human senses. The buyer had long familiarity with the products through prior purchase and use. Hence the buyer did assure that the products were fit for use. Mostly the buyer gained this assurance from inspection of the product prior to purchase. Alternatively, the buyer might rely on the known quality reputation of the seller.

Attaining an undoubted quality reputation was of the utmost importance to a seller. The seller's income, family security, and status in the community as a reliable "craftsman" all were directly affected by the quality of the product. These were high stakes and they exerted a powerful influence on sellers to do their utmost to make their products fit for use.

The growth of cities and of intercity trade created new quality problems which the village marketplace could not solve. Many sellers and buyers no longer met face to face, owing to intervention by intermediate materials suppliers and merchants. Many quality characteristics could no longer be judged by the unaided human senses, because of intervention of a growing number of unnatural materials and processes. New tools and quality tasks were needed to deal with these new quality problems.

Some of these new tools were of a technological nature, involving development and use of material and product specifications (either by sample or in written form), test specifications, and measuring instruments. Other tools were of a commercial and legal nature, e.g., warranties implied by the law of sales and warranties agreed on by contract. In addition, some associations of producers, e.g., the guilds, imposed quality controls on their members as a means of upholding the quality reputation of the city.

The Industrial Revolution opened the way for the growth of the modern corporation with its great capacity to produce and distribute goods and services. Corporations have created specialized departments to carry out certain functions (product design, manufacture, inspection and test, etc.) which are essential to launching any new or changed product. Morover, these functions follow a relatively unvarying sequence of events, much as is depicted in Figure 1-1, the *spiral.*

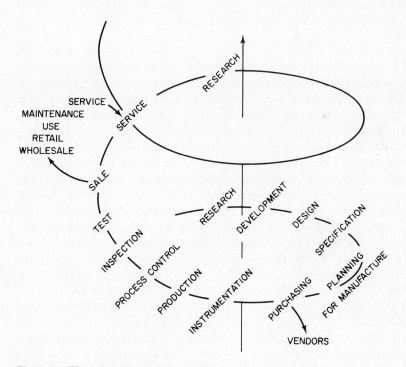

Figure 1-1 The spiral of progress in quality.

It is evident from the spiral that many activities and tasks must be performed to attain fitness for use. Some of these are performed within the manufacturing or service companies. Others are performed elsewhere, e.g., by vendors, merchants, regulators, etc. It is convenient to have a shorthand name for this collection of activities, and the term *quality function* is used for this purpose. The quality function is *the entire collection of activities through which we achieve fitness for use, no matter where these activities are performed.*

Some practitioners look upon the spiral or the quality function as a *system*, i.e., a network of activities or *subsystems*. Some of these subsystems correspond to segments of the spiral. Others, although not shown on the spiral, are nevertheless present and active, e.g., data processing, standardization. These subsystems, when well designed and coordinated, become a unified system which carries out the intended quality objectives, as we will see in the next section.

1-4 THE SYSTEMS CONCEPT

In primitive societies, coordinating the quality activities around the spiral is the job of one person, e.g., usufacturer, farmer, artisan. The proprietor of the small shop is also personally well placed to do such coordination through observing all activities, through deciding what actions should be taken, and through having the most compelling personal reasons for attaining good coordination.

As enterprises grow in size and complexity, they reach a stage where it is no longer possible to retain personal coordination by the leader. The company is now organized into specialized departments, each of which carries out some specialty of the sort shown in the spiral, Figure 1-1. Of course each of these specialized departments can aid in attaining fitness for use in ways that outperform the predecessor proprietors of the small shops. However, these specialized departments must collectively coordinate their activities so as to meet the goals of the company. This interdepartmental coordination has turned out to be difficult to achieve. In part this difficulty is due to sheer complexity arising from the multiplicity of goals pursued by or imposed on the company. In part the difficulty is organizational in nature, since the departments usually exhibit strong tendencies to pursue departmental goals to the detriment of company goals.

There are several approaches which the large company may use for coordinating the quality function. One of these is through use of the *systems concept*. Under this concept, managers collectively agree on what are to be the broad quality "policies" (or guides for managerial conduct) as well as the specific quantitative quality goals or "objectives" to be met. In addition, the managers prepare "plans" for meeting these objectives. These plans include agreement on how to "organize," i.e., definition of what tasks are to be performed and who is to be held responsible for carrying out these tasks.

Because all this coordination is of an interdepartmental nature, it requires the participation and agreement of the respective departmental managers. Some of it requires the agreement of upper management as well. In addition, since a great deal of analytical study is involved, it is increasingly the practice to make use of specialists who possess experience and skills relative to the quality function. These specialists (e.g., quality engineers) collect and analyze the pertinent data, draft proposals, and otherwise assist the managers to attain coordination.

The systems concept is widely used though under a variety of names. Its principal features include:

1. *Broad scope.* It is intended to achieve coordination of the entire quality function.
2. *Definition of the organizational mechanisms.* It defines the work to be done and what departments are to be responsible for doing it.
3. *Quantitative standards and measures.* It sets out measurable goals and provides for review of progress against goals.

In later chapters we will see in greater detail how the systems concept is carried out.

1-5 LIFE BEHIND THE QUALITY DIKES

Prior to industrialization the great bulk of humanity lived in villages under primitive conditions of transport, communication, energy sources, health care, etc. The life span was short and life itself was grim and exhausting, with wide prevalence of poverty, disease, and hunger.

In many countries the Industrial Revolution has changed all this. Mass production of goods and services has enabled hundreds of millions of people to reorganize their lives in ways which can take advantage of the benefits of industrialization: central energy sources, modern transport and communication, improved health, longer life, reduction of toil, opportunity for travel, time for cultural activities.[3] These are important benefits, yet the continuity, safety, and convenience of every one of them depends on the quality of manufactured products and services.

This dependence is much more widespread and serious than is generally realized. For example, in the United States over 80 percent of the work force uses privately owned automobiles for transportation to the workplace. If the vehicle fails, the motorists cannot simply walk to work—they no longer live within walking distance of their work. So they must arrange to have service restored and to find alternative transport in the interim. All this is time-consuming and costly, and interferes with the orderly routines they had established. At the

---

[3] There are serious disadvantages as well: dangerous products, damage to the environment, etc. We will look at these in subsequent chapters.

other extreme are the massive power failures which can paralyze entire cities, and disasters such as an unsafe drug being put on the market.

One of the authors has coined the phrase "life behind the quality dikes" to describe this dependence on quality. It is similar to the Dutch way of life—about a third of their lands lie below sea level. The land confers great benefits but to use it requires that massive sea walls (dikes) be built and maintained so as to keep the sea out. In like manner, the modern products and services confer great benefits but also demand protective dikes in the form of adequate quality controls.

The concept of life behind the dikes imposes ever broader obligations on the manufacturers of goods and services. These broader obligations go beyond those voluntarily assumed by contract and *run directly to the public*. They relate to matters such as product safety, continuity of service, the environment, etc. This list will probably continue to grow for the foreseeable future, and into new areas of responsibility. Possible extensions include:

Pricing based on the users' cost of ownership.
Service contracts that extend over the useful life. of the product.
Penalties for exaggerated claims of what the product will do.
Payment for time lost by the user to secure satisfaction.

1-6 THE FACTUAL APPROACH

In the modern quality function there is a continuing procession of questions requiring answers:

Does this specification reflect fitness for use?
Can this process hold the tolerance?
Does this lot of product conform to specification?

It would seem to be obvious that the answers to such questions should be based on data rather than on opinion. Yet in practice we find that many such questions are answered based on the "experience" of designers, manufacturing engineers, inspectors, etc., in the absence of data, i.e., based on "opinion" rather than on "fact." Such persons defend their actions on various grounds: a good prior record of decision making, lack of time to dig fully into the facts, etc.

For example, in a watch factory one of the processes had for years operated at a costly level of waste with associated high costs for sorting good products from bad. Over these same years there had been much earnest debate among the managers as to whether the battery of machines in that process was able to hold the tolerances.

Then came a time when a quality control specialist armed himself with a precise gage and measured the pieces as they emerged from one machine.

When he charted the measurements in relation to the tolerances, the question was settled once and for all. (See Figure 11-2 and associated discussion.)

How is it that adults can for years continue debating an important question for which a factual answer can "easily" be provided? There are many reasons: they are blocked by their axiomatic beliefs; they lack the time or skills to take on the study; they lack the tools but are not aware of this (in the study mentioned above a key factor in providing the answer was use of a precise laboratory gage rather than the coarser shop gage); they are afraid the answer might deny what they have said for years. For these and other reasons, it often turns out that the missing facts are so easy to provide that some managers are stunned—"That should have been obvious." At the other extreme, supplying the missing facts requires so heroic an effort that no one thinks of the word "obvious."

Students who are to take on the role of quality control specialist should grasp fully the importance of the factual approach. They become advocates of change in an environment where they may be the least experienced as to the technology. The factual approach is their major tool for raising themselves to a state of equality in contribution to the problem at hand.

1-7 CONCEPTUAL PAST AND PROLOGUE

The proliferation of new concepts in commerce and industry has been paralleled by the periodic emergence of something "new" in the quality function: new concepts, tools, techniques, etc. Some of these concepts are very old, going back many centuries before the Christian era: metrology, product specifications, process specifications, full-time inspectors. Independent product certification was in use by A.D. 1000. The concept of the central inspection department was employed, although sparingly, before the twentieth century.

The pace of these developments has quickened during the twentieth century, which has seen a lengthy procession of "new" activities and ideas launched under a bewildering array of names, among which the following have been the most widely publicized: quality control; inspection planning; quality planning; statistical quality control; field complaint analysis; defect prevention; quality control engineering; reliability engineering; quality cost analysis; zero defects; total quality control; vendor surveillance; quality assurance; quality audit; QC circles; quality information systems.

There has been no standardization of meanings of these terms. Some are merely new labels for old activities under new management. In some cases the germ of a sound idea when combined with skillful promotion succeeded in creating a "movement"—a national wave of activity. Then, when the enthusiasm and overenthusiasm died down, the residue quietly took its place with other useful tools and ideas in the industrial collection.

We can safely predict that this procession will continue without end as long as commerce and industry continue to grow in size and complexity. Already, numerous additional concepts are emerging: quality control of computer programming and automated processes; responses to government regulation and threats of liability suits; employee participation in quality problem solving; professionalism; etc.

PROBLEMS

1-1 Our schools are an industry supplying a service (education). Schools start with raw material (students), apply a process (teaching), and turn out a finished product (graduates), although with some rejects. There are raw material specifications (minimum entrance requirements) and incoming inspection (entrance examinations). There is a process specification (curriculum, course outlines); process facilities (faculty, laboratories, textbooks); process controls (reports, recitations, quizzes); and final product testing (examinations).

It is easy to identify the elements through which this educational service achieves fitness for use. They include:

1. The service rendered.
2. The specifications established for "raw materials" entering the process.
3. The nature of the process specifications.
4. The nature of the "finished product" specifications.
5. The nature of the quality controls in use during the various stages of progression from raw material to finished product.

For each institution listed below, identify the elements (a) through (e):

(a) The neighborhood laundry
(b) The U.S. Postal Service
(c) The local shoe repair shop
(d) The public bus company
(e) The public library
(f) The local newspaper
(g) The "gas" station
(h) The supermarket
(i) The bank
(j) The telephone company

1-2 Figure 1-1 identifies the more usual activities through which a manufacturing company achieves fitness for use. Identify, for each institution listed in Problem 1-1, the activities through which it achieves fitness for use. For each of the identified activities, determine who carries them out, i.e., the boss, a specific individual assigned to that activity (full time or part time), a specialized department, an outside service, etc.

SUPPLEMENTARY READING

Fitness for use: *Quality Control Handbook,* 3rd ed. (QCH3), McGraw-Hill Book Company, New York, 1974, pp. 2-2, 2-3.
Parameters of fitness for use: QCH3, pp. 2-6 to 2-9.
Control and quality control: QCH3, pp. 2-11, 2-12
Life behind the quality dikes: J. M. Juran, "Life Behind the Quality Dikes," European Organization for Quality Control, 22nd Annual Conference, Dresden, 1978.

EXAMPLES OF EXAMINATION QUESTIONS USED IN FORMER ASQC QUALITY ENGINEER CERTIFICATION EXAMINATION AS PUBLISHED IN *QUALITY PROGRESS* MAGAZINE

1 A quality program has the best foundation for success when it is initiated by: (*a*) a certified quality engineer; (*b*) contractual requirements; (*c*) chief executive of company; (*d*) production management; (*e*) an experienced quality manager.

2 The most important measure of outgoing quality needed by managers is product performance as viewed by: (*a*) the customer; (*b*) the final inspector; (*c*) production; (*d*) marketing.

QUALITY COSTS

2-1 THE QUALITY COST CONCEPT

Virtually all institutions make use of financial controls which include a comparison of actual costs with budgeted costs, plus associated action on the difference, or "variance." In large organizations it is usual to extend this principle to the recognized departments. To this end, departmental budgets are established and departmental costs are measured. The heads of the departments are then held responsible for meeting their budgets.

These departmental costs are incurred to carry out the assigned special mission of the department, including its contribution to quality. However, until the 1950s there was no special accounting procedure to evaluate the cost of the quality function. The costs of achieving fitness for use were scattered widely among numerous departments. For most of them, the quality costs were a minority of their expenditures. (An obvious exception was the inspection and test department.)

Beginning in the 1950s, various forces converged to urge companies to evaluate the costs associated with the quality function. These forces included:

1. Growth of quality costs due to growth in volume of complex products, which demanded higher precision, greater reliability, etc.
2. The influence of the great growth of long-life products with resulting high costs due to field failures, maintenance labor, spare parts, etc. (The costs of

keeping such products in service often exceeded the original purchase price.)
3. The pressures arising from the phenomenon of "life behind the quality dikes" (Section 1-5).
4. The need for quality specialists to express their findings and recommendations in the language of upper management—the language of money.

What has emerged is a concept of defining and measuring *quality costs* and then using the resulting figures for two different but interrelated purposes:

1. To provide *a new scoreboard* as an added form of cost control.
2. To *identify opportunities* for reducing quality costs. Here the emphasis is not on meeting some historical standard but on challenging the validity of that standard.

The interrelation of these purposes is seen in Table 2-1.

Because the costs of attaining fitness for use have become huge—of the order of 10 percent of the economy—the opportunities for cost reduction are also huge. These potentialities, plus the published success stories of some companies, have stimulated a keen interest in study of quality costs.

Note that the term "quality costs" is *associated solely with defective product*—the costs of making, finding, repairing, or avoiding defects. The costs of making good products are not a part of quality costs. We will return to this distinction later.

Table 2-1 Phases in quality cost programs

	Selling phase	Project phase	Control phase
Objectives of the phases	To justify launching a program of quality improvement and cost reduction	To observe and stimulate progress during the improvement program	To hold gains made during the improvement program and to provide data for continuing control of quality costs
Sources of information	Estimates made by QC specialists, supplemented by accounting data	Accounting data supplemented by estimates made by QC specialists	Accounting data
Information published by	Quality control	Quality control, with verification by accounting	Accounting, with charting and commentary by quality control
Frequency of publication	One-time or infrequently, e.g., annually	At least annually; sometimes monthly	Monthly or quarterly

2-2 QUALITY COST CATEGORIES

The first step toward quantifying quality costs is to agree on what is meant by "quality costs." This is done by identifying and defining those *categories* of costs which are associated with making, finding, repairing, or avoiding (preventing) defects. Many manufacturing companies have gone through this process, resulting in a rather standardized set of *core* categories. The core categories and their typical definitions are as follows:[1]

Internal Failure Costs

These are costs which would disappear if no defects existed in the product prior to shipment to the customer. They include:

Scrap. The net loss in labor and material resulting from defectives which cannot economically be repaired or used.

Rework. The cost of correcting defectives to make them fit for use. Sometimes this category is broadened to include extra operations created to solve an epidemic of defects, or special piece rates provided for a similar purpose.

Retest. The cost of reinspection and retest of products which have undergone rework or other revision.

Downtime. The cost of idle facilities resulting from defects (e.g., printing press down due to paper breaks, aircraft idle due to unreliability). In some industries this category is very large and hence is quantified. In most companies, this is ignored.

Yield losses. The cost of process yields lower than might be attainable by improved controls. Includes "overfill" of containers (going to customers) due to variability in filling and measuring equipment.

Disposition. The effort required to determine whether nonconforming products are usable and to make final disposition. Includes the time of individuals and material review boards, no matter what the department of origin of the workers involved, e.g., a designer preparing a deviation authorization.

External Failure Costs

These costs also would disappear if there were no defects. They are distinguished from the internal failure costs by the fact that the defects are found after shipment to the customer. They include:

Complaint adjustment. All costs of investigation and adjustment of justified complaints attributable to defective product or installation.

[1] A more elaborate list of categories, together with sources of cost figures and some "cautions in use," is contained in the publication "Quality Costs—What and How," 2nd ed., American Society for Quality Control, 1971.

Returned material. All costs associated with receipt and replacement of defective product returned from the field.

Warranty charges. All costs involved in service to customers under warranty contracts.

Allowances. Costs of concessions made to customers due to substandard products being accepted by the customer as is. Includes loss in income due to downgrading products for sale as seconds.

Appraisal Costs

These are the costs incurred to discover the condition of the product, mainly during the "first time through." The costs include:

Incoming material inspection. The cost of determining the quality of vendor-made products, whether by inspection on receipt, by inspection at the source, or by surveillance methods.

Inspection and test. The costs of checking the conformance of the product throughout its progression in the factory, including final acceptance, and check of packing and shipping. Includes life, environmental, and reliability tests. Also includes testing done at the customer's premises prior to turning the product over to the customer. (It is usual to keep separate subaccounts for inspection, laboratory testing, and field testing.) In collecting these costs, what is decisive is the kind of work done and not the department name (i.e., the work may be done by chemists in a Technical Department laboratory, by sorters in the Production Department, by testers in the Inspection Department, or by outside services engaged for the purpose of testing).

Maintaining accuracy of test equipment. Includes the cost of operating the system that keeps the measuring instruments and equipment in calibration.

Materials and services consumed. Includes the costs of products consumed through destructive tests, materials consumed (e.g., X-ray film), and services (e.g., electric power) where significant.

Evaluation of stocks. Includes the costs of testing products in field storage or in stock to evaluate degradation.

Prevention Costs

These costs are incurred to keep failure and appraisal costs to a minimum. The usual categories are as follows:

Quality planning. This includes the broad array of activities which collectively create the overall quality plan, the inspection plan, the reliability plan, the data system, and the numerous specialized plans. It includes also preparation of the manuals and procedures needed to communicate these plans to all concerned.

As in the case of inspection and test, some of this work may be done by personnel who are not on the payroll of a department called Quality Control. The decisive criterion is again the type of work, not the name of the department performing the work.

New-products review. Includes preparation of bid proposals, evaluation of new designs, preparation of test and experimental programs, and other quality activities associated with the launching of new designs.

Training. The costs of preparing training programs for attaining and improving quality performance, no matter which department is to be the recipient of the training. Includes the cost of conducting formal training programs as well.

Process control. Includes that part of process control which is conducted to achieve fitness for use, as distinguished from achieving productivity, safety, etc. (Separating these is often difficult.)

Quality data acquisition and analysis. This is the work of running the quality data system to acquire continuing data on quality performance. It includes analysis of these data to identify the quality troubles, to sound the alarms, stimulate study, etc.

Quality reporting. Includes the work of summarizing and publishing quality information to the middle and upper management.

Improvement projects. Includes the work of structuring and carrying out programs for breakthrough to new levels of performance, i.e., defect prevention programs, motivation programs, etc.

2-3 EXAMPLES OF QUALITY COST STUDIES

Table 2-2 shows the results of a quality cost study made for a large printing company. Several major conclusions became obvious:

1. The total of $1.7 million was of an order of magnitude sufficient to attract the attention of upper management.
2. The bulk of the costs were concentrated in three categories: proofreading, press downtime, and typographical errors. The quality costs for these three categories (which were somewhat interrelated) accounted for over 80 percent of the total. Hence any major improvement in the total would require major improvements in these categories.
3. The prevention costs were less than 2 percent of the total. This raised questions as to whether increased prevention effort might yield a good return on the investment.

At the other extreme in size is the study for a small chemical plant shown in Table 2.2b.

Table 2-2a Quality costs: printing company ($000)

Losses due to quality failures	
Press downtime	404
Correction of typos	309
Bindery waste	74
Plate revision	40
Cover-making waste	56
Customer complaint remakes	41
Total	924
Appraisal expenses	
Proofreading	709
Other checking and inspection	62
Total	771
Prevention expenses	
Quality improvement project	20
Quality planning	10
Total	30
Total quality costs	1,725

Table 2.2b Chemical plant

Quality cost category	Annual quality cost
Rework	$48,804
Scrap	7,594
Retesting	7,100
Processing rejection forms	1,410
Customer complaints	280
Total	$65,188

For most quality cost studies the original scope is less than company-wide. More typically the early studies are limited to specific divisions, plants, processes, product lines, functions, etc. For example, Table 2-3 shows the cost of time lost in searching for gages in a machine shop.

Quality cost studies can be made for service companies as well as for manufacturing companies. For example, a railroad found the following costs associated with derailments (damage to equipment and tracks, damage to goods, and cost of clearing the tracks):

Year	Number of derailments	Total cost	Cost per derailment
19--	88	$97,604	$1,109
19--	126	86,248	684

Table 2-3 Cost of time lost in searching for gages

Machine type	Number of machines	Hours lost per year*
Automatic chucking	249	18,052
Boring	147	10,658
Drilling	481	34,872
Grinding	169	12,252
Total	1,046	75,834

For 257 inspectors, hours lost = 2.1 h per inspector per week for 50 weeks per year = 26,985 h.

Cost of lost time:

Operators: 75,834 at $15.00 (worker and machine) =	$1,137,510
Inspectors: 26,984 at $6.00 (worker)	161,910
Gages lost annually	40,000
Total cost of time lost	$1,339,420

* Estimated at 1.45 h per machine operator per week, 50 weeks per year.

In like manner the annual cost to airlines due to lost or mishandled baggage was reported[2] to be as follows:

Airline	$000,000
Eastern	$6.0
Pan American	1.0
United	3.6

2-4 SECURING THE COST FIGURES

Most quality cost categories are not reflected in the charts of accounts of the prevailing cost accounting systems. Hence the accountants are unable to provide figures on what are the costs incurred with respect to such categories. What the accountants can provide readily are figures for those quality cost categories which coincide with accounts that are elements of departmental budgets, e.g., product testing done by the test department. In addition, some companies have, over the years, evolved ways of quantifying some of their categories of failure costs. However, the first efforts to secure quality cost figures typically disclose that the bulk of the categories cannot be evaluated from the accounts regularly maintained by the cost accountants.

The approach used to supply the missing figures depends on what is the purpose of quantifying quality costs in the first place. If the main purpose is to identify opportunities for reducing the costs, the missing figures are supplied by digging into the accounting figures, by estimates, and in still other makeshift

[2] *Newsweek*, September 3, 1973, p. 73.

ways. If the main purpose is to create a new scoreboard, the approach used to supply the missing figures is to revise the chart of accounts so that each agreed quality cost category is assigned an account number. Thereafter, the regular cost accounting process follows through to secure the cost data associated with the new accounts.

In some programs both of these approaches are employed in a time-phased sequence. The phases and their interrelation are shown in Table 2-1. The associated levels and trends of quality costs are shown in Figure 2-1.

The methods used to supply the missing figures depend on what is missing and what the available resources are. The cases most commonly encountered involve:

1. *Analysis of the ingredients of established accounts.* For example, an account called "Customer Returns" may report the cost of all goods returned. However, returns are made to reduce inventories as well as to send back defective product. Hence, it may be necessary to go back to the basic return documents to separate the quality costs from the rest.
2. *Resort to basic accounting documents.* For example, some product inspection is done by Production Department employees. By securing their

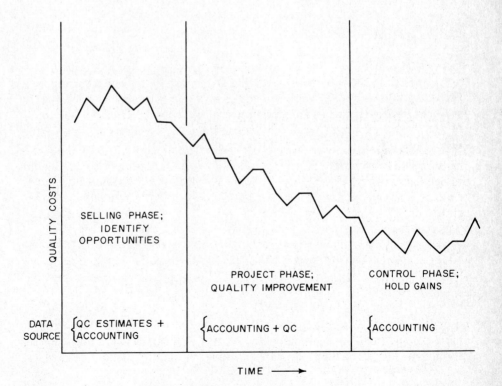

Figure 2-1 Schematic of phases in quality cost programs.

names and the associated payroll data, it is feasible to quantify these quality costs.

3. *Creating temporary records.* For example, some production workers spend part of their time repairing defective product. It may be feasible to arrange with their supervisor to create a temporary record so as to evaluate the repair time and thereby the repair costs.

4. *Estimates.* For example, in one of the engineering departments some of the engineers are engaged part time in making product failure analyses. However, the department makes no provision for charging engineering time to multiple accounts. It may be adequate to ask each engineer to make an estimate of time spent on product failure analysis.

Managers and accountants tend to be reluctant to use a mixture such as the foregoing as the basis for a scoreboard. (To the accountant, the word "estimate" is a dirty word.) However, managers have no such reluctance to use estimates as a basis for decision making. The waste in a certain process might be estimated as $100,000 per year; the true figure might be as low as $80,000 or as high as $120,000. Yet the managers' decision would probably be identical for all three. A typical comment would be: "Every one of those three figures is too high, so let's get on with reducing it, whatever the figure."

2-5 PARETO ANALYSIS

Quality costs are always "maldistributed." Without exception, relatively few of the contributors (divisions, plants, products, defects, etc.) account for the bulk of the costs. For example, Table 2-4 shows how in a paper mill the accounting category "broke" (the paper mill term for scrap) accounted for $556,000, or 61 percent of the total quality costs. This single category is more costly than all the rest combined.

Continuing with this analysis, Table 2-5 shows how the broke losses are maldistributed over the 53 different types of paper being made. It is evident

Table 2-4 Quality losses in a paper mill

Accounting category	Annual quality loss, $000	Percent of total quality loss	
		This category	Cumulative
Broke	556	61	61
Customer claim	122	14	75
Odd lot	78	9	84
High material cost	67	7	91
Downtime	37	4	95
Excess inspection	28	3	98
High testing cost	19	2	100

Table 2-5 "Broke" losses in a paper mill

Product type	Annual "broke" loss, $000	Cumulative "broke" loss, $000	Percent of broke loss	Cumulative percent of broke loss
A	132	132	24	24
B	96	228	17	41
C	72	300	13	54
D	68	368	12	66
E	47	415	8	74
F	33	448	6	80
47 other types	108	556	20	100
Total 53 types	556		100	

that the worst six types of paper account for $448,000, which is 80 percent of the broke.

Continuing the analysis still further, Table 2-6 shows the estimated quality costs for the principal defects found in these six types of paper. Now some likely "projects" have begun to make themselves evident. (A project is a problem scheduled for solution.) For example, the defect "tear" in product type B has an estimated cost of $61,200—the highest quality cost of any combination in the matrix. Thereby it becomes a likely candidate for cost reduction.

These tables exemplify the principle of the "vital few and trivial many"—a universal rule which one of the authors once misnamed the Pareto principle.[3] It is one of the most powerful of all management tools and is widely used as a means of attacking the bulk of the problem areas with the least amount of analytical study.

[3] For numerous additional examples of the Pareto principle, see the cases listed in the index of *Quality Control Handbook*, 3rd ed., McGraw-Hill Book Company, New York, 1974.

Table 2-6 Matrix of quality costs

Type	Trim	Visual defects*	Caliper	Tear	Porosity	All other causes	Total
A	$27,000	$ 9,400	None†	$ 16,200	$43,000	$36,400	$132,000
B	12,000	3,300	None†	61,200	5,800	13,700	96,000
C	9,500	7,800	$38,000	3,100	7,400	6,200	72,000
D	8,200	10,300	None†	9,000	29,700	10,800	68,000
E	5,400	10,800	None†	24,600	None†	6,200	47,000
F	5,100	4,900	3,900	1,600	3,300	14,200	33,000
Total	$67,200	$46,500	$41,900	$115,700	$89,200	$87,500	$448,000

* Slime spots, holes, wrinkles, etc.
† Not a specified requirement for this type.

2-6 INTERPRETATION AND PRESENTATION TO MANAGEMENT

As quality costs are collected, they must be analyzed to understand their significance, to identify the opportunities they offer, and to present the findings to the cognizant managers. If these managers accept the findings, their support of the proposals will simplify greatly the job of securing the budgets, personnel, and legitimacy needed to make the proposals effective.

The form of presentation depends largely on whether the basic purpose is to create a new scoreboard or to embark on an improvement program. (It is possible to present both purposes as a time-phased program, but it is difficult to communicate so complex a concept.)

The Grand Total

The most significant figure in a quality cost study is the total of the quality costs. The total may be so small as to fail to compete for managerial priority. For example, in a confectionery company the avoidable quality costs totaled $44,500 per year. The managers decided that any program to reduce these costs would have to wait, since numerous other problems had higher priority.

More usually, managers are stunned by the size of the total—they had no idea the amount was so big. One memorable example was a leading manufacturer of aircraft engines. When the total quality costs were made known to the then Managing Director, he promptly convened his senior executives to discuss a broad plan of action.

Comparisons

Interpretation is aided by relating total quality costs to other figures with which managers are familiar. The relationships which have the greatest impact on upper management are:

1. *Quality costs as a percent of sales.* The financial reports to upper managers and even to shareholders make extensive use of sales as a basis for comparison. When quality costs are similarly related to sales, it becomes easier for upper management to grasp the significance of the numbers.
2. *Quality costs compared to profit.* It comes as a shock to managers to learn that quality costs exceed the company's profit (which sometimes they do).
3. *Quality costs compared to the magnitude of current problems.* While money is the universal language of upper management,[4] there are addi-

---

[4] Two universal languages are spoken in the company. At the "bottom" the language is that of things and deeds: square feet of floor space, schedules of 400 tons per week, rejection rates of 3.6 percent. At the "top" the language is that of money: sales, profits, taxes, investment. The middle managers and the technical specialists *must be bilingual.* They must be able to talk to the "bottom" in the language of things, and to the "top" in the language of money.

tional ways of conveying significance to these managers. In one company which was preoccupied with meeting delivery schedules, the quality costs were translated into equivalent added production. Since this coincided with the chief current goals of the managers, their interest was aroused. In another company, the total quality costs of $76,000,000 were shown to be equivalent to one of the company plants employing 2900 people, occupying 1.1 million square feet of space and requiring $6,000,000 of inventory.

Interrelation of Categories

Additional useful comparisons are available from the interrelationship among the subtotals of the quality costs for the major categories. In many companies the appraisal costs have long been budgeted and hence have long been a subject for discussion. However, the typical quality cost study will show that the previously underemphasized failure costs are several times the appraisal costs. This comes as a surprise to most managers and forces them to reconsider their emphasis.

In like manner, when managers discover that prevention costs are pitifully low in relation to the total, their instinctive reaction is to look more attentively at the possibilities of increasing preventive efforts. The relationship between internal failure costs and external failure costs likewise has significance. The former generally point to the need for programs involving manufacturing planning and production, whereas the latter generally point to programs involving product design and field service.

The ratios of category costs to total costs vary widely among industries and even among companies in the same industry. However, many companies exhibit ratios which fall within the following ranges:

Quality cost category	Percent of total
Internal failures	25–40
External failures	20–40
Appraisal	10–50
Prevention	0.5–5

Presentation Pitfalls

Presentations to managers should be done in a way such that what remains to be discussed is the merits of the proposals, not the validity of the data. Nevertheless, many presentations of quality cost data have resulted only in a debate on the validity of the figures. The challenges to the data have mainly been due to:

Inclusion of nonquality costs For example, the word "waste" has multiple meanings. Material which is so defective as to be unsalvageable is sometimes called "waste." However, the word "waste" is also used to designate skeleton scrap from the press room, lathe turnings, trim from coils, kettle residues, etc. If the value of such materials is included in the quality cost figures, the presentation will be challenged. The challenge will be quite in order since such categories of waste are unrelated to quality and hence are not quality costs.

Implications of reducing quality costs to zero It is not economic to reduce quality costs to zero. Before that stage is reached, the incremental control and prevention efforts rise more rapidly than the resulting cost reductions. Practicing managers are quite sensitive on this point and are quick to challenge any presentation which even remotely implies that it is feasible to reduce the quality costs to zero. The presentation must take the initiative in pointing out that perfection is an uneconomic goal.

Reducing quality costs but increasing total company costs In proposing reductions in quality costs care must be taken to avoid disproportionate increases in other costs. For example, a proposal to reduce dimensional defects in a machine operation required a redesign of tools which, if done, would have an impact on several other aspects of company costs: material usage, productivity, tool breakage, and tool maintenance. It became necessary to quantify the effect of all these variables in order to assure that the reduction in quality costs would not result in an increase in total costs.[5]

Understatement of quality costs There are also ways of understating quality costs. By far the most usual form is to omit proposals for dealing with specific costs on the basis that they are "usual," "standard," "regular," etc. This line of reasoning is widely used as the basis for the scoreboard approach to cost control. In the scoreboard approach the emphasis is not on the standard level of costs but on the variances from that standard. However, in the prevention approach, the emphasis is one of challenging the standard level itself. This latter emphasis is entirely valid if the costs in question are "avoidable," i.e., associated with defective product.

2-7 COST-REDUCTION PROGRAMS—RETURN ON INVESTMENT

The *Pareto analysis* identifies the "vital few" concentrations of quality costs with respect to certain product types, processes, defect types, etc. Some of these concentrations become logical nominations for cost reduction projects. One of the most productive results of a study of quality costs is the preparation of a quality cost reduction "program" consisting of an organized attack on the most promising projects.

Effective presentation of such a program to upper management normally

[5] See *Quality Control Handbook*, 3rd ed., p. 16–36.

includes an estimate of *return on investment* for each project. Preparation of this estimate requires several subestimates, as follows:

1. The present annual quality costs being incurred.
2. The anticipated reduction in annual cost, assuming successful completion of the project.
3. The cost of diagnosis, i.e., the cost of discovering the causes of the outward symptoms of poor quality.
4. The cost of remedy, i.e., the cost of eliminating the causes.
5. The resulting return on investment.

In its simplest form, the return on investment is the ratio of estimated reduction (item 2 above) to the estimated investment (item 3 plus item 4). For example, suppose that ($000):

$$\text{Estimated reduction} = 32$$

$$\text{Estimated investment} = 80$$

Then estimated return on investment = $32 \div 80 = 40$ percent. This means that 40 percent of the investment will be recovered in the first full year of the improvement. The reciprocal of $1 \div 0.4$ means that it will take 2.5 years to recover the investment.[6]

All of these estimates are surrounded with uncertainty. "There is a long fringe around the numbers." None of this is frightening to experienced managers. In launching new products, adopting new processes, promoting new managers, and in still other untried ventures, managers know they must make decisions based on estimates. They know also that they can make better decisions with well-prepared estimates than in the absence of estimates. Moreover, with experience the estimates become more and more reliable. The estimate of return on investment is especially valuable because it helps managers in choosing from among competing projects when it is not possible to undertake them all.

How much cost reduction can be attained by these programs? In the experience of one of the authors, these programs have the capability of cutting the quality costs in half over a period of several years, provided that the costs have not previously been attacked in an organized way. The 50 percent reduction also follows the Pareto principle, i.e., the bulk of the cost reduction comes from the vital few concentrations of quality costs. The "trivial many" contribute very little.

Management approval of the program opens the way to an attack on the

---

[6] Return on investment is more complex than the simple example given. Two kinds of money are involved (capital and operating expenditures) at different tax rates. Time is a factor, i.e., money in the future has a different value than does present money. Each company usually has specialists (in finance, industrial engineering, etc.) available to assist in preparing the estimates of return on investment.

vital few sources of high quality costs. The detailed approach to this is covered in Chapter 5.

2-8 CONCEPT OF OPTIMUM COST OF CONFORMANCE

The total quality costs are strongly influenced by the interplay among the various categories. Table 2-7 is a model demonstrating this interplay.

In step A, the absence of appraisal and prevention costs results in very high external failures. (There are many defects and there is little to stop them from going on to the users, resulting in the highest possible failure costs.) In step B, a sorting operation is introduced. This stops most of the defects from going out to the field and hence reduces external failures. Of course, this reduction has its price. The appraisal costs are increased and the defects found during sorting now show up as internal failures. However, the total quality costs are less than in step A.

In step C, process controls are introduced to find the defects at still earlier stages of product progression. This further increase in appraisal costs nevertheless again reduces the total quality costs. In step D, prevention costs are increased and this has the most beneficial effect of all.[7]

This interrelation among the cost categories can be shown to lead to an optimum level of total quality costs. Figure 2-2 shows this model graphically. The sum of appraisal and prevention costs rises from zero to infinity as perfection is approached. The failure costs drop from infinity to zero as perfection is approached. The total quality costs necessarily have a minimum or optimum between the two infinities. (Note that the vertical scale is cost per *good* unit of product.)

This concept of the optimum has wide practical application. Figure 2-3

---

[7] Adapted from B. Veen, "Quality Costs," *Quality (EOQC Journal),* vol. 17, no. 2, Summer 1974, pp. 55–59.

Table 2-7 Model of interplay among quality cost categories

Quality cost category	Steps in quality cost reduction			
	A. Minimal appraisal and prevention costs	B. Increase in appraisal cost (product sorting)	C. Increase in appraisal cost (process controls)	D. Increase in prevention costs
External failures	20	3	2	1
Internal failures	1	12	8	4
Sorting	1	3	2	1
Process controls	1	1	4	2
Prevention	1	1	1	2
Total	24	20	17	10

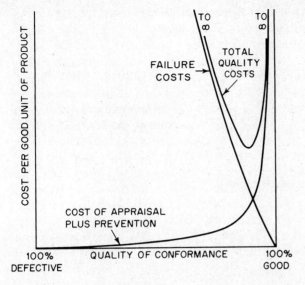

COST PER GOOD UNIT OF PRODUCT

TO ∞   TO ∞

FAILURE COSTS

TOTAL QUALITY COSTS

COST OF APPRAISAL PLUS PREVENTION

100% DEFECTIVE   QUALITY OF CONFORMANCE   100% GOOD

Figure 2-2 Model for optimum quality costs.

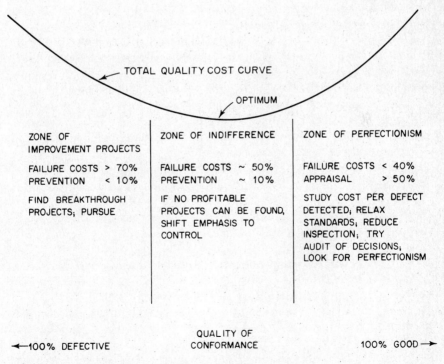

TOTAL QUALITY COST CURVE

OPTIMUM

ZONE OF IMPROVEMENT PROJECTS	ZONE OF INDIFFERENCE	ZONE OF PERFECTIONISM
FAILURE COSTS > 70% PREVENTION < 10%	FAILURE COSTS ~ 50% PREVENTION ~ 10%	FAILURE COSTS < 40% APPRAISAL > 50%
FIND BREAKTHROUGH PROJECTS; PURSUE	IF NO PROFITABLE PROJECTS CAN BE FOUND, SHIFT EMPHASIS TO CONTROL	STUDY COST PER DEFECT DETECTED; RELAX STANDARDS; REDUCE INSPECTION; TRY AUDIT OF DECISIONS; LOOK FOR PERFECTIONISM

◄—100% DEFECTIVE   QUALITY OF CONFORMANCE   100% GOOD —►

Figure 2-3 Optimum segment of quality cost model.

shows an annotated enlargement of the area of minimum total quality costs. When the failure costs dominate (left-hand zone), the main opportunities for quality cost improvement lie in reducing failure costs through attack on the main defect concentration areas. When the appraisal costs dominate (right-hand zone), the main opportunities for profitable projects lie in reduction of perfectionism in standards, more effective inspection and test procedures, more efficient sampling, etc. If no profitable projects can be identified, the total quality costs are probably optimal, and the need is to control—to hold them at that optimal level.

2-9 QUALITY COST SCOREBOARDS

There are two species of these scoreboards. One is designed to follow the progress of an improvement program. The other is a cost control scoreboard, designed to report costs against standards and to sound the alarm when there are variances.

Scoreboard on Program Progress

In those companies that follow a time-phased program (Figure 2-1), the scoreboard is also time-phased. The first compilation of figures is to secure a basis for identifying projects and for securing approval of a program for improvement. These figures are largely based on estimates. Then, as the improvement program gets under way, the managers want to know whether results are being achieved. This requires periodic reports on progress. In part these progress reports deal with the ongoing deeds—meetings held, data presented, recommendations made, actions taken, etc. In addition, the reports estimate the financial results achieved. Such financial figures tend to become also a basis for judging the performance of those involved with the improvement program, including the managers themselves. Understandably, those being judged want such scoreboards to be based on good data, not on estimates. Hence they insist that the accounting system be extended to permit quality costs to be collected and summarized in a manner paralleling that used for cost accounting generally.

The control scoreboard The approach is similar to preparation of any scoreboard on costs. The usual ingredients include:

1. *A chart of accounts* corresponding to the various quality cost categories.
2. *A data collection system* to enable the basic data to be recorded and then converted into money equivalents.
3. *Summary of the data* in total and by various logical subtotals, e.g., by product type, departmental responsibility, quality cost category, time-to-time trend, etc.
4. *A unit of measure.* Managers invariably want the quality cost scoreboard

to be expressed in a way which compares quality costs with the opportunity for quality costs. The result is an index in which the numerator is quality cost dollars and the denominator is any of a variety of measures of activity:

Hours of direct production labor
Dollars of direct production labor
Dollars of processing cost
Dollars of manufacturing cost, i.e., materials cost plus processing cost
Dollars of sales
Units of product, e.g., per 1000 pieces, per ton, etc.

5. *A standard* against which to compare the prevailing quality cost figures. The usual standard is past performance, so that the scoreboards are, in effect, reports of variances from past performance.

Some managers, especially upper managers, inquire as to "What is par?", i.e., what are the quality cost levels of other companies in the same industry. Such data are seldom available due to lack of adequate research studies.

In the case of appraisal costs it is feasible to establish engineered standards. The amount of inspection, test, etc., needed is determined by conventional quality control engineering methods. Then the number of hours needed to perform such work is determined by conventional industrial engineering methods. The end result is a budgeted standard for inspection and test, with periodic reports of actual vs. budget, again in the conventional manner.

The quality scoreboard is useful primarily as a device for detecting departures from standard (variances) and bringing these to the attention of the managers. However, the scoreboard is not very useful as a device for challenging the standard. That challenge comes from identification of potential quality improvement projects and from organizing specially to secure those improvements.

In the final "control" phase there emerges an added reason for a good scoreboard. As cost improvements are made, there is a residual problem of holding the gains. Once the attention associated with improvement projects is relaxed, there is the risk that some of the improvements will be lost—there will be a reversion to former practices. A good scoreboard helps to identify such tendencies because the rising costs will show up as variances.

Editing and publication This, again, is conventional. The accounting data are summarized and published by the accountants in the usual format—columns of numbers. These numbers show, for the various categories, the actual charges, the budgeted values, and the variances. There are subtotals in various appropriate ways—by product line, by departmental responsibility, by quality cost category, etc.

In some companies these figures are presented in chart form rather than in tabular form. In such cases it is usual for the quality specialists to design the charts and to publish them together with supplemental analysis and comments as to trends, alarms, news of progress, etc.

2-10 WHY QUALITY COST PROGRAMS FAIL

A great many companies have undertaken to study their quality costs. Many have gotten good results and some have attained spectacular improvements. However, there have also been many failures. These failures have resulted in extensive abandonment of quality cost programs. Examination of some of these failures suggests that there are a few principal causes for the bulk of the failures.

Scoreboard Only

Many quality cost study programs start with the premise that publication of the quality cost scoreboard will by itself energize supervisors and managers into finding ways to reduce the costs. However, in most companies this premise is not valid. What is missing is an organized approach (1) to identify the promising improvement projects and (2) to undertake diagnosis and remedy in the manner described in Chapter 5. Lacking this organized approach, there will be no significant improvement. Instead, the new scoreboard will be used (like any other scoreboard) for *control* rather than for improvement. As long as the quality costs are no worse than they used to be, the scoreboard will give no alarm signal demanding action. As a result, the quality costs remain at their traditional levels. The effort used to create the new scoreboard does provide an added tool for control but fails to provide a tool for improvement.

Transfer of Charges

In some companies the effort to stimulate reduction of quality costs emphasizes a *transfer of charges*. Under this concept, studies are conducted to fix responsibility for specific categories of quality costs, i.e., to identify the departments that appear to have an obvious opportunity to reduce or eliminate the costs so categorized. Arrangements are then made to transfer the costs associated with such categories to the respective responsible departments. For example, if one category of field failure costs is discovered to have its origin in assembly department errors, those costs will be transferred to the assembly department and will become a part of their score of actual costs vs. budgeted costs. The premise is that the transfer of charges will stimulate the managers (those being charged) to find ways to reduce the costs in question.

As in "Scoreboard Only" (above), the decisive factor in securing improvement is the organized approach to identify projects, followed by diagnosis and remedy. Mere transfer of charges does not create this organized approach for improvement. The usual result, instead, is a temporary budget deficit for the departments charged. The departmental managers then contest the validity of transferring such charges without corresponding transfer of the associated budgets. This argument has merit, and in subsequent years the departmental budgets are revised to reflect the increased costs resulting from the transfers, after which life goes on as before.

Perfectionism in the Figures

In some companies the effort to create a new scoreboard gets stalled through the urge for uneconomic precision in the figures. There are lengthy debates on how to classify certain costs, on the validity of estimates, and on completeness of the figures. The latter is known as "the illusion of totality" and is usually concerned with borderline cases. An example is tool maintenance, which is needed for good quality and also for good productivity, prompt delivery, low production costs, etc. In some companies an inordinate amount of time is spent debating whether such cases belong in quality costs or not, when the real point is that it is quite unimportant which way the matter is decided.

Other companies, while exhibiting a basic orientation toward improvement (rather than toward a new scoreboard), attempt to identify projects based entirely on accounting data rather than on estimates. This attempt greatly increases the length of time required to present a proposal to management, and also increases the cost of preparing the figures. It might take only 2 weeks and X dollars to prepare estimates which are (say) 80 percent accurate. Such accuracy is adequate for most managerial decision making. However, to raise this accuracy to (say) 90 percent could readily take 2 months and $3X$ dollars. To raise the accuracy to (say) 95 percent could readily take 6 months and $15X$ dollars. As the time stretches out, the risk increases that managers become impatient, since a good deal of effort is being consumed without outward evidence of some return on the investment. Such programs give the appearance of being on dead center and hence become readily vulnerable to the periodic retrenchment programs undertaken by all companies.

Corporate Totals

In some companies the proponents of the quality cost studies become so preoccupied with corporate totals that years are spent trying to make the figures complete. Meanwhile the preoccupation with the figures delays the undertaking of improvement projects. For example, in one large company, a proposal for conducting quality cost studies across the entire corporation was approved by corporate management. Actually, one division liked the idea, one was tolerant, and the rest were resistant in varying degrees. Three years later, there were still several divisions whose quality costs had not yet been adequately studied. Meanwhile the estimated corporate quality costs had gone from 10.2 percent of corporate sales to 9.9 percent of sales, clearly not a statistically significant change. Then an economic recession resulted in the entire effort being wiped out on the ground of not having justified its costs. Had the proponents limited their studies to the interested and tolerant divisions, they would probably have gotten useful project work accomplished within 1 year. The results achieved could then have been used as a means of enlisting the interest of other divisions, and the concept would have taken firm root.

A similar problem of preoccupation with totals can take place at the division level if there are multiple plants. Even at the plant level, there may be a similar problem due to multiple departments.

PROBLEMS

2-1 Identify the quality cost elements associated with any of the institutions listed below. Define each of the elements, and suggest how each might be quantified in practice: (a) a university; (b) a hospital; (c) the local bus line; (d) a bank; (e) a manufacturer of (any of these): wooden furniture, cotton cloth, men's shoes, glass bottles, castings, drugs; (f) a textbook publisher.

2-2 Conduct a study of the applicability of the Pareto principle to any of the following: (a) causes of human mortality; (b) persons committing crimes; (c) population of countries; (d) population of American cities; (e) sales of American companies.

2-3 The Federated Screw Company manufactures a wide variety of screws for industrial companies to designs usually supplied by customers. Total manufacturing payroll is 260 people with sales of about $4,000,000. Operations are relatively simple but geared to high-volume production. Wire in rolls is fed to heading machines at high speed, where the contour of the screw is formed. Pointers and slotters perform secondary operations. The thread-rolling operation completes the screw configuration. Heat treatment, plating, and sometimes baking are the final steps and are performed by an outside contractor located nearby.

You have been asked to prepare a quality cost summary for the company and have made the following notes:

1. The Quality Control Department is primarily a Final Inspection Department (eight inspectors), who also inspect the incoming wire. Another inspector performs patrol inspection in the Heading Room, checking first and last pieces. The Quality Control Department also handles the checking and setting of all ring, snap, and plug gages used by themselves and production personnel. Salaries of inspectors are approximately $12,000 per year.
2. Quality during manufacture is the responsibility of the operator-setup teams assigned to batteries of about four machines. It is difficult to estimate how much of their time is spent checking setups or checking the running of the machines, so you have not tried to do this as yet. Production has two sorting inspectors, earning $9000 each, who sort lots rejected by Final Inspection.
3. The Engineering Department prepares quotations, designs tools, plans the routing of jobs, and establishes the quality requirements, working from customers' prints. They also do troubleshooting, at a cost of about $10,000 a year. Another $8000 is spent in previewing customers' prints to identify critical dimensions, trying to get such items changed by the customer, and interpreting customers' quality requirements into specifications for use by Federated inspectors and manufacturing personnel.
4. Records of scrap, rework, and customer returns are meager, but you have been able to piece together a certain amount of information from records and estimates.
   a. Scrap from Final Inspection rejections and customer returns amounted to 438,000 and 667,000 pieces, respectively, for the last 2 months.
   b. Customer returns requiring rework average about 1,000,000 pieces per month.

    c. Scrap generated during production is believed to be about half of the total floor scrap (the rest not being quality-related) of 30,000 lbs per month.

    d. Final Inspection rejects an average of 400,000 reworkable pieces per month. These are items that can be flat-rolled or rerolled.

5. Rough cost figures have been obtained from the accountants, who say that scrap items can be figured at $6.00 per thousand pieces, floor scrap at $400 per thousand pounds, reworking of customer returns at $2.00 per thousand pieces, and flat-rolling or rerolling at $0.60 per thousand pieces. All of these figures are supposed to include factory overhead.

    Prepare a quality cost summary on an annual basis. (This example was adapted from one originally prepared by L. A. Seder.)

SUPPLEMENTARY READING

Quality costs in general

1. *Quality Control Handbook,* 3rd ed. (QCH3), sec. 5, "Quality Costs," McGraw-Hill Book Company, New York, 1974.
2. "Quality Costs—What and How," 2nd ed., prepared by Quality Cost-Cost Effectiveness Technical Committee, American Society for Quality Control, 1971. This 54-page booklet is oriented mainly to the scoreboard concept. There is much detail (13 pages) on defining the cost categories. There are also examples of scoreboard format and presentation.
3. "Guide for Reducing Quality Costs," prepared by Quality Costs Technical Committee, American Society for Quality Control, 1977. This 46-page pamphlet is mainly oriented to cost reduction and stresses a formal, procedural approach.
4. *The Cost of Quality* by J. M. Groocock, Pitman Publishing Corporation, New York, 1974. This book by an official of ITT reflects the approach used by that multinational company to reduce its quality costs.
5. "The Quality World of ITT," *Quality Management and Engineering,* January 1975. A journalist's report of the ITT approach.

The Pareto principle

QCH3:

1. The basic concept, pp. 2-16 to 2-19.
2. Use in identifying cost reduction projects, pp. 16-4 to 16-6.
3. For further case examples, see the index under Pareto analysis.

    For examples of application to many types of management activity, see J. M. Juran, *Managerial Breakthrough,* McGraw-Hill Book Company, New York, 1964, chap. 4, "The Pareto Principle." For some history respecting the discovery of the Pareto principle, see J. M. Juran, "The Non-Pareto Principle; Mea Culpa," *Quality Progress,* May 1975, pp. 8, 9.

EXAMPLES OF EXAMINATION QUESTIONS USED IN FORMER ASQC QUALITY ENGINEER CERTIFICATION EXAMINATIONS AS PUBLISHED IN *QUALITY PROGRESS* MAGAZINE

1 When looking for existing sources of internal failure cost data, which of the following is usually the best source available? (*a*) operating budgets; (*b*) sales-personnel field reports; (*c*) labor and material cost documents; (*d*) returned material reports; (*e*) purchase orders.

2 Of the following, which are typically appraisal costs? (*a*) vendor surveys and vendor faults; (*b*) quality planning and quality reports; (*c*) drawing control centers and material dispositions; (*d*) quality audits and final inspection; (*e*) none of the above.

3 When analyzing quality cost data gathered during the *initial* stages of a new management emphasis on quality control and corrective action as part of a product improvement program, one normally expects to see: (*a*) increased prevention costs and decreased appraisal costs; (*b*) increased appraisal costs with little change in prevention costs; (*c*) decreased internal failure costs; (*d*) decreased total quality costs; (*e*) all of these.

4 Quality costs are best classified as: (*a*) cost of inspection and test, cost of quality engineering, cost of quality administration and cost of quality equipment; (*b*) direct, indirect, and overhead; (*c*) cost of prevention, cost of appraisal, and cost of failure; (*d*) unnecessary; (*e*) none of the above.

5 Operating quality costs can be related to different volume bases. An example of volume base that could be used would be: (*a*) direct labor cost; (*b*) standard manufacturing cost; (*c*) processing cost; (*d*) sales; (*e*) all of the above.

6 When operating a quality cost system, excessive costs can be identified when: (*a*) appraisal costs exceed failure costs; (*b*) total quality costs exceed 10 percent of sales; (*c*) appraisal and failure costs are equal; (*d*) total quality costs exceed 4 percent of manufacturing costs; (*e*) there is no fixed rule—management experience must be used.

7 Analyze the following cost data:

$ 10,000	equipment design
150,000	scrap
180,000	reinspection and retest
45,000	loss or disposition of surplus stock
4,000	vendor quality surveys
40,000	repair

Considering only the quality costs shown above, we might conclude that: (*a*) prevention costs should be decreased; (*b*) internal failure costs can be decreased; (*c*) prevention costs are too low a proportion of the quality costs shown; (*d*) appraisal costs should be increased; (*e*) nothing can be concluded.

8 The percentages of total quality cost are distributed as follows:

Prevention	12%
Appraisal	28%
Internal failure	40%
External failure	20%

We conclude: (*a*) We should invest more money in prevention; (*b*) Expenditures for failures are excessive; (*c*) The amount spent for appraisal seems about right; (*d*) Nothing.

THREE

PROBABILITY DISTRIBUTIONS

3-1 STATISTICAL TOOLS IN QUALITY CONTROL

Statistics is the collection, organization, analysis, interpretation, and presentation of data. The application of statistics to engineering (and other fields) has resulted in the recognition that statistics is a complete field in itself. Unfortunately, some people have become so involved in statistics that they have unknowingly become "technique-oriented" instead of remaining "problem-oriented." The student is warned that statistics is just one of many *tools* necessary to solve quality problems. Statistical methods may or may not be required for the solution of a problem. Our objective is to solve problems and not to promote the statistical method as an end in itself.

3-2 THE CONCEPT OF VARIATION

The concept of *variation* states that no two items will be perfectly identical. Variation is a fact of nature and a fact of industrial life. For example, even "identical" twins vary slightly in height and weight at birth. Cans of tomato soup vary slightly in weight from can to can. The overall weight of a particular model of automobile varies slightly from unit to unit on the same model. To disregard the existence of variation (or to rationalize falsely that it is small) can lead to incorrect decisions on major problems. Statistics helps to analyze data properly and draw conclusions, taking into account the existence of variation.

Data summarization can take several forms: tabular, graphical, and numerical indices. Sometimes, one form will provide a useful and complete summarization. In other cases, two or even three forms are needed for complete clarity.

3-3 TABULAR SUMMARIZATION OF DATA: FREQUENCY DISTRIBUTION

A *frequency distribution* is a tabulation of data arranged according to size. The raw data of the electrical resistance of 100 coils are given in Table 3-1. Table 3-2 shows the frequency distribution of these data with all measurements tabulated at their actual values. For examples, there were 14 coils, each of which had a resistance of 3.35 ohms (Ω); there were 5 coils, each of which had a resistance of 3.30 Ω, etc. The frequency distribution spotlights where most of the data are grouped (the data are centered about a resistance of 3.35) and how much variation there is in the data (resistance runs from 3.27 to 3.44 Ω). Table 3-2 shows the conventional frequency distribution and the cumulative frequency distribution in which the frequency values are accumulated to show the number of coils with resistances equal to or less than a specific value. The particular problem determines whether the conventional or cumulative or both distributions are required.

When there are a large number of highly variable data, the frequency distribution can become too large to serve as a summary of the original data. The data may be grouped into *cells* to provide a better summary. Table 3-3 shows the frequency distribution for these data grouped into six cells, each 0.03 wide. Grouping the data into cells condenses the original data, and therefore some detail is lost.

The following is a common procedure for constructing a frequency distribution:

1. Decide on the number of cells. Table 3-4 provides a guide.
2. Calculate the approximate cell interval i. The cell interval equals the larg-

Table 3-1 Resistance (ohms) of 100 coils

3.37	3.34	3.38	3.32	3.33	3.28	3.34	3.31	3.33	3.34
3.29	3.36	3.30	3.31	3.33	3.34	3.34	3.36	3.39	3.34
3.35	3.36	3.30	3.32	3.33	3.35	3.35	3.34	3.?2	3.38
3.32	3.37	3.34	3.38	3.36	3.37	3.36	3.31	3.33	3.30
3.35	3.33	3.38	3.37	3.44	3.32	3.36	3.32	3.29	3.35
3.38	3.39	3.34	3.32	3.30	3.39	3.36	3.40	3.32	3.33
3.29	3.41	3.27	3.36	3.41	3.37	3.36	3.37	3.33	3.36
3.31	3.33	3.35	3.34	3.35	3.34	3.31	3.36	3.37	3.35
3.40	3.35	3.37	3.35	3.32	3.36	3.38	3.35	3.31	3.34
3.35	3.36	3.39	3.31	3.31	3.30	3.35	3.33	3.35	3.31

Table 3-2 Tally of resistance values of 100 coils

Resistance, Ω	Tabulation	Frequency	Cumulative frequency
3.45			
3.44	|	1	1
3.43			
3.42			
3.41	||	2	3
3.40	||	2	5
3.39	||||	4	9
3.38	卌 |	6	15
3.37	卌 |||	8	23
3.36	卌 卌 |||	13	36
3.35	卌 卌 ||||	14	50
3.34	卌 卌 ||	12	62
3.33	卌 卌	10	72
3.32	卌 ||||	9	81
3.31	卌 ||||	9	90
3.30	卌	5	95
3.29	|||	3	98
3.28	|	1	99
3.27	|	1	100
3.26			
Total		100	

Table 3-3 Frequency table of resistance values

Resistance	Frequency
3.415–3.445	1
3.385–3.415	8
3.355–3.385	27
3.325–3.355	36
3.295–3.325	23
3.265–3.295	5
Total	100

Table 3-4 Number of cells in frequency distribution

Number of observations	Recommended number of cells
20–50	6
51–100	7
101–200	8
201–500	9
501–1000	10
Over 1000	11–20

est observation minus the smallest observation divided by the number of cells. Round this result to some convenient number (preferably the nearest *uneven* number with the same amount of significant digits as the actual data).

3. Construct the cells by listing cell boundaries.
   a. The cell boundaries should be to one more significant digit than the actual data and should end in a 5.
   b. The cell interval should be constant throughout the entire frequency distribution.
4. Tally each observation into the appropriate cell and then list the total frequency *f* for each cell.

This procedure should be adjusted when necessary to provide a clear summary of the data and to reveal the underlying pattern of variation.

3-4 GRAPHICAL SUMMARIZATION OF DATA: THE HISTOGRAM

A *histogram* is a vertical bar chart of a frequency distribution. Figure 3-1 shows the histogram for the electrical resistance data. Note that as in the frequency distribution, the histogram highlights the center and amount of variation in the sample of data. The simplicity of construction and interpretation of the histogram makes it an effective tool in the elementary analysis of data.

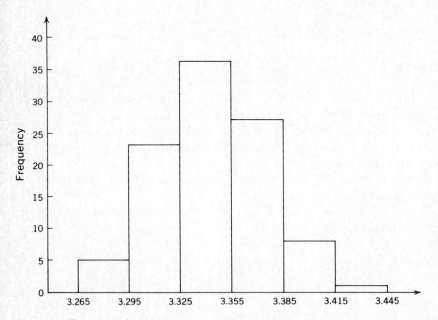

Figure 3-1 Histogram of resistance.

Many problems in quality control have been solved with this one elementary tool alone. Section 3-8 demonstrates how the shape of the histogram provides insights into a manufacturing process that would not otherwise be apparent.

3-5 QUANTITATIVE METHODS OF SUMMARIZING DATA: NUMERICAL INDICES

Data can also be summarized by computing (1) a measure of central tendency to indicate where most of the data are centered, and (2) the measure of dispersion to indicate the amount of scatter in the data. Often these two measures provide an adequate summary.

The key measure of the central tendency is the arithmetic *mean* or *average*.[1] The definition of the average is

$$\bar{X} = \frac{\Sigma X}{n}$$

where $\bar{X}$ = sample mean
X = individual observations
n = number of observations

There are two measures of dispersion commonly calculated. When the number of data are small (10 or fewer observations) the *range* is useful. The range is the difference between the maximum value and the minimum value in the data. As the range is based on only two values, it is not as useful when the number of observations is large.

In general, the *standard deviation* is the most useful measure of dispersion. Like the mean, the definition of the standard deviation is a formula:

$$s = \sqrt{\frac{\Sigma(X - \bar{X})^2}{n - 1}}$$

where s is the sample standard deviation. The square of the standard deviation, s^2, is called the *variance*.

There is usually difficulty in understanding the "meaning" of the standard deviation. The only definition is a formula. There is no hidden meaning to the standard deviation, and it is best viewed as an arbitrary index which shows the amount of variation in a set of data. Later applications of the standard deviation to making predictions will help clarify its meaning.

With data in frequency distribution form, shortcut calculations (particularly with the use of calculators) can be employed to find the average and the standard deviation.[2]

A problem that sometimes arises in the summarization of data is that one or

---

[1] In this book, the terms "mean" and "average" will have the same meaning and will be used interchangeably.

[2] See *Quality Control Handbook*, 3rd ed. (QCH3), pp. 22-7 and 22-8.

more extreme values are far from the rest of the data. A simple (but not necessarily correct) solution is available, i.e., drop such values. The reasoning is that a measurement error or some other unknown factor makes the values "unrepresentative." Unfortunately, this may be rationalizing to eliminate an annoying problem of data analysis. The decision to keep or discard extreme values rests with the investigator. However, statistical tests are available to help make the decision.[3]

3-6 PROBABILITY DISTRIBUTIONS: GENERAL

A distinction is made between a sample and a population. A *sample* is a limited number of items taken from a larger source. A *population* is a large source of items from which the sample is taken. Measurements are made on the items. Many problems are solved by taking the measurement results from a sample and based on these results making predictions about the defined *population* containing the sample. It is usually assumed that the sample is a random one; i.e., each possible sample of *n* items has an equal chance of being selected (or the items are selected systematically from material that is itself random due to mixing during processing).

A *probability distribution function* is a mathematical formula that relates the values of the characteristic with their probability of occurrence in the *population*. The collection of these probabilities is called a *probability distribution*. Some distributions and their functions are summarized in Figure 3-2. Distributions are of two types:

1. *Continuous* (for "variables" data). When the characteristic being measured can take on any value (subject to the fineness of the measuring process), its probability distribution is called a continuous probability distribution. For example, the probability distribution for the resistance data of Table 3-1 is an example of a continuous probability distribution because the resistance could have any value, limited only by the fineness of the measuring instrument. Experience has shown that most continuous characteristics follow one of several common probability distributions, i.e., the "normal" distribution, the "exponential" distribution, and the "Weibull" distribution. These distributions find the probabilities associated with occurrences of the *actual values* of the characteristic. Other continuous distributions (e.g., t, F, and chi square) are important in data analysis but are not helpful in directly predicting the probability of occurrence of actual values.

2. *Discrete* (for "attributes" data). When the characteristic being measured can take on only certain specific values (e.g., integers 0, 1, 2, 3, etc.), its probability distribution is called a discrete probability distribution. For example, the distribution for the number of defectives r in a sample of five items is

---

[3] See QCH3, p. 22-43.

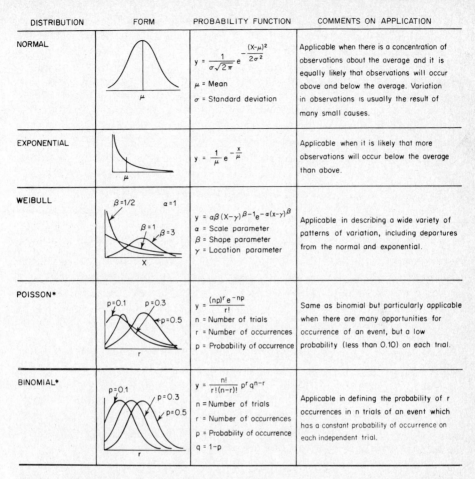

DISTRIBUTION	FORM	PROBABILITY FUNCTION	COMMENTS ON APPLICATION
NORMAL		$y = \dfrac{1}{\sigma\sqrt{2\pi}}\, e^{-\frac{(X-\mu)^2}{2\sigma^2}}$ μ = Mean σ = Standard deviation	Applicable when there is a concentration of observations about the average and it is equally likely that observations will occur above and below the average. Variation in observations is usually the result of many small causes.
EXPONENTIAL		$y = \dfrac{1}{\mu}\, e^{-\frac{x}{\mu}}$	Applicable when it is likely that more observations will occur below the average than above.
WEIBULL		$y = \alpha\beta\,(X-\gamma)^{\beta-1} e^{-\alpha(x-\gamma)^{\beta}}$ α = Scale parameter β = Shape parameter γ = Location parameter	Applicable in describing a wide variety of patterns of variation, including departures from the normal and exponential.
POISSON*		$y = \dfrac{(np)^r e^{-np}}{r!}$ n = Number of trials r = Number of occurrences p = Probability of occurrence	Same as binomial but particularly applicable when there are many opportunities for occurrence of an event, but a low probability (less than 0.10) on each trial.
BINOMIAL*		$y = \dfrac{n!}{r!(n-r)!}\, p^r q^{n-r}$ n = Number of trials r = Number of occurrences p = Probability of occurrence q = 1-p	Applicable in defining the probability of r occurrences in n trials of an event which has a constant probability of occurrence on each independent trial.

Figure 3-2 Summary of common probability distributions. (Asterisks indicate that these are discrete distributions, but the curves are shown as continuous for ease of comparison with the continuous distributions.)

a discrete probability distribution because *r* can only be 0, 1, 2, 3, 4, or 5. The common discrete distributions are the Poisson and binomial (see Figure 3-2).

The following paragraphs explain how probability distributions can be used with a sample of observations to make predictions about the larger population.

3-7 THE NORMAL PROBABILITY DISTRIBUTION

Many engineering characteristics can be approximated by the *normal distribution function*:

$$y = \frac{1}{\sigma\sqrt{2\pi}}\, e^{-(X-\mu)^2/2\sigma^2}$$

where $e = 2.718$
$\pi = 3.141$
μ = population mean
σ = population standard deviation

Problems are solved with a table, but note that the distribution requires only the average μ and standard deviation σ of the population.[4] The curve for the normal probability distribution is related to a frequency distribution and its histogram. As the sar.., e becomes larger and larger, and the width of each cell becomes smaller and smaller, the histogram approaches a smooth curve. If the entire population[5] were measured, and if it were normally distributed, the result would be as shown in Figure 3-2. Thus the *shape* of a histogram of sample data provides some indication of the probability distribution for the population. If the histogram resembles[6] the "bell" shape shown in Figure 3-2, this is a basis for assuming that the population follows a normal probability distribution.

Making Predictions Using the Normal Probability Distribution

Predictions require just two estimates and a table. The estimates are:

$$\text{Estimate of } \mu = \bar{X} \qquad \text{Estimate of } \sigma = s$$

The calculations of the sample $\bar{X}$ and s are made by the methods previously discussed.

For example, from past experience, a manufacturer concludes that the burnout time of a particular light bulb follows a normal distribution. A sample of 50 bulbs has been tested and the average life found to be 60 days with a standard deviation of 20 days. How many bulbs in the entire population of light bulbs can be expected to be still working after 100 days of life?

The problem is to find the area under the curve beyond 100 days (see Figure 3-3). The area under a distribution curve between two stated limits represents the probability of occurrence. Therefore, the area beyond 100 days is the probability that a bulb will last more than 100 days. To find the area, calculate the difference Z between a particular value and the average of the curve in units of standard deviation:

$$Z = \frac{X - \mu}{\sigma}$$

In this problem $Z = (100 - 60) \div 20 = +2.0$. Table A in the Appendix shows a

---

[4] Unless otherwise indicated, Greek symbols will be used for population values and Roman symbols for sample values.

[5] In practice, the population is usually considered infinite, e.g., the potential production from a process.

[6] It is *not* necessary that the sample histogram look as if it came from a normal population. The assumption of normality is applied only to the population. Small deviations from normality are expected in random samples.

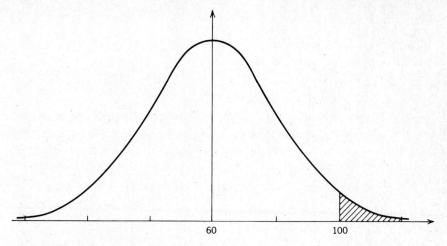

Figure 3-3 Distribution of light bulb life.

probability of 0.9773 for $Z = 2$. The statistical distribution tables in this edition provide probabilities that cover the span from $-\infty$ up to and including the value of X included in the formula. Thus 0.9773 is the probability that a bulb will last 100 days or less. The normal curve is symmetrical about the average and the total area is 1.000. The probability of a bulb lasting more than 100 days then is $1.0000 - 0.9773$, or 0.0227, or 2.27 percent of the bulbs in the population will still be working after 100 days.

Similarly, if a characteristic is normally distributed and if estimates of the average and standard deviation of the population are obtained, this method can estimate the total percent of production that will fall within engineering specification limits.

Figure 3-4 shows representative areas under the normal distribution curve.[7] Thus 68.26 percent of the *population* will fall between the average of the population plus or minus 1 standard deviation of the population, 95.46 percent of the population will fall between the average of $\pm 2\sigma$, and finally, $\pm 3\sigma$ will include 99.73 percent of the population. The percentage of a *sample* within a set of limits can be quite different from the percentage within the same limits in the population.

3-8 THE NORMAL CURVE AND HISTOGRAM ANALYSIS

As many manufacturing processes produce results which reasonably follow a normal distribution, it is useful to combine the histogram concept and the normal curve concept to yield a practical working tool known as *histogram analysis*.

---

[7] These can be derived from Table A in the Appendix.

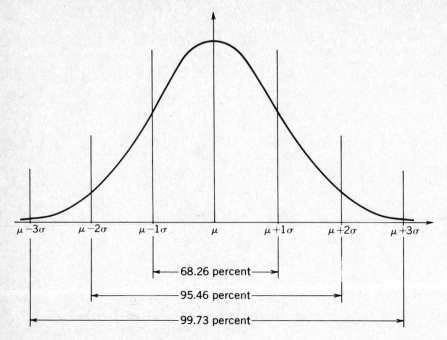

Figure 3-4 Areas of the normal curve.

A random sample is selected from the process and measurements are made for the selected quality characteristics. A histogram is prepared and specification limits are added. Knowledge of the manufacturing process is then combined with insights provided by the histogram to draw conclusions about the ability of the process to meet the specifications.

Figure 3-5 shows 12 typical histograms. The student is encouraged to interpret each of these pictures by asking two questions:

1. Does the process have the ability to meet the specification limits?
2. What action, if any, is appropriate on the process?

These questions can be answered by analyzing:

1. *The centering of the histogram.* This defines the aim of the process.
2. *The width of the histogram.* This defines the variability about the aim.
3. *The shape of the histogram.* When a normal or bell-shaped curve is expected, then any significant deviation or other aberration is usually caused by a manufacturing (or other) condition that may be the root of the quality problem. For example, histograms with two or more peaks may reveal that several "populations" have been mixed together.

Histograms illustrate how variables data provide much more information

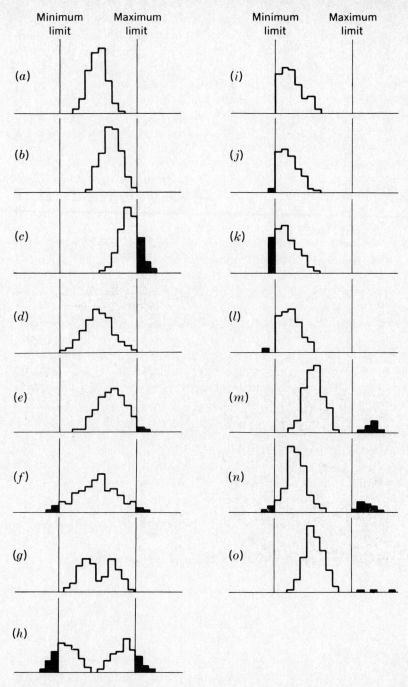

Figure 3-5 Distributions patterns related to tolerances. (Adapted from G. R. Armstrong and P. C. Clarke, "Frequency Distribution vs. Acceptance Table," *Industrial Quality Control,* vol. 3, no. 2, September 1946, pp. 22–27.)

than do attributes data. For example, Figure 3-5*b*, *d*, *g*, and *i* warn of potential trouble even though all units in the sample are within specification limits. With attributes measurement, all the units would simply be classified as acceptable and the inspection report would have stated "50 inspected, 0 defective"—therefore no problem. One customer had a dramatic experience based on a lot which yielded a sample histogram similar to Figure 3-5*i*. Although the sample indicated that the lot met quality requirements, the customer realized that the vendor must have made much scrap and screened it out before delivery. A rough calculation indicated that full production must have been about 25 percent defective. The histogram enabled the customer to deduce this *without ever having been inside the vendor's plant*. Note how the "product tells on the process." As the customer would eventually pay for this scrap (in the selling price), he wanted the situation corrected. The vendor was contacted and advice was offered in a constructive manner.

As a general rule, at least 50 measurements are needed for the histogram to reveal the basic pattern of variation. Histograms based on too few measurements can lead to incorrect conclusions, because the shape of the histogram may be incomplete without the observer realizing it. Note that the discussion here is based on the assumption of normality.

Histograms have limitations. Since the samples are taken at random rather than in the order of manufacture, the time to time process trends during manufacture are not disclosed. Hence the seeming central tendency of a histogram may be illusory—the process may have drifted substantially. In like manner, the histogram does not disclose whether the vendor's process was operating at its best, i.e., whether it was in a state of statistical control (see Chapter 12).

In spite of these shortcomings, the histogram is an effective analytical tool. The key to its usefulness is its simplicity. It speaks a language that everyone understands—comparison of product measurements against specification limits. To draw useful conclusions from this comparison requires little experience in interpreting frequency distributions, and no formal training in statistics. The experience soon expands, to include applications in development, manufacturing, vendor relations, and field data.

3-9 THE EXPONENTIAL PROBABILITY DISTRIBUTION

The *exponential probability function* is

$$y = \frac{1}{\mu} e^{-X/\mu}$$

Figure 3-2 shows the shape of an exponential distribution curve. Note that the normal and exponential distributions have distinctly different shapes. An examination of the tables of areas shows that 50 percent of a normally distributed population occurs above the mean value and 50 percent below. In an exponential population, 36.8 percent are above the mean and 63.2 percent below the mean. This refutes the intuitive idea that the mean is always associated with a 50 percent probability. The exponential describes the loading pattern for some structural members because smaller loads are more numerous than are larger loads. The exponential is also useful in describing the distribution of failure times of complex equipments.

Making Predictions Using the Exponential Probability Distribution

Predictions based on an exponentially distributed population require only an estimate of the population mean. For example, the time between successive failures of a complex piece of repairable equipment is measured and the resulting histogram is found to resemble the exponential probability curve. For the measurements made, the *mean time between failures* (commonly called MTBF) is 100 h. What is the probability that the time between two successive failures of this equipment will be at least 20 h?

The problem is one of finding the area under the curve beyond 20 h (Figure 3-6). Table B in the Appendix gives the area under the curve beyond any particular value X that is substituted in the ratio X/μ. In this problem,

$$\frac{X}{\mu} = \frac{20}{100} = 0.20$$

From Table B the area under the curve beyond 20 h is 0.8187. The probability that the time between two successive failures is greater than 20 hours is 0.8187; i.e., there is about an 82 percent chance that the equipment will operate without failure continuously for 20 or more hours. Similar calculations would give a probability of 0.9048 for 10 or more hours.

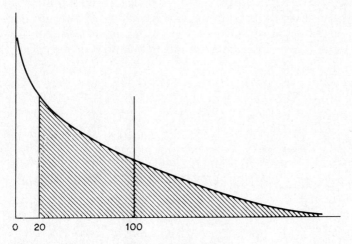

Figure 3-6 Distribution of time between failures.

3-10 THE WEIBULL PROBABILITY DISTRIBUTION

The *Weibull distribution* is a family of distributions having the general function

$$y = \alpha\beta(X - \gamma)^{\beta-1} e^{-\alpha(X-\gamma)\beta}$$

where α = scale parameter
β = shape parameter
γ = location parameter

The curve of the function (Figure 3-2) varies greatly depending on the numerical values of the parameters. Most important is the shape parameter β, which reflects the pattern of the curve. Note that when β is 1.0, the Weibull function reduces to the exponential and that when β is about 3.5 (and $\alpha = 1$ and $\gamma = 0$), the Weibull closely approximates the normal distribution. In practice, β varies from about $\frac{1}{3}$ to 5. The scale parameter α is related to the peakedness of the curve; i.e., as α changes, the curve becomes flatter or more peaked. The location parameter γ is the smallest possible value of X. This is often assumed to be 0, thereby simplifying the equation. It is often unnecessary to determine the values of these parameters because predictions are made directly from Weibull probability paper, but King[8] gives procedures for graphically finding α, β, and γ.

The Weibull covers many shapes of distributions. This makes it popular in practice because it reduces the problems of examining a set of data and deciding which of the common distributions (e.g., normal or exponential) fits best.

Making Predictions Using the Weibull Probability Distribution

An analytical approach for the Weibull distribution (even with tables) is cumbersome, and the predictions are usually made with Weibull probability paper. For example, seven heat-treated shafts were stress-tested until each of them failed. The fatigue life (in terms of number of cycles to failure) was as follows:

11,251	40,122
17,786	46,638
26,432	52,374
28,811	

The problem is to predict the percent of failures of the population for various values of fatigue life. The solution is to plot the data on Weibull paper, observe

---

[8] James R. King, *Probability Charts for Decision Making,* The Industrial Press, New York, 1971.

Table 3-5 Table of mean ranks

Failure number (i)	Mean rank
1	0.125
2	0.250
3	0.375
4	0.500
5	0.625
6	0.750
7	0.875

if the points fall approximately in a straight line, and if so, read the probability predictions (percentage failure) from the graph.

In a Weibull plot, the original data are usually[9] plotted against *mean ranks*. (Thus the mean rank for the ith value in a sample of n ranked observations refers to the mean value of the percent of the population that would be less than the ith value in repeated experiments of size n.) The mean rank is calculated as $i/(n + 1)$. The mean ranks necessary for this example are based on a sample size of seven failures and are as shown in Table 3-5. The cycles to failure are now plotted on the Weibull graph paper against the corresponding values of the mean rank (see Figure 3-7). These points fall approximately in a straight line, so it is assumed that the Weibull distribution applies. The vertical axis gives the cumulative percent of failures in the population corresponding to the fatigue life shown on the horizontal axis. For example, about 50 percent of the population of shafts will fail in fewer than 32,000 cycles. About 80 percent of the population will fail in fewer than 52,000 cycles. By appropriate subtractions, predictions can be made of the percent of failures between any two fatigue life limits.

It is tempting to extrapolate on probability paper, particularly to predict life. For example, suppose that the minimum fatigue life were specified as 8000 cycles and the seven measurements displayed earlier were from tests conducted to evaluate the ability of the design to meet 8000 cycles. As all seven tests exceeded 8000 cycles, the design seems adequate and therefore should be released for production. However, extrapolation on the Weibull paper predicts that about 5 percent of the *population* of shafts would fail in less than 8000 cycles. This suggests a review of the design before release to production. Thus the small *sample* (all *within* specifications) gives a deceiving result, but the Weibull plot acts as an alarm signal by highlighting a potential problem.

Extrapolation can go in the other direction. Note that a probability plot of life-test data does *not* require that all tests be completed before the plotting starts. As each unit fails, the failure time can be plotted against the mean

---

[9] There are other plotting positions. See, for example, QCH3, p. 22-16.

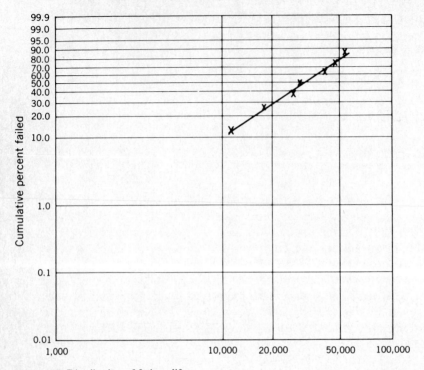

Figure 3-7 Distribution of fatigue life.

rank. If the early points appear to be following a straight line, it is tempting to draw in the line *before* all tests are finished. The line can then be extrapolated beyond the actual test data and life predictions can be made without accumulating a large amount of test time. The approach has been applied to predicting *early* in a warranty period the "vital few" components of a complex product that will be most troublesome. However, extrapolation has dangers. It requires the judicious melding of statistical theory and engineering experience and judgment.

To make a valid Weibull plot, at least seven points are needed. Any less casts doubt on the ability of the plot to reveal the underlying pattern of variation. When the plot is prepared, it is hoped that the points will approximate a straight line. This then implies a single stable population and the line can be used for predictions. However, non-straight-line plots are often extremely valuable (in the same way as nonnormal histograms) in suggesting that several populations have been mixed together.

Probability graph paper is available for the normal, exponential, Weibull, and other probability distributions.[10] Although the mathematical functions and tables provide the same information, the graph paper reveals *relationships* be-

[10] A source is Technical and Engineering Aids for Management, Lowell, Massachusetts 01852.

tween probabilities and values of X that are not readily apparent from the calculations. For example, the reduction in percent defective in a population as a function of wider and wider tolerance limits can be easily portrayed by the graph paper.

3-11 THE POISSON PROBABILITY DISTRIBUTION

If the probability of occurrence p of an event is constant on each of n independent trials of the event, the probability of r occurrences in n trials is

$$\frac{(np)^r e^{-np}}{r!}$$

where n = number of trials
p = probability of occurrence
r = number of occurrences

Making Predictions Using the Poisson Distribution

The Poisson is useful in calculating probabilities associated with sampling procedures. Appendix C directly gives cumulative Poisson probabilities, i.e., the probability of r or fewer occurrences in n trials of an event having probability p. For example, suppose that a lot of 300 units of product is submitted by a vendor whose past quality has been about 2 percent defective. A random sample of 40 units is selected from the lot. Table C in the Appendix provides the probability of r or less defectives in a sample of n units.[11] Entering the table with a value of np equal to 40(0.02), or 0.8, for various values of r results in Table 3-6. Individual probabilities can be found by subtracting cumulative probabilities. Thus the probability of exactly 2 defectives is $0.953 - 0.809$, or 0.144. Of course, the probabilities in Table 3-6 could also be found by substituting into the formula six times ($r = 0, 1, 2, 3, 4, 5$).

The Poisson is an approximation to more exact distributions and applies when the sample size is at least 16, the population size is at least 10 times the

[11] The application of these probabilities is explained in Chapter 18.

Table 3-6 Table of Poisson probabilities

r	Probability of r or fewer in sample
0	0.449
1	0.809
2	0.953
3	0.991
4	0.999
5	1.000

sample size, and the probability of occurrence p on each trial is less than 0.1. These conditions are often met.

3-12 THE BINOMIAL PROBABILITY DISTRIBUTION

If the conditions of the Poisson distribution are not met, the binomial distribution may be applicable. If the probability of occurrence p of an event is constant on each of n independent trials of the event, then the probability of r occurrences in n trials is:

$$\frac{n!}{r!(n-r)!} p^r q^{n-r}$$

where $q = 1 - p$.

In practice, the assumption of a constant probability of occurrence is considered reasonable when the population size is at least 10 times the sample size.[12] (Note that the binomial has fewer conditions than the Poisson.)

Tables for the binomial are available.[13]

Making Predictions Using the Binomial Probability Distribution

A lot of 100 units of product is submitted by a vendor whose past quality has been about 5 percent defective. A random sample of 6 units is selected from the lot. The probabilities of various sample results are given in Table 3-7.

In using the formula, note that $0! = 1$.

---

[12] Under this condition, the change in probability from one trial to the next is negligible. If this condition is not met, the hypergeometric distribution should be used. See *Quality Control Handbook*, 3rd ed., p. 22-19.

[13] See QCH3, app II, pp. 13–15.

Table 3-7 Table of binomial probabilities

r	P (exactly r defectives in 6) $=$ $[6!/r!(6-r)!](0.05)^r(0.95)^{6-r}$
0	0.7351
1	0.2321
2	0.0306
3	0.0021
4	0.0001
5	0.0000
6	0.0000

3-13 TESTING A DISTRIBUTION ASSUMPTION

In practice, a distribution is assumed by evaluating a sample of data. Often, it is sufficient to evaluate the shape of the histogram or the degree to which a plot on probability paper follows a straight line. These convenient methods do require judgment (e.g., how "straight" must the line be?) because the sample is never a perfect fit. Be suspicious of the data if the fit is "perfect." *Goodness-of-fit tests* evaluate any distribution assumption using quantitative criteria.[14]

3-14 BASIC THEOREMS OF PROBABILITY

Probability is expressed as a number which lies between 1.0 (certainty that an event will occur) and 0.0 (impossibility of occurrence).

A convenient definition of probability is one based on a frequency interpretation: If an event A can occur in s cases out of a total of n possible and equally probable cases, the probability that the event will occur is

$$P(A) = \frac{s}{n} = \frac{\text{number of successful cases}}{\text{total number of possible cases}}$$

Example A lot consists of 100 parts. A single part is selected at random, and thus, each of the 100 parts has an equal chance of being selected. Suppose that a lot contains a total of 8 defectives. Then the probability of drawing a single part that is defective is then 8/100, or 0.08.

The following theorems are useful in solving problems:

Theorem 1 If $P(A)$ is the probability that an event A will occur, then the probability that A will not occur is $1 - P(A)$.

Theorem 2 If A and B are two events, then the probability that either A or B occurs is

$$P(A \text{ or } B) = P(A) + P(B) - P(A \text{ and } B)$$

A special case of this theorem occurs when A and B cannot occur simultaneously (i.e., A and B are *mutually exclusive*). Then the probability that either A or B occurs is

$$P(A \text{ or } B) = P(A) + P(B)$$

Example The probabilities of r defectives in a sample of 6 units from a 5 percent defective lot were found previously by the binomial. The probabil-

[14] See QCH3, p. 22-44.

ity of 0 defectives was 0.7351; the probability of 1 defective was 0.2321. The probability of 0 or 1 defective is then 0.7351 + 0.2321, or 0.9672.

Theorem 3 If A and B are two events, then the probability that events A and B occur together is

$$P(A \text{ and } B) = P(A) \times P(B|A)$$

where $P(B|A)$ = probability that B will occur assuming A has already occurred.

A special case of this theorem occurs when the two events are independent, i.e., when the occurrence of one event has no influence on the probability of the other event. If A and B are independent, then the probability of both A and B occurring is

$$P(A \text{ and } B) = P(A) \times P(B)$$

Example A complex system consists of two major subsystems that operate independently. The probability of successful performance of the first subsystem is 0.95; the corresponding probability for the second subsystem is 0.90. Both subsystems must operate successfully in order to achieve total system success. The probability of the successful operation of the total system is therefore $0.95 \times 0.90 = 0.855$.

The theorems above have been stated in terms of two events but can be expanded for any number of events.

PROBLEMS

Note: Many of the statistical problems in the book have intentionally been stated in industrial language. Thus the specific statistical technique required will often *not* be specified. Hopefully, the student will then gain some experience in translating the industrial problem to a statistical formulation and then choosing the appropriate statistical technique.

3-1 The following data consist of 80 potency measurements of the drug streptomycin.

4.1	5.0	2.0	2.6	4.5	8.1	5.7	2.5
3.5	6.3	5.5	1.6	6.1	5.9	9.3	4.2
4.9	5.6	3.8	4.4	7.1	4.6	7.4	3.5
4.9	5.1	4.6	6.3	8.3	6.3	8.8	1.0
5.3	5.4	4.4	2.9	7.5	5.7	5.3	3.0
4.2	5.2	7.0	3.7	6.7	5.8	6.9	2.8
6.0	8.2	6.1	7.3	8.2	6.2	4.3	2.2
5.2	5.5	3.5	7.1	7.9	5.6	5.4	3.9
6.8	8.2	4.2	4.2	5.5	6.2	3.5	3.4
6.8	4.7	4.6	4.1	4.7	5.0	3.4	7.1

(*a*) Summarize the data in tabular form.
(*b*) Summarize the data in graphical form.

3-2 The data below are 50 measurements on the pitch rating of pulp.

95	87	110	113	85
78	92	101	115	78
81	81	61	109	103
73	74	122	60	102
101	66	109	77	93
91	84	116	87	107
93	74	123	100	80
102	95	115	81	94
99	124	93	60	93
93	108	90	95	64

   (*a*) Summarize the data in tabular form.
   (*b*) Summarize the data in graphical form.

3-3 Compute a measure of central tendency and two measures of variation for the data given in Problem 3-1.

3-4 Compute a measure of central tendency and two measures of variation for the data given in Problem 3-2.

3-5 From past data, a manufacturer of a photographic film base knows that the tensile modulus of the film base follows the normal distribution. Data show an average modulus of 521,000 psi with a standard deviation of 13,000 psi.

   (*a*) The lower specification limit is 495,000 psi. If there is no upper specification limit, what percent of the film base will meet the specification?
   (*b*) What percent of the film base will have a modulus exceeding 550,000 psi?
   (*c*) What recommendations would you make?
   Answer: (*a*) 97.72 percent. (*b*) 1.29 percent.

3-6 A company has a filling machine for low-pressure oxygen shells. Data collected over the past 2 months show an average weight after filling of 1.433 g with a standard deviation of 0.033 g. The specification for weight is 1.460 ± 0.085 g. Weight is normally distributed.

   (*a*) What percent will not meet the weight specification?
   (*b*) Would you suggest a shift in the aim of the filling machine? Why or why not?

3-7 A company that makes fasteners has government specifications on a self-locking nut. The locking torque has both a maximum and a minimum specified. The offsetting machine used to make these nuts has been producing nuts with an average locking torque of 8.62 in-lb, and a variance σ^2 of 4.49 in-lb. Torque is normally distributed.

   (*a*) If the upper specification is 13.0 in-lb and the lower specification is 2.25 in-lb, what percent of these nuts will meet the specification limits?
   (*b*) Another machine in the offset department can turn out the nuts with an average of 8.91 in-lb and a standard deviation of 2.33 in-lb. In a lot of 1000 nuts, how many would have too high a torque?
   Answer: (*a*) 97.95 percent. (*b*) 40 nuts.

3-8 A power company defines service continuity as providing electric power within specified frequency and voltage limits to the customer's service entrance. Interruption of this service may be caused by equipment malfunctions or line outages due to planned maintenance or to unscheduled reasons. Records for the entire city indicate that there were 416 unscheduled interruptions in 1967 and 503 in 1966.

   (*a*) Calculate the mean time between unscheduled interruptions assuming power is to be supplied continuously.
   (*b*) What is the chance that power will be supplied to all users without interruption for at least 24 h? For at least 48 h? Assume an exponential distribution.

3-9 An analysis was made of repair time for an electrohydraulic servovalve used in fatigue test equipment. Discussions concluded that about 90 percent of all repairs could be made within 6 h.

(a) Assuming an exponential distribution of repair time, calculate the average repair time.

(b) What is the probability that a repair would take between 3 and 6 h?

Answer: (a) 2.6 h. (b) 0.217.

3-10 Three designs of a certain shaft are to be compared. The information on the designs is summarized as:

	Design I	Design II	Design III
Material	Medium-carbon alloy steel	Medium-carbon unalloyed steel	Low-carbon special analysis steel
Process	Fully machined before heat treatment, then furnace-heated, oil-quenched, and tempered	Fully machined before heat treatment, then induction-scan-heated, water-quenched, and tempered	Fully machined before heat treatment, then furnace-heated, water-quenched, and tempered

	Design I	Design II	Design III
Equipment cost	Already available	$125,000	$500
Cost of finished shaft	$57	$53	$55

Fatigue tests were run on six shafts of each design with the following results (in units of thousands of cycles to failure):

I	II	III
180	210	900
240	360	1400
100	575	1500
50	330	340
220	130	850
110	575	600

(a) Rearrange the data in ascending order and make a Weibull plot for each design.

(b) For each design, estimate the number of cycles at which 10 percent of the population will fail. (This is called the B_{10} life.) Do the same for 50 percent of the population.

(c) Calculate the average life for each design based on the test results. Then estimate the percentage of the population that will fail within this average life. Note that it is not 50 percent.

(d) Comment on replacing the current design I with II or III.

3-11 Life tests on a sample of 5 units were conducted to evaluate a component design before release to production. The units failed at the following times:

Unit number	Failure time, h
1	1200
2	1900
3	2800
4	3500
5	4500

Suppose that the component was guaranteed to last 1000 h. Any failures during this period must be replaced by the manufacturer at a cost of $200 each. Although the number of test data is small, management wants an estimate of the cost of replacements. If 4000 of these components are sold, provide a dollar estimate of the replacement cost.

SUPPLEMENTARY READING

The *Quality Control Handbook,* 3rd ed., McGraw-Hill Book Company, New York, 1974, includes a number of sections devoted to statistical methods. Pages 22-1 to 22-20 discusses methods of summarizing data and also probability distributions.

A good source of statistical methods as applied to quality control is provided in Acheson J. Duncan, *Quality Control and Industrial Statistics,* 4th ed., Richard D. Irwin, Inc., Homewood, Ill., 1974.

EXAMPLES OF EXAMINATION QUESTIONS USED IN FORMER ASQC QUALITY ENGINEER CERTIFICATION EXAMINATIONS AS PUBLISHED IN *QUALITY PROGRESS* MAGAZINE

1 The sum of the squared deviations of a group of measurements from their mean divided by the number of measurements equals: (*a*) σ; (*b*) σ^2; (*c*) zero; (*d*) $\overline{X}$; (*e*) the mean deviation.

2 The mean of either a discrete or a continuous distribution can always be visualized as: (*a*) the point where 50 percent of the values are to the left side and 50 percent are to the right side; (*b*) its center of gravity; (*c*) the point where the most values in the distribution occur; (*d*) all of the above.

3 The lengths of a certain bushing are normally distributed with mean $\overline{X}'$. How many standard deviation units, symmetrical about $\overline{X}'$, will include 80 percent of the lengths? (*a*) ± 1.04; (*b*) ± 0.52; (*c*) ± 1.28; (*d*) ± 0.84.

4 An inspection plan is set up to randomly sample 3 ft of a 100 ft cable and accept the cable if no flaws are found in the 3 ft length. What is the probability that a cable with an average of 1 flaw per foot will be rejected by the plan? (*a*) 0.05; (*b*) 0.95; (*c*) 0.72; (*d*) 0.03; (*e*) 0.10.

5 When using the Poisson as an approximation to the binomial the following conditions apply for the best approximation: (*a*) larger sample size and larger fraction defective; (*b*) larger sample size and smaller fraction defective; (*c*) smaller sample size and larger fraction defective; (*d*) smaller sample size and smaller fraction defective.

6 A process is producing material which is 40 percent defective. Four pieces are selected at random for inspection. What is the probability of exactly one good piece being found in the sample? (*a*) 0.870; (*b*) 0.575; (*c*) 0.346; (*d*) 0.130; (*e*) 0.154.

7 The probability of observing at least one defective in a random sample of size 10 drawn from a population that has been producing, on the average, ten percent defective units is: (a) $(0.10)^{10}$; (b) $(0.90)^{10}$; (c) $1 - (0.10)^{10}$; (d) $1 - (0.90)^{10}$; (e) $(0.10)(0.90)^9$.

8 A process is turning out end items that have defects of type A or type B or both in them. If the probability of a type A defect is 0.10 and of a type B defect is 0.20, the probability that an end item will have no defects is: (a) 0.02; (b) 0.28; (c) 0.30; (d) 0.72; (e) 0.68.

9 A trip is contemplated with an automobile equipped with four well-used tires on the wheels plus an equally well-used spare. Because of the poor condition of the five tires, the probability that any tire will experience a blowout during the trip is estimated to be 0.50. What is the expected probability of successful trip completion (in the sense that no more than one blowout will occur which would necessitate the purchase of a tire enroute)? (a) 0.0625; (b) 0.5000; (c) 0.0313; (d) 0.3125.

STATISTICAL AIDS FOR ANALYZING DATA

4-1 SCOPE OF DATA ANALYSIS

Here are some types of problems that can benefit from statistical analysis:

1. Determination of the usefulness of a limited number of test results in estimating the true value of a product characteristic.
2. Determination of the number of tests required to provide adequate data for evaluation.
3. Comparison of test data between two alternative designs, or comparison of test data from one design with the specification values.
4. Planning of experiments to determine the significant variable influencing a performance characteristic.
5. Determination of the quantitative relationship between two or more variables.

This chapter presents the statistical methods for handling these problems.

4-2 STATISTICAL INFERENCE

Drawing conclusions from a small number of data can be notoriously unreliable. The "gossip" of a small sample size can be dangerous. Examine the following problems concerned with the evaluation of test data. For each, give a yes or no answer based on your intuitive analysis of the problem. (Write your answers on a piece of paper *now* and then check for the correct answers at the end of this chapter.) Some of the problems are solved in the chapter.

Examples of Engineering Problems That Can Be Solved Using the Concepts of Statistical Inference

1. A single-cavity molding process has been producing insulators with an average impact strength of 5.15 ft-lb [6.9834 Newton-meters (N-m)]. A group of 12 insulators from a new lot shows an average of 4.952 ft-lb (6.7149 N-m). Is this enough evidence to conclude that the new lot is lower in average strength?

2. Past data show the average hardness of brass parts to be 49.95. A new design is submitted and claimed to have higher hardness. A sample of 61 parts of the new design shows an average of 54.62. Does the new design actually have a different hardness?

3. Two types of spark plugs were tested for wear. A sample of 10 of design 1 showed an average wear of 0.0049 in (0.0124 cm). A sample of 8 of design 2 showed an average wear of 0.0064 in (0.0163 cm). Are these enough data to conclude that design 1 is better than design 2?

4. Only 11.7 percent of the 60 new-alloy blades on a turbine rotor failed on test in a gas turbine where 20 percent have shown failures in a series of similar tests in the past. Are the new blades better?

5. 1050 resistors supplied by one manufacturer were 3.71 percent defective. 1690 similar resistors from another manufacturer were 1.95 percent defective. Can one reasonably assert that the product of one plant is inferior to that of the other?

You probably had some incorrect answers. The statistical methods used to properly analyze these problems are called *statistical inference*. We shall start with the concept of sampling variation and sampling distributions.

4-3 SAMPLING VARIATION AND SAMPLING DISTRIBUTIONS

Suppose that a battery is to be evaluated to assure that life requirements are met. A mean life of 30 h is desired. Preliminary data indicate that life follows a normal distribution and that the standard deviation is equal to 10 h. A sample of four batteries is selected at random from the process and tested. If the mean of the four is close to 30 h, it is concluded that the battery meets the specification. Figure 4-1 plots the distribution of *individual* batteries from the population assuming that the true *mean* of the population is exactly 30 h.

If a sample of four is life-tested, the following lifetimes might result: 34, 28, 38, and 24, giving a mean of 31.0. However, this is a random sample selected from the many batteries made by the same process. Suppose that another

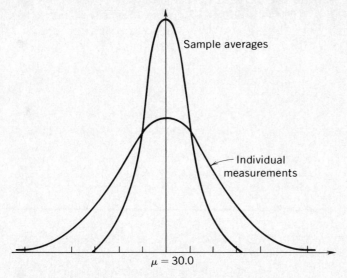

Figure 4-1 Distributions of individuals and sample means.

sample of four were taken. The second sample of four would likely be different from the first sample. Perhaps the results would be 40, 32, 18, and 29, giving a mean of 29.8. If the process of drawing many samples (with four in each sample) were repeated over and over, different results would be obtained in most samples. This is significant because *all* the samples were drawn from the *same* process. This outcome of different sample results illustrates the concept of sampling variation.

Returning to the problem of evaluating the battery, a dilemma exists. In the actual evaluation, only one sample of four can be drawn (because of time and cost limitations). Yet the experiment of drawing many samples indicates that samples vary. The question is how reliable is that sample of four that will be the basis of the decision. The final decision can be influenced by the luck of which sample is chosen. The key point is that the existence of sampling variation means that any one sample cannot be relied upon to always give an adequate decision. The statistical approach analyzes the results of the sample, *taking into account the possible sampling variation that could occur.* Formulas have been developed defining the expected amount of sampling variation. Knowing this, a valid decision can be reached based on evaluating the one sample of data.

The problem, then, is to define how means of samples vary. If sampling were continued and for each sample of four the mean calculated, these means could be compiled into a histogram. Figure 4-1 shows the resulting probability curve, superimposed on the curve for the population. The narrow curve represents the distribution of life for the sample *means* (where each average includes four individual batteries). This is called the *sampling distribution of means.*

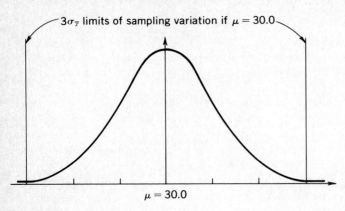

Figure 4-2 Distribution of sample means.

The curve for means is narrower than the curve for individuals because in calculating means, extreme individual values are offset. The mathematical properties for the curve for averages have been studied and the following relationship developed:

$$\sigma_{\bar{x}} = \frac{\sigma}{\sqrt{n}}$$

where $\sigma_{\bar{x}}$ = standard deviation of means of samples (sometimes called the standard error of the mean)

σ = standard deviation of individual items

n = number of items in *each* sample

This relationship is significant because if an estimate of the standard deviation of *individual* items can be obtained, then the standard deviation of sample means can be calculated from the foregoing relationship instead of running an experiment to generate sample averages. The problems of evaluating the battery can now be portrayed graphically (Figure 4-2).

This concept of a sampling distribution is basic to the two major areas of statistical inference, i.e., estimation and tests of hypotheses, which will be discussed next.

4-4 STATISTICAL ESTIMATION: CONFIDENCE LIMITS

Estimation is the process of analyzing a sample result in order to predict the corresponding value of the population parameter. For example, the sample of four batteries previously mentioned had a mean life of 31.0 h. If this is a representative sample from the process, what estimate can be made of the true life of the entire population of batteries?

The estimation statement has two parts:

1. The *point estimate* is a single value used to estimate the population parameter. For example, 31.0 h is the point estimate of the average life of the population.
2. The *confidence interval* is a range of values which includes (with a preassigned probability called *confidence level*) the true value of a population parameter. *Confidence limits* are the upper and lower boundaries of the confidence interval. Confidence level is the probability that an assertion about the value of a population parameter is correct.

Duncan[1] provides a thorough discussion of confidence limits. The explanation here indicates the concept behind the calculations.

If the population mean is μ, the probability that the sample mean will lie between

$$\mu \pm 1.96 \frac{\sigma}{\sqrt{n}}$$

is equal to 0.95: or

$$P\left(\mu - 1.96 \frac{\sigma}{\sqrt{n}} \leq \bar{X} \leq \mu + 1.96 \frac{\sigma}{\sqrt{n}}\right) = 0.95$$

The multiple of 1.96 is obtained by entering Table A in the Appendix at $1 - 0.025$ and $1 - 0.975$. This is equivalent to saying that the probability that the sample mean plus 1.96 standard deviations of the mean lies above μ and the sample mean minus 1.96 standard deviations of the mean lies below μ equals 0.95:

$$P\left(\mu \leq \bar{X} + 1.96 \frac{\sigma}{\sqrt{n}} \text{ and } \bar{X} - 1.96 \frac{\sigma}{\sqrt{n}} \leq \mu\right) = 0.95$$

Combining yields

$$P\left(\bar{X} - 1.96 \frac{\sigma}{\sqrt{n}} \leq \mu \leq \bar{X} + 1.96 \frac{\sigma}{\sqrt{n}}\right) = 0.95$$

Or the 95 percent confidence interval on μ is $\bar{X} \pm 1.96(\sigma/\sqrt{n})$. This interval has a 0.95 probability of including the population value. Strictly speaking, 95 percent of the sets of such intervals would include the population value. In practice, this is interpreted to mean that there is a 95 percent probability that the confidence limits based on one sample will include the true value.

For the sample of four batteries, suppose that $\sigma = 10.0$. Then the 95 per-

---

[1] Acheson J. Duncan, *Quality Control and Industrial Statistics*, 4th ed., Richard D. Irwin, Inc., Homewood, Ill., 1974, pp. 510–524.

cent confidence limits are

$$\bar{X} \pm 1.96 \ \frac{\sigma}{\sqrt{n}} = 31.0 \pm 1.96 \ \frac{10.0}{\sqrt{4}} = 21.2 \text{ and } 40.8$$

This is interpreted to mean that there is 95 percent confidence that μ is between 21.2 and 40.8. The 95 percent is the confidence level[2] and 21.2 and 40.8 are the limits of the confidence interval. A confidence level is associated with an assertion based on actual measurements and measures the probability that the assertion is true. Confidence limits are limits which include the true value with a preassigned degree of confidence (the confidence level).

Table 4-1 summarizes confidence limit formulas for common parameters. The following examples illustrate some of these formulas.

Example (mean of a normal population) Twenty-five specimens of brass have a mean hardness of 54.62 and an estimated standard deviation of 5.34. Determine the 95 percent confidence limits on the mean.

SOLUTION Note that when the standard deviation is unknown and is estimated from the sample, the t distribution (Table D in the Appendix) must be used. The t value for 95 percent confidence is found by entering the table at 0.975 and $25 - 1$, or 24, degrees of freedom[3] and reading a t value of 2.064.

$$\text{Confidence limits} = \bar{X} \pm t \ \frac{s}{\sqrt{n}}$$

$$= 54.62 \pm (2.064) \ \frac{5.34}{\sqrt{25}}$$

$$= 52.42 \text{ and } 56.82$$

There is 95 percent confidence that the true mean hardness of the brass is between 52.42 and 56.82.

Example (mean of an exponential population) A repairable radar system has been operated for 1200 h, during which time eight failures occurred. What are the 90 percent confidence limits on the mean time between failures for the system?

---

[2] Confidence levels of 90, 95, or 99 percent are usually assumed in practice.

[3] A mathematical derivation of degrees of freedom is beyond the scope of this handbook, but the underlying concept can be stated. *Degrees of freedom* (DF) is the parameter involved when, e.g., a sample standard deviation is used to estimate the true standard deviation of a universe. DF equals the number of measurements in the sample minus some number of constraints estimated from the data in order to compute the standard deviation. In this example, it was necessary to estimate only one constant (the population mean) in order to compute the standard deviation. Therefore, DF $= 25 - 1 = 24$.

Table 4-1 Summary of confidence limit formulas

Parameters	Formulas
1. Mean of a normal population (standard deviation known)	$\bar{X} \pm Z_{\alpha/2} \dfrac{\sigma}{\sqrt{n}}$

where $\bar{X}$ = sample average
Z = normal distribution coefficient
σ = standard deviation of population
n = sample size

2. Mean of a normal population (standard deviation unknown)	$\bar{X} \pm t_{\alpha/2} \dfrac{s}{\sqrt{n}}$

where t = distribution coefficient (with $n - 1$ degrees of freedom)
s = estimated σ

3. Standard deviation of a normal population	Upper confidence limit $= s\sqrt{\dfrac{n-1}{\chi^2_{\alpha/2}}}$
	Lower confidence limit $= s\sqrt{\dfrac{n-1}{\chi^2_{1-\alpha/2}}}$

where χ^2 = chi-square distribution coefficient with $n - 1$ degrees of freedom
$1 - \alpha$ = confidence level

4. Population fraction defective	See Table F in the Appendix.
5. Difference between the means of two normal populations (standard deviations σ_1 and σ_2 known)	$(\bar{X}_1 - \bar{X}_2) \pm Z_{\alpha/2}\sqrt{\dfrac{\sigma_1^2}{n_1} + \dfrac{\sigma_2^2}{n_2}}$
6. Difference between the means of two normal populations ($\sigma_1 = \sigma_2$ but unknown)	$(\bar{X}_1 - \bar{X}_2) \pm t_{\alpha/2}\sqrt{\dfrac{1}{n_1} + \dfrac{1}{n_2}}$ $\times \sqrt{\dfrac{\Sigma(X - X_1)^2 + \Sigma(X - X_2)^2}{n_1 + n_2 - 2}}$
7. Mean time between failures based on an exponential population of time between failures	Upper confidence limit $= \dfrac{2rm}{\chi^2_{\alpha/2}}$
	Lower confidence limit $= \dfrac{2rm}{\chi^2_{1-\alpha/2}}$

where r = number of occurrences in the sample (i.e., number of failures)
m = sample mean time between failures
DF = $2r$

SOLUTION

$$\text{Estimated } m = \frac{1200}{8} = 150 \text{ h between failures}$$

$$\text{Upper confidence limit} = 2(1200)/7.962 = 301.4$$

$$\text{Lower confidence limit} = 2(1200)/26.296 = 91.3$$

The values 7.96 and 26.30 are obtained from the chi-square table (Table E in the Appendix). There is 90 percent confidence that the true mean time between failures is between 91.3 and 301.4 h.

Confusion has arisen on the application of the term "confidence level" to a reliability index such as mean time between failures. Using a different example, suppose that the numerical portion of a reliability requirement reads as follows:

"The MTBF shall be at least 100 h at the 90 percent confidence level." This means:

1. The minimum MTBF must be 100 h.
2. Actual tests shall be conducted on the product to demonstrate with 90 percent confidence that the 100-h MTBF has been met.
3. The test data shall be analyzed by calculating the observed MTBF and the lower one-sided 90 percent confidence limit on MTBF. The true MTBF lies above this limit with 90 percent of confidence.
4. The lower one-sided confidence limit must be ≥ 100 h.

The term "confidence level" from a statistical viewpoint has great implications on a test program. The observed MTBF must be *greater* than 100 if the lower confidence limit is to be ≥ 100. Confidence level means that sufficient tests must be conducted to demonstrate, with statistical validity, that a requirement has been met. Confidence level does *not* refer to the qualitative opinion about meeting a requirement. Also, confidence level does *not* lower a requirement, i.e., a 100-h MTBF at a 90 percent confidence level does *not* mean that 0.90 × 100, or 90 h, is acceptable. Such serious misunderstandings have occurred. When the term "confidence level" is used, a clear understanding should be verified and not assumed.

4-5 IMPORTANCE OF CONFIDENCE LIMITS IN PLANNING TEST PROGRAMS

Additional tests will increase the accuracy of estimates. Accuracy here refers to the agreement between an estimate and the true value of the population parameter. The increase in accuracy does not vary linearly with the number of tests—doubling the number of tests usually does *not* double the precision. Examine the graph (Figure 4-3) of the confidence interval for the mean against sample size (a standard deviation of 50.0 was assumed): when the sample size is small, an increase has a great effect on the width of the confidence interval; after about 30 units, an increase has a much smaller effect. The inclusion of the cost parameter is vital here. The cost of additional tests must be evaluated against the value of the additional accuracy.

Further, if the sample is selected randomly and if the sample size is less than 10 percent of the population size, accuracy depends primarily on the

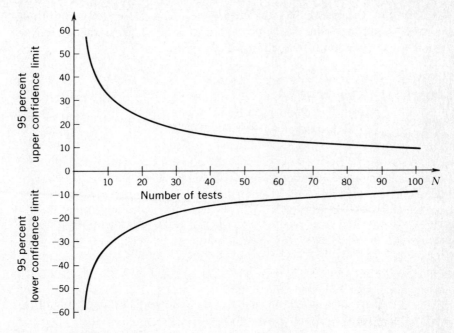

Figure 4-3 Width of confidence interval versus number of tests.

absolute size of the sample rather than the sample size expressed as a percent of the population size. Thus a sample size which is 1 percent of the population of 100,000 may be better than a 10 percent sample from a population of 1000.

4-6 DETERMINATION OF THE SAMPLE SIZE REQUIRED TO ACHIEVE A SPECIFIED ACCURACY IN AN ESTIMATE

Confidence limits can help to determine the size of test program required to estimate a product characteristic within a specified accuracy. It is desired to estimate the true mean of the battery previously cited where $\sigma = 10$. The estimate must be within 2.0 h of the true mean if the estimate is to be of any value. A 95 percent confidence level is desired on the confidence statement. The desired confidence interval is ± 2.0 h, or

$$2.0 = \frac{(1.96)(10)}{\sqrt{n}} \qquad n = 96$$

A sample of 96 batteries will provide an average which is within 2.0 h of the true mean (with 95 percent confidence). Notice the type of information required for estimating the mean of a normal population: (1) desired width of the confidence interval (the accuracy desired in the estimate), (2) confidence level desired, and (3) variability of the characteristic under investigation. The number of tests required cannot be determined until the engineer furnishes these items of information. Past information may also have a major role in designing a test program (see Section 4-11).

4-7 TESTS OF HYPOTHESIS

Basic Concepts

Hypothesis as used here is an assertion made about a population. Usually, the assertion concerns the numerical value of some parameter of the population. For example, a hypothesis might state that the mean life of a population of batteries equals 30.0 h, written as $H:\mu_0 = 30.0$. This assertion may or may not be correct. A *test of hypothesis* is a test of the validity of the assertion, and is carried out by analysis of a sample of data.

There are two reasons why sample results must be carefully evaluated. First, there are many other samples which, by chance alone, could be drawn from the population. Second, the numerical results in the sample actually selected can easily be compatible with several different hypotheses. These points are handled by recognizing the two types of sampling error.

The two types of sampling error In evaluating a hypothesis, two errors can be made:

1. *Reject* the hypothesis when it is *true*. This is called the *type I error* or the *level of significance*. The probability of the type I error is denoted by α.
2. *Accept* the hypothesis when it is *false*. This is called the *type II error* and the probability is denoted by β.

These errors are defined in terms of probability numbers and can be controlled to desired values. The results possible in testing a hypothesis are summarized in Table 4-2.

The type I error is shown graphically in Figure 4-4 for the hypothesis $H_0:\mu_0 = 30.0$. The interval on the horizontal axis between the vertical lines represents the *acceptance region* for the test of hypothesis. If the sample result (e.g., the mean) falls within the acceptance region, the hypothesis is accepted.

Table 4-2 Type I (α) error and Type II (β) error

Suppose decision of analysis is:	Suppose the *H* is:	
	True	False
Accept *H*	Correct decision $P = 1 - \alpha$	Wrong decision $P = \beta$
Reject *H*	Wrong decision $P = \alpha$	Correct decision $P = 1 - \beta$
	$\Sigma P = 1.0$	$\Sigma P = 1.0$

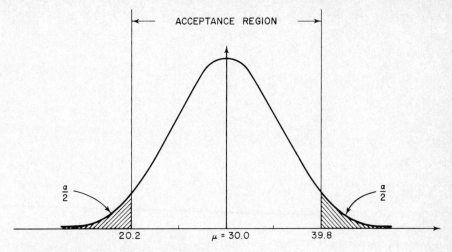

Figure 4-4 Acceptance region for $H:\mu = 30.0$.

Otherwise, it is rejected. The terms "accepted" and "rejected" require careful interpretation. The meanings are explained in a later section of this chapter. Notice that there is a small portion of the curve which falls outside the acceptance region. This area (α) represents the maximum probability of obtaining a sample result outside the acceptance region, even though the hypothesis is correct.

Suppose it has been decided that the type I error must not exceed 5 percent. This is the probability of rejecting the hypothesis when, in truth, the true mean life is 30.0. The acceptance region can be obtained by locating values of mean life which have only a 5 percent chance of being exceeded when the true mean life is 30.0. Further, suppose a sample n of four measurements is taken and $\sigma = 10.0$.

Remember that the curve represents a population of sample means because the decision will be made on the basis of a sample mean. Sample means vary less than individual measurements according to the relationship $\sigma_{\bar{x}} = \sigma/\sqrt{n}$ (see Section 4-3).

Further, the distribution of sample means is approximately normal even if the distribution of the individual measurements (going into the means) is not normal. The approximation holds best for large values of n but is adequate for n as low as 4.

Table A in the Appendix shows that a 2.5% area in each tail is at a limit which is 1.96 standard deviations from 30.0. Then under the hypothesis that $\mu_0 = 30.0$, 95 percent of sample means will fall within $\pm 1.96\sigma_{\bar{x}}$ of 30.0, or

$$\text{Upper limit} = 30.0 + 1.96\,\frac{10}{\sqrt{4}} = 39.8$$

$$\text{Lower limit} = 30.0 - 1.96\,\frac{10}{\sqrt{4}} = 20.2$$

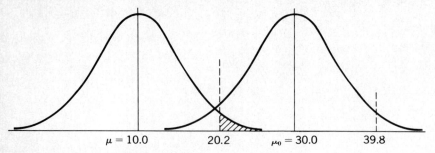

Figure 4-5 Type II or β error.

The acceptance region is thereby defined as 20.2 to 39.8. If the mean of a random sample of four batteries is within this acceptance region, the hypothesis is accepted. If the mean falls outside the acceptance region, the hypothesis is rejected. This decision rule provides a type I error of 0.05.

The type II or β error, the probability of accepting a hypothesis when it is false, is shown in Figure 4-5 as the shaded area. Notice that it is possible to obtain a sample result within the acceptance region, even though the population has a true mean which is *not* equal to the mean stated in the hypothesis. The numerical value of β depends on the true value of the population mean (and also on n, σ, and α). The various probabilities are depicted by an *operating characteristic* (OC) *curve*.

The problem now is to construct an operating characteristic curve to define the magnitude of the type II (β) error. As β is the probability of *accepting* the original hypothesis ($\mu_0 = 30.0$) when it is *false*, the probability that a sample mean will fall between 20.2 and 39.8 must be found when the true mean of the population is something other than 30.0.

Suppose that the true mean is equal to 35.0. Figure 4-6 shows the distribution of sample means under this hypothesis (called $H_1: \mu = 35.0$) and the location of the acceptance region for the hypothesis being tested, H_0.

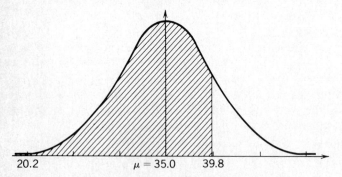

Figure 4-6 Acceptance region when $\mu = 35.0$.

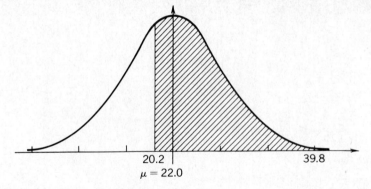

Figure 4-7 Acceptance region when $\mu = 22.0$.

The type II error is the shaded area in Figure 4-6. The area is found by the following calculations:

$$\frac{39.8 - 35.0}{10/\sqrt{4}} = +0.96 \qquad \text{Area} > 39.8 = 0.1685$$

$$\frac{20.2 - 35.0}{10/\sqrt{4}} = -2.96 \qquad \text{Area} < 20.2 = \frac{0.0015}{0.1700}$$

These calculations indicate that if the true mean life in the population is 35.0, the probability of selecting a sample of four batteries having a mean within the acceptance region is 0.830 $(1 - 0.1700)$. This means there is an 83 percent chance of incorrectly accepting the hypothesis (that the mean of the population is equal to 30.0).

Now suppose that the true mean is 22.0. Figure 4-7 shows the distribution of sample means under this hypothesis and the location of the acceptance region for the original hypothesis.

The shaded area again indicates the type II error, calculated as follows:

$$\frac{39.8 - 22.0}{10/\sqrt{4}} = +3.56 \qquad \text{Area} > 39.8 = 0 \text{ (approx.)}$$

$$\frac{20.2 - 22.0}{10/\sqrt{4}} = -0.36 \qquad \text{Area} < 20.2 = \frac{0.3594}{0.3594}$$

There is a 64 percent $(100 - 35.94)$ chance that, if the true mean of the population is 22.0, a mean of four will fall between 20.2 and 39.8. Or, there is a 64 percent chance of incorrectly accepting the hypothesis that the true population mean is 30.0.

Calculations such as those above are repeated for all possible values of the true mean of population. The results form the operating characteristic (OC) curve shown in Figure 4-8. The OC curve is a plot of the probability of accepting the original hypothesis as a function of the true value of the population

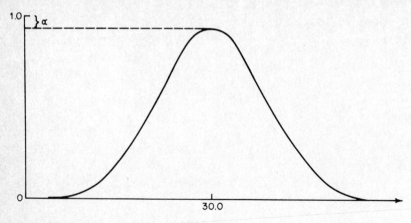

Figure 4-8 Operating characteristic curve.

parameter (and the given values of n, σ, and α). Note that for a mean equal to the hypothesis (30.0), the probability of acceptance is $1 - \alpha$. This curve should not be confused with that of a normal distribution of measurements. In some cases, the shape is similar, but the meanings of an OC curve and a distribution curve are entirely different.

The Use of the Operating Characteristic Curve in Selecting an Acceptance Region

The acceptance region was determined by dividing the 5 percent allowable α error into two equal parts (see Figure 4-4). This is called a *two-tail test*. The entire 5 percent error could also be placed at either the left or the right tail of the distribution curve. These are *one-tail tests*.

Operating characteristic curves for tests having these one-tail acceptance regions can be developed following the approach used for the two-tail region. Although the α error is the same, the β error varies depending on whether a one-tail or two-tail test is used.

In some problems, knowledge is available to indicate that if the true mean of the population is *not* equal to the hypothesis value, then it is on one side of the hypothesis value. For example, a new material of supposedly higher mean strength will have a mean equal to or *greater than* that of the present material. Such information will help select a one-tail or two-tail test to make the β error as small as possible. The following guidelines are based on the analysis of OC curves:

Use a one-tail test with the entire α risk on the right tail if (1) it is suspected that (if μ_0 is not true) the true mean is $> \mu_0$ or (2) values of the population mean $< \mu_0$ are acceptable and we only want to detect a population mean $> \mu_0$.
Use a one-tail test with the entire α risk on the left tail if (1) it is suspected that

(if μ_0 is not true) the true mean is $<\mu_0$ or (2) values of the population mean $>\mu_0$ are acceptable and we only want to detect a population mean $<\mu_0$.
Use a two-tail test if (1) there is no prior knowledge on the location of the true population mean or (2) we want to detect a true population mean $<$ or $>$ the μ_0 stated in the original hypothesis.[4]

The selection of a one- or two-tail test will be illustrated by some examples in a later section. Every test of hypothesis has an OC curve. Both Duncan and Natrella[5] are good sources of OC curves. (Some references present "power" curves, but power is simply 1 minus the probability of acceptance, or $1 - \beta$.)

With this background, the discussion now proceeds to the steps for testing a hypothesis.

4-8 TESTING A HYPOTHESIS WHEN THE SAMPLE SIZE IS FIXED IN ADVANCE

Ideally, desired values for the type I and type II errors are defined in advance and the required sample size determined (see Section 4-10). If the sample size is fixed in advance because of cost or time limitations, then usually the desired type I error is defined and the following procedure is followed:

1. State the hypothesis.
2. Choose a value for the type I error. Common values are 0.01, 0.05, or 0.10.
3. Choose the test statistic for testing the hypothesis.
4. Determine the acceptance region for the test, i.e., the range of values of the test statistic which result in a decision to accept the hypothesis.
5. Obtain a sample of observations, compute the test statistic, and compare the value to the acceptance region to make a decision to accept or reject the hypothesis.
6. Draw an engineering conclusion.

Table 4-3 summarizes some common tests of hypotheses. The procedure is illustrated through the following examples. In these examples, a type I error of 0.05 will be assumed.

1. Test for a population mean, μ. (Standard deviation of the population is known.)

---

[4] With a two-tail test, the hypothesis is sometimes stated as the original hypothesis $H_0:\mu_0 = 30.0$ against the alternative hypothesis $H_1:\mu_0 \neq 30.0$. With a one-tail test, $H_0:\mu_0 = 30.0$ is used against the alternative $H_1:\mu_1 < 30.0$ if α is placed in the left tail, or $H_1:\mu_1 > 30.0$ is used if α is placed in the right tail.

[5] Further sources of OC curves are Duncan, *Quality Control*, and Mary G. Natrella, "Experimental Statistics," *National Bureau of Standards Handbook 91*, Government Printing Office, Washington, D.C., 1963.

Table 4-3 Summary of formulas on tests of hypotheses

Hypothesis	Test statistic and distribution
1. $H : \mu = \mu_0$ (the mean of a normal population is equal to a specified value μ_0; σ is known)	$Z = \dfrac{\bar{X} - \mu_0}{\sigma/\sqrt{n}}$ Normal distribution
2. $H : \mu = \mu_0$ (the mean of a normal population is equal to a specified value μ_0; σ is estimated by s)	$t = \dfrac{\bar{X} - \mu_0}{s/\sqrt{n}}$ t distribution with $n - 1$ degrees of freedom (DF)
3. $H : \mu_1 = \mu_2$ (the mean of population 1 is equal to the mean of population 2; assume that $\sigma_1 = \sigma_2$ and that both populations are normal)	$t = \dfrac{\bar{X}_1 - \bar{X}_2}{\sqrt{1/n_1 + 1/n_2}\ \sqrt{[(n_1 - 1)s_1{}^2 + (n_2 - 1)s_2{}^2]/(n_1 + n_2 - 2)}}$ t distribution with $\text{DF} = n_1 + n_2 - 2$
4. $H : \sigma = \sigma_0$ (the standard deviation of a normal population is equal to a specified value σ_0)	$\chi^2 = \dfrac{(n - 1)s^2}{\sigma_0{}^2}$ Chi-square distribution with $\text{DF} = n - 1$
5. $H : \sigma_1 = \sigma_2$ (the standard deviation of population 1 is equal to the standard deviation of population 2; assume that both populations are normal)	$F = \dfrac{s_1{}^2}{s_2{}^2}$ F distribution with $\text{DF}_1 = n_1 - 1$ and $\text{DF}_2 = n_2 - 1$
6. $H : p = p_0$ (the fraction defective in a population is equal to a specified value p_0; assume that $np_0 \geq 5$)	$Z = \dfrac{p - p_0}{\sqrt{p_0(1 - p_0)/n}}$ Normal distribution
7. $H : p_1 = p_2$ (the fraction defective in population 1 is equal to the fraction defective in population 2; assume that $n_1 p_1$ and $n_2 p_2$ are each ≥ 5)	$Z = \dfrac{X_1/n_1 - X_2/n_2}{\sqrt{\hat{p}(1 - \hat{p})(1/n_1 + 1/n_2)}} \qquad \hat{p} = \dfrac{X_1 + X_2}{n_1 + n_2}$ Normal distribution

Example A single-cavity molding press has been producing insulators with a mean impact strength of 5.15 ft-lb (6.98N-m) and with a standard deviation of 0.25 ft-lb (0.34 N-m). A new lot shows the following data from 12 specimens:

Specimen	Strength
1	5.02
2	4.87
3	4.95
4	4.88
5	5.01
6	4.93
7	4.91
8	5.09
9	4.96
10	4.89
11	5.06
12	4.85
	$\bar{X} = 4.95$

Is the new lot from which the sample of 12 was taken different in mean impact strength from the past performance of the process?

SOLUTION $H_0 : \mu_0 = 5.15$ ft-lb (6.98 N-m). (The mean of the population from which the sample was taken is the same as the past process average.)

Test statistic

$$Z = \frac{X - \mu_0}{\sigma / \sqrt{n}}$$

Acceptance region Assuming no prior information and that a deviation on either side of the hypothesis average is important to detect, a two-tail test (Figure 4-9) is applicable. From Table A in the Appendix, the acceptance region is Z between -1.96 and $+1.96$.

Analysis of sample data

$$Z = \frac{4.95 - 5.15}{0.25 / \sqrt{12}} = -2.75$$

Conclusion Since Z is outside the acceptance region, the hypothesis is rejected. Therefore, sufficient evidence is present to conclude that the mean impact strength of the new process is significantly different from the

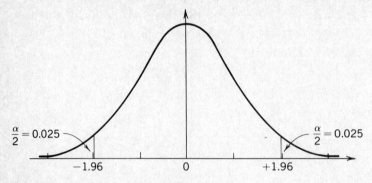

Figure 4-9 Distribution of Z (two-tail test).

mean of the past process. The answer to the first question in Section 4-2 is yes.

2. Test for two population means, μ_1 and μ_2, when the standard deviation is unknown but believed to be the same for the two populations. (This assumption can be evaluated by test 4.)

Example Two makes of spark plugs were operated in the alternate cylinders of an aircraft engine for 100 h and the following data obtained:

	Make 1	Make 2
Number of spark plugs tested	10	8
Average wear per 100 h ($\overline{X}$), in	0.0049	0.0064
Variability (s), in	0.0005	0.0004

Can it be said that make 1 wears less than make 2?

SOLUTION $H:\mu_1 = \mu_2$.

Test statistic

$$t = \frac{X_1 - X_2}{\sqrt{1/n_1 + 1/n_2}\ \sqrt{[(n_1 - 1)s_1^2 + (n_2 - 1)s_2^2]/(n_1 + n_2 - 2)}}$$

with degress of freedom $= n_1 + n_2 - 2$.

Acceptance region We are concerned only with the possibility that make 1 wears less than make 2; therefore, use a one-tail test (Figure 4-10) with the entire α risk in the left tail. From Table D in the Appendix, the acceptance region is $t > -1.746$.

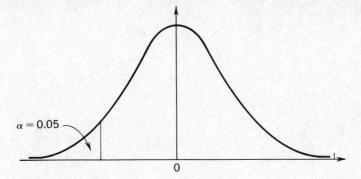

Figure 4-10 Distribution of t with α on left tail.

Analysis of sample data

$$t = \frac{0.0049 - 0.0064}{\sqrt{1/10 + 1/8}\ \sqrt{[(10-1)(0.0005)^2 + (8-1)(0.0004)^2]/(10 + 8 - 2)}}$$
$$= -7.0$$

Conclusion Since t is outside the acceptance region, the hypothesis is rejected. Therefore, sufficient evidence is present to conclude that make 1 wears less than make 2. The answer to the third question in Section 4-2 is yes.

3. Test for a population standard deviation, σ.

Example For the insulator strengths tabulated in the first example, the sample standard deviation is 0.036 ft-lb (0.049 N-m). The previous variability, recorded over a period, has been established as a standard deviation of 0.25 ft-lb (0.34 N-m). Does the low value of 0.036 indicate that the new lot is significantly more uniform (i.e., standard deviation less than 0.25)?

SOLUTION $H:\sigma_0 = 0.25$ ft-lb (0.34 N-m).

Test statistic

$$\chi^2 = \frac{(n-1)s^2}{\sigma_0^2}$$

with degrees of freedom $= n - 1$.

Acceptance region We believe that the standard deviation is smaller; therefore, we will use a one-tail test (Figure 4-11) with the entire risk on the left tail. From Table E in the Appendix the acceptance region is $\chi^2 \geq 4.57$.

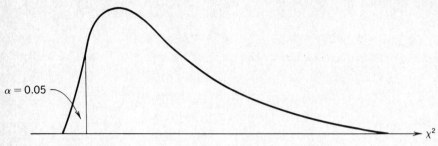

Figure 4-11 Distribution of χ^2 with α on left tail.

Analysis of sample data

$$\chi^2 = \frac{(12 - 1)(0.036)^2}{(0.25)^2} = 0.23$$

Conclusion Since χ^2 is outside the acceptance region, the hypothesis is rejected. Therefore, sufficient evidence is present to conclude that the new lot is more uniform.

4. Test for the difference in variability (s_1 versus s_2) in two samples.

Example A materials laboratory was studying the effect of aging on a metal alloy. They wanted to know if the parts were more consistent in strength after aging than before. The data obtained were:

	At start (1)	After 1 year (2)
Number of specimens (n)	9	7
Average strength ($\bar{X}$), psi	41,350	40,920
Variability (s), psi	934	659

SOLUTION $H: \sigma_1 = \sigma_2$.

Test statistic

$$F = \frac{s_1^2}{s_2^2} \qquad \text{with } DF_1 = n_1 - 1, \, DF_2 = n_2 - 1$$

Acceptance region We are concerned with an improvement in variation; therefore, we will use a one-tail test (Figure 4-12) with the entire α risk in the right tail.

From Table G in the Appendix, the acceptance region is $F \leq 4.15$.

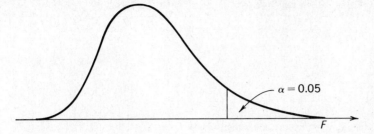

Figure 4-12 Distribution of F with α on right tail.

Analysis of sample data

$$F = \frac{(934)^2}{(659)^2} = 2.01$$

Conclusion Since F is inside the acceptance region, the hypothesis is accepted. Therefore, there is not sufficient evidence to conclude that the parts were more consistent in strength after aging.

In this test and other tests that compare two samples, it is important that the samples be independent to assure valid conclusions.

4-9 DRAWING CONCLUSIONS FROM TESTS OF HYPOTHESES

The payoff for these tests of hypotheses comes from reaching useful conclusions. The meaning of "reject the hypothesis" or "accept the hypothesis" is shown in Table 4-4, together with some analogies to explain the subtleties of the meanings.

When a hypothesis is rejected, the practical conclusion is: "the parameter value specified in the hypothesis is wrong." The conclusion is made with strong conviction—roughly speaking at a confidence level of $(1 - \alpha)$ percent. The key question then is: Just what is a good estimate of the value of the parameter for the population? Help can be provided on this question by calculating the confidence limits for the parameter. This was discussed in Section 4-4.

When a hypothesis is accepted, the numerical value of the parameter stated in the hypothesis has not been proved, but it has not been disproved. It is not correct to say that the hypothesis has been proved as correct at the $(1 - \alpha)$ percent confidence level. Many other hypotheses could be accepted for the given sample of observations and yet only one hypothesis can be true. Therefore, an acceptance does not mean a high probability of proof that a specific hypothesis is correct. (All other factors being equal, the smaller the sample size, the more likely it is that the hypothesis will be accepted. Less evidence certainly does not imply proof.)

Table 4-4 The meaning of a conclusion from tests of hypotheses

	If hypothesis is rejected	If hypothesis is accepted
Adequacy of evidence in the sample of observations	Sufficient to conclude that hypothesis is false	Not sufficient to conclude that hypothesis is false. Hypothesis is a reasonable one but has not been proved to be true
Difference between sample result (e.g., $\bar{X}$) and hypothesis value (e.g., μ_0)	Unlikely that difference was due to chance (sampling) variation	Difference could easily have been due to chance (sampling) variation
Analogy of guilt or innocence in a court of law	Guilt has been established beyond a reasonable doubt	Have not established guilt beyond a reasonable doubt
Analogy of a batting average in baseball	If player got 300 base hits out of 1000 times at bat, this is sufficient to conclude that his overall batting average is about 0.300	If player got 3 hits in 10 times, this is not sufficient to conclude that his overall average is about 0.300

With an acceptance of a hypothesis, a key question then is: What conclusion, if any, can be drawn about the parameter value in the hypothesis? Two approaches are suggested:

1. *Construct and review the operating characteristic curve for the test of hypothesis.* This defines the probability that other possible values of the population parameter could have been accepted by the test. Knowing these probabilities for values relatively close to the original hypothesis can help draw further conclusions about the acceptance of the original hypothesis. For example, Figure 4-8 shows the OC curve for a hypothesis which specified that the population mean is 30.0. Note that the probability of accepting the hypothesis when the population mean is 30.0 is 0.95 (or $1 - \alpha$). But also note that if μ really is 35.0, then the probability of accepting $\mu = 30.0$ is still high (about 0.83). If μ really is 42.0, the probability of accepting $\mu = 30.0$ is only about 0.33.

2. *Calculate confidence limits on the sample result.* These confidence limits define an interval within which the true population parameter lies. If this interval is small, an acceptance decision on the test of hypothesis means that the true population value is either equal to or close to the value stated in the hypothesis. Then, it is reasonable to act as if the parameter value specified in the hypothesis is in fact correct. If the confidence interval is relatively wide, this is a stern warning that the true value of the population might be far different from that specified in the hypothesis. For example, the confidence limits of 21.2 and 40.8 on battery life in Section 4-4 would lead to an acceptance of the hypothesis of $\mu = 30.0$, but note that the confidence interval is relatively wide.

Care must always be taken in drawing engineering conclusions from the statistical conclusions, particularly when a hypothesis is accepted.

A test of hypothesis tests to see if there is a statistically significant difference between the sample result and the value of the population parameter stated in the hypothesis. A decision to reject the hypothesis means that there is a statistically significant difference. However, this does not mean that the difference has practical significance. Large sample sizes, although not generally available, can detect small differences that may not have practical importance. Conversely, "accept hypothesis" means that a statistically significant difference was not found but this may have been due to a small sample size. A larger sample size could result in a "reject hypothesis" and thus detect a significant difference.

4-10 DETERMINING THE SAMPLE SIZE REQUIRED FOR TESTING A HYPOTHESIS

The previous sections assumed that the sample size was fixed by nonstatistical reasons and that the type I error only was predefined for the test. The ideal procedure is to predefine the desired type I and II errors and calculate the sample size required to cover both types of errors.

The sample size required will depend on (1) the sampling risks desired (α and β), (2) the size of the smallest true difference that is to be detected, and (3) the variation in characteristic being measured. The sample size can be determined by using the operating characteristic curve for the test.

Curves[6] are given (Figure 4-13) for a two-tail test of the hypothesis that the mean is equal to a specified value. Suppose that it was important to detect the fact that the mean of the battery cited previously was 35.0. Specifically, we want to be 80 percent sure of detecting this change ($\beta = 0.2$). Further, if the true mean was 30.0 (as stated in the hypothesis), we want to have only a 5 percent risk of rejecting the hypothesis ($\alpha = 0.05$). In using Figure 4-13, d is defined as

$$d = \frac{\mu - \mu_0}{\sigma} = \frac{35.0 - 30.0}{10.0} = 0.5$$

Entering with $d = 0.5$ and $P_a = 0.2$ (the beta risk), the curves indicate that a sample size of about 30 is required.

In practice, however, one is often not sure of desired values of α and β. Reviewing the operating characteristic curves for various sample sizes can help to arrive at a decision on the sample size required to reflect the relative importance of both risks.

4-11 USE OF PRIOR INFORMATION IN PLANNING TESTS

The previous sections have assumed that statements concerning product performance would be based strictly on actual tests conducted on the product. Recently, attention has been drawn to the possibility of using past ("prior") in-

[6] See footnote 5.

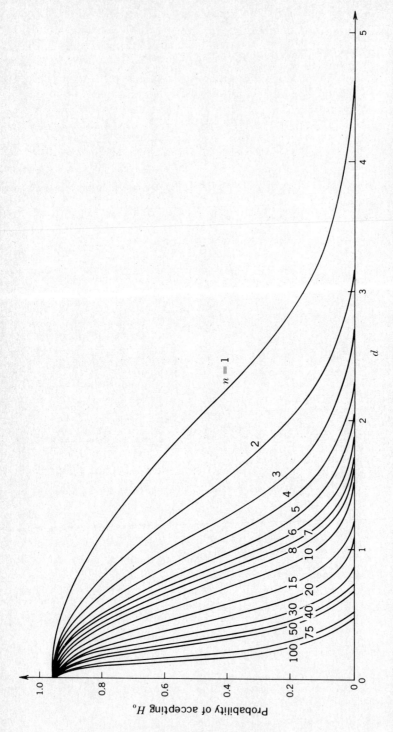

Figure 4-13 Operating characteristics of the two-sided normal test for a level of significance equal to 0.05. (From Charles D. Ferris, Frank E. Grubbs, and Chalmers L. Weaver, "Operating Characteristics for the Common Statistical Tests of Significance," *Annals of Mathematical Statistics*, June 1946.)

formation to supplement the actual test data. The approach is based on a theorem originally proposed by Rev. Thomas Bayes in 1763. The theorem may be stated as follows: If $\mu_1, \mu_2, \ldots, \mu_n$ are mutually exclusive events (i.e., they cannot happen simultaneously) of which one must occur, and if these events can be associated with another event A, then

$$P(\mu_i|A) = \frac{P(\mu_i)P(A|\mu_i)}{\sum_{\text{all } i} [P(\mu_i)P(A|\mu_i)]}$$

An oversimplified example will illustrate the concept. Suppose it is desired to evaluate the average life of an engine. The requirement is 5000 h. The wealth of experience in the development department on similar engines has been summarized as follows:

We are fairly certain (80 percent) that the new engine will have a mean life of 5000 h.

There is a small chance (15 percent) that the new engine will have a mean life of only 2500 h.

There is a smaller chance (5 percent) that the new engine will be poor and only achieve a mean life of 1000 h.

The three values of mean life are the events μ_1, μ_2, and μ_3. The percentages are the values of $P(\mu_i)$, i.e., the probability that the mean life of the population will be μ_i.

The following test program has been proposed: run 11 engines each for 1000 h; if four or fewer failures occur conclude that the design meets the 5000-h requirement. In this case, the event A is the passing of the above program (i.e., running 11 engines and having four or fewer failures). Assuming an exponential distribution, calculations for an operating characteristic curve can be made (see Chapter 17) to find the probability of passing the test given that the true mean is μ_i.

These probabilities are $P(A|\mu_i)$ in Bayes' theorem. Summarizing:

μ_i	$P(\mu_i)$	$P(A|\mu_i)$
5000	0.80	0.95
2500	0.15	0.71
1000	0.05	0.10

Suppose that the test program is conducted and passed. The probability that the 5000-h mean life requirement has been met may be calculated as

$$P(\mu = 5000 \text{ test passed}) = \frac{0.8(0.95)}{0.8(0.95) + 0.15(0.71) + 0.05(0.1)} = 0.86$$

Thus the test program would give reasonably high assurance (86 percent) that the design meets the requirement (if the test is passed). Simultaneously, if the design is extremely poor ($\mu = 1000$), there is only a small chance (10 percent) that it will pass the test. (The adequacy of a 71 percent chance of passing a design with a mean of only 2500 h is a subject of discussion.)

The controversial question in all this is the determination of the values of $P(\mu_i)$; for example, what is the basis of saying that there is an 80 percent chance that the engine will achieve the 5000-h mean life? The writers believe that it *may* often be possible to synthesize such probabilities from past experience on similar products or parts of products.

This experience may be test data or proven scientific principles. As a simple example, suppose it is desired to predict the probability that an object will not break if it is dropped from a specified height. Six such objects are dropped and none break. Confidence limit calculations (based on the binomial distribution, not on Bayes' theorem) predict, with 90 percent confidence, that the probability of success on a seventh trial is at least 0.68. However, if scientific principles (e.g., the law of gravity and strength of material principles) tell us that the object should not break, then the prediction is conservative. Ideally, conclusions should be based only on tests of the current product. However, this is often impossible and engineering managers have used and will continue to use past experience in drawing conclusions on current products. They often do this in an informal and qualitative manner.

The Bayes approach, when applicable, may provide an opportunity to evaluate this extremely valuable past experience in a more methodical manner. Judgment will be needed and danger will exist. Bonis[7] discusses the advantages of the Bayes approach as applied to demonstration of reliability.

There is controversy on the Bayes versus the conventional approach to analysis of data. The viewpoints as applied to evaluating a new design are summarized in Table 4-5.

Another dimension in planning test programs is to incorporate the consequences of costs and revenues on decisions. When the Bayesian approach of prior probabilities is combined with the recognition of economic consequences, the resulting methods are called *statistical decision theory*. An illustrative example is given in Section 17-19.

4-12 THE DESIGN OF EXPERIMENTS

Experiments can have a wide variety of objectives and the best strategy depends on the objective. In some experiments, the objective is to find the most important variables affecting a quality characteristic. The plan for conducting such experiments is called the *design of the experiment*. We will first cover an example that presents several alternative designs and defines basic terminology and concepts.

Suppose that three detergents are to be compared for their ability in clean-

---

[7] Austin J., Bonis, "Why Bayes Is Better," *Proceedings, Annual Reliability and Maintainability Symposium*, January 1975, pp. 340–348.

Table 4-5 Bayes versus conventional statistical approach in evaluating a new design

	Bayes	Conventional
Role of past experience	Past experience is valuable in helping to predict performance of a new design	Not applicable because the new design is different. Evaluation of new design must be based solely on test results of new design
Purpose of development test program on new design	Confirm or deny expected performance of new design as predicted from past experience	Supply the data for evaluating the new design
Validity of conclusions about the new design	Depends on ability to quantitatively relate past experience to new design	Usually more conservative than Bayes because evaluation is based solely on test results of new design
Number of tests required on new design	Bayes approach requires less than conventional approach because it makes use of applicable past data	

ing clothes in an automatic washing machine. The "whiteness" readings obtained by a special measuring procedure are called the *dependent* or *response variable*. The variable under investigation (detergent) is a *factor* and each variation of the factor is called a *level*; i.e., there are three levels. A factor may be qualitative (different detergents) or quantitative (water temperature). Finally, some experiments have a *fixed-effects model*; i.e., the levels investigated represent all levels of concern to the investigator (e.g., three brands of washing machines). Other experiments have a *random-effects model*; i.e., the levels chosen are just a sample from a larger population (e.g., three operators of washing machines). A *mixed-effects model* has both fixed and random factors.

Figure 4-14 outlines six designs of experiments starting with the classical design in Figure 4-14*a*. Here all factors except detergent are held constant. Thus nine tests are run, i.e., three with each detergent with the washing time, make of machine, water temperature, and all other factors held constant. One drawback of this design is that the conclusions about detergent brands would only apply to the specific conditions run in the experiment.

Figure 4-14*b* recognizes a second factor at three levels, i.e., washing machines brand I, II, and III. However, in this design it would not be known whether an observed difference was due to detergents or washing times.

In Figure 4-14*c*, the nine tests are assigned completely at random and thus the name *completely randomized design*. However, detergent A is not used with machine brand III and detergent B is not used with machine brand I, thus complicating the conclusions.

Figure 4-14*d* shows the *randomized block design*. Here, each block is a

(a)

A	B	C
—	—	—
—	—	—
—	—	—

(b)

I	II	III
A	B	C
A	B	C
A	B	C

(c)

I	II	III
C	B	B
A	C	B
A	A	C

(d)

I	II	III
B	A	C
C	C	A
A	B	B

(e)

	I	II	III
1	C	A	B
2	B	C	A
3	A	B	C

(f)

	I A B C	II A B C	III A B C
1	— — —	— — —	— — —
2	— — —	— — —	— — —
3	— — —	— — —	— — —

Figure 4-14 Some experimental designs.

machine brand and the detergents are run in random order within each block. This guards against any possible bias due to the order in which the detergents are used. This design has advantages in the subsequent data analysis and conclusions. First, a test of hypothesis can be run to compare detergents and a separate test run to compare machines and all nine observations are used in both tests of hypothesis. Second, the conclusions concerning detergents apply for the three machines and vice versa, thus providing conclusions over a wider range of conditions.

Now suppose that another factor such as water temperature was also to be studied. This could be done with the *Latin square design* shown in Figure 4-14e. Note that this design requires that each detergent is used only once with each machine and only once with each temperature. Thus three factors can be evaluated (by three separate tests of hypothesis) with only nine observations. However, there is a danger. This design assumes no "interaction" between the factors. No interaction between detergent and machine means that the effect of changing from detergent A to B to C does not depend on which machine is used, and similarly for the other combinations of factors. The concept of interaction is shown in Figure 4-15.

Finally, the main factors and possible interactions could be investigated by

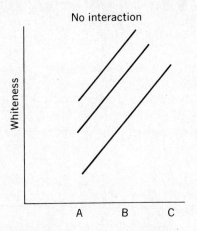

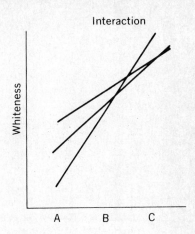

Figure 4-15 Interaction.

the *factorial design* in Figure 4-14*f*. "Factorial" means that at least one test is run at every combination of the main factors, in this case 3 × 3 × 3 or 27 combinations. Separate tests of hypothesis can be run to evaluate the main factors and also the possible interactions. Again, all the observations contribute to each comparison.

Several key tools used in this example will now be explained.

4-13 SOME TOOLS FOR SOUND EXPERIMENTATION

Planned Grouping or Blocking

Beyond the factors selected for study, there are other "background" variables which may affect the outcome of the experiments. Where the experimenter is aware of these variables, it is often possible to plan the experiment so that:

1. Possible effects due to background variables do not affect information obtained about the factors of primary interest.
2. Some information about the effects of the background variables can be obtained.

In designing experiments, wide use is made of the uniformity within blocks to minimize the effect of unwanted variables and to accentuate the effect of the variables under study. Designs that make use of this uniformity within blocks are called *block designs*, and the process is called *planned grouping*.

Randomization The assignment of specimens to treatments in a purely chance manner is called *randomization* in the design of experiments. Such assignment increases the likelihood that the effect of uncontrolled variables will balance out. It also improves the validity of estimates of experimental error and makes possible the application of statistical tests of significance and the construction of confidence intervals.

There are many famous examples of experiments where failure to randomize at a crucial stage led to completely misleading results. However, the beneficial effects of randomization are obtained in the long run, not in a single isolated experiment. Randomization may be thought of as insurance and, like insurance, may sometimes be too expensive. If a variable is thought unlikely to have an effect, and if it is difficult to randomize with respect to the variable, we may choose not to randomize.

Replication Replication is the repetition of an observation or measurement. It is done to increase precision and to provide the means for measuring precision. (In some kinds of experiments there is no outside source for measuring precision, so that the measure must come from the experiment itself.) In addition, replication provides an opportunity for the effects of uncontrolled factors to balance out, and thus aids randomization as a bias-decreasing tool. (In successive replications, the randomization features must be independent.) Replication also helps to detect gross errors in the measurements.

In designing the experiment, some key questions that arise are:

1. How large a difference in the conditions being compared is considered significant from an engineering point of view? (How large a difference do we want the experiment to detect?)
2. How much variation has been experienced in the quality characteristics under investigation?
3. What risk do we want to take that the experiment incorrectly concludes that a significant difference exists when the correct conclusion is that no significant difference exists? (This is the type I error.)
4. What risk do we want to take that the experiment fails to detect the difference that really does exist? (This is the type II error.)
5. Do we have any knowledge about possible interactions of the factors? Do we wish to test for these interactions?

Many experimental problems can be handled with one of the standard experimental designs.[8]

4-14 CONTRAST BETWEEN THE CLASSICAL AND MODERN METHODS OF EXPERIMENTATION

The contrast between the classical method of experimentation (vary one factor at a time, hold everything else constant) and the modern approach is striking. Table 4-6 compares these two approaches for an experiment in which there are

[8] For a list of experiment designs and associated applications, see *Quality Control Handbook*, 3rd ed., table 27-2.

Table 4-6 Comparison of the classical and the modern methods of experimentation

Criteria	Classical	Modern
Basic procedure	Hold everything constant except the factor under investigation. Vary that factor and note the effect on the characteristic of concern. To investigate a second factor, conduct a separate experiment in the same manner	Plan the experiment to evaluate both factors in one main experiment. Include, in the design, measurements to evaluate the effect of varying both factors simultaneously
Experimental conditions	Care taken to have material, workers, and machine constant throughout the entire experiment	Realizes difficulty of holding conditions reasonably constant throughout an entire experiment. Instead, experiment is divided into several groups or blocks of measurements. Within each block, conditions must be reasonably constant (except for deliberate variation to investigate a factor)
Experimental error	Recognized but not stated in quantitative terms	Stated in quantitative terms
Basis of evaluation	Effect due to a factor is evaluated with only a vague knowledge of the amount of experimental error	Effect due to a factor is evaluated by comparing variation due to that factor with the quantitative measure of experimental error
Possible bias due to sequence of measurements	Often assumed that sequence has no effect	Guarded against by "randomization"
Effect of varying both factors simultaneously ("interaction")	Not adequately planned into experiment. Frequently assumed that the effect of varying factor 1 (when factor 2 is held constant at some value) would be the same for any value of factor 2	Experiment can be planned to include an investigation for "interaction" between factors
Validity of results	Misleading and erroneous if "interaction" exists and is not realized	Even if "interaction" exists, a valid evaluation of the main factors can be made
Number of measurements	For a given amount of useful and valid information, more measurements needed than in the modern approach	Fewer measurements needed for useful and valid information

Table 4-6 Comparison of the classical and modern methods of experimentation (*continued*)

Criteria	Classical	Modern
Definition of problem	Objective of experiment frequently not defined as necessary	In order to design experiment, it is necessary to define the objective in detail (how large an effect do we want to determine, what numerical risks can be taken, etc.)
Application of conclusions	Sometimes disputed as only applicable to "the controlled conditions under which the experiment was conducted"	Broad conditions can be planned into the experiment, thereby making conclusions applicable to a wider range of actual conditions

two factors (or variables) whose effects on a characteristic are being investigated. (The same conclusions hold for an experiment with more than two factors.)

This discussion has been restricted to the *design* or planning of the experiment. Extensive literature[9] is available on both the design of the experiment and the analysis of the data.

4-15 REGRESSION ANALYSIS

Quality control problems sometimes require a study of the relationship between two or more variables. This is called *regression analysis*. The uses of regression analysis include forecasting and prediction, determining the important variables influencing some result, and locating optimum operating conditions.

The steps in a regression study are:

1. Clearly define the objectives of the study. This must include a definition of the dependent or response variable and the independent variables that are thought to be related to the dependent variable.
2. Collect the data.
3. Prepare scatter diagrams (plots of one variable versus another).
4. Calculate the regression equation.
5. Study the equation to see how well it fits the data.
6. Provide measures of the precision of the equation.

---

[9] See *Quality Control Handbook*, 3rd ed., sec. 27, for a discussion with many references.

Table 4-7 Cutting speed (X, in feet per minute) versus tool life (Y, in minutes)

X	Y	X	Y	X	Y	X	Y
90	41	100	22	105	21	110	15
90	43	100	35	105	13	110	11
90	35	100	29	105	18	110	6
90	32	100	18	105	20	110	10

These steps will be illustrated with an example.

Suppose it is thought that the life of a tool varies with the cutting speed of the tool and it is desired to predict life based on cutting speed. Thus life is the dependent variable (Y) and cutting speed is the independent variable (X). Data are collected at four different cutting speeds (Table 4-7).

The plot of the data is called a *scatter diagram* (Figure 4-16). This plot should *always* be prepared before making any further analysis. The graph *alone* may provide sufficient information on the relationship between the variables to draw conclusions on the immediate problem, but the graph is also useful in suggesting possible forms of an estimating equation. Figure 4-16 suggests that life does vary with speed (i.e., life decreases with an increase in speed) and that it varies in a linear manner (i.e., increases in speed result in a certain decrease in life that is the same over the range of the data). Note that the relationship is not perfect—the points scatter about the line.

Often it is valuable to determine a regression equation. For linear relationships, this can be done approximately by drawing a straight line by eye and then graphically estimating the Y intercept and slope. The linear regression model is

$$Y = \beta_0 + \beta_1 X + \epsilon$$

where β_0 and β_1 are the unknown population intercept and slope and ϵ is a random-error term that may be due to measurement errors and/or the effects of other independent variables. This model is estimated from sample data by the form

$$\hat{Y} = b_0 + b_1 X$$

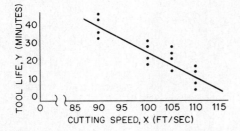

Figure 4-16 Tool life Y versus cutting speed X.

where $\hat{Y}$ is the predicted value of Y for a given value of X and b_0 and b_1 are the sample estimates of β_0 and β_1.

These estimates are usually found by the least squares method, so named because it minimizes the sum of the squared deviations between the observed and predicted values of Y. The least squares estimates are

$$b_1 = \frac{\Sigma(X_m - \bar{X})(Y_m - \bar{Y})}{\Sigma(X_m - \bar{X})^2}$$

$$b_0 = \bar{Y} - b_1\bar{X}$$

The summations range from $m = 1$ to $m = N$, where N is the total number of sets of values of X and Y.

The sums, sums of squares, and sum of cross products for the data ($N = 16$) given in Table 26-1 are

$$\Sigma X_m = 90 + 90 + \cdots + 110 = 1620$$

$$\Sigma Y_m = 41 + 43 + \cdots + 10 = 369$$

$$\Sigma X_m^2 = 8100 + 8100 + \cdots + 12{,}000 = 164{,}900$$

$$\Sigma Y_m^2 = 1681 + 1849 + \cdots + 100 = 10{,}469$$

$$\Sigma X_m Y_m = 3690 + 3870 + \cdots + 1100 = 36{,}170$$

which can be computed in one pass on many desk calculators. It is worthwhile to note here that whenever doing calculations of this type it is advisable to repeat the calculations as a check.

The summary statistics are computed from the raw statistics using the following computational forms:

$$\bar{X} = \frac{\Sigma X_m}{N} = 101.25 \qquad \bar{Y} = \frac{\Sigma Y_m}{N} = 23.06$$

$$\Sigma(X_m - \bar{X})^2 = \Sigma X_m^2 - \frac{(\Sigma X_m)^2}{N} = 164{,}900 - \frac{(1620)^2}{16} = 875.00$$

$$\Sigma(Y_m - \bar{Y})^2 = \Sigma Y_m^2 - \frac{(\Sigma Y_m)^2}{N} = 10{,}469 - \frac{(369)^2}{16} = 1958.94$$

$$\Sigma(X_m - \bar{X})(Y_m - \bar{Y}) = \Sigma X_m Y_m - \frac{\Sigma X_m \Sigma Y_m}{N}$$

$$= 36{,}170 - \frac{(1620)(369)}{16}$$

$$= -1191.25$$

From these results the least squares estimates can be calculated as

$$b_1 = \frac{-1191.25}{875} = -1.3614$$

$$b_0 = 23.06 - (-1.3614)(101.25) = 160.9018$$

and hence the prediction equation is

$$\hat{Y} = 160.90 - 1.3614X$$

After estimating the coefficients of the prediction equation, the equation should be plotted over the data to check for gross calculation errors. Roughly half the data points should be above the line and half below it. In addition, the equation should pass exactly through the point $\bar{X}, \bar{Y}$.

A number of criteria exist for judging the adequacy of the prediction equation. One common measure of the adequacy of the prediction equation is R^2, the proportion of variation explained by the prediction equation. R^2 is called the *coefficient of determination*. This is the ratio of the variation due to the regression, $\Sigma(\hat{Y}_m - \bar{Y})$, to the total variation, $\Sigma(Y_m - \bar{Y})^2$. $\bar{Y}_m$ is the predicted Y value for X_m. The calculation formula is

$$R^2 = \frac{b_1 \Sigma(X_m - \bar{X})(Y_m - \bar{Y})}{\Sigma(Y_m - \bar{Y})^2}$$

$$= \frac{(-1.3614)(-1191.25)}{1958.94} = 0.828$$

Thus for this example the prediction equation explains 82.8 percent of the variation of the tool life. The coefficient of determination and *all* other measures of the precision of a regression relationship must be interpreted with great care. This is not an area for the amateur.

This brief treatment of regression is just an introduction to a complex subject. Further topics include confidence intervals and other measures of precision, multiple regression, and nonlinear regression. The literature provides more information.[10]

4-16 STATISTICAL COMPUTATION DEVICES

The advent of time-sharing computers and programmable calculators has greatly simplified complex statistical analyses. The practitioner can now use many statistical techniques that were not previously considered because of difficulty in understanding the techniques or doing the calculations. Now, procedures define the input to a computer or calculator and the final result is then presented. With all this, accessibility is a danger. The practitioner using these systems must understand the assumptions behind the methods and what the final results do and do not mean. In the haste to obtain an answer and avoid tedious detail, there is a danger of wrong application of a technique or misinterpretation of a result. The serious consequences dictate a need for understanding.

[10] See *Quality Control Handbook*, 3rd ed., sec. 26.

Answers to questions at the beginning of the chapter:

1. Yes
2. Yes
3. Yes
4. No
5. Yes

PROBLEMS

Note: The specific questions have purposely been stated in nonstatistical language to provide the student with some practice in choosing techniques and making assumptions. When required, use a type I error of 0.05 and a confidence level of 95 percent. State any other assumptions needed.

4-1 In the casting industry, the pouring temperature of metal is important. For an aluminum alloy, past experience shows a standard deviation of 15°. During a particular day, five temperature tests were made during the pouring time.

    (a) If the average of these measurements was 1650°, make a statement about the average pouring temperature.

    (b) If you had taken 25 measurements and obtained the same results, what effect would this have on your statement? Make such a revised statement.

4-2 At the casting firm mentioned in problem 4-1, a new aluminum alloy is being poured. During the first day of pouring, five pouring temperature tests were made, with these results:

1705°
1725°
1685°
1690°
1715°

Make a statement about the average pouring temperature of this metal.

4-3 A manufacturer pressure-tests gaskets for leaks. The pressure at which this gasket leaked on nine trials was (in psi):

4000	3900	4500
4200	4400	4300
4800	4800	4300

Make a statement about the average "leak" pressure of this gasket.

4-4 In a test of 500 electronic tubes, 427 were found to be acceptable. Make a statement concerning the true proportion that would be acceptable.

4-5 In a meat packing firm, out of 600 pieces of beef, 420 were found to be Grade A. Make a statement about the true proportion of Grade A beef.

4-6 A specification requires that the average breaking strength of a certain material be at least 180 psi. Past data indicate the standard deviation of individual measurements to be 5 psi. How many tests are necessary to be 99 percent sure of detecting a lot that has an average strength of 170 psi?

4-7 Tests are to be run to estimate the average life of a product. Based on past data on similar products, it is assumed that the standard deviation of individual units is about 20 percent of the average life.

(a) How many units must be tested to be 90 percent sure that the sample estimate will be within 5 percent of the true average?

(b) Suppose funds were available to run only 25 tests. How sure would we be of obtaining an estimate within 5 percent?

Answer: (*a*) 44. (*b*) 78.8 percent.

4-8 A manufacturer of needles has a new method of controlling a diameter dimension. From many measurements of the present method, the average diameter is 0.076 cm with a standard deviation of 0.010 cm. A sample of 25 needles from the new process shows the average to be 0.071. If a smaller diameter is desirable, should the new method be adopted? (Assume that the standard deviation of the new method is the same as that for the present method.)

4-9 In the garment industry, the breaking strength of cloth is important. A heavy cotton cloth must have at least an average breaking strength of 200 psi. From one particular lot of this cloth, these five measurements of breaking strength (in psi) were obtained:

206
194
203
196
192

Does this lot of cloth meet the requirement of an average breaking strength of 200 psi?

Answer: $t = -0.67$.

4-10 In a drug firm, the variation in the weight of an antibiotic, from batch to batch, is important. With our present process, the standard deviation is 0.11 g. The research department has developed a new process that they believe will produce less variation. The following weight measurements (in grams) were obtained with the new process:

7.47
7.49
7.64
7.59
7.55

Does the new process have less variation?

4-11 A paper manufacturer has a new method of coating paper. The less variation in the weight of this coating, the more uniform and better the product. The following 10 sample coatings were obtained by the new method:

**Coating
weights (in
weight/unit
area × 100)**

223	234
215	229
220	223
238	235
230	227

If the standard deviation in the past was 9.3, is this proposed method any better? Should they switch to this method?

Answer: $\chi^2 = 5.43$.

4-12 A manufacturer of rubber products is trying to decide which "recipe" to use for a particular rubber compound. High tensile strength is desirable. Recipe 1 is cheaper to mix, but he is not sure if its strength is about the same as that of recipe 2. Five batches of rubber were made by each recipe and tested for tensile strength. These are the data collected (in psi):

Recipe 1	Recipe 2
3067	3200
2730	2777
2840	2623
2913	3044
2789	2834

Which recipe would you recommend that he use?

4-13 Test runs with five models of an experimental engine showed that they operated, respectively, for 20, 18, 22, 17, and 18 min with 1 gal of a certain kind of fuel. A proposed specification states that the engine must operate for a mean of at least 22 min.

(a) What can we conclude about the ability of the engine to meet the specification?

(b) What is the probability that the sample mean could have come from a process whose true mean is equal to the specification mean?

(c) How low would the mean operating minutes (of the engine population) have to be in order to have a 50 percent chance of concluding that the engine does not meet the specification?

Answer: (a) $t = -3.4$. (b) Approx. 0.03. (c) 20.1.

4-14 A manufacturer claims that the average length in a large lot of parts is 2.680 in. A large amount of past data indicates the standard deviation of individual lengths to be 0.002 in. A sample of 25 parts shows an average of 2.678 in. The manufacturer says that the result is still consistent with his claim because only a small sample was taken.

(a) State a hypothesis to evaluate his claim.

(b) Evaluate his claim using the standard hypothesis testing approach.

(c) Evaluate his claim using the confidence limit approach.

4-15 An engineer wants to determine if the type of test oven or temperature has a significant effect on the average life of a component. She proposes the following design of experiment:

	Oven 1	Oven 2	Oven 3
550°	1	0	1
575°	0	1	1
600°	1	1	0

The numbers in the body of the table represent the number of measurements to be made in the experiment. What are two reasons why interaction cannot be adequately evaluated in this design?

4-16 The molding department in a record manufacturing plant has been making too many defective records. There are many opinions about the reasons. One opinion states that the molding time per record has a cause-and-effect relationship with the number of defectives produced per 100 records. Several trial lots of 100 records each were made with various mold times. The results were:

Time, s	Number defective
2	16
4	13
5	8
7	8
10	4
11	6
13	5
17	3
17	5
20	3

Graph the data and find the least squares estimate of the linear regression line. How much of the variation in the number of defectives does the prediction equation explain?

SUPPLEMENTARY READING

Sections 22–28 of the *Quality Control Handbook,* 3rd ed., McGraw-Hill Book Company, New York, 1974, discuss the statistical methods useful in quality control.

A good source covering statistical methods in further depth is provided in Acheson J. Duncan, *Quality Control and Industrial Statistics,* 4th ed., Richard D. Irwin, Inc., Homewood, Ill., 1974.

EXAMPLES OF EXAMINATION QUESTIONS USED IN FORMER ASQC QUALITY ENGINEER CERTIFICATION EXAMINATIONS AS PUBLISHED IN *QUALITY PROGRESS* MAGAZINE

1 In determining a process average fraction defective using inductive or inferential statistics, we use _____ computed from _____ to make inferences about _____.
(*a*) statistics, samples, populations; (*b*) populations, samples, populations; (*c*) samples, statistics, populations; (*d*) samples, populations, samples; (*e*) statistics, populations, statistics.

2 If in a *t* test, α is 0.01: (*a*) 1 percent of the time we will say that there is a real difference, when there really is not a difference; (*b*) 1 percent of the time we will make a correct inference; (*c*) 1 percent of the time we will say that there is no real difference, but in reality there is a difference; (*d*) 99 percent of the time we will make an incorrect inference; (*e*) 99 percent of the time the null hypothesis will be correct.

3 Suppose that, given $\overline{X} = 50$, and $Z = \pm 1.96$, we established 95 percent confidence limits for μ of 30 and 70. This means that: (*a*) the probability that $\mu = 50$ is 0.05; (*b*) the probability that $\mu = 50$ is 0.95; (*c*) the probability that the interval contains μ is 0.05; (*d*) the probability that the interval contains μ is 0.95; (*e*) none of the above.

4 If it was known that a population of 30,000 parts had a standard deviation of 0.05 s, what size of sample would be required to maintain an error no greater than 0.01 s with a confidence level of 95 percent? (*a*) 235; (*b*) 487; (*c*) 123; (*d*) 96; (*e*) 78.

5 Determine whether the following two types of rockets have significantly different variances at the 5 percent level.

Rocket 1	Rocket 2
61 readings	31 readings
1346.89 mi^2	2237.29 mi^2

6 "A Latin square design is noted for its straightforward analysis of interaction effects." This statement is:(a) true in every case; (b) true sometimes, depending on the size of the square; (c) true only for Greco-Latin squares; (d) false in every case; (e) false except for Greco-Latin squares.

7 A factorial experiment has been performed to determine the effect of factor A and factor B on the strength of a part. An F test shows a significant interaction effect. This means that: (a) either factor A or factor B has a significant effect on strength; (b) both factor A and factor B affect strength; (c) the effect of changing factor B can be estimated only if the level of factor A is known; (d) neither factor A nor factor B affect strength; (e) strength will increase if factor A is increased while factor B is held at a low level.

QUALITY IMPROVEMENT — MANAGEMENT-CONTROLLABLE DEFECTS

5-1 SPORADIC AND CHRONIC QUALITY PROBLEMS

Quality improvement activities are concerned with both sporadic and chronic quality problems (see Figure 5-1). A *sporadic problem* is a sudden adverse change in the status quo, requiring remedy through *restoring* the status quo (e.g., changing a worn cutting tool). A *chronic problem* is a long-standing adverse situation, requiring remedy through *changing* the status quo (e.g., revising a set of unrealistic tolerances).

The distinction is important for two reasons:

1. The approach for solving sporadic problems differs from that for solving chronic problems. Sporadic problems are attacked by the *control* sequence defined in Section 1-2 and developed in Chapters 11 through 14. Chronic problems use the breakthrough sequence discussed in this chapter.
2. Sporadic problems are dramatic (e.g., an irate customer reacting to a shipment of bad parts) and receive immediate attention. Chronic problems are not dramatic because they have been occurring for a long time (e.g., 2 percent scrap has been typical for the past 5 years), are often difficult to solve, and are accepted as inevitable. The danger is that the firefighting on sporadic problems may take continuing priority over effort where larger savings are possible, i.e., on chronic problems.

This chapter takes a quality cost study (Chapter 2) as the starting point for an improvement program on chronic problems and discusses the principles and

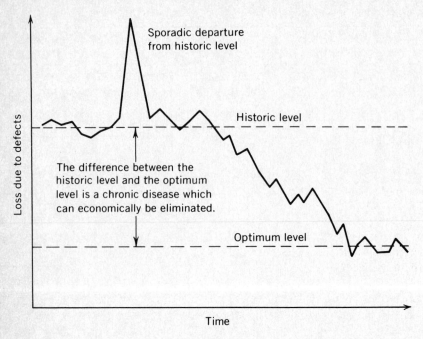

Figure 5-1 Sporadic and chronic quality troubles.

techniques needed to achieve a *breakthrough* to an improved level of quality. The breakthrough achieved not only reduces quality costs but provides input for the quality planning on new products. We start with a definition of the breakthrough sequence.

5-2 BREAKTHROUGH SEQUENCE

The breakthrough sequence[1] for solving chronic quality problems is this:

1. Convince others that a breakthrough is needed—convince those responsible that a change in quality level is desirable and feasible.
2. Identify the vital few projects—determine which quality problem areas are most important.
3. Organize for breakthrough in knowledge—define the organizational mechanisms for obtaining missing knowledge.
4. Conduct the analysis—collect and analyze the facts that are required and recommend the action needed.
5. Determine the effect of proposed changes on the people involved and find ways to overcome the resistance to change.

[1] For a complete development of this theme, see J. M. Juran, *Managerial Breakthrough,* McGraw-Hill Book Company, New York, 1964.

6. Take action to institute the changes.
7. Institute controls to hold the new level.

Thus breakthrough as used in this book is not due to luck but to the effective execution of the foregoing step sequence. Each step will be explained and then two case examples presented to show the integrated sequence.

5-3 BREAKTHROUGH IN ATTITUDES

Step 1 Prove that a breakthrough is needed and create an attitude favorable for embarking on an improvement program.

Chronic problems often require a far-reaching investigation. If the solution were easy, the problem would not be chronic. Investigation may mean that substantial time and resources will be required.

To gain management approval:

1. Collect factual information to show the size of the problem.
   a. Data in terms of quality, cost, or delivery parameters. This might include percent defectives produced, dollar value of scrap, and rework or delays in delivering product. The choice of units of measure varies with the orientation of management, but a most potent way is quality costs (Chapter 2).
   b. Data to show an actual or potential loss of sales income due to quality. This might include customer complaints or a decrease in the market share.
   c. Other information, such as a study of quality of competition or new government legislation.
2. Show the benefits possible from an improvement program and use this to justify the resources requested for the program. This might take the form of percent return on investment, time required to pay back the investment through savings, or other measures.

Even when there is agreement on the importance of a problem, it is still helpful to quantify the size of the quality loss and the potential savings, because it can justify a sufficient investment to solve the problem.

5-4 IDENTIFY THE VITAL FEW PROJECTS—THE PARETO PRINCIPLE

Step 2 A "vital few" contributors to a problem account for most of the total size of the problem. The remaining contributors (the "trivial many") account for a small part of the total problem.

Table 5-1 Medication errors in a hospital

Error type	Number of errors	Percent Of opportunities for errors	Of all errors
Dose administered at wrong time	808	8.3	55
Wrong amount administered	253	2.6	17
Dose omitted	188	1.9	13
Extra dose	113	1.2	8
Unordered drug	88	0.9	6
Wrong dosage form	11	0.1	1
Total	1461	15.0	100

This is the Pareto concept presented in Section 2-5. The example of the paper mill quality problem in that section showed how three successive applications of the Pareto concept narrowed the quality problem to certain defects on six types of paper. An example of the Pareto principle to medication errors in a hospital is shown in Table 5-1. Figure 5-2 shows a graphical example.

The Pareto principle defines priorities for the improvement projects and

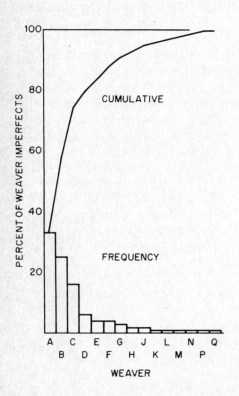

Figure 5-2 Pareto analysis of weaving imperfects.

dramatizes that improvement effort should be deployed unequally over all departments, products, defects, or machines.

5-5 ORGANIZE FOR BREAKTHROUGH IN KNOWLEDGE

Step 3 Organize to secure the new knowledge needed to achieve the improvement.

The investigation of a chronic quality problem can be aided by organizing a steering arm and a diagnostic arm.

A *steering arm* is a person or persons from various departments who give direction and advice on the improvement program. The chairman is often the line manager who will take the bulk of the ultimate action, and the secretary is usually the head of the staff department doing the diagnosis work. The steering arm provides:

1. *Definition and agreement on the specific aims of the improvement program.* For example, consider the vaguely defined problem of "excessive quality costs in a paper mill." A Pareto analysis could reveal the vital few six products. A steering arm might then define that an improvement program would be restricted to these six products and that quality costs on these would be reduced by 50 percent within the next 2 years.
2. *Ideas on possible causes of the problem.* As breakthrough problems are often interdepartmental, a steering arm representing different areas can generate a list of theories on causes.
3. *Authority to experiment.* Part of the investigation of causes involves conducting experiments and/or collecting existing data. If the steering arm includes managers of those departments where the experiments are to be conducted, this will expedite the investigations.
4. *Information and advice on overcoming the "resistance to change" inherent in proposing new approaches.*
5. *Action on implementing the solution to the problem.* If the managers affected have been on the steering arm, it will be more likely that they will agree with the solution and use it.

A *diagnostic arm* is a person or persons brought together to determine the causes, not remedies, of a problem. The diagnostic arm provides:

1. *The time required for the investigation.* Chronic problems require investigation time that the steering arm or other line managers simply do not have.
2. *The diagnostic skills.* The investigation often requires technical skills that line managers do not possess.
3. *Objectivity of analysis.* The steering arm and other line managers all have

loyalties to their own departments, and thus they may not be completely objective in conducting analyses and drawing conclusions.

In the United States, the diagnostic arm is usually a group of professional specialists, although line supervisors also do diagnosis. In contrast, the Japanese make extensive use of line supervisors as well as nonsupervisors (see Section 6-11) for diagnosis.

5-6 CONDUCT THE PROBLEM ANALYSIS (DIAGNOSIS)

Step 4 Conduct the analysis to determine the cause of the problem and a remedy.

The solution to the problem involves two "journeys"—diagnostic and remedial (see step 6).
The diagnostic journey consists of:

1. Study of the symptoms surrounding the defects to serve as a basis for theorizing about causes.
2. Theorizing on the causes of these symptoms.
3. Analysis and experiment to establish the true causes.

We start by defining some critical terms:

A *defect* is any state of unfitness for use, or nonconformance to specification, e.g., oversize, low mean time between failures, poor appearance.

A *problem* is a potential task resulting from the existence of defects. The defects may be so minor that nothing will be done. At the other extreme, the defects may constitute so significant a problem that an organized approach will be structured for solution.

A *project* is a problem selected for solution through an organized approach of diagnosis and remedy.

A *symptom* is an observable phenomenon arising from and accompanying a defect. Sometimes, but not always, the same word is used both as a defect description and as a symptom description, e.g., "open circuit." More usually, a defect will have multiple symptoms, e.g., "insufficient torque" may include the symptoms of vibration, overheating, erratic function, etc.

A *theory* is an unproved assertion as to reasons for the existence of defects and symptoms. Usually, multiple theories are advanced to explain the presence of the observed phenomena.

A *cause* is a proved reason for the existence of the defect. Often there are multiple causes, in which case they follow the Pareto principle, i.e., one or two causes will dominate all the rest.

A *dominant cause* is a major contributor to the existence of defects and one which must be remedied before there can be an adequate solution.

Diagnosis is the process of studying symptoms, taking and analyzing data, conducting experiments to test theories, and establishing relationships between causes and effects.

A *remedy* is a change that can successfully eliminate or neutralize a cause of defects. Usually, there are multiple proposals for remedy, and the remedial process must choose from the alternatives. In some cases, remedy takes place without knowledge of causes; e.g., take back the defective unit and give the customer a new one; cut away the rotten spot on the apple.

Of these two journeys, the diagnostic is the main source of confusion. The reason for this is in part organizational. For sporadic defects—i.e., troubleshooting—the responsibility for diagnosis is usually clear and usually rests with the line supervisor. For chronic defects this responsibility is seldom clear, with the result that no one makes the diagnostic journey.

However, an additional source of confusion is in concepts and terminology. In particular, managers tend to do the following:

1. *Confuse symptom with cause.* For example, internal scrap data sheets often have a column headed "cause," under which are listed such terms as "undersize," "broken," etc. The word "cause" is used in the sense of "reason for scrapping." However, such usage leads managers to assume that the cause of the defects is really known and that hence no diagnosis is needed—only remedy.

2. *Confuse theory with cause.* In discussing causes of defects, it is common for numerous theories to be advanced earnestly and even heatedly. "I *know* this is the cause." What the advocate means is that he or she personally is convinced. However, he or she lacks the data which can convince colleagues in the face of all those other competing theories. Actually, until the diagnosis is complete, it is not known which is the dominant cause. In addition, since many theories had been advanced, only a small minority of the theories turn out to be decisive in the solution. (What all chronic defects have in common is that we do not *know* the causes. Lacking this knowledge, the defect goes on and on, which is what makes it chronic.)

A major fork on the diagnostic journey is to conduct one or both of two analyses:

1. A study to determine whether defects are primarily operator-controllable or management-controllable.
2. A study, for the management-controllable defects, to determine the distribution of the problem causes over design, manufacturing, or usage factors.

Table 5-2 Summary of causes of failure

Classification of failures		Percent of total
1. Engineering		43
Electrical	33	
Mechanical	10	
2. Operational		30
Abnormal or accidental conditions	12	
Manhandling	10	
Faulty maintenance	8	
3. Manufacturing		20
4. Other		7
		100

Source: R. M. C. Greenidge, "The Case of Reliability versus Defective Components et al.," *Electronic Applications Reliability Review,* no. 1, p. 12, 1953.

Such studies can furnish important basic direction to the improvement program.

A classic example of the distribution of causes is shown in Table 5-2. In this example, extensive field failures were occurring on electronic products supplied by a number of companies. A group of 850 failures were thoroughly examined and the failures classified by basic cause. The dramatic percentages in "Engineering" and "Operational" were contrary to the belief that most quality problems were due to manufacturing causes. This dictated an improvement effort aimed at functional areas that had previously not been part of a "quality program." (This and similar studies revealing design as important resulted in the "reliability" movement.)

A *controllable study* is used to learn if the defects are operator-controllable or management-controllable. What is decisive here is whether the criteria for operator self-control have been met. A defect is operator-controllable if *all* the following criteria have been met:

Operators have the means of knowing what they are supposed to do.
Operators have the means of knowing what they are actually doing.
Operators have available to them the means for regulating their performance.

Controllability can be quantified by analyzing the major defects to see whether the foregoing criteria have all been met. Such an analysis was conducted for a textile mill process. In this process, there were 37 different types of defects in the product. However, the top six defects accounted for 75 percent of all the defectiveness. A team consisting of the foreman and an engineer studied these six principal defects, with results as shown in Table 5-3.

Table 5-3 shows that the controllability was clear for two of these defects, uncertain for one of them, and divided as to the other three. (The team es-

Table 5-3 Quantification of controllability

Defect	Percent of total	Percent controllable by:		
		Operator	Uncertain	Management
Leader end off shade	17			17
Start marks	16	8		8
Broken ends	14		14	
Creases	12	2		10
Dirt	11	7		4
Coarse filling	5			5
31 other defects	25		25	
Total	100	17	39	44

timated the allocation as best they could.) With the "trivial many" defects unanalyzed, Table 5-3 indicates that the management-controllable defects dominated by about $2\frac{1}{2}$ to 1.

The box score on defects in most controllability studies indicates that over 80 percent are management-controllable and 20 percent are operator-controllable. This ratio does not appear to vary greatly from one industry to another, but it does vary considerably from one process to another. Obviously, no one needs to accept such figures as applying to his or her own company. Any particular situation can be clarified by making a controllability study.

Many managers harbor deep-seated beliefs that the bulk of defects are due to operator errors, i.e., that defects are mainly operator-controllable. The facts seldom bear this out but the belief persists. In one printing company the managers had traditionally regarded keyboarding errors (the major component of the total error rate) as operator-controllable despite operator protests that the linotype machines made mistakes. When a program was undertaken to improve quality, the managers concluded that this issue needed to be resolved before wholehearted operator support could be enlisted. A tape-operated attachment was used to test several machines by repeat casting 25 lines in succession. It was found that machine-caused errors contributed about half of the keyboarding errors and about a third of the total error rate.[2]

The controllability study is important because the approach to eliminating management-controllable errors is different from that used to eliminate operator-controllable errors. To oversimplify, the former requires a considerable contribution from each of a few people (managers and specialists), whereas the latter requires a small contribution from each of many people.

The approach to diagnosis of operator-controllable defects is discussed in Chapter 6. The approach to diagnosis of management-controllable defects is discussed in the following paragraphs.

Crucial to all of these initial studies is a thorough analysis of the observed defects. These studies should not be based on opinions but on sufficient in-

[2] See *Quality Control Handbook*, 3rd ed., p. 40-13.

depth technical analysis to gain the agreement of all people concerned. This means an analysis of the symptoms of the problem.

The first diagnostic step is to understand the symptoms. Unless the terminology has been precisely defined, the steering arm can be misled. Understanding is derived from reports and autopsies but with cautions as indicated below.

Meanings of words used to describe symptoms Some descriptive words, e.g., "oversize," may cover several degrees of seriousness. In such cases it is quite helpful in diagnosis of symptoms to use several terms to describe these degrees, e.g., "Oversize (critical)," "Oversize (major)," "Oversize (minor)." Other descriptive words are really generic in nature, e.g., "malfunction." Such a word may be used to describe several very different symptoms (e.g., open circuit, reversed wiring, dead battery), each of which arises from very different causes.

A widespread source of confusion is variation in departmental dialect. For example, to the accountant, "scrap" may mean anything thrown away, no matter what the reason; to the quality specialist, "scrap" is something thrown away because of nonconformance or unfitness for use.

This lack of standardization in the meanings of words can confuse managers as to the effect of defects. For example, in an optical company, the term "beauty defect" was company dialect for damaged surfaces on lenses, prisms, etc. This term failed to distinguish among several different aspects of fitness for use:

1. Damage in the focal plane, which significantly impairs fitness for use.
2. Damage which does not significantly impair fitness for use but which is visible to the user during normal use.
3. Damage which does not significantly impair fitness for use and which is not visible to the user during normal use.

The lack of standardization can also confuse managers as to the causes of defects. In a plant making rubber products, there were several sources of torn product: the stripping operation, the machine cutting ("click") operation, and the assembly operation. The single word "tears" failed to distinguish among strip tears, click tears, and assembly tears. One of these categories was largely operator-controllable but involved only 15 percent of all tears. However, one important manager had assumed all the defects to be operator-controllable.

Autopsy of product An essential device for cutting through the confusion in terminology is the autopsy or (seeing with one's own eyes) failed-parts analysis. The steering team (and of course the diagnosticians) should get their hands on the product and learn at first hand how the words used relate to observed conditions of the product. This seeing with one's own eyes is of added value in stimulating realistic theories of causation.

Quantification The frequency and intensity of symptoms is of great signifi-

**Table 5-4 Pareto analysis of defect
types in an optical company**

Defect type	Percent of all defects	Cumulative percent
Scratches	27	27
Chips	25	52
Digs	10	62
Thickness	7	69
Poor film	7	76
All other	24	100

cance in pointing to directions for analysis. The Pareto principle, applied to the records of past performance, can be of great aid in quantifying the symptom pattern. For example, an optical company undertook a project to reduce quality losses in the precision components department. Table 5-4 shows the Pareto study of the defects within the department, based on 3 months' prior data. The top five defects account for 76% of all rejections. Information is of obvious aid to the steering arm in directing the priorities of the study.

Theories: formulation and arrangement To the question "What causes defect X?," the responses are mainly assertions or theories. Such theories are essential if diagnosis is to proceed. The main sources for theories are the steering arm, the diagnostic arm, and the work force.

When the number of theories is small, their interrelation may be understood from seeing the written list. However, as the list grows in size, it also grows in complexity, to a point where the interrelations are difficult to grasp. Now it becomes desirable to create an orderly arrangement of the list of theories. There are two principal ways to create this arrangement.

One method is to reduce the list to writing by identifying the likely major variables. Each of these major variables has "satellites" (i.e., contributing minor variables), which are then grouped under their respective major variables. Table 5-5 shows this method used to depict the variables affecting yield of fine powder chemicals.

The second method is to use a graphic form to show the arrangement of theories. The most highly developed is the *cause-and-effect diagram*.[3] Figure 5-3 shows this diagram presenting the same information as is listed in Table 5-5.

Test of Theories

Theories of causes must be tested, some disproved and some affirmed, until a cause-and-effect relationship is defined so that a remedy can be developed.

[3] See *Quality Control Handbook*, 3rd ed., p. 16-20.

Table 5-5 Orderly arrangement of theories

Raw material	Moisture content
Shortage of weight	Charging speed of wet powder
Method of discharge	Dryer, rpm
Catalyzer	Temperature
Types	Steam pressure
Quantity	Steam flow
Quality	Overweight of package
Reaction	Type of balance
Solution and concentration	Accuracy of balance
B solution temperature	Maintenance of balance
Solution and pouring speed	Method of weighing
pH	Operator
Stirrer, rpm	Transportation
Time	Road
Crystallization	Cover
Temperature	Spill
Time	Container
Concentration	
Mother crystal	
Weight	
Size	

Theories can be tested in three ways: (1) using past data, (2) using current production, and (3) conducting tests and experiments.

Test of theories using past data Some theories can be tested from available records without the need for experimentation or even for study of current production. This type of analysis involves relating product quality data to some theory of causation—process, tools, operators, etc. The relationship may be examined using various statistical tools, such as ranking, correlation, and matrixes.

Ranking An automobile parts plant made 23 types of torque tubes. When tested for dynamic unbalance, the tubes ranged from 52.3 percent defective down to 12.3 percent, the average being 22.1 percent. One of the theories advanced was that a swaging operation was a dominant cause of dynamic unbalance. Since only the large-diameter tubes were swaged, it was an easy matter to prepare a ranking of tubes in order of percent defective and to identify which were swaged. Table 5-6 shows this ranking. The result was dramatic—the worst seven types were all swaged, the best seven all unswaged.[4] The support thus given to the swaging theory resulted in a study of the swaging process. This study showed that the swaging did not closely control the coaxial relationship between the swaged and unswaged diameters, and that the specifi-

[4] A similar approach is described in C. H. Kepner and B. B. Tregoe, *The Rational Manager*, McGraw-Hill Book Company, New York, 1965, chaps. 6–8.

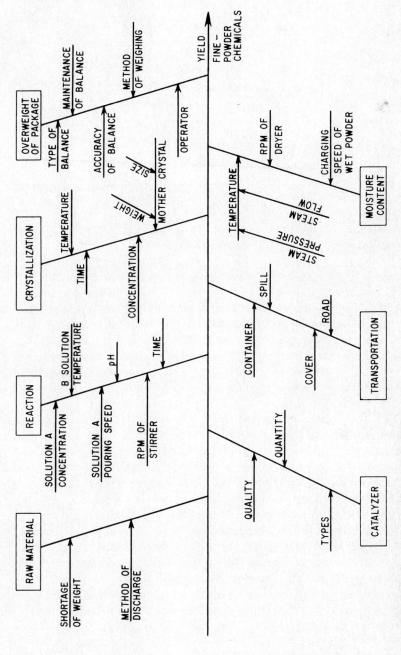

Figure 5-3 Ishikawa cause-and-effect diagram.

Table 5-6 Test of theories by ranking

Type	Percent defective	Swaged (marked ×)	Type	Percent defective	Swaged (marked ×)
A	52.3	×	M	19.2	×
B	36.7	×	N	18.0	×
C	30.8	×	O	17.3	
D	29.9	×	P	16.9	×
E	25.3	×	Q	15.8	
F	23.3	×	R	15.3	
G	23.1	×	S	14.9	
H	22.5		T	14.7	
I	21.8	×	U	14.2	
J	21.7	×	V	13.5	
K	20.7	×	W	12.3	
L	20.3				

cation imposed no limit on this. (See the book by Ott in the Supplementary Reading for a similar diagnostic approach.)

Correlation In one foundry, it was theorized that the dominant cause of pitted castings was too large a "choke" in the pattern. (The choke is a narrow orifice designed to permit free flow of the molten metal and at the same time to obstruct the passage of lumps of sand.) Prior data were available on the percent defective of many lots of castings made from a variety of patterns. It was easy to measure the choke thickness on the physical patterns and then to correlate choke thickness against pit scrap. A positive correlation became evident (Figure 5-4). Subsequent experimentation established 0.050 in as the optimum choke thickness.

Matrixes A plant making hunting guns experienced over 10 percent rejections of the assembled guns as a result of "open hard after fire." Assembly was an intricate operation, requiring about 1 h of the time of a skilled workman. One theory of cause of the defect was poor workmanship. This theory was vigorously opposed by the production supervision, who asserted that there were times when the defect virtually disappeared of its own accord.

Past records were available, showing, for each gun, the operator who assembled it and the results of the tests. When these data were organized into a matrix (Table 5-7a), it became evident that there were drastic month-to-month changes in percent rejections, confirming the assertions of the production supervision. Clearly, the assemblers had not suddenly learned in January (1.8 percent defective) how to do this job and then suddenly forgotten it in February (22.6 percent defective).

Still more information was derived from this same matrix by summing up the defects for the five "best" and five "worst" assemblers (Table 5-7b). This analysis showed that during all months, good, bad, or indifferent, the five

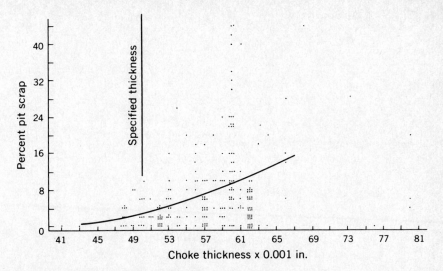

Figure 5-4 Test of theories by correlation.

Table 5-7*a* Matrix analysis

Assembly operator rank	Nov.	Dec.	Jan.	Feb.	Mar.	Apr.	Total
1	4	1	0	0	0	0	5
2	1	2	0	5	1	0	9
3	3	1	0	3	0	3	10
4	1	1	0	2	2	4	10
5	0	1	0	10	2	1	14
6	2	1	0	2	2	15	22
7	2	4	1	11	1	7	26
8	2	0	0	7	23	7	39
9	6	3	0	18	9	4	40
10	13	4	0	10	10	9	46
11	15	8	2	11	10	3	49
12	6	6	5	18	6	10	51
13	7	2	1	28	25	1	64
14	16	8	1	14	11	15	65
15	2	16	8	22	8	23	79
16	22	18	1	33	7	13	94
17	18	8	3	37	9	23	98
18	16	17	0	22	36	11	102
19	27	13	4	62	4	14	124
20	6	5	2	61	22	29	125
21	39	10	2	45	20	14	130
22	26	17	4	75	31	35	188
Total	234	146	34	496	239	241	1390
% defective	10.6	6.6	1.8	22.6	10.9	11.0	10.5

Table 5-7b Matrix analysis

	Nov.	Dec.	Jan.	Feb.	Mar.	Apr.	Total
5 best	9	6	0	20	5	8	48
5 worst	114	62	12	265	113	103	669
Ratio	13	10	∞	13	23	13	14

"worst" assemblers had consistently more than 10 times as many defects as the five "best." This suggested that the best operators possessed some "knack" or form of secret knowledge not known to the "worst." (Alternatively, the "worst" operators possessed some form of secret ignorance.) It was found on shop study that the "best" assemblers filed away one of the critical piece part dimensions and that this constituted the knack. The managers then embodied the knack into the official technology, and the defect virtually disappeared.

In these cases, simple techniques (ranking, correlation, matrixes) were combined with other readily available data (type of process, characteristics of tools, identity of workers) to affirm the validity of theories. These examples do not exhaust the list of techniques available or the kind of job information available to make good use of past data. However, they do demonstrate how it is possible to make a good deal of diagnostic progress "in the office," with minimal effort and without experimentation.

Test of theories using current production In most projects, there is need to secure information beyond that available from past data. Much of this missing information comes from the study of current production. There are multiple forms of such study, including process-capability studies, dissection of process and product, cutting new "windows" in the process, and experiments. All these forms of study except process-capability studies are discussed below under their respective headings.

Process-capability studies are one of the most widely used forms, since one of the theories most widely encountered is "the process can't hold the tolerances." Testing this theory requires a study of current production to determine the process capability. Once this capability has been measured, it can be compared with the tolerances to determine whether the process can hold the tolerances. Process capability is discussed in Chapter 12.

Dissection: Process and Product

The collections of products known as "lots" commonly result from numerous arrays of variables, as shown in Figure 5-5. In most projects it is feasible and useful to "dissect" these multiple variables into their components so as to quantify their size and to discover which is dominant. This dissection takes various forms, as we now discuss.

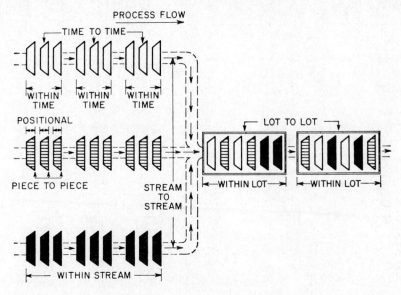

Figure 5-5 The anatomy of lot formation.

Stream-to-stream analysis Often "lots" are the result of the confluence of several separate streams of product, as shown in Figure 5-5. These streams differ from each other because of being processed by different machines, from different material batches, by different operators, etc. When a study is made of the nature of the product coming from each stream, the results are of value in affirming or denying the validity of theories.

Common examples of stream-to-stream differences are the cases of multiple-spindle metal cutting machines; multiple-cavity molding operations (plastic, glass, metal, etc.); multiple-spindle textile machines. In all such cases the special effort required in the analysis is to segregate the product to avoid the mixtures created during normal production. Sometimes this segregation is made simple by preplanning the identification, e.g., using cavity numbers in the molding dies. In other cases, the segregation can become tedious.

For example, a polishing operation conveyed the parts to the polishing wheel in an endless chain of 138 holding fixtures. The polished pieces exhibited defects in the form of unpolished areas, and these defects seemed to present no orderly pattern. When a diagnostician dissected the product into 138 separate streams, each stream consisting of product held by only one of the fixtures, the "random" patterns immediately became identifiable with the respective fixtures (Figure 5-6).

Time-to-time analysis Within many streams, there is a time-to-time "drift"; e.g., the processing solution gradually becomes more dilute, the tools gradually

Order of production

Successive holding fixtures

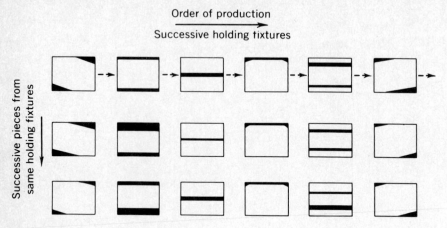

Figure 5-6 Dissection—train of fixtures.

wear, the operator becomes fatigued. Such drifts can often be quantified to determine the magnitude of the effect.

In a textile carding operation, there was a cyclic rise and fall of yarn weights, the cycle being about 45 min in length (Figure 5-7). The reaction of the production superintendent was immediate: "The only thing we do every 45 minutes or so is to stuff that feed box." In like manner, a process for making asbestos roofing shingles was found to produce abnormal weights every 6 min, on a precise timetable. Six minutes was also the interval for dumping a new load of material into the machine.

Products also may exhibit piece-to-piece variation or within-piece variation,

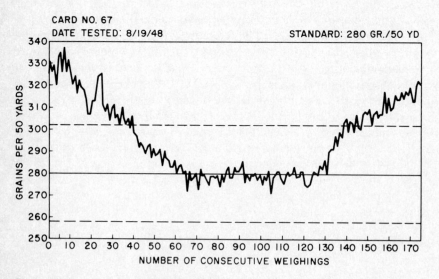

Figure 5-7 Consecutive weighings of card yarn.

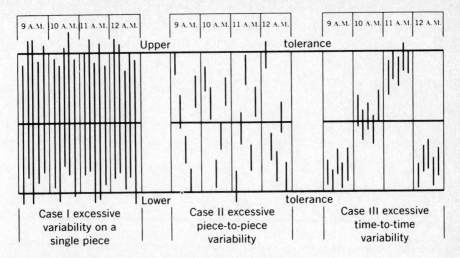

Figure 5-8 Multi-Vari chart.

variations which are independent of stream-to-stream or time-to-time variations. The *Multi-Vari chart*[5] is a very useful tool for analyzing such situations. A vertical line depicts the range of variation within a single piece of product. In Figure 5-8, the left-hand case is one in which the within-piece variation alone is too great in relation to the tolerance. Hence there is no solution unless within-piece variation is reduced. The middle example is a case in which within-piece variation is comfortable, occupying only about 20 percent of the tolerance. The problem is piece-to-piece variation. In the right-hand example, the problem is excess time-to-time variability.

Defect-concentration analysis A totally different form of piece-to-piece variation is the defect-concentration study used for attribute types of defects. The purpose is to discover whether defects are located in the same physical area. The technique has long been used by shop personnel when they observe that *all* pieces are defective, and in precisely the same way. However, when the defects are intermittent or become evident only in later departments, the analysis can be beyond the unaided memory of the shop personnel.

For example, a problem of pitted castings was analyzed by dividing the castings into 12 zones and tallying up the number of pits in each zone over many units of product. The concentration at the gates became evident, as did areas which were remarkably free of pits (Figure 5-9).

Tests of theories by cutting new windows In some cases, the diagnosis of causes requires further digging to obtain additional measurements or other knowledge not currently available. This is called *cutting new windows* and it can take several forms:

---

[5] See *Quality Control Handbook*, 3rd ed., pp. 16-31, 16-32.

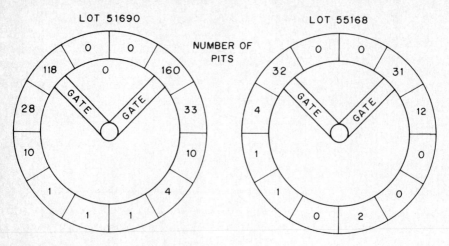

Figure 5-9 Concentration of pits in cast rings.

1. *Measurement at intermediate stages of a single operation.* An example concerned a defect known as "voids" in welded joints of pressure vessels. Initial diagnosis established six sources of variation: operator, time-to-time, joint-to-joint, layer-to-layer, within-layer, and within one welding "bead." Past data were available to permit analysis of the first three sources as possible causes of voids. The remaining three could not be analyzed since the critical X-ray test was performed only when a joint was completely finished. The answer was to "cut a new window" by making an X ray after each of the several beads needed to make a joint. The data established that the main variable was within-bead variation and that the problem was concentrated at the start of the bead.

2. *Measurement following noncontrolled operations.* A simple example was a process for machining the inside of gun barrels, consisting of a sequence of operations of drill, redrill, and ream. There was no measurement after the first two operations. However, after reaming, the inside diameters were measured with an air gage. Regularly, some of the barrels were found to have inside diameters with severe gouges in one or more locations.

Did the gouging take place during the drill, redrill, or ream operation? There was no way of knowing, since the air gage head could measure only the ream diameter. When additional gaging heads were made to fit the drill and redrill diameters, the way was open to solving the problem.

3. *Measurement of additional or related properties.* In the production of phonograph records it was necessary to cut new windows to understand the variability of the pressing process. Data collected on pressure and temperature in the record mold and the viscosity of the record material established these three variables as important to final record quality. The process was then changed from relying on automatic timers (to control the pressing cycle) to computer-controlled processes that monitor the three variables and analyze the data to decide when any given record has reached optimum molding conditions.

4. *Study of workers' methods.* In some situations involving management-controllable defects (and many more involving operator-controllable defects), there are *consistent* differences in the defect levels coming from various production operators. Month after month, some operators are "good" and others are "poor." In such situations, there must be a cause for this consistent difference in observed performance. The managers know only that the difference is there and that improvement—by bringing all workers up to the level of the best—is possible.

There are two main approaches to discovering the cause of worker-to-worker differences:

1. *Ask the workers.* In a centrifugal casting operation, one team of melters was found to have significantly and consistently less pitted castings than all other melters. On inquiry, the "best" melter volunteered that each morning, before pouring any castings, he cleaned out the accumulated metal adhering to the inside surfaces of the spout used to transfer molten metal from the ladle to the casting machines. None of the other melters did this. This difference in practice provided a vital clue to bringing all melters up to the level of the best.

2. *Study the work methods.* Where the secret knowledge is not available from personal disclosure by the worker, it may be discovered anyway by studying the methods used by the "good" and "poor" workers. These studies will always disclose differences in method, and often one or two of these differences are found to be decisive. They constitute the "knack"—a small difference in method which accounts for a large difference in results. In some cases it is necessary to videotape the activity of operators to discover the knack.

Cutting new windows obtains new knowledge in the laboratory, shop, or field for diagnosis in the same way that a physician gets additional knowledge through tests on patients. Obtaining the knowledge requires additional time and funds. Here a steering arm of management-level people can use its power to supply the time and funds.

Test of theories through experiments Experiments in the laboratory or outside world may be necessary to determine and analyze the dominant causes of a quality problem.

Four types of diagnostic experiments are summarized in Table 5-8.

Experiments for evaluating one or two suspected variables are sometimes called *rifleshot experiments.* An example from a foundry is shown in Figure 5-10. The purpose was to test the theory that the gating design was a major cause of excess eccentricity in the castings and of poor tension of the final product (rings). Note the effective way of graphing the results in the form of a frequency distribution for each design.

In the exploratory experiment, the dominant variables are not known but

Table 5-8 Types of diagnostic experiments

Type of experiment	Purpose and approach
Evaluating suspected dominant variables	Evaluate changes in values of a variable by dividing a lot into several parts and processing each portion at some different value, e.g., temperature
Exploratory experiments to determine dominant variables	Statistically plan an experiment in which a number of characteristics are carefully varied in a manner to yield data for quantifying each dominant variable and the interactions among variables
Production experiments (evolutionary operation)	Make small changes in selected variables of a process and evaluate the effect to find the optimum combination of variables
Simulation	Use the computer to study the variability of several dependent variables which interact to yield a final result

must be pursued by a formal experiment. This is called an *unbridled experiment*.

A well-organized exploratory experiment has a high probability of identifying the dominant causes of variability. However, there is a risk of overloading the experimental plan with too much detail. A check on overextension of the experiment is to require that the analyst prepare a written plan to be reviewed by the steering arm. This written plan must define:

1. The characteristics of material, process, environment, and product to be observed.
2. The control of these characteristics during the experiment. A characteristic may be:

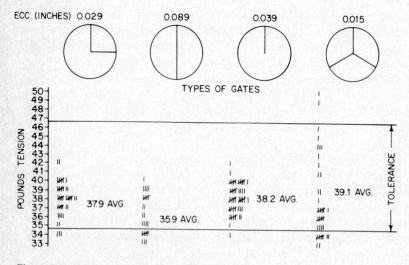

Figure 5-10 Trial run to discover optimum gating.

  a. Allowed to vary as it will, and measured as is (M).
  b. Held at a standard value (S).
  c. Deliberately randomized (R).
  d. Deliberately varied, in several classes or treatments (V).
3. The means of measurement to be used (if different from standard practice).

If the plan shows that the experiment may be overloaded, a "dry run" in the form of a small-scale experiment is in order. A review of the dry-run experiment can then help decide the final plan.

Production experiments Experimentation is often regarded as an activity that can only be performed under laboratory conditions. To achieve maximum performance from some manufacturing processes, it is necessary to determine the effect of key process variables on process yield or product properties under shop conditions. Laboratory experimentation to evaluate these variables does not always yield conclusions that are completely applicable to shop conditions. When justified, a "pilot plant" may be set up to evaluate process variables. However, the final determination of the effect of process variables must often be done during the regular production run by informally observing the results and making changes if these are deemed necessary. Thus informal experimentation *does* take place on the manufacturing floor.

To systematize informal experimentation and provide a methodical approach for process improvement, G. E. P. Box developed a technique known as *evolutionary operations* (EVOP). EVOP is based on the concept that every manufactured lot has information to contribute about the effect of process variables on a quality characteristic. Although such variables could be analyzed by a design of experiment (Section 4-12), EVOP introduces *small* changes into these variables according to a planned pattern of changes. These changes are small enough to avoid nonconformance but large enough to gradually establish (1) what variables are important, and (2) the optimum process values for these variables. Although this approach is slower than a formal design of experiment, results are achieved in a production environment without the additional costs of a special experiment.

The steps are:

1. Select two or three independent process variables which are likely to influence quality. For example, time and temperature were selected as variables affecting the yield of a chemical process.
2. Change these steps according to a plan (see Figure 5-11). This diagram shows the *plan*, not any data. For example, a reference run was made with the production process set to run at 130°C for $3\frac{1}{2}$ h. The next batch (point 1 in Figure 5-11) was run at 120°C for 3 h. The first *cycle* contains five runs, one at each condition. Samples were taken from each batch and analyses made.

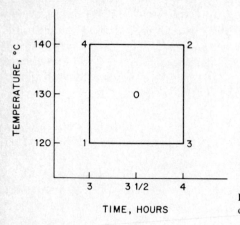

Figure 5-11 An EVOP plan. Numbers are in run order. O is the reference run.

TIME, HOURS

3. After the second repetition of the plan (cycle 2) and each succeeding cycle, calculate the effects.[6]
4. When one or more of the effects is significant, change the midpoints of the variables and perhaps their ranges.
5. After eight cycles, if no variable has been shown to be effective, change the ranges or select new variables.
6. Continue moving the midpoint of the EVOP plan and adjust the ranges as necessary.
7. When a maximum has been obtained, or the rate of gain is too slow, drop the current variables from the plan and run a new plan with different variables.

EVOP is a highly structured form of production experimentation. Ott (see Supplementary Reading) presents a variety of practical design and analysis techniques for solving production quality problems.

Simulation experiments From the field of operations research comes a technique called *simulation* that can be useful in analyzing quality problems. Simulation provides a method of studying the effect of a number of variables on a final quality characteristic—but all of this is done on paper without conducting experiments! A simulation study requires the following inputs:

1. Definition of the output variable(s).
2. Definition of the input variable(s).
3. Description of the complete system relating the input and output variables.
4. Data on the distribution of each input variable. Thus variability is accepted as inherent to the process.

In simulation, a system model is developed and translated into a computer

[6] See *Quality Control Handbook*, 3rd ed., sec. 27A.

program. This program not only defines the relationship between input and output variables but makes provision for storing the distribution of each input variable. The computer then selects values at random from each input distribution and combines these values, using the relationship defined, to generate a simulated value of the output variable. Each repetition of this process results in a simulated output result. These can then be formed into a frequency distribution. The payoff is to make *changes* in the input variables or the relationships, run another simulation, and observe the effect of the change. Thus the significance of variables can be evaluated "on paper," and this provides one more way of evaluating theories on causes of problems.

Simulation has been applied to many quality problems, including interacting tolerances, circuit design, and reliability.

Diagnosis for Nondissectible Characteristics

A characteristic is *dissectible* if it is measurable during the process of manufacture, e.g., a shaft diameter as it progresses through a series of mechanical operations, or the viscosity of a resinous material as it is processed into a varnish.

A characteristic is *nondissectible* if it cannot be measured during such progression. Examples are the taste of a whiskey blend, the sharpness of a razor blade, the tensile strength of a casting, and the electrical output of an electron tube. These examples are all alike in that the characteristics do not even exist until a whole series of manufacturing operations has been performed.

Most of the examples cited in this chapter have consisted of dissectible characteristics. For such cases, the diagnostician is greatly aided by the opportunity to make measurements at successive process stages or even to cut new windows for this purpose. The nondissectible characteristic lacks this feature, so the diagnostician must use other approaches. There are several of these:

1. Convert nondissectible characteristics to dissectible ones through:
   a. Measurement of related but dissectible properties, e.g., hardness used as a measure of tensile strength or viscosity used as a measure of polymerization.
   b. Creation of a new instrument, e.g., the airflow instrument for measuring uniformity of textile sliver.
   c. Use of a parallel pilot plant, i.e., samples are processed in a laboratory-controlled pilot plant, thereby providing an early control against the results of production in the regular departments.
2. Correlate process variables with product results. A common approach is to take data on current production for those process variables believed to influence the product characteristic under study. The resulting product is also measured, following which use is made of statistical analysis to test for cause-and-effect relationships.
3. Experiment using trail lots. This differs from approach 2 because the trial

lot is deliberately designed to be processed specially. This special design reduces the work of experimentation and permits drawing conclusions which have a wider range of application than would result from letting nature take its course.

Remedy

Once the diagnosis has established the cause-and-effect relationships, next comes the remedy. This section discusses the remedy for management-controllable defects and Chapter 6 discusses remedy for operator-controllable defects. Remedies may be proposed and tested by the steering arm and diagnostic arm, but they must be implemented by those responsible for the causes of the problem as determined by diagnosis.

Remedy through change in technology Many remedies involve changes in processes, instruments, methods, etc. The diagnosis for cause often points to these and clarifies the economics as well.

Cases of conflicting terminology, incomplete information, vague orders, or lack of standards are all forms of failure to provide the work force with knowledge of what they are supposed to do. They are usually economical to remedy.

As the cost of remedy rises (new tools, processes), the need for return-on-investment calculations becomes acute. Here it is useful to secure the aid of industrial engineering and finance personnel, who are skilled in preparing such studies and whose "certifications" tend to carry weight with upper management.

The greatest risk involves the cases where the process variability exceeds the necessary tolerable range yet *the process is the best known*. To improve the process would involve a form of research, with all the uncertainties associated with such a journey into the unknown. However, a solution in such cases constitutes a breakthrough (often patentable) and thereby a competitive advantage.

Remedy through change in standards One of the possible remedies for chronic defects is to change the standards. In consequence, one of the directions for diagnosis should be to look at the validity of the standards. Challenging the standards is repugnant to some people on the grounds that any widening of standards represents a degradation of quality. Sometimes this resistance may be valid, but often it is not.

The alarm signals which point to a review of standards include:

1. A lack of correlation between (a) the principal defects which stimulate field complaints and returns and (b) the principal defects found by the factory inspectors.
2. A situation in which the personnel who set the standards have no clear knowledge of the needs of fitness for use. These situations abound in the

case of sensory qualities and require field studies on panels of users to establish realistic standards.

3. Cases in which nonconforming components discovered in-house are regularly repaired or discarded but have never been subjected to trial of fitness for use. The need here may be to set up an experiment in collaboration with the users. Through such experiments it may be found that the nonconforming product is in fact fit for use or that the economics of use are more favorable than the economics of nonuse.

    Figure 5-12 shows the trend of percent scrap on a mechanical component over a 2-year period. In September of the first year, a process change was made, and during the following 8 months the scrap levels fell from 32 percent to 24 percent. Meanwhile, through collaboration with the users, a change in standards was made, resulting in a drop from 24 percent to 10 percent. The gain from change in standards (14 percent) exceeded the gain from change in process (8 percent).

4. Cases in which the user is overspecifying, to his or her detriment. For example, a company bidding on specifications for an instrumentation system noted that there were requirements for interchangeability not only on the subsystems but also on the components entering the subsystems. The former was obviously an essential requirement for field use; the latter was not, since the components were of a nature such that any repairs involving replacement of components could be made only at the factory site and not in the field.

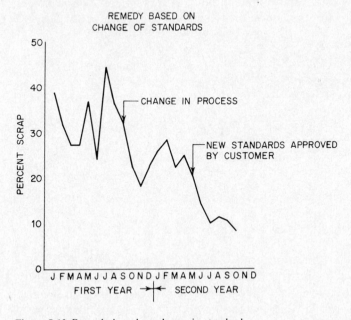

Figure 5-12 Remedy based on change in standards.

The response to the foregoing alarm signals is to set up experiments which can validly establish the needs of fitness for use. A common road block to such experiments is the assumption that the designers had established their tolerances by experiment. For most tolerances this assumption is not valid.

A more valid objection arises under the following set of facts. The prevailing product acceptance standards do not reflect the needs of fitness for use and can be relaxed. However, there is objection to this relaxation on the grounds that the process controls will then also be relaxed, thereby making the product worse and "crowding" the new (relaxed) product acceptance standards. This objection is well founded in plants, where this "crowding" has been a way of life, and it is a plausible reaction in any case, even if the real resistance has its origins in the cultural pattern. A sensible response to such an objection is to establish and publish a scoreboard on process performance. Such publication provides assurance to the objectors that the process is in fact being kept in control. Alternatively, it sounds a public alarm in cases of lack of control.

Remedy by enduring the defects This solution is not merely a matter of "suffer and sort," although such is sometimes the economical solution. The economics of cost of avoiding defects versus cost of enduring are largely controlling in the case of internal defects which are endured at one stage to be caught at another.

Even when the defects make the product clearly unfit for use, they may be endured if they occur rarely. In such cases, the cost of finding a defect through sorting soars as the percent defective declines. The cost of finding a defect compared to the sales value of the unit of product is another useful comparison.

This then completes the journeys of symptom to cause and cause to remedy.

5-7 DEAL WITH RESISTANCE TO CHANGE

Step 5 Deal with the cultural resistance to the needed technical changes.

The purpose of breakthrough is change—to solve a chronic problem. Change has two facets:

1. *Technological change:* the effect on the machines, products, procedures, etc.
2. *Social change:* the effect on the people involved.

People often voice objections to *technological* change, although the true reason for their objection is the *social* effect. Thus those proposing the change can be misled by the objections stated. For example, an industrial engineer once proposed a change in work method that involved moving the storage of finished parts from a specific machine to a central storage area. The engineer was confused by the worker's resistance to the new method. The method seemed to benefit all parties concerned, but the worker argued that it "would not work." The foreman was perceptive enough to know the true reason for resistance—the worker's production was superb and many people stopped at his machine to admire and compliment him. Who would want to give up that pleasure?

Social change strongly depends on the "culture" of the people involved. Culture is a body of learned behavior, a collection of beliefs, habits, practices, and traditions shared by a group of people. To achieve change we must:

1. Be aware that we are dealing with a pattern of human habits, beliefs, and traditions (culture) that may differ from our own.
2. Discover just what will be the social effects of the proposed technological changes.

Some Recommendations

1. Establish the *need* for the change in terms that are important to the people involved rather than on the basis of the logic of the change.
2. Use participation to get ideas on both the technical and social aspects of the change.
   a. Know the people for whom the change is intended. What are their short- and long-range goals, their problems, etc.?
   b. Announce the need for a change and provide for participation of those concerned as early as possible.
   c. Use the members of the culture (maybe the steering arm) to furnish advice on the possible social effects of a technological change.
   d. Where a change is to be made in the work system for a group of workers, allow the workers to create as much of the change as possible.
   e. Consider using a "change catalyst" to help in the planning and implementation of the change. The change catalyst is a respected person who can supply objectivity to the analysis and implementation.
   f. Answer suggestions from workers promptly and in a manner that shows respect for the worker.
   g. Treat all people with dignity.
   h. Keep the change relatively small so it can be introduced gradually and modified as experience dictates. Build major programs on a foundation of previous successes.
   i. Produce rewarding results early.
   j. Guard against surprises by keeping everyone informed.
3. Gain agreement on the change.
   a. Try persuasion to secure change. Much depends here on the extent of prior participation and on the extent to which the individual is "treated with dignity."
   b. Change the environment in a way that makes it easy for the individual to change his point of view.

   c. Remedy the causes of resistance from any of the line personnel.
   d. Create a social climate that favors the new habits.
   e. Explain what each person must do under the new procedure. What must they do "different"?
   f. Eliminate technical jargon in explaining the change.
   g. Reduce the impact of changes by weaving them into an existing broader pattern of behavior, or by letting them ride in on the back of some acceptable change.
   h. Put yourself in the other person's place.

Dealing with resistance to change will always be an art!

5-8 INSTITUTE THE CHANGE

Step 6 Convince the necessary departments to take action to institute the changes.

This involves (*a*) gaining the approval of management (if required) for instituting the solution, and (*b*) installing the solution in a way that will make it effective.

The presentation to management should explain the size of the current problem (breakthrough step 1), the proposed solution together with a summary of alternative solutions, the cost of the remedy and the expected benefits, the efforts taken to anticipate the effects of the solution on the people involved, and the restrictions on the applicability of the solution.

Installing the proposed solution requires adequate training and evaluating the solution in practice. The approach should:

1. Present a clear definition of the new procedure and provide sufficient training to learn the new steps.
2. Seek out opinion leaders in a group but also work with the groups as a whole in gaining acceptance.
3. Allow time for reflection on a proposed change and choose the right time for implementing the change.

This leads to the last step in the breakthrough sequence.

5-9 INSTITUTE CONTROLS

Step 7 Institute controls to hold the new level of performance.

The final step in breakthrough is to follow progress on the problem solution to make sure that (*a*) the solution continues to be effective, and (*b*) unforeseen problems are resolved.

In many cases, the follow-up can simply be a periodic audit of the new procedures. An audit will probably detect any serious deviation from the selected solution. However, such periodic audits must be scheduled, else they will be forgotten (and never conducted). All organizations abound with cases in which documented procedures are *not* being followed. Sometimes, of course, the procedures may be wrong, but often they are correct and simply not being followed.

A formal follow-up on the solution found by breakthrough is the full control sequence for sporadic problems (see Chapter 1).

5-10 CASE EXAMPLES OF THE BREAKTHROUGH PROCESS

The sequence of steps in the breakthrough process will now be traced by an example. A plant making piston rings for aircraft engines was experiencing high scrap in the foundry.

Step 1: Breakthrough in attitude The physical volume of scrap, and the accounting reports on continuing unfavorable variances from standard costs, had already made the defect problems notorious. A quality cost study showed that the total quality costs came to about $1.2 million per year, of which $871,000 were internal failures. These figures sharpened management's determination to find ways to reduce the loss.

Step 2: Discover the vital few A Pareto analysis of the quality costs (Table 5-9) showed that the principal problem was "pits," involving quality costs of $315,000 per year. All agreed that this should be the first project.

Step 3: Organize for breakthrough The scrap problem was so severe in relation

Table 5-9 Pareto analysis by defects—estimated defect costs in a foundry

Defect name	Annual cost, $000	Percent of all defect costs		Annual cost 3 years later, $000
		This defect	Cumulative	
Pits	315	36	36	55
Light	78	9	45	30
Physical excess	73	8	53	40
Hard	41	5	58	20
Wide gaps	39	4	62	30
Thin face	32	4	66	8
Rough sides	30	3	69	16
Broken (foundry)	30	3	72	15
Casting	24	3	75	13
Broken (machining)	23	3	78	18
All other	186	22	100	144
Total	871	100		389

to the size of the factory that the principal managers collectively became the steering arm—an informal team to guide the projects. They consisted of the factory manager, technical manager, foundry manager, machine shop manager, quality manager, and an outside consultant. The diagnostic arm consisted of the quality control engineer. (Later this was increased to three engineers.)

Step 4: Diagnose the causes The piston rings start out as centrifugal castings made on 12 identical machines. As the heated mold spins on a horizontal axis, molten metal is poured in and this solidifies as a hollow cylinder or "pot." The pot then goes to the machine shop to be cut into rings, turned and ground to precise size, etc.

The journey from symptom to cause started with a list of the theories as to what caused pits. About 40 theories were proposed, e.g., metal temperature, time required to pour the metal, the melters' adherence to procedure, rotational speed of the centrifugal casting machine, etc.

After much deliberation and no agreement on the validity of the various theories, it was concluded that new knowledge was needed about the process. The steering arm authorized such a study to be made by recording process conditions and subsequent product quality for 2400 pots as they progressed through the various shop operations. The quality control engineers were directed to record the process data and the subsequent inspection findings on the completed piston rings. The resulting information was a statistician's dream.

The data on pouring time were plotted against the subsequent scrap (Figure 5-13). This simple scatter diagram suggested that scrap seemed to increase with pouring time, so the theory of time as a major cause looked promising. This was supported by an "autopsy" of some defective piston rings which revealed a premature freezing of metal—possibly due to lengthy pouring time.

When the data sheets were sorted for another variable—the foundry melter—a new relationship emerged. One of the melters—Mr. Knight—had a product with far fewer pits than any other melter. Analysis of the data failed to disclose why, so the steering arm decided to interview Knight. (This required that some steering-arm members swallow their professional pride.) Among Knight's disclosures was his habit at startup (each morning) of ramming a metal rod through each spout to clean out any metal adhering to the inside surfaces. (Again the time variable shows up—a clean spout permits a swifter flow of the molten metal.) The regular procedures did not require this cleaning; Knight did it because he was naturally a tidy housekeeper. (The engineers who recorded the process data had missed this because they started work an hour later than Knight!)

This discovery finally led to a full remedy, which included larger pouring spouts and the use of scales by melters to weigh out the amount of metal being poured.

Step 5: Breakthrough in the cultural pattern There was no cultural resistance from the managers. They were a part of the study plan from the beginning, so it

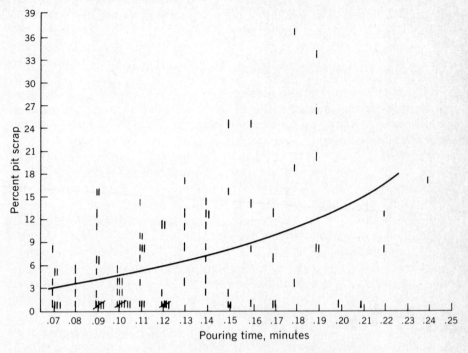

Figure 5-13 Percent pit scrap versus pouring time: Unit A, Machines 1, 2, and 3.

was their plan and they acted on the findings. However, there was some cultural resistance from the workforce. The managers tried to keep this resistance to a minimum; e.g., they asked Knight to serve part time as a trainer to teach the findings to the other melters. Nevertheless, there was some cultural resistance. For example, some of the melters would not use the scales to weigh the metal. They preferred to use the old method of estimate by eye.

Step 6: Take action to institute the improvements In this case, the data and analysis resulted in agreement by the steering arm on the numerous actions needed. They directed that these actions be taken.

Step 7: Institute controls to hold the new level It was decided to report the percent scrap on a monthly basis. The reduction was dramatic, but then the scrap rate started to increase. It was found that the melters had strayed from their new instructions; e.g., they were no longer using scales to measure out the metal. To assure adherence to process procedures, a process audit was instituted. This audit soon enabled the managers to restore the percent scrap to the levels reached by the improvement studies.

The entire study required 9 person-years of diagnostic time spread over 3 calendar years. The cost of this engineering time plus the cost of added tools and instruments totaled $150,000. The resulting savings (on pits and other vital few defects) came to about $600,000 year after year—a very large return on the investment.

Another Case Example of the Breakthrough Sequence

Breakthrough does not have to involve the formal organization and investigation described in the example of pits. This example comes from a small manufacturer of capacitors. The plant manager had been exposed to the breakthrough process and decided to try it.

He started by making the first quality cost study at the plant. The "cost of rejects" was $170,000 per year and this convinced him and the quality control manager to embark on a breakthrough project (step 1). A Pareto analysis (step 2) revealed that dielectric strength failures alone accounted for $71,100 per year. In this case, the plant manager and quality control manager were the steering arm and also did much of the diagnosis with help from their subordinates as needed (step 3).

In diagnosis (step 4), they began looking for "jobs that normally ran well" to be compared to "consistently poor runners." This comparison led to two surprises:

1. The electrical quality of the Kraft insulating tissue used in the capacitors varied significantly among the three suppliers (dissection into streams). Further, incoming inspection tests could not detect this. In one instance tissue from one supplier yielded less than 1 percent dielectric strength failures, whereas the same design from another supplier yielded 9 percent failures.
2. The standard method for dielectric strength testing was destroying good capacitors by testing to unnecessarily severe levels that were not required for fitness for use.

It was decided to change suppliers and change the level of testing. In addition, suppliers were asked to help find a more meaningful way of assessing dielectric strength of the material before it was made into a capacitor.

These changes were instituted without any problems and a saving of about $65,000 per year was achieved (steps 5 and 6). Controls for the future include monitoring of field returns and having suppliers monitor their process to correlate it with the rate of dielectric strength failures in capacitors for individual lots of paper (step 7).

PROBLEMS

5-1 A quality problem has been traced to variation in the thickness of 2-in-wide incoming steel, and the sampling plan used to check the steel is being questioned. The steel carries a tolerance of ±0.001 in, which must be met, since parts punched from the steel are later stacked up on one another and the cumulative error of over- or undersize pieces cannot be tolerated.

The present sampling plan is based on measuring the first lap of the selected coils. But the question arises: "Are the measurements on the first lap of a coil an adequate representation of the thickness of the coil?"

To answer this question, it is necessary to study the nature of the thickness variability, from coil to coil, within a coil, and across the coil. Accordingly, a study has been made by unrolling 12 coils. Each coil was measured on the first lap and at three other randomly selected spots along the length. At each such spot, three thickness measurements were made, one in from each edge ¾ in and one in the middle of the strip.

The measurements were recorded as follows. All data in excess of 0.0600 in are in 0.0001 in. Tolerance limits are 0.0620 and 0.0640. The first set of entries for each coil is the measurement on the first lap; the other three are at randomly selected spots along the length.

Coil no.	Edge	Middle	Edge	Coil no.	Edge	Middle	Edge
1	30	30	28	7	25	28	24
	35	32	35		27	28	29
	35	35	38		32	32	33
	39	35	39		29	29	31
2	30	29	30	8	28	27	26
	27	31	31		26	26	24
	29	28	30		39	38	42
	30	32	33		30	30	32
3	28	28	28	9	22	27	24
	30	32	30		21	27	27
	28	30	30		32	32	35
	40	39	45		29	27	30
4	29	30	29	10	26	28	28
	30	34	33		29	29	30
	27	27	30		22	23	23
	30	30	33		28	27	29
5	28	27	28	11	32	30	33
	18	18	18		37	35	37
	23	23	24		30	31	31
	24	24	30		28	27	28
6	39	40	40	12	22	22	23
	30	32	30		32	35	23
	30	30	30		31	31	31
	30	30	29		37	30	38

(a) Draw a Multi-Vari chart representing the data.

(b) Is the principal source of variation in steel thickness across coil, within coil, or coil to coil?

(c) Can the proposed sampling plan be based on measurements made on first laps? If so, explain why. If not, on what basis *should* the sampling plan be set up?[7]

Answer: (b) Within coil.

5-2 Trouble has been experienced in assembling magnetron tubes because of oversize cathode poles. About 5 percent of the cathode poles are too big to fit into the assembly fixtures, even though the fixtures are made to take poles 0.001 to 0.002 in larger than the 0.9980 in/1.0020 in pole specification. The cathode poles are expensive and the 5 percent loss is well worth reducing.

[7] Course notes for Management of Quality Control, U.S. Air Force School of Logistics, 1959.

Size	As made	After plating	After first braze	After second braze
1.0042-3				1
1.0040-2				2
1.0038-9				4
1.0036-7			1	5
1.0034-5			1	8
1.0032-3			3	9
1.0030-1			6	6
1.0028-9			11	3
1.0026-7			7	1
1.0024-5			6	
1.0022-3			4	
1.0020-1			1	
1.0018-9		2		
1.0016-7		4		
1.0014-5		6		
1.0012-3	1	9		
1.0010-1	3	8		
1.0008-9	6	5		
1.0006-7	10	4		
1.0004-5	8	2		
1.0002-3	5			
1.0000-1	3			
0.9998-9	2			
0.9996-7	1			
0.9994-5				
0.9992-3				
0.9990-1				
0.9988-9				
0.9986-7				
0.9984-5				
0.9982-3				
0.9980-1				

A considerable hassle has been brewing between the assembly foreman and the inspection group in the pole-making department. The foreman blames the inspectors for accepting lots with oversize poles, while the inspectors steadfastly maintain that they do no such thing, that it is probably the subsequent plating or brazing operations that make the poles too big. The foreman retorts that there is only 0.0002 in of plating put on and that the brazing could not possibly swell the poles.

The need to get facts is imperative; a lot of 40 cathode poles is taken as manufactured and followed through the plating and two brazing operations, measured at each stage. The measurements are shown in the table. ("Size" represents cell boundaries.)

What conclusions can be drawn?[8]

5-3 The width of a slot is a critical dimension on an eccentric cam. The specification calls for 0.500 in ± 0.002 in. A large sample was measured with the following results:

$$\text{Average} = 0.499 \text{ in}$$
$$\text{Standard deviation} = 0.001 \text{ in}$$

[8] Ibid.

The width is normally distributed. Suppose that the average value can be changed easily by adjusting the aim of the machine but that the variation about any given average cannot be reduced. If a change is made to minimize the percent defective, predict the percent defective that will result. Why might the present process setup be preferred to the revised setup to lower the total percent defective?

Answer: 4.54 percent.

5-4 Visit a local plant and find two examples of each of the following: (*a*) a dissectible characteristic; (*b*) a nondissectible characteristic; (*c*) a quantity of product coming from several streams. Report your findings.

5-5 Draw an Ishikawa diagram for one of the following: (*a*) the quality level of a specific activity at a university, bank, or automobile repair shop; (*b*) the quality level of *one* important characteristic of a product at a local plant. Base the diagram on discussions with the organization involved.

5-6 The following data summarize the total number of defects for each operator over the past 6 months:

Operator	Number of defects	Operator	Number of defects
A	46	H	9
B	22	I	130
C	64	J	10
D	5	K	125
E	65	L	39
F	79	M	26
G	188	N	94

A quality cost study indicates that the cost of these defects is excessive. There is much discussion about the type of quality improvement program. Analysis indicates that the manufacturing equipment is adequate, the specifications are clear, and operators are given periodic information about their quality record. What do you suggest as the next step?

5-7 An engineer in a research organization has twice proposed that the department be authorized to conduct a research project. The project involves a redesign of a component to reduce the frequency of failures. The research approach has been meticulously defined by the engineer and verified as valid by an outside expert. Management has not authorized the project because "other projects seem more important." What further action should the engineer consider?

5-8 A company that manufactures small household appliances has experienced high scrap and rework for several years. The total cost of the scrap and rework was recently estimated on an annual basis. The number shocked top management. Discussions by the management team degenerated into arguments. Finally, top management has proposed that all departments reduce scrap and rework costs by 20 percent in the coming year. Comment on this proposal.

5-9 A small steel manufacturing firm has had a chronic problem of scrap and rework in the wire mill. The costs involved have reached a level where they are a major factor in the profits of the division. All levels of personnel in the wire mill are aware of the problem and there is agreement on the vital few product lines that account for most of the problem. However, no reduction in scrap and rework costs has been achieved. What do you propose as a next step?

5-10 The medical profession makes the journey from symptom to cause and cause to remedy for medical problems on human beings. Contrast this with the task of diagnosing quality problems on physical products. If possible, speak with a physician to learn the diagnostic approach used in medicine.

5-11 You are a QC engineer in a plant making refrigerators. A troublesome problem has been the "cosmetic"-type defect, e.g., scratches, blemishes, and other surface imperfections on refrigerator parts that are visible to the consumer. Management first ordered a motivation program to convince workers of the importance of refrigerator appearance. Next, the quality of the paint was improved. Neither of these actions helped, so it was decided to add a special "touch-up" operation at the end of the production line to correct any surface defects. This extra operation is costly and inconvenient (space, storage, etc.), so management is still searching for another approach. What do you suggest?

SUPPLEMENTARY READING

The *Quality Control Handbook,* 3rd ed., McGraw-Hill Book Company, New York, 1974, has a section on quality improvement (sec. 16). In addition, the topic is discussed in several of the industry sections, specifically secs. 29, 30, 33, 34, 38, 39, 45, 46, and 47.

The concepts of breakthrough and control are discussed in J. M. Juran, *Managerial Breakthrough,* McGraw-Hill Book Company, New York, 1964.

A book with many examples of data analysis is E. R. Ott, *Process Quality Control,* McGraw-Hill Book Company, New York, 1975.

A discussion of many unusual data analysis techniques is given in John W. Tukey, *Exploratory Data Analysis,* Addison-Wesley Publishing Company, Inc., Reading, Mass., 1977.

QUALITY IMPROVEMENT —
OPERATOR-CONTROLLABLE DEFECTS;
MOTIVATION FOR QUALITY

6-1 INTRODUCTION

Human beings evidently possess an instinctive urge to attain quality—to make good products rather than bad. Outside of the workplace this instinct is widely evident, e.g., in the projects of children or in the hobbies of adults. The museums and archaeological sites are filled with evidence of the ancient origins of this instinct.

Within the workplace this instinct can face strong competition from other parameters. The enterprise needs high productivity, low costs, prompt delivery, etc., as well as good quality. These competing needs vary with the economic climate. For example, during a time of shortages, the need to meet customer demands for delivery will result in cost overruns and in shipment of nonconforming products. In contrast, as goods become plentiful, there are "drives" to reduce costs and improve quality.

The industrial manager would like to meet *all* parameters. (Life would be much more comfortable that way.) But this ideal is hard to attain in an economy based on competition in the marketplace. Hence the manager resorts to "trade-offs." These trade-offs can push quality down or up depending on the state of the economic cycle, the actions of competitors, etc.

There are also company-imposed limits on the managers' freedom to trade off. These limits arise from the presence of the various controls imposed by upper management. One of these controls is oriented to quality and takes the form of a quality-oriented department equipped with inspectors, analysts, auditors, etc. Such a quality-oriented department can readily become embroiled in confrontations with the line managers on specific actions and decisions affecting quality. These confrontations can then lead to accusations that the line manager lacks quality-mindedness. Such accusations are resented, with resulting recriminations and antagonisms.

This competition among parameters extends to all departments and all levels of the hierarchy, including the nonsupervisors. These workers are also asked to meet multiple standards, i.e., productivity, quality, safety, etc. As in the case of the managers, all workers are "for" quality. (Trade unions have stressed quality for centuries.) But workers, like managers, find it difficult to meet all standards simultaneously, and hence must resort to trade-offs so as to strike a balance.

For the village artisan the controls were mainly through the forces of the marketplace rather than through the actions of control departments. Income and reputation depended on making goods fit for use. Solvency required control of costs plus attainment of high productivity. The artisan was personally in a position to make the critical decisions and thereby to strike a balance (among the competing parameters) so as to optimize the performance of the little enterprise.

In the modern factory it is different. The various standards are set by the line managers in collaboration with the control departments. The balance struck by the workers is based not on an interaction with the forces of the marketplace but by interaction with the control departments and especially with the boss. The priorities and actions of the boss are a major influence on the course taken by the worker.

6-2 SUBSPECIES OF OPERATOR ERROR

Defects can be classified as management-controllable or operator-controllable, depending on whether the criteria for operator controllability have been met.[1] The approach to reduction of management-controllable errors was set out in Section 5-6. The approach to reduction of operator-controllable errors will be taken up in the present chapter.

In theory, a worker in a state of self-control has no reason to make errors (defects). Yet in practice all human beings make errors to such an extent that human fallibility has long been taken for granted—"to err is human." This contradiction between theory and practice was one of the ingredients of a widespread and lively debate which took place during the 1960s. The most controversial aspect of that debate was the assertion by *zero defects* (ZD) advocates that if workers are properly motivated they will make no errors—lit-

---

[1] See Sections 13-1 through 13-4; also Section 5-6.

erally zero defects. Many companies, mainly in defense industries (and under the urging of the Department of Defense), undertook to establish quality motivation programs for workers.[2] Many of these programs consisted solely of motivational propaganda. Such programs had little effect on quality—their main effect was on customer relations. Some programs went beyond propaganda—they included a type of suggestion system oriented to quality. These programs were often beneficial to quality.

The fatal assumptions of the ZD movement were (1) that operator errors are the main source of quality troubles, and (2) that all operator errors can be remedied by proper motivation. These assumptions found favor with some managers but had no basis in fact. What the facts show is that:

1. The bulk of defects (over 80 percent) are management-controllable, not operator-controllable.
2. There are multiple subspecies of operator-controllable error; the matter is not as simplistic as motivation alone.

The fallacy of "motivation alone" becomes obvious when we study the "operation" of playing golf. Such study makes it clear that the golfer is in a state of self-control (see Section 13-1). Yet some golfers make few errors while other golfers make many errors despite the fact that the tools used may be identical. To explain the difference on the theory of a difference in motivation is ludicrous—few people are as intensely motivated as are golfers. The explanation lies somewhere else—in the concept of subspecies of operator error. There are at least three such subspecies:

1. *Inadvertent errors.*
2. *Errors due to lack of technique* (skill, knowledge, etc.). These will be referred to as *technique errors.*
3. *Willful errors.*

A simple demonstration of multiple subspecies of operator error is provided by Table 6-1. This example involves an office "operation" of preparing insurance policies. The operator or "policy writer" starts with the sales agent's order plus the data in the company manuals. Using a typewriter, the policy writer then fills in the printed blank policy form which later becomes an official insurance contract. Upon completion, the work is examined 100 percent by an inspector. Table 6-1 shows a summary of the inspection findings over a 3-month period. The right-hand column of the table shows the total number of errors for each of the 29 types encountered. There were a total of 19 errors of type 3. Of these 19 errors, 16 were made by policy writer B. A study of the vertical columns shows that except for error type 3, policy writer B did

---

[2] See *Quality Control Handbook*, 3rd ed., McGraw-Hill Book Company, New York, 1974, pp. 18-24 to 18-34.

Table 6-1 Matrix of errors by insurance policy writers

Error type	Policy writer						Total
	A	B	C	D	E	F	
1	0	0	1	0	2	1	4
2	1	0	0	0	1	0	2
3	0	(16)	1	0	2	0	(19)
4	0	0	0	0	1	0	1
5	2	1	3	1	4	2	(13)
6	0	0	0	0	3	0	3
.							
.							
.							
27							
28							
29							
Totals	6	(20)	8	3	(36)	7	80

an excellent job. It is easy to come up with a train of reasoning somewhat as follows:

1. Since five of the six policy writers have no serious problem with error type 3, there exists a state of self-control with respect to that error type.
2. Since policy writer B has no serious problem with 28 of the 29 error types, there is nothing wrong with the selection, training, motivation, etc., of policy writer B.
3. Since policy writer B does have a problem with error type 3, the likely cause is a misinterpretation of that part of the procedure which relates to error type 3 (hence a technique error).[3]

A second "lump" in the matrix is the 13 errors of type 5. Here the errors are distributed rather evenly among all policy writers. The fact that all policy writers are susceptible to this error suggests there is a lack of self-control and that the error is management-controllable rather than operator-controllable.

A third lump is the total of 36 errors made by policy writer E. Closer study of the data shows that policy writer E makes errors in virtually all categories, and is the only operator to do so. Further study would be needed to discover why policy writer E exhibits such outward evidence of being so defect-prone.

Each of the three subspecies of operator error (inadvertent, technique, and willful) has its own set of outward symptoms. (The nature of these symptoms will be discussed in detail shortly.) Discovery of the outward symptoms is done through use of three principal tools for data collection and summary:

[3] For elaboration, see *Quality Control Handbook*, 3rd ed., pp. 18-5, 18-6.

Table 6-2 Pareto analysis of weaving imperfects

Weaver	Defective yardage	Percent of all defective yardage	Cumulative defective yardage	Cumulative percent
A	106	33	106	33
B	81	25	187	58
C	51	16	238	74
D	21	6	259	80
E	14	4	273	84
F	13	4	286	88
G	9	3	295	91
H	8	2	303	93
J	5	2	308	95
K	3	1	311	96
L	3	1	314	97
M	3	1	317	98
N	2	1	319	99
P	2	1	321	100
Q	2	1	323	100

1. *Pareto analysis.* For example, Table 6-2 shows a list of 15 weavers in a textile mill, together with the extent of imperfect cloth woven by each. It is evident that three of the weavers account for 74 percent of the imperfect cloth. In contrast, the eight best weavers account for only 10 percent of the imperfect cloth. Additional data (not shown in Table 6-2) establish the further fact that this wide difference in operator performance is consistently present month after month. This consistency, along with data on defect types (not shown in Table 6-2), points strongly to errors arising from differences in technique.[4]
2. *Matrix of operators versus defect types.* Table 6-1 is an example of such a matrix.
3. *Matrix of operators versus time.* Table 5-7 is an example of this type of matrix.

6-3 INADVERTENT ERRORS

The literal meaning of inadvertent is "not paying attention." Failure to pay attention is an important source of human error. Inadvertent errors exhibit several distinguishing features. They are typically:

Unintentional. The operator does not want to make errors.

[4] See Figure 5-2 for a graphical presentation of the data of Table 6-2.

Unwitting. At the time of making an error the operator has no knowledge of having made an error.

Unpredictable. No one knows beforehand just when the worker will make an error, or what type of error will be made. In addition, no one knows at any one time who will be the next operator to make an error.

The result of such a pattern of features is *randomness.* In turn, this randomness is evident in the data. For example, in Table 6-1 the pattern of defect occurrences for defect type 3 is nonrandom, whereas for most other types the pattern is random. Similarly, for most of the policy writers the pattern of occurrence of defect types is random.

Among the various subspecies of operator error, only the inadvertent errors exhibit randomness. In consequence, when data on operator error do exhibit randomness, it is highly probable that the errors are of the inadvertent type. The fact of randomness has a further effect—it precludes a concentration of defect types in the form exhibited by the "vital few" of the Pareto principle. Hence it is quite usual to find that the "trivial many" errors are the result of inadvertence.

Remedy for inadvertent errors involves two major approaches:

1. *Reducing the extent of dependence on human attention.* The methods used are usually termed "foolproofing." They are similar to those discussed in Section 11-3 relative to planning manufacturing processes and in Section 15-10 relative to inspector accuracy.
2. *Making it easier for human beings to remain attentive.* This approach employs psychological tools (e.g., job rotation, rest periods) as well as technological tools (e.g., sense multipliers, templates, masks, overlays, etc.) such as are discussed in Section 15-10.

A large-scale program of finding remedies for inadvertent errors is contained in the Japanese QC circle movement. Many of the projects tackled involve inadvertent defects, and the bulk of the solutions consist either of foolproofing or of making it easier to remain attentive.

There are of course some residual contentions that attentiveness can be improved by motivation. Where the lack of attention is deliberate, this contention is valid, but such deliberate inattention properly falls in the category of willful errors. Inattention that is involuntary is the result of limitations in the human organism and hence is presumably not responsive to motivation.

6-4 TECHNIQUE ERRORS

Technique errors arise because the worker lacks some essential technique (or skill, knowledge, etc.) which is needed to avoid making the error. The resulting technique errors possess certain common features. Technique errors are:

Unintentional. The worker wants to do good work, not bad work.

Selective. The errors are confined to those error types for which the missing technique is essential.

Consistent. Workers who possess the technique can consistently avoid the associated error type; workers who lack the technique will consistently make errors of that type.

Witting and unwitting. Technique errors are of both kinds. The golfer knows very well whether he is consistently slicing the ball. In contrast, a welder may not know, at the time of welding, that lack of some technique will result in a future failure of the weld.

Unavoidable by the unaided worker. The worker lacking the technique does not know "what to do different from what I am doing now." Hence the error can go on and on.

The outward evidence of technique errors is the presence of consistent differences in error rates among workers. These consistent differences are selective—they apply to specific defect types. They are most readily disclosed by a data matrix showing the time-to-time error rates of various workers. Table 5-9 is an example of such a matrix.

In Table 5-9 the month-to-month incidence of the defect "open hard after fire" shows great and consistent differences among the gun assemblers. These differences are made more dramatic by summing up the defects for the five best and the five worst assemblers for each of the 6 months. In each month, without exception, the five worst performances add up to at least 10 times as many defects as the sum of the five best performances. Such a consistent difference relative to a specific defect is clear evidence of a difference in technique.

(Table 5-9*b* shows that the total of defects for all 22 assemblers varied widely from month to month. Since this phenomenon is evident in best and worst assemblers alike, its cause must be management-controllable rather than operator-controllable.)

It is quite common to discover, from a matrix such as Table 5-9, the evidence of the existence of technique errors. The next step is to discover the precise cause of the errors, i.e., the nature of the technique which is so critical to good work. This discovery requires a study (which should include asking the workers) of the work methods used by both successful and unsuccessful workers. Such a study will disclose various differences in technique. Further study will disclose which technique(s) constitutes the *knack*—that small difference in method which is responsible for a large difference in results. In the case of the gun assemblers, the knack was found. The superior performers were using a file to reduce one of the dimensions on a complex component; the inferior performers did not file the component.

Once the knack has been identified, the way is open to bring all workers up to the level of the best. The managers have several options, such as:

1. Train the inferior performers to adopt the knack. Note that this training

provides the needed answer to the question: "What should I do different from what I am doing now?"

2. Change the technology so that the process itself embodies the knack. In the gun assembly case, this would mean making that dimension smaller and abolishing the practice of filing.
3. Foolproof the operation in ways that require use of the knack (or that prohibit some technique which is damaging to the product).

Usually, the difference in worker performance is traceable to some superior knack used by the successful performers to benefit the product. In the case of the gun assemblers, the knack consisted of filing that component. In other cases the difference in worker performance is traceable to unwitting *damage* done to the product by the inferior performers. The three inferior weavers (Table 6-2) were damaging the product in this way—a sort of "negative knack."

There is a useful rule for judging whether the difference in operator performance is due to a beneficial knack or a negative knack. If the strikingly superior performers are in the minority, the difference is probably due to a beneficial knack. For example, in the piston rings case (Section 5-10), one of the nine melters (Knight) was instinctively a neat housekeeper. This urge for neatness extended to care of his tools. This care included a daily early morning cleanup, including removal of any metal adhering to the inside surfaces of the spouts used to transfer molten metal from the ladle to the casting machines. No other melter did this—only one in nine was employing this knack. In the case of the gun assemblers, the strikingly superior performers were also in the minority. However, in the case of the weavers, the strikingly *inferior* workers were in the minority, suggesting a negative knack.

Note also that the existence of the knack may be unknown to the very workers who have it! The melter Knight knew he cleaned the spouts, but he had no knowledge that the resulting product had a lower scrap rate than that of any other melter. In like manner, the superior gun assemblers knew that they were filing the components but they had no knowledge that this filing greatly reduced the incidence of "open hard after fire." Not until Table 5-9 was prepared had anyone ever made an analysis to discover worker-to-worker differences.

Cases such as these make clear the dangers of assuming that workers can eliminate defects by becoming more interested, better motivated, etc. The entire category of technique errors is doomed to go on and on until someone is able to provide the inferior workers with an answer to the question: "What should I do different from what I am doing now?" It is sometimes possible for workers themselves to find an answer to this question, as in the case of the Japanese QC circles. More usually the answer cannot be provided without a considerable degree of management commitment and participation.

We can now summarize the sequence of events through which we identify, analyze, and remedy technique errors.

1. For the defect type under study, collect data which can disclose any significant worker-to-worker differences.
2. Analyze the data on a time-to-time basis to discover whether consistency is present.
3. Identify the consistently best and consistently worst performances.
4. Ask the workers, and study the work methods used by the best and worst performers to identify their differences in technique.
5. Study these differences further to discover the beneficial knack which produces superior results (or the negative knack which is damaging the product).
6. Bring everyone up to the level of the best through appropriate remedial action, such as:
   a. Training inferior performers in use of the knack or in avoidance of damage.
   b. Changing the technology so that the process embodies the knack.
   c. Foolproofing the process.

6-5 WILLFUL ERRORS

Willful errors are those which workers know they are making and which they (usually) intend to keep on making. The distinguishing features of willful errors include:

Witting. At the time the error is made, the worker knows that an error has been made.
Intentional. The error is the result of a deliberate intention by the worker to commit an error.
Consistent. The workers who cause willful errors usually do so on a continuing basis.

Because of these features, the outward evidences of willful errors differ from those of inadvertent errors or technique errors. Willful errors do not exhibit randomness. They exhibit a pattern of consistency, since the workers involved regularly make more errors than other workers. However, this error proneness is not necessarily restricted to specific defect types—it can extend over many defect types.

Willful errors committed by workers are sometimes traceable to management-initiated actions. Such actions are often due to the trade-offs which managers make under the pressure of trying to meet multiple standards and of trying to keep up with changes in the marketplace (as discussed above in Section 6-1). These trade-offs can transmit corresponding pressures to the work force, who, in turn, may resort to trade-offs to meet *their* multiple standards. Some of these worker trade-offs are in the form of willful violation of the quality standards in order to meet other standards which seem to have managerial priority.

Still other management-initiated cases have their origin in managerial mistakes. For example, a misguided drive on factory scrap creates an atmosphere of blame. The workers discover that if they make out scrap tickets, they risk being criticized for having made the scrap despite the fact that in many cases they are not to blame. Hence the workers stop making out scrap tickets. They know they are violating the rules but they feel justified because of having been blamed unjustly.

Many willful errors are operator-initiated, and some of these make dismal reading. Workers may have real or fancied grievances (against the company or the boss) and get their revenge by neglect of quality. They may be rebels against society and strike back by sabotaging the product. Some of the instances encountered are so obviously antisocial that no one, including the union, will defend such actions.

In still other cases the willful error seems to be worker-initiated but the responsibility is confused because of inadequate communication. Managers may ship out nonconforming product without explaining the reasons to the work force. Managers may publish reports of performance against schedule but not on performance against quality standards. These and other cases (see Table 6-3) can lead the work force to conclude that management does not regard quality to be as important as the other standards.

Table 6-3 Operator's views of actions taken by managers

Conditions as seen by the managers	Conditions as they look to the shop operators	Probable shop interpretation
Nonconforming material judged to be fit for use after discussion with customer.	Material outside of specification was rejected by inspectors but was accepted by managers.	Management does not regard the specification as important.
Machine needs repair, but in view of a new machine being on order, it would be a waste to repair the old machine with only a few months to go.	Defects are being produced by a machine in need of repair, but management will not repair the machine.	Management is not willing to spend money to get quality.
Operator suggestion for improving quality was investigated and found to be uneconomic.	Operator suggestion for improving quality has not been answered.	Management is not interested in improving quality.
We are badly behind in delivery to customers and must act to catch up on schedules.	Scoreboards on quantity receive much more attention than scoreboards on quality.	Management is more interested in quantity than quality.
A process cannot hold the tolerances, but there is no better process known. Hence the process must be closely watched to minimize defects.	The process cannot hold the tolerances but the operators are urged to reduce the defects.	Management does not know what it is doing.

Remedy for willful errors takes several forms:

1. *Improve communications.* Steps are taken to enable the managers to understand better how things look to the workers, and to enable the workers to understand better why the managers take certain actions. Table 6-3 gives some examples of how the managers and workers can reach different conclusions from identical factual situations.
2. *Establish accountability.* Human beings act more responsibly if their identity is known. In one company there was periodic damage to costly bales of product due to being punctured by the prongs of the forklift trucks used for internal transport. When the company introduced a simple means of identifying which trucker moved which bale, the amount of damage dropped dramatically.
3. *Foolproof the operation.* Analysis of the defect pattern may show that it is feasible to use foolproofing as to some defect types. The methods for such foolproofing are discussed in Section 11-3 (as to production workers) and Section 15-10 (as to inspectors).
4. *Remove the offender.* This option is often open to managers and in severe cases may be the only real solution.
5. *Motivate the worker.* See Section 6-7.

6-6 INTERRELATIONSHIP AMONG SUBSPECIES OF OPERATOR ERROR

Table 6-4 on page 148 summarizes the interrelationship among subspecies of operator error. It makes evident how analysis of data on operator error can point to likely sources of causation and then to likely solutions. The starting point is data on operator errors in a form that permits analysis by operator, by defect type, and on a time-to-time basis.

6-7 WORKER MOTIVATION FOR QUALITY

Motivation may be defined as the process of stimulating behavior. Applied to quality, motivation consists of discovering and applying the stimuli needed to induce employees to meet their responsibilities with respect to quality.

Motivation for What?

Motivation for workers is not merely for the purpose of reducing willful errors. It includes securing worker willingness to:

1. Follow the control plan and meet the established standards.
2. Accept training and retraining in methods for doing the job.

Table 6-4 Interrelationships among subspecies of operator error

Pattern disclosed by analysis of operator error	Likely subspecies of error causing this pattern	Likely solution
On certain defects, no one is error-prone; defect pattern is random.	Errors are due to inadvertence.	Foolproof the process.
On certain defects, some operators are consistently error-prone while others are consistently "good."	Errors are due to lack of technique (ability, know-how, etc.). Lack of technique may take the form of secret ignorance. Technique may consist of known knack or of secret knowledge.	Discovery and propagation of knack. Discovery and elimination of secret ignorance.
Some operators are consistently error-prone over a wide range of defects.	There are several potential causes:	Solution follows the cause:
	Willful failure to comply with standards	Motivation
	Inherent incapacity to perform this task	Transfer to work for which operator is qualified.
	Lack of training	Supply training.
On certain defects, all operators are error-prone.	Errors are management-controllable.	Meet the criteria for self-control.

3. Adopt new technology as it is evolved.

In addition, it is highly desirable if workers can be induced to:

1. Provide feedback to management on problems encountered.
2. Assist in troubleshooting to restore the status quo.
3. Participate in projects for quality improvement.

Pride of Workmanship

Many, many managers deplore what they regard as a loss in pride of workmanship or a decline in the spirit of "craftsmanship" which once prevailed among workers. The implication is that workers once were self-motivating with respect to quality and that this self-motivation has been lost. There is a good deal of outward evidence which supports this complaint. However, there is much confusion as to the reasons behind the loss in pride of workmanship. Prior to the Industrial Revolution, craftsmanship was a primary concern and constituted a major source of quality assurance for the buyer. In the villages and towns of that era

the proprietors of the small shops . . . had a personal and major stake in the quality of their products . . . the quality performance of specific suppliers became known or notorious. The resulting reputation of the supplier became an important and even decisive factor in his ability to sell his products, and thus became an aid or a threat to his personal livelihood. His reputation as an honest and competent craftsman was inseparable from his social status in the community and thereby that of his family.[5]

Since those village craftsman days, the practice of craftsmanship has been eroded extensively, owing principally to three changes:

1. The factories of the Industrial Revolution transferred work from village craftsmen to factory employees. The factory workers were thereby deprived of the functions of product design, marketing, finance, etc., formerly carried out by independent proprietors. What remained was the function of manufacture.
2. Factory work was typically divided up into numerous specialized operations. As a result, the worker typically performed a highly repetitive task which comprised only a tiny part of the job of building an entire product.
3. The Taylor system (see Section 6-8) went further by separating work planning from execution. As a result, the workers were left only with the job of executing plans prepared by someone else, usually the industrial engineers.

Collectively, these and other job changes have had a remarkable effect on the workers' breadth of understanding and on their depth of responsibility. The village artisan performed all the functions associated with a business. The factory worker typically performs only the function of manufacture, and even this is usually limited to execution of plans prepared by someone else. The artisan was concerned with an entire product or service; the factory worker is typically concerned with a narrow operation. The artisan dealt with customers and users of the product, and hence had to think in terms of fitness for use. The factory worker has no contact with customers or users, and is required to think only in terms of conformance to standard. (Note that in certain skilled trades, e.g., toolmaker, the worker still plans and completes an entire product. Hence the tradition of craftsmanship remains strong.)

It is evident then that when we compare today's pride in one's work with that prevailing in the past, we are not talking about the same work. This difference in breadth of work and in extent of worker involvement is central to many of the problems of worker motivation for quality. Certainly, there is serious doubt that the factory worker's *attitude* (i.e., state of mind) can be expected to be the same as that of the village craftsman. However, it may well be possible to secure adequate worker *behavior* (i.e., state of action) despite the changed conditions.

6-8 THEORIES OF MOTIVATION

It would be of obvious value if we had scientific knowledge on just how various stimuli affect human behavior. The professionals in this field are the behavioral

---

[5] Quoted from J. M. Juran, "Quality and Its Assurance—An Overview," NATO Symposium on Quality Assurance, London, 1977.

Table 6-5 Hierarchy of human needs, and forms of quality motivation

McGregor's list of human needs	Usual forms of quality motivation
Physiological needs; i.e., need for food, shelter, basic survival. In an industrial economy this translates into minimum subsistence earnings.	Opportunity to increase earnings by bonus for good work.
Safety needs: i.e., once a subsistence level is achieved, the need to remain employed at that level.	Job security: e.g., quality makes sales; sales make jobs.
Social needs: i.e., the need to belong to a group and be accepted.	Appeal to the employee as a member of the team—he or she must not let the team down.
Ego needs: i.e., the need for self-respect and for the respect of others.	Appeal to pride of workmanship, to achieving a good score. Recognition through awards, publicity, etc.
Self-fulfillment needs: i.e., the urge for creativity, for self-expression.	Opportunity to propose creative ideas, to participate in creative planning.

scientists. (The managers are merely experienced amateurs.) Studies by these behavioral scientists have provided us with some useful theories which help us to understand how human behavior responds to various stimuli.

Hierarchy of Human Needs

Under this theory, human needs fall into five fundamental categories, under a predictable order of priorities.[6] Table 6-5 shows this "hierarchy of human needs," together with the associated forms of motivation for quality.

Job Dissatisfaction and Satisfaction

Under this theory, job dissatisfaction and job satisfaction are *not* opposites. Job dissatisfaction is the result of specific dislikes—the pay is low, the working conditions are poor, the boss is unpleasant. It is possible to eliminate these dislikes—raise the pay, change the working conditions, reform the boss. The revised conditions are then accepted as normal but do not motivate behavior.

[6] This theory was originated by A. H. Maslow and popularized by Douglas McGregor. See A. H. Maslow, *Motivation and Personality*, Harper & Bros., New York, 1954. See also Douglas McGregor, *The Human Side of Enterprise*, McGraw-Hill Book Company, New York, 1960.

In contrast, job satisfaction is dependent on what the worker *does*. The satisfaction comes from the doing—the motivation comes from such things as job challenges, opportunities for creativity, identification with groups, responsibility for planning, etc.[7] To illustrate: at the end of the day the assembly line worker is happy to leave that monotonous job and go home to something more interesting. In that same company the researcher does not leave precisely at closing time—the research project may be more interesting than the outside hobby.

Theory X and Theory Y

Two theories bring us back to the controversy about whether workers have lost their pride in their work. Is the change in the worker or in the work? These two alternatives have been given names—Theory X and Theory Y, respectively.

Under Theory X, the modern worker has become lazy, uncooperative, etc. Hence the managers must combat this decline in worker motivation through skillful use of incentives and penalties.

Under Theory Y there has been no change in human nature. What has changed is the way in which work is organized. Hence the solution is to create new job conditions which permit the normal human drives to assert themselves.[8]

Managers are not unanimous in adhering to one or the other of these theories. It is common to find, even within the same company, some managers who support Theory X and others who support Theory Y. This support is not merely philosophical—it is reflected in the operating conditions that prevail in the respective departments, as exemplified in Table 6-6.

Both the X theory and the Y theory have their advocates. However, there seems to be no conclusive evidence that either can outperform the other in economic terms, i.e., productivity, cost, etc. There is some evidence to suggest that the Y theory approach makes for better human relations, but even this evidence is blurred. Some studies have shown that a proportion of workers regards repetitive, routine work as less stressful than a broader range of work with its demands for decision making and creativity.

The Taylor System

Frederick W. Taylor was a mechanical engineer who had worked as a machinist, foreman, and plant manager. He concluded from his experience that the supervisors and workers of his day (late nineteenth and early twentieth centuries) lacked the education needed to make various essential decisions, e.g., what work methods should be used, what constitutes a day's work, etc.

---

[7] This theory is attributable to Frederick Herzberg. See Frederick Herzberg, Bernard Mausman, and B. Snyderman, *The Motivation to Work*, 2nd ed., John Wiley & Sons, Inc., New York, 1959.

[8] This theory was evolved by Douglas McGregor. See McGregor, *The Human Side of Enterprise*.

Table 6-6 Shop operation under Theory X versus Theory Y

Operation under Theory X	Operation under Theory Y
Extensive use of piecework rates as an incentive to meet the standard	Less emphasis on piecework rates; greater use of supervisory leadership
Emphasis on wage-penalty clauses or disciplinary measures to punish poor quality performance	Emphasis on the "why" and "how" to improve poor quality performance
Reliance mainly on inspection personnel for tool control	Reliance mainly on production personnel for tool control
Reliance mainly on patrol inspectors to see that setups are correct	Reliance mainly on operators and setup personnel for correctness of setup
Reliance on patrol inspectors to stop machines which are found by inspectors to be producing defects	Reliance on operators to stop machines which are found by inspectors to be producing defects
Extensive use of formal inspection approval for piecework payment, movement of material, etc.	Limited use of formal inspection approval
Debates on the factory floor center on authority to shut down machines, and on motives	Debates on the factory floor center on the interpretation of specifications and measurements
Relationships between operators and inspectors tense, often hostile and acrimonious	Relationships between operators and inspectors businesslike, often good-natured
Upper-management criticism for high scrap losses directed at Inspection as much as Production	Upper-management criticism for high scrap losses directed at Production
Operators exhibit no outward desire to do a quality job	Operators do exhibit the outward desire to do a quality job
Operators largely ignored as a source of ideas for improvement	Operators frequently consulted for ideas for improvement

Taylor's remedy was to separate planning from execution. He assigned engineers and specialists to do the planning, and he left to the supervisors and workers the job of executing the plans.

Taylor's system achieved spectacular increases in productivity. The resulting publicity stimulated further application of his ideas. The outcome was a widespread adoption of the concept of separating planning from execution. Through this adoption, the Taylor system (later called Scientific Management) became widely used and deeply rooted in the United States and, to a lesser degree, among the industrialized countries of the West.[9]

Meanwhile, Taylor's major premise—lack of worker education—has been made obsolete by the remarkable rise in education levels. As a consequence, the major *under*employed asset in the United States is the education, experience, and creativity of the work force. Other cultures, notably the Japanese, have found ways to employ this asset and have attained remarkable results. (See QC circles, Section 6-11.)

It is seen that the Taylor system is both a philosophy of management and an approach to worker motivation (through piecework incentives). The philosophy of separating planning from execution has endured, but the motivation through piecework has been in a long-range decline. This decline appears to be closely related to the rise in worker affluence.

6-9 MOTIVATION—CONTINUING PROGRAMS

Most motivation for quality is determined by the company's employee relations practices during the various stages of the employment cycle. These practices may or may not include certain essential quality-oriented activities as discussed below.

Job Design and Planning

The most critical need in job design and planning is to meet the criteria for worker self-control so that the worker has the means needed to make a good product. Where this self-control is not feasible, worker responsibility should be based on "best effort" or on meeting process control criteria rather than product criteria.

Recruitment

Even before recruitment, quality-oriented companies try to project an outward image of attention to quality. They do this through emphasis on quality in product advertising and public relations propaganda, sponsorship of quality-related activities, exhibits of products, publication of brochures, etc. A similar emphasis on quality then carries over into the recruitment process. The recruiters, the "Welcome to the X Company" brochures, etc., all carry the message. The actual induction process then follows through by explaining the "why" of quality through product use demonstrations, plant tours, etc.

Training

Training for quality includes technological information on specifications, standards, facilities, processes, tools, materials, products. It includes the

---

[9] For elaboration, see *Quality Control Handbook*, 3rd ed., pp. 18-17, 18-18.

information needed to make clear the worker's responsibility for taking actions and making decisions. It should also include information on the reasons behind the instructions. When these reasons are understood, the orders to do good work are depersonalized—they come from an understood need as much as from a boss.

Training should also be provided with respect to "knack." Knack becomes the answer to the worker's logical question: "What should I do different from what I am doing now?" In addition, where it is feasible to enlist worker participation in problem solving, there is an added need for worker training in problem solving.

Supervision

Subsequent to induction, the worker's behavior is strongly influenced by supervisory and managerial conduct. This conduct relates to such matters as: seeing that facilities are kept in good repair; giving adequate priority to quality in relation to other parameters; listening to worker ideas with an open mind; praising good work as well as criticizing poor work; setting a good example.

Communication to Employees

Communication is an essential part of motivation, and the company employs various media:

1. Manuals of procedure, which include aids to doing a good-quality job.
2. Journals, bulletins, and posters for general communication direct to the work force.
3. Meetings, e.g., scrap conferences to discuss quality of work.
4. Specific aids, e.g., quality "cues" to provide information about the knack to be used in specific operations.

Quality Incentives

Until the mid-1930s numerous companies in the United States employed a financial type of quality incentives for production operators. Most of these incentives were of a penalty nature. Poor work was paid for at lower rates or not at all. Alternatively, the worker was required to perform some remedial work on his or her own time, e.g., sort or repair. These financial incentives and penalties were swept away by the wave of industrial unionism of the 1930s and have only rarely been reinstated.

Except for the socialist countries of Eastern Europe, most quality incentives are now nonfinancial in nature. They take such forms as:

1. Recognition through publicity, awards of prizes, etc.
2. Delegation of special responsibility, e.g., self-inspection (see Section 13-6).

3. Presentation of certificates of qualification. These may enlarge the range of job opportunities as well as becoming inputs to the system of appraising the work of employees.
4. Providing opportunity for further training at company expense, or on company time, etc.
5. Providing opportunities for participation in work projects, planning, etc. (see below).

In the socialist countries of eastern Europe, incentives for quality are both financial and nonfinancial in nature. The chief measure of quality is the percent of work that is done right the first time.[10]

6-10 MOTIVATION CAMPAIGNS

Many companies encounter quality deficiencies or opportunities which appear to require a major change in motivation for quality. To secure such a change by restructuring the basic "continuing program" involves waiting patiently for results. Some companies decide not to wait. Instead, they go into a motivation "campaign"—an attempt to secure a swift change in behavior toward quality. Their decision may be influenced by such factors as a spate of field troubles, prevailing publicity about some "new" form of motivation, pressure from important customers, etc.

During the 1960s the defense and aerospace industries made wide use of such campaigns, the major influence being the insistence of government officials that such campaigns be undertaken. (The typical name was "zero defects" campaign, or just ZD.) Most of these campaigns accomplished nothing but meeting the demands of the government officials. However, some campaigns succeeded also in improving quality. On analysis, the difference in results was traceable mainly to the contents of the campaign—whether the campaign contained both or only one of the following "packages":

1. A *motivation* package, aimed at stimulating employees to reduce their own (operator-controllable) errors.
2. A *prevention* package, aimed at stimulating employees to assist in reducing management-controllable errors.

Campaigns that contained only the motivation package achieved no significant results in improving quality.

Purposes and Prerequisites

Before launching a campaign, it is well to understand clearly the purposes to be achieved. These purposes are common to most campaigns and are well known:

---

[10] See *Quality Control Handbook*, 3rd ed., pp. 18-37 to 18-39.

1. To make all employees aware that the company's quality performance is important to their well-being; e.g., quality makes sales, sales make jobs.
2. To convince all workers that there is something they can do in their daily work to contribute to quality performance.
3. To show each worker just what to do to make this contribution on the regular job.
4. To establish and record the best way of doing each job, as a reference for future training and audit.
5. To provide a means for receiving and acting on employee ideas and suggestions for improving quality.
6. To provide a scoreboard for measuring performance and progress.

In addition, it is well to look to the background conditions to see whether the essential prerequisites have been met. They are generally as follows:

1. The company has already done a respectable job of reducing management-controllable defects and hence is coming to the employee body with clean hands.
2. The employee-controllable defects are substantial enough, for economic or use reasons, to warrant a serious motivational effort.
3. The extent of mutual confidence between management and employees is such that employee participation in a campaign is likely to be genuine.
4. The top managers are willing to show personal interest, especially to set an example by changing their priority of emphasis on quality in relation to other company goals.
5. The intermediate supervision is sufficiently open-minded to be willing to listen seriously to the ideas and suggestions of the employees.
6. Management is willing to provide the staff manpower needed to conduct the numerous detailed studies (discovering the knack of superior operators, investigating employee proposals, etc.).

Organization and Planning

This takes a form similar to that used for quality improvement programs, as discussed in Chapter 5. Committees are appointed to plan and guide the campaign. Budgets and time schedules are established. Diagnostic support is provided to carry out the detailed work of setting goals, investigating ideas, reporting results, etc.

The Motivational Package

The campaigns of the 1960s developed much sophistication in design and execution of the motivational package. Wide and skillful use was made of product exhibits, slogan contests, pledge cards, etc. Publicity and propaganda were equally well organized, including a dramatic spectacle for launching the campaign. The literature of that period describes the techniques used in complete detail.[11]

Design of a motivation package for any specific company should keep in mind just what kinds of worker behavior are sought. Such behavior applies primarily to operator-controllable defects and includes principally:

1. Reduction of willful errors.
2. Acceptance of retraining to improve technique and to acquire the knack of superior performers.
3. Acceptance of technological changes such as foolproofing.

Prevention Package

The purpose of this package is to secure worker behavior with respect to management-controllable errors. (These are generally the major part of the error problem.) By definition, management-controllable errors are the result of management failure to meet the criteria for operator self-control. Hence a potentially useful role of the worker is to help identify with precision the nature of these failures to meet the criteria for self-control.

In the campaigns of the 1960s wide use was made of a sort of quality-oriented suggestion system employing a special suggestion form called *error cause removal* (ECR). Workers were asked to fill in such ECR forms and to submit them to the supervisor or the "ZD Administrator." (The companies had previously agreed in the dramatic launching meeting to investigate all ECRs.) Generally, the companies that employed ECRs secured benefits greater than the effort required to investigate them.

6-11 MOTIVATION—"NEW" APPROACHES

During most of the twentieth century the major direction of company motivation of workers was to attain and improve productivity. To this end companies designed their worker motivation programs to include such concepts as work study, setting standards of a day's work, piecework incentives, etc. In the United States the basic model for such concepts was the Taylor system.

More recently, attainment and improvement in productivity have been achieved through technology, e.g., process redesign, automation, computerized controls, etc. These new aids to productivity have reduced the emphasis on traditional worker motivation forms. In the United States less than 25 percent of the work force is now on piecework incentives.

Meanwhile, quality has continued to grow in importance while the attainment of adequate quality has become progressively more difficult. These developments have resulted in a search for new forms of motivation which could stimulate worker contribution to quality and which could be built into the basic

[11] See *Quality Control Handbook*, 3rd ed., pp. 18-24 to 18-34, and references cited.

motivation structure of the company. (The Taylor system is inherently a poor motivator for quality.) In discussing these new forms it is well to realize that some are not so new—they are applications of earlier ideas to a new situation. In most respects they are in the nature of making use of that underemployed asset—the education, experience, and creativity of the work force.

Explanation of "Why"

In most modern work situations the worker does not understand the real reasons behind the quality standards. The worker's motivation to meet the standards comes from such stimuli as faith in the company's procedures, leadership of the boss, fear of penalties, etc. Yet in some cases the understanding of the "why" can become a more powerful motivator than all other stimuli combined.

> **Example** In one textile mill the new girls recently hired in the spinning room were failing to tie the specified "weaver's knot" when tying two ends of yarn together. This persisted despite supervisory pleas and threats. The personnel director got into the problem, hunted up the unofficial leader of the new girls, and asked for an explanation. The annoyed response was "What difference does it make?" He escorted her to the weaving department and showed her how much trouble the weavers and the machines were having due to incorrect knots. The girl then burst into tears—"Why didn't someone tell us about this?" It turned out that the new spinners were quite willing to tie weaver's knots once they realized that it was necessary. They had not been willing to do so just on orders from a supervisor they disliked.

Motivation by explaining the "why" can be restated as "depersonalizing the order." Under this concept one person does not give orders to another person. Instead, all persons take their orders from knowledge of the needs.

Participation—Worker-initiated

In this form the company creates a suggestion system or similar means for receiving and investigating worker ideas. Thereafter the initiative for participation rests with the workers. However, the company commonly urges participation through offers of attractive awards for valuable ideas, by publicizing successful cases, etc. The company can also influence the choice of subject matter by offer of special awards, e.g., for suggestions on improving quality.

Participation—Management-initiated

In this form the supervisors and managers take the initiative by asking workers for their ideas on specific problems. The daily or weekly scrap conference is an obvious example.

In addition, there are many projects in which managers find it worthwhile to make use of the knowledge that workers derive from long association with the process.

Example In the piston ring case (see Section 5-10) the melter Knight was found to be making castings which yielded a finished product superior in quality to that of any other melter. Discussion with Knight brought out the fact that each morning he cleaned out the spouts used for pouring the metal. (No other melter did this.) The studies of the quality control engineers had failed to discover this practice because of a difference in starting time between office and shop personnel.

On a more elaborate scale are the joint planning meetings in which workers are invited to sit with supervisors and managers to discuss ways of dealing with problems which are of concern to all. "We are no longer competitive in this product line. All of our jobs are at stake unless we can find ways to become more competitive." Such joint planning is still in the experimental stages in the United States. It may well increase under the pressure of competition from abroad. However, such increase will require a considerable break with traditional concepts about management's right to manage.

Worker Study Teams

In this approach workers are encouraged to take training courses in problem solving. Subsequently, teams of workers are organized to engage in discussion and solution of departmental problems.

While this concept is still in the experimental stage in the United States, it is a regular part of the motivational approach used in the socialist countries of Eastern Europe. However, the most spectacular use of the worker team concept is that of the Japanese QC circles.

The Japanese QC circles A *QC circle* comprises a group of about 10 workers and work leaders within a single company department. It is created for the purpose of conducting studies to improve the effectiveness of work in their department. The studies are not restricted to quality. Many projects involve productivity, cost, safety, etc.

Participation in QC circles is voluntary. (Typically about half the company workers do volunteer.) The work of the circle begins with a training course, which consists of three major elements:

1. Training "by the book" in various techniques of data collection and analysis, i.e., statistical tools, Pareto analysis, Ishikawa diagram, etc.
2. Study of successful projects worked out by other QC circles. A major reference source is the monthly journal *FQC* (Quality Control for the Foreman), which publishes many prize-winning project reports.
3. Proving the effectiveness of the training by completion of an actual project, using such assistance as may be needed from outside the circle. This aspect

of the training includes preparation of the final report and recommendations for action.

In Japan the QC circle movement has been stunningly successful.[12] By the end of 1978, about 7 million workers had undergone the training and participated in project studies. The cumulative projects completed since 1962 (the beginning of the movement) had risen to over 10 million. The financial gains (at an estimated average of about $5000 per project) have been enormous. The effect on product quality has been significant. In turn, these experiences have prepared the workers to be better supervisors and managers in the years ahead.

As of 1978 the developed countries of the West had produced no effective equivalent of the QC circle as their means for utilizing the education, experience, and creativity of the work force. Only the developing countries of Southeast Asia (and Brazil) had organized QC circles in any significant numbers.

Whether the QC circle can be adapted to the culture of the West remains to be seen. The limitation is not technological—it is cultural. In the West the cultural resistance arises from two major sources:

1. Managers and engineers are reluctant to delegate to the work force the functions and prerogatives to which they have clung so tenaciously in the past.
2. The work force does not consider that it has a responsibility to help the managers improve the company's performance.

Job Redesign

Still another "new" approach is to redesign the workplace to increase the variety of work done by the worker as well as to restore functions previously taken away by the Taylor system.

For example, a Swedish company redesigned its method of assembling automotive engines to enable a team of 10 (or so) workers to assemble the entire engine. Such teams are virtually self-supervising. They decide which member is to perform which operations. They also carry out various other functions, such as tending to the materials supply, conducting some of tool maintenance, performing some of the inspections, keeping some of the records, etc. Such reorganization of work obviously enlarges the job and delegates much planning and decision making to the work force.[13] The education and creativity of the workers are clearly being utilized to an extent far greater than that which

---

[12] See *Quality Control Handbook*, 3rd ed., pp. 18-34 to 18-37; also special bibliography, pp. 18-51, 18-52.

[13] For elaboration, see Jan-Peder Norstedt and Stefan Aguren, "The Saab-Scania Report," Swedish Employers' Confederation, Technical Department, Box 16-120, S-103-23, Stockholm 16, Sweden.

prevailed when each worker was limited to performing a highly repetitive short-cycle operation on a long assembly line.

Job redesign is not limited to factory work. A telephone company reorganized its method of preparing telephone directories for publication. Previously, the work had been broken down into 21 separate clerical steps, each carried out by one or more workers. The revised approach was to let each worker prepare an entire telephone directory, i.e., to perform all 21 clerical operations. In this case the company published the "before" and "after" results:

	Before	After
Employees lost annually through turnover	28	0
Absenteeism rate, %	2.8	0.6
Errors per 1000 lines	3.9	1.1

6-12 MOTIVATION FOR MANAGERS

All managers, without exception, want good product quality. (They also want low costs, prompt deliveries, etc.) Despite their universal desire for quality, these same managers are sometimes accused (by quality specialists) of lacking quality-mindedness or of not being interested in quality. The accused managers resent this—they feel they *are* quality-minded. The seeming contradiction is due to a variety of reasons, principally as follows:

1. *Nonconforming products which are fit for use.* Line managers regard fitness for use as the ultimate criterion for judging quality. However, quality specialists believe from their experience that repeated acceptance of nonconforming products weakens the entire discipline of attaining quality.
2. *Multiple standards.* When line managers are unable to meet all standards (quality, cost, delivery, etc.) simultaneously, they conclude that they must resort to trade-offs. To make these trade-offs, the line managers must contest with several specialist departments (such as Quality Control), each one of which regards its own specialty as having top priority.
3. *Orientation: technique versus results.* Quality specialists often propose adoption of specific quality-oriented systems, techniques, practices, etc. When the line managers reject such proposals, the quality specialists tend to regard the rejections as evidence of lack of interest in quality.
4. *Jurisdictional differences.* Many quality specialists resent being excluded from participation in certain activities and/or decisions which affect product quality, e.g., new product development. The quality specialists may regard this exclusion as a form of lack of quality-mindedness on the part of the line managers. The line managers do not see it that way—they regard it as just another problem in organizational jurisdiction.

Trade-offs—Economic and Other

To the line manager who must meet multiple standards, the need for trade-offs seems obvious. In most cases these trade-offs are concerned only with money, e.g., finding how to reduce losses to a minimum.

> **Example** A new product model is being launched but there remains an unsolved problem of excessive failures. It is estimated that 3 months will be required to solve the problem. The quality manager urges that the model be held up until the problem can be solved. Such action (argues the quality manager) would not only avoid the resulting field failures; it would avoid damage to the company's quality reputation outside and to quality morale inside. The marketing manager nevertheless urges going ahead because the merchants have meanwhile been clearing out the old model and hence will be left with no replacement product to sell. The general manager upholds the marketing manager on the ground that it will cost less to make the extra service calls than to delay shipment. The quality manager resents the decision. He feels that as quality manager he should have the last word on a quality question.

It is quite possible that the general manager is mistaken. However, the quality manager is certainly mistaken in believing that this is solely a quality problem. It is also a problem in keeping a customer supplied with goods to sell as well as a problem in overall economics. As to such matters, the quality manager does not have the last word.

A more difficult problem is presented when matters of public health and safety are involved.

> **Example** Two reliability engineers are assigned to a project of developing a brake for a military vehicle. The product design is inadequate, and all prototypes have failed the laboratory test. The delivery time is fast approaching. When still another prototype is tested in the laboratory, the project manager deliberately departs from the specified test conditions. Nevertheless, the test results are only on the borderline of acceptability. The project manager then orders the reliability engineers to bias the test performance curves so as to make it seem that the test has been fully successful. The reliability engineers are unwilling to do this. They go over the head of the project manager to the chief project manager, to the technical manager, and to the general manager, none of whom is willing to countermand the order. The reliability engineers now find themselves in an impossible position. They must commit an offense against society or risk severe economic sanctions.

Increasingly, various national laws are imposing obligations on company managers to report such situations to regulatory bodies or to risk criminal penalties. (These same laws also protect employees from discrimination if they choose to report asserted violations.) However, the companies have not yet fully worked out the measures needed to protect subordinate managers and specialists from pressures that place them in impossible positions. The company's policies should provide means to enable the pressured employees to reach some special protective mechanism (legal department, ombudsman, etc.) without fear of subsequent disciplinary action.

Note that such a policy is needed in cases that involve the safety and health of human beings or adherence to regulatory laws. In such cases each employee has a personal obligation to society with the risk of personal criminal liability in the event of violations. In cases that involve only the company's economics, there is as yet no such personal obligation to society. Hence the employee, as part of his or her employment contract, must carry out the decisions of the hierarchy even if he or she disagrees with them.

Motivation for Improvement

The weakest area of quality motivation for managers is that of motivation for improvement of quality—for "breakthrough" to new levels of performance. This weakness arises primarily because the problem of control—of meeting this year's goals—has a much higher priority.

Control sets its own priorities. When the alarm bells ring they demand corrective action then and there. The alarms must be heeded or the current goals will not be met. The manager wants to meet these current goals—managerial performance is judged mainly by measuring results against these same goals.

In contrast, improvement of quality is not needed to meet this year's goals—it is needed to attain leadership in some future year, or at least to remain competitive. Hence improvement can be deferred, whereas control cannot. Moreover, improvement to new levels (breakthrough) requires special organization machinery such as is described in Chapter 5. Such special machinery is not needed for maintaining current control.

Ideally, managers should be engaged in both control and improvement, and should be equally comfortable whether doing one or the other. Preferably, the leadership for such a way of life should come from the upper management, but in many companies it does not. Where it does not, the leadership, if any, comes from some of the venturesome middle managers, whose job is all the harder since it lacks top-management support.

PROBLEMS

6-1 For any process acceptable to the instructor:

    (a) Identify the multiple standards faced by the workers.

    (b) List the principal operator-controllable defects.

    (c) Classify these defects as to whether they are inadvertent, willful, or due to lack of technique.

    (d) Propose a program for reducing the error level.

6-2 For any organization acceptable to the instructor, study the prevailing continuing program of motivation for quality. Report your findings as to:

(*a*) Ingredients of the program.

(*b*) Effectiveness in carrying out the various aspects of the program.

6-3 Look about your community to identify some of the on-going drives or campaigns, such as for traffic safety, fund raising, political elections, keep-your-city-clean, etc. For any campaign acceptable to the instructor, analyze and report on:

(*a*) The methods used for securing attention.

(*b*) The methods used for securing interest and identification with the program.

(*c*) The methods used for securing action.

6-4 For any motivational campaign acceptable to the instructor, study the plan of organization used to achieve results, and report on the organization plan used.

6-5 In one electronics plant there was a requirement that certain subassemblies (mounts) made in department A should be inspected 100 percent before going to the final assembly department B. From time to time department B would run short of mounts and would request rush deliveries. To meet such requests, department A would omit the inspection so as to give prompt service. To the surprise of department A's manager, the final product quality did not seem to be affected adversely by the use of uninspected mounts. However, except for such emergencies, the manager continued the 100 percent inspection.

Then came a drop in the economy and a top-management drive on cost reduction. As in previous drives, severe and arbitrary budget cuts were made. Now the manager made use of what he had been saving for such a rainy day. He quietly eliminated the costly 100 percent inspection without telling anyone.

What do you think of the actions taken by the manager of department A? What would you have done? Why?

6-6 You are the general manager of the X Division. A large batch of product has been made up and is discovered to contain 0.2 percent of units which are unfit for use. The quality manager proposes to test the product 100 percent to remove the unfit units before shipment to clients. The manufacturing manager objects on the ground that it would be less costly to make replacements in the field when and if defective units are returned by the consumers. The marketing manager supports the quality manager.

You ask for a cost analysis and the facts are found to be as follows:

Percent defective = 0.2 percent.

Cost to test = $3 per 100 units.

About 500 units must be tested to find one defect, or $15.00 spent per defect found.

Selling price of the product = $6.00.

Probable frequency of consumer complaints per 100 field failures—about 20 percent.

Cost to adjust a field complaint including replacement of the defective unit—about $25.00.

What do you decide? Why?

6-7 In *The Wartime Journals of Charles A. Lindbergh* (Harcourt Brace Jovanovich, New York, 1970), under the entry for September 4, 1942, Lindbergh describes an incident at the Ford Motor Company's bomber factory at Willow Run, Michigan. (Lindbergh was at the time an adviser on the military aircraft program; Sorensen was Ford's production chief. Henry Ford was the founder of the Ford Motor Company.)

Sorensen brought up the question of our production schedule and the quality of workmanship at Willow Run—said we were ahead of schedule and that our workmanship was just as good as that of other companies. He tried to get me to agree with him and put me in a corner where I had to say bluntly that we were *not* making schedule and that the workmanship on the first bombers that went through Willow Run was the worst I had ever seen. Sorensen is not used to having anyone oppose him, and I have seen him bluff his way through a difficult situation time and time again. He tries to get a man to agree with him either out of fear or courtesy, and then constantly reminds him of the fact that he once agreed. The only way to handle Sorensen is to say exactly what you believe when he asks a question, and I did. Henry Ford listened quietly and apparently enjoyed the situation very much!

(*a*) What do you think of Lindbergh's manner of handling the situation?

(*b*) What would you have done if you were a subordinate of Sorensen's under similar circumstances?

6-8 A pharmaceutical company has been forced to recall from the market all of a certain type of product because of an error on the label. A missing decimal point resulted in the amount of medication being shown as 11 ml instead of 1.1 ml. The procedure for making labels includes a detailed proofreading by a member of the Quality Control Department to compare the text on the first printed label with the original text as approved by the Research Department. The inspector failed to find the error.

Because of the seriousness of such a recall, there is discussion of what discipline to apply to the inspector. In this connection a look is taken at what other errors were detected or not detected. It is found that in the last 3 years the inspector found 47 errors on labels and other printed materials. The missing decimal point is the only known instance during this time of a failure to detect an error. What is your conclusion as to the disciplinary action to be taken?

SUPPLEMENTARY READING

Controllability

See *Quality Control Handbook*, 3rd ed., McGraw-Hill Book Company, New York, 1974, pp. 11-5 to 11-11; also pp. 16-16, 16-17.

Japanese QC circles

QC Circles: Applications, Tools, and Theory, American Society for Quality Control, 161 West Wisconsin Ave., Milwaukee, Wisconsin 53203, 1976. A good collection of papers, both Japanese and American.

Proceedings, International Quality Conference, Tokyo, 1978. Japanese Union of Scientists and Engineers.

Proceedings, International Conference on Quality Control, Tokyo, 1978. Japanese Union of Scientists and Engineers.

The Taylor system

Juran, J. M., "The Taylor System and Quality Control." A series of eight papers, published in *Quality Progress* (American Society for Quality Control), May to December 1973.

Socialist countries

Quality Control Handbook, 3rd ed., sec. 48 A.

EXAMPLES OF EXAMINATION QUESTIONS USED IN FORMER ASQC QUALITY ENGINEER CERTIFICATION EXAMINATIONS AS PUBLISHED IN *QUALITY PROGRESS* MAGAZINE

1 McGregor's Theory X manager is typified as one who operates from the following basic assumption about subordinates (select the one best answer): (*a*) performance can be improved through tolerance and trust; (*b*) people have a basic need to produce; (*c*) status is more important than money;

(*d*) self-actualization is the highest order of human need; (*e*) people are lazy and are motivated by reward and punishment.

2 Quality motivation in industry should be directed at: (*a*) manufacturing management; (*b*) procurement and engineering; (*c*) the quality assurance staff; (*d*) the work force; (*e*) all of the above.

3 To instill the quality control employee with the desire to perform to his or her utmost and optimum ability, which of the following recognition for sustaining motivation has been found most effective? (*a*) recognition by issuance of monetary award; (*b*) verbal recognition publicly; (*c*) private verbal recognition; (*d*) public recognition plus nonmonetary award; (*e*) no recognition; salary is sufficient motivation.

4 Which of the following methods used to improve employee efficiency and promote an atmosphere conducive to quality and profit is the most effective in the long run? (*a*) offering incentives such as bonus, praise, profit sharing, etc.; (*b*) strict discipline to reduce mistakes, idleness, and sloppiness; (*c*) combination of incentive and discipline to provide both reward for excellence and punishment for inferior performance; (*d*) building constructive attitudes through development of realistic quality goals relating to both company and employee success; (*e*) all of the above provided that emphasis is placed on attitude motivation, with incentive and discipline used with utmost caution.

5 The famous Hawthorne study provided which of the following clinical evidence regarding the factors that can increase work group productivity? (*a*) attention and recognition is more important than working conditions; (*b*) productivity did not change significantly under any of the test conditions; (*c*) informal group pressures set a production "goal"; (*d*) people with higher capabilities are bored with routine jobs; (*e*) work-station layout is critical to higher productivity.

DESIGNING FOR QUALITY

7-1 INTRODUCTION

The evolution of a product includes the activities of design, manufacture, and use. At one time, all of these activities were performed by the same person, i.e., to provide what was needed for one's own use. As industry evolved, separate departments doing design, manufacture, and planning for field use were created within companies. Each department developed and refined its activity. Within each department there evolved various specialists who became expert in performing certain specialized activities within that department.

In the design department the central figures were obviously the designers. They were primarily responsible for creating a design that would meet the "performance" requirements. For example, the pump should do the needed pumping at good efficiency. In addition, all good designers tried to design the product to be reliable (perform without failure). They also tried to design the product so that it would be economic to make (producible), safe during use, easy to maintain in case of failure (maintainable), etc. There were no separate specialists assigned to help designers with these parameters. Whether the parameters were well met depended on the capability and breadth of the specific designer involved. However, designers were strongly influenced by the fact that the *performance* requirements were usually quantified and hence subject to verification by company inspectors or customers' inspectors. In contrast, parameters such as reliability were not quantified and hence not subject to rigorous verification.

Starting in the 1950s a movement got under way to quantify reliability, availability, maintainability, etc. It soon became evident that this quantification would not be made effective if left to the traditional designers. Hence specialists were created to help the company enter the era of quantification of these parameters. In some cases the need for these specialists was large enough to warrant the creation of new specialist departments.

Times have changed. A comparison of traditional and modern products is shown in Table 7-1. The traditional product is a reciprocating pump, a garden tool, a bicycle, or an aspirin. The modern product is a printed circuit board, a computer, an electronic component, or a nuclear reactor. In practice, products are really on a continuous spectrum from extremely traditional to extremely modern. Some products move on the spectrum; e.g., the earliest automobiles and telephones were traditional but they no longer are.

For the traditional products, the old design process, centered on the unaided designer, was adequate to arrive at good designs, and still is. For modern products, many companies have adopted a new design process involving various aids to the designer:

Design review by various specialists to provide early warning of potential trouble.
Assistance from specialists in the form of data collection and analysis.
New design disciplines which require the designer to replace empirical ways with formalized, quantified approaches.
Expanded facilities—laboratories, pilot plants, trial lots.

For modern products, attainment of fitness for use involves a balance among competing parameters and costs. The aggregation of these parameters

Table 7-1 Traditional versus modern products

Aspects of products	Traditional	Modern
Simplicity	Simple, static	Complex, dynamic
Precision	Low	High
Need for interchangeability	Limited	Extensive
Consumables or durables	Mainly consumables	Mainly durables
Environment in which used	Natural	Unnatural
User understanding of product	High	Low
Importance to human health, safety, and continuity of life	Seldom important	Often important
Life-cycle cost to user	Similar to purchase price	Much greater than purchase price
Life of a new design	Long; decades, even centuries	Short; less than a decade
Scientific basis of design	Largely empirical	Largely scientific
Basis of reliability, maintainability, etc.	Vague: "best effort"	Quantified
Volume of production	Usually low	Often high
Usual cause of field failures	Manufacturing errors	Design weaknesses

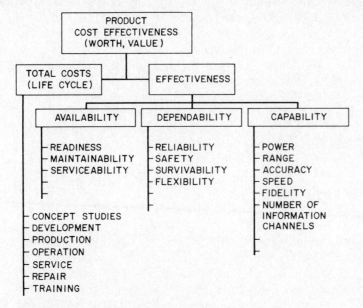

Figure 7-1 Elements of cost effectiveness.

and costs, from the inception of the design to the end of the operational life, is called the *cost-effectiveness concept* (see Figure 7-1). Some of these parameters do *not* apply to all products. However, the model does provide a framework to analyze (1) modern products and (2) traditional products which may be walking the path toward the modern arena. Life-cycle costs are discussed in Section 18-9. The availability and dependability parameters will be discussed in this chapter and the next. The capability parameter represents the collection of performance parameters unique to each product.

In practice, the "design," "manufacture," and "use" classification is an oversimplification. For many products (traditional and modern) it is useful to visualize an evolution through many phases. Typically, these phases are the design concept, feasibility, experimental, preproduction, production release, production, maintenance, and use. For many products, some of these phases are brief or even combined with other phases. Increasingly, even companies making traditional products are finding it useful to plan the launching of a new product by recognizing the need for a series of phases before going into full production.

The need for careful evolution of a new product is not restricted to products having complex hardware. The evolution of a new antiperspirant is an example.[1] It started with a formal market research study that established the need for a new product, i.e., one that "did not go on wet and make you wait to get dressed." First, a volatile silicone was used as a substitute for water, but the silicone dissolved part of the applicator. The next model corrected the problem

---

[1] This summary is based on "Sweating It Out," *Wall Street Journal,* November 17, 1978, p. 1.

but was "too oily." The next model looked promising until it became a rock-hard gel that could not be removed from the package. The next model had several problems: (1) it leaked out of most containers, (2) the new dispenser was too confusing, and (3) users felt the product was *too* dry on application and therefore they were not sure that the product was working properly. After other futile attempts to develop a new applicator (including one with a clicking noise to assure users that it was working), a conventional applicator was chosen and the new product released for production. The cost of this development was $18 million over a 2-year period—and the product was a simple one with just a few moving parts.

7-2 ELEMENTS OF A TYPICAL RELIABILITY PROGRAM

In the 1950s, costly failure problems were experienced on military electronic equipment and space products. Initially, it was suspected that most of the failures were due to manufacturing or inspection errors. The facts revealed otherwise. Design was the major problem. For moderate to highly complex products, fitness-for-use problems in the field show this breakdown: 40 percent due to design, 30 percent due to manufacturing, and 30 percent due to field conditions. (Examples of causes due to field conditions are faulty maintenance and improper operation of a product.) This is based on the early studies of product failures and the experience of Frank M. Gryna, Jr.

As the problem was analyzed, the term *reliability* emerged. In a historic report,[2] reliability was defined as "the probability of a product performing without failure a specified function under given conditions for a specified period of time." (More simply, reliability is the chance that a product will work.) If this definition is dissected, four implications become apparent:

1. The quantification of reliability in terms of a probability.
2. A statement defining successful product performance.
3. A statement defining the environment in which the equipment must operate.
4. A statement of the required operating time between failures. (Otherwise, the probability is a meaningless number for time-oriented products.)

To achieve high reliability, it is necessary to define the specific tasks required. This task definition is called the *reliability program*. The early development of reliability programs emphasized the *design* phase of the product life cycle. However, it soon became apparent that the manufacturing and field-usage phases could not be handled separately. This resulted in reliability programs that spanned the full product life cycle, i.e., "cradle to grave."

---

[2] *Reliability of Military Electronic Equipment*, report by Advisory Group on Reliability of Electronic Equipment, Office of the Assistant Secretary of Defense (R&D), June 1957. (This was the historic "AGREE" report.)

Such broad-scope reliability programs are identical to broad-scope quality programs aimed at fitness for use.

A reliability program typically includes the following activities: .

Setting overall reliability goals
Apportionment of the reliability goals
Stress analysis
Identification of critical parts
Failure mode and effect analysis
Reliability prediction
Design review
Selection of suppliers (Chapter 9)
Control of reliability during manufacturing (Chapters 11 through 14)
Reliability testing
Failure reporting and corrective action system (Chapter 20)

Except as indicated, these activities will be discussed in this chapter and the following one.

Some elements of a reliability program are *old* (e.g., stress analysis, part selection). The significant *new* aspect is the *quantification* of reliability. The act of quantification makes reliability a design parameter just like weight and tensile strength. Thus reliability can be submitted to specification and verification. Quantification also helps to refine certain traditional design tasks such as stress analysis and part selection.

Many of the tasks in a reliability program are really applications of a long-standing aid for launching new products, i.e., the early warning concept. Under this concept, activities are introduced into the product development cycle as a means of detecting and alerting people to trouble ahead. Some forms of early warning for various phases of the product life cycle are shown in Table 7-2.

The tasks in a reliability program require actions from many functions. Securing these actions commonly requires positive, formal planning if the

Table 7-2 Forms of early warning of new-product problems

Phases of new-product progression	Forms of early warning of new-product troubles
Concept and feasibility study	Concept review
Prototype design	Design review, reliability prediction, failure mode and effect analysis
Prototype construction	Prototype test, environmental test, overstressing
Preproduction	Pilot production lots
Early full-scale production	In-house testing (e.g., kitchen, road), consumer use panels, limited marketing area
Full-scale production, marketing, and use	Employees as test panels, special provisions for prompt feedback
All phases	Failure analysis, data collection and analysis

Table 7-3 Excerpts from the Martin reliability management (MRM) program for the ——— project

Task	Primary responsibility	Other functions concerned	Procedure approved		Controls	Schedule	
			Date	By		Start	Completion
Perform reliability predictions based on circuit and component analyses and use of reliability handbook. Compare to reliability budgets. If any design revisions are made, review reliability prediction and revise as required	Design engineer	Quality	Completed	Technical director	1. Reliability predictions to be included on page and line schedule 2. Analyses to be reviewed by group engineer 3. All analyses must be submitted to reliability engineer for his approval	7/1/58	10/1/59
Review all designs to determine component part and assembly limitations with respect to reliability requirements using economical processes and procedures	Electrical manufacturing	Quality	8/15/58	Manufacturing manager	1. All drawings must be reviewed by manufacturing representative prior to engineering release	9/1/58	1/1/59
Establish failure reporting and problem resolution system from first development test through service use. 1. Establish and maintain failure reporting in test areas and service use 2. Establish and maintain failure reporting in selected vendors' plants	Quality	Engineering, manufacturing, procurement, logistics support	2/15/59	Quality manager	1. Assign specific reliability and assurance engineer and corrective action team to find problems and assure correction 2. Monitor reporting through assigned personnel in reporting areas	3/1/59	Completion of service use

deeds are to be done, and done on time. Moreover, since many departments and individuals are involved, it is useful to set out in detail the tasks to be performed, who is to do them, the timetable, etc. Table 7-3 gives a *small* portion of an example of such a formalized approach.[3] For organizations that are involved in "modern" products, the written definition of tasks into one overall program is essential. Often such a definition (as illustrated in Table 7-3) is missing. This lack of definition presents a major opportunity for someone to orchestrate the program. Typically, quality control managers can "make the rounds" of all company functions and help get agreement on tasks and responsibilities. Some companies prepare such a reliability task definition for each major new product to be launched. This definition helps to assure that adequate funds are available for the tasks to be accomplished during the product life cycle.

Before embarking on a discussion of reliability tasks, a remark on the application of the tasks is in order:

1. These tasks are clearly not warranted for simple products. However, many products that were originally simple are now becoming more complex. When this is the case, the various reliability tasks should be examined to see which, if any, might be justified to use.
2. Reliability techniques were originally developed for electronic and space products, but the adaptation to mechanical products has now achieved success.
3. These techniques not only apply to products the company markets but also to the capital equipment the company purchases, e.g., numerically controlled machines. A less obvious application is to chemical processing equipment.[4]

7-3 SETTING OVERALL RELIABILITY GOALS

The original development of reliability quantification consisted of a probability and a mission time along with a definition of performance and usage conditions. This proved confusing to many people, so the index was abbreviated (using a mathematical relationship) to mean time between failures. Many people believe this to be the only reliability index. This is not so; no single index applies to most products. A summary of common indices (often called *figures of merit*) is presented in Table 7-4.

As experience is gained in quantifying reliability, many companies are learning that it is best to create an index that uniquely meets the needs of those who will use the index. Users of the index not only include internal technical

---

[3] F. M. Gryna, "Total Quality Control Through Reliability," *1960 ASQC Annual Technical Conference Transactions*, p. 295.

[4] For a collection of articles showing the application of reliability techniques to the chemical industry, see the December 1970 issue of *Chemical Engineering Progress*.

Table 7-4 Reliability figures of merit

Figure of merit	Meaning
Mean time between failures (MTBF)	Mean time between successive failures of a repairable product
Failure rate	Number of failures per unit time
Mean time to failure (MTTF)	Mean time to failure of a nonrepairable product or mean time to first failure of a repairable product
Mean life	Mean value of life ("life" may be related to major overhaul, wear-out, etc.)
Mean time to first failure (MTFF)	Mean time to first failure of a repairable product
Mean time between maintenance (MTBM)	Mean time between a specified type of maintenance action
Longevity	Wear-out time for a product
Availability	Operating time expressed as a percentage of operating and repair time
System effectiveness	Extent to which a product achieves the requirements of the user
Probability of success	Same as reliability (but often used for "one-shot" or non-time-oriented products)
b_{10} life	Life during which 10% of the population would have failed
b_{50} life	Median life, or life during which 50% of the population would have failed
Repairs/100	Number of repairs per 100 operating hours

personnel but also marketing personnel and users of the product. Examples of reliability indices and goals are:

1. For a telephone system: The downtime of each switching center should be a maximum of 24 h per 40 years.
2. For an engine manufacturer: 70 percent of the engines produced should pass through the warranty period without generating a claim. The number of failures per failed engine should not exceed 1.
3. For an automobile manufacturer: Repairs per 100 vehicles.
4. For a locomotive manufacturer:[5]
   Reliability goals. These will be normally expressed as a failure rate in terms of a multiple of warranty periods. For example, 3 percent failure rate in two warranty periods is expressed as

$$W2 = 3\%$$

   Service conditions
   a. Locomotive to have 95 percent availability, and therefore, to have a total operating time of 8350 h per year.
   b. Time spent at each throttle notch is as follows:

[5] M. Emphrain, Jr., and A. B. Hamilton, "Locomotive Reliability," Paper 73-DGP-14, Diesel and Gas Engine Power Division, American Society of Mechanical Engineers, New York, 1973.

Throttle	8	7	6	5	4	3	2	1	Idle	Dynamic brake	("8" is full speed)
% of time	30	3	3	3	3	3	3	3	41	8	= 100%

    c. Outside ambient temperature limits to be $-40°F$ to $+115°F$.

    d. Throttle handling to be from 10 to 100 throttle changes per hour, but a maximum "throttle wipe" from the number eight notch to the number one notch, or vice versa, to occur four times per hour.

    e. Locomotive to run 10 percent of the operating time at the continuous speed rating and 20 percent of the operating time at the maximum rated speed.

Note that all three of these examples quantify reliability.

Setting overall reliability goals requires a meeting of the minds on (1) reliability as a number, (2) the environmental conditions to which the numbers apply, and (3) a definition of successful product performance. This is *not* easily accomplished. However, the act of requiring designers to define with precision both environmental conditions and successful product performance forces the designer to understand the design in greater depth.

7-4 RELIABILITY APPORTIONMENT, PREDICTION, AND ANALYSIS

The process of reliability quantification involves three phases:

Apportionment (or budgeting): i.e., the process of allocating reliability objectives among various elements which collectively make up a higher-level product.

Prediction: i.e., use of prior performance data plus probability theory to calculate the expected failure rates for various circuits, configurations, etc.

Analysis: i.e., identification of the strong and weak portions of the design to serve as a basis for improvements, trade-offs, and similar actions.

These phases are illustrated in Table 7-5.

In the top section of the table, an overall reliability requirement of 95 percent for 1.45 h is apportioned to the six subsystems of a missile. The second section of the table apportions the budget for the explosive subsystem to the three units within the subsystem. The allocation for the fusing circuitry is 0.998 or, in terms of mean time between failures, 725 h. In the final section of the table, the proposed design for the circuitry is analyzed and a reliability prediction made, using the method of adding failure rates. As the prediction indicates an MTBF of 1398 h as compared to a budget of 725 h, the proposed design is acceptable. The prediction technique not only provides a quantitative evaluation of a design or a design change but can also identify design areas having the largest potential for reliability improvement. Thus the "vital few" will be obvi-

Table 7-5 Establishment of reliability objectives*

		System breakdown			
Subsystem	Type of operation	Relia- bility	Unrelia- bility	Failure rate per hour	Reliability objective†
Air frame	Continuous	0.997	0.003	0.0021	483
Rocket motor	One-shot	0.995	0.005		1/200 operations
Transmitter	Continuous	0.982	0.018	0.0126	80.5 h
Receiver	Continuous	0.988	0.012	0.0084	121 h
Control system	Continuous	0.993	0.007	0.0049	207 h
Explosive system	One-shot	0.995	0.005		1/200 operations
System		0.95	0.05		

	Explosive subsystem breakdown			
Unit	Operating mode	Relia- bility	Unrelia- bility	Reliability objective
Fusing circuitry	Continuous	0.998	0.002	725 h
Safety and arming mechanism	One-shot	0.999	0.001	1/1,000 operations
Warhead	One-shot	0.998	0.002	2/1,000 operations
Explosive subsystem		0.995	0.005	

Fusing circuitry component part classification	Unit breakdown Number used, n	Failure rate per part, λ (%/1000 h)	Total part failure rate, $n\lambda$ (%/1000 h)
Transistors	93	0.30	27.90
Diodes	87	0.15	13.05
Film resistors	112	0.04	4.48
Wirewound resistors	29	0.20	5.80
Paper capacitors	63	0.04	2.52
Tantalum capacitors	17	0.50	8.50
Transformers	13	0.20	2.60
Inductors	11	0.14	1.54
Solder joints and wires	512	0.01	5.12
			71.51

$$\text{MTBF} = \frac{1}{\text{failure rate}} = \frac{1}{\Sigma\, n\lambda} = \frac{1}{0.0007151} = 1398 \text{ h}$$

*Adapted by F. M. Gryna, Jr., from G. N. Beaton, "Putting the R&D Reliability Dollar to Work," *Proceedings of the Fifth National Symposium on Reliability and Quality Control,* 1959, Institute of Electrical and Electronics Engineers, Inc., p. 65.

†For a mission time of 1.45 hours.

ous by noting the components with the highest failure rates. In this example, the transistors, diodes, and tantalum capacitors account for about 70 percent of all the unreliability.

The approach of adding failure rates to predict system reliability is analogous to the control of weight in aircraft structures, where a running record is kept of weight as various parts are added to the design. Another analogy is the continuous record that is kept of the increased costs as complexity is added to a design. The reliability engineer, then, is asking that a continuous record be kept of the increasing failure rate as complexity and higher performance requirements are demanded of products.

Rich, Smith, and Korte[6] show the application of reliability apportionment to a vehicle (see Table 7-6). A reliability goal is to be set for a new vehicle. The overall goal on the complete vehicle and the apportionment (to the power train, engine, hitch and hydraulics, electrical components, and chassis) is determined by evaluating actual data on a similar vehicle and setting new goals based on expected improvements. The reliability goal on the complete vehicle is set in terms of average hours per failure and repair cost as a percent of price.

Reliability apportionment and prediction methods are still evolving. The present status is about comparable to the early days of quantifying basic properties of materials. Prediction methods based on different statistical distributions are discussed in Chapter 8.

To date, experience with reliability apportionment and reliability prediction has been that:

1. The *process* of using these tools is usually most helpful in identifying design weaknesses and strengths, and reaching a meeting of the minds among those concerned.
2. The precision of reliability prediction has a long way to go. Kern[7] studied 16 different pieces of avionics equipment and compared the field reliability with (a) the reliability predicted by a paper analysis, and (b) the reliability

[6] Barrett G. Rich, O. A. Smith, and Lee Korte, "Experience with a Formal Reliability Program," SAE Paper 670731, Farm, Construction and Industrial Machinery Meeting, 1967.

[7] George A. Kern, "Operational Influences on Avionics Reliability," *Proceedings, Annual Reliability and Maintainability Symposium*, January 1978, pp. 231–242.

Table 7-6 Example of reliability apportionment

Development of reliability goal for complete vehicle		
	Hours/failure (MTBF)	Repair cost (% of price)
Past experience	245	1.8
Past experience adjusted for improvements	305	1.0
Goal for new design	300	1.0

Development of reliability apportionment [hours/failure (MTBF)]		
	Past experience	Past experience adjusted	New goal
Power train	1200	1960	1650
Engine	900	1260	1250
Hitch and hydraulics	836	870	900
Electrical components	1260	1460	1500
Chassis	6580	6580	6500

demonstrated by tests. The predicted and demonstrated reliability were both generally higher than the actual field reliability.

Reliability prediction is a continuous process starting with paper *predictions* based on a design analysis, plus historical failure-rate information. The evaluation ends with reliability *measurement* based on data from customer use of the product. Table 7-7 lists some characteristics of the various phases.

7-5 SELECTION OF TOLERANCES

The selection of tolerances has a dual effect on economics of quality. The tolerance affects:

1. Fitness for use and hence the salability of the product
2. Costs of manufacture (facilities, tooling, productivity) and quality costs (equipment, inspection, scrap, rework, material review, etc.)

In theory, the designer should, by scientific study, establish the proper balance between the value of precision and the cost of precision. In practice, the designer is unable to do this for each tolerance—there are too many quality characteristics. As a result, only a minority of tolerances are set scientifically. Scientific tools for tolerancing include:

1. *Regression studies.* For example, a thermostat may be required to turn on and shut off a power source at specified low and high temperature values, respectively. A number of thermostat elements are built and tested. The prime recorded data are (1) turn on temperature, (2) shut off temperature, and (3) physical characteristics of the thermostat elements. These data permit scatter diagrams to be prepared (Figure 7-2) and regression equations to be computed to aid in establishing critical component tolerances on a basis which is scientific within the confidence limits for the numbers involved.
2. *Tolerances for interacting dimensions.* Numerous designs involve "interacting dimensions." An electronic circuit may consist of 11 elements in series; a mechanical assembly may consist of a buildup of 8 elements; a single complex piece part may include a chain of 10 dimensions, starting from a baseline. What these designs have in common is the existence of interaction among these elements or dimensions. Each element or dimension has its own tolerances. However, the variation of the composite (the circuit, the assembly, or the chain) will be related to the variations of the elements according to the laws of probability; i.e., it is very unlikely that all the extremes will come together simultaneously.

   This unlikelihood makes it possible to establish wider tolerances on el-

Table 7-7 Stages of reliability prediction and measurement*

	1 Start of design	2 During detailed design	3 At final design	4 From system tests	5 From customer usage
Basis	Prediction based on approximate part counts and part failure rates from previous product usage; little knowledge of stress levels, redundancy, etc.	Prediction based on quantities and types of parts, redundancies, stress levels, etc.	Prediction based on types and quantities of part failure rates for expected stress levels, redundancies, external environments, special maintenance practices, special effects of system complexity, cycling effects, etc.	Measurement based on the results of tests of the complete system; appropriate reliability indices are calculated from the number of failures and operating time	Same as step 4 except calculations are based on customer usage data
Primary uses	1. Evaluate feasibility of meeting a proposed numerical requirement 2. Help in establishing a reliability goal for design	1. Evaluate overall reliability 2. Define problem areas	1. Evaluate overall reliability 2. Define problem areas	1. Evaluate overall reliability 2. Define problem areas	1. Measure achieved reliability 2. Define problem areas 3. Obtain data for future designs

*System tests in steps 4 and/or 5 may reveal problems that result in a revision of the "final" design. Such changes can be evaluated by repeating steps 3, 4, 5.

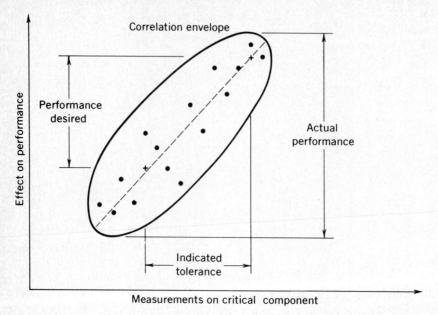

Figure 7-2 Approach to functional tolerancing.

ements of such designs without significantly increasing the extent of non-conformance. The scientific approach to this is discussed in Section 12-15.

Most tolerances are established by methods which, in varying degrees, are less than scientific. The principal methods include: precedent, bargaining, and standard tolerance systems defined at the company, industry, national, and international levels.

In most companies, the accumulated specifications contain an extensive array of unduly tight tolerances, i.e., tolerances not really needed to achieve fitness for use. When this condition creates shop troubles, the shop often responds by exceeding the tolerances to meet delivery dates. This is a situation of "unrealistic tolerances loosely enforced." Such a situation has evolved from many historic forces and in some companies unfortunately results in distrust between the design and manufacturing departments. Recently, the companies have tried to reduce the distrust in order to convert to a situation of "realistic tolerances rigidly enforced."

A conservative approach for the short run is to make provisions for handling current specifications having unrealistic tolerances. In the long run, the evolutionary solution to unrealistic tolerances lies in providing designers with the information they need to set realistic tolerances. This includes process capability data (see Section 12-10) and data on the cost of achieving various levels of tolerances. A useful step requires the designer (or someone else) to indicate the relative seriousness of the various product characteristics (see Section 15-4).

In Japan,[8] designers acquire knowledge about setting realistic tolerances as part of an extensive training program. This program provides the designer with practical experience and knowledge of producibility, field service work, and quality control methodology.

7-6 DESIGN REVIEW

Design review is a technique for evaluating a proposed design to assure that the design (1) will perform successfully during use, (2) can be manufactured at low cost, and (3) is suitable for prompt, low-cost field maintenance.

Design review is not new. However, in the past the term has referred to an informal evaluation of the design. Modern products often require a more formal program. A formal design review recognizes that many individual designers do not have specialized knowledge in reliability, maintainability, safety, producibility, and the other parameters that are important in achieving an optimum design. The design review aims to provide such knowledge.

For modern products, design reviews are based on the following concepts:

1. Design reviews are made mandatory, either through customer demand or through upper-management policy declaration.
2. The design reviews are conducted by a team consisting mainly of specialists who are not directly associated with the development of the design. These specialists must be highly experienced and bring with them the reputation of being objective. The combination of competence, experience, and objectivity is present in some people but these people are in great demand. The success of design reviews largely depends on the degree to which management supports the program by insisting that the best specialists be made available for design review work. The program deteriorates into superficial activity if (a) inexperienced people are assigned to design reviews or (b) those on the design review team are not given sufficient time to study product information prior to design review meetings.
3. Design reviews are formal. They are planned and scheduled like any other legitimized activity. The meetings are built around prepared agendas and documentation sent out in advance. Minutes of meetings are prepared and circulated. Follow-ups for action are likewise formalized.
4. Design reviews cover all quality-related parameters and others as well. The parameters can include reliability, maintainability, safety, producibility, weight, packaging, appearance, cost, etc.
5. As much as possible, design reviews are made to defined criteria. Such cri-

[8] J. M. Juran, "Japanese and Western Quality—A Contrast," *Quality Progress,* December 1978, pp. 10–18.

teria may include customer requirements, internal goals, or experience with previous products.

6. Design reviews are conducted at several phases of the progression of the design, such as design concept, prototype design and test, and final design. Reviews are made at several levels of the product hierarchy, such as system and subsystem.

A universal obstacle to design review has been the cultural resistance of the design department. It has been common practice for this department to hold a virtual monopoly on design decisions; i.e., these decisions have historically been immune from challenge unless actual product trouble was being encountered. With such a background, it was not surprising that the designers resisted the use of design reviews to challenge their designs. The designers contended that such challenges were based purely on grounds of theory and analysis (at which they regarded themselves as the top experts) rather than on the traditional grounds of "failed hardware." This resistance was further aggravated in those companies which permitted the reliability engineers to propose competing designs. The designers resisted the idea of having competitors even more than they resisted the idea of design review.

The emerging purpose of the design review is one of bringing to the designer inputs from the best experts available (on various essential specialties) so that the designer can optimize the design. In the design review meetings, the designer must listen to these inputs and respond constructively. The designer retains the benefit of the doubt and the last word on matters of structural integrity.

7-7 FAILURE MODE/FAILURE EFFECT AND FAULT TREE ANALYSES

Two techniques provide a methodical way to examine a design for possible ways in which failures can occur. In the *failure mode and effect analysis* (FMEA), a product (at the system and/or lower levels) is examined for all the ways in which a failure may occur. For each potential failure, an estimate is made of its effect on the total system and of its seriousness. In addition, a review is made of the action being taken (or planned) to minimize the probability of failure or to minimize the effect of failure. Figure 7-3 shows a portion of an FMEA for a traveling lawn sprinkler. Each hardware item is listed on a separate line. Note that the failure "mode" is the symptom of the failure, as distinct from the cause of failure, which consists of the proved reasons for the existence of the symptoms. The analysis can be elaborated to include such matters as:

Safety. Injury is the most serious of all failure effects. In consequence, safety is handled through special programs (Section 7-14).

1 = Very low (<1 in 1000)
2 = Low (3 in 1000)
3 = Medium (5 in 1000)
4 = High (7 in 1000)
5 = Very high (>9 in 1000)

T = Type of failure
P = Probability of occurrence
S = Seriousness of failure to system
H = Hydraulic failure
M = Mechanical failure
W = Wear failure
C = Customer abuse

Product   HRC-1

Date   Jan. 14, 1978

By   S.M.

Component part number	Possible failure	Cause of failure	T	P	S	Effect of failure on product	Alternatives
Worm bearing 4224	Bearing worn	Not aligned with bottom housing	M	1	4	Spray head wobble or slowing down	Improve inspection
Zytel 101		Excessive spray head wobble	M	1	3	DITTO	Improve worm bearing
Bearing stem 4225	Excessive wear	Poor bearing/ material combination	M	5	4	Spray head wobbles and loses power	Change stem material
Brass		Dirty water in bearing area	M	5	4	DITTO	Improve worm seal area
		Excessive spray head wobble	M	2	3	DITTO	Improve operating instructions
Thrust washer 4226	Excessive wear	High water pressure	M	2	5	Spray head will stall out	Inform customer in instructions
Fulton 404		Dirty water in washers	M	5	5	DITTO	Improve worm seal design
Worm 4527	Excessive wear in bearing area	Poor bearing/ material combination	M	5	4	Spray head wobbles and loses power	Change bearing stem material
Brass		Dirty water in bearing area	M	5	4	DITTO	Improve worm seal design
		Excessive spray head wobble	M	2	3	DITTO	Improve operating instructions

Figure 7-3 Failure mode and effect analysis.

Effect on downtime: i.e., must the system stop until repairs are made, or can repairs be made during an off-duty time?

Access: i.e., what hardware items must be removed to get at the failed component?

Repair planning: i.e., repair time, special repair tools, etc.

Recommendations for changes in designs or specifications; for added tests; for instructions to be included in manuals of inspection, operation, or maintenance.

In Figure 7-3, a ranking procedure has been applied in order to assign priorities to the failure modes for further study. The ranking is twofold: (1) the probability of occurrence of the failure mode, and (2) the severity of the effect. For each of these, a scale of 1 to 5 is used. If desired, a risk-priority number can be calculated as the product of the ratings. Priority is then assigned to investigating failure modes with high risk-priority numbers.

In this example, the analysis revealed that about 30 percent of the expected failures were in the worm and bearing stem area and that a redesign could easily be justified.

For most products, it is not economic to conduct the analysis of failure mode and failure effect for each component. Instead, engineering judgment is used to single out those items which are critical to the operation of the product. As the FMEA proceeds for these selected items, the designer will discover that ready answers are lacking for some of the failure modes and that further analysis is necessary.

Generally, failure mode and effect analysis on one item is helpful to designers of other items in the system. In addition, the analyses are useful in the planning for inspection, assembly, maintainability, and safety.

In *fault tree analysis* (e.g., for safety), the starting point is the list of hazards or undesired events for which the designer must provide some solution. This list is prepared from records of actual accidents or "near-misses." Each hazard on the list then becomes a failure mode requiring analysis. The analysis then considers the possible direct causes that could lead to the event. Next, it looks for the origins of these causes. Finally, it looks for ways to avoid these origins and causes. The branching out of origins and causes is what gives the technique the name "fault tree" analysis. The approach is the reverse of failure mode and failure effect analysis, which starts with origins and causes and looks for any resulting bad effects. (For complex products, failure mode and failure effect analysis becomes a huge undertaking.) An example of fault tree analysis is given in Section 7-15.

7-8 PARTS SELECTION AND CONTROL

In Table 7-5 we saw how system reliability rests on a base of reliability of the component parts.

The vital role played by part reliability has resulted in programs for thorough selection, evaluation, and control of parts. These programs include mainly:

1. *Parts application study.* The specification and design information supplied by parts manufacturers generally provides guidelines for application. If previous history is available from parts used in similar products, this history becomes an essential input. New applications must be subjected to qualification tests, including overstress, to determine safety factors. The analyses include derating (see below), stress analysis, thermal analysis, and other forms appropriate to each product.

2. *Approved parts list.* Preliminary component-parts lists are reviewed as early in the design phase as possible to:

Verify that proved parts (i.e., proved in previous usage) are being utilized wherever possible.
Verify that unproved or questionable parts are actually capable of meeting reliability or environmental ratings.

Compare ratings or qualification test data with anticipated environmental (life) stresses.

3. *Critical components list.* A component part is considered "critical" if any of the following conditions apply:

It has a high population in the equipment.
It has a single source of supply.
It must function to special, tight limits.
It has not been proved to the reliability standard, i.e., no test data, insufficient usage data.

The critical components list should be prepared early in the design effort. It is common practice to formalize these lists, showing, for each critical component, the nature of the critical features, the plan to quantify reliability, the plan for improving reliability, etc. The list becomes the basic planning document for (1) test programs to qualify parts, (2) design guidance in application studies and techniques, and (3) design guidance for application of redundant parts, circuits, or subsystems.

4. *Derating practice.* Derating is the assignment of a product to operate at stress levels below its normal rating, e.g., a capacitor rated at 300 V is used in a 200-V application. For many components, data are available showing failure rate as a function of stress levels (see Section 8-7). The conservative designer will use such data to achieve reliability by using the parts at low power ratios and low ambient temperatures.

Some companies have established internal policies with respect to *derating.* Derating is a form of quantifying the factor of safety and hence lends itself to setting guidelines as to the margins to be used. Derating may be considered as a method of determining more scientifically the factor of safety which engineers have long provided on an empirical basis. For example, if the calculated load was 20 tons, the engineers might design the structure to withstand 100 tons as a protection against unanticipated loads, misuse, hidden flaws, deterioration, etc.

7-9 EVALUATING DESIGNS BY TESTS

Although reliability prediction, design review, failure mode and effect analyses, and other techniques are valuable as early warning devices, they cannot be a substitute for the ultimate proof, i.e., use of the product by the customer. However, field experience comes too late and must be preceded by a substitute— various forms of testing the product to simulate field use.

Long before reliability technology was developed, several types of tests (performance, environmental, stress, life) were made to evaluate a design. The

Table 7-8 Summary of tests used to evaluate a design

Type of test	Purpose
Performance	Determine ability of product to meet basic performance requirements
Environmental	Evaluate ability of product to withstand defined environmental levels; determine internal environments generated by product operation; verify environmental levels specified
Stress	Determine levels of stress that a product can withstand in order to determine the safety margin inherent in the design; determine modes of failure that are not associated with time
Reliability	Determine product reliability and compare to requirements; monitor for trends
Maintainability	Determine time required to make repairs and compare to requirements
Life	Determine wear-out time for a product and failure modes associated with time
Pilot run	Determine if fabrication and assembly processes are capable of meeting design requirements; determine if reliability will be degraded

advent of reliability, maintainability, and other parameters resulted in additional types of tests.

A summary of types of tests for evaluating a design is given in Table 7-8. It is often possible to plan a test program so that one type of test can serve several purposes, e.g., evaluate both performance and environmental capabilities.

Accelerated testing is a common form of securing reliability test data at reduced testing cost. In this form of testing, the products are made to perform at abnormally high levels of stress and/or environments in order to make them fail sooner. (Earlier failures mean less test equipment, lower testing costs, and earlier answers.) Extrapolation is then used to convert the short life under severe conditions into expected life under normal conditions. Great care is needed to assure that the accelerated test time is properly correlated to normal usage time to avoid overstating the expected life. A further problem is that accelerated testing can introduce new failure modes which do not occur during normal product usage. Taking such failure modes seriously has sometimes led to major redesigns which provided no benefit from the standpoint of the original product requirements. While the benefits from accelerated testing can be substantial, there are serious risks of being misled. It is obviously essential to apply engineering judgment in such tests.

The accelerated-testing concept can be combined with probability-paper analysis to relate test results with field results. Stanton[9] describes how this was done for two models of room air conditioners. The field data and data from accelerated tests were plotted on Weibull probability paper as shown in Figure 7-4. As the lines were essentially parallel, it was concluded that the basic mode of failure was the same on the test as in the field. In Figure 7-4, the field data are

---

[9] Burr Stanton, "Consumer Appliance Reliability: Closing the Feedback Loop," *Proceedings, Annual Reliability and Maintainability Symposium*, January 1974, pp. 30–34.

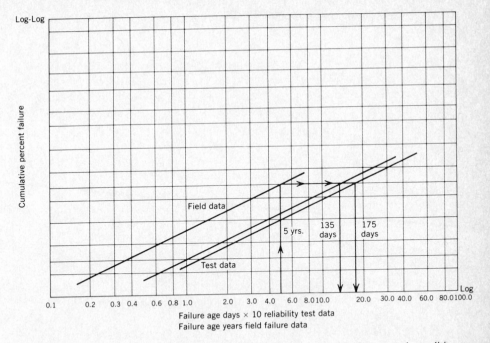

Figure 7-4 Superposed plot of field failure data over test data for two different room air conditioner models.

plotted in *years* of service. The test data are plotted in *tens of days*. The field data line shows the cumulative percent failure. The 5-year warranty period is represented by a heavy vertical line. Moving up on this line to intersect the field data line and then moving horizontally from the field data line to the lines for the accelerated test data, the accelerated time equivalent to the 5-year period can be read. For example, on one model the cumulative percent failed in 135 days of accelerated testing is equivalent to 5 years of field use. On the other model, the equivalent accelerated test time is 175 days.

Reliability Data Systems

Reliability data serve several important purposes:

1. To detect current reliability problems and assist in their solution.
2. To provide managers with quantitative information on product performance and on the status of problems.
3. To assist in reliability improvement programs.
4. To provide failure history and other reference data for use in product changes and in future products. This is the *data bank* concept and serves the needs of reliability in a manner analogous to that served by handbooks

of properties of materials (when choosing materials for specific applications).

Reliability data banks The term "data bank" implies an organized approach to data collection, classification, analysis, summary, and retrieval. Despite the seeming advantages of such an organized approach, it is difficult and costly to execute. In practice, companies make only limited use of the available data. These data originate from:

1. Engineering, preproduction, production, or special tests (e.g., test track, test kitchen) under the manufacturer's control. These tests are usually conducted on the premises but may include "captive" usage tests, e.g., employee homes, consumer panels, captive sales outlets.
2. Vendors and major subcontractors.
3. Field performance data, including customer returns.
4. Independent data banks. These are springing up in recognition of the fact that basic failure data can be used by many companies. For such multiple use, it may be more economic to maintain a central data bank instead of numerous duplicating company data banks. The more prominent of these banks are discussed in Section 9-6. In addition, there are laboratories devoted mainly to testing products for safety, and these laboratories develop test data which have wide application.

Many reliability programs are built with emphasis on field performance data and with inadequate use of in-plant test data. It is a mistake to structure programs in this way. Not only do they lose much of the advantage of early warning, but the field data are often unreliable and incomplete, for reasons noted above. The most cost-effective data system is that which has a positive influence on end-product quality through actions taken *early* in the development or production phases.

7-10 METHODS FOR IMPROVING RELIABILITY DURING DESIGN

The general approach to quality improvement (Chapter 5) is widely applicable to reliability improvement as far as economic analysis and managerial tools are concerned. The differences are in the technological tools used for diagnosis and remedy. Projects can be identified through reliability prediction, design review, failure mode and effect analysis, or other reliability evaluation techniques.

Action to improve reliability during the design phase is best taken by the designer. The designer understands best the engineering principles involved in the design. The reliability engineer can help by defining areas needing improvement and by assisting in the development of alternatives. The following actions indicate some approaches to improving a design:

1. *Review the users' needs* to see if the *function* of the unreliable parts is real-

ly necessary to the user. If not, eliminate those parts from the design. Alternatively, look to see if the reliability index (figure of merit) correctly reflects the real needs of the user. For example, availability (see below) is sometimes more meaningful than reliability. If so, a good maintenance program might improve availability and hence ease the reliability problem.

2. *Consider trade-offs* of reliability for other parameters, e.g., functional performance, weight. Here again it may be found that the customers' real needs may be better served by such a trade-off.

3. *Use redundancy* to provide more than one means for accomplishing a given task in such a way that all the means must fail before the system fails. This is discussed in Section 8-3.

4. *Review the selection of any parts* that are relatively new and unproven. Use standard parts whose reliability has been proven by actual field usage. (However, be sure that the conditions of previous use are applicable to the new product.)

5. *Use derating* to assure that the stresses applied to the parts are lower than the stresses the parts can normally withstand.

6. *Control the operating environment* to provide conditions that yield lower failure rates. Common examples are (a) potting electronic components to protect them against climate and shock, and (b) use of cooling systems to keep down ambient temperatures.

7. *Specify replacement schedules* to remove and replace low-reliability parts before they reach the wear-out stage. In many cases the replacement is made contingent on the results of checkouts or tests which determine whether degradation has reached a prescribed limit.

8. *Prescribe screening tests* to detect infant-mortality failures and to eliminate substandard components. The tests take various forms: bench tests, "burn in," accelerated life tests.

9. *Conduct research and development* to attain an improvement in the basic reliability of those components which contribute most of the unreliability. While such improvements avoid the need for subsequent trade-offs, they may require advancing the state of the art and hence an investment of unpredictable size.

Although none of the foregoing actions provides a perfect solution, the range of choice is broad. In some instances the designer can arrive at a solution single-handedly. More usually it means collaboration with other company specialists. In still other cases the customer and/or the company management must concur because of the broader considerations involved.

7-11 CORRECTIVE ACTION SYSTEM

A *corrective action system* is a company-wide coordinated effort that has several objectives:

1. Collect information from all sources on product failures and discrepancies. These sources include in-plant testing, field testing, and customer use.
2. Detect and assure resolution of problems affecting reliability. This objective includes problem selection, problem definition, and follow-up.
3. Keep management aware of the status of problems affecting the product.
4. Disseminate failure history and other reference data for use in preventing similar problems in product modifications and in future products.

The corrective action system is discussed further in Section 20-5.

7-12 AVAILABILITY

One of the major parameters of fitness for use is availability. Availability is the probability that a product, when used under given conditions, will perform satisfactorily when called upon. The total time in the operative state (also called *uptime*) is the sum of the time spent (1) in active use and (2) in the standby state. The total time in the nonoperative state (also called *downtime*) is the sum of the time spent (3) under active repair, and (4) waiting for spare parts, paperwork, etc. These categories are illustrated in Figure 7-5. The quantification of availability (and unavailability) dramatizes the extent of the problems and the areas for potential improvements. Formulas for quantifying availability are presented in Section 8-8.

The proportion of time that a product is available for use depends on (1)

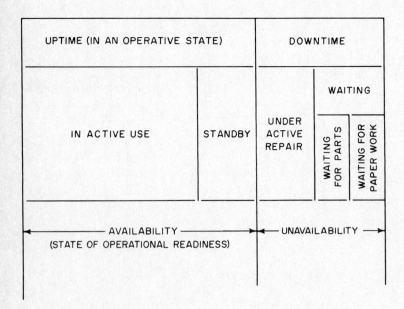

Figure 7-5 Ingredients of availability.

freedom from failures, i.e., reliability, and (2) the ease with which service can be restored after a failure. The latter factor brings us to the subject of maintainability.

7-13 MAINTAINABILITY

For many decades, designers have done their best to create designs that will be reliable and maintainable. However, the rise of complex products has resulted in the development of some new tools for improving reliability and maintainability during design. The tools for reliability have been described previously. The tools for maintainability follow the same basic pattern as those for reliability; i.e., there are tools for specifying, predicting, analyzing, and measuring maintainability. The tools apply to both preventive maintenance (i.e., maintenance to reduce the number of failures) and corrective maintenance (i.e., maintenance to restore a product to operable condition).

The specification of maintainability is occasionally in quantitative form. As with reliability, there is no one maintainability index that applies to most products. A summary of some common figures of merit for maintainability is given in Table 7-9. Helland[10] presents an example for a duplicating machine:

For machine usage below 80 h per month, preventive maintenance (P.M.) calls will be scheduled at 2-month intervals. At usage of 80 to 200 h, one P.M. call per month will be allowed. At more than 200 h, two P.M. calls per month are acceptable. P.M. calls must not exceed 2.3 h of active maintenance time.

[10] Kris L. Helland, Jr., "Motivating Management on Maintainability," *Proceedings, Annual Reliability and Maintainability Symposium*, January 1978, p. 34.

Table 7-9 Maintainability figures of merit

Figure of merit	Meaning
Mean time to repair (MTTR)	Mean time to perform the repair work assuming a spare part and technician are available
Mean downtime	Mean time during which a system is not in operative condition for any reason
Mean preventive maintenance time	Mean time for scheduled preventive maintenance
Repair hours per 100 operating hours	Number of hours required for repairs per 100 product operating hours
Rate of preventive maintenance actions	Number of preventive maintenance actions required per period of operative or calendar hours
Downtime probability	Probability that a failed product is restored to operative condition in a specified downtime
Maintainability index	Score for a product design based on evaluation of defined maintainability features
Rate of maintenance cost	Cost of preventive and corrective maintenance per unit of operating or calendar time

Mean maintenance time for corrective maintenance must not exceed 160 h of machine operating time. MTBF must exceed 80 h.

Following the approach used in reliability, a maintainability goal for a product can be apportioned to the various components of the product. Also, maintainability can be predicted based on an analysis of the design.

The methods differ widely. For example, one prediction method extrapolates past experience on maintainability of similar equipment to make predictions on a new design. Another method breaks down the maintenance task into elemental maintenance tasks and uses past data on these elemental tasks to build up a predicted maintainability time for a total repair. This method is analogous to predicting the time required for manufacturing operation by working with standard elemental times from a time study handbook. Still another method of maintainability prediction uses a checklist to score significant features of a system and then uses the scores in a regression equation to predict average repair time. These methods predict the absolute value of repair time.

Another approach evaluates a design by using a rating system that calculates (for routine and preventive maintenance) a comparative, rather than an absolute, measure of maintainability. Miller[11] explains this approach for earth-moving equipment. A scale of point values is applied to each of five categories: (1) *frequency* of the maintenance operation, (2) physical position of the technician's body in reaching the *location*, (3) an assessment of the maintenance *operation*, (4) what must be done to achieve *access*, and (5) *miscellaneous* actions. Specific examples of the point system for each category are shown in Table 7-10. The score for the design is the sum of the points for all categories. Low scores mean better maintainability. Although the score has no absolute meaning, it is useful in comparing alternative designs, e.g., a new design versus the present design. When sufficient experience is gained with such a system, a numerical value of the index can be used as a maintainability goal for the design department.

Approaches for improving the maintainability of a design are both general and specific. General approaches include:

1. *Reliability versus maintainability.* For example, given an availability requirement, should the response be an improvement in reliability or in maintainability?
2. *Modular versus nonmodular construction.* Modular design requires added design effort but reduces the time required for diagnosis and remedy in the field. The fault need only be localized to the module level, after which the defective module is unplugged and replaced. This concept is being rapidly extended to consumer products such as television sets.
3. *Repair versus throwaway.* For some products or modules, the cost of field

[11] E. W. Miller, "Maintenance Index—A Design Tool," SAE Paper 710680, Society of Automotive Engineers, 1971.

Table 7-10 Comparative maintenance index

1. Frequency of scheduled maintenance	
2000 h	1 point
.	
.	
.	
Less than 10 h	20 points
2. Location	
Within normal reach while standing on ground	1 point
.	
.	
Any position under machine	8 points
3. Access	
Exposed	1 point
.	
.	
Belly guard removal	25 points
4. Operation (complexity of service operation)	
Check visual gage	1 point
.	
.	
5. Miscellaneous	
Drainage requires hose	2 points
.	
.	
Two workers required	10 points

repair exceeds the cost of making new units in the factory. In such cases, design for throwaway is an economic improvement in maintainability.

4. *Built-in versus external test equipment.* Built-in test features reduce diagnostic time but usually at an added investment.

5. *Person versus machine.* For example, should the operation/maintenance function be highly engineered with special instrumentation and repair facilities, or should it be left to skilled technicians with general-use equipment?

Specific approaches are based on detailed checklists that are used as a guide to good design for maintainability.

Maintainability can also be demonstrated by test. The demonstration consists of measuring the time needed to locate and repair malfunctions or to perform selected maintenance tasks.

Ekings[12] presents an overview of the technical and managerial aspects of a combined reliability and maintainability program.

[12] J. Douglas Ekings, "Commercial and Military Applications of Reliability and Maintainability Engineering," *Transactions of Seminar on Quality Motivation,* ASQC North Jersey Section and Newark College of Engineering, April 14, 1971.

7-14 SAFETY IN NEW-PRODUCT DESIGN

Safety has always been considered of paramount importance during all phases of the product life cycle—starting with the design phase. Recently, a collection of social forces has resulted in a dramatic increase in emphasis on product safety. The background for this new emphasis is discussed in Section 21-6.

The evolution of modern reliability, maintainability, and safety techniques has followed an identical pattern. In the past, these parameters were recognized as important but were treated in an empirical, qualitative way. As with reliability and maintainability techniques, the modern techniques for product safety attempt to treat safety in a more formal, quantitative way. With the increased complexity of many products, the techniques emphasize the effects of interactions of components on overall product performance.

The terms "hazard" and "risk" are used extensively in the literature. A *hazard* is an attribute of a product that is capable of a harmful result. *Risk* is the probability of injury occurring due to a hazard when the product is being operated by the user.

The general approach to safety analysis is as follows:

1. *Review available historical data on safety of similar and predecessor products.* These data obviously should include complaints, claims, and lawsuits. In addition, data are available from regulators, independent laboratories, and still other sources.
2. *Study the ways in which the product has actually been used and misused.* This study is especially important for products which are used by a wide spectrum of the population, e.g., consumer products or those military products which are used directly by the foot soldier. Such a wide spectrum of humanity inevitably misuses products or finds uses for which the products were never designed.

   Products for children (or to which children have access) are a special case because of the inexperience of youngsters and because "logic" becomes academic when injured children are displayed before a jury. A child's building block has a very high reliability. Yet the child may fall and injure himself on a corner of the block; he may throw the block and injure another child. Manufacturers may turn to the use of plastic foam for making the blocks, but now new questions arise: Could a child bite off a piece and choke on it? Would the material be toxic? Obviously, a child is misusing a block when he bites off a piece. Yet the standards on electric lamp cord have been revised to minimize the danger to a child who may bite through the insulation.
3. *Assess the risk that damage will actually occur.* This likelihood is the resultant of several probabilities:
   a. That the product will fail in a way which creates a hazard (this probability may be available through failure-rate analysis).
   b. That the existence of the hazard will result in damage.

    c. That despite no failures in the product, it will be misused so as to result in damage.
4. *Quantify the exposure (time, cycles, etc.) of the product and the users to hazardous conditions.*
5. *Determine the severity of the effect of hazards on product or user.*

    While safety analyses are of long standing, the empirical, qualitative approaches of the past are giving way to more formalized, quantitative studies, as discussed below.

7-15 SAFETY TECHNIQUES DURING DESIGN

During the design phase, both qualitative and quantitative techniques can be helpful. These include fault tree analysis, fail-safe concepts, in-house and field testing, data analysis, designation of safety-oriented characteristics and components, and publication of product ratings.

    Recht[13] describes some specific techniques by application to a hot water heater. Figure 7-6 is a diagram of the product and its principal components. The Gas Supply Subsystem is blocked out for more detailed analysis.

[13] J. L. Recht, "System Safety Analysis: Failure Mode and Effect," *National Safety News*, vol. 93, no. 2, 1965, pp. 24–26.

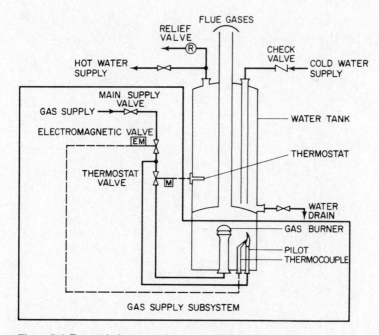

Figure 7-6 Domestic hot water heater—product diagram.

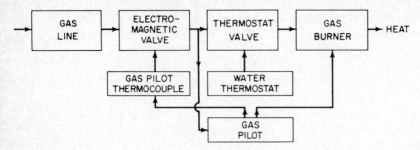

Figure 7-7 Gas supply subsystem—block diagram.

Figure 7-7 is a block diagram showing the sequence and interaction of the gas supply subsystem components. Sometimes called a *functional flow diagram*, it is an essential step in all engineering analyses for whatever subsequent purpose.

Figure 7-8 illustrates a hazard analysis. The possible modes of failure and their probable effect from a safety viewpoint are enumerated. The relative seriousness of the hazard is indicated in the last column of the figure:

Figure 7-8 Gas supply subsystem—hazard analysis.

Item	Function	Hazard involved	Hazard effect on system	Hazard class
I Gas supply subsystem				
1.1 Gas line	To supply gas	1. Line leakage	Gas explosion	IV
1.2 Electromagnetic valve (normally closed)	Controls gas supply	1. Internal leakage or failure to close	Gas explosion	IV
		2. Failure to open	System inoperative	II
1.3 Gas pilot thermocouple	Actuates electromagnetic valve	1. Fails to actuate	System inoperative	II
		2. Premature actuation	None	I
1.4 Thermostat valve (normally open)	Controls gas supply	1. External leakage	Gas explosion	IV
		2. Internal leakage or failure to close	System continues to heat up until relief valve opens	III
		3. Failure to open	System inoperative	II
1.5 Water thermostat	Actuates thermostat valve	1. Fails to actuate	System continues to heat up until relief valve opens	III
		2. Premature actuation	None	I
1.6 Gas pilot	Ignites gas	1. Pilot lit	None	I
		2. Pilot extinguished	System inoperative	II
1.7 Gas burner	Heats water	1. Clogged	System inoperative	II
		2. Open	None	I

Class I. *Negligible*. Will not result in personnel injury or product damage.

Class II. *Marginal*. Can be counteracted or controlled without injury to personnel or major product damage.

Class III. *Critical*. Will cause personnel injury or major product damage, or will require immediate corrective action for personnel or product survival.

Class IV. *Catastrophic*. Will cause death, severe injury to personnel, or product loss.

Figure 7-9, a fault tree analysis, groups related failure events by class or relative seriousness. A numerical risk analysis may now be performed for each of the hazard classes, using the following expressions:

$$p = Kft$$

where p = probability of occurrence of an unsafe event

K = severity effect of the occurrence, e.g., class I = 0; class II = 0.1; class III = 0.5; class IV = 1.0

f = frequency of occurrence, i.e., event occurrence rate (probability), failure rate, and/or personnel injuries per time exposure (occurrences per hour)

t = time of operation or exposure, hours

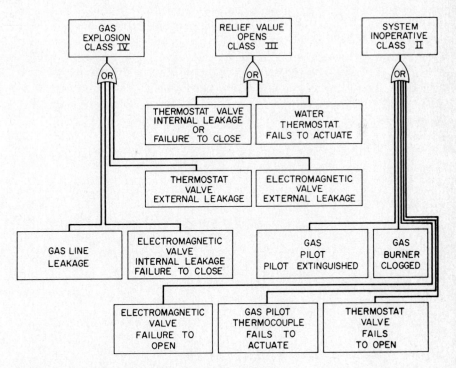

Figure 7-9 Gas supply subsystem—fault tree analysis.

For a gas explosion, $K = 1$. Let us assume that the summation of failure rates, including cycle-time adjustments, for those events that could cause gas explosion (obtained from a reliability analysis) is 0.06×10^{-6}. This is the f term of the equation above. Let us further assume that a 10-year warranty period is the design requirement. During this period the exposure time, t, is 87,000 h. Therefore,

$$p = (1)\, \frac{0.06}{1,000,000}\, (87,000) = 0.005$$

Since S, the safety of the system, is merely $1 - p$, it follows that

$$S = 1 - 0.005 = 0.995$$

In a similar manner, the probability of less serious events may be derived and an overall safety index calculated.

Based on field experience with specific products, detailed checklists are often developed to provide the designer with information on potential hazards, the injuries that can result, and design actions that can be taken to minimize the risk.[14]

7-16 THE HUMAN FACTOR

As the human being using a product has a direct effect on reliability, maintainability, and safety, the human element has received much analysis. This subject, called *human factors engineering* or *ergonomics,* is the study of the interaction between the human being and the product. The scope of activity ranges from the broad (e.g., analyzing what tasks are best performed by the human being versus the machine) to the narrow (e.g., determining how to prevent the installation of a plug-in device upside down). The methodology that has been developed follows the familiar pattern of specifying, predicting, and analyzing.

Drevenka[15] presents an example of ergonomical requirements for a household sewing machine. The requirements, in part, are:

2.1 Ergonomical requirements

The structural parts, or their effects qualified as dangerous during operation, are, according to this standard, the following: external execution, needle handwheel and flywheel, machine lamp and lighting, electric motor and other installations, drive belt, frame or portable case, noise and vibration.

Machine lamp and lighting

The lighting intensity, as measured at any point of the sewing process, i.e., at a distance of 20 mm in front of the needle and within a semicircle of 180 degrees, must be 500 lux minimum.

---

[14] See *Quality Control Handbook,* 3rd ed., pp. 8-53 to 8-56.
[15] R. Drevenka, "Ergonomics, Quality and Standard," *Quality* (European Organization for Quality Control), vol. 21, no. 5, 1977, p. 8.

Noise and vibration

The noise level emitted by the sewing machine, as measured in the octave bands corresponding to the specification, must not exceed the decibel (dB) values of hearing-damage audiogram N70.

The vibration of the head of the sewing machine must not exceed the values specified in clause 3.165.

A variety of methods have been developed for quantitatively predicting human performance. These methods develop predictive indices either by using data banks on human performance or by simulating behavior processes with a computer. Meister[16] reviews eight of the methods.

The following general approach to analyzing the human element during design is summarized from Swain:[17]

1. Prepare a time-based flowchart showing the allocations of system functions between the human being and the machine for the complete cycle from factory to end use.
2. List the likely *operational* uses and use conditions for the system.
3. List the likely *training* uses and conditions for the system.
4. Estimate the personnel factors (skills, experience, training, and motivation).
5. Prepare a time-based detailed analysis of tasks based on the flowchart of step 1.
6. Analyze the behavior process for potential sources of human error.
7. Identify specific error-likely situations and estimate error rates.
8. Estimate the likelihood that errors will be undetected or uncorrected.
9. Estimate the consequences of undetected errors.
10. Recommend changes to the system.

Another approach to evaluation is based on simulated or actual hardware operated by typical users. Cornog and Ruder[18] describe the field evaluation of keyboards for three letter-sorting machines. No significant difference was found in the error rate, but the operators overwhelmingly favored a particular machine.

7-17 COST AND PRODUCT PERFORMANCE

Designing for reliability, maintainability, safety, and other parameters must be done with a simultaneous objective of minimizing cost. Formal techniques to

[16] David Meister, "A Critical Review of Human Performance Reliability Predictive Methods," *IEEE Transactions on Reliability*, vol. R-22, no. 3, August 1973, pp. 116–123.

[17] Alan D. Swain, "The Human Element in System Development," *Proceedings, Annual Reliability and Maintainability Symposium*, January 1970, pp. 20–28.

[18] Douglas Y. Cornog and Arthur H. Ruder, "A Postal Service Field Evaluation of Letter Sorting Machine Keyboards," *Proceedings, Annual Reliability and Maintainability Symposium*, January 1977, pp. 43–48.

Table 7-11 Cost-effectiveness comparison of alternative designs

	Design			
	1	2	3	4
Mean time between failures (MTBF)	100	200	500	500
Mean downtime (MDT)	18	18	15	6
Availability	0.847	0.917	0.971	0.988
Life-cycle cost ($)	51,000	49,000	50,000	52,000
Number of effective hours	8470	9170	9710	9880
Cost/effective hour ($)	6.02	5.34	5.15	5.26

$$\text{Availability} = \frac{\text{MTBF}}{\text{MTBF} + \text{MDT}}$$

Number of effective hours = 10,000 h of life × availability

achieve an optimum balance between performance and cost include both quantitative and qualitative approaches.

The quantitative approach makes use of a ratio relating performance and cost. Such a ratio tells "what we get for each dollar we spend." The ratio is particularly useful in comparing alternative design approaches for accomplishing a desired function.

A cost-effectiveness comparison of four alternative designs is shown in Table 7-11. Note that design 3 is the optimum design even though design 4 has higher availability.

Several approaches have been developed to achieve a balance between performance and cost. Value engineering is a technique for evaluating the *design* of a product to assure that the *essential functions* are provided at *minimum overall cost* to the manufacturer or user. A complementary technique is the "design to cost" approach. This starts with a definition of (1) a cost target for the product, and (2) the function desired. Alternative design concepts are then developed and evaluated.

PROBLEMS

7-1 In Section 5-6 we defined the concept of self-control. For a design department with which you are familiar, state whether the engineers "know what they are supposed to do, know how they are actually doing, and have the means to regulate."

7-2 Make a failure mode/failure effect analysis for one of the following products: (1) a product acceptable to the instructor; (2) a flashlight; (3) a toaster; (4) a vacuum cleaner.

7-3 Make a fault tree analysis for one of the products mentioned in Problem 7-2.

7-4 Visit a local plant and determine whether any formal or informal numerical reliability and maintainability goals are issued to the design function for their guidance in designing new products.

7-5 Obtain a schematic diagram on a product for which you can also obtain a list of the components that fail most frequently. Show the diagram to a group of engineering students most closely associated with the product (e.g., a mechanical product would be shown to mechanical engineering students). Have the students *independently* write their opinion of the most likely components to fail by ranking the top three.

   (*a*) Summarize the results and comment on the agreement among the students.

   (*b*) Comment on the student opinions versus actual product history.

7-6 A reliability prediction can be made by the designer of a product or by an engineer in a staff reliability department which might be a part of the design function. One advantage of the designer making the prediction is that his or her knowledge of the design will likely make possible a faster and more thorough job.

   (*a*) What is one other advantage in having the designer make the prediction?

   (*b*) Are there any disadvantages to having the designer make the prediction?

7-7 Prepare a formal presentation to gain adoption of one of the following: (1) quantification of reliability goals, apportionment, and prediction; (2) formal design reviews; (3) failure mode/failure effect analysis; (4) critical components program. You will make the presentation to one or more people who will be invited into the classroom by the instructor. These people may be from industry or may be other students or faculty. (The instructor will announce time and other limitations on your presentation.)

7-8 Outline a reliability test for one of the following products: (1) a product acceptable to the instructor; (2) a household clothes dryer; (3) a motor for a windshield wiper; (4) an electric food mixer; (5) an automobile spark plug. The testing must cover performance, environmental, and time aspects.

7-9 Speak with some practicing design engineers and learn the extent of feedback of field information to them on their own design work.

7-10 You are the design engineering manager for a refrigerator. Most of your day is spent on administrative work. You do not have the time to get into details on new or modified designs. However, you must approve (by sign-off) all new designs or changes. In reality, your sign-off consists of a brief review of the design, but you rely basically on the competence of your individual designers. You do not want to institute a formal reliability program for designers or set up a reliability group at this time. What action could you take to give yourself some assurance that a design presented to you has been adequately examined by the designer with respect to reliability? It is not possible to increase the testing, and any action you take must involve a minimum of additional costs.

7-11 You work for a public utility and your department employs outside contractors who design and build various equipment and building installations. You have just finished a value engineering seminar at a university and you wonder if your utility should consider establishing such a function to evaluate contractor designs. Someone in your management group has heard that value engineering can reduce costs but "by lowering the performance or reliability of a design." Comment.

7-12 The chapter discusses a number of concepts (e.g., reliability prediction, design review, etc.). Select several concepts and outline a potential application of the concept to an actual problem on a specific product. The outline should state: (1) the name of the concept, (2) a brief statement of the problem, (3) application of the concept to the problem, (4) potential advantages, (5) obstacles to the actual implementation, and (6) an approach to use to overcome each obstacle. The outline for each concept should be about one page.

SUPPLEMENTARY READING

Quality Control Handbook, 3rd ed., McGraw-Hill Book Company, New York, 1974, sec. 8, provides further details on many of the subjects discussed in this chapter. For application to various industries, see secs. 29, 32, 33, 34, 36A, 37–39, 41–45, and 47. Various aspects of testing are discussed in secs. 32–34, 37, 38, 42, and 43. Safety as applied to specific industries is discussed in secs. 42 and 43.

A complete reference on reliability is Grant Ireson, *Reliability Handbook*, McGraw-Hill Book Company, New York, 1966. A reference providing many details for the high-technology industries is B. W. Marguglio, *Quality Systems in the Nuclear Industry*, American Society for Testing and Materials, Philadelphia, 1977. A reference on maintainability and associated topics is Benjamin S. Blanchard, *Logistics Engineering and Management*, Prentice-Hall, Inc., Englewood Cliffs, N.J., 1974. Value engineering is discussed by Arthur E. Mudge, *Value Engineering—A Systematic Approach*, McGraw-Hill Book Company, New York, 1971.

History is instructive on the development of new products. For some fascinating reading on the airplane, see Marvin W. McFarland, *The Papers of Wilbur and Orville Wright, Vols. 1 and 2*, McGraw-Hill Book Company, New York, 1952.

EXAMPLES OF EXAMINATION QUESTIONS USED IN FORMER ASQC RELIABILITY ENGINEER CERTIFICATION EXAMINATIONS AS PUBLISHED IN *QUALITY PROGRESS* MAGAZINE

1 From the definition of reliability, it follows that in any reliability program there must be: (*a*) a quantification of reliability in terms of probability; (*b*) a clear statement defining successful performance; (*c*) a definition of the environment in which the equipment must operate; (*d*) a statement of the required operating times between failures; (*e*) all of the above.

2 When reliability people say they are breaking the monopoly of the designer, they mean: (*a*) they are relieving the designer of responsibility for the design; (*b*) they intend to review the design in conjunction with other experts; (*c*) they insist on having final approval of the design; (*d*) they intend to put the reliability engineer one level higher than the design engineer in the organization.

3 It is Reliability's job to see that all the tasks outlined in the reliability program are: (*a*) carried out by reliability engineers; (*b*) carried out by the department having the primary responsibility; (*c*) defined, making sure that quality control does its job; (*d*) done, including those jobs that the primary responsible departments are incapable of doing.

4 The process of dividing up or budgeting the final reliability goal among the subsystems is known as: (*a*) reliability estimation; (*b*) reliability prediction; (*c*) reliability apportionment; (*d*) all of the above.

5 Reliability prediction is: (*a*) a one-shot estimation process; (*b*) a continuous process starting with paper predictions; (*c*) a process to be viewed as an end in itself in fulfillment of a contract; (*d*) none of the above.

6 Reliability prediction and measurement is primarily useful in: (*a*) evaluating feasibility; (*b*) establishing reliability goals; (*c*) evaluating overall reliability; (*d*) defining problem areas; (*e*) all of the above.

7 Preventive maintenance is defined as: (*a*) actions performed as a result of failure; (*b*) repair of an item to a specified condition; (*c*) actions performed on a scheduled or routine basis to retain an item in a specified condition; (*d*) maintenance performed for detection and prevention of incipient failure.

8 Reliability testing of parts is performed to yield which of the following types of information? (*a*) application suitability; (*b*) environmental capability; (*c*) measurement of life characteristics; (*d*) all of the above.

9 Human factors inputs: (*a*) should be incorporated during the detailed design phase; (*b*) are not necessary until the hardware has been field-tested; (*c*) are most costly to incorporate during the detailed design phase; (*d*) will cause schedule slippage whenever they are incorporated.

EIGHT

DESIGNING FOR QUALITY — STATISTICAL AIDS

8-1 FAILURE PATTERNS FOR COMPLEX PRODUCTS

Methodology for quantifying reliability was first developed for complex products. Suppose that a piece of equipment is placed on test, is run until it fails, and the failure time is recorded. The equipment is repaired, again placed on test, and the time of the next failure recorded. The procedure is repeated to accumulate the data shown in Table 8-1. The *failure rate* is calculated, for equal time intervals, as the number of failures per unit time. When the failure rate is plotted against time, the result (Figure 8-1) often follows a familiar pattern of failure known as the *bathtub curve*. Three periods are apparent. These periods differ in the frequency of failure and in the failure causation pattern:

1. *The infant-mortality period.* This is characterized by high failure rates which show up early in use (see the lower half of Figure 8-1). Commonly, these failures are the result of blunders in design or manufacture, misuse, or misapplication. Usually, once corrected, these failures do not occur again, e.g., an oil hole that is not drilled. Sometimes it is possible to "debug" the product by a simulated use test or by overstressing (in electronics this is known as burn-in). The weak units still fail, but the failure takes place in the test rig rather than in service.
2. *The constant-failure-rate period.* Here the failures result from the limitations inherent in the design, changes in the environment, and accidents

Table 8-1 Failure history for a unit of electronic ground support equipment

Time of failure, infant-mortality period		Time of failure, constant-failure-rate period		Time of failure, wear-out period	
1.0	7.2	28.1	60.2	100.8	125.8
1.2	7.9	28.2	63.7	102.6	126.6
1.3	8.3	29.0	64.6	103.2	127.7
2.0	8.7	29.9	65.3	104.0	128.4
2.4	9.2	30.6	66.2	104.3	129.2
2.9	9.8	32.4	70.1	105.0	129.5
3.0	10.2	33.0	71.0	105.8	129.9
3.1	10.4	35.3	75.1	106.5	
3.3	11.9	36.1	75.6	110.7	
3.5	13.8	40.1	78.4	112.6	
3.8	14.4	42.8	79.2	113.5	
4.3	15.6	43.7	84.1	114.8	
4.6	16.2	44.5	86.0	115.1	
4.7	17.0	50.4	87.9	117.4	
4.8	17.5	51.2	88.4	118.3	
5.2	19.2	52.0	89.9	119.7	
5.4		53.3	90.8	120.6	
5.9		54.2	91.1	121.0	
6.4		55.6	91.5	122.9	
6.8		56.4	92.1	123.3	
6.9		58.3	97.9	124.5	

caused by use or maintenance. The accidents can be held down by good control on operating and maintenance procedures. However, a reduction in the failure rate requires a basic redesign.

3. *The wear-out period.* These are failures due to old age; e.g., the metal becomes embrittled or the insulation dries out. A reduction in failure rates requires preventive replacement of these dying components before they result in catastrophic failure.

The top portion of Figure 8-1 shows the corresponding Weibull plot when $\alpha = 2.6$ was applied to the original data (see Section 3-10). The values of the shape parameter, β, were approximately 0.5, 1.0, and 6.0, respectively. A shape parameter of less than 1.0 indicates a decreasing failure rate, a value of 1.0 a constant failure rate, and a value greater than 1.0 an increasing failure rate (see Figure 8-1).

The Distribution of Time between Failures

Together with concern for low failures during the infant-mortality period, users are concerned with the length of time that a product will run without failure. For repairable products, this means that the *time between failures* (TBF) is a

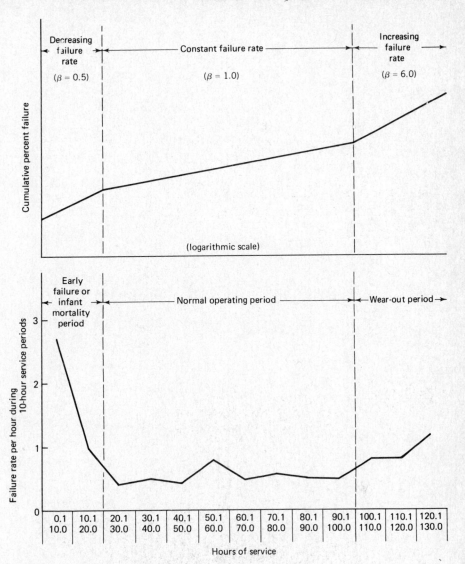

Figure 8-1 Failure rate versus time.

critical characteristic. The variation in time between failures can be studied statistically. The corresponding characteristic for nonrepairable products is usually called the *time to failure*.

When the failure rate is constant, the distribution of time between failures is distributed exponentially. Consider the 42 failure times in the constant-failure-rate portion of Table 8-1. The time between failures for successive failures can be tallied, and the 41 resulting TBFs can then be formed into the frequency distribution shown in Figure 8-2a. The distribution is roughly ex-

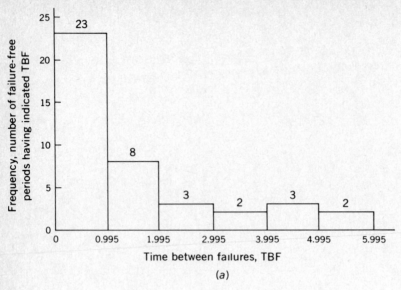

(a)

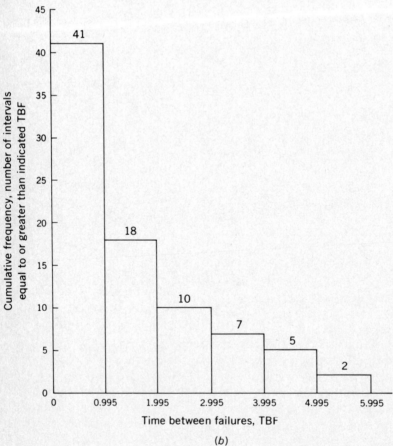

(b)

Figure 8-2 (a) Histogram of time between failures. (b) Cumulative histogram of time between failures.

ponential in shape, indicating that when the failure rate is constant, the distribution of time between failures (not *mean* time between failures) is exponential. This is the basis of the *exponential formula for reliability*.

8-2 THE EXPONENTIAL FORMULA FOR RELIABILITY

The distribution of time between failures indicates the chance of failure-free operation for the specified time period. The chance of obtaining failure-free operation for a specified time period *or longer* can be shown by changing the TBF distribution to a distribution showing the number of intervals equal to or greater than a specified time length (Figure 8-2b). If the frequencies are expressed as relative frequencies, they become estimates of the probability of survival. When the failure rate is constant, the probability of survival (or reliability) is

$$P_s = R = e^{-t/\mu} = e^{-t\lambda}$$

where $P_s = R$ = probability of failure-free operation for a time period equal to
        or greater than t
    $e = 2.718$
    t = specified period of failure-free operation
    μ = mean time between failures, or MTBF (the mean of TBF distribution)
    λ = failure rate (the reciprocal of μ)

Note that this formula is simply the exponential probability distribution rewritten in terms of reliability.

> **Example** A washing machine requires 30 min to clean a load of clothes. The mean time between failures of the machine is 100 h. Assuming a constant failure rate, what is the chance of the machine completing a cycle without failure?
>
> $$R = e^{-t/\mu} = e^{-0.5/100} = 0.995$$
>
> There is a 99.5 percent chance of completing a washing cycle.

How about the assumption of a constant failure rate? In practice, sufficient data are usually not available to evaluate the assumption. However, experience suggests that the assumption is often a fair one to make. This is particularly true when (1) infant-mortality types of failures have been eliminated before delivery of the product to the user, and (2) the user replaces the product or specific components before the wear-out phase begins.

The Meaning of "Mean Time between Failures"

Confusion surrounds the meaning of "mean time between failures" (MTBF). Further explanation is warranted:

1. The MTBF is the mean (or average) time between successive failures on a product. This definition assumes that the product in question can be repaired and placed back in operation after each failure.
2. If the failure rate is constant, the probability that a product will operate without failure for a time equal to or greater than its MTBF is only 37 percent. This is based on the exponential distribution. (R is equal to 0.37 when t is equal to the MTBF.) This is contrary to the intuitive feeling that there is a 50–50 chance of exceeding an MTBF.
3. MTBF is not the same as "operating life," "service life," or other indices which generally connote overhaul or replacement time.
4. An increase in an MTBF does not result in a proportional increase in reliability (the probability of survival). If $t = 1$ h, the following table shows the mean time between failures required in order to obtain various reliabilities:

MTBF	R
5	0.82
10	0.90
20	0.95
100	0.99

A fivefold increase in MTBF from 20 to 100 h is necessary to increase the reliability by 4 percentage points as compared with a doubling of the MTBF from 5 to 10 h to get 8 percentage points' increase in reliability.

MTBF is a useful measure of reliability, but it is *not* correct for all applications. Section 7-3 includes a list of other reliability indices.

8-3 THE RELATIONSHIP BETWEEN PART AND SYSTEM RELIABILITY

It is often assumed that system reliability (i.e., the probability of survival P_s) is the product of the individual reliabilities of the n parts within the system:

$$P_s = P_1 P_2 \cdots P_n$$

For example, if a communications system has four subsystems with reliabilities of 0.970, 0.989, 0.995, and 0.996, the system reliability is 0.951. The formula assumes (1) that the failure of any part causes failure of the system, and (2) that the reliabilities of the parts are independent of each other; i.e., the reliability of one part does not depend on the functioning of another part.

These assumptions are *not* always true but, in practice, the formula serves two purposes. First, it shows the effect of increased complexity of equipment on overall reliability. As the number of parts in a system increases, the system reliability decreases drastically (see Figure 8-3). Second, the formula is often a

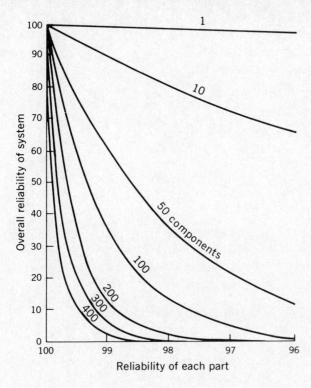

Figure 8-3 Relation of part and system reliability.

convenient approximation that can be refined as information becomes available on the interrelationships of the parts.

Sometimes, designs are planned so that the failure of one part will not cause system failure, e.g., the use of redundancy.

Redundancy is an old design technique invented long before the advent of reliability prediction techniques. However, the designer can now predict in *quantitative* terms the effect of redundancy on system reliability.

Redundancy is the existence of more than one element for accomplishing a given task, where all elements must fail before there is an overall failure to the system. In *parallel redundancy* (one of several types of redundancy), two or more elements operate at the same time to accomplish the task, and any single element is capable of handling the job itself in case of failure of the other elements. When parallel redundancy is used, the overall reliability is calculated as follows:

$$P_s = 1 - (1 - P_1)^n$$

where P_s = reliability of the system

P_1 = reliability of the individual elements in the redundancy

n = number of identical redundant elements

Example Suppose that a unit has a reliability of 99.0 percent for a specified mission time. If two identical units are used in parallel redundancy, what overall reliability will be obtained?

$$R = 1 - (1 - 0.99)(1 - 0.99) = 0.9999, \text{ or } 99.99 \text{ percent}$$

When it can be assumed that (1) the failure of any part causes system failure, (2) the parts are independent, and (3) each part follows an exponential distribution, then

$$P_s = e^{-t_1 \lambda_1} e^{\lambda 1} e^{-t_2 \lambda_2} \cdots e^{-t_n \lambda_n}$$

Further, if t is the same for each part,

$$P_s = e^{-t \Sigma \lambda}$$

Thus, when the failure rate is constant (and therefore the exponential distribution applied), a *reliability prediction* of a system can be made based on the addition of the part failure rates. This is illustrated in Section 8-5.

8-4 PREDICTING RELIABILITY DURING DESIGN

In Section 7-4 we introduced the reliability prediction method. Reliability prediction is still in the early stages of development. Several methods will be discussed in this chapter. Kapur and Lamberson[1] provide an extensive discussion of reliability prediction.

While the visible result of the prediction procedures is to quantify the reliability numbers, the process of prediction is usually as important as the resulting numbers. This is so because the prediction cannot be made without obtaining rather detailed information on product missions, environments, critical component histories, etc. Acquiring this information often gives the designer knowledge previously not available. Even if the designer is unable to secure the needed information, this inability nevertheless identifies the areas of ignorance in the design.

The following steps make up a reliability prediction method:

1. *Define the product and its functional operation.* The system, subsystems, and units must be precisely defined in terms of their functional configurations and boundaries. This precise definition is aided by preparation of a functional block diagram (see Figure 8-4) which shows the subsystems and lower-level products, their interrelation, and the interfaces with other systems.

Given a functional block diagram and a well-defined statement of the functional requirements of the product, the conditions that constitute failure or unsatisfactory performance can be defined.

2. *Prepare a reliability block diagram.* For systems in which there are

[1] K. C. Kapur and L. R. Lamberson, *Reliability in Engineering Design,* John Wiley & Sons, Inc., New York, 1977.

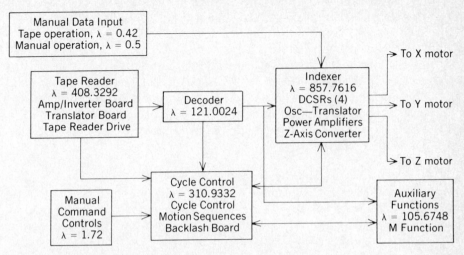

Figure 8-4 Functional block diagram (system failure rates/10^6).

redundancies or other special interrelationships among parts, a reliability block diagram is useful. This diagram is similar to a functional block diagram, but the reliability block diagram shows exactly what must function for successful operation of the system. The diagram shows redundancies and alternative modes of operation. The reliability block diagram is the foundation for developing the probability model for reliability. The book *Reliability Engineering* (see Supplementary Reading) provides further discussion.

3. *Develop the probability model for predicting reliability.* This may simply be the addition of failure rates or a complex model to care for redundancies and other conditions.

4. *Collect information relevant to part reliability.* This includes information such as part function, part ratings, stresses, internal and external environments, and operating time. Many sources of failure-rate information state failure rates as a function of operating parameters. For example, MIL-HDBK-217B[2] provides failure rates for fixed ceramic capacitors as a function of (1) expected operating temperature, and (2) the ratio of the operating voltage to the rated voltage. Such data show the effect of derating (see Section 7-8) on reducing the failure rate.

5. *Select part reliability data.* The required part data consist of information on catastrophic failures and on tolerance variations with respect to time under known operating and environmental conditions. Acquiring these data is a major problem for the designer, since there is no single reliability data bank comparable to handbooks such as those that are available for physical properties of materials. Instead, the designer must build up a data bank by securing reliability data from a variety of sources:

[2] MIL-HDBK-217B, *Reliability Prediction of Electronic Equipment*, 1974, U.S. Government Printing Office, Washington, D.C.

Field performance studies conducted under controlled conditions.

Specified life tests.

Data from parts manufacturers or industry associations.

Customers' part-qualification and inspection tests.

Government publications such as MIL-HDBK-217B (mentioned above), which contains a large amount of failure-rate data together with stress-analysis procedures essential to its use.

Government agency data banks such as the Government Industry Data Exchange Program (GIDEP).[3]

6. *Combine all of the above to obtain the numerical reliability prediction.* An example[4] of a relatively simple reliability prediction method is shown in Table 8-2. An electromechanical subsystem that is currently being used in the field is to be redesigned. A prediction of the reliability of the new design is desired. Reliability is measured in terms of repairs per 100 ($R/100$) at 12 months or 12,000 mi (12/12) and at 50,000 mi. Three steps are involved:

a. Using field data on the current design, establish the $R/100$ value for the current design.

b. Show the breakdown of the $R/100$ value into the various failure modes.

c. Decide which of the failure modes will be eliminated by the new design. Estimate the reduction in repairs ($\Delta R/100$) and calculate the predicted $R/100$ of the new design.

Table 8-2 indicates an improvement in reliability from 1.7 repairs/100 to 1.1 repairs/100 for the 12/12 warranty period.

Other prediction methods are based on various statistical distributions, as explained in the following sections.

8-5 PREDICTING RELIABILITY BASED ON THE EXPONENTIAL DISTRIBUTION

This method will be illustrated for a unit of numerical control equipment. The specific unit is a controller—from the tape reader to the output pulses that drive some servomotors. The controller can be operated either automatically or manually. A reliability prediction for each mode of operation is desired.

The functional block diagram is shown in Figure 8-4. A study of the schematic diagrams of the various subsystems reveals that all parts must function

[3] For a series of four papers describing GIDEP, see the *Proceedings of the 1976 Annual Reliability and Maintainability Symposium,* pp. 42–62. Complete information can be obtained from the GIDEP Operations Center, Naval Fleet Missile Systems Analysis and Evaluation Group, Corona, Calif. 91720

[4] *Reliability Methods—Reliability Predictions, Module XIII,* Ford Motor Company, 1972, p. 6.

Table 8-2 Electromechanical subsystem reliability prediction

Failure mode	Customer complaint	Causal factor	Current R/100		ΔR/100 (−)/+		Predicted R/100		Change and variance description
			12/12	50,000	12/12	50,000	12/12	50,000	
Design									
Shorted stator	Inoperative	Insulation breakdown due to heat cycling	0.0	2.5	—	(1.5)	0.0	1.0	Improved insulation—lab tests show 60% reduction in failure rate
Loose bearing	Noisy	Bearing wear	0.2	1.0	(0.1)	(0.5)	0.1	0.5	Bearing change—vendor data shows B_{10} life of new bearing double present
Manufacturing									
Shorted stator	Inoperative	Insulation scratched in assembly	0.4	0.5			0.4	0.5	
Open solder joint	Inoperative	Contamination & improper processing	0.2	0.3			0.2	0.3	
Assembly									
Loose drive belt	Erratic operation	Insufficient tension in assembly	0.5	0.6	(0.4)	(0.5)	0.1	0.1	Provide tensioning fixtures—audit shows 80% improvement
Service									
Misdiagnosis	Various	Service procedure not clear	0.4	0.8	(0.1)	(0.2)	0.3	0.6	New service procedure—20% improvement on judgment basis
			1.7	5.7	(0.6)	(2.7)	1.1	3.0	

Step 1   Step 2   Step 3

Table 8-3 Reliability prediction of decoder board

Parts	Number of parts	Failure rate per 10^6 h	Total failure rate
Composition resistors, fixed	108	0.0048	0.5184
Transistors	23	3.00	69.00
Diodes	50	1.00	50.00
Capacitors—paper	13	0.11	1.43
Button mica capacitor	1	0.054	0.054
			121.0024

for overall system success. Thus, in this case, it is not necessary to prepare a reliability block diagram. The probability model is the simple addition of failure rates.

As an example of a subsystem prediction, the prediction for the decoder board is shown in Table 8-3. Similar predictions are made for 17 subsystems. The resulting failure rates for subsystems are shown in Figure 8-4.

The overall predictions are made by adding appropriate failure rates as shown in Table 8-4. The mean time between failures (MTBF) is calculated as the reciprocal of the total failure rate.

8-6 PREDICTING RELIABILITY DURING DESIGN BASED ON THE WEIBULL DISTRIBUTION

Prediction of overall reliability based on the simple addition of component failure rates is valid only if the failure rate is constant. When this assumption can-

Table 8-4 Overall reliability predictions

Subsystem	Mode of operation	
	Manual	Automatic
Manual data input	0.5	0.42
Tape reader	—	408.3292
Decoder	—	121.0024
Indexer	857.7616	857.7616
Manual command controls	1.72	1.72
Cycle control	310.9332	310.9332
Auxiliary functions	—	105.6748
Total failure rate (failures/10^6 h)	1170.9148	1805.8412
MTBF (h)	854	554

Table 8-5 Reliability prediction for a variable displacement pump

	First analysis			Analysis after changes		
	Percent failure at		$/tractor at	Percent failure at		$/tractor at
Part name*	500 h	1500 h	500 h	500 h	1500 h	500 h
Pump drive coupling						
special screws	0.6	3.0	0.21	0.2	1.0	0.07
Pump drive coupling	0.07	0.8	0.01	0.07	0.8	0.01
Hydraulic pump shaft	0.02	0.06	0.01	0.02	0.06	0.01
Pump shaft oil seal	3.7	20.0	0.41	1.0	5.0	0.10
Pump shaft bushing	0.75	2.25	0.30	0.25	0.75	0.10
O-ring packings (11)						
(evaluated separately)	0.63	2.10	0.08	0.63	2.10	0.08
Stroke control valve	13.0	38.0	0.77	0.05	0.15	0.02
Assembly reliability (68 parts)						
At 500 h (%)		80			97.3	
At 1500 h (%)		49			92.0	
Cost at 500 h ($)		$2.18			$0.77	

*Only parts with significant percent failure are listed.

not be made, an alternative approach, based on the Weibull distribution, can be used.

1. Graphically, use the Weibull distribution to predict the reliability R for the time period specified. $R = 100 - \%$ failure. Do this for each component.
2. Combine the component reliabilities using the product rule and/or redundancy formulas to obtain the prediction of system reliability.

Table 8-5 shows an example[5] of predicting the reliability of a tractor pump for a 500-h period and a 1500-h period. The first analysis is on a proposed design. Note how the prediction highlights the "vital few" parts such as the oil seal and control valve. The analysis after some design changes on these parts shows a significant increase in reliability and decrease in failure cost per tractor. (Table 8-5 lists data for important items only and then summarizes reliability and cost for the complete assembly of 68 parts.)

8-7 RELIABILITY AS A FUNCTION OF APPLIED STRESS AND STRENGTH

Failures are not always a function of time. In some cases, a part will function indefinitely if the strength is greater than the stress applied to it. The terms

[5] Barrett G. Rich, O. A. Smith, and Lee Korte, "Experience with a Formal Reliability Program," SAE Paper 670731, Farm, Construction and Industrial Machinery Meeting, 1967.

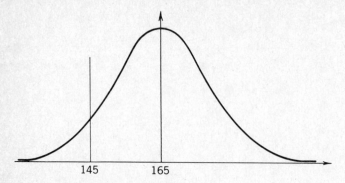

Figure 8-5 Distribution of strength.

strength and *stress* here are used in the broad sense of inherent capability and operating conditions applied to a part, respectively.

For example,[6] operating temperature is a critical parameter and the maximum expected temperature is 145°F (63°C). Further, the capability is indicated by a strength distribution having a mean of 165°F and a standard deviation of 13°F (7°C) (see Figure 8-5). With knowledge of only the maximum temperatures, the *safety margin* is

$$\frac{165 - 145}{13} = 1.54$$

The safety margin says that the average strength is 1.54 standard deviations above the maximum expected temperature of 145°F (63°C). Table A in the Appendix can be used to calculate a reliability of 0.938 [the area beyond 145°F (63°C)].

This calculation illustrates the importance of *variation* in addition to the *average* value during design. Designers have always recognized the existence of variation by using a *safety factor* in design. However, safety factor is often defined as the ratio of average strength to the worst stress expected.

Note that in Figure 8-6, all the designs have the same safety factor. Also note that the reliability (probability of a part having a strength greater than the stress) varies considerably. Thus the uncertainty often associated with this definition of safety factor is in part due to its failure to reflect the *variation* in strength and *variation* in stress. Such variation is partially reflected in a safety margin, defined as

$$\frac{\text{average strength} - \text{worst stress}}{\text{standard deviation of strength}}$$

This recognizes the variation in strength but is conservative because it does not recognize a variation in stress.

[6] *Reliability for the Engineer, Book Five: Testing for Reliability*, Martin Marietta Corp., Orlando, Fla., 1966, pp. 29–31.

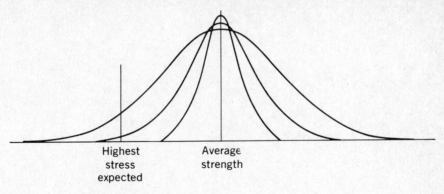

Figure 8-6 Variation and safety factor.

Lusser[7] proposed the use of safety margins in specifications for critical products such as guided missiles (Figure 8-7). He suggested safety margins for strength and stress. Specifically, the *reliability boundary* (maximum stress) is defined as 6 standard deviations (of stress) above the average stress. He also proposed that the average strength should be at least 5 standard deviations (of strength) above the reliability boundary. These multiples of standard deviation were proposed for products requiring extremely high reliability. However, use of a safety margin between the stress and strength distributions is wise for all products.

8-8 AVAILABILITY

Availability has been defined as the probability that a product, when used under given conditions, will perform satisfactorily when called upon. Availability considers the operating time of the product and the time required for repairs. Idle time, during which the product is not needed, is excluded.

Availability is calculated as the ratio of operating time to operating time plus downtime. However, downtime can be viewed in two ways:

1. *Total downtime.* This includes the active repair time (diagnosis and repair), preventive maintenance time, and logistics time (time spent waiting for personnel, spare parts, etc.). When total downtime is used, the resulting ratio is called *operational availability* (A_o).
2. *Active repair time.* The resulting ratio is called *intrinsic availability* (A_i).

Under certain conditions, the availability can be calculated as

$$A_o = \frac{\text{MTBF}}{\text{MTBF} + \text{MDT}} \quad \text{and} \quad A_i = \frac{\text{MTBF}}{\text{MTBF} + \text{MTTR}}$$

[7] R. Lusser, "Reliability through Safety Margins," United States Army Ordnance Missile Command, Redstone Arsenal, Alabama, October 1958.

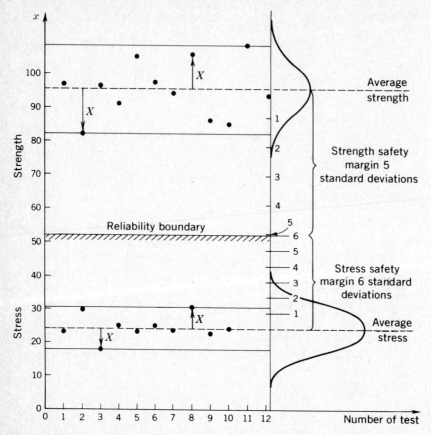

Figure 8-7 Illustrating how scatterbands of stresses and strengths should be separated by a reliability boundary.

where MTBF = mean time between failures
MDT = mean downtime
MTTR = mean time to repair

This is known as the *steady-state* formula for availability.

Garrick and Mulvihill[8] present data on certain subsystems of a mechanized bulk mail system (see Table 8-6). If estimates of reliability and maintainability can be made during the design process, availability can be evaluated before the design is released for production.

The steady-state formula for availability has the virtue of simplicity. However, the formula has several assumptions that are not always met in the real

[8] B. John Garrick and Robert J. Mulvihill, "Reliability and Maintainability of Mechanized Bulk Mail Systems," *Proceedings, 1974 Annual Reliability and Maintainability Symposium*, January 1974, Institute of Electrical and Electronics Engineers.

Table 8-6   Availability data for mail system equipment

Equipment	MTBF, h	MTTR, h	Availability (%)
Sack sorter	90	1.620	98.2
Parcel sorter	160	0.8867	99.4
Conveyor, induction	17,900	1.920	100.0
Deflector, traveling	3,516	3.070	99.9

world. The assumptions are:

1. The product is operating in the constant-failure-rate period of the overall life. Thus, the failure time distribution is exponential.
2. The downtime or repair time distribution is exponential.
3. Attempts to locate system failures do not change the overall system failure rate.
4. No reliability growth occurs. (Such growth might be due to design improvements or through debugging of bad parts.)
5. Preventive maintenance is scheduled outside the time frame included in the availability calculation.

More precise formulas for calculating availability depend on operational conditions and statistical assumptions. These formulas are discussed by Locks.[9]

The availability concept is also useful in analyzing the performance of capital equipment, e.g., manufacturing equipment. Often, production schedules are developed using an assumed value of availability of manufacturing equipment. The assumed value is based on past history but with the further assumption that personnel and spare parts are always available when repairs must be made. In practice, it is useful to measure the actual availability. For example, production schedules in a heat-treatment department were developed assuming a 90 percent availability of the furnaces. Great difficulty was experienced in meeting the schedules. After many months of argument about the causes of failing to meet schedules, data were collected and the availability calculated. The intrinsic availability was 95 percent but the operational availability was only 85 percent. This revelation resulted in a decision to (1) increase the preventive maintenance program on equipment, (2) increase the supply of spare parts, and (3) periodically measure availability of other critical equipment and make adjustments to availability standards used in preparing production schedules.

Availability analysis has also been applied to chemical plants. Such analysis applied the steady-state availability formula to processes involving a series of operations.[10]

[9] Mitchell O. Locks, *Reliability, Maintainability and Availability,* Hayden Book Company, Inc., Rochelle Park, N.J., 1973, pp. 172–185.

[10] D. H. Cherry, J. C. Grogan, W. A. Holmes, and F. A. Perris, "Availability Analysis for Chemical Plants," *Chemical Engineering Progress,* January 1978, pp. 172–185.

8-9 SYSTEM EFFECTIVENESS

The concept of cost effectiveness was introduced in Section 7-1. The quantification of cost effectiveness involves the development of mathematical models for both cost and effectiveness.

A useful model for effectiveness defines *system effectiveness* as

$$P_{SE} = P_A \times P_R \times P_C$$

where P_{SE} = probability of overall system effectiveness
P_A = probability that the system will be available for use (i.e., "availability")
P_R = probability that the system will be reliable (i.e., "reliability")
P_C = probability that the system has the design capability to perform the function required

Once such a model is developed, it can be used to (1) evaluate a design against user requirements; (2) compare alternative designs; and (3) evaluate trade-offs among availability, reliability, and capability.

As an example, this model is used to compare a proposed new circuit design with the existing production circuit design. A summary of the information on the two designs is given in Table 8-7. The MTBF and MTTR values are based on predictions and operating data. In this case, both designs have a 100 percent capability of performing the function assuming that the parts operate without failure. Thus the capability is 1.0.

System effectiveness is calculated for a 5000-h mission time as:
Present design:

$$P_{SE} = \left(\frac{29,000}{29,000 + 8} \right) \left(e^{-5000/29,000} \right) \left(1.0 \right) = 0.841$$

New design:

$$P_{SE} = \left(\frac{37,500}{37,500 + 2} \right) \left(e^{-5000/37,500} \right) \left(1.0 \right) = 0.875$$

Table 8-7 Summary of information on two circuit designs

	Present design	New design
MTBF, h	29,000	37,500
MTTR, h	8	2
Capability	1.0	1.0
Costs, $		
Parts	85	60
Assembly	170	60
Overhead	25	12
Profit	56	26
Price, $	336	158

Table 8-8 Value comparison of food-waste disposers

	Company design	Competitor designs B	G
Grinding time	9/1.73 = 5.2	9/0.87 = 10.3	6/2.14 = 2.8
Fineness of grind	4/9.18 = 0.4	4/7.82 = 0.5	4/11.88 = 0.3
Frequency of jamming	9/2.25 = 4.0	9/1.98 = 4.6	9/2.46 = 3.7
Noise	4/0.40 = 10.0	4/0.45 = 8.9	4/0.52 = 7.7
Self-cleaning	4/0.62 = 6.5	2/0.49 = 4.1	4/0.58 = 6.9
Electrical safety	16/0.58 = 27.6	16/0.52 = 30.8	16/0.43 = 37.2
Particle protection	6/0.29 = 20.7	6/0.30 = 20.0	2/0.37 = 5.4
Ease of servicing	6/0.70 = 8.6	4/0.52 = 7.7	6/0.98 = 6.1
Cutter life	9/0.96 = 9.4	9/0.83 = 10.8	9/1.32 = 6.8
Ease of installation	9/0.54 = 16.7	9/0.33 = 27.3	9/0.70 = 11.8
Total	76/17.25 = 4.4	72/14.11 = 5.1	69/21.44 = 3.2

Ordinarily, the cost parameter is defined as life-cycle costs (i.e., the purchase price plus all other costs over the product life). In this case, price is used instead of life-cycle costs and an effectiveness cost index is calculated as effectiveness/$100:

$$\text{Present design:} \quad 0.825/\$3.36 = 0.25$$
$$\text{New design:} \quad 0.875/\$1.58 = 0.55$$

The designer who made this analysis used it to justify the new design to management. In addition, the reliability prediction on the new design pointed out that the potentiometers and the fixed wirewound high-wattage resistors had high failure rates. These high failure rates demanded changes.

Another approach for comparing several different designs over a number of attributes is shown in Table 8-8. A design for a food-waste disposer is compared to the designs of two competitor models for 10 attributes describing fitness for use. For each combination of attribute and design, an effectiveness cost ratio is calculated. For example, for design G and the grinding time characteristic, the ratio is 6/2.14, or 2.8. The value of 6 is the product of a weighting factor of 3 for grinding time and a score of 2 for design G on grinding time. The value of $2.14 is the estimated cost of achieving the grinding time of design G using the design G concept in production. The total of the ratios for each company provides a cost-effectiveness type of index.

Designers have long tried to achieve a balance between effectiveness and cost. This balance may involve increasing cost in one phase to reduce cost and increase effectiveness elsewhere. Self-lubricating bearings, stainless steel, and redundant circuits all involve greater original cost, but can result in lower overall costs and greater effectiveness. This process of balancing costs and effects is known as *trade-off analysis*. The quantification provided by system-effectiveness models can spearhead the trade-off analysis.

PROBLEMS

8-1 A radar set has a mean time between failures of 240 h based on the exponential distribution. Suppose that a certain mission requires failure-free operation of the set for 24 h. What is the chance that the set will complete a mission without failure?

Answer: 0.91.

8-2 A piece of ground support equipment for a missile has a specified mean time between failures of 100 h. What is the reliability for a mission time of 1 h? 10 h? 50 h? 100 h? 200 h? 300 h? Graph these answers by plotting mission time versus reliability. Assume an exponential distribution.

8-3 The average life of subassembly A is 2000 h. Data indicate that this life characteristic is exponentially distributed.

(*a*) What percent of the subassemblies in the population will last at least 200 h?

(*b*) The average life of subassembly B is 1000 h and the life is exponentially distributed. What percent of the subassemblies in the population will last at least 200 hours?

(*c*) These subassemblies are independently manufactured and then connected in series to form the total assembly. What percent of assemblies in the population will last at least 200 hours?

Answer: (*a*) 90.5 percent. (*b*) 81.9 percent. (*c*) 74.1 percent.

8-4 It is expected that the average time to repair a failure on a certain product is 4 h. Assume that repair time is exponentially distributed. What is the chance that the time for a repair will be between 3 and 5 h?

8-5 The following table summarizes basic failure-rate data on components in an electronic subsystem:

Component	Quantity	Failure rate per hour
Silicon transistor	40	74.0×10^{-6}
Film resistor	100	3.0×10^{-6}
Paper capacitor	50	10.0×10^{-6}

Estimate the mean time between failures. (Assume an exponential distribution. All components are critical for subsystem success.)

Answer: 267 h.

8-6 A system consists of subsystems A, B, and C. The system is primarily used on a certain mission that lasts 8 h. The following information has been collected:

Subsystem	Required operating time during mission, h	Type of failure distribution	Reliability information
A	8	Exponential	50% of subsystems will last at least 14 h
B	3	Normal	Average life is 6 h with a standard deviation of 1.5 h
C	4	Weibull with $\beta = 1.0$	Average life is 40 h

Assuming independence of the subsystems, calculate the reliability for a mission.

8-7 A hydraulic subsystem consists of two subsystems in parallel, each having the following components and characteristics:

Components	Failures/10^6 h	Number of components
Pump	23.4	1
Quick disconnect	2.4	3
Check valve	6.1	2
Shutoff valve	7.9	1
Lines and fittings	3.13	7

The components within each subsystem are all necessary for subsystem success. The two parallel subsystems operate simultaneously and either can perform the mission. What is the mission reliability if the mission time is 300 h? (Assume an exponential distribution.)

8-8 The following estimates, based on field experience, are available on three subsystems:

Subsystem	Percent failed at 1000 mi	Weibull beta value
A	0.1	2.0
B	0.2	1.8
C	0.5	1.0

If these estimates are assumed to be applicable for similar subsystems which will be used in a new system, predict the reliability (in terms of percent successful) at the end of 3000 mi, 5000 mi, 8000 mi, and 10,000 mi.

8-9 It is desired that a power plant be in operating condition 95 percent of the time. The average time required for repairing a failure is about 24 h. What must be the mean time between failures in order for the power plant to meet the 95 percent objective?

Answer: 456 h.

8-10 A manufacturing process runs continuously 24 h per day and 7 days a week (except for planned shutdowns). Past data indicate a 50 percent probability that the time between successive failures is 100 h or more. The average repair time for failures is 6 h. Failure times and repair times are both exponentially distributed. Calculate the availability of the process.

8-11 The following table summarizes data on components in a hydraulic system:

Component	Quantity	Failure rate per hour
Relief valve	1	200×10^{-6}
Check valve	1	150×10^{-6}
Filter	1	100×10^{-6}
Cylinder	1	50×10^{-6}

Assume that all components must operate for system success and that the system is used continuously throughout the 8760 h in a year with no shutdowns except for failures. Repair time varies with the type of failure but 50 percent of the repairs require 3 h or more. The following average cost estimates apply:

$$\text{Material cost/failure} = \$100.00$$

$$\text{Repair labor cost/hour} = \$ \quad 5.00$$

Assume that failure time and repair time are exponentially distributed. Calculate the average cost of repairing failures per year.

Answer: $532.

8-12 The following table summarizes data on components in a proposed hydraulic system:

Component	Quantity	Failure rate per hour
Check valve	1	8.1×10^{-6}
Filter	1	7.1×10^{-6}
Relief valve	1	4.2×10^{-6}
Transfer valve	1	22.9×10^{-6}
Cylinder	1	8.7×10^{-6}

The failure of any component results in system failure. Assume a constant failure rate. Management has set a goal that no more than 3 percent of the systems will fail during a warranty period of 1000 h.

(*a*) Can the goal be met?

(*b*) Although the 1000-h warranty period is the contractual requirement, management would like an estimate of the average time to failure that the customer could expect.

8-13 The following data applied to a proposed hydraulic subsystem:

Part	Failure rate per hour
Check valve	70×10^{-6}
Filter	300×10^{-6}
Relief valve	30×10^{-6}
Transfer valve	1480×10^{-6}
Cylinder	40×10^{-6}
Lines and fittings	80×10^{-6}

(*a*) If all parts are in series and critical for subsystem success, what is the probability that the subsystem will run without failure for at least 20 h?

(*b*) Suppose that the predicted probability in (*a*) is considered too low. What would be the overall reliability if parallel redundancy of the entire subsystem is used?

(*c*) Suppose that it is decided to institute a parts-improvement program instead of using redundancy. Do you have any suggestion on the direction of this effort?

Answer: (*a*) 0.96. (*b*) 0.998.

8-14 A system has a required mission time of 10 h. Past data indicate a 90 percent probability that the desired function can be accomplished by the system design when it is manufactured in accordance with specifications. There is a 50 percent probability that the time between successive failures will be 100 h or more. Average repair time for failure is 6 h. Failure and repair times are both exponentially distributed. Calculate the system effectiveness for the required mission time.

8-15 Extensive design analyses and tests have been run to evaluate the design of a clothes dryer. One series of tests was run to evaluate the basic capability to get the clothes clean without damaging them or leaving too much lint on the clothes. Of 50 loads put in the dryer, 48 were judged by a consumer panel as acceptable on the capability test. The remaining two loads were judged unacceptable. Paper analyses made of the reliability indicate a mean time between failures of about 500 h. A typical load cycle takes about 1 h.

A quality objective of 95 percent has been set. This must reflect the likelihood that the machine will be ready for use at any random time, the capability of the machine to get clothes clean without damage or lint, and the ability of the dryer to run through a cycle without failure of the dryer. What mean repair time objective should be set for the design?

Answer: 4.2 h.

8-16 The following table summarizes data on a certain product that a contractor proposes to install in your company:

Component	Quantity	Failure rate per hour
A	12	22×10^{-6}
B	22	5×10^{-6}
C	8	12×10^{-6}
D	10	17×10^{-6}

The failure rates apply for *one* of each component. A sample of prototypes has been run through a maintainability evaluation. A group of 15 failures were timed for repair time and the *total* repair time for the 15 failures was 52.0 h. It appears that the repair times are exponentially distributed.

(*a*) Assuming a constant failure rate, what is the predicted mean time between failures? All components are required for system success.

(*b*) What is the chance that a repair will take less than 3 h?

(*c*) As the customer, you desire that this product be in operating condition at least 95 percent of the time. Is it likely that this desire can be met?

8-17 Consider a product which you expect to purchase. Choose three alternative brands. Select five factors and define an importance rating value for each factor. Compare the three brands using the quantitative method described in this chapter.

SUPPLEMENTARY READING

Further discussion of reliability and maintainability quantification is provided in *Quality Control Handbook*, 3rd ed., McGraw-Hill Book Company, New York, 1974, pp. 8-16 to 8-44, 22-21 to 22-33.

Reliability in Engineering Design (see footnote 1) describes a wide range of quantitative reliability techniques. *Reliability Engineering* by ARINC, Prentice-Hall, Inc., Englewood Cliffs, N.J., 1964, emphasizes applications to electronic products. *Reliability Handbook* by W. G. Ireson, McGraw-Hill Book Company, New York, 1966, discusses both quantitative and other techniques for many types of products.

EXAMPLES OF EXAMINATION QUESTIONS USED IN FORMER ASQC RELIABILITY ENGINEER CERTIFICATION EXAMINATIONS AS PUBLISHED IN *QUALITY PROGRESS* MAGAZINE

1 If the mean time between failure is 200 h, what is the probability of surviving for 200 h? (*a*) 0.20; (*b*) 0.90; (*c*) 0.10; (*d*) 0.63; (*e*) 0.37.

2 If a system reliability of 0.998 is required, what reliability of two components in series is required? (*a*) $R_c = 0.99$; (*b*) $R_c = 0.999$; (*c*) $R_c = 0.98$; (*d*) $R_c = 0.9999$; (*e*) $R_c = 0.998$.

3 Given mean time to failure of 200 h for each of two components, what is the probability of failure if both components operate in series for 1 h? (a) $P = 0.010$; (b) $P = 0.990$; (c) $P = 0.001$; (d) $P = 0.0025$; (e) $P = 0.000025$.

4 The reliability of a device comprised of various parts functionally in series is: (a) the sum of the probabilities of the unreliabilities; (b) the product of the unreliabilities; (c) the sum of the reliabilities; (d) the product of the reliabilities; (e) the sum of the combinations and permutations.

5 The flat portion of the bathtub curve is a region of chance failures; therefore, the reliability equation, $R = e^{-t\lambda}$: (a) does not apply to this region; (b) only applies to this region; (c) applies to the wear-out region as well as the flat region; (d) applies to the entire bathtub curve.

6 If a component has a known constant failure rate of 0.0037 failure per hour, the reliability of two of these components in a series arrangement would be: (a) less than 99 percent; (b) dependent on the wear-out rate of a mating subsystem; (c) insufficient information to solve the problem; (d) 99.63 percent.

7 Assuming an exponential failure distribution, the probability of surviving an operating time equal to twice the MTBF is: (a) practically zero; (b) about 14 percent; (c) about 36 percent; (d) none of the above.

8 Unless repair or maintenance action is taken, the probability of failure of a device which has progressed to the point of wear-out will: (a) decrease; (b) increase; (c) not change.

9 System effectiveness: (a) is a measure of the extent to which a system may be expected to achieve a set of specific mission requirements; (b) may be expressed as a function of availability, dependability, and capability; (c) provides a decision criterion for system selection and justification; (d) is all of the above; (e) is none of the above.

NINE

VENDOR RELATIONS

9-1 SCOPE OF VENDOR QUALITY PROBLEMS

In many companies the cost of purchased materials, parts, and services is over 50 percent of the manufacturing costs of the company. Thus the overall program for quality in a company must extend to the "vendors" (or "suppliers") from whom the purchases are made.

In defining vendor quality activities, it is important to recognize that most companies purchase a variety of items for their final product and other items which are not product-related, such as supplies. This chapter deals only with product-related purchases.

The traditional purchase is a material, e.g., a standard steel, a simple chemical, or a standard component. The modern product involves buying more than standard materials. It involves also product designs, manufacturing and test capability, and other forms of expertise.

The existence of these two classes of purchases (Table 9-1) results in the need for two types of vendor quality programs—one for traditional purchases and one for modern purchases. Simple purchases usually require a minimum of formal quality activities by the buyer, while modern purchases often need some of the activities discussed in this chapter. Thus the topics in this chapter are normally recommended only for those products or situations where the cost of instituting formal controls can be justified by potential savings.

In many companies, a controversial question often arises: Who is responsi-

Table 9-1 Contrast in purchases

Traditional	Modern
Natural or semiprocessed materials	Purchases of designs, plans, and technical service in addition to materials
Tolerances wide, quality variable	High precision, high reliability
Specifications rudimentary	Sophisticated designs, quantified design parameters
Independent usage, low interchangeability	High interdependence, high interchangeability
Incoming inspection practical	Incoming inspection impractical
Limited subcontracting, geographic proximity, short feedback loop	Multiple tiers of subcontracting, wide geographic dispersion, long feedback loop
Secrecy concept by both parties	Mutual disclosures essential
Single line of communication	Multiple lines of communication
Vendor supplies goods only	Vendor supplies goods plus proof of compliance

Source: J. M. Juran, "Vendor Relations—An Overview," *Quality Progress,* July 1968, pp. 10-16.

ble for vendor quality? Discussions on this question are usually futile. Instead, it is much more constructive to define a list of specific actions and decisions and then discuss responsibility separately for each item. There is usually agreement on most of the items. This narrows the area of controversy to a few specific items that can be intelligently discussed. Table 9-2 shows a typical list with responsibilities as assigned in one company. These activities are discussed in this chapter and the next one.

9-2 VENDOR QUALITY POLICY

Policies are often useless generalities; i.e., "we will only buy from capable vendors." However, policies can be specific and provide useful guidance both internal and external to the company. Examples are:

1. Multiple sources of supply will be developed for all important purchases (see Section 9-3).
2. Vendors will be required to review all requirements and accept them before a purchasing contract is finalized.
3. Where appropriate, the facilities and personnel of our company will be made available to vendors to assist them in achieving mutual objectives.

Table 9-2 Responsibility matrix—vendor relations

Activity	Participating departments*		
	Product design	Purchasing	Quality control
1. Establish a vendor quality policy	×	×	××
2. Use multiple vendors for major procurements		××	
3. Evaluate quality capability of potential vendors	×	×	××
4. Specify requirements for vendors	××		×
5. Conduct joint quality planning	×		××
6. Conduct vendor surveillance		×	××
7. Evaluate delivered product	×		××
8. Conduct improvement programs	×	×	××
9. Use vendor quality ratings in selecting vendors		××	×

*×× = principal responsibility.
 × = collateral responsibility.

4. Data on vendor quality will be collected and used to determine priorities on incoming inspection of purchased items.
5. Vendor quality ratings will be prepared for use in selecting vendors.

A Quality Control Department can contribute to policy generation by nominating specific subjects for vendor quality policies and discussing them with appropriate functions in order to prepare a draft policy for review and approval by higher management.

Vendor quality policies for modern products must face up to the interdependence of the vendor and buyer. Interdependence takes three major forms:

Technological For traditional and proprietary products, the vendor is usually self-sufficient; for modern products, he or she often is not. The more complex the product, the greater is the need to give the vendor the type of technological assistance given to an in-house department.

Technological assistance is a two-way street. In *all* cases the buyer can learn from the vendor. (In some cases it is the vendor who is the technological giant, selling to buyers who lack engineers and laboratories.)

Technological assistance usually requires "exchange visiting," i.e., mutual visits to see each other's operations. These visits create the risk that the visitors will make unauthorized use of the knowledge obtained during the visit. For modern products, the need to take these risks is far greater than for traditional products.

Economic In modern products, the life-cycle-cost concept requires that the vendor understand the buyer's costs over the entire useful life of the product. This is a revolutionary change from the relationship prevailing in traditional products and creates a new level of economic interdependence.

Managerial Because modern products involve purchase of a wide range of vendor capabilities, the planning for use of these capabilities must be coordinated with the capabilities of the buyer. A major effect of this form of interdependence is that the assurance of good quality can no longer be derived from incoming inspection. Instead, the assurance must come from placing responsibility on the vendor to (1) make the product right, and (2) furnish the proof that it is right.

Details of making effective these three forms of interdependence are discussed later in this chapter.

9-3 MULTIPLE VENDORS

For important purchases it is well to use multiple sources of supply. A single source can more easily neglect to sharpen its competitive edge in quality, cost, and service. (A single source is also risky for continuity, e.g., strikes, fire.)

Despite the evident advantages of multiple sources, there is an enormous extent of use of single sources. The most dramatic cases are the huge multidivisional companies in which some divisions are vendors to others, e.g., large, integrated steel, oil, chemical, automotive, and electronic companies. These operations are quite successful in using monopolistic sources of supply because they solve their quality problems through a combination of managerial tools:

1. Joint quality planning.
2. Prompt feedback of deviations.
3. Upper-management insistence on corrective action.
4. Threat of breaking the monopoly if the vendor division will not act.

At the other extreme, the expense of qualifying additional sources results in use of single sources for small-volume purchases. Single sources may actually offer price advantages if the volume is not split among multiple vendors.

When companies find themselves restricted to a single source, steps can be taken to create a competitor:

1. Provide financial and technical assistance to a new company as an inducement to manufacture the needed product.
2. Make the product internally.
3. Add an operation internally to replace that being poorly performed by the vendor.

It may also be possible to redesign the final product to eliminate the need for the purchased product available from the single source.

In the short run, living with a single source of supply means that technical cooperation with the vendor must be stressed. This can be done (1) by thoroughly explaining the fitness-for-use needs to the vendor; (2) by showing how the product functions in the overall product; and (3) by translating this information into formal requirements, including a classification of the relative seriousness of different requirements so that the vendor can set proper priorities during manufacturing. It also means providing technical assistance to the vendor. For example, modern products often have numerical reliability and maintainability requirements. The methodologies discussed in Chapters 7 and 8 are often unknown to vendors. In such cases, the buyer may have to provide technical assistance to the vendor.

9-4 EVALUATING VENDOR QUALITY CAPABILITY

In a typical journey for a vendor to do business with a buyer (Figure 9-1), the evaluation of vendor quality involves two facets:

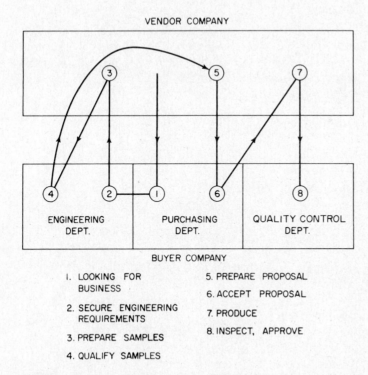

Figure 9-1 Product qualification process. This may be supplemented by surveys and visits to the facility.

1. Qualifying the vendor's design through the evaluation of product samples.
2. Qualifying the vendor's capability to meet quality requirements on production lots. This is done by vendor quality surveys (see Section 9-5).

Qualification Testing

As shown in Figure 9-1, the procedure here is for the vendor to make up samples of the product and submit these to the buyer's engineers for testing. These tests are not merely for instantaneous conformance to specification; they extend to life, failure rate, maintainability, and other environmental aspects of use.

Much lead time is needed for this qualification testing, and this in turn requires good advance planning. The procedure is costly enough to limit its use to mass-production or high-reliability projects. The validity of the results is heavily influenced by the integrity of the samples. They should be made by the same production process as will be used in regular production. They should not be made by hand in the laboratory. (Nevertheless, sometimes they are.)

9-5 VENDOR QUALITY SURVEY

A vendor quality survey is an evaluation of a vendor's ability to meet quality requirements on production lots. The results of the survey are used in the vendor selection process or, if the vendor has already been chosen, the survey alerts the purchaser to areas where the vendor may need help in meeting requirements. The survey can vary from a simple questionnaire mailed to the vendor to a visit to the vendor's facility.

The questionnaire poses explicit questions such as these submitted to vendors of a manufacturer of medical devices:

1. Has your company received the quality requirements on the product and agreed that they can be fully met?
2. Are your final inspection results documented?
3. Do you agree to provide the purchaser with advance notice of any changes in your product design?
4. What protective garments do your employees wear to reduce product contamination?
5. Describe the air-filtration system in your manufacturing areas.

The more formal quality survey consists of a visit to the vendor's facility by a team of observers from departments such as Quality Control, Engineering, Manufacturing, and Purchasing. Such a visit may be part of a broader survey of the vendor covering the financial, managerial, and technological competence. Depending on the product involved, the activities included in the quality control portion of the survey can be chosen from the following list:

Management: philosophy, quality policies, organization structure, indoctrination, commitment to quality.

Design: organization, systems in use, caliber of specifications, orientation to modern technique, attention to reliability, engineering change control, development laboratories.

Manufacture: physical facilities, maintenance, special processes, process capability, production capacity, caliber of planning, lot identification, and traceability.

Purchasing: specifications, vendor relations, procedures.

Quality control: organization structure, availability of quality control and reliability engineers, quality planning (materials, in-process, finished goods, packing, storage, shipping, usage, field service), audit of adherence to plan.

Inspection and test: laboratories, special tests, instruments, measurement control.

Quality coordination: organization for coordination, order analysis, control over subcontractors, quality cost analysis, corrective action loop, disposition of nonconforming product.

Data systems: facilities, procedures, effective use reports.

Personnel: indoctrination, training, motivation.

Quality results: performance attained, self-use of product, prestigious customers, prestigious subcontractors.

Following the survey, the team reports its findings. These consist of (1) some objective findings as to facilities possessed or lacked by the vendor, (2) some subjective judgments on the effectiveness of the vendor's operations, (3) a further judgment on the extent of assistance needed by the vendor, and (4) a highly subjective prediction as to whether the vendor will deliver good product if he is awarded a contract.

Although the objectives of vendor surveys are sound, objectives are not always achieved. Brainard[1] compared the actual product quality of 151 currently active vendors to their ratings (predictions) made in surveys.

1. There was no difference in product quality for vendors with acceptable ratings versus unacceptable ratings.
2. The surveyors could not reliably predict vendor quality performance (see Figure 9-2). Thus 74 of 151 surveys incorrectly predicted product quality. As a survey costs several hundred dollars, a penny coin may have been an adequate substitute for a prediction.
3. The significant elements of a quality system "were not required, were not measured, or were not measurable by the Company's system." Further, there was no relationship between the elements required of the vendor and the quality of his or her product.
4. The survey program did *not* result in reduced inspection.

[1] Edgar H. Brainard, "Just How Good Are Vendor Surveys?" *Quality Assurance,* August 1966, pp. 22–25.

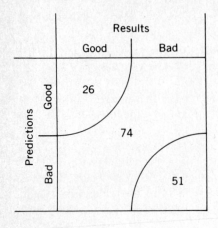

Figure 9-2 Ability of surveys to predict actual product quality.

In view of these conclusions, the company revised the survey program and substituted a simpler program. Prospective suppliers were asked to submit written information on test equipment, certifications, organization charts, and operating procedures. This uncovers obvious deficiencies. In addition, the first article delivered comes with a form showing the actual results of vendor measurements. This indicates if the vendor is aware of all characteristics, is able to measure them, and if his or her results check with the company results.

On balance, on-site surveys can be useful in evaluating tangible matters such as facilities, existence of written procedures, and documentation of results. However, such surveys are weak in evaluating intangibles, such as the attitude of key personnel in quality matters. Until surveys can reliably predict performance, the best means of evaluating a vendor is past performance through use of a quality data bank.

9-6 DATA BANKS FOR VENDOR EVALUATION

In a quality data bank, vendor performance and survey data on quality from various buyers are pooled and a summary is made available to those with a need to know.

The data bank can be organized in several ways:

1. *Pooling of data from several divisions within one large company.* This may include the pooling of both quality performance data and survey data. Multidivisional companies publish a handbook showing the field failure rate and cost of remedying the failure for specific purchased components. Such information is valuable in negotiating new or renewal contracts with vendors.
2. *Pooling of data by a governmental agency.* Much effort has been expended in developing such programs, particularly for reliability data of new com-

ponents. A recent effort is known as the Government Industry Data Exchange Program (GIDEP).
3. *Pooling of data to serve a specific industry.* An example is Coordinated Aerospace Supplier Evaluation (CASE).[2] This started as an informal association of aerospace prime contractors with the objective of reducing redundant surveys of suppliers in the industry. Survey data are received by the bank and summarized. The summaries, including backup data, are issued on request to members of the association.

The results of a vendor survey are sometimes combined with actual product history to form a "vendor certification" program. If a survey approves the vendor's quality system and if incoming inspection data show an acceptable level of quality, a vendor can be established as a *certified vendor*. A certified vendor is one who is an approved source of supply for unlimited quantities. The certification can also result in a reduction or elimination of incoming inspection of the vendor's goods.

9-7 SPECIFYING QUALITY REQUIREMENTS FOR VENDORS

For modern products, quality planning starts *before* a contract is signed. Such planning must recognize two issues:

1. The buyer must transmit to the vendor a full understanding of the use to be made of the product.
2. The buyer must obtain information to be sure that the vendor has the capability to provide a product that meets all fitness-for-use requirements. Communicating usage requirements can be difficult even for a simple product.

Example A vendor (manufacturer) of metal tubing sells through distributors. The customers buy the tubings for a wide variety of applications. Some of these applications require further processing on the tubing, e.g., redrawing, thread rolling. These various applications require variations in input materials. However, the vendor, not the distributor, is the expert in choice of tubing to be used for a given application. The vendor therefore takes positive steps to discover what the end use of the product will be. The vendor also has established a Material/Specification Review Board (MSRB) to review inquiries and orders for potential trouble for the vendor or buyer. The resulting classifications includes:

1. Easy to make.
2. Think we could make but need a trial order.

[2] John W. Shappard, Sr., "CASE Is Now 12 Years Old," *Quality Progress,* November 1977, pp. 38–39.

3. Would be surprised if we could make to the specifications as written.[3]

The complexity of many modern products makes it difficult to communicate usage needs to a vendor in a specification. Not only are the field usage conditions sometimes poorly known in a complex product, the internal environments surrounding a particular component may not be known until the complete product is designed and tested. For example, specifying accurate temperature and vibration requirements to a vendor supplying an electric component may not be feasible until the complete system is developed. Such cases require, at the least, continuous cooperation between vendor and buyer. In special cases, it may be necessary to award separate development and production contracts to discover how to finalize requirements.

It should be noted that circumstances may require two kinds of specifications:

1. Specifications defining what the product must do.
2. Specifications defining, in addition, what activities the vendor is expected to do to make the product fit for use.

The second type of specification is a departure from traditional practice of refraining from telling a vendor "how to run his plant." Defining required activities within a vendor's plant is sometimes necessary to assure that a vendor does have the expertise to conduct the full program needed to result in a satisfactory product. For some products, government regulations require that a buyer impose certain processing requirements (e.g., sanitary conditions for manufacturing pharmaceutical products) on vendors. For other products, such as a complex mechanical or electronic subsystem, the overall system requirements may result in a need for a vendor to meet a numerical reliability or maintainability requirement and to conduct certain activities (see Chapter 7) to assure that such requirements are met.

Example Several vendors were asked to submit bids on a battery needed in a space program. They were given a numerical reliability goal and asked to include in their bid proposal a description of the reliability activities that would be conducted to help meet the goal. Most of the prospective vendors included a reliability program consisting of appropriate reliability activities for a battery. However, one vendor apparently had no expertise in formal reliability methodology and submitted a surprising write-up. That vendor made a word-for-word copy of the complete reliability program write-up previously published for a complete missile system (the word "battery" was substituted for "missile"). This led to suspicion, later confirmed, that the vendor knew little about reliability programs.

[3] Harry W. Poole, "Customer/Supplier or Supplier/Customer—It Works Both Ways," *Quality Assurance*, October 1970, pp. 32, 33.

For complex products where a vendor is asked to design and manufacture a product, the vendor can be required to include *in the proposal* a preliminary reliability prediction, a failure mode and effect analysis, a reliability test plan, or other reliability analyses (see Chapter 7). The vendor's response will not only provide some assurance on the design concept but also show that the vendor has the reliability expertise to conduct the program and has provided the funds and schedule time in the proposal.

A special form of precontract planning is the *design-to-cost approach* (see Section 7-17). Here, the prospective bidder is given a statement of the mission or function to be provided by the product along with a cost target. The vendor is then asked to submit a design concept and also to define trade-offs in performance and delivery to meet the cost target.

9-8 THREE TYPES OF JOINT QUALITY PLANNING

The finalization and execution of the contract between vendor and buyer requires that detailed quality planning cover three elements: economic, technological, and managerial.

Joint Economic Planning

The economic aspects of joint quality planning concentrate on two major approaches:

1. *Buying value rather than conformance to specification.* The technique used is to analyze the value of what is being bought and to try to effect an improvement. The organized approach is known as *value engineering* (see Section 7-17). Applied to vendor quality relations, value analysis looks for excessive costs due to:

   Overspecification for the use to which the product will be put, e.g., special products ordered when a standard product would do.
   Emphasis on original price rather than on cost of use over the life of the product.
   Emphasis on conformance to specification, not fitness for use.

2. *Optimizing quality costs.* To the purchase price the buyer must add a whole array of quality-related costs: incoming inspection, material review, production delays, downtime, extra inventories, etc. However, the vendor also has a set of costs which he or she is trying to optimize. The buyer should put together the data needed to understand the life-cycle costs or the cost of use and then press for a result that will optimize these.

   Example A heavy-equipment manufacturer bought castings from several vendors. It was decided to calculate the "total cost of the purchased casting" as the original purchase price plus incoming inspection costs plus the costs of rejections detected later in assembly. The unit purchase price on a contract given to the lowest bidder was $19. The inspection and rejection costs amounted to an additional $2.11. The variation among bid prices was $2.

Joint Technological Planning

The more usual elements of such planning include:

1. Agreement on the meaning of performance requirements in the specifications.
2. Quantification of reliability and maintainability requirements.

   Example A vendor was given a contract to provide an air-conditioning system with a mean time between failures of at least 2000 h. As part of joint planning, the vendor was required to submit a detailed reliability program early in the design phase. The program write-up was submitted and included a provision to impose the same 2000-h requirement on each supplier of parts for the system. This revealed a complete lack of understanding by the vendor of the multiplication rule (see Section 8-3).

3. Definition of reliability and maintainability tasks to be conducted by the vendor.
4. Definition of special efforts to be made during manufacture to assure that sanitary and other aspects of "good manufacturing practices" are met.
5. Seriousness classification of defects to help the vendor understand where to concentrate his efforts (see Section 15-4).
6. Establishment of sensory standards for those qualities which require use of the human being as an instrument (see Section 12-18).

   Example The federal government was faced with the problem of defining the limits of color on a military uniform. It was finally decided to prepare physical samples of the lightest and darkest acceptable colors. Such standards were then sent to the field with the provision of replacing the standards periodically because of color fading.

7. Standardization of test methods and test conditions between vendor and buyer to assure their compatibility.

   Example A carpet manufacturer repeatedly complained to the yarn vendor about the yarn weight. Finally, the vendor visited his customer to verify the test methods. The mechanics of the test methods were alike. Next, an impartial testing lab was hired and it verified the tests at the carpet plant. Finally, the mystery was solved. The supplier was spinning (and measuring) the yarn at bone-dry conditions, but the carpet manufacturer measured at standard conditions. During this period, $62,000 more was spent for yarn than if it had been purchased at standard weight.

8. Establishment of sampling plans and other criteria relative to inspection and test activity. From the vendor's viewpoint, the plan should usually accept lots having the usual process average. For the buyer, the critical factor is the amount of damage caused by one defect getting through the sampling screen. Balancing the cost of sorting versus sampling can be a useful input in designing a sampling plan (see Chapter 17). In addition to sampling criteria, the error of measurement can also be a problem.

9. Establishment of a system of lot identification and traceability. This concept has always been present in some degree, e.g., heat numbers of steel, lot numbers of pharmaceutical products. More recently, with intensified attention to product and reliability, this idea is more acutely needed to simplify localization of trouble, to reduce the volume of product recall and to fix responsibility. These traceability systems, while demanding some extra effort to preserve the order of manufacture and to identify the product, can be decidedly helpful in quality control, since preserving the order makes possible greater precision in sampling.

10. Establishment of a system of timely response to alarm signals resulting from defects. In many contracts, the buyer and vendor are yoked to a common timetable for completion of the final product. Usually, a separate department called Production Control (or Materials Management, etc.) presides over major aspects of scheduling. However, the upper management properly looks to the people associated with the quality function to set up alarm signals to detect quality failures and to act positively on these signals to avoid deterioration, whether in quality, cost, or delivery.

The Department of Defense and the National Aeronautics and Space Administration have found it useful to prepare specifications for quality and reliability programs for their contractors. Although these specifications contain certain requirements that go beyond the needs of conventional products, they do provide a valuable source of advanced ideas for *all* companies to consider.[4]

Joint Managerial Planning

Achieving the economic and technological goals requires use of the conventional management tools of planning. These should be applied on a joint basis, as though buyer and vendor were all part of the same management team. The more usual elements of this planning include:

Definition of responsibility: buyer versus vendor When multiple departments of

[4] See *Quality Control Handbook*, 3rd ed., p. 6-22.

both companies are involved in a joint effort, it becomes important to clear up the assignment of duties as between buyer and vendor. The assignments are spelled out partly in the contracts, partly in the vendor relations manual, and partly in the conferences and other communications between the parties.

In modern products some innocent-looking tasks turn out to be quite demanding, e.g., those associated with achieving reliability. These tasks should be clearly defined, and should be clearly assigned as to responsibility, before the contract is signed.

Definition of responsibility: within buyer Responsibilities within the buying organization are often more difficult to straighten out than those between buyer and vendor. Table 9-2 shows a typical assignment of some common responsibilities. In practice, this needs to be expanded to cover greater detail.

Documentation and reporting In many contracts the vendor is required to provide documented proof that the product conforms to specification and is fit for use. (The buyer uses these proofs in lieu of incoming inspection of the product.)

Achieving this compatibility requires that a whole array of details be made compatible, details such as designs of forms, code numbers for defects, seriousness classification, data processing systems, key aspects of terminology, target dates for reports, computer programs, and still other aspects of systems and procedures.

All this compatibility is used for other essential purposes as well, e.g., data feedback, quality certifications, audits.

Multiple communication channels The need for multiple forms of joint planning can be met only by setting up multiple channels of communications: designers must communicate directly with designers, quality specialists with quality specialists, etc. These multiple channels are a drastic departure from the single channel, which is the method in common use for purchase of traditional products (see Figure 9-3.) The multiple channels also create a risk of confusion unless coordination is provided. One form of such coordination is to provide Purchasing and Sales with copies of all letters, minutes, etc. However, in many cases this is not enough and needs to be supplemented with conferences at which members from the key departments of both companies are present. It is easier to arrive at necessary understandings and trade-offs through such conferences than through multiple isolated channels.

9-9 COOPERATION WITH VENDORS DURING EXECUTION OF THE CONTRACT

With the end of the planning stage there is a need for providing continual two-way communication during the execution of the contract. The purpose is to supply essential information, provide performance data, identify troubles

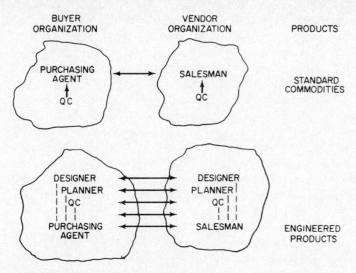

Figure 9-3 Vendor communication channels.

which arise, stimulate corrective action, and improve the ability of the parties to work together. The amount of effort may range from simple analysis of receiving inspection data to extensive "vendor surveillance" (covered later in this chapter).

The cooperation usually concentrates on the following activities:

Design information and changes Industry has made great strides in learning how to communicate design information at the beginning of a contract, but the record on communicating design *changes* is less impressive.

Design changes may take place either at the initiative of the buyer or the vendor. Either way, there is need to treat the vendor like an in-house department in the procedures for processing design changes and in configuration control (see Section 19-5). This need is especially acute for modern products, where design changes can affect products, processes, tools, instruments, stored materials, procedures, etc. Some of these effects are obvious, but others are subtle, requiring the opportunity for complete analysis to identify the effects. Failure to provide adequate design change information to vendors has been a distinct obstacle to good vendor relations.

Deviations During the performance of the contract there will arise instances of nonconformance. These may be on the product itself or on process requirements or procedural requirements. Such deviations need to be resolved, but priority effort should go to cases where product is unfit for use.

Product unfitness for use These cases may be discovered through product testing, Material Review Board decisions, field complaints, service calls, returns, etc. The impact on the manufacturer is direct and severe, since the ability to sell the product is jeopardized. Despite the importance of these feedbacks, the manufacturer may have difficulty in relaying the necessary alarm signals to the vendor. Some of this difficulty is technological; i.e., there are problems in securing adequate field data and in working out the data processing needed to separate out the information required by the various vendors. However, some of the inadequacies in communication have been due to lack of buyer awareness of the usefulness of good feedback to the vendors.

Corrective action Communications to the vendor on nonconformance must include precise description of the symptoms of the defects. The best description is in the form of samples, but if this is not possible, the vendor should have the opportunity to visit the site of the trouble. There are numerous related questions: What disposition is to be made of the defectives? Who will sort or repair? Who will pay the costs? What were the causes? What steps are needed to avoid a recurrence? These questions are outside the scope of pure defect detection; they require joint discussion among departments within each company and further joint discussions between buyer and vendor. On modern products it is no longer feasible to settle these matters through the single communication link of purchasing agent and salesperson. Instead, conferences are held and attended by those who can make the main contribution to the problem at hand.

A final note concerns "positive communication." Buyers usually quickly communicate to vendors the data defining nonconformance, unfitness for use, and other troubles encountered. In contrast, the vendor is usually not given product data when the situation is trouble-free. When communication is limited to reports of a negative nature, the atmosphere for constructive improvement can also become negative.

There is increasing awareness of this problem. Positive communication can include letters of praise, vendor awards, and recognition in vendor ratings. When successfully done, it can help change the vendor's attitude from a defensive one to one of constructive cooperation on a problem needing quality improvement. The general approach to quality improvement (Chapter 5) also applies to vendors. The Pareto analysis to identify the vital few problems is particularly important as an alternative to broad attempts to tighten up all procedures on a vendor.[5]

9-10 EVALUATING DELIVERED PRODUCT

Buyers secure their assurance of product conformance to fitness for use in several ways:

1. *Reliance solely on the vendor.* In this case, no incoming inspection of the vendor product is made. This form is in wide use for small purchases, for

[5] See *Quality Control Handbook*, 3rd ed., p. 10-29.

purchase of standard materials, and for purchase of goods not used in the product, e.g., office furniture. The assurance is secured during the subsequent processing or use of the product.

2. *Incoming inspection.* This consists of a physical inspection of the product, usually before the buyer authorizes payment to the vendor. When the inspection occurs at the buyer's plant, it is called incoming inspection. In some cases the *incoming inspection* is conducted by the buyer at the vendor's plant and this is called *source inspection.*

Incoming inspection on a product can vary from 100 percent inspection of all product to a simple identity inspection (see Table 9-3).

Example The experience of a clothing manufacturer is pertinent here. One of its purchased items was ready for customer use; i.e., it was price tagged, bagged, and sent to stock for distribution. The vendor had an outgoing inspection and the buyer duplicated this with a 100 percent receiving inspection. About 6 percent of the items were not "first quality." These items were sold to employees as seconds and a claim made (and honored) against the vendor. The buyer initiated discussions with the vendor to eliminate the double cost of inspection. The discussions (as is typical) uncovered different views on what was acceptable, but these were resolved. Finally, it was agreed that the buyer would pay the vendor to fold, tag, and bag the items. Except for a spot check, the receiving inspection was discontinued and the items are sent directly to stock.

In previous decades, incoming inspection often consumed a large amount of effort. With the advent of modern complex products, many companies have found that they do not have the necessary inspection skills or equipment to inspect the new breed of incoming product. This has forced them to rely more on

Table 9-3 Types of incoming inspection

Type	Approach	Application
100% inspection	Every item in a lot is evaluated for all or some of the characteristics in the specification	Critical items where the cost of inspection is justified by the cost of risk of defectives; also used to establish quality level of new vendors
Sampling inspection	A sample of each lot is evaluated by a predefined sampling plan and a decision made to accept or reject the lot.	Important items where the vendor has established an adequate quality record by the prior history of lots submitted
Identity inspection	The product is examined to assure that the vendor sent the correct product; no inspection of characteristics is made	Items of less importance where the reliability of the vendor laboratory has been established in addition to the quality level of the product

the vendor's quality system or inspection and test data as discussed later in this chapter. However, even companies making traditional products have reexamined the nature of their incoming inspection effort.

> **Example** An equipment manufacturer has a stable line of products where design changes are evolutionary rather than revolutionary. In past decades, their incoming inspection effort consisted 95 percent of inspection personnel and 5 percent for administrative and clerical personnel. As the business has grown, a careful look has been taken at the productivity of the incoming inspection function to assure that it was cost-effective. This look included an analysis of past vendor performances to develop sampling plans that will put the inspection effort where it is most needed. Now the incoming inspection effort splits into 70 percent for actual inspection, 25 percent for analysis of vendor data and development of sampling plans, and 5 percent for administrative and clerical effort.

3. *Vendor surveillance* (see below).
4. *Use of vendor data* (see below).

The choice of evaluation methods depends in part on the prevailing economic conditions in the country at a given time. Cost-reduction efforts brought about by adverse economic conditions or material shortages caused by high demand can result in a quality deterioration of purchased product. Weaver[6] discusses an example.

When incoming inspection is used as the sole means of evaluating the vendor's product, much valuable information about the vendor's process is ignored. This may include process capability information (see Chapter 12), process controls, outgoing inspection results, and other information. Such information can significantly reduce or even eliminate incoming inspection by the buyer. Lacking this information, incoming inspection sampling plans must be determined by the probability laws governing random sampling, and the resulting sample sizes can be quite large.

9-11 VENDOR SURVEILLANCE

For many modern products, only the vendor has sufficient product knowledge and inspection skills and facilities to evaluate the final product. In these cases the contract may require the vendor to present (1) a written plan for controlling quality, and (2) proof that the plan has been followed.

The contracts permit the buyer to exercise a "surveillance" over all the vendor activities to achieve conformance to specifications and fitness for use.

---

[6] Henry Weaver, "Quality Deterioration (Economic Marketplace)," *Quality Progress*, February 1978, pp. 28–30.

This surveillance includes procedural, process, and product audits, as well as inspection conducted by the buyer. Surveillance can take place through periodic visits to the vendor's plant. Alternatively, the buyer may maintain a resident auditor at the vendor's plant to provide for a continuing surveillance. This same auditor may also conduct source inspection, although this is not universal. For vendors who must do considerable design and development, the surveillance may include periodic reviews of the reliability engineering efforts.

A specific approach is *first-piece inspection.* This requires that the first piece manufactured be inspected and accepted by the buyer before production continues. An extension of this is a *preproduction quality evaluation* which stresses the active cooperation of buyer and vendor during manufacturing planning. The automobile industry illustrates the concept.

Every new model of automobile is quite an exercise in teamwork, since both buyer and vendor are yoked to a severe timetable. The crux of it is a joint venture on several fronts: engineers work directly with engineers; other specialists work directly with their opposite numbers. The manufacturing planning is a joint venture in providing an adequate process, machines, and tools. The quality planning is a joint venture, down to avoiding duplication of gages. The first samples go through a prove-in procedure which includes assembly into prove-out vehicles. Through such joint planning and execution, not only is the preparation intrinsically better done; the personnel of the two companies are brought to work together face to face. The confidence born of such relationships can often outperform the most precisely drawn procedures. Juran[7] provides further discussion.

Vendor surveillance can provide the buyer (and the vendor) with early warning of problems prior to product nonconformance or unfitness for use. However, surveillance is difficult to administer to the satisfaction of both parties. The buyer emphasis must be on whether or not the product is fit for use rather than on minor product deviations, process deviations, or procedural deviations. Concurrently, the vendor must understand the need for the buyer to insist on a certain level of documentation that may go beyond the ordinary needs of the vendor.[8]

9-12 USES OF VENDOR QUALITY DATA—AUDIT OF DECISIONS

A buyer who receives a vendor's test data has an opportunity to eliminate incoming inspection through use of the concept of the *audit of decisions.* Under the concept, the following sequence of events takes place:

1. Along with product shipments, the vendor arranges to transmit test data.
2. The buyer performs a lot-by-lot incoming inspection on the product and compares the test data with the vendor's test data to determine if the ven-

[7] J. M. Juran, "Vendor Relations—An Overview," *Quality Progress,* July 1968, p. 13.
[8] See *Quality Control Handbook,* 3rd ed., pp. 10-24, 10-25.

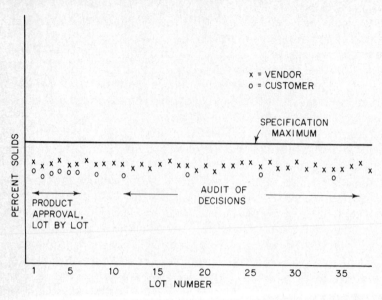

Figure 9-4 Concept of audit of decisions.

dor's laboratory can be relied on to make good product conformance decisions.

3. As the buyer develops confidence in the vendor's laboratory, the buyer stops making lot-by-lot incoming inspections. Instead, the test results of the vendor are accepted as valid. However, the buyer initiates a periodic check (every tenth lot or so) to verify that the vendor's laboratory continues to make good product acceptance decisions. It is this periodic check which constitutes the audit of decisions.

Figure 9-4 shows in simplified graphic form how the concept operates. Comparative data for the first six lots has established the following:

1. The vendor has a process which is capable of holding the tolerances.
2. The lot-to-lot variability of the vendor's process is low enough to avoid jeopardizing product conformance through inherent variation.
3. The laboratory gives results which are a sound basis for decision making.
4. There is an unexplained consistent difference in test procedures, the vendor's test being the more severe.

Under these circumstances, the buyer begins to rely on the vendor's laboratory at lot 7. The buyer progressively increases this reliance by reducing incoming testing further and further and finally converts to a full audit of decisions. This constitutes a drastic change in philosophy of testing. At the outset, the purpose of testing was to determine "Is the product good or bad?" Any information about the vendor's laboratory was incidental. At the final state, the purpose of the buyer's testing is to determine "Does the vendor's laboratory continue to make good decisions?" Any information about the program is incidental.

Companies that contemplate use of the concept of audit of decisions are always concerned about what to do when the audit check shows a failure by the vendor's laboratory. Usually, these companies insist that means be set up for tracing the identity and rechecking of all lots not tested by the buyer since the previous audit check. This is quite a sensible requirement and calls for joint planning that will establish clear lot identification and traceability.

Use of the concept of audit of decision requires that the vendor supply test data to the buyer on a continuing basis. In simple cases such as shown in Figure 9-4, the vendor commonly does this upon request by the buyer. However, many cases are not as simple, involving frequency distributions, control charts, computer printouts, etc. As a result, some vendors make a charge for the copies of the data, especially if the buyer wants these data specially processed. In other cases, e.g., a large vendor selling a small order to a buyer, the vendor may resist the request altogether. In still other cases, the vendor takes the initiative and supplies the data automatically as a selling device; i.e., he hopes to enlist the support of the buyer's technical and quality control people. An early example was that of Hunter Spring Company, which initiated the practice of supplying the frequency distributions of tests on lots of springs to their customers in the early 1940s. Other test data or reliability analyses can also be offered to customers as part of an initial marketing package.

PROBLEMS

9-1 Visit the purchasing agent of some local institution to learn the overall approach to vendor selection and the role of vendor quality performance in this selection process. Report your findings.

9-2 Visit a sampling of local vendors (printer, merchant, repair shop, etc.) to learn the role of quality performance in their relationship with their clients. Report your findings.

9-3 Visit a local manufacturing company and create a table similar to Table 9-2.

9-4 Outline a potential application of several concepts in this chapter. Follow the instructions given in Problem 7-12.

9-5 A government agency contracted with a company to design and build a satellite system.[9] Months after the contract was signed, it was discovered that the design would not be immune to certain types of radar interference. The agency claimed that they did describe the performance desired for the satellites. The company disagreed (with respect to the radar interference). If this need had been realized at the start of the project, it would have been relatively simple to create an appropriate design. The satellites are in an advanced stage of design and construction and the necessary changes would require $100 million. There was further confusion. The company chose a supplier to manufacture the satellites. This supplier had previous experience on such products, and some people claimed that the supplier should have been aware of the radar interference problem. Comment on the actions that should be taken by three such organizations to prevent such a situation on a future project.

[9] "A $100 Million Satellite Error," *Business Week*, August 7, 1978, p. 52.

9-6 During World War II, many manufacturers made products that were totally new to them. For example, the Ford Motor Company was asked to produce fuselage sections for B-24 aircraft. To do this, Ford had to work closely with the Consolidated Company, which was responsible for the manufacture of the entire aircraft. Thus Ford was a vendor for Consolidated. There was much friction between the companies. Lindbergh[10] describes the background:

> In short, if the Consolidated men were carrying a chip on one shoulder, the Ford men arrived with a chip on each shoulder. Instead of taking the attitude that they had come to San Diego to learn how to build Consolidated bombers from the company that had developed those bombers, they took the attitude that they were there only as a preliminary to showing Consolidated how to build Consolidated bombers better and on mass production. The inevitable result was a deep-rooted antagonism which still exists.

The first article delivered by Ford was "not only as bad but considerably worse than the aviation people said it would be—rivets missing · · · badly formed skin · · · cracks *already* started · · · etc." However, this article had been passed by both Ford inspection and by the Army inspector stationed at Ford. Lindberg concluded:

> What has happened is clear enough: under pressure, and encouraged by the desire to get production under way at Willow Run, and more than a little due to lack of experience, both Army and Ford inspection passed material that should have been rejected (and which was rejected by the more experienced and impartial inspectors at Tulsa).

Describe the *specific* actions that you would recommend to correct the immediate problem and prevent a recurrence in the future.

SUPPLEMENTARY READING

The *Quality Control Handbook,* 3rd ed., McGraw-Hill Book Company, New York, 1974, includes a section on vendor relations (sec. 10).

A booklet that discusses many aspects of vendor relations is *Procurement Quality Control,* 2nd ed., American Society for Quality Control, Milwaukee, Wis., 1976.

EXAMPLES OF EXAMINATION QUESTIONS USED IN FORMER ASQC QUALITY ENGINEER CERTIFICATION EXAMINATIONS AS PUBLISHED IN *QUALITY PROGRESS* MAGAZINE

1 Good housekeeping is an important quality factor in a supplier's plant because: (*a*) it promotes good working conditions; (*b*) it minimizes fire hazards; (*c*) it enhances safer operations; (*d*) it reflects favorably on the efficiency and management of a company; (*e*) all of the above.

2 A preaward survey of a potential supplier is best described as a _____ audit. (*a*) compliance; (*b*) assessment; (*c*) quantitative; (*d*) all of these; (*e*) none of these.

3 The most desirable method of evaluating a supplier is: (*a*) history evaluation; (*b*) survey evaluation; (*c*) questionnaire; (*d*) discuss with quality manager on phone; (*e*) all of the above.

---

[10] Charles A. Lindbergh, *The Wartime Journals of Charles A. Lindbergh,* Harcourt Brace Jovanovich, New York, 1970, pp. 644, 646.

4 The most important step in vendor certification is to: (*a*) obtain copies of vendor's handbook; (*b*) familiarize vendor with quality requirements; (*c*) analyze vendor's first shipment; (*d*) visit the vendor's plant.

5 During the preaward survey at a potential key supplier, you discover the existence of a quality control manual. This means: (*a*) that a quality system has been developed; (*b*) that a quality system has been implemented; (*c*) that the firm is quality conscious; (*d*) that the firm has a quality manager; (*e*) all of the above.

6 A vendor must perform tests on parts to determine which of the following? (*a*) functional capabilities under specified environmental conditions; (*b*) materials and processes; (*c*) configuration and size; (*d*) cost.

TEN

VENDOR RELATIONS — STATISTICAL AIDS

10-1 DEFINITION OF NUMERICAL QUALITY AND RELIABILITY REQUIREMENTS FOR LOTS

Beyond the quality and reliability requirements imposed on individual units or product (see Section 9-7), there is usually need for added numerical criteria to judge conformance of *lots* of products.

These criteria are typically needed in acceptance sampling procedures (see Chapter 17), which makes it possible to accept or reject an entire lot of product based on the inspection and test results of a random sample from the lot. The application of sampling procedures is facilitated if lot quality requirements are defined in numerical terms. Examples of numerical indices are shown in Table 10-1.

The selection of numerical values for these criteria depends on several factors and also on probability considerations. These matters are discussed in Chapter 17 and by Hogan.[1] These criteria are also a means of indexing sampling plans developed from statistical concepts. Unfortunately, many vendors do not understand the statistical concepts and make incorrect interpretations of the quality level requirement and also the results of sampling inspection (see Table 10-1). Also, these criteria can be a source of confusion in product li-

---

[1] Paul J. Hogan, "Specifying AQLs and LQs in Procurement Documents," *Quality Progress,* June 1975, pp. 13–15.

Table 10-1 Forms of numerical sampling criteria

Form of numerical sampling criteria	Meaning	Typical values, %	Common misinterpretations
Acceptable quality level (AQL)	That percent defective which has a high probability (say ≥ 0.90) of being accepted by the sampling plan*	0.01–10.0	All accepted lots are at least as good as the AQL; all rejected lots are worse than the AQL
Lot tolerance percent defective (LTPD)	That percent defective which has a low probability (say ≤ 0.10) of being accepted by the sampling plan	0.5–10.0	All lots better than the LTPD will be accepted; all lots worse than the LTPD will be rejected
Average outgoing quality limit (AOQL)	Worse average percent defective over many lots after sampling inspection has been performed and rejected lots 100% inspected	0.1–10.0	All accepted lots are at least as good as the AOQL; all rejected lots are worse than the AOQL

*Some sampling tables and other sources define AQL as the maximum percent defective considered satisfactory as a process average.

ability discussions. Thus, although an Acceptable Quality Level or other index is sometimes specified in vendor purchasing documents, buyers must exercise caution in using these terms with vendors.

For complex and/or time-oriented products, numerical reliability requirements can be defined in vendor purchasing documents. Sometimes, such requirements are stated in terms of mean time between failures. Numerical reliability requirements can help to clarify what a customer means by "high reliability."

Example A capacitor manufacturer requested bids on a unit of manufacturing equipment that was to perform several manufacturing operations. Reliability of the equipment was important to maintain production schedules, so a numerical requirement on "mean time between jams" (MTBJ) was specified to prospective bidders. (Previously, reliability was not treated quantitatively. Equipment manufacturers always promised high reliability, but results were disappointing.) After several rounds of discussion with bidders it was concluded that the desired level of reliability was unrealistic if the machine was to perform several operations. The capacitor manufacturer finally decided to revise the requirement for several operations and thereby reduce the complexity of the equipment. The effort to specify a numerical requirement in the procurement document forced a clear understanding of "reliability." Vendors can also be required to demonstrate, by test, specified levels of reliability (see Chapter 7).

10-2 QUANTIFICATION OF VENDOR SURVEYS

The vendor quality survey is a technique for evaluating the vendor's ability to meet quality requirements on production lots (see Section 9-5). The evaluation of various quality activities can be quantified by a scoring system.

A scoring system that includes importance weights for activities is illustrated in Figure 10-1. This system is used by a manufacturer of electronic assemblies. In this case, the importance weights (W) vary from 1 to 4 and must total to 25 for each of the three areas surveyed. The weights show the relative importance of the various activities in the overall index. The actual ratings (R) of the activities observed are assigned as follows:

10: The specific activity is satisfactory in every respect (or does not apply).
 8: The activity meets minimum requirements but improvements could be made.
 0: The activity is unsatisfactory.

Figure 10-1 Scoring of a vendor quality survey

Activity	Receiving inspection			Manufacturing			Final inspection		
	R	W	$R \times W$	R	W	$R \times W$	R	W	$R \times W$
1. Quality management	8	3	24	8	3	24	8	3	24
2. Quality planning	8	4	32	8	4	32	10	4	40
3. Inspection equipment	10	3	30	10	3	30	10	3	30
4. Calibration	0	3	0	10	3	30	0	3	0
5. Drawing control	0	3	0	10	2	20	10	2	20
6. Corrective action	10	3	30	8	3	24	8	3	24
7. Handling rejects	10	2	20	8	2	16	10	3	30
8. Storage and shipping	10	1	10	10	1	10	10	1	10
9. Environment	8	1	8	8	1	8	8	1	8
10. Personnel experience	10	2	20	10	3	30	10	2	20
			Area total = 174			Area total = 224			Area total = 206

R = rating; W = weight

Interpretation of area totals:
  Fully approved: Each of the three area totals is 250.
  Approved: None of the three area totals is less than 200.
  Conditionally approved: No single area total is less than 180.
  Unapproved: One or more of the area totals is less than 180.

Scoring schemes can be made simpler,[2] or more complicated as illustrated by a probabilistic approach described by Shilliff and Bodis.[3]

10-3 EVALUATING VENDOR PRODUCT AT INCOMING INSPECTION

Incoming inspection of a vendor's product can assume several forms:

1. *100 percent inspection.* Every item in the lot is inspected for some or all of the specification requirements.
2. *Sampling inspection.* A portion of each lot is inspected and a decision made on the entire lot (see Chapter 17).
3. *Identity check.* The lot is examined to determine if the correct product has been received. No inspections for conformance to requirements are made.
4. *No inspection.* The lot is directly sent to a storeroom.
5. *Use of vendor data.* The vendor provides a copy of the results of outgoing inspection and test at the vendor's plant and this is used in place of incoming inspection at the buyer's plant. The general concept is explained in Section 9-12. A later section of the present chapter discusses the verification of the vendor data.

A difficult problem at incoming inspection is distributing the limited inspection resources available over the large number of parts and vendors. Generally, the resources are not sufficient for 100 percent inspection on all parts or even sampling inspection of all lots using sample sizes from the conventional tables discussed in Chapter 17. Judgments must then be made on how to allocate the inspection effort to part numbers and vendors. The factors to be considered include:

1. Prior quality history on the part and vendor.
2. Criticality of the part on overall system performance.
3. Criticality on later manufacturing operations.
4. Warranty or use history.
5. Vendor process capability information.
6. Nature of the manufacturing process. For example, a press operation primarily depends on the adequacy of the setup. Information on the first few pieces and last few pieces in a production run is usually sufficient to draw conclusions about the entire run.
7. Product homogeneity. For example, fluid product is homogeneous and reduces the need for large sample sizes.

[2] American Society for Quality Control, *Procurement Quality Control*, 2nd ed., 1976, app. C.
[3] Karl A. Shilliff and Milan Bodis, "How to Pick the Right Vendor," *Quality Progress*, January 1975, pp. 12–14.

8. Availability of required inspection skills and equipment.

Often the volume of part numbers and vendors is so large that judgments on the amount of inspection are made in a cursory manner that result in a poor distribution of effort at incoming inspection. A balance must be reached between a simple incoming inspection system and one that formally recognizes the factors listed.

Example A spare-parts distribution center reviewed its approach to incoming inspection. Inspection ranged from 100 percent to almost no inspection. Special sampling tables had been created because the conventional tables required sample sizes that were judged to be uneconomically large. Prior history of vendors was documented but only periodically used to determine the amount of inspection. Also, it was felt that *all* lots should have some inspection and therefore the minimum sample size was 1 unit.

Seven years of data were readily available (stored in a computer) on lot decisions by vendor and part number, but no continuous system was used to evaluate the data and adjust the amount of inspection. A preliminary analysis revealed:

1. 30 percent of the vendor/part number combinations had not had a single lot rejected in 21 or more consecutive lots.
2. Most of the rejected lots were on part numbers with recent lot rejections, i.e., 93 percent of rejected part numbers had 4 or less accepted lots since the last rejected lot.

A system was devised to provide inspection personnel with updated pertinent information to properly allocate inspection effort. History on each vendor/part number combination was compiled using an arbitrary scoring system:

Lot rejection: 20 points
Rejection discovered later: 10 points
Borderline acceptance: 5 points
Dealer complaint: 10 points
Warranty claim: 10 points

The score for a part number was the sum of the points. Each accepted lot resulted in a subtraction of 8 points. Other adjustments restricted the range of the score to 0 to 50.

The sampling tables are now related to the current score, thereby providing inspection personnel with a simple way to reallocate effort on the basis of product history. The system also contains provisions for critical parts in other special situations.

This system has been implemented and 30 percent of inspection hours were saved initially with additional savings expected later. In some cases inspection was eliminated (except for an audit inspection), but in other cases inspection was increased to provide more protection on troublesome part numbers or vendors.

Allocation of incoming inspection effort is usually done with oversimplified procedures having high or unknown risks. The future need is to develop reasonably simple procedures that incorporate information, including prior vending history and the effect of a defective part entering the buyer's production process.

10-4 USE OF HISTOGRAM ANALYSIS ON VENDOR DATA

A useful tool for learning about a vendor's process and comparing several vendors' manufacturing product to the same specification is the histogram (see Section 3-8). A random sample is selected from a lot and measurements are made on the selected quality characteristics. The data are charted as frequency histograms. The analysis consists of comparing the histograms to the specification limits.

An application of histograms to evaluating the hardenability of a particular grade of steel from four vendors is shown in Figure 10-2. The specification was a maximum Rockwell C reading of 43 measured at Jominy position J8. Histograms were also prepared for carbon, manganese, nickel, and chromium content. Analysis revealed:

1. Vendor 46 had a process without any strong central tendency. The histogram on nickel for this vendor was also rectangular in shape, indicating a lack of control of the nickel content and resulting in several heats of steel with excessively high Rockwell values.
2. Vendor 27 had several heats above the maximum, although the process had a central value of about 28. The histograms for manganese, nickel, and chromium showed several values above and apart from the main histogram.
3. Vendor 74 showed much less variability than the others. Analysis of other histograms for this vendor suggested that about half of the original heats of steel had been screened out and used for other applications.

Note how these analyses can be made without visiting the vendor plants, i.e., the "product tells on the process." Histograms have limitations (see Chapter 3), but they are an effective tool for incoming inspection.

10-5 THE LOT PLOT PLAN

Lot plot is a sampling plan that uses histograms to make acceptance and rejection decisions on lots.

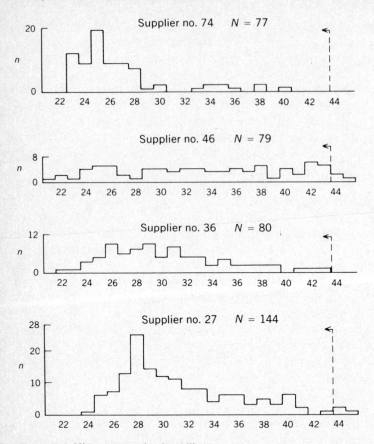

Figure 10-2 Histograms on hardenability.

A minimum sample of 50 units is taken at random and is measured with a variables gage precise enough to subdivide product variability into about 10 cells. The data are recorded on a special form to form a histogram and calculations are made of $\bar{X}$ and σ. Then, under the assumption of a normal distribution, and by using a graphic "lot plot card," it is readily possible to compute the percent defective and still other features of the lot. A decision to accept or reject the lot can then be made.

The simplified mechanics of predicting the percent defective by making a lot plot of data should not overshadow the valuable information for quality improvement supplied by the histogram plot itself. Analysis of a plot (see Chapter 3) often helps in determining the corrective action needed. For this reason the plot should be discussed with the vendor. Comparisons of lot plots are also revealing, e.g., the plots of several vendors supplying the same part, the plots of one vendor supplying lots periodically, the plots from one vendor before and after material or other design changes, etc.

The lot plot plan was originally developed by Dorian Shainin. Grant and Leavenworth[4] provide a more detailed discussion.

10-6 VERIFICATION OF VENDOR-SUBMITTED DATA

Section 9-12 explains how buyers can achieve economies in incoming inspection by using the vendor's inspection and test data. Such an audit of decisions is often complicated because of sampling variation. Suppose a vendor uses a sampling plan that requires a random sample of 80 from a lot of 1000 units with 2 or fewer defectives allowed in the sample. Now suppose the vendor found 2 defectives in the sample. The lot would be accepted and shipped to the customer. The latter also takes a random sample of 80 but finds 5 defectives and would, therefore, reach a rejection decision. This difference in number of defectives could readily have been the result of sampling variation (see Section 4-3). If so, the vendor results are valid.

Table H in the Appendix provides a table for evaluating the difference in sample results. The table provides critical values at the 5 percent level of statistical significance. In the example above, the ratio of sample sizes is 1.0, while 2 defectives were found in the vendor's sample. The table shows a critical value of 7; i.e., sampling variation could result in as many as 7 defectives even when the two inspection systems are really the same. As the 5 defectives found by the vendor are within the limit of 7, there is not sufficient evidence to doubt the validity of the vendor's inspection for the lot in question.

10-7 PARETO ANALYSIS OF VENDORS

Vendor improvement programs can fail because the vital few problems are not identified and attacked. Instead, the programs consist of broad attempts to tighten up all procedures. The Pareto analysis (see Section 2-5) can be used to identify the problem in a number of forms:

1. Analysis of losses (or defects, lot rejections, etc.) by material number or *part number*. Such analysis serves a useful purpose as applied to catalog numbers involving substantial or frequent purchases.
2. Analysis of losses by *product family*. This identifies the vital few product families present in small but numerous purchases of common product families, e.g., fasteners, resistors, paints.
3. Analysis of losses by *process*, i.e., classifying the defects or lot rejections in terms of the process to which they relate, e.g., plating, swaging, coil winding, etc.

[4] Eugene L. Grant and Richard S. Leavenworth, *Statistical Quality Control*, 4th ed., McGraw-Hill Book Company, New York, 1972, pp. 505–512.

4. Analysis by *vendor* across the entire spectrum of purchases. This can help to identify weaknesses in the vendor's managerial approach as contrasted to the technological, which more usually is correlated with products and processes. In one company there were 222 vendors on the active list. Of these, 38 (or 17 percent) accounted for 53 percent of the lot rejections and 45 percent of the bad parts.
5. Analysis by *cost* of the parts. In one company, 37 percent of the part numbers purchased accounted for only 5 percent of the total dollar volume of purchases, but for a much higher percent of the total incoming inspection cost. The conclusion was that these "trivial many" parts should be purchased from the best vendors, even at top prices. The alternative of relying on incoming inspection would be even more costly.
6. Analysis by *failure mode*. This technique is used to discover major defects in the management *system*. For example, suppose that studies disclose multiple instances of working to the wrong issue of the specification. In such cases, the *system* used for specification revision should be reexamined. If value analysis discovers multiple instances of overspecification, the design *procedures* for choosing components should be reexamined. These analyses by failure mode can reveal how the buyer is contributing to his own problems.

Example A manufacturer[5] of industrial switches and controls had a significant quality problem with purchased printed circuit boards. A study was made of 1092 lots received over 11 months from the 5 vendors supplying the boards. Overall, 45.1 percent of the lots were rejected and this varied, by vendor, from 39.0 percent to 68.8 percent. The cost to process the rejected lots totaled $19,680. A Pareto analysis of the results at receiving inspection is shown in Table 10-2.

Of 27 requirements checked, 7 accounted for 70.4 percent of the defects. For many requirements (e.g., hole size and board dimensions), a large percent of defects were finally accepted as a deviation to the specification. Based on an engineering review certain specifications were changed. The study was instrumental in alerting management on the size of the vendor problem, defining a main cause, and returning product to vendors that was not fit for use.

10-8 QUALITY RATING OF VENDORS

Product quality submitted by vendors has always been evaluated and used as a factor in making purchasing decisions. Recently, the evaluation has been formalized by the use of vendor rating formulas which provide a quantitative

---

[5] Virgil L. Bowers, "Procurement Quality Assurance of PC Boards," *1978 ASQC Annual Technical Conference Transactions*, pp. 69–72.

Table 10-2 Pareto analysis of incoming inspection

	Pareto distribution			Defects accepted under deviation	
Requirement	Number of defects	Percent defective	Cumulative percent	Number accepted	Percent accepted
Hole size	165	19.0	19.0	150	90.9
Board dimensions	110	12.7	31.7	96	87.3
Cond. defects	79	9.1	40.8	23	29.1
Cold thickness	69	8.0	48.8	31	44.9
Plating visual	66	7.6	56.4	31	50.8
Cold visual	61	7.0	63.4	27	44.3
PTH thickness	61	7.0	70.4	10	16.4
20 other	257	29.6	100.0	158	61.4
	868			526	60.6

measure of vendor quality. These ratings are primarily meant to provide comparative measures of overall vendor quality for use in deciding how to allocate purchases among vendors.

To create a single numerical quality score is difficult because there are several units of measure, such as:

1. The quality of multiple lots expressed as lots rejected versus lots inspected.
2. The quality of multiple parts expressed as percent defective.
3. The quality of specific characteristics, expressed in numerous natural units, e.g., ohmic resistance, percent active ingredient, MTBF, etc.
4. The economic consequences of bad quality, expressed in dollars.

Because these units of measure vary in importance among different companies, the published rating schemes differ markedly in emphasis.

Some vendor rating formulas evaluate the vendor on quality alone. In one such plan,[6] the rating is determined by multiplying the percent of defective lots received (for each of three action categories) by a weighting factor. The products are then totaled and subtracted from 100 percent. This is illustrated in Figure 10-3. A rating of 95 through 100 is considered excellent, 90 to 94.9 is acceptable, and below 90 unacceptable.

Vendor performance is, of course, not limited to quality. It includes delivery against schedule, price (or effective price), and still other performance categories. These multiple needs suggest that vendor rating should include overall vendor performance rather than just vendor quality performance. The purchasing department is a strong advocate of this principle and has valid grounds for this advocacy.

[6] Rockwell International (Admiral Group), "Supplier Quality Control Manual," Galesburg, Ill., 1976.

Figure 10-3 Vendor rating example.

Number of lots received during period from vendor: 50

Action on lots	Number of lots	Percent of lots	Weight	Percent × weight
Use "as is"	2	2/50 = 4%	1	4%
Sort/rework	1	1/50 = 2%	5	10%
Reject and return	1	1/50 = 2%	2	4%
				18%

Vendor rating = 100 − 18 = 82%

The purchasing people have themselves been active in creating vendor rating plans which embody these multiple performances of the vendor. The National Association of Purchasing Management has published[7] three alternative plans:

1. *Categorical plan.* This is a nonquantitative evaluation. The buyers meet monthly and rate the vendors as plus, neutral, or minus.
2. *Weighted-point plan.* The three principle vendor performances are rated in accordance with the following plan:

Factor	Unit of measure	Weight
Quality	Percent of lots accepted	40
Cost	Low price ÷ actual price	35
Service	Percent of promises kept	25

Figure 10-4 illustrates this plan.
3. *Cost-ratio plan.* This plan compares vendors on the total dollar cost for a specific purchase. Total costs includes quoted price plus quality costs (defect prevention, detection, and correction) and delivery costs (follow-up and expediting costs). A ratio of these costs to the value of materials purchased is calculated. The supplier technical service capability is also rated numerically but not in cost units.

The extensive literature[8] on vendor quality rating schemes makes clear that differences in products and in purchasing patterns require differences in rating plans. For products whose qualities are clearly identified at incoming inspection, a plan based on summarizing results of incoming inspection is adequate. For purchased components that create substantial excess processing costs, the

[7] *Guide to Purchasing,* National Association of Purchasing Agents, Inc., New York, 1967, sec. 1-6.

[8] For additional vendor quality rating formulas, see *Quality Control Handbook,* 3rd ed., pp. 10-30 to 10-34.

Figure 10-4 Weighted-point plan of vendor rating. (From *Evaluation of Supplier Performance*, National Association of Purchasing Agents, New York, 1964.)

	Supplier A	Supplier B	Supplier C
1 Lots received	60	60	20
2 Lots accepted	54	56	16
3 Percent accepted $\frac{2}{1} \times 100$	90.0	93.3	80.0
4 Quality rating 3×0.40	36.0	37.3	32.0
5 Net price*	0.93	1.12	1.23
6 $\dfrac{\text{Lowest price}\dagger}{\text{Net price}} \times 100$	100	83	76
7 Price rating 6×0.35	35.0	29.1	26.6
8 Delivery promise kept	90%	95%	100%
9 Service rating 8×0.25	22.5	23.8	25.0
10 Total rating $4 + 7 + 9$	93.5	90.2	83.6

*Net price = unit price − discount + transportation.

†Lowest price = minimum net price.

plan should reflect the existence of these costs. For purchased components that affect the buyer's warranty and service costs, the vendor rating plan should (ideally) reflect these field troubles as well.

10-9 USING VENDOR RATINGS

Because we have not yet learned how to reduce all vendor quality data to a single index on which all can agree, it is necessary to use the ratings as a servant and not as a master for decision making. The single index hides important detail; the decision maker should understand what is hidden. The single index, being numerical, has a pseudo-precision, but the decision maker should not be deceived. The decision maker should understand the fringe around the numbers. The purpose should be kept clearly in mind—product rating (for which the specification is usually the standard) should not be confused with vendor rating (for which other vendors may be the standard).

Vendor rating is an important defect prevention device if it is used in an atmosphere of interdependence between vendor and customer (see Chapter 9). This means that the customer must:

1. Make the investment of time, effort, and special skills to help the poor vendors improve.
2. Be willing to change the specification when warranted. In some companies, 20 to 40 percent of rejected purchases can be used without any quality compromise. The customer must search for these situations and change the specifications.

Some organizations use a periodic vendor rating to determine the share of future purchases given to each vendor. The rating system and effect on share of market is fully explained to vendors. The approach has been used successfully by both automotive and appliance manufacturers to highlight the importance of quality to their vendors.

Finally, in the cases of consistently poor vendors who cannot respond to help, the vendor rating highlights them as candidates to be dropped as vendors.

PROBLEMS

10-1 Apply the weighted-point plan of vendor rating (Section 10-8) to compare three vendors for one of the following: (1) any product acceptable to the instructor; (2) an automatic washing machine; (3) a new automobile; (4) a lawn mower.

10-2 Can you think of a situation other than 100 percent screening inspection that would result in the histogram shown in Figure 10-5?

10-3 Can you describe what caused the unusual histogram plots in Figure 10-6?

10-4 You have been asked to propose a specific vendor quality rating procedure for use in one of the following types of organizations: (1) a company acceptable to the instructor; (2) a large municipal government; (3) a manufacturer of plastic toys; (4) a manufacturer of earth-moving equipment; (5) a manufacturer of whiskey. Research the literature for specific procedures and select (or create) a procedure for the organization.

10-5 Visit a local manufacturing organization and learn how it determines the quality of purchased items. Define the specific procedures used and what use is made of the information compiled.

10-6 Outline a potential application of several concepts in this chapter. Follow the instructions given in Problem 7-12.

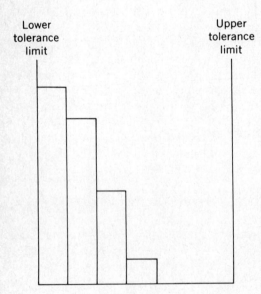

Figure 10-5 Sample histogram.

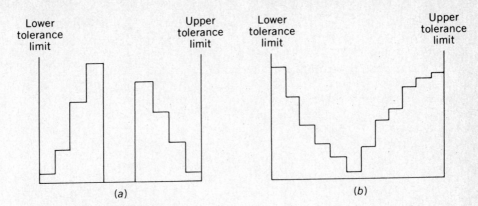

Figure 10-6 Sample histograms.

SUPPLEMENTARY READING

The *Quality Control Handbook*, 3rd ed., McGraw-Hill Book Company, New York, 1974, includes a discussion of vendor relations (sec. 10). In addition, the application of the material to particular industries is included in secs. 29, 30, 37, 42, and 43.

Another source that discusses a wide variety of techniques is *Procurement Quality Control*, 2nd ed., American Society for Quality Control, Milwaukee, Wis., 1976.

ELEVEN

MANUFACTURE

The word *manufacture* as used here includes both planning for manufacture and the subsequent carrying out of the plan, which we will call *production*.

Manufacture is one of the key activities needed to attain fitness for use (see the spiral, Figure 1-1), and numerous safeguards are employed to help assure that the resulting product is indeed fit for use. Designs are reviewed to assure that they are "producible." Process controls help to assure that there will be conformance to the designs. Still other controls minimize the possibility of making defective product inadvertently. In addition, numerous "systems" are used to provide product identity and traceability, prepare documentation, etc.

11-1 MANUFACTURING PLANNING

Manufacturing planning comprises the activities needed to put the factory in a state of readiness to produce to quality and other standards. These activities are listed in Table 11-1, which also shows the usual end result of conducting such activities.

Responsibility for carrying out these planning activities varies widely and depends mainly on:

Technological complexity of the product.
Anatomy of the process; i.e., is it highly concentrated within one autonomous department or is it divided among many departments?

Table 11-1 Manufacturing planning: activities and results

Planning activity	End result of planning
1. Review design for clarity of specifications and for producibility; recommend change	Producible design; revised product specification
2. Choose process for manufacture: operations, sequences	Economic, feasible process; process specification
3. Provide machines and tools capable of meeting tolerances	Capable machines and tools
4. Provide instruments of accuracy adequate to control the process	Capable instrumentation
5. Provide manufacturing information: methods, procedures, cautions	Operation sheets
6. Provide system of quality controls: data collection, feedback, adjustment	Control stations equipped to provide feedback
7. Define responsibilities for quality	Agreed pattern of responsibilities
8. Select and train production personnel	Qualified production operators
9. Prove adequacy of planning; tryouts; trial lots	Proof of adequacy

The technological training of the line supervisors and workers.

The extent of a managerial commitment to the philosophy of separating planning from execution.

In the United States a typical assignment of principal responsibilities for the activities in Table 11-1 would be to staff technical departments (Manufacturing Planning, Process Development, etc.) for activities 1, 2, 3, 4, 5, and 9; to a staff quality control department for activity 6; and to line production supervisors for activities 7 and 8.

The managers of the Manufacturing Planning and Production departments have the responsibility of meeting multiple standards: quality, cost, delivery schedule, factory safety, employee relations, etc. Some of these standards are so critical that companies set up special safeguards to assure that compliance with these critical standards does not suffer from efforts to meet other essential standards. In the case of quality, the manufacturing managers are concerned with the parameter of quality of conformance, and a major responsibility is one of complying with the quality specifications. To safeguard this compliance, companies have established Inspection and Test departments and, more recently, staff quality specialist departments. These latter departments, e.g., Quality Control Engineering, have increasingly become involved in manufacturing planning activities. They often play a leading role in planning the system of process quality controls and in quantifying process capability. They are usually members of the teams who review designs, choose the instrumentation, and plan the trial lots for proving the adequacy of the manufacturing planning activities.

11-2 TOLERANCE REVIEW

An important aspect of manufacturing planning is participation in the design reviews, as discussed in Chapter 7. A major reason for this participation is to assure that the product tolerances and the "process capabilities" (see Section 11-5) are compatible. If the processes are unable to hold the product tolerances, the consequences can be severe. There will be many defects, with associated scrap and rework. There will be inspections to separate good lots from bad and to sort good units of product from bad. There will be nonconforming lots, with associated need for determining their disposition. Some of these nonconforming lots may escape the inspection screen and get out to customers. All this is costly in tangible terms. In addition, there are the intangible costs of the delays, the friction between departments, and still other consequences of asking human beings to achieve a result with inadequate tools.

For most products the number of quality characteristics is very large. As a result, the number of tolerances is also very large. Such large numbers make it uneconomic to review all tolerances individually. Instead, the reviews concentrate on the relatively few tolerances, which are potentially the greatest trouble makers.

Some of the quality characteristics are "functional"; i.e., they are essential to product safety, critical to the users' economics, necessary to make the product marketable, etc. For such cases it is most useful to learn in advance about any inordinately high costs which might be needed to hold the tolerances. Such high costs should be made known to the business departments of the company in view of the implications for pricing and marketing the product.

Most quality characteristics are nonfunctional. However, some of them carry tolerances which may also involve inordinately high costs. The design review is one means of looking for these, through comparing the tolerances with the known process capabilities. Alternatively, the identification may come from past experience with similar designs and tolerances; i.e., such tolerances have generated high internal failure rates, high inspection costs, high vendor costs, etc. It is most helpful if the design review can identify potential recurrences of such difficulties. In some cases the designer will be able to provide relief. In other cases it may be possible to modify the process in ways which make it easier to meet the tolerances economically.

In some companies these design reviews are aided by use of some well-known tools:

1. *Seriousness classification of characteristics.* Such classification is typically into three or four categories, e.g., critical, major, minor, incidental. Availability of such a classification simplifies the job of identifying the vital few tolerances. (For elaboration, see Section 15-4.)
2. *Tables of process capability.* In some companies the accumulated studies of process capability are organized into tables which show, for the prin-

cipal processes, their inherent uniformity.[1] Such tables greatly simplify the job of predicting whether those processes can hold the proposed tolerances.

3. *Charts of cost of precision.* In many companies data are available showing the costs of performing operations at various levels of precision on materials, components, products, etc. Sometimes it is possible to organize these data in ways which show the correlation between precision and cost.[2] Such relationships are of obvious value in tolerance review.

In tolerance review, as in all design review, there are human problems as well as technological problems. A major human problem has been the impact of the concept of design review on the traditional "monopoly" of the designers. Traditionally, they consulted manufacturing planners, etc., only as they felt the need—the choice was with the designers. Under the new concept of mandatory design review the choice is made for the designers—there will be design review, and you will participate. There has been extensive "cultural resistance" to the breaking of this traditional monopoly.[3]

11-3 PROCESS DESIGN; TRYOUTS; FOOLPROOFING; TRACEABILITY

The complexity and volume of modern products usually requires a manufacturing process which is multidepartmental in scope. Design of the physical facilities for this process involves:

1. A *systems design*, which contemplates the entire progression of the product from purchased materials and components through finished goods.
2. A set of designs for the various departmental processes, i.e., *unit processes,* which collectively carry out the broad concept of manufacture. Each unit process, in turn, can consist of multiple *work stations*, each of which carries out one or more production *operations*.

These designs of the physical facilities involve choice of types of machines, equipment, tools, transport, storage, etc. In addition, there are supplementary decisions as to organization of work stations, sequence of operations, limits for process variables, schedules for facilities maintenance, etc. These decisions are almost always recorded in a formal planning document known as Master Route Sheet, Operation Sheet, etc. In many companies the leading role in designing

[1] For an example, see *Quality Control Handbook,* 3rd ed., p. 9-8, table 9-2.
[2] For an example, see *Quality Control Handbook,* 3rd ed., p. 9-7, fig. 9-4.
[3] For added discussion, see *Quality Control Handbook,* 3rd ed., pp. 8-7 to 8-9; also p. 8-64, "Cultural Resistance of Designers."

these physical facilities is played by specialized departments such as Manufacturing Engineering or Process Development.

Beyond the design of the physical facilities are the designs of the quality controls. These likewise involve a system design of a multidepartmental nature plus designs for the unit processes. The details of these designs deal with such matters as standardization of methods of inspection and test; choice of instruments and test equipment; schedules for extent and frequency of test; data recording and analysis systems for process control and product evaluation; audits to provide assurances or alarms with respect to the continuing effectiveness of the quality controls. In many companies the leading role in designing these quality controls is played by a specialized department such as Quality Control Engineering.

These two designs—the physical facilities and the quality controls—must of course be well coordinated. To this end, use is made of a number of quality control concepts which have demonstrated their applicability to a wide variety of products and processes. (Some of these same concepts are also of aid in planning for high productivity, prompt delivery, etc.)

At both the unit process level and the system level, wide use is made of the concept of "tryout." Under this concept, provision is made at the unit process level to test new machines and tools to see if they can meet the quality standards for the process and product. It is quite common for the planning schedules to provide for securing early deliveries of materials specifically to make such tryouts possible.

At the system level a major form of tryout is the "preproduction lot." Ideally, such a lot is processed through the entire system with associated evaluation of quality, productivity, etc. Changes are then made in the light of this evaluation so that the system will be improved before all concerned become preoccupied with full-scale production. In practice, the urge to go to market promptly can force compromises with this ideal unless the newness of the product poses a severe risk of wide exposure to unknown levels of field failures.

In some companies the transfer of responsibility from Process Development to Manufacture is formalized through a "Release to Manufacture" document. Completion of this formality is then made contingent on the results of the trial lots along with follow-through to make the indicated needed changes.

Foolproofing

Well-designed manufacturing processes may nevertheless result in some degree of defective product due to human fallibility in operating or maintaining the process. When the resulting defects are not critical to human safety or to the ability to sell the product, the solution may be purely one of factory economics—inspect the product 100 percent or pay for the consequences of shipping the defects. However, when the defects are critical to human safety, inspecting the product may be an inadequate solution since human inspection is also fallible. (Human inspectors will typically find 80 percent of the defects present but will miss the remaining 20 percent.) Instead, resort must be had to "foolproofing" the process or to nonhuman sorting of the product.

A widely used form of foolproofing is through design (or redesign) of the machines and tools (the "hardware") so as to make human error improbable or even impossible. For example, components and tools may be designed with lugs and notches to achieve a key-and-lock effect, which makes it impossible to misassemble. Tools may be designed to sense automatically the presence and correctness of prior operations or to stop the process on sensing depletion of the material supply. For example, in the textile industry a break in the thread releases a spring-loaded device which stops the machine. Protective systems, e.g., fire detection, can be designed to "fail safe" and to sound alarms as well as all-clear signals.

The second major form of foolproofing is through redundancy—to require multiple improbable events to occur simultaneously before a defect can be made or can escape. Important process setups typically require multiple approval. For example, the weighing out of the ingredients for a pharmaceutical batch must be done independently by each of two registered pharmacists. Look-alike products may bear multiple identity codes (numbers, colors, shapes, etc.). Automated 100 percent testing may be superimposed on the process controls. The "countdown" so well dramatized during the prelaunch phases of a space vehicle is also a form of redundancy.

A third approach is one of aiding human beings to reduce their fallibility. Some of this involves magnifying the natural human muscles and senses through programmed indexing of fixtures, optical magnification, viewing through closed-circuit television, simultaneous signals to multiple senses, etc. For example, ampoules of medicine are dumped into a dye bath and left there overnight to simplify the discovery of cracks in the glass. Even in the review of documents there has recently emerged an awareness that there are two kinds of review—active and passive. The former requires so positive a participation, e.g., reading a number out loud, that full attention is indispensable. The passive review, e.g., silently looking or listening, does not make full attention indispensable.

Finally, some foolproofing is done by eliminating error-prone elements in the basic system design. Some aircraft have been lost due to easy-to-misread altimeters. Other disasters have taken place because the knobs on control levers were look-alikes or feel-alikes. Good planning includes review of prior failure modes to detect such error-prone systems. For example, a study of damage due to dropping of expensive electronic equipment found solutions through such changes as: reducing the number of handlings, reducing traffic congestion, improving containers and transport vehicles, provision and redesign of handles, etc.[4]

[4] Lynn V. Rigby, "Why Do People Drop Things?" *Quality Progress*, September 1973, pp. 16–19.

Traceability

A further need in process planning is to provide *traceability* so that the product and its origins ("genealogy") can be mutually identified. This traceability is needed for many reasons: to assure lot uniformity in products such as pharmaceuticals; to avoid mixup of look-alike products; to aid in proper sequential usage of perishable materials; to simplify investigation of product failures; to minimize the extent of product recalls.

Attaining complete traceability for complex products (made of many materials and components and employing numerous processes) can be a formidable job, involving extensive paperwork, records, bonded stock rooms, physical markings on the products, etc. Yet this is actually done for many products in the drug, aerospace, and nuclear industries.

In commercial products complete traceability is limited to safety-oriented qualities and to those components which are decisive in achieving overall fitness for use. For example, in one semiconductor product line the component chiefly responsible for final product quality was the semiconducting wafer. The company therefore structured the traceability system around the wafer lot numbers. The finished products were then coded with the wafer lot number rather than with a weekly dating code, which might involve the same code number for products made from multiple wafer lots.[5]

11-4 PLANNING PROCESS CONTROLS: FLOWCHARTS; DOMINANCE

Most process controls take place at the unit process level, and are planned to meet the needs of specific unit processes and operations. Some of these process controls are designed to be carried out at the work stations by the production work force. Other controls are designed to be exercised at separate "control stations" which are usually a part of the Quality Control Department. Still other controls may be exercised by laboratories or specialists who are not a part of the factory organization.

Flowcharts

For complex products it is useful to prepare a *flowchart* depicting how the streams of materials move and converge during the processing stages. Such a flowchart makes it easier for all concerned to understand the system design and thereby makes it easier to identify and agree on the logical places to locate the control stations. Figure 11-1 is an example of such a flowchart as applied to the manufacture of refrigerator cabinets.

---

[5] Richard A. Staffiery, "A Semiconductor Traceability Plan That Avoids Confusion," *Quality Management and Engineering*, April 1975, pp. 20, 21.

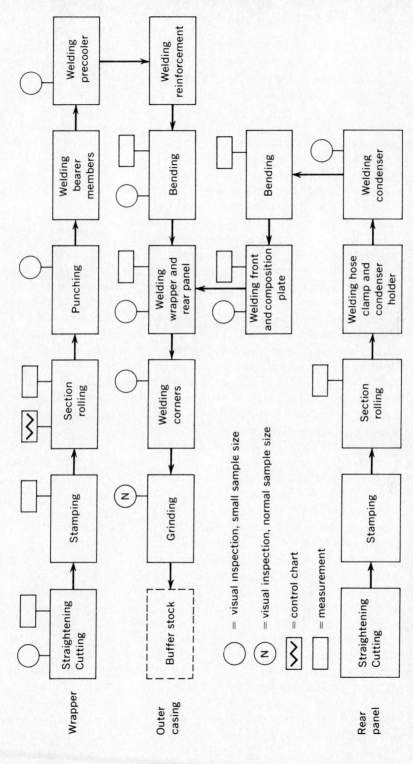

Figure 11-1 Flowchart showing control stations in manufacturing of refrigerator cabinets. (From L. Sandholm, "Program to Reduce the Need for Servicing Domestic Appliances," First Scandinavian Conference on Quality and Reliability, Gothenburg, Sweden, May 22–28, 1968.)

Dominance

Processes exhibit numerous variables, but these are not equally important. Often one variable "dominates," and as a result the planning activity emphasizes that dominant variable. In manufacturing planning there are several forms of dominance which occur over and over again:

1. *Setup-dominant.* The process is so highly reproducible that if the setup is correct the lot will be correct. Hence the process controls formalize the procedure for creating and verifying the setup.
2. *Machine-dominant.* The process is "instantaneously uniform" but has an inherent rate of change with the passing of time, e.g., wear of tools, depletion of reagents. The process controls therefore emphasize sampling on a scheduled basis and resetting the process to compensate for the drift.
3. *Operator-dominant.* The process is not fully engineered and hence much depends on the skill of the workers. The process controls emphasize keeping data on operator performance, analysis to discover the "knack" which gives some workers consistent superiority, and foolproofing the operations against operator errors.
4. *Component-dominant.* The quality of the final product depends to a large degree on the quality of purchased components. Now the process controls emphasize component quality and failure-rate data collection, plus feedback, to improve vendor selection and performance.
5. *Information-dominant.* In some types of job shop manufacture, it is essential that all departments understand with precision just how this customer's order differs from all previous orders. Hence the process controls emphasize foolproofing of transmission of the customer order information.

11-5 PROCESS CAPABILITY

In planning the quality aspects of manufacture nothing is more important than advance assurance that the processes will be able to hold the tolerances. Until our century this prediction was derived from empirical or indirect means to an extent such that there was little true prediction prior to actual tryout. In recent decades there has emerged a concept of *process capability* which provides a quantified prediction of process adequacy. This ability to predict quantitatively has resulted in widespread adoption of the concept as a major element of quality planning.

Process capability is a measure of the inherent uniformity of the process. Normally, it is not feasible to determine this process capability by direct measurements on the process under operating conditions. What is done instead is to measure the process indirectly by measuring the *product* uniformity.

Example An example is shown in Figure 11-2. In this company the turning operations on the screw machines, making tiny watch parts, are of great im-

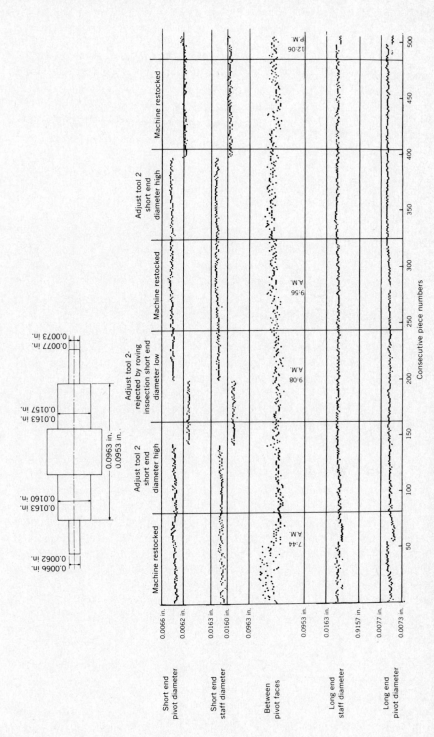

Figure 11-2 Process capability study of automatic screw machine.

273

portance. A study was conducted of the capability of one of the screw machines. The machine was studied for several hours, the personnel on the job having been asked to follow their usual practices. A diary, or "log," was kept of the actual happenings on the job. Meanwhile, the order of the pieces was carefully preserved so that the 500 pieces shown on the chart are in the actual manufacturing sequence. Then the pieces were carefully measured for each of the five critical dimensions, using a very precise gage. These 2500 observations are shown on the chart, together with the log of what transpired during the day. The disclosures of the chart are many:

1. Progressive changes in diameter were very slight. During the run of 500 pieces, the average diameter changed about 0.0001 in, this being about a third of the narrowest tolerance range. This uniformity exceeded the expectations of most of the supervisors.
2. Changes caused by restocking the machine were less than expected, and of short duration. Note the effect of pieces no. 55 and no. 493. The effect at piece no. 271 is negligible.
3. The operators' gages were inadequate to "steer" the machines. Note at piece no. 140 how both short-end diameters dropped suddenly (these diameters are controlled by a single toolholder). The explanation was that the operator, from his gage, had concluded that the parts were becoming oversize and had adjusted the machine downward. At piece no. 197 he restored the adjustment following a check by the patrol inspector. At piece no. 392 the operator was again misled by his gage.
4. The machine capability for the pivot-shoulder distance was easily adequate. (The greater variability of the first 50 parts was due to the investigator's unfamiliarity with the precise gage.)

From these disclosures, the supervisors concluded that (1) the process was uniform enough for the job, (2) the gages were inadequate for the job, (3) it was possible to make more pieces with less frequent adjustment and with less frequent checking than had been realized, and (4) a number of other beliefs were unfounded. By providing better gages and by periodic measurement at the machines, the company reduced the level of defects in this department substantially, while also increasing production. An associated detailed gaging could thereupon be minimized. The consequence was a better product at substantially lower cost.

The example above shows how it is possible, by measurements on the product, to discover:

1. The natural or inherent variability of the process, i.e., the "instantaneous reproducibility."
2. The time-to-time variability.

Both of these forms of variability can be quantified in statistical terms, and this quantification is discussed in Chapter 12.

The example above also suggests the multiple purposes to which these capabilities can be put to use:

1. To predict the extent to which the process will be able to hold tolerances.
2. To choose from among competing processes that which is most appropriate for the tolerances to be met.
3. To plan the interrelation of sequential processes. For example, one process may distort the precision achieved by a predecessor process, as in hardening of gear teeth. Quantifying the respective process capabilities often points the way to a solution.
4. To provide a quantified basis for establishing a schedule of periodic process control checks and readjustments.
5. To assign machines to classes of work for which they are best suited.
6. To test theories of causes of defects during quality improvement programs.
7. To serve as a basis for specifying the quality performance requirements for purchased machines.

These are worthwhile purposes and account for the growing use of the process capability concept.

11-6 THE CONTROL STATION

The control station differs from the work station in several important respects.

1. The work station is concerned with multiple performance parameters: quality, productivity, delivery rate, etc. The control station is concerned primarily with the parameter of quality.
2. The quality-oriented decisions of the work station are primarily directed at the question: Should the process continue to run, or undergo adjustment, or stop? The quality-oriented decisions of the control station are directed mainly at the question: Does the product conform to specification?
3. To make its process decisions the work station uses its observations of the process plus data acquired from process instruments and from measurements on the product. Some of these product measurements come from the control stations, which in addition make the supplemental measurements needed for the product conformance decision.
4. The personnel at the work station are normally responsible to the Production Department; the personnel at the control station are normally responsible to the Quality Control Department.

The extensive use of separate control stations is due to two main reasons:

1. For some critical characteristics it is not economic or even technologically possible for the work stations to measure the product and make product conformance decisions.
2. Experience has shown that in complex product manufacture involving critical qualities, it is too risky to rely solely on the work stations to assure product conformance. Hence a separate control station is superimposed as an added form of assurance of product quality.

Planning for the control stations follows a sequence quite similar to that followed in planning for the work stations. The flowchart is prepared and agreement is reached on where to locate the control stations. Analysis is then made to determine what tasks are to be carried out at each control station. Figure 11-3 shows an example of a formal control plan as established for one of the control stations in the refrigerator cabinet plant. Such plans always list the quality characteristics to be controlled, the tolerances to be observed, the instruments to be used, and the sampling plans to be followed. The control plans sometimes include the types of data to be recorded, cautions to be observed, supplemental surveillance over the process, etc.

11-7 DESIGN OF THE FEEDBACK LOOP

All control systems embody a feedback of information from "sensor" to "effector." The sensor is any means of evaluating actual performance, e.g., a production worker, an inspector, an automated instrument. The effector is any means of taking action on the information (closing the feedback loop), e.g., a production worker, an automated mechanism. Figure 11-4 shows the schematic of the feedback loop as applied to quality generally.

At the operation and unit process level, the feedback loop may be designed on any of several bases:

1. *Automated control.* In such cases the feedback loop is closed without human intervention (see Section 11-8).
2. *Operator self-control.* Here the worker personally observes or measures and then takes action in the light of the information (see Chapter 13).
3. *Feedback of inspection data.* Here the measurements are made by inspectors, who give the information to the workers, who then close the loop (see Chapter 13).

Choice among these (or even more elaborate loops) is a unique decision for each process depending on such variables as complexity of the technology, extent of worker education and training, state of mutual confidence between managers and workers, economics of automation, etc.

Part name Casing	Part No. 200 10 68	Dwg. index 1	Rev. 1
Intended for Bending of outer casing	Insp. group alt. op. KAT	Date issued 10/10/70	Issued by RZ
Item No.	Characteristic	Inspection method	Sample size
1.1	Corner cut undamaged	Visual inspection	5 per day
1.2	Corner cut slit not exceeding 0.5 mm	Visual inspection	
1.3	Tube holders intact close to bending points	Visual inspection	
1.4	Height 1190 ± 1, 1490 ± 1, 1690 ± 1	Steel measuring tape	
1.5	Width 595 ± 0.5. 800 ± 0.5	Sliding caliper	
1.6	Lower hinge hole position 1106, 1406, 1606 ± 1	Steel measuring tape	
1.7	Intermediate bearer member position 800.5 ± 0.5 or 300.5 ± 0.5, 38.8 ± 0.5, 16.4	Fixture V-41071	
1.8	35 ± 0.5	Sliding caliper	
1.9	Tube flattening in bending minute 5.5	Sliding caliper	

Figure 11-3 Example of a control plan for a control station. (From L. Sandholm, "Program to Reduce the Need for Servicing Domestic Appliances," First Scandinavian Conference on Quality and Reliability, Gothenburg, Sweden, May 22–28, 1968.)

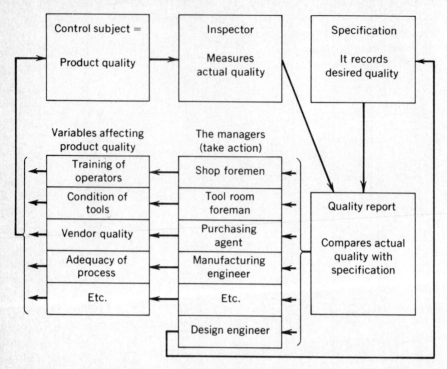

Figure 11-4 Servomechanism diagram for quality control. (Adapted from those first published in J. M. Juran, "Universals in Management Planning and Control," *The Management Review,* November 1954, pp. 748–761.)

11-8 AUTOMATIC PROCESS REGULATION

There are two basic designs of automated control. In the analog design the sensor creates action without the need for creating intervening information. In the flyball governor mechanism, the speed of rotation is converted directly into a motion of the control valves. In the automated centerless grinder, the attainment of the desired dimension shuts off any further grinding. The analog design is quite simple, but it is also limited to the performance of that simple task.

In the digital design, the sensor creates information, not action. The information must then be processed before the feedback loop can be closed. A widespread example is the computer-controlled process. This separation of information and analysis from action provides a wider range of possible actions, such as:

Make decisions on whether the product conforms to specification.
Adjust the process to restore conformance.
Stop the process if conformance cannot be restored.
Sound the alarm to secure human assistance.

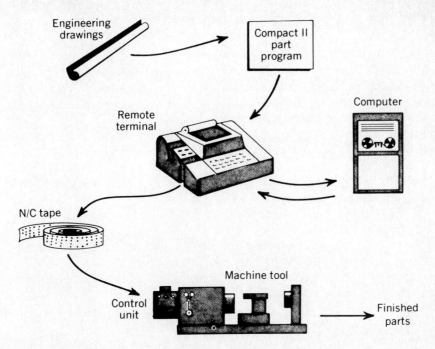

Figure 11-5 Schematic of operation for numerically controlled (N/C) machine. (From John A. Silva, "Computer Assisted N/C Programming," *Industrial Engineering,* April 1973, p. 16.)

Analyze for causes of nonconformance and provide the results to the process regulators.

Summarize the data and prepare reports for managerial control.

At the operation level, these automated designs can be comparatively simple. (Some are not simple at all.) At the unit process and system level, the designs grow in complexity, and demand extensive coordination among:

The processing machines, tools, and equipment, along with their controlling mechanisms.

The instruments that sense the process variables and product characteristics.

The computer hardware (the computer itself with its peripheral equipment).

The computer programs which receive the inputs and close the feedback loop by issuing the commands to the effector mechanisms.

Figure 11-5 is a schematic showing one form of automatic process regulation—the numerically controlled (N/C) machine.[6]

---

[6] From John A. Silva, "Computer Assisted N/C Programming," *Industrial Engineering,* April 1973, pp. 16–18.

11-9 QUALITY PLANNING IN SERVICE INDUSTRIES

The service industries' equivalent of "manufacture" is usually the term "operations"—running the trains, preparing and serving the restaurant meals, etc. These operations are planned at several levels—system, unit process, and operation. (In large companies the resulting plans are written out and published as "product" and process specifications.)

Operations planning for the service industries differs from manufacturing planning for the manufacturing industries in several important respects:

The planning is to a high degree done by the line managers, with relatively less use of full-time staff planners.

Extensive use is made of planning contributed by vendors—suppliers of equipment, systems, materials.

With a lower availability of specialized planners, less use is made of various planning techniques of the sort discussed in this chapter.

The line managers in the service industries have the advantage of much direct feedback of fitness for use since the service industries sell extensively to the ultimate consumer.

Carrying out the plans is of course a line function, as it is in manufacturing industries. However, the check on whether there is conformance with specifications is generally done by the work force itself and by the line supervision. In contrast, such checking in manufacturing industries is to a significant degree supplemented by a separate Quality Control Department. As a corollary, the creation of quality data systems and use of such data for control and improvement is still in the early stages of development in the service industries.

PROBLEMS

11-1 For any manufacturing process acceptable to the instructor, prepare a plan for attaining and controlling quality during manufacture, including flow diagram, selection of control stations, definition of work to be performed at each control station, and criteria to be used.

11-2 For any manufacturing process acceptable to the instructor, prepare an analysis of the foolproofing which has been built into the planning, including your ideas for improving the foolproofing.

11-3 For any product acceptable to the instructor, prepare an analysis of the system of traceability employed.

11-4 Visit a local manufacturing company and identify the departments that have the principal and collateral responsibilities for carrying out the planning activities set out in Table 11-1.

11-5 For any process to which you can gain ready access, determine what form of "dominance" constitutes the major variable affecting attainment of quality.

11-6 Speak with several designers in your company and find out from each their approach to setting tolerances for quality characteristics. Summarize your findings and make recommendations.

SUPPLEMENTARY READING

The "industry" sections of *Quality Control Handbook*, 3rd ed. (QCH3), McGraw-Hill Book Company, New York, 1974, contain much case material on manufacture. Each of these sections shows the approach to process control planning for its specific industry, process, or product. In addition, there is case material for specialized topics, as follows:

Topic	Sections in QCH3
Process development	29, 34, 35, 36A, 42
Flow diagrams	29, 32, 33, 35, 37, 39, 43
Process capability	34, 35, 43
Trial lots	33, 35, 42, 43, 44
Traceability	32, 33, 35, 38

Some added references include:

Tolerance review: QCH3, pp. 9-6, 9-7
Process design: QCH3, pp. 9-9 to 9-11
Foolproofing: QCH3, pp. 9-39 to 9-41
Traceability: QCH3, pp. 9-41, 9-42
Dominance: QCH3, pp. 9-11 to 9-14
Process capability: QCH3, pp. 9-14 to 9-39; "A Guide to Process Capability Analysis," published jointly by the Institution of Production Engineers and The Institute of Quality Assurance, London.
The feedback loop: J. M. Juran, *Managerial Breakthrough*, McGraw-Hill Book Company, New York, 1964, chap. 12.
Automatic process regulation: QCH3, pp. 9-48 to 9-51; P. A. McKeown, "The Place of Quality Control in Automated Manufacturing," *Quality Assurance*, December 1977, pp. 109–115.

EXAMPLES OF EXAMINATION QUESTIONS USED IN FORMER ASQC QUALITY ENGINEER CERTIFICATION EXAMINATIONS AS PUBLISHED IN *QUALITY PROGRESS* MAGAZINE

1 In recent months, several quality problems have resulted from apparent change in design specifications by engineering, including material substitutions. This has only come to light through Quality Engineering's failure-analysis system. You recommend which of the following quality system provisions as the best corrective action? (*a*) establishing a formal procedure for initial design review; (*b*) establishing a formal procedure for process control; (*c*) establishing a formal procedure for specification change control (sometimes called an ECO or SCO system); (*d*) establishing a formal system for drawing and print control; (*e*) establishing a formal material review (MRB) system.

2 When a quality engineer wants parts removed from a line which is operating for tolerance checking, he or she should: (*a*) request the operator and/or supervisor to get them while being observed; (*b*) request the operator and/or supervisor to sample the line and bring them to the engineer's office; (*c*) get the samples personally without notifying either the operator and/or supervisor; (*d*) go out to the line, stop it, take the part, start it, and leave as quickly as possible.

3 The quality engineer should be concerned with the human factors of a new piece of in-house manufacturing equipment as well as its operational effects because it: (*a*) may speed the line to the point where a visual operator inspection is impossible; (*b*) may require the operator's undivided attention at the controls so the product cannot be fully seen; (*c*) may remove an operator formerly devoting some portion of time to inspection; (*d*) all of the above.

TWELVE

MANUFACTURE—STATISTICAL AIDS

12-1 THE ROLE OF STATISTICAL TOOLS IN MANUFACTURING PLANNING

Statistical tools can be helpful prior to manufacturing by analyzing data to quantify process variation and compare the variation to engineering tolerance limits (a "process capability" study). In addition, the tools can be used to evaluate proposed tolerance limits on several interacting characteristics to assure that the manufacturing function is permitted the maximum possible variation consistent with overall product requirements.

This chapter discusses process capability and the statistical analysis of data for both individual and interacting dimensions.

12-2 STATISTICAL APPROACHES TO PROCESS CAPABILITY

Chapter 11 introduced the concept of process capability as a measure of the inherent uniformity of a manufacturing process. The measure is useful in evaluating new equipment, reviewing tolerances, assigning equipment to product, and planning process control checks and adjustments during manufacture. Chapter 11 also presented a process capability study in which 500 consecutive units of a watch part were plotted, in their order of production, against tolerance limits. This simple plot of individual units against tolerance limits, with *no* statistical analysis, is sometimes sufficient to draw conclusions. At other times, however, statistical techniques are often required and include:

1. Frequency distribution.
2. Probability paper.
3. Control chart.
4. Advanced techniques.

These techniques will be covered shortly.

Prior to data collection, the following steps should be taken:

1. *Choose the machine(s) to be used to establish capability.* If the results of a study on one screw machine are to be used to define capability of all screw machines of that type, the machine selected must be representative of that type. In addition, a "machine" may actually consist of several machines within it, i.e., a machine with multiple spindles often shows different results for supposedly identical spindles. In such cases the study should quantify the spindle to spindle variation.
2. *Define the process conditions.* For mechanical processes, conditions will include machine feeds, speeds, coolant, fixtures, cycle time, and any other aspect that could influence the final dimension. For a chemical process, examples of conditions are temperature and pressure. Process capability numbers are meaningless unless they are related to a defined set of conditions that will repeat in the future.
3. *Select a representative productive operator.* Where variability depends mainly on the operator, the study may really be one of operator variability.
4. *Provide sufficient raw material for uninterrupted study.* A sample of about 50 units is preferred. Smaller samples are sometimes necessary, but they may not clearly show the statistical distribution of the characteristic under study.
5. *Provide adequate gaging and a defined measurement method.*
6. *Make provisions for keeping track of the order in which the units are made.*

12-3 PROCESS CAPABILITY ANALYSIS USING A FREQUENCY DISTRIBUTION AND HISTOGRAM

A sample of about 50 consecutive units is taken, during which time no adjustments are made on the machines or tools. The units are all measured, the data are tallied in frequency distribution form, and the standard deviation calculated and used as an estimate of σ. The characteristic is assumed to follow a normal probability distribution where ± 3 standard deviations includes 99.73 percent of the population (these matters are discussed in Chapter 3). The process capability is then defined as $\pm 3\sigma$ or 6σ.

The process capability is a measure of the inherent variability of the process. The planner must relate this capability to the tolerance. Usually, he or she does this by an index known as the *capability ratio*:

$$\text{Capability ratio} = \frac{6\sigma \text{ variation}}{\text{total tolerance}}$$

Some companies use as a rule of thumb for adequacy the following maxima for the capability ratio:

	Bilateral tolerance %	Unilateral tolerance %
Existing processes	75	88
New processes	67	83

Thus a dimension with a bilateral tolerance should be assigned to an existing process having process variation of less than 75 percent of the tolerance range. For a unilateral tolerance, e.g., a maximum-only tolerance, the value of $\bar{X} + 3\sigma$ should be less than 88 percent of the tolerance limit. Such rules of thumb stem from the histogram approach discussed in Section 3-4.

For example, the histogram for a sample of 60 measurements is shown in Figure 12-1 (machine N-5). Analysis of the 60 measurements yielded:

$$\bar{X} = 9.6 \qquad s = 2.5$$

The process capability is calculated as $\pm 3(2.5)$ or ± 7.5, or a total of 15.0. The product has a specification of 0.258 ± 0.005. The data have been recorded in units of 0.001 in above 0.250 and thus the tolerance limits (LTL and UTL) are indicated as 3 and 13, or a tolerance of 10.0. This tolerance is narrower than the process capability of 15.0. Hence the process is not capable of meeting the tolerance. Using the rule of thumb for bilateral tolerances on an existing process, this machine should only be assigned to parts with a total tolerance of 20.0 or a bilateral tolerance of ± 10.0. Note that the process capability is a property of

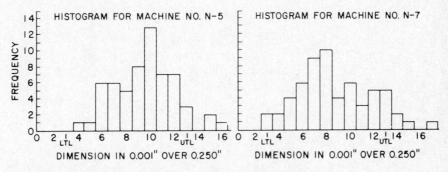

Figure 12-1 Two machines with similar frequency distributions.

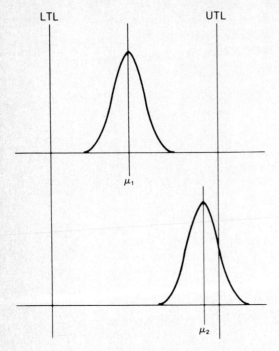

LTL   UTL

μ_1

μ_2

Figure 12-2 Processes with equal process capability but different aim.

the process and is independent of the tolerance (the process does not know what is the tolerance).

The process capability refers to the *variation* in a process about some aim. This is illustrated in Figure 12-2. The two processes have equal capabilities because 6σ is the same for the two, as indicated by the widths of the distribution curves. The process aimed at μ_2 is producing defectives because the aim is off center, not because of the inherent variation about the aim (i.e., the capability).

Defining process capability as $\pm 3\sigma$ is in common use. The concept of a statistical distribution in describing process variation is far superior to nonstatistical approaches, but the assumptions involved need to be recognized:

1. *The characteristic follows a normal probability distribution.* This is often the case, but it is not universally true. For example, dimensions that are close to a physical limit, such as the amount "out of round" (where a value of zero is desired), tend to show "skewed" distributions. In such cases, $\pm 3\sigma$ does not include 99.73 percent of the population. However, it is possible to use special probability tables to derive a measure of process capability.
2. *The process is operating with its minimum possible variation.* The word "capability" implies best potential and a frequency distribution and histogram *cannot* evaluate whether the process is operating with minimum

variation. The answer to this situation is the control chart discussed later in this chapter.

3. The effect of tool wear or other time-dependent parameters is not included. This will be covered later in the chapter.

12-4 PROCESS CAPABILITY ANALYSIS USING PROBABILITY PAPER

The use of probability paper was introduced in Section 3-10. Probability paper can also be used to determine process capability—without any calculation of the standard deviation.

An example on a shaft diameter is shown in Figure 12-3.[1] Here probability paper for the normal distribution is used, but the procedure for plotting the data is identical to that described in Chapter 3 for the Weibull distribution. The points are plotted and can be approximated by a single straight line (indicating that the population is normally distributed). The line is then extended to the upper and lower horizontal lines on the grid. These lines represent probabilities of 99.86 and 0.13 percent, respectively, or a difference of 99.73 percent. Thus 99.73 percent of the population will have diameters between 0.9965 and 1.0115 or a process capability of 0.015. This yields a capability ratio of 0.015/0.020, or 75 percent. Also, note how the plot predicts that about 1 percent of the diameters will be above the upper tolerance limit. Process capability is not the problem—the process aim is too high.

The probability-paper approach has a few advantages. The term "standard deviation" (still a mystery to most people even after it is explained) is avoided. The plot provides an approximate test of normality. When data are limited, the probability-paper plot may be more valuable than comparing a histogram to the theoretical "bell shape" because small samples frequently yield histograms having many peaks and valleys, making it difficult to judge the underlying shape. Finally, Weibull probability paper could be used to care for skewed or other unusual distributions.

12-5 PROCESS CAPABILITY ANALYSIS USING CONTROL CHARTS

Process capability based on $\pm 3\sigma$ from a histogram or probability-paper analysis represents the *performance* but not necessarily the full *potential* capability of the process. This can occur if the data include measurements from several populations, such as different machine settings or different stations on the same machine (i.e., supposedly identical cutting tools on a metal cutting machine or filling heads on a food packaging machine). In addition, there may be other

---

[1] "Reliability Methods, Module No. II," p. 13, Ford Motor Company, January 1972.

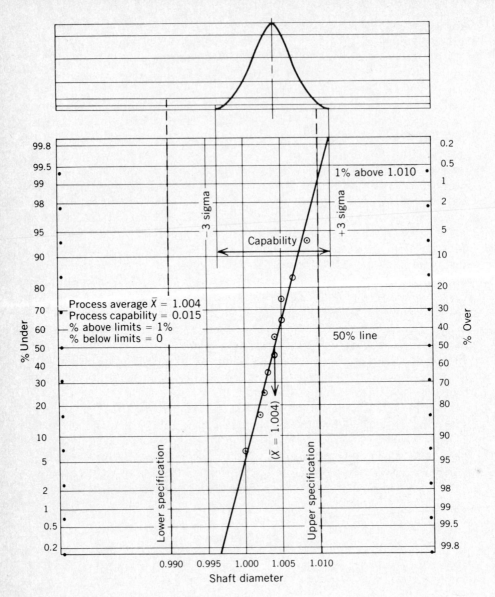

Figure 12-3 Solution of sample problem.

sources of variation, such as within the sample, sample to sample, time to time, or unusual causes that result in an unstable process. This leads to the need for a more powerful analysis tool—the control chart.

A *control chart* is a graphic comparison of process performance data to computed "control limits" drawn as limit lines on the chart. The process performance data usually consist of groups of measurements ("rational subgroups") selected in regular sequence of production while preserving the order.

A prime use of the control chart is to detect *assignable causes* of variation in the process. The term "assignable causes" has a special meaning, and it is essential to understand this meaning in order to understand the control-chart concept (see Table 12-1).

Process variations are traceable to two kinds of causes: (1) random, i.e., due solely to chance, and (2) assignable, i.e., due to specific "findable" causes. Ideally, only random causes should be present in a process, because this represents the minimum possible amount of variation. A process that is operating without assignable causes of variation is said to be "in a state of statistical control," which is usually abbreviated to "in control." As a state of control means minimum possible process variation, a control-chart analysis should be made and assignable causes eliminated from the process prior to calculating 6σ as a measure of process capability. When this is done, 6σ then represents the true inherent process capability. If 6σ is calculated without first making a control-chart analysis, the 6σ will probably be inflated because many control-chart

Table 12-1 Distinction between random and assignable causes of variation

Random (chance) causes	Assignable causes
Description	
Consists of many individual causes	Consists of one or just a few individual causes
Any one random cause results in a minute amount of variation (but many random causes act together to yield a substantial total)	Any one assignable cause can result in a large amount of variation
Examples are human variation in setting control dials; slight vibration in machines; slight variation in raw material	Examples are operator blunder, a faulty setup, or a batch of defective raw material
Interpretation	
Random variation cannot economically be eliminated from a process	Assignable variation can be detected; action to eliminate the causes is usually economically justified
When only random variation is present, the process is operating at its best; if defectives are still being produced, a basic process change must be made or the specifications revised in order to reduce the defectives	If assignable variation is present, the process is not operating at its best
An observation within the control limits of random variation means the process should not be adjusted	An observation beyond control limits usually means the process should be investigated and corrected
With only random variation, the process is sufficiently stable to use sampling procedures to predict the quality of total production or make process optimization studies (e.g., EVOP—see p. 297)	With assignable variation present, the process is not sufficiently stable to use sampling procedures for prediction

analyses reveal the presence of assignable causes even though production people profess that the process is operating with the minimum possible variation.

The control chart distinguishes between random and assignable causes of variation through its choice of the control limits. These are calculated from the laws of probability in such a way that highly improbable random variations are presumed to be due not to random causes, but to assignable causes. When the actual variation exceeds the control limits, it is a signal that assignable causes entered the process and the process should be investigated. Variation within the control limits means that only random causes are present and the process should be left alone. Each point on a control chart represents a test of hypothesis (see Section 4-7), but the chart simplifies the calculations and presents a graphic method for doing hypothesis testing continuously.

Control charts may be classified by the characteristic being tested:

1. The average of the measurements in the sample. This is known as an $\bar{X}$ *chart*. Averages are used because they are more sensitive to change than individual values. The average measures the *aim* or centering of a process.
2. The range of the measurements in the sample. This is known as an *R chart*. The range measures variability about the aim of the process.
3. The percent defective in the sample. This is known as a *p chart*.
4. The number of defects in the sample. This is known as a *c chart*.

There are many variations of these four basic charts. The $\bar{X}$ and *R* charts will be discussed in this chapter because of the tie-in to process capability. The *p* and *c* charts are covered in Chapter 14.

The control chart was invented by Walter A. Shewhart in 1924.[2] A complete discussion of various control charts is given by Grant and Leavenworth[3] and ASTM.[4]

12-6 ESTABLISHING AN $\bar{X}$ AND *R* CONTROL CHART

A small sample (e.g., 5 units) is taken periodically from the process, and the average ($\bar{X}$) and range (*R*) are calculated for each sample. A total of at least 50 individual measurements (e.g., 10 samples of 5 each) should be collected before the control limits are calculated. The control limits are set at $\pm 3\sigma$ for sample averages and sample ranges. The $\bar{X}$ and *R* values are plotted on separate charts against their $\pm 3\sigma$ limits.

[2] W. A. Shewhart, *The Economics of Control of Quality of Manufactured Product*, D. Van Nostrand Company, Inc., New York, 1931.

[3] E. L. Grant and R. S. Leavenworth, *Statistical Quality Control*, 4th ed., McGraw-Hill Book Company, New York, 1972.

[4] *ASTM Manual on Presentation of Data and Control Chart Analysis STP15D*, American Society for Testing and Materials, Philadelphia, 1976.

Methods have been developed to simplify the calculations by eliminating the need to calculate standard deviations. Standard deviations are readily computed by modern calculators, but calculations can be avoided by using shortcuts.

The shortcut formulas for the control limits on sample averages are

$$\text{Upper control limit} = \bar{\bar{X}} + A_2\bar{R}$$

$$\text{Lower control limit} = \bar{\bar{X}} - A_2\bar{R}$$

where $\bar{\bar{X}}$ = grand average = average of the sample averages
$\bar{R}$ = average of the sample ranges
A_2 = constant found from Table I in the Appendix

The shortcut consists of (1) computing, for each sample, the range (difference between largest and smallest) of the individuals; (2) averaging the ranges thus obtained; and (3) then multiplying the average range by a conversion factor to get the distance from the expected average to the limit line. The central line is merely the average of all the individual observations.

The shortcut formulas for control limits on sample ranges are:

$$\text{Upper control limit} = D_4\bar{R}$$

$$\text{Lower control limit} = D_3\bar{R}$$

where D_3 and D_4 are constants found in Table I in the Appendix. A partial tabulation of the A_2, D_3, and D_4 factors is reproduced in Table 12-2 for the convenience of the reader in following the text.

As an example, the data from Figure 12-1 will be used to illustrate the control-chart concept. Originally the data were presented as one large sample of 60 units. Now suppose this had been 10 samples with 6 units in each sample. This is shown together with the $\bar{X}$ and R values for each sample in Figure 12-4 for machine N-5.

Table 12-2 Constants for $\bar{X}$ and R chart

n	A_2	D_3	D_4	d_2
2	1.880	0	3.268	1.128
3	1.023	0	2.574	1.693
4	0.729	0	2.282	2.059
5	0.577	0	2.114	2.326
6	0.483	0	2.004	2.534
7	0.419	0.076	1.924	2.704
8	0.373	0.136	1.864	2.847
9	0.337	0.184	1.816	2.970
10	0.308	0.223	1.777	3.078

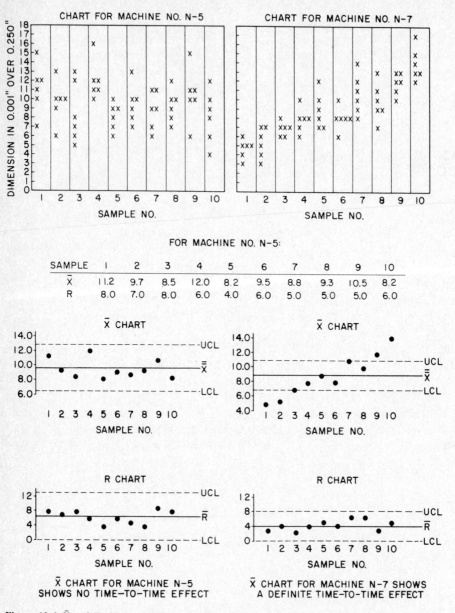

FOR MACHINE NO. N-5:

SAMPLE	1	2	3	4	5	6	7	8	9	10
$\bar{X}$	11.2	9.7	8.5	12.0	8.2	9.5	8.8	9.3	10.5	8.2
R	8.0	7.0	8.0	6.0	4.0	6.0	5.0	5.0	5.0	6.0

$\bar{X}$ CHART FOR MACHINE N-5
SHOWS NO TIME–TO–TIME EFFECT

$\bar{X}$ CHART FOR MACHINE N-7 SHOWS
A DEFINITE TIME–TO–TIME EFFECT

Figure 12-4 $\bar{X}$ and R charts confirm suspected machine differences.

The upper and lower control limits (UCL and LCL) are calculated as *Averages*

$$\text{UCL} = \bar{\bar{X}} + A_2\bar{R} = 9.59 + 0.483(6.0) = 12.48$$

$$\text{LCL} = \bar{\bar{X}} - A_2\bar{R} = 9.59 - 0.483(6.0) = 6.68$$

Ranges

$$UCL = D_4\bar{R} = 2.004(6.0) = 12.02$$

$$LCL = D_3\bar{R} = \quad 0(6.0) = 0$$

As all points fell within the control limits, it is concluded that the process is free of assignable causes of variation.

12-7 DETERMINATION OF PROCESS CAPABILITY FROM A CONTROL-CHART ANALYSIS

Control limits for a chart for averages represent 3 standard deviations of sample *averages* (not individual values). As tolerance limits usually apply to *individual* values, the control limits *cannot* be compared to tolerance limits, because averages inherently vary less than the individual measurements going into the averages (Figure 4-1). Therefore, tolerance limits should *not* be placed on a control chart for averages. The only valid comparison that can be made is to convert $\bar{R}$ to the standard deviation, calculate the natural tolerance limits, and compare to product tolerances.

If a process is in statistical control, it is operating with the minimum amount of variation possible (the variation due to chance causes). If, and only if, a process is in statistical control, the following relationship holds:

$$\text{estimate of } \sigma = s = \frac{\bar{R}}{d_2}$$

Table I in the Appendix and Table 12-2 provide values of d_2. Knowing the standard deviation, process capability limits can be set at $\pm 3s$ and this used as an estimate of 3σ.

For the data of Figure 12-1,

$$s = \frac{\bar{R}}{d_2} = \frac{6.0}{2.534} = 2.37$$

and $$\pm 3s = \pm 3(2.37) = 7.11$$

or $$6s = 14.22$$

This value of process capability is close to the value of 15.0 found for the same data by the frequency distribution method. The estimate of σ using the control chart is based on $\bar{R}$, the average of the range *within* each sample about the process aim. The estimate of σ using the frequency distribution method includes both *within*-sample variation and *between*-sample variation. This will be discussed in a later section of the chapter.

Note a special case of the $s = \bar{R}/d_2$ calculation. When $n = 10$, $d_2 = 3.078$. Then

$$3s = \frac{3\bar{R}}{3.078} = \text{approximately } 1\bar{R}$$

or the 6σ process capability is about $2\bar{R}$. If it were necessary to make a quick approximation of process capability, a *single* sample of 10 could be measured, the range calculated, and process capability estimated as $2R$. Of course, this would lose the advantage of the control chart.

Another example is presented in Figure 12-4 for machine N-7. This machine has both within-sample variation shown by the range chart and between-sample variation as illustrated by the chart for sample averages. The $\bar{X}$ chart indicates that some factor such as tool wear is present that results in larger values of the characteristic with the passing of time (note the importance of preserving the order of the measurements). In such cases, measures of process capability should reflect both sources of variation. The inherent capability can be estimated in the usual way as 6σ (where $\sigma = \bar{R}/d_2$), and this will depict the variation about a given process aim. In addition, the time-to-time variation can be expressed separately as the difference in process aim over the time period covered by the averages plotted on the control chart.

12-8 THE ASSUMPTION OF STATISTICAL CONTROL AND ITS EFFECT ON PROCESS CAPABILITY

All statistical predictions assume a stable population. In a statistical sense, a stable population is one which is repeatable and therefore free of large causes of variation—that is, a population that is in a state of statistical control. The statistician rightfully insists that this be the case before predictions can be made. The manufacturing engineer also insists that the process conditions (feeds, speeds, etc.) be fully defined.

In practice, the original control-chart analysis will often show the process to be out of statistical control. (It may or may not be meeting product specifications.) However, an investigation may show that the causes cannot be *economically* eliminated from the process. Strictly speaking, a process capability prediction should not be made until a process is in statistical control. However, some comparison of capability to product tolerances must be made. The danger in delaying the analysis is that the assignable causes may *never* be eliminated from the process and the indecision will thereby prolong the interdepartmental bickering on whether the "tolerance is too tight" or "manufacturing too careless."

A good way to start is by plotting *individual* measurement against *tolerance* limits (see Section 11-5). This may show that the process can meet the product tolerances even with assignable causes present. If a process has assignable causes of variation, but is able to meet the product tolerances, no *economic* problem exists. The statistician will properly point out that a process with assignable variation is unpredictable. This point is well taken but in establishing *priority* of quality control efforts, processes that are meeting tolerances simply cannot be given high priority.

If a process is out of control and the causes cannot be economically eliminated, the standard deviation and process capability limits can be computed (with the out-of-control points included). *These limits will be inflated because the process will not be operating at its best. In addition, the instability of the process means that the prediction is approximate.*

12-9 OTHER METHODS OF PROCESS CAPABILITY ANALYSIS

As the process becomes complex, the analysis to measure process capability also becomes complex. The product lots are in reality composed of multiple streams, each of which can exhibit time-to-time drift and other changes. In addition, even at instantaneous time, there are piece-to-piece and within-piece variations.

Several methods of analysis are available to assist the planner in quantifying these components of total variation.

Graphic analysis. An example is the Multi-Vari graph discussed in Section 5-6.
SPAN plan. This is a structured approach to analysis.[5]
Design of experiment and analysis of variance. This is a generalized approach, with flexibility to fit any combination of variables. For each such combination, there is prepared a tailor-made *design of experiment* for collecting the data which will permit resolution of the composite variation into its components. The resulting data are analyzed by the technique of *analysis of variance*, which provides, in standardized format, the determination of significance of the variables under experiment as well as their interaction.[6]

12-10 USE OF PROCESS CAPABILITY DATA IN MANUFACTURING PLANNING

The measurement and publication of machine capability for different operations and different materials is of great importance in prevention of quality problems. For example, the design engineer, acquainted with the attainable tolerances of the available equipment, has a more rational basis for the specification of tolerances. Many plants use these data as the basis for a complete review of all engineering tolerances. The planning engineer or dispatch clerk can assign the jobs with the most rigid tolerances to the most capable machines and the less exacting work to the poorer machines. The tool designer is provided with a measure of the effectiveness of changes in his tooling; he can

---

[5] L. A. Seder and D. Cowan, "The SPAN Plan Method of Process Capability Analysis," *ASQC General Publication 3*, September 1956.
[6] See *Quality Control Handbook*, 3rd ed., sec. 27.

also spot the places where tooling improvements must be made. Capability information helps the foreman by highlighting individual machines that may require overhaul. The machine setup person learns which machines require the most attention to set up and which ones need only normal care. The purchasing agent has a means of comparing the actual performance of equipment with the manufacturer's claims. The patrol inspector and the machine operator have a better index to show which machines need the closest watching in production.

Beyond the general uses above, there are problems arising from the relationship of machine capability to product tolerance.

1. *If the machine capability is inadequate to meet the tolerance:*
   a. Try to shift the job to another machine with more adequate capability. If the order already is completed, make provisions for proper assignment when the job occurs again.
   b. Try to improve the machine capability. This is particularly advisable if the value obtained differed markedly from that of similar machines. The machine may require overhauling or the tooling may need to be reviewed. For multispindle machines, the causes for spindle differences may need to be pinpointed. Control-chart analysis may be helpful. If the machine is in a state of statistical control, a major change such as an overhaul will be required to improve the capability. If the machine is not in statistical control, the assignable causes should be identified for the out-of-control points, and this can result in improved capability.
   c. Try to get a review of the tolerance. The availability of specific information showing what tolerance can be achieved may soften the engineer's attitude on liberalizing the tolerance.
   d. Sort the good product from the bad. The economics of this alternative should be brought to the attention of management.
2. *If the machine capability is equal to the tolerance:* This usually should be treated as in (1) above, since it means that tools must be set exactly at the nominal point and gives no allowance for tool wear. However, if tool wear is negligible or where a small percentage of parts just outside the tolerance can be tolerated, this should be treated as in (3) below.
3. *If the machine capability is adequate to meet the tolerance:*
   a. If the machine capability is of the order of two-thirds to three-fourths of the tolerance or less, it is the acceptable situation. The machine should produce practically all good work over a long period of time if periodic samples are taken to check the setting of tools.
   b. If the machine capability is less than one-half of the tolerance, do nothing unless reducing the tolerance will achieve some gain. The ability to tighten the tolerance on one part in an assembly may permit loosening a difficult tolerance on another part. Closer guarantee of tolerances may also have competitive sales advantage.
   c. One hundred percent inspection of the product is not needed and a sampling procedure should be considered.

12-11 DETERMINATION OF OPTIMUM CONDITIONS FOR A PROCESS

Allied to process capability analyses are techniques for determining the set of manufacturing process conditions that yields the optimum result for some quality characteristic.

Response surface methodology[7] (RSM) is a technique in which selected important variables of the process are varied in a carefully chosen way. Measurements are made on the operating capabilities of the process, and the data are analyzed to indicate in what ways the variables should be adjusted to improve the performance. These steps are repeated to find the combination of variables for optimum results. RSM is usually applied in development laboratories for the purpose of finding an optimum process.

Evolutionary operation[8] (EVOP) is similar to RSM but is conducted during actual manufacturing operations. Successive lots are made under process conditions which vary from one lot to another. Process conditions are deliberately changed to provide needed data for determining optimum conditions without jeopardizing the product. Special analysis techniques then derive the relationships to find the optimum set of process conditions.

Sometimes, the relationship of process variation and process economics can be evaluated to determine the most profitable target value for a process. Hunter and Kartha[9] have developed a technique for determining the best target value for a process with a single specification limit that simultaneously produces (1) product conforming to specification, (2) product not conforming but which can be sold at a lower selling price, and (3) product that results in a "giveaway" cost, as when a minimum weight specification is exceeded and product is given away.

In an example cited by Hunter and Kartha, suppose that a food package has a minimum weight requirement of 1.00 lb (4.448 N). The selling price of an accepted package is 67.5 cents and the cost of material is 55 cents per pound. A rejected package is sold for 37 cents. The standard deviation of the process is about 0.00563. Let:

a = net selling price of an accepted item

r = net selling price of a rejected item

g = giveaway cost

σ = process standard deviation

The value of $g/(a - r)$ is calculated and Table J in the Appendix is used to determine the value of δ^*/σ. The value of δ^* is then calculated and added to a

---

[7] See *Quality Control Handbook*, 3rd ed., sec. 28.

[8] See *Quality Control Handbook*, 3rd ed., sec. 27A.

[9] William G. Hunter and C. P. Kartha, "Determining the Most Profitable Target Value for a Production Process," *Journal of Quality Technology*, vol. 9, no. 4, October 1977, pp. 176–181.

lower specification limit L (or subtracted from an upper specification limit T) to yield the most profitable target value of the process.

For this example:

$$\frac{g\sigma}{a - r} = \frac{55.0(0.00563)}{67.5 - 37.0} = 0.0102$$

From Table J, $\delta^*/\sigma = 2.71$ and therefore $\delta^* = 0.0153$. The most profitable target value is

$$T = L + \delta^*$$

$$= 1.00 + 0.0153 = 1.0153$$

12-12 ANALYZING PROCESS DATA TO SET LIMITS ON DISCRETE COMPONENTS OR PARTS

Generally, designers will not be provided with information on process capability. Their problem will be to obtain a sample of data from the process, calculate the limits that the process can meet, and compare these to the limits they were going to specify. (If they do not have any limits in mind, the capability limits calculated from process data provide them with a set of limits that are realistic from the viewpoint of producibility. These must then be evaluated against the functional needs of the product.)

Statistically, the problem is to predict the limits of variation of individual items in the total *population* based on a *sample* of data. For example, suppose that a product characteristic is normally distributed with a population average of 5.000 in (12.7 cm) and a population standard deviation of 0.001 in (0.00254 cm). Limits can then be calculated to include any given percentage of the population. Figure 12-5 shows the location of the 99 percent limits. Table A in the Appendix indicates that ± 2.575 standard deviations will include 99 percent of the population. Thus, in this example, a realistic set of tolerance limits would be

$$5.000 \pm 2.575(0.001) = \begin{array}{c} 5.003 \\ 4.997 \end{array}$$

Ninety-nine percent of the individual pieces in the population will have values within 4.997 and 5.003.

In practice, the average and standard deviation of the population are *not* known but must be estimated from a sample of product from the process. As a first approximation, tolerance limits are sometimes set at

$$\bar{X} + 3s$$

Here the average $\bar{X}$ and standard deviation s of the sample are used directly as estimates of the population values. If the true average and standard deviation of the population happen to be equal to those of the sample, and if the characteristic is normally distributed, then 99.73 percent of the pieces in the population

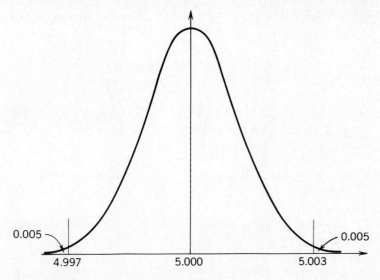

Figure 12-5 Distribution with 99 percent limits.

will fall within the limits calculated above. These limits are frequently called *natural tolerance limits* (limits that recognize the actual variation of the process and therefore are realistic). This approximation ignores the possible error in both the average and standard deviation as estimated from the sample.

Methodology has been developed for setting tolerance limits in a more precise manner.[10] For example, formulas and tables are available for determining tolerance limits based on a normally distributed population. Table K in the Appendix provides factors for calculating tolerance limits that recognize the uncertainty in the sample mean and sample standard deviation. The tolerance limits are determined as

$$\bar{X} \pm Ks$$

The factor K is a function of the confidence level desired, the percent of the population to be included within the tolerance limits, and the amount of data in the sample.

For example, suppose that a sample of 10 resistors from a process yielded an average and standard deviation of 5.04 Ω and 0.016 Ω, respectively. The tolerance limits are to include 99 percent of the population, and the tolerance statement is to have a confidence level of 95 percent. Referring to Table K in the Appendix, the value of K is 4.433, and tolerance limits are then calculated as

$$5.04 \pm 4.433(0.016) = \begin{matrix} 4.97 \\ 5.11 \end{matrix}$$

[10] See *Quality Control Handbook*, 3rd ed., pp. 22–53 to 22–56.

We are 95 percent confident that at least 99 percent of the resistors in the population will have a resistance between 4.97 and 5.11 Ω. Tolerance limits calculated in this manner are often called statistical tolerance limits. This approach is more rigorous than the $\pm 3s$ natural tolerance limits, but the two percentages in the statement are a mystery to those without a statistical background.

Statistical tolerance limits can also be calculated using the range instead of the standard deviation.[11] This method also assumes normality and is an approximation to the method using the standard deviation.

Another method is distribution-free, i.e., does not assume a normal or any other distribution. In this approach, a sample of n units are measured and the tolerance limits are defined as the rth smallest and sth largest values in the sample. The distribution-free concept is appealing but generally requires high sample sizes. An abbreviated table that provides sample sizes for both the normal distribution case and the distribution-free case for specified levels of precision is given in Table L in the Appendix. Suppose that it was desired to set statistical tolerance limits to include 99 ± 0.99 percent of the population with a 95% confidence level. Assuming normality, Table L shows that a sample of 32 units should be measured, $\bar{X}$ and s calculated, and a $K = 3.158$ used to set the limits. That is, there is 95 percent confidence that 99 ± 0.99 percent of the population will be included in the limits $\bar{X} \pm 3.1585$. In the distribution-free case, the sample size required is 278 and $r + s$ (called m) is 2. This means measure a sample of 278 units and define the limits as the smallest ($r = 1$) and the largest ($s = 1$) values. Then there is 95 percent confidence that 99 ± 0.99 percent of the population will be included with the smallest and largest values observed in the sample.

All methods of setting tolerance limits based on process data assume that the sample of data is representative of a process that is sufficiently stabilized to be predictable. In practice, the assumption is often accepted without any formal evaluation. If sufficient data are available, the assumption can be checked with a control chart.

Statistical tolerance limits are sometimes confused with other limits used in engineering and statistics. Table 12-3 summarizes the distinction among five types of limits. Hahn[12] gives an excellent discussion with examples and tables to illustrate the differences among several types of limits.

12-13 CONCEPT OF POSITION TOLERANCE

Of relatively recent origin is the concept of position tolerance or true position tolerance. This is usually applied to mating parts where function and in-

---

[11] See *Quality Control Handbook*, 3rd ed., pp. 22–54.

[12] G. J. Hahn, "Statistical Intervals for a Normal Population, Part I, Tables, Examples and Applications; Part II, Formulas, Assumptions, Some Derivations," *Journal of Quality Technology*, vol. 2, no. 3, July 1970; vol. 2, no. 4, October 1970. See also G. J. Hahn and Wayne Nelson, "A Survey of Prediction Intervals and Their Applications," *Journal of Quality Technology*, vol. 5, no. 4, October 1973.

Table 12-3 Distinction among limits

Name of limits	Meaning
Tolerance limits	Set by the engineering design function to define the minimum and maximum values allowable for the product to work properly
Statistical tolerance limits	Calculated from process data to define the amount of variation that the process exhibits; these limits will contain a specified proportion of the total population
Prediction limits	Calculated from process data to define the limits which will contain all of k future observations
Confidence limits	Calculated from data to define an interval within which a population parameter lies
Control limits	Calculated from process data to define the limits of chance (random) variation around some central value

terchangeability are vital. It can result in (1) larger tolerances than those possible from conventional tolerancing, and (2) more efficient inspection techniques.

The concept can be explained using the example of a hole to be made in a part. In conventional tolerancing, the location of the center of the hole would be determined by distance specifications from two other locations on the part. However, these distance specifications include tolerance ranges resulting in a zone restriction on the center of the hole as indicated by the square zone in Figure 12-6. As a cylindrical hole should normally have a cylindrical tolerance zone, the square zone restriction is not as realistic as the true position tolerance zone indicated by the circle. Thus, under position tolerancing, all of the dots in Figure 12-6 would be acceptable locations of the centerline of the hole but under conventional tolerancing only three of the five locations would be acceptable. The mating of the shaft and hole depends on the location of the center and the diameter of the hole. Therefore, the tolerance on the *position* of a hole depends on the *size* of the hole. In this tolerancing system, the position toler-

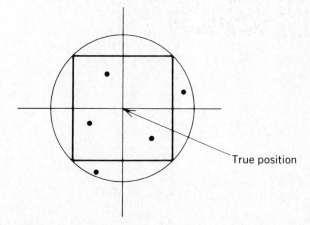

True position

Figure 12-6 Concept of position tolerance.

ance is normally stated for the condition containing the maximum amount of material, i.e., the smallest hole.

This tolerancing system will probably become increasingly important in the future. Further discussion is provided by Frank[13] and MIL-STD-8C.[14]

12-14 SETTING TOLERANCE LIMITS FOR BULK (OR COALESCED) PRODUCTS

For discrete products (e.g., bolts, pumps, toasters) the setting of tolerance limits on a quality characteristic includes several aspects that are clear:

1. The definition of a unit of product is a discrete piece (a bolt).
2. The product is tested and used on a unit basis. Therefore, tolerance limits apply to individual units of product and all units should meet the tolerances.

Bulk or coalesced products (gasoline, sheet steel, coal) are different:

1. The definition of a unit of product is a mass (e.g., a tank car of chemicals).
2. The product is evaluated by testing specimens from the mass. The measurement on a single specimen is of little importance because the product is not used in the form of specimens. However, the measurement of a number of specimens is important in determining the characteristic of the mass.

For coalesced products, the specification must first define the mass in physical terms, set limits on the quality characteristics of the mass, and finally set limits on the measurement of specimens from the mass. The quality limits are usually defined in terms of average and standard deviation. For example, Rockwell C scale hardness limits for a *mass* might be

Average $= 58 \pm 1$; standard deviation $=$ maximum of 1.5

The limits on the specimens from the mass must recognize the sampling variation within the mass. The formula for sampling variation of the average states that the variation depends on (1) the size of the sample, and (2) the intrinsic variation of the mass itself. Thus the test limits specified must be related to a defined number of measurements. (This is distinctly different from test limits for discrete products which apply to each unit of product.) The determination of the number of specimens to be tested and the corresponding limits is based on the concept of variables sampling plans.[15]

---

[13] G. R. Frank, "Tolerance Challenge," *1977 ASQC Annual Technical Conference Transactions*, p. 72.

[14] MIL-STD-8C, Dimensions and Tolerancing, 1963.

[15] See *Quality Control Handbook*, 3rd ed., sec. 25A.

The special problems of coalesced products can be a source of serious confusion. One company had a problem on the percent impurities in a chemical product. The specification stated that the percent impurities "shall not exceed 12 percent." Unfortunately, the manufacturing and quality people differed on the interpretation of the term "12 percent." The quality people interpreted it to mean that any *single* measurement of impurity in the product must be equal to or less than 12 percent. The manufacturing people felt it meant that the *average* of the measurements taken over a 1-day period should be equal to or less than 12 percent. This lack of agreement had been going on for *months* because neither function fully realized the significance of the distinction between the mass and specimens.

12-15 TOLERANCE LIMITS FOR INTERACTING DIMENSIONS

Interacting dimensions are those which mate or merge with other dimensions to create a final result. Consider the simple mechanical assembly shown in Figure 12-7. The lengths of components A, B, and C are interacting dimensions because they determine the overall assembly length.

Suppose the components were manufactured to the specifications indicated in Figure 12-7. A logical specification on the assembly length would be 3.500 ± 0.0035, giving limits of 3.5035 and 3.4965. The logic of this may be verified from the two extreme assemblies:

Maximum	Minimum
1.001	0.999
0.5005	0.4995
2.002	1.998
3.5035	3.4965

The approach of adding component tolerances is mathematically correct but is often too conservative. Suppose that about 1 percent of the pieces of component A are expected to be below the lower tolerance limit for component A and suppose the same for components B and C. If a component A is selected

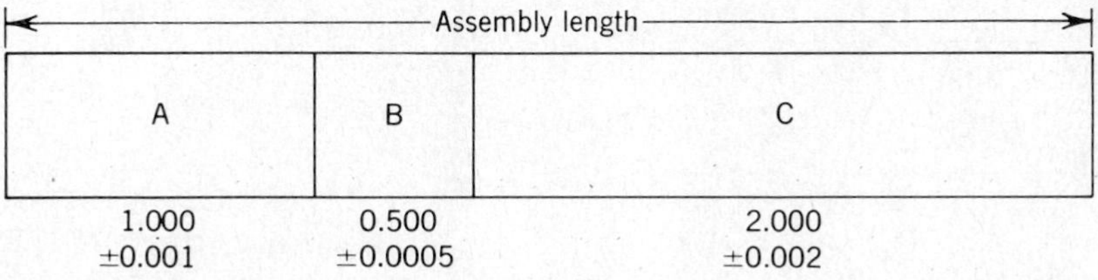

◄─────────────────── Assembly length ───────────────────►		
A	B	C
1.000	0.500	2.000
±0.001	±0.0005	±0.002

Figure 12-7 Mechanical assembly.

at random, there is, on the average, 1 chance in 100 that it will be on the low side, and similarly for components B and C. The key point is this: If assemblies are made at random and if the components are manufactured independently, then the chance that an assembly will have all *three* components simultaneously below the lower tolerance limit is

$$\frac{1}{100} \times \frac{1}{100} \times \frac{1}{100} = \frac{1}{1,000,000}$$

There is only about one chance in a million that all three components will be too small, resulting in a small assembly. Thus, setting component and assembly tolerances based on the simple addition formula is conservative in that it fails to recognize the extremely low probability of an assembly containing all low (or all high) components.

The statistical approach is based on the relationship between the variances of a number of independent causes and the variance of the dependent or overall result. This may be written as

$$\sigma_{result} = \sqrt{\sigma_{cause\ A}^2 + \sigma_{cause\ B}^2 + \sigma_{cause\ C}^2 + \cdots}$$

In terms of the assembly example, the formula is

$$\sigma_{assembly} = \sqrt{\sigma_A^2 + \sigma_B^2 + \sigma_C^2}$$

Now suppose that, for each component, the tolerance range is equal to ± 3 standard deviations (or any constant multiple of the standard deviation). As σ is equal to T divided by 3, the variance relationship may be rewritten as

$$\frac{T}{3} = \sqrt{\left(\frac{T_A}{3}\right)^2 + \left(\frac{T_B}{3}\right)^2 + \left(\frac{T_C}{3}\right)^2}$$

or

$$T_{assembly} = \sqrt{T_A^2 + T_B^2 + T_C^2}$$

Thus the *squares* of tolerances are added to determine the square of the tolerance for the overall result. This compares to the simple addition of tolerances commonly used.

The effect of the statistical approach is dramatic. Listed below are two possible sets of component tolerances which when used with the formula above will yield an assembly tolerance equal to ± 0.0035.

Component	Alternative 1	Alternative 2
A	± 0.002	± 0.001
B	± 0.002	± 0.001
C	± 0.002	± 0.003

With alternative 1, the tolerance for component A has been doubled, the tolerance for component B has been quadrupled, and the tolerance for component C has been kept the same as the original component tolerance based on the simple addition approach. If alternative 2 is chosen, similar significant increases in the component tolerances may be achieved. This formula, then, may result in a larger component tolerance with *no* change in the manufacturing processes and *no* change in the assembly tolerance.

A risk is involved with this approach. It is possible that an assembly will result which falls outside the assembly tolerance. However, the probability of this occurring can be calculated by expressing the component tolerances as standard deviations, calculating the standard deviation of the result, and finding the area under the normal curve outside the assembly tolerance limits. For example, if each of the component tolerances was equal to 3σ, then 99.73 percent of the assemblies would be within the assembly tolerance, i.e., a 0.27 percent risk or about 3 assemblies in 1000 made at random would fail to meet the assembly tolerance. The risk could be eliminated if components were changed for these few assemblies that did not meet the assembly tolerance.

The tolerance formula is not restricted to outside dimensions of assemblies. Generalizing, the left side of the equation contains the dependent variable or *physical result*, while the right side of the equation contains the independent variables of *physical causes*. If the result is placed on the left and the causes on the right, the formula always has *plus* signs under the square root—even if the result is an internal dimension (such as the clearance between a shaft and hole). The causes of variation are *additive* wherever the physical result happens to fall.

The formula has been applied to a variety of mechanical and electronic products. The concept may be applied to several interacting variables in an engineering relationship. The nature of the relationship need not be additive (assembly example) or subtractive (shaft and hole example). The tolerance formula can be adapted to predict the variation of results that are the product and/or the division of several variables.[16]

12-16 ASSUMPTIONS OF THE FORMULA

The formula is based on several assumptions:

1. The component dimensions are independent and the components are assembled randomly. This assumption is usually met in practice.
2. Each component dimension should be normally distributed. Some departure from this assumption is permissible.
3. The actual average for each component is equal to the nominal value stated in the specification. For the original assembly example, the actual averages for components A, B, and C must be 1.000, 0.500, and 2.000, respectively.

[16] G. Mouradian, "Tolerance Limits for Assemblies and Engineering Relationships," *1966 ASQC Annual Technical Conference Transactions*, p. 598.

Otherwise, the nominal value of 3.500 will not be achieved for the assembly, and tolerance limits set about 3.500 will not be realistic. Thus it is important to control the average value for interacting dimensions. This means that process control techniques are needed using variables measurement.

Use caution if any of the assumptions are violated. Reasonable departures from the assumptions may still permit the concept of the formula to be applied. Notice that the formula resulted in the doubling of certain tolerances in the illustrative example. This much of an increase may not even be necessary from the viewpoint of process capability.

Bender[17] has studied these assumptions for some complex assembly cases and concluded based on a "combination of probability and experience" that a factor of 1.5 should be included to care for the assumptions, i.e.,

$$T_{result} = 1.5\sqrt{T_A^2 + T_B^2 + T_C^2 + \cdots}$$

A summary of conventional and statistical tolerancing is given in Table 12-4.

12-17 OTHER SOLUTION METHODS FOR STATISTICAL TOLERANCING

In a series of three papers, Evans[18] discusses four methods of statistical tolerancing covering both linear and nonlinear cases. One of the methods is a Monte Carlo simulation.

Simulation is one of the most useful of the techniques of operations research and is directly applicable to the problem of statistical tolerancing. It is particularly useful when the component distributions are nonnormal and the relationship between the components and the final result is complex and difficult to analyze with conventional statistical methods.

A simulation is usually made using a computer model. The distribution of each component is defined in terms of the form of the distribution and numerical parameters, e.g., a normal distribution with a mean of 2.000 and standard deviation of 0.004 or an exponential distribution with a mean of 1.000. The relationship between the components and the final result is then expressed in a model equation. This may be a simple or complex combination of component dimensions.

In a Monte Carlo simulation, the computer uses a "random-number generator" to draw values at random from each component distribution and combine them (using the model equation) to obtain a simulated value of the overall result. This process is repeated many times and represents a simulation of what

[17] Art Bender, "Statistical Tolerancing As It Relates to Quality Control and the Designer," *Automotive Division Newsletter of ASQC*, April 1975, p. 12.

[18] David H. Evans, "Statistical Tolerancing: The State of the Art, Part I: Background; Part II: Methods for Estimating Moments; Part III: Shifts and Drifts," *Journal of Quality Technology*, vol. 6, no. 4, October 1974; vol. 7, no. 1, January 1975; and vol. 7, no. 2, April 1975.

Table 12-4 Comparison of conventional and statistical tolerancing

Factor	Conventional	Statistical
Risk of items not interacting properly	No risk; 100% interchangeability of items	Small percent of final results will fall outside limits (but these can sometimes be corrected with selective assembly)
Utilization of full tolerance range	Method is conservative; tolerances on interacting dimensions are smaller than necessary	Permits larger tolerances on interacting dimensions
Special process control techniques	None	Average of each interacting dimension must be controlled using variables measurement
Statistical assumptions	None	Interacting dimensions must be independent and each must be normally distributed
Lot size for components	Any size	Lot size should be moderately large (to assure balancing effect on extreme interacting dimensions)

would happen if many assemblies were made at random from components having the characteristics described in the computer simulation model. The simulated assembly dimensions can then be summarized in a histogram or other form and used to set assembly tolerances or to evaluate previously defined assembly tolerances. With a simulation model, component distributions can be changed and the effect on the overall result immediately predicted by running additional simulation runs.

Further discussion of simulation as applied to statistical tolerancing is provided by Gugel[19] and Choksi.[20]

12-18 SETTING LIMITS FOR SENSORY QUALITIES

Sensory qualities are those for which we lack technological measuring instruments and for which the senses of human beings must be used as measuring instruments. Examples of sensory qualities include adhesion of a protective coating, appearance of carpets, and taste of food.

The lack of measuring instruments also complicates the task of setting the standards of acceptance, i.e., the product specifications. Setting this standard should be done by those who have knowledge of the economic and marketing factors involved. Otherwise, the standards will, by default, be set by factory inspectors who lack this knowledge.

[19] H. W. Gugel, "Monte Carlo Simulation with Interactive Graphics," *Research Publication GMR-1531*, General Motors Corporation, Warren, Mich., October 1974.

[20] Suresh Choksi, "Computer Can Optimize Manufacturing Tolerances for an Economical Design," *1966 ASQC Annual Technical Conference Transactions*, p. 598.

An organized approach to setting sensory standards includes:

1. *Definition of various levels of sensory quality* along some scale of evaluation. These levels are used as reference points throughout the organized procedure.
2. *Study of yield of the company's manufacturing process at each of these levels* to discover the effect, on company cost, of the various potential decisions on sensory standards. (See Figure 12-8; level 1 is highest quality.) This determines the percentage of product being produced at the various defined levels. For example, about 4 percent of production is at level 7 or worse. If the specification limit were set at level 6, the 4 percent at level 7+ would mean a loss of $30,000.

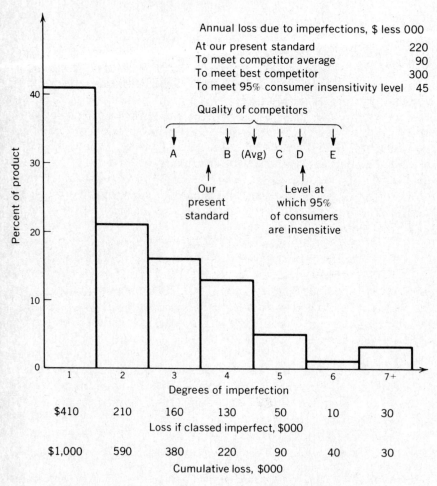

Figure 12-8 Summary for executive decision on sensory standards.

3. *Study of consumer sensitivity* to discover the effect, on consumer acceptance, of a decision on sensory standards.
4. *Study of competitor quality* to discover what is "market quality" in relation to the various defined levels.
5. *Analysis and summary of the foregoing* for executive decision. The data on cost of setting standards at various levels, consumer sensitivity at various levels, and competitor performance can all be brought together for executive convenience (Figure 12-8). Note that the present standard is set at level 3, which is better than the industry average and second only to competitor A. However, 95 percent of the consumers were insensitive to differences in levels through level 5.

The group (whether a committee or a single department) charged with recommending a sensory standard should provide for full and early participation by all departments affected. A recommendation on sensory standards prepared through such participation will seldom be upset by the higher supervision.

6. *Executive decision on sensory standards.* The making of the executive decision should itself be formalized. The signature of the responsible executive(s) should be secured on the recommendations or on the samples themselves to clear the air on the fact of decision making, as well as to identify the standards unmistakably.
7. *Recording the sensory standard.* For stable products the sensory standard can be selected, approved, and filed like any other master reference standard. Duplicates can be prepared for everyday use, and these can be checked against the master under a scheduled plan.

For unstable products there is a continuing problem of creating new masters at intervals which are shorter than the interval of deterioration. Sometimes special storage or preservatives can be employed to retard deterioration.

Another method of recording the standard is to standardize the conditions of inspection rather than the condition of the product. In this plan, a defect is an objectionable flaw that can be seen by the inspector (under the standard inspection conditions) at a specified distance from the product and within a specified interval of time.

8. *Training the personnel* in use of the standards.
9. *Follow-up* to ensure adequate use.

Another approach to reducing the judgment involved in sensory inspection involves specifying the *conditions* of inspection instead of limits of acceptability on the product. Riley[21] describes a special inspection procedure for cosmetic (appearance) defects of electronic calculators.

Part drawings indicate the relative importance of different surfaces using

---

[21]Frederic D. Riley, "Visual Inspection—Time and Distance Method," *1979 ASQC Annual Technical Conference Transactions,* p. 483.

a system of category numbers and class letters. Three categories identify the surface being inspected:

I. Plastic window (critical areas only)
II. External
III. Internal

Three classes indicate the frequency that the surface will be viewed by the user:

A. Usually seen by user.
B. Seldom seen by user.
C. Never seen by user (except during maintenance).

For example, a sheet-metal part that will seldom be seen carries a grade of Coating IIB.

The conditions of inspection are stated in terms of viewing distance, viewing time, and lighting conditions. The distance and time are specified for each combination of surface being inspected and the frequency of viewing by the user. Lighting conditions are required to be between 75 and 150 footcandles from a nondirectional source.

The guidelines help to establish cosmetic gradings on part drawings. However, a judgment must still be made by the inspector as to whether or not the end user would consider the flaw(s) objectionable, using the specified time and distance.

PROBLEMS

12-1 A large manufacturer of watches makes some of their own parts and buys some other parts from a vendor. The vendor submits lots of parts that meet the specifications of the horologist. The vendor thus wishes to keep a continuous check on their production of watch parts. One gear has been a special problem. A check of 25 samples of 5 pieces gave the following data on a key dimension:

$$\bar{\bar{X}} = 0.3175 \text{ cm} \qquad \bar{R} = 0.00508 \text{ cm}$$

What criterion should be set up to determine when the process is out of control? How should this criterion compare with the specifications? What are some alternatives if the criterion is not compatible with the specification?

12-2 A manufacturer of dustless chalk is concerned with the density of the product. Previous analysis has shown that the chalk has the required characteristics only if the density is between 4.4 g/cm^2 and 5.0 g/cm^2. If a sample of 100 pieces gives an average of 4.8 and a standard deviation of 0.2, is the process aimed at the proper density? If not, what should the aim be? Is the process capable of meeting the density requirements?

12-3 The head of an automobile engine must be machined so that both the surface that meets the engine block and the surface that meets the valve covers are flat. These surfaces must also be 4.875 in ± 0.001 in apart. Presuming that the valve-cover side of the head is finished correctly, compare the capability of two processes for performing the finishing of the engine-block side of the head. A broach set up to do the job gave an average thickness of 4.877 in with an average range of 0.0005 in for 25 samples of 4 each. A milling machine gave an average of 4.875 in and average range of 0.001 in for 20 samples of 4 each.

Answer: Broach $\pm 3s = \pm 0.00072$, milling machine $\pm 3s = 0.00144$.

12-4 A critical dimension on a double-armed armature has been causing trouble and the designer has decided to change the specification from 0.033 ± 0.005 in to 0.033 ± 0.001 in. To evaluate the proposed change, the manufacturing planning department has obtained the following coded data from the process:

Time	Left arm			Right arm			Comments
8:00	331	330	331	329	330	328	
8:30	332	331	329	327	331	329	
9:00	330	329	329	330	329	327	
9:30	332	330	331	331	332	328	
10:00	333	332	333	326	331	326	
10:30	332	331	332	329	330	331	
11:00	333	331	331	330	326	327	
11:30	332	332	333	327	326	329	
12:00	331	332	334	337	328	337	Adjustment
12:30	335	334	336	326	325	325	
1:00	333	332	332	329	332	330	
1:30	336	331	330	331	328	329	
2:00	332	334	329	332	330	329	
2:30	336	336	330	329	329	327	
3:00	329	335	338	333	330	331	Adjustment
3:30	341	333	330	329	331	332	

Comment on the proposal to change the specification

12-5 A company manufactures an expensive chemical. The net package weight has a minimum specification value of 25.0 lb. Data from a control-chart analysis show (based on 20 samples of 5 each):

$$\bar{\bar{X}} = 26.0 \qquad \bar{R} = 1.4$$

The points on both the average and range chart are all in control.

(a) Draw conclusions about the ability of the process to meet the specification.

(b) What action, if any, would you suggest on the process? If any action is suggested, are there any disadvantages to the action?

12-6 Samples of four units were taken from a manufacturing process at regular intervals. The width of a slot on a part was measured and the average and range computed for each sample of four. After 25 samples of four, the following coded results were obtained:

	Averages	Ranges
Upper control limit	UCL $= 626$	UCL $= 37.5$
Average	$\bar{\bar{X}} = 614$	$\bar{R} = 16.5$
Lower control limit	LCL $= 602$	LCL $= 0$

All points on the $\bar{X}$ and R charts fell within control limits. The specification requirements are 610 ± 15. If the width is normally distributed and the distribution centered at $\bar{X}$, what percentage of product would you expect to fall outside the specification limits?

Answer: 9.4 percent.

12-7 (*a*) What kind of conclusion (about a process) can be made from an average and range control chart that cannot be made from a histogram?

(*b*) What kind of conclusion can be made from a histogram that cannot be made from a control chart?

12-8 Measurements were made on the bore dimension of an impeller. A sample of 20 from a pilot run production showed a mean value of 25.038 cm and a standard deviation of 0.000381 cm. All the units functioned properly, so it was decided to use the data to set specification limits for regular production.

(*a*) Suppose it was assumed that the sample estimates were exactly equal to the population mean and standard deviation. What specification limits should be set to include 99 percent of production?

(*b*) There is uncertainty that the sample and population values are equal. Based on the sample of 20, what limits should be set to be 95 percent sure of including 99 percent of production?

(*c*) Explain the meaning of the difference in (*a*) and (*b*).

(*d*) What assumptions were necessary to determine both sets of limits?

12-9 A circuit contains three resistors in series. Past data show these data on resistance:

Resistor	Mean, Ω	Standard deviation, Ω
1	125	3
2	200	4
3	600	12

(*a*) What percent of circuits would meet the specification on total resistance of 930 ± 30 Ω?

(*b*) Inquire from a local distributor if it is reasonable to assume that the resistance of a resistor is normally distributed.

12-10 A manufacturer of rotary lawn mowers received numerous complaints concerning the effort required to push its product. Studies soon found that the small clearance between the wheel bushing and shaft was the cause. Designers chose to make the clearance large enough for easy rotation of the wheel (or for a heavy grease coating), but still "tight enough" to prevent wobbling. Because of a large inventory of wheels and shafts, a decision was made to ream the bushings to a larger inside diameter (I.D.) and retain the shafts. The following specifications were proposed:

$$\text{Shaft diameter} = 0.800 \pm 0.002 \text{ in}$$
$$\text{New clearance} = 0.008 \pm 0.003 \text{ in}$$
$$\text{Bushing I.D.} = 0.808 \pm 0.001 \text{ in}$$

Production people claimed that they could not economically hold the tolerance on the bushing I.D. What comment would you make about this claim?

Answer: I.D. tolerance of ± 0.0022 could be allowed.

12-11 An assembly consists of two parts (A and B) which mate together "end to end" to form an overall length, C. It is desired that the overall length, C, meet a specification of 3.000 ± 0.005 cm. The nominal specification on A is 2.000 and on B it is 1.000. The manufacturing process for B has much more variability than the process for A. Specifically, the tolerance for part B should be twice as large as for part A. Assemblies are to be made at random and parts A and B are independently manufactured. Assuming that we want only a small risk of not meeting the specification on C, what tolerances should be set on A and B?

12-12 A canning factory decided to set tolerance limits for filling cans of a new product by sampling a pilot run of 30 cans. The results of that run yielded an average of 446 g with a standard deviation of 1.25 g. What tolerance limits should be set which would be 95 percent certain of including 99 percent of production? The label of the can states that it contains 453 g of the product. How many grams of product should the average can contain if the company is to be 95 percent certain that 99 percent of production contains at least 453 g?

SUPPLEMENTARY READING

The *Quality Control Handbook,* 3rd ed., McGraw-Hill Book Company, New York, 1974, discusses manufacturing planning (sec. 9). The application of the concepts to various industries is included in secs. 29–45.

A thorough discussion of evaluating a complex new process is provided by John L. Bemesderfer, "Approving a Process for Production," *Journal of Quality Technology,* January 1979, pp. 1–12.

EXAMPLES OF EXAMINATION QUESTIONS USED IN FORMER ASQC QUALITY ENGINEER CERTIFICATION EXAMINATIONS AS PUBLISHED IN *QUALITY PROGRESS* MAGAZINE

1 When used together for variables data, which of the following is the most useful pair of quantities in quality control? (a) $\bar{X}$, R; (b) $\bar{X}$, η; (c) R, σ; (d) $\bar{p}$, η; (e) AQL, p'.

2 If X and Y are distributed normally and independently, the variance of $X - Y$ is then equal to (a) $\sigma_x^2 + \sigma_y^2$; (b) $\sigma_x - \sigma_y^2$; (c) $\sqrt{\sigma_x^2 + \sigma_y^2}$; (d) $\sqrt{\sigma_x^2 - \sigma_y^2}$.

3 An $\bar{X}$ and R chart was prepared for an operation using 20 samples with five pieces in each sample. $\bar{X}$ was found to be 33.6 and R was 6.2. During production a sample of five was taken and the pieces measured 36, 43, 37, 34, and 38. At the time this sample was taken: (a) both average and range were within control limits; (b) neither average nor range was within control limits; (c) only the average was outside control limits; (d) only the range was outside control limits; (e) the information given is not sufficient to construct an $\bar{X}$ and R chart using tables usually available.

4 When an initial study is made of a repetitive industrial process for the purpose of setting up a Shewhart control chart, information on the following process characteristic is sought. (a) process capability; (b) process performance; (c) process reliability; (d) process conformance; (e) process tolerance.

THIRTEEN

MANUFACTURE—PROCESS CONTROL CONCEPTS

13-1 CONCEPT OF CONTROLLABILITY; SELF-CONTROL

The concept of controllability was introduced in Section 5-6. Creating a state of self-control for a human being requires that we meet several essential criteria. We must provide people with the means for:

1. Knowing what they are supposed to do.
2. Knowing what they are actually doing.
3. Taking regulatory action.

These criteria for self-control make possible a separation of defects into various categories of "controllability," of which the most important are

1. *Operator-controllable.* A defect is operator-controllable if all three criteria for self-control have been met.
2. *Management-controllable.* A defect is management-controllable if any one or more of the criteria for self-control have not been met.

The theory behind these categories is that only the management can provide the means for meeting the criteria for self-control. Hence any failure to meet these criteria is a failure of management, and the resulting defects are therefore beyond the control of the operators. This theory is not 100 percent sound. Operators commonly have the duty to call management's attention to

greatly among operations. Other investigators, in Japan, Sweden, The Netherlands, and Czechoslovakia, have reached similar conclusions.

While the available quantitative studies make clear that defects are mainly management-controllable, many industrial managers do not know this, or are unable to accept the data. Their long-standing beliefs are that most defects are the result of operator carelessness, indifference, and even sabotage. Such managers are easily persuaded to embark on operator motivational schemes which, under the usual state of facts, aim at a small minority of the problem and hence are doomed to achievement of minor results at best. The issue is *not* whether quality problems in industry are management-controllable. The need is to determine the answer in a given plant. This cannot be answered authoritatively by opinions but requires solid facts through a controllability study of actual defects.

13-2 KNOWLEDGE OF "SUPPOSED TO DO"

This knowledge commonly consists of the following:

1. The product standard, which may be a written specification, a product sample, or other definition of the end result to be attained.
2. The process standard, which may be a written process specification, a verbal instruction, or other definition of the "means to an end."
3. A definition of responsibility, i.e., what decisions to make and what actions to take (discussed later in this chapter).

The obstacles to knowledge of what the operator is supposed to do are legion. Singly or in combination these obstacles result in numerous quality failures.

The specification may be vague. For example, when fiberglass tanks are to be transported in vehicles, the surface of the supporting cradles should be smooth. It was recognized that weld spatter would be deposited on the cradle surface, so an operation was specified to scrape the surface "smooth." However, there was no definition of "how smooth," and many rejections resulted.

There may be conflicting specifications. The foreman's "black book" has had a long, durable career. Changes in specifications may fail to be communicated, especially when there is a constant parade of changes. In one instance, an inspector rejected product which lacked an angle cut needed for clearance in assembly. It was discovered that the inspector was using drawing revision D, the production floor had used revision B, and the design office had issued revision E just 3 days ago.

In another case, a new method was developed for coding terminals and wire size of drawings. The designers began using the new method on the drawings before the new system was explained to the production people, with much resulting confusion and guesswork.

There are also failures to provide operators with the means for interpretation. Lack of seriousness classification is widespread, so that the operator lacks complete knowledge of what is vital and what is trivial. To the same effect is lack of training in the "why" of the specifications.

With respect to the process, sometimes the specific process conditions and work methods are not adequately defined. There may be a need to specify temperature, pressure, and time cycle in addition to the sequence of steps to be taken by the operator. As products become more complex, the definition of process conditions and work methods is critical.

A checklist to evaluate this first criterion could include questions such as:

1. Are there written product specifications and work-method instructions? If written in more than one place, do they all agree? Are they legible? Are they conveniently accessible to the operator?
2. Does the specification define the relative importance of different quality characteristics? Are advisory tolerances on a process distinguished from mandatory tolerances on a product? If control charts or other control techniques are to be used, is it clear how these relate to product specification?
3. Are standards for visual defects displayed in the work area?
4. Are the written specifications given to the operator the same as the criteria used by inspectors? Are deviations from the specification often allowed?
5. Does the operator know how the product is used?
6. Has the operator been adequately trained to understand the specification and perform the steps needed to meet the specification? Has the operator been evaluated by test or other means to see if he or she is qualified?
7. Does the operator know the effect on future operations and product performance if the specification is not met?
8. Does the operator receive specification changes automatically and promptly?
9. Does the operator know what to do with defective raw meterial and defective finished product?

We proceed now to the second criterion of self-control.

13-3 KNOWLEDGE OF "IS DOING"

For self-control, one must have the means of knowing whether the performance conforms to standard. For some operations, the normal human senses are sufficient. The stenographer can see whether the typed letter follows the draft; the assembly operator can see whether the lock washer is in place. However, in most modern operations, the human senses are not adequate, and they must be supplemented by instrumentation.

Example In highway construction, the personnel operating the earth-compacting rollers are told to achieve a certain percentage of earth compaction.

On some jobs they are given no means for measuring compaction. Only after the rolling is finished are they told whether the compaction is acceptable.

Where the operator is to use the instruments, it is necessary to provide training in: how to measure, what sampling criteria to use, how to record, how to chart, what kinds of corrective action to take. Motivating the operators to follow these instructions is so widespread a problem that many companies go to great lengths to minimize the need for operator action by providing instruments which require little or no human effort to measure, record, and control.

When instruments are provided to operators, it is also necessary to ensure that these instruments are compatible with those used by inspectors and in other operations later in the progression of events.

On one construction project, the "form setters" were provided with carpenter levels and rulers to set the height of forms prior to the pouring of concrete. The inspectors were provided with a complex optical instrument. The differences in measurement led to many disputes.

Where the operator does not have access to the instruments, provision must be made for feedback of the essential data from someone who does the actual measuring.

Feedback of Quality Data to Operators

The needs of production operators (as distinguished from supervisors or technical specialists) require that the data feedback:

Read at a glance.
Deal only with the *few important defects.*
Deal only with *operator-controllable defects.*
Provide *prompt information,* both as to symptom and cause.
Provide enough information to *guide corrective action.*

To meet these criteria for good feedback, use is made of modern communication technology: large departmental scoreboards; departmental loudspeakers or "bullhorns"; individualized signals (e.g., lights, flags) for specific processes, machines, or stations; computers for analyzing and summarizing quality data and presenting the results on individualized instruments (these instruments can be wired into the private offices as well).

Well-chosen feedback has both an informative and an incentive effect on production and laboratory personnel. Stok[1] describes interviews with workers to discover their attitude toward quality feedback in visible forms. The response was strongly positive. Examples of comments were: "it brings more variety into the work," "the bosses can see whether you're doing your best,"

[1] Thomas L. Stok, *The Worker and Quality Control,* University of Michigan, Ann Arbor, Mich., 1965, p. 73.

"you become more involved in the production process," and "everybody wants to know how he has done."

Charts as a Feedback to Operators

The criterion of "read at a glance" is normally met by use of indicating or recording instruments. However, in many situations, more sensitive detection can be provided through multiple measurements and through observations of trends. To meet these needs requires statistical processing of data plus a presentation of the statistics in their time-to-time relationship.

Charts can provide an excellent form of such sensitive feedback provided that they are designed to be consistent with the assigned responsibility of the operator, as in the four situations listed in Table 13-2.

Feedback Related to Operator Action

Inspection data are the result of measuring the *product*, whereas operator action is commonly to make changes in the *process*. In consequence, the operator needs to know what kind of process change to make to respond to a product deviation. This knowledge can be secured in one of several ways:

1. From the planners, who provide information relating process variables to product characteristics.
2. From cut-and-try experience by the operator.
3. From the fact that the units of measure for product and process are identical.

Lacking all these, the operators can only cut-and-try further or stop the process and sound the alarm.

Sometimes it is feasible for the data feedback to be converted into a form which makes easier the operator's decision of what action to take on the process.

Table 13-2 Operator responsibility versus chart design

Responsibility of the operator is to	Chart should be designed to show
1. Make individual units of product meet a product specification	The measurements of individual units of product compared to product specification limits
2. Hold process conditions to the requirements of a process specification	The measurements of the process conditions compared with the process specification limits
3. Hold averages and ranges to specified statistical control limits	The averages and ranges compared to the statistical control limits
4. Hold percent defective below some prescribed level	Actual percent defective compared to the limiting level

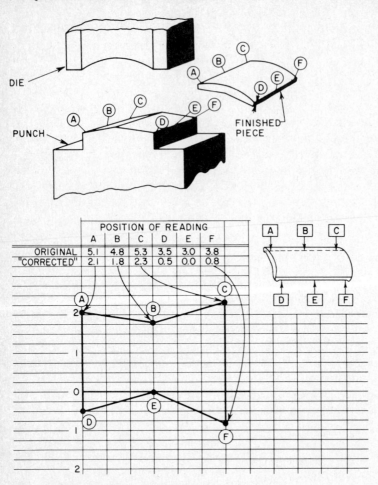

Figure 13-1 Method of drawing P-D diagram.

For example, a copper cap had six critical dimensions. It was easy to measure the dimensions and to discover the nature of product deviation. However, it was difficult to translate the product data into process changes. To simplify this translation, use was made of a *position-dimension* (P-D) *diagram*. The six measurements were first "corrected" (i.e., coded) by subtracting the thinnest from all the others. These corrected data were then plotted on a P-D diagram as shown in Figure 13-1.

Feedback to Supervisors

Beyond the need for feedback at the work stations, there is need to provide supervisors with short-term summaries. These take several forms.

Matrix summary A common form of matrix is operators versus defects; i.e., the vertical columns are headed up by operator names and the horizontal rows by the names of defect types. The matrix makes clear which defect types predominate, which operators have the most defects, and what the interaction is. Other matrices might be of machine number versus defect type or defect type versus calendar week.

When the summary is published, it is usual to circle the matrix cells to highlight the vital few situations which call for attention (see Table 6-1 for an example).

An elaboration of the matrix is to split the cell diagonally, permitting the entry of two numbers, e.g., number defective and number produced.

Pareto analysis Some companies prefer to minimize the detail given to the supervisor. Instead, they merely give information on the total defects for the day plus a list of the top three (or so) defects encountered, and how many of each. The logic is that the supervisor cannot in any case deal with more than a few defects. A lengthy list dilutes the attention given to any one defect type, including the important ones.

Computer data analysis and reporting In situations with many work stations and quality characteristics, it may be justified to mechanize both the recording of data and the analysis of data. Direct feedback can even include printing of summaries at typewriters located in the offices of the supervisors involved.

In some industries, a "chart room" is used to display performance by product and department against goals.

A checklist to evaluate the second criterion of self-control could include questions such as:

1. Are gages provided to the operator? Do they provide numerical measurements rather than sort good from bad? Are they precise enough? Are they regularly checked for accuracy?
2. Is the operator told how often to sample work and is sufficient time allowed?
3. Is the operator told how to evaluate measurements to decide when to adjust the process and when to leave it alone?
4. Is there a check to see that the operator does follow instructions on sampling work and making process adjustments?
5. Are inspection results provided to the operator, and are these results reviewed by the supervisor with the operator?

We proceed now to the third criterion of self-control.

[2] Jay W. Leek and Fred H. Riley, "Product Quality Improvement through Visibility," *1978 ASQC Annual Technical Conference Transactions*, p. 229.

13-4 ABILITY TO REGULATE

Whenever the product or process fails to conform to specification, the operator should be able to regulate or adjust the process. This may consist either of:

1. Varying process conditions, e.g., increasing the air pressure, adding more concentrate, or turning the feedwheel.
2. Varying the "human component," e.g., using lighter blows of the mallet.

Regulating the process depends on a number of management-controllable factors, including:

1. The process must be capable of meeting the tolerances (see Chapter 12).
2. The process must be responsive to the regulatory action in a predictable cause-and-effect relationship.

Example In a process for making an electronic component, the means for centering a winding mechanism lacked provision for adjustment. The mechanic could cut-and-try, i.e., disassemble and reassemble the setup, but with no assurance that the revised setup would be an improvement. As a result it became common practice for the mechanics to avoid changes in setup.

3. The operator should be trained in how to use the regulatory mechanisms and procedures. This training should cover the entire spectrum of action: under what conditions to act, what kind and extent of changes to make, how to use the regulatory devices (sometimes the operators must be certified), why these things need to be done.

Example In one food plant, there were three qualified operators on a certain process. One of the three operated the process every week and became proficient. The other two operators were used only for relief when the primary operator was on vacation or was ill, and thus they never became proficient. Continuous training of the relief people was considered uneconomical, and agreements with the union prohibited their use except under the situations cited above. This problem is management-controllable; i.e., additional training or a change in union agreements is necessary.

4. The act of adjustment should not be personally distasteful to the operator, e.g., require undue physical exertion.

Example In a plant making glass bottles, one adjustment mechanism was located next to a furnace area. During the summer months this area was so hot that operators tended to keep out of there as much as possible.

When the regulation consists of varying the human component of the operation, the question of process capability arises in a new form; i.e., does the operator have the capability to regulate? This important question is discussed in Chapter 6, which includes some examples of discovering operator "knack."

A checklist to evaluate the third criterion of self-control could include such questions as:

1. Has the quality capability of the process been measured to include both inherent variability and variability due to time? Is the capability periodically checked?
2. Has the operator been told how often to reset the process or how to evaluate measurements to decide when the process should be reset?
3. Is there a process adjustment that the operator can make to eliminate defects? Under what conditions should the operator adjust the process? When should the operator shut down the machine and seek more help? Whose help?
4. Have the operator actions which cause defects, and the necessary preventive action, been given to the operator, preferably in written form?
5. Is there an adequate preventive maintenance program on the process?
6. Is there a hidden "knack" possessed by some operators that needs to be discovered and transmitted to all operators?

The ability to regulate a process is often the weakest of the three criteria of self-control. Some specific techniques are discussed in Chapter 14.

13-5 DEFINING QUALITY RESPONSIBILITIES ON THE FACTORY FLOOR

In many organizations, the responsibility for product quality on the production floor is unclear. This can become apparent from (1) the actions or lack of actions by various functions, and (2) the lack of agreement between functions (and even within a function) on current responsibilities for quality.

When the situation becomes serious enough, it gains attention because the question is raised: "Who is responsible for quality?" Discussion of this question is generally futile and a waste of time because the question covers too broad a scope. It is like asking "Who is responsible for cost?" or "Who is responsible for safety?" Such broad questions result in a haphazard discussion of many issues or conclude with a panacea that "everyone is responsible for quality."

The way toward constructive discussion of responsibility is to become specific. This can be done by defining the *decisions and actions* that collectively determine quality on the factory floor and then discussing the responsibility question *separately* for each decision and action. A useful tool is a responsibility matrix showing the decisions/actions and those available to make them (Figure 13-2).

Figure 13-2 Responsibility matrix.

Decision/action	Manufacturing engineering	Setup technician	Operator	Supervisor	Inspector	QC engineer
Review designs						
Assign machines						
Make setup						
Approve setup						
Run machine						
Monitor machine						
Inspect parts						
Decide disposition of rejects						
Diagnose causes of rejects						
Determine corrective action						

The supervisors associated with the department under study convene for the purpose of arriving at a meeting of the minds on "Who should do what?" As one step in reaching an agreement, they may first tally up on the matrix "Who *now* does what?" From the study of the present pattern of "who does what," they move to discussion of what *should* be the pattern.

Often this is done by "ballot." Each person executes a copy of the matrix in accordance with their views of who now does what. All these views are then tallied on the blackboard to see what are the points of agreement and what are the areas of lack of agreement. The differences are then talked out to arrive at a meeting of the minds.

Managers often ask: "Is there a right way to organize?" The answer is no. The pattern of responsibility must be designed to fit the local conditions. In one department it is convenient to assign to the same person the jobs of set up and operate; in another department setup is best done by a special setup person. In one department the process is so stable that the original setup will endure for the length of the lot; in another department the setup requires check and readjust during the life of the lot. There are differences in the extent of training, in the level of morale, etc., of the work force. The permutations of these and other differences make each department unique and require a made-to-measure design of responsibility for decision making.

13-6 PRODUCT ACCEPTANCE BY OPERATORS (SELF-INSPECTION)

Recently, one aspect of the responsibility for quality on the factory floor has received much attention, i.e., product acceptance by operators. In the past, decisions on whether the *process should run or stop* have been made mainly by the production department. Decisions on whether the *product conforms or not* have been made mainly by the inspection department. Sometimes it is possible to have the production operators perform both of these functions.

In practice, most managers have the conviction that they dare not delegate the decision of product conformance to the operators. The belief is that some or many of the operators will solve their production quota problems by accepting poor product. This belief is based on long-standing tradition buttressed by some bitter experience, plus the contentions of the inspection and quality control specialists.[3] All this has given rise to a sizable inspection function in many companies.

The point in question is whether the production operators should make the conformance decisions on the product they make. They are already in the mainstream of product flow, know the product characteristics, and usually measure the product. To require a second person (an inspector) to make measurements and judge conformance is a partial duplication of the measurement process and incurs additional handling, all resulting in added cost. Thus product acceptance by operators often has cost-reduction opportunities. Proponents of the concept also cite another advantage. A separate inspection function is sometimes viewed as a "crutch" that inevitably reduces Production's sense of responsibility for quality and shifts the responsibility to the inspection or quality control function.

What has evolved in some companies is the concept of audit of decisions. Under this concept, all inspection and all conformance decisions, both on the process and on the product, are made by the production operator. (Decisions on the action to be taken on a nonconforming product are *not* delegated to the operator.) However, an independent audit of these decisions is made. The quality control department inspects a random sample periodically to ensure that the decision-making process used by operators to accept or reject a product is still valid. The audit verified the *decision-making process*. Note that, under a pure audit concept, the inspectors are not transferred to do inspection work in the production department. Except for the audits, the inspection positions are eliminated.

Several ways of organizing responsibility on the factory floor are shown in Table 13-3. The upper part shows organizational approaches and the lower part shows the criteria for each. In the case of audit of decisions, several criteria must be met. The defects must be mainly operator-controllable, the cost of defects must be low, the operators must be trained in process control, there must be mutual confidence between managers and operators, and the operators must have a high degree of motivation to meet quality requirements. Many companies do *not* meet these criteria, and risks would be involved if product conformance decisions were given to production operators. However, the po-

---

[3] For some of the contesting views see J. M. Juran. "Inspectors—Headed for Extinction?" *Industrial Quality Control*, October 1965, pp. 198–199; E. G. D. Paterson, "Stop, Look, Inspect," *Industrial Quality Control*, August 1967, pp. 86–89. See also J. M. Juran. "A Challenge to the Extinction of 'Homo Inspectiens,'" *Industrial Quality Control*, December 1967, pp. 298–299. See also Letters to the Editor, *Quality Progress*, March 1968, pp. 33, 43, 44.

Table 13-3 Organizing responsibility on the production floor

	Extent of inspection intervention			
	Full control	Semicontrol	Product approval	Audit control
Control decisions				
Setup approval	×	×		
Running approval	×			
Product approval	×	×	×	
Audit of decisions				×
Criteria for plan of decision making				
Defects mainly operator-controllable?	Yes or no	Yes or no	Yes or no	Yes
Cost of nonconformance	High	High	Moderate	Low
Operators trained in measurement and use of data?	No	No	Partial	Yes
Mutual confidence between managers and operators	No	No	Partial	Yes
Operator motivation	Low	Low	Adequate	High

tential advantages have prompted some companies to adopt the concept prematurely. As with all complex problems in society, solutions that are dramatic and amenable to immediate action are usually not as effective as embarking on the long road of diagnosing basic causes and determining remedies. Harrington[4] gives a description of steps taken by one company in transferring the inspection responsibility (and other responsibilities) to the production department.

If operators are to be given the product conformance decision, it is necessary to decide whether the responsibility should be given to all operators or only to those operators who have demonstrated their ability to make good decisions. The latter approach is preferable and should proceed as follows:

1. Train the operators in how to make product conformance decisions.
2. Set up the necessary system of product identification and preserving the order to assure that product decisions can be traced readily back to the operator who made them.
3. Institute a trial period during which operators make conformance decisions while duplicate decision making by inspectors is retained. The purpose of this dual acceptance is to discover, through data, which operators consistently make good product conformance decisions.
4. Issue "licenses" (for making product conformance decisions) only to those operators who demonstrate their competence.
5. For the licensed operators, institute an audit of decisions (see below). For the operators who do not qualify, retain the regular inspection.
6. Based on the results of the audits, continue or suspend the licenses.

[4] H. James Harrington, "Are You Ready for Integration?" *1973 ASQC Annual Technical Conference Transactions*, p. 196.

7. Periodically conduct new trials in an effort to qualify the unlicensed operators.

If an audit reveals that wrong decisions were made by the operators, then the product evaluated since the last audit is reinspected—often by the operators.

Operator response to the delegation is generally favorable, the concept of job enlargement being a significant factor. However, operators who do qualify for the license commonly demand some form of compensation for this achievement, e.g., higher grade, more pay, etc. The companies invariably make a constructive response to these demands, since the economics of making the delegation are very favorable. In addition, the resulting differential tends to act as a stimulus to the nonlicensed operators to qualify themselves.

Results Achieved

Published reports of results of delegating product acceptance decisions to Production claim quality improvements as well as sharp reductions in inspection costs.

Folloni[5] describes the results at a naval rework facility where defects per 1000 labor-hours were reduced from 26.9 to 15.8; quarterly rework costs were reduced from $19,800 to $10,200; average defects per aircraft discrepancy report were reduced from 10.0 to 4.0. This occurred over a 5-year period. It took several years for the production force to attain a high level of percent licensed.

In several cases[6] reductions in inspectors ranged from 30 to 7 percent. There were also reductions in supervision and in maintenance personnel as well as in reject rates.

13-7 PROCESS CONTROL IN THE SERVICE INDUSTRIES

The service industries cover a wide spectrum, from those which are primarily equipment-based, such as automatic car washes, to those which are primarily people-based, such as hotels and restaurants.[7] The approach to process control is heavily influenced by the industry's degree of dependence on equipment versus people.

Increasingly, service industries are becoming more technological by the

---

[5] See John R. Folloni, Jr., "Production Certifies Quality of Its Work," *Industrial Engineering*, November 1971, pp. 11–16. See also, for subsequent data, John R. Folloni, Jr., "Employee Certification and Motivation," *1972 ASQC Annual Technical Conference Transactions*, pp. 397–401, from which Figure 11-9 is taken.

[6] "It Pays to Wake Up the Blue Collar Worker," *Fortune*, September 1970, p. 168.

[7] Dan R. E. Thomas, "Strategy Is Different in Service Industries," *Harvard Business Review*, July/August 1978, p. 158.

use of (1) equipment to perform manual tasks, (2) a systems approach to more thoroughly plan and integrate manual tasks, or (3) a combination of both equipment and systems. The original incentive for the adoption of technology was to provide service at a low cost, but of equal importance was to provide service in a short *time,* because in many service industries time is a fitness-for-use parameter. Because of the problems of recruiting, training, and holding people, service work was often engineered so as to permit it to be performed by unskilled labor. The substitution of equipment for some manual tasks and the explicit definition of work methods for other tasks also helped to achieve a *consistency* of the quality of service provided. The fast-food establishments are an example of this concept.[8]

The three criteria of self-control can help bring focus to process control problems in service industries. With respect to the first criterion, the task of defining what is meant by "quality" is a difficult one. Some innovative approaches are being tried, as illustrated by the airline that has defined 47 quantitative indices covering customer service (see Section 14-10). With respect to the second criterion, the service organization does have the benefit of possible immediate feedback because the service is usually provided directly to the ultimate consumer. However, the feedback is often weak unless the service is extremely poor. Thus market research may be needed to provide adequate information on fitness for use. With respect to the third criterion, the ability to "regulate the process" applies particularly to equipment-based service industries but can also be used to analyze the human tasks that are cardinal in people-based service industries.

PROBLEMS

13-1 For any of the following processes, list the defects commonly encountered, estimate the frequency of each, and estimate the controllability of the principal defects. Tabulate your results and prepare your conclusions.

  1. A man playing golf
  2. A foursome playing bridge
  3. A regular on the football team
  4. A trucker driving in traffic
  5. A department store salesclerk waiting on a customer
  6. A stenographer transcribing notes
  7. A bricklayer on a construction job

13-2 In a certain operation involving the high-volume manufacture of discrete pieces from continuous lengths of material, the following is the system of controlling quality on the manufacturing floor:

  1. The *operator* makes initial roll adjustments for each new length of material by examining

[8] Theodore Levitt, "The Industrialization of Service," *Harvard Business Review,* September/October 1976, p. 63. Also, "Production-Use Approach to Service," *Harvard Business Review,* September/October 1972, p. 41.

sample pieces, and subsequently continues to make such examinations and adjustments while the machine is running.

2. The *patrol inspector* (reporting to the chief inspector) also periodically examines sample pieces directly from the machine and, if he or she thinks it necessary, asks the operator to make adjustments.

3. Usually, the operator complies with such requests, but on occasion remonstrates. If he or she feels very strongly about it appeal may be made to the *foreman*, who may decide to let the machine run without making the requested adjustment.

4. If this happens, the patrol inspector may appeal to the *chief inspector* (through his or her supervisor), who may then order the machine to be shut down. Such an order is complied with.

5. All the pieces from the machine, in lots of 1000, go to a *bench inspector*, who samples them according to a prescribed plan. He or she passes some lots to the next operation on the basis of a good sample and sorts those lots which fail the sampling plan if they contain particular types of defects (i.e., easily identifiable and removable). Other rejected lots (containing defects not so easily identifiable) are routed to the next operation, marked to indicate the nature of defects to be removed.

6. The next operation is final inspection, where a *final inspector* reexamines all lots 100 percent (accepted, sorted, and rejected lots) and is supposed to remove all types of defects, including some attributable to operations preceding the one we have been considering.

Using the following form, place the necessary check marks to indicate who has authority to make the decisions indicated.

	Operator	Foreman	Patrol inspector	Bench inspector	Final inspector	Chief inspector
Make setup						
Accept setup						
Operate process						
Accept process						
Correct process						
Accept lots						
Accept pieces						

Are the responsibilities clear-cut? Explain your answer.[9]

13-3 Study the system of performance feedback available to any of the following categories of "operator" and report your conclusions on the adequacy of this feedback for controlling quality of performance.

1. The motorist in city traffic
2. The student at school
3. The supermarket cashier

13-4 Your plant has just conducted a "controllability study" by analyzing the causes of a large sample of defective parts. The results showed that 45 percent of the causes were operator-controllable and 55 percent management-controllable. One program (diagnosis of specific causes, determination of remedies, etc.) is planned for the management-controllable problems. For the operator-controllable, a motivation program for the operators producing poor work is planned. You are asked to comment on this approach.

[9] Course notes for Management of Quality Control, U.S. Air Force School of Logistics, 1959.

13-5 For a specific manufacturing operation with which you are familiar, describe how you would make a controllability study.

SUPPLEMENTARY READING

The *Quality Control Handbook*, 3rd ed., McGraw-Hill Book Company, New York, 1974, includes two sections discussing the overall approach to quality during production. Section 11 discusses the topic as applied to manufacturing organizations and Section 47 provides an approach for the service industries.

FOURTEEN

MANUFACTURE—PROCESS CONTROL TECHNIQUES

14-1 CONCEPT OF DOMINANCE

In Section 11-4 we introduced the concept of dominance. This recognizes that process variables are not equally important in their effect on quality characteristics and that one variable, or one type of variable, often dominates the others. For example, in presswork it has long been known that the die is dominant, and process controls have been built around this fact. In other cases, the dominant variable may or may not be obvious but is not acted upon, for many reasons. Identifying the dominant subsystem in a manufacturing system has value in both process control and process improvement because it focuses on those variables that will provide the highest return on an investment in process control techniques.

It is useful to categorize manufacturing systems as having four forms of dominance: setup, machine, operator, and component. Some examples of each are given for manufacturing and service industries in Table 14-1.

The dominant system is not the sole source of defects for the process in question, but is the main source. For example, a printing operation is setup-dominated as to defects such as spelling or color of ink. It is operator-dominated as to fingerprints on the sheets. In planning process controls, it is helpful to list the important quality characteristics and define the dominance. An example for a textile product is given in Table 14-2.

Table 14-1 Process dominance categories

Setup dominant	Machine dominant	Operator dominant	Component dominant
		Typical operations	
Punching	Packaging	Arc welding	Watch assembly
Drilling	Screw machining	Hand soldering	Auto assembly
Cutting	Automatic cutting	Blanchard grinding	Other mechanical
Broaching	Volume filling	Steel rolling	assembly
Die cutting	Weight filling	Turret-lathe	Plastics assembly
Molding	Paper making	running	Electronics
Coil winding	Wool carding	Spray painting	assembly
Labeling	Resistance welding	Hand packing	Food formulation
Heat sealing	Chemical processes	Repairing	Vegetable packing
Printing	Transportation	Food serving	Retailing
Data processing	Electric utilities	Clerical	Fast food
		Typical control systems during manufacture	
First-piece	Patrol inspection	Patrol inspection	Vendor rating
inspection	X chart	p chart	Incoming inspection
Lot plot	Median chart	c chart	Prior operation
PRE-Control	$\bar{X}$ and R chart	Operator certification	control
Narrow-limit	PRE control	Systems audits	Acceptance
gaging	Narrow-limit		inspection
Attributes visual	gaging		
inspection	p chart		
	Systems audits		

Table 14-2 Dominant causes of quality characteristics

Process or product quality	Setup dominant	Machine dominant	Operator dominant	Material dominant
Proper thread-up	—	—	×	—
Denier of yarn	—	×	—	—
Tenacity of yarn	—	×	—	—
Elongation of yarn	—	×	—	—
Filament cross-section shape	—	×	—	—
Filament cross-section size variation	—	—	—	×
Wind of yarn on packages	—	×	—	—
Stops	—	—	—	×
Tension on end	—	×	—	—
Lay of yarn on beam	—	×	—	—
Broken filaments on beam	—	—	—	×
Soil on beam	—	—	×	—
Beam circumference	×	—	—	—
Beam hardness	×	—	—	—

For each form of dominance there is an appropriate kit of control tools. Table 14-1 lists the most usual tools associated with the four forms of dominance. This chapter will discuss these tools.

14-2 SETUP-DOMINANT OPERATIONS

When the setup is the dominant cause of defects, the process setup should be formally approved before production starts. The evaluation of a process setup can vary from a first-piece inspection for a simple mechanical operation to an evaluation of a pilot plant for a complex chemical process.[1] Often the evaluation is conducted for several reasons, including quality, and may require the participation and approval of the Quality Control, Manufacturing, Industrial Engineering, and Product Engineering departments.

The concept of self-control can be applied to the setup of a process. Those making a setup must:

1. *Know where to center the setup.* Sometimes this is evident from the product or process specification. If not, special knowledge must be provided to the setup person. For example, a company making metal containers ("tin cans") found that while the process was highly reproducible, it was essential that certain dimensions of the setup be precisely centered. For this purpose the planners prepared a narrow limit scheme and provided the setup personnel with suitable narrow limits to meet. These became a mandatory requirement of the setup. Narrow limit gaging is explained in this chapter.
2. *Know whether the setup is actually centered.* The necessary instruments, standards, etc., should be provided to the setup personnel for this purpose. Alternatively, patrol inspectors who are so provided should do the measuring and feed these data back to the setup staff. In some cases it is feasible to make use of product data to show clearly the nature of the setup, as in the example in Section 13-3.
3. *Be able to adjust the setup with precision.* (This is often a neglected aspect of process design.) In conventional metal cutting, calibrated feed wheels accomplish this purpose. However, for many other processes, the setup personnel are left on a cut-and-try basis. Since they are also responsible for meeting cost and delivery standards, the cut-and-try adjustments become a temptation to "settle for a close one," since a new try may be no better.

Setup acceptance criteria have historically been based on rule-of-thumb methods, exemplified by first-piece inspection. Here the process is set up and the first piece produced is inspected. If acceptable, the setup is approved and production begins. Unfortunately, one measurement provides little information on the centering of the process. That measurement could have come from any

---

[1] See *Quality Control Handbook,* 3rd ed., p. 29-7.

deficiencies in the system of control and sometimes they do not do so. (Sometimes they do, and it is management who fails to act.) However, the theory is much more right than wrong.

Whether the defects in a plant are mainly management-controllable or operator-controllable is a fact of the highest order of importance. To reduce the former requires a program in which the main contributions must come from the managers, supervisors, and technical specialists. To reduce the latter requires a different kind of program in which much of the contribution comes from the operators. The great difference between these two kinds of programs suggests that managers should quantify their knowledge of the state of controllability before embarking on major programs.

An example of a controllability study was given in Section 5-6. Another example is given in Table 13-1. Here a diagnostic team was set up to study the scrap and rework reports in 6 machine shop departments for 17 working days. The defect cause was entered on each report by the foreman and verified by the team chairman. When the cause was not apparent, the team reviewed the defect and, when necessary, contacted other specialists (who had been alerted by management about the priority of the project) to identify the cause. The purpose of the study was to resolve a lack of agreement on the causes of chronically high scrap and rework. It did the job. The study was decisive in obtaining agreement on the focus of the improvement program. In less than one year over $2 million was saved and important strides made in reducing production backlogs.

One of the authors has made extensive studies in controllability and has found that the defects encountered are about 80 percent management-controllable. This figure does not vary much from industry to industry, but varies

Table 13-1 Controllability study in a machine shop (%)

Management-controllable	
Inadequate training	15
Machine inadequate	8
Machine maintenance	8
Other process problems	8
Materials handling	7
Tool, fixture, gage (T, F, G) maintenance	6
T, F, G inadequate	5
Wrong material	3
Operation run out of sequence	3
Miscellaneous	5
Total	68
Operator-controllable	
Failure to check work	11
Improperly operated	11
Other (e.g., piece mislocated)	10
Total	32

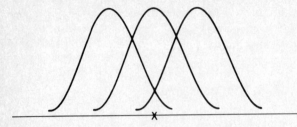

Figure 14-1 Different distributions having the same result at first-piece inspection.

one of many distribution curves, and thus the single measurement is not a good indicator of the true process center (see Figure 14-1). Further, one measurement provides no information on the *variation* of the process.

Two possible mistakes can be made in evaluating a setup—disapproving a correct setup or approving an incorrect setup. Formal techniques are available for choosing sample sizes and interpreting data for evaluating setups. These are summarized in Table 14-3 and explained in this chapter and elsewhere in the book.

14-3 MACHINE-DOMINANT OPERATIONS

Machine-dominant processes undergo a continuing time-to-time change (e.g., depletion of reagents, wear of tools, heat buildup) of such magnitude that defective units will eventually be made. To prevent this, provision must be made for periodic check and adjustment. This is often called *patrol inspection.*

Table 14-3 Techniques for evaluating process setup

Technique	Application to setup evaluation
Measurable characteristics	
Frequency distribution (Chaps. 3 and 12), probability paper (Chap. 12), lot plot (Chap. 10)	Sample is taken and $\bar{X}$ and 6σ calculated to evaluate process aim and capability. Sample size varies from 7 to 50 depending on technique.
PRE-Control and narrow-limit gaging (see this chapter)	Sample of 5 units is judged against special limits to evaluate process aim and capability.
Variables sampling plans (Chap. 17)	Desired risks of disapproving a correct setup and approving an incorrect setup are defined and sampling procedures developed to meet these risks. Sample size depends on risk levels.
Nonmeasurable characteristics	
Attributes sampling	Sample is inspected for visual defects. Sample size varies from 1 to 50 depending on stability of process and seriousness of defect.

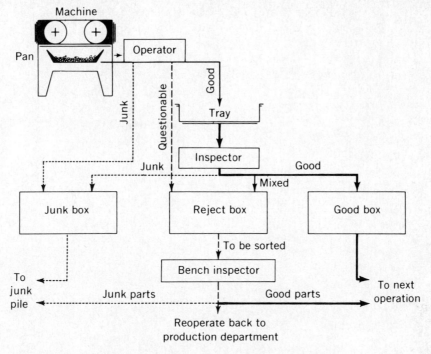

Figure 14-2 Patrol inspection plan based on preserving the order.

The numerous plans of patrol inspection in use consist mainly of the following four types:

1. Preserve the order of manufacture under an arrangement such as that depicted in Figure 14-2. In this example, the machine discharges its production into a small container called a "pan." The production operator periodically empties the pan into one of three larger containers.
   a. Into the junk box if the parts are junk.
   b. Into the reject box if the parts are questionable or are mixed good and bad.
   c. Into the "tray" if the parts are presumably good.
   When the patrol inspector comes to the machine, he or she checks the last few pieces being made (and may also sample the tray). Based on this check, he or she disposes of the tray in one of three ways:
   a. Into the junk box if the parts are junk.
   b. Into the reject box if the parts are questionable or mixed good and bad.
   c. Into the "good box" if the parts are O.K. The good box goes on to the next operation.
   Only the inspector may dispose of the tray, and only the inspector may place any product in the good box.

The reject box is gone over by a sorter, who makes three dispositions:

a. Junk to junk department.

b. Reoperates back to production department.

c. Good parts on to next operation.

2. This method is similar to (1), but the inspection data from the last few pieces are posted to a control chart. If the process remains in control, all product made since the last check is accepted.
3. The accumulated product (e.g., in the tray of Figure 14-2) is sampled at random using some standard sampling plan, and acceptance is based on the sampling criteria.
4. The process variables are checked against a process specification, and the product is accepted provided the process conforms to specification. This method is usually restricted to cases in which there is to be a direct check on the product at later stages.

This chapter will discuss two specific techniques, i.e., control charts and narrow-limit gaging, including PRE-Control.

14-4 STATISTICAL CONTROL CHARTS

The control-chart concept was introduced in Chapter 12 in conjunction with process capability. The following steps are taken to set up a control chart:

1. Choose the characteristic to be charted.
   a. Give high priority to characteristics that are currently running defective. A Pareto analysis can establish priorities.
   b. Identify the process variables and conditions that contribute to the end product characteristics, so as to define potential charting applications, from raw material through processing steps to final characteristics. For example, pH, salt concentration, and temperature of plating solution are process variables contributing to plating smoothness.
   c. Choose measurement methods which will provide the kind of data needed for diagnosis of problems. Attribute data (e.g., percent defective) provide summary information but may need to be supplemented by variables data (e.g., numerical diameter of individual pieces) to diagnose causes and determine action.
   d. Determine the earliest point in the production process at which testing can be done to get information on assignable causes so that the chart can serve as an effective early warning device to prevent defectives.
2. Choose the type of control chart. Table 14-4 compares three basic control charts.
3. Decide the centerline to be used and the basis of calculating the limits. The centerline may be the average of past data, or it may be a desired average

Table 14-4 Comparison of some control charts

Statistical measure plotted	Average $\bar{X}$ and range R	Percent defective (p)	Number of defects (c)
Type of data required	Variable data (measured values of a characteristic)	Attribute data (number of defective units of product)	Attribute data (number of defects per unit of product)
General field of application	Control of individual characteristics	Control of overall fraction defective of a process	Control of overall number of defects per unit
Significant advantages	1. Provides maximum utilization of information available from data 2. Provides detailed information on process average and variation for control of individual dimensions	1. Data required are often already available from inspection records 2. Easily understood by all personnel 3. Provides an overall picture of quality	Same advantages as p chart but also provides a measure of defectiveness
Significant disadvantages	1. Not understood unless training is provided; can cause confusion between control limits and tolerance limits 2. Cannot be used with go/no go type of data	1. Does not provide detailed information for control of individual characteristics 2. Does not recognize different degrees of defectiveness in units of product	Does not provide detailed information for control of individual characteristics
Sample size	Usually 4 or 5	Use given inspection results or samples of 25, 50, or 100	Any convenient unit of product such as 100 ft of wire or one television set

(i.e., a standard value). The limits are usually set at ± 3 standard deviations, but other multiples may be chosen for different statistical risks.[2]

4. Choose the "rational subgroup." Each point on a control chart represents a subgroup (or sample) consisting of several units of product. For process control purposes, subgroups should be chosen so that the units *within* a subgroup have the greatest chance of being alike and the units *between* subgroups have the greatest chance of being different.

5. Provide the system for collecting the data. If the control chart is to serve as a day-to-day shop tool, it must be made simple and convenient for use.

[2] Acheson J. Duncan, *Quality Control and Industrial Statistics*, 4th ed., Richard D. Irwin, Inc., Homewood, Ill., 1974, p. 381.

Table 14-5 Control-chart limits—attaining a state of control

Chart for	Central line	Lower limit	Upper limit
Averages, $\bar{X}$	$\bar{\bar{X}}$	$\bar{\bar{X}} - A_2\bar{R}$	$\bar{\bar{X}} + A_2\bar{R}$
Ranges, R	$\bar{R}$	$D_3\bar{R}$	$D_4\bar{R}$
Percent defective, p	$\bar{p}$	$\bar{p} - 3\sqrt{\dfrac{\bar{p}(1-\bar{p})}{n}}$	$\bar{p} + 3\sqrt{\dfrac{\bar{p}(1-\bar{p})}{n}}$
Number of defects, c	$\bar{c}$	$\bar{c} - 3\sqrt{\bar{c}}$	$\bar{c} + 3\sqrt{\bar{c}}$

Measurement must be simplified and kept free of error. Indicating instruments must be designed to give prompt and reliable readings. Better yet, instruments should be designed which can record as well as indicate. Recording of data can be simplified by skillful design of data or tally sheets. The working conditions are a factor. A machine department which abounds in cutting oil cannot keep respectable records with ordinary pencil and paper. Protective covers can be made, special paper and crayons provided. Copying of day-to-day data should be avoided.

6. Calculate the control limits and provide specific instructions on the interpretation of the results and the actions which are to be taken by various production personnel (see subsequent paragraphs). Control limit formulas for the three basic types of control charts are given in Table 14-5. These formulas are based on ± 3 standard deviations and use a central line equal to the average of the data used in calculating the control limits. Values of the A_2, D_3, and D_4 factors used in the formulas are given in Table I in the Appendix. (A generalized control chart for averages is given in Figure 14-3.)

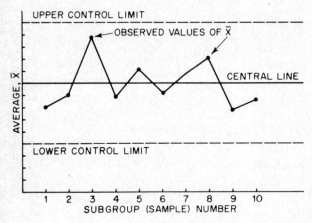

Figure 14-3 Generalized control chart for averages.

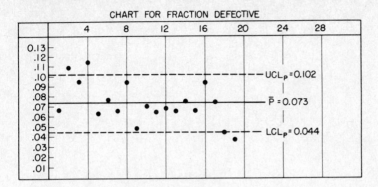

Figure 14-4 p chart for permanent magnets.

14-5 EXAMPLES OF CONTROL CHARTS

An example of an average and range ($\bar{X}$ and R) control chart was included in Section 12-5. An example of a percent defective (p) control chart will be presented next, and an example of a number-of-defects control chart will be presented later in the chapter. Additional examples can be found in Grant.[3]

The p chart will be illustrated with data on magnets used in electrical relays. For each of 19 weeks, the number of magnets inspected and the number of defective magnets were recorded. The total number of magnets tested was 14,091. The total number found to be defective was 1030. The average sample size was

$$\bar{n} = \frac{14,091}{19} = 741.6$$

The average fraction defective was

$$\bar{p} = \frac{1,030}{14,091} = 0.073$$

Control limits for the chart were placed at

$$\bar{p} \pm 3\sigma_p = \bar{p} \pm 3\sqrt{\frac{\bar{p}(1-\bar{p})}{\bar{n}}} = 0.073 \pm 3\sqrt{\frac{0.073(1-0.073)}{741.6}}$$

$$= 0.073 \pm 0.0287 = 0.102 \text{ and } 0.044$$

The resulting control chart is shown in Figure 14-4. Note that the last sample is below the lower control limit, indicating a significantly low fraction defective. Although this might mean that there is some assignable cause result-

[3] E. L. Grant, *Statistical Quality Control*, 4th ed., McGraw-Hill Book Company, New York, chaps. 3 through 9.

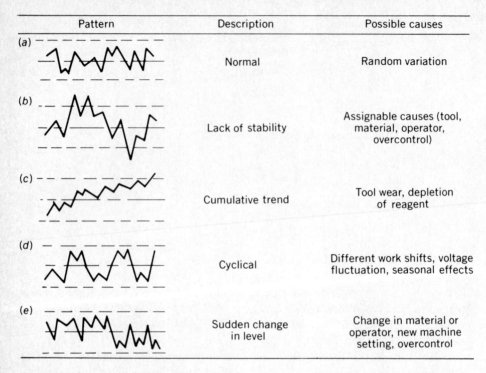

Pattern	Description	Possible causes
(a)	Normal	Random variation
(b)	Lack of stability	Assignable causes (tool, material, operator, overcontrol)
(c)	Cumulative trend	Tool wear, depletion of reagent
(d)	Cyclical	Different work shifts, voltage fluctuation, seasonal effects
(e)	Sudden change in level	Change in material or operator, new machine setting, overcontrol

Figure 14-5 Patterns on control charts.

ing in better quality, such points can also be due to an inspector's accepting some defective units in error.

A few of the many patterns and possible explanations are shown in Figure 14-5. Note that assignable causes can be present even though all points are within control limits (see Figure 14-5c, d, and e). Figure 14-5e includes a succession of points on one side of the centerline (called a *run*).

A set of rules to evaluate runs is given below (see Figure 14-6):

Divide each of the two areas between the centerline and the two control limits mentally into three equal zones. Since the control limits are at ±3 standard deviations from the centerline, each zone will be 1 standard deviation wide. Instability in the process is indicated if:

```
                        CONTROL LIMIT
──→ ──────────────────────────────────────────
──→ ZONE  A
──→ ZONE  B
──→ ZONE  C
──→ ──────────────────────────────────────────
──→ ZONE  C
──→ ZONE  B
──→ ZONE  A
──→ ──────────────────────────────────────────
                        CONTROL  LIMIT
```

Figure 14-6 Zones for applying tests for instability.

1. A single point falls outside the 3σ limit (beyond zone A).
2. Two out of three successive points fall in zone A or beyond. (The odd point may be anywhere.)
3. Four out of five successive points fall in zone B or beyond. (The odd point may be anywhere.)
4. Eight successive points fall in zone C or beyond.

A further discussion of runs and various other patterns on control charts is given in the literature.[4]

The three basic types of control charts have many variations. A comparison of alternative control charts for variables measurement is provided by Jackson[5] and Gibra.[6]

The control chart is a powerful statistical concept but its use should be kept in perspective. The ultimate purpose of a manufacturing process is to make product that is fit for use—and not to make product that meets statistical control limits. Considering the vast number of quality characteristics present in a modern plant, *control charts are justified for only a small minority of the quality characteristics.* Furthermore, once they have served their purpose (for problem analysis for breakthrough or control), most should be taken down and the effort shifted to other characteristics needing improvement.

14-6 NARROW-LIMIT GAGING: PRE-CONTROL

PRE-Control is a statistical technique for detecting process conditions and changes which may cause defects (rather than changes which are statistically significant). PRE-Control starts a process centered between specification limits and detects shifts that might result in making some of the parts outside a print limit. PRE-Control requires no plotting and no computations and it needs only three pieces to give control information. The technique utilizes the normal distribution curve in the determination of significant changes in the aim or the spread of a production process that could result in the increased production of defective work.

The principle of PRE-Control is demonstrated by assuming the worst condition that can be accepted from a process capable of quality production, i.e., when the natural tolerance is the same as the print allows, and when the process is precisely centered and any shift would result in some defective work.

If we draw in two PRE-Control (PC) lines, each one-fourth of the way in from each print-tolerance limit (Figure 14-7), it can be shown that 86 percent of

[4] Western Electric Company, *Statistical Quality Control Handbook,* Mack Printing Co., Easton, Pa., 1956, p. 161.

[5] J. Edward Jackson, "Evaluate Control Procedures by Examining Errors in Process Adjustment," *Journal of Quality Technology,* vol. 9, no. 2, April 1977, p. 47.

[6] Isaac Gibra, "Recent Developments in Control Chart Techniques," *Journal of Quality Technology,* vol. 7, no. 4, October 1975, p. 183.

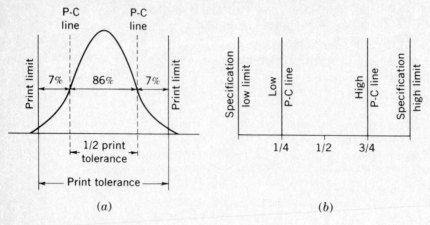

Figure 14-7 (*a*) Assumptions for underlying PRE-Control. (*b*) Location of PRE-Control lines.

the parts will be inside the PC lines, with 7 percent in each of the outer sections. In other words, 7 percent, or 1 part in 14, will occur outside a PC line under normal circumstances.

The chance that two parts in a row will fall outside a PC line is $\frac{1}{14}$ times $\frac{1}{14}$, or $\frac{1}{196}$. This means that only once in about every 200 pieces could we expect to get two parts in a row in a given outer band. When two in a row do occur, there is a much greater chance ($\frac{195}{196}$) that the process has shifted. It is advisable, therefore, to reset the process to the center. It is equally unlikely to get a piece beyond one given PC line and the next piece outside the other PC line. In this case, the indication is not that the process has shifted but that some factor has been introduced which has widened the pattern to an extent that defective pieces are inevitable. An immediate remedy of the cause of the trouble must be made before the process can safely continue.

These principles lead to the following set of rules[7] that summarize the technique of PRE-Control:

1. Divide the specification tolerance band with PC lines at $\frac{1}{4}$ and $\frac{3}{4}$ of the tolerance, as in Figure 14-7.
2. Start job.
3. If piece is outside specification limits, reset.
4. If one piece is inside specification limit but outside a PC line, check next piece.
5. If second piece is also outside same PC line, reset.

[7] This set of rules applies when 1 to 3 percent defective is permissible and the 6σ process dispersion is a maximum of 88 percent of the tolerance range. For other rules covering different quality levels and process dispersion, see D. Shainin, "Techniques for Maintaining a Zero Defects Program," *American Management Association Bulletin 71*, 1965; also, N. Raymond Brown, "Zero Defects the Easy Way with Target Area Control," *Modern Machine Shop*, July 1966, pp. 96–100.

6. If second piece is inside PC line, continue process and reset only when two pieces in a row are outside a given PC line.
7. If two successive pieces show one to be outside the high PC line and one below the low PC line, action must be taken immediately to reduce variation.
8. When five successive pieces fall between the PC lines, frequency gaging may start. While waiting for five, if one piece goes over a PC line, start count over again.
9. When frequency gaging, let process alone until a piece exceeds a PC line. Check the very next piece and proceed as in 6 above.
10. When machine is reset, five successive pieces inside the PC lines must again be made before returning to frequency gaging.
11. If the operator checks more than 25 times without having to reset, the gaging frequency may be reduced so that more pieces are made between checks. If, on the other hand, the operator must reset before 25 checks are made, increase the gaging frequency. An average of 25 checks to a reset is indication that the gaging frequency is correct.

The PRE-Control technique indicates changes in process aim and process variation. It is simple to use, can use go/no go gages, and can guarantee a specified percent defective if corrections are made when required.

PRE-Control is an example of a concept known as *narrow-limit gaging.* The broader concept provides sampling procedures (sample size, location of the narrow limits, and allowable number of units outside the narrow limits) to meet predefined risks of accepting bad product. Narrow-limit gaging is discussed by Ott.[8] Another approach is the acceptance control chart. This reflects both consumer and producer risks.[9]

14-7 OPERATOR-DOMINANT OPERATIONS

In operator-dominant operations, quality problems are caused by inadvertence, lack of skill, or willful action. Sections 6-2 to 6-5 discuss these causes.

Performance can be presented in control-chart form. Charts can be plotted using one of the following as sample index:

1. *Percent defective.* Usually, the inspection scheme is designed to serve both for product acceptance and for supplying operator control data. This method is used in attributes cases when the product is either good or bad.
2. *Number of defects.* This method is used for more elaborate products in which multiple errors can occur on a single unit of product, e.g., a television set, a large roll of woven carpeting.
3. *Defects per opportunity.* Each job is given a rating, prior to production, based on its complexity, or on the "number of opportunities for a defect." In electronics assembly work, for example, the rating is the sum of all com-

---

[8] Ellis R. Ott, *Process Quality Control,* McGraw-Hill Book Company, New York, 1975, chap. 7.

[9] Raymond F. Woods, "Effective, Economic Quality through the Use of Acceptance Control Charts," *Journal of Quality Technology,* vol. 8, no. 2, April 1976, p. 81.

ponents, solder connections, hardware insertions, etc., for the operations to be performed by a given operator. The operator's error rate is then the actual number of defects found in a sample divided by the total number of opportunities for a defect (i.e., units inspected times opportunities per unit for that job). This denominator more nearly puts all operators on the same basis, so that fair comparisons can be made between them.

4. *Defects per characteristic.* For mechanical parts or assemblies, "opportunities for a defect" may more conveniently be defined as the total number of quality characteristics for a given operation. This is used as the denominator. Such a scoring method is readily adapted to cumulative "pyramiding" for higher-management reporting.

Example The number of defects on paper sheets was plotted on a number-of-defects (c) chart. Specimen sheets 11 by 17 in in size were taken from production at intervals, and colored ink was applied to one side of the sheet. Each individual inkblot which appeared on the other side of the sheet within 5 min was counted as a defect. Twenty-five sheets were inspected and a total of 200 defects found.

The centerline of the chart is located at $\bar{c} = 200/25 = 8.0$ defects per sheet. Control limits were calculated as $8.0 \pm 3\sqrt{8.0}$, or 0 and 16.5. The c chart is shown in Figure 14-8.

Control charts for p or c are often plotted without statistical control limits. When such charts are installed on a process, a dramatic and quick improvement in quality sometimes occurs. There can be several reasons for such an improvement. First, the chart may provide tangible evidence

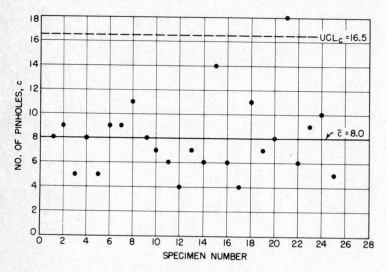

Figure 14-8 c chart for pinholes in paper.

that management is truly concerned with quality. Second, the chart may provide the operator with useful information that was not available before.

An example of a primarily operator-dominated process in a service industry comes from the Internal Revenue Service.[10] Here the "operator" is of two types: the original taxpayer preparing the form, and the government personnel examining the form. The control process here is threefold. First, each return is reviewed by an examiner and the tax information transferred to a computer, where the arithmetic is verified and other validity checks made. Second, employee quality is evaluated by drawing a sample of work from each employee once a week. This makes use of the MIL-STD-105D sampling tables (see Section 17-11) and a classification of defects into critical and noncritical defects. Acceptable quality standards, "alert" levels, and "critical" levels are defined based on desired results and past accomplishments. Third, computer-generated letters and other documents are reviewed for accuracy. Standard sampling tables are used weekly and if a rejection decision is made, the entire lot is reworked.

Another technique for operator-dominated processes is the systems audit. This is discussed later in this chapter.

14-8 COMPONENT-DOMINANT OPERATIONS

In component-dominant operations, the prime cause of poor quality is in the input materials to the operations. Defects may occur in epidemics (a lot of wrong material or out-of-specification material) or they may occur at random (a lot containing partially defective material). Assembly and subassembly, many chemical and food-processing operations, and packaging operations are typical examples.

The solution lies in establishing control systems for the earlier operations producing the material. For in-plant operations, the control system needed will depend on whether the particular operation producing the defect is setup-, machine-, or operator-dominant, all of which have been treated in this section. For vendor material, a vendor control system employing incoming inspection, corrective-action follow-up, vendor rating, and similar features may be needed (see Chapters 9 and 10). For internally produced material or components, a temporary system of lot-by-lot acceptance of components, before they enter the component-dominant operation, may be beneficial.

The development of automated testing equipment has made it possible to justify 100 percent inspection of components for some applications, particularly those used in complex products. One defective found at receiving inspec-

---

[10] David L. Gaugler, "Controlling Quality at an Internal Revenue Center," *1975 ASQC Annual Technical Conference Transactions*, p. 288.

tion can save a large amount of rework as compared to finding that same defective later in the assembly of a complex product.

In contrasting American versus Japanese quality control on color television sets, an important factor was the Japanese emphasis on sorting purchased components. A large investment in equipment personnel was necessary but the benefits were spectacular—a reduction in the number of line inspection and repair personnel from about 15 to 1 or 2 per assembly line.[11] These and other process control measures have resulted in a defect rate (for the entire production cycle) of one-half defect per *100* sets versus an industry score of about one defect per *single* set.[12]

14-9 AUTOMATION OF PROCESS CONTROL

The computer age has indeed arrived. The expanded use of computers has been made possible by breakthroughs in computer hardware. Such breakthroughs have given rise to a variety of computer systems. These are described in Section 25-5.

An example of a control chart used in an automated or complex process is the adaptive quality control chart. It goes beyond the conventional control chart by signaling not only when process action is required but the *amount* by which the process should be adjusted. An example[13] involving viscosity control in a continuous reactor is given in Figure 14-9. Viscosity is to be held between 86 and 98, with a target of 92. The amount of gas injected is a key process variable, and it was experimentally determined that a change in gas rate of 50 lb per minute eventually produced a viscosity change of 10 centipoise, i.e., $g = 10/50 = 0.2$. Further, the viscosity change occurred exponentially.

In Figure 14-9, the proportional (P) chart is a plot of hourly readings as a deviation from the target. On the difference (D) chart, the difference between successive readings is plotted; e.g., the first D is $94 - 90$, or 4. The action (A) chart first requires that the values from the P and D charts be added and then the process factor g applied. Thus for hour 2, $A + D = 2 + 4$, or 6. This is then multiplied by $-1/g$ to determine the amount of process adjustment, i.e., $6 \times 1/0.2 = 30$.

The technique is ideal for chemical and process industries, where the effect of variation of inputs can be measured and corrective action taken and where the full effect of a process change occurs over a period of time. The dynamics of the process must be known to generate the relationships needed for these charts. Adaptive control charts provide faster response to unexpected process variation, achieve a closer match to a process target, and eliminate overcontrol of a process due to improper adjustments.

[11] J. M. Juran, "Japanese and Western Quality—A Contrast," *Quality Progress*, December 1978, pp. 10–18.

[12] "No Miracle—Just Good Management," *Quality*, February 1978, p. 22.

[13] Adapted from G. E. P. Box and G. M. Jenkins. *Time Series Analysis, Forecasting and Control*, Holden-Day, Inc., San Francisco, 1970.

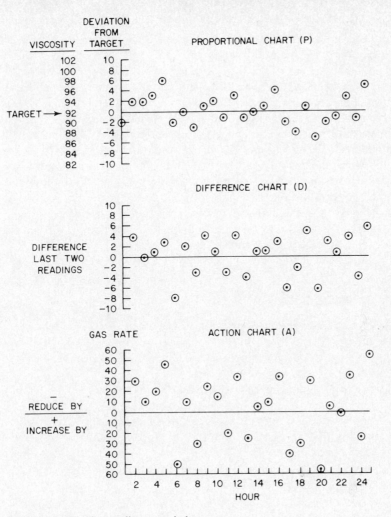

Figure 14-9 Adaptive quality control charts.

In using computers for process quality control, the quality control practitioner must work closely with the computer specialist. When the computer interfaces with production operators, several precautions are suggested:[14]

1. Avoid overwhelming the operator with too much display of data. Emphasize the data that are actually required by the operator.
2. Organize the data to parallel the operations of the natural subsystems.
3. Provide for manual operation of control valves.
4. Provide information on trends (no need for documents).

[14] Theodore J. Williams, "Trends in the Development of Process Control Computer Systems," *Journal of Quality Technology*, vol. 8, no. 2, April 1976, p. 69.

5. Analog displays (e.g., a diagram of surface imperfections) should be used for qualitative information and digital displays (e.g., a frequency tally of inspection results) for quantitative information.

The future of computer systems in the automation of processes appears unlimited. Automated chemical processes and numerically controlled machine tools have been proven feasible both technically and economically. Product designs can be stored in a computer and revisions entered as they are prepared. When reference must be made to the design, the computer can then furnish the latest edition. Entry of inspection data by voice rather than writing is now leading to changes in the inspection function. Among the future possibilities are transmission of information on the manufacturing floor by fiber optics rather than by copper wires. Data analyses that were considered too time-consuming in the past are trivial for the new breed of inexpensive computers, and unfold opportunities for new process control techniques.

14-10 PROCESS QUALITY AUDITS

A *quality audit* is an independent evaluation of various aspects of quality performance for the purpose of providing information to those in need of assurance with respect to that performance. A full discussion of quality audits is given in Chapter 22.

Application to manufacturing has been extensive and includes both audit of activities (systems audit) and audit of product (product audit).

Systems audit includes any activity that can affect final product quality. The major activities that are usually audited for process quality are listed in Section 22-4. The checklists presented in Chapter 13 for the three criteria of self-control can suggest useful subjects for audit. Priority should be assigned to subjects that affect product fitness for use.

The audit (as contrasted to a broad survey) is usually made on a specific activity, such as the system for calibrating measuring equipment. The audit is made by one or more persons and consists of an on-site observation of the activity. Adherence to existing procedures is often emphasized, but audits often uncover situations of inadequate or nonexistent procedures. Audits must be based on a foundation of hard facts that are presented in the audit report in a way that will help those responsible to determine and execute the required corrective action. A discussion of systems audit for an assembly manufacturer is given by Zeccardi and Radigan.[15]

A major airline uses audits to evaluate customer service in three areas:

1. Airport arrival and departure.
2. Aircraft interior and exterior.
3. Airport facilities.

[15] Joseph J. Zeccardi and Robert A. Radigan, "Auditing Systems Which Affect Product Quality: Increasing the Management Visibility of Quality Systems Performance," *1976 ASQC Annual Technical Conference Transactions*, p. 323.

Table 14-6 Example of a monthly audit report

Department number	Defect cost per operator per day, $	Predominant defect	Demerits per statistical unit
450	1.96	Grounded windings	98
462	0.42	Oversize dimension	21
465	1.20	Defective paint finish	60
479	2.34	Transposed wire	117

A total of 47 specific activities are periodically audited, then performance measurements made and compared to numerical goals. A few examples of goals are as follows:

1. At least 95 percent of public contact transactions are positive overall. (The term "positive" is defined in terms of actions expected of agents when serving customers.)
2. On ticketing, at least 80 percent of all passengers encounter line waits of not more than 5 min.
3. Carpets inside the planes should be at least 85 percent acceptable.
4. Adhesion of paint to planes should be at least 80 percent acceptable.
5. At airport security, at least 90 percent of all passengers should be processed within 3 min.
6. At least 90 percent of agents should be acceptable in personal appearance and grooming. (Specific local guidelines are defined to reflect passenger perception of agent appearance.) Detailed reports are available to all station personnel and a monthly summary is provided to several levels of management.

Product audit involves the reinspection of product to verify the adequacy of acceptance and rejection decisions made by inspection and test personnel. In theory, such audits should not be needed. In practice, they can often be justified by field complaints. Such audits can take place at each inspection station for the product or after final assembly and packing. Sometimes an audit is required before product may be moved to the next operation.

Product audits often must reflect the varying seriousness of different types of defects. An example[16] is shown in Table 14-6. In this example, demerits are assigned to the different types of defects and a unit of product requiring 8 h of labor to produce is called a *statistical unit*. Audit results are then summarized in terms of *demerits per statistical unit* (DPSU). The goal on DPSU is 50 and the allowable defect cost per operator is $1.00.

A manufacturer of consumer products classifies defects found at a final product audit as visual (V), electrical (E), and performance (P) and then predicts service costs on products in the field. This is done by first establishing

[16] Sidney L. Emons, "Auditing for Profit and Productivity," *1977 ASQC Annual Technical Conference Transactions*, p. 206.

Table 14-7 Audit data

Class of defect	Probability	Number of defects found in audit	Cost per service call, $	Expected cost, $
V1	1.00	1	15.00	15.00
V2	0.60	3	15.00	27.00
E1	1.00	2	30.00	90.00
E2	0.60	4	30.00	72.00
P1	1.00	1	25.00	25.00
P2	0.60	2	25.00	30.00
P3	0.20	2	25.00	10.00
				269.00

classes for each type of defect in terms of the probability of receiving a field complaint, e.g., a class 2 visual defect has a 60 percent probability. Service call costs are then combined with the audit data. For example, assume the data in Table 14-7 for a sample of 50. The expected cost is the product of the probability, number of defects, and cost per service call. The expected service cost per unit is then estimated as $269.00/50 = $5.38.

PROBLEMS

14-1 The percent of water absorption is an important characteristic of common building brick. A certain company occasionally measured this characteristic of its product but records were never kept. It was decided to analyze the process with a control chart. Twenty-five samples of four bricks each yielded these results:

Sample number	$\bar{X}$	R	Sample number	$\bar{X}$	R
1	15.1	9.1	14	9.8	17.5
2	12.3	9.9	15	8.8	10.5
3	7.4	9.7	16	8.1	4.4
4	8.7	6.7	17	6.3	4.1
5	8.8	7.1	18	10.5	5.7
6	11.7	9.1	19	9.7	6.4
7	10.2	12.1	20	11.7	4.6
8	11.5	10.8	21	13.2	7.2
9	11.2	13.5	22	12.5	8.3
10	10.2	6.9	23	7.5	6.4
11	9.6	5.0	24	8.8	6.9
12	7.6	8.2	25	8.0	6.4
13	7.6	5.4			

(a) Plot the data on an average and range control chart with control limits.

(b) During the manufacturing process, water is added to a clay paste to produce a workable mass. The amount of water added depended on the feel of the clay paste to the "pug mill" operator.

Several process changes were made after the original data were taken. A key change was the installation of a flowmeter to better control the quantity of water added. Twenty-five new samples of four bricks each were taken with the revised process:

Sample number	$\bar{X}$	R	Sample number	$\bar{X}$	R
1	6.7	4.0	14	9.6	6.9
2	7.7	8.4	15	11.1	2.9
3	8.0	4.0	16	13.2	13.2
4	10.9	8.3	17	8.7	8.7
5	8.7	2.2	18	4.7	4.7
6	8.2	4.1	19	6.1	6.1
7	9.9	3.7	20	4.8	4.8
8	11.1	8.0	21	2.3	2.3
9	10.5	6.1	22	4.2	4.2
10	7.3	2.7	23	4.5	4.5
11	8.8	2.2	24	2.0	2.0
12	10.8	6.3	25	2.9	2.9
13	10.4	7.7			

Plot these data on an average and range control chart with limits calculated from the new data. Comment on the charts for both sets of data.

Answer: (a) 15.8 and 3.97; 18.4 and 0. (b) 12.9 and 5.9; 13.4 and 0.

14-2 The specification on a certain dimension is 3.000 ± 0.004 in. A large sample from the process indicates an average of 2.998 in and a standard deviation of 0.002 in. Suppose that controls are instituted to shift the process average to the nominal specification of 3.000. Each part outside specification limits results in a loss of $5.00. In a lot of 1000 parts, how much monetary saving would be achieved by shifting the average as compared to keeping it at 2.998?

Answer: $573.

14-3 A statistical control chart for averages and ranges has been used to help control a manufacturing process. The sample data are consistently within control limits and the control limits are inside the engineering tolerance limits. The supervisor is confused because a high percentage of product is outside the tolerance limits even though the process is within control limits. What is your explanation?

14-4 The following data represent the number of defects found on each sewing machine cabinet inspected:

Sample number	Number of defects	Sample number	Number of defects
1	8	14	6
2	10	15	4
3	7	16	7
4	7	17	5
5	8	18	8
6	6	19	6
7	9	20	4
8	8	21	5
9	4	22	7
10	7	23	4
11	9	24	5
12	6	25	5
13	5		

Plot a control chart with control limits. Comment on the chart.

14-5 A sample of 100 electrical connectors was inspected each shift. Three characteristics were inspected on each connector but each connector was classified simply as defective or acceptable. The results follow:

Sample number	Percent defective	Sample number	Percent defective
1	4	14	4
2	3	15	4
3	5	16	5
4	6	17	3
5	7	18	0
6	5	19	3
7	4	20	2
8	2	21	1
9	5	22	3
10	6	23	4
11	4	24	2
12	3	25	2
13	3		

(a) Plot a control chart with control limits. Comment on the chart.

(b) If the inspection results had been recorded in sufficient detail, what other type of chart could also have been plotted?

Answer: (a) 9.2%, 0.

14-6 An average and range chart based on a sample size of five has been run, with the following results:

	Averages	Ranges
Upper control limit	78.0	8.0
Average value	75.8	3.8
Lower control limit	73.6	0

How large an increase in the overall process average would have to occur in order to have a 30 percent chance that a sample average will exceed the upper control limit?

Answer: 1.83.

14-7 As a part of a quality improvement program, a textile manufacturer decides to use a control chart to monitor the number of imperfections in bolts of cloth. The data from the last 25 inspections are recorded in the following table. From these data, compute control limits for an appropriate type of control chart. Plot the chart.

Bolt of cloth	Number of imperfections	Bolt of cloth	Number of imperfections
1	14	14	22
2	5	15	1
3	10	16	6
4	19	17	14
5	0	18	8
6	6	19	6
7	2	20	9
8	9	21	7
9	8	22	1
10	7	23	5
11	3	24	12
12	12	25	4
13	1		191
			(for 25 bolts)

Answer: Limits are 15.93 and 0.

14-8 Control-chart data were collected for the softening point (in degrees) in a polymerization process. Based on 25 samples of 4 each, the following control limits were calculated:

	Averages	Ranges
Upper control limit	12.9	13.4
Average	9.4	5.9
Lower control limit	5.9	0

Suppose that the population average shifts to 12.4. How large a sample would be necessary to have a 25 percent probability that the control chart for averages will signal out of control?

14-9 A p chart is to be used to analyze the September record for 100 percent inspection of certain radio components. The total number inspected during the month was 2196, and the total number of defectives was 158. Compute $\bar{p}$. Compute control limits for the following 3 days, and state whether the fraction defective falls within control limits for each day.

Date	Number inspected	Number of defectives
Sept. 14	54	8
15	162	24
16	213	3

SUPPLEMENTARY READING

Section 23 of the *Quality Control Handbook,* 3rd ed., McGraw-Hill Book Company, New York, 1974, discusses statistical process control methods. In addition, the industry sections contain much case material on process control. These sections, 29 through 47, explain process control techniques for the specific industry, process, or product. In addition, there is specialized material as follows:

Topic	Sections in QCH3
Setup-dominant operations	36A, 40, 45
Machine-dominant operations	29–33, 35, 36B, 39, 43
Operator-dominant operations	30, 34, 41, 46, 47
Component-dominant operations	33, 34, 37, 38, 42
Automation of process control	29, 32, 38, 42
Process quality audits	39, 40, 42, 43

A discussion of automatic testing as applied to process control is provided in Roy Knowles, *Automatic Testing*, McGraw-Hill Book Company, New York, 1976.

EXAMPLES OF EXAMINATION QUESTIONS USED IN FORMER ASQC QUALITY ENGINEER CERTIFICATION EXAMINATIONS AS PUBLISHED IN *QUALITY PROGRESS* MAGAZINE

1 A p chart is a type of control chart for: (*a*) plotting bar-stock lengths from receiving inspection samples; (*b*) plotting fraction-defective results from shipping inspection samples; (*c*) plotting defects per unit from in-process inspection samples; (*d*) answers (*a*), (*b*), and (*c*); (*e*) answers (*a*) and (*c*) only.

2 The sensitivity of a p chart to changes in quality is: (*a*) equal to that of a range chart; (*b*) equal to that of a chart for averages; (*c*) equal to that of a c chart; (*d*) equal to that of a u chart; (*e*) none of the above.

3 A p chart has exhibited statistical control over a period of time. However, the average fraction defective is too high to be satisfactory. Improvement can be obtained by: (*a*) a change in the basic design of the product; (*b*) instituting 100 percent inspection; (*c*) a change in the production process through substitution of new tooling or machinery; (*d*) all of the answers above are correct except (*b*); (*e*) all of the answers above are correct except (*c*).

4 In control-chart theory, the distribution of the number of defects per unit follows very closely the: (*a*) normal distribution; (*b*) binomial distribution; (*c*) chi-square distribution; (*d*) Poisson distribution.

5 You determine that it is sometimes economical to permit X to go out of control when: (*a*) the individual R's exceed R; (*b*) the cost of inspection is high; (*c*) 6σ is appreciably less than the difference between specification limits; (*d*) the $\bar{X}$ control limits are inside the drawing tolerance limits; (*e*) never.

6 An electronics firm was experiencing high rejections in their multiple connector manufacturing departments. p charts were introduced as part of a program to reduce defectives. Control limits were based on prior history, using the formula

$$p' \pm 3\sqrt{\frac{p'(100 - p')}{N}}$$

where p' is the historical value of percent defective and N is the number of pieces inspected each week. After six weeks the following record was accumulated:

Department number	p'	Percent defective					
		Week 1	Week 2	Week 3	Week 4	Week 5	Week 6
101	12	11	11	14	15	10	12
102	17	20	17	21	21	20	13
103	22	18	26	27	17	20	19
104	9	8	11	6	13	12	10
105	16	13	19	20	12	15	17
106	15	18	19	16	11	13	16

600 pieces were inspected each week in each department. Which department(s) exhibited a point or points out of control during the period? (*a*) dept. 101; (*b*) dept. 102; (*c*) dept. 103; (*d*) dept. 104; (*e*) dept. 105; (*f*) dept. 106.

7 You have just returned from a 2-week vacation and are going over with your QC manager the control charts that have been maintained during your absence. The manager calls your attention to the fact that one of the X charts shows the last 50 points to be very near the centerline. In fact, they all seem to be within about 1 σ of the centerline. What explanation would you offer? (*a*) "Somebody 'goofed' in the original calculation of the control limits"; (*b*) "The process standard deviation has decreased during the time the last 50 samples were taken and nobody thought to recompute the control limits"; (*c*) "This is a terrible situation. I'll get on it right away and see what the trouble is. I hope we haven't produced too much scrap"; (*d*) "This is fine. The closer the points are to the centerline, the better our control."

8 You look at a process and note that the chart for averages has been in control. If the range suddenly and significantly increases, the mean will: (*a*) always increase; (*b*) stay the same; (*c*) always decrease; (*d*) occasionally show out of control of either limit; (*e*) none of the above.

9 On the production floor, parts being produced measure 0.992 to 1.011. The specification requires the parts to be 0.995 to 1.005. Which of the following techniques would *not* be particularly useful in trying to improve and control the process? (*a*) PRE-Control; (*b*) MIL-STD-105 charts; (*c*) Multi-Vari charts; (*d*) $\bar{X}$ and R charts; (*e*) machine capability analysis.

CHAPTER FIFTEEN

INSPECTION AND TEST; PRODUCT ACCEPTANCE

15-1 PURPOSES OF INSPECTION

It is possible to visualize a company in which all functions are carried out with perfect attention to quality, cost, delivery schedule, etc. In such a company, market research would discover precisely the needs of fitness for use. Product designs would correctly reflect these needs. Specifications would correctly describe the intentions of the designs. Manufacturing planning would provide processes able to meet the specifications. Production personnel would operate and maintain the processes so as to produce products which conform to specification and thereby to the needs of fitness for use.

In practice, none of these things is done perfectly—there are deficiencies in market research, design, specification, manufacturing planning, production, etc. In addition, there are deficiencies in coordination. As a result, there is always present some tangible extent of nonconformance to specifications as well as some unfitness for use. The concept of inspection and test has evolved to help all concerned—vendors, processors, finished-goods makers, merchants, users, consumers, regulators, etc.—to secure improved quality performance.

All inspection (and test) involves some form of evaluation of product, comparing this evaluation with some standard, and judging whether there is conformance. However, inspection is now done for a wide variety of purposes (Table 15-1). Each of these purposes has its special influence on the nature of the inspection and on the manner of doing it.

15-2 CONFORMANCE TO SPECIFICATION AND FITNESS FOR USE

A major purpose of inspection is product acceptance, i.e., disposition of product based on its quality. This disposition involves several cardinal decisions:

Name	Purpose
Conformance decision	To judge whether the product conforms to specification
Fitness-for-use decision	To decide whether nonconforming product is fit for use
Communication decision	To decide what to communicate to outsiders and insiders

The Conformance Decision

Except in small companies, the number of conformance decisions made per year is simply huge. There is no possibility for the supervisory body to become involved in the details of so many decisions. Hence the work is so organized that the inspectors or production operators can make these decisions. To this end they are trained to understand the products, the standards, and the instruments. Once trained they are given the job of making the inspections and of judging conformance. (In many cases the delegation is to automated instruments.)

Associated with the conformance decision is the disposition of conforming product. What is done is to authorize the inspector to identify the product ("stamp it up") as acceptable product. This identification then serves to inform the packers, shippers, etc., that the product should proceed to its next destination (further processing, storeroom, customer). Strictly speaking, this decision to "ship" is made not by the inspectors but by the management. With some exceptions, product that conforms to specification is also fit for use. Hence the company procedures (which are established by the managers) provide that conforming products should be shipped as a regular practice.

The Fitness-for-Use Decision

In the case of nonconforming products, a new question arises: Is this nonconforming product fit for use or unfit? In some cases the answer is obvious—the nonconformance is so severe as to make the product clearly unfit. Hence it is scrapped or, if economically repairable, brought to a state of conformance. However, in many cases the answer as to fitness for use is not obvious. In such cases, if enough is at stake, a study is made to determine fitness for use. This study involves securing inputs such as the following:

1. *Who will be the user?* A technologically sophisticated user may be able to deal successfully with the nonconformance; a consumer may not. A nearby

Table 15-1 Purposes of inspection

Inspection includes, in all instances, (1) interpretation of the specification, (2) measurement of the product, and (3) comparison of (1) with (2). Inspection also includes additional elements depending on the purpose (see below). Section numbers in table refer to section numbers in *Quality Control Handbook*, 3rd ed.

Purpose	Usually called	Distinguishing features
a. To distinguish good lots from bad lots.	Acceptance sampling or sampling inspection; also called:	Prime purpose is to classify lots of product as to whether they are acceptable or nonacceptable. Results of the sampling are used to make this classification. Data from sampling usually made available to producing department.
	Vendor (or incoming) inspection	If done by purchaser on material bought from another company
	Process inspection	If done between departments of the same company
	Final inspection	If done by seller prior to shipment of finished goods to the customer
b. To distinguish good pieces from bad pieces.	Detail inspection, 100% inspection, or sorting; also called:	Prime purpose is to sort the product between good pieces and bad. Any data are incidental but are usually made available to producer.
	Classification	If process is inadequate to meet tolerances
		If process is adequate, but shop difficulties have created defects "needlessly"
c. To determine if the process is changing. See Sec. 23.	Control sampling	Prime purpose is to see if the process is changing. Usually done through Shewhart control charts which compare averages of samples to statistical limit lines. Detects the entrance of significant causes of variation. Any classification of product is incidental.

d. To determine if the process is approaching the specification limits. See Sec. 23.	Narrow-limit control	Prime purpose is to see if the trend of change within the process is such that there is danger of producing defective product. Usually done through charts which compare measurements on individual units of product to narrowed specification limits
e. To rate the quality of product. See Sec. 21, under Product Auditing.	Product auditing or quality rating	Prime purpose is to "photograph" the quality of product. Usually the seriousness of defects is recognized by assigning demerits or weights depending on the severity of defects. Results are usually charted as demerits per unit of product.
f. To rate the accuracy of inspectors. See the section on Measure of Inspector Accuracy.	Accuracy inspection, or overinspection, or accuracy rating, or check inspection	Prime purpose is to measure the effectiveness of inspectors in finding defects. Comparison is made between (1) defects found by the inspector and (2) defects which should have been found by the inspector. The ratio of (1) to (2) is the accuracy of the inspector.
g. To measure the precision of the measuring instrument. See Sec. 13.		Prime purpose is to measure the ability of the instrument to reproduce its own readings under like conditions. Usually involves repeat checks by the same instrument on the same unit of product. May involve checks by more than one instrument on the same unit of product
h. To secure product-design information.	Qualification testing	Prime purpose is to judge the service capability of the product. Sometimes involves tests of increased severity
i. To measure process capability. See Sec. 9, under Process Capability Measurement.	Process-capability measurement	Quantifies inherent variation of process

user may have easy access to field service; a distant or foreign user may lack such easy access.

2. *How will this product be used?* For many materials and standard products the specifications are broad enough to cover a variety of possible uses, and it is not known at the time of manufacture just what will be the actual use to which the product will be put. For example, sheet steel may be cut up to serve as decorative plates or as structural members; the television receiver may be stationed at a comfortable range or at an extreme range; chemical intermediates may be employed in numerous formulas.

3. *Are there risks to human safety or to structural integrity?* Where such risks are significant, all else is academic.

4. *What is the urgency?* For some applications, the client cannot wait, because the product in question is critical to putting some broader system into operation. Hence they may demand delivery now, and make repairs in the field.

5. *What are the company's and the users' economics?* For some nonconformances the economics of repair are so forbidding that the product must be used as is, although at a price discount. In some industries, e.g., textiles, the price structure formalizes this concept by use of a separate grade—"seconds."

6. *What are the users' measures of fitness for use?* These may differ significantly from those available to the manufacturer. For example, a manufacturer of abrasive cloth used a laboratory test to judge the ability of the cloth to polish metal; a major client evaluated the cost per 1000 pieces polished.

These and other inputs may be needed at several levels of fitness for use, i.e., the effects on: the economics of subsequent processors; the marketability requirements of the merchants; the qualities that determine fitness for the ultimate user; the qualities that influence field maintenance.

The job of securing such inputs is often assigned to a staff specialist, e.g., quality control engineer. He "makes the rounds," contacting the various departments which are able to provide pertinent information. There may be need to contact the customer, and even to conduct an actual tryout. A typical list of sources is as follows:

Input	Usual sources
Who will be the user?	Marketing
How will the nonconforming product be used?	Marketing; client
Are there risks to human safety or structural integrity?	Product research and design
What is the urgency?	Marketing; client
What are the company's and the users' economics?	All departments; client
What are the users' measures of fitness for use?	Market research; marketing; client

Once all the information has been collected and analyzed, the fitness-for-use decision can be made. If the amount at stake is small, this decision will be delegated to a staff specialist, to the Quality Control Manager, or to some continuing decision-making committee such as a Material Review Board (see Section 15-6). If the amount at stake is large, the decision will usually be made by a team of upper managers.

The Communication Decision

Inspection serves not only to make decisions on the product; it serves also to generate data which provide essential information for a wide variety of purposes, such as those listed in Table 15-1. The conformance and fitness-for-use decisions likewise are a source of essential information, although some of this is not well communicated.

Data on nonconforming products are usually communicated to the producing departments to aid them in preventing a recurrence. In more elaborate data collection systems there may be periodic summaries to identify "repeaters," which then become the subject of special studies.

When nonconforming products are sent out as fit for use, there arises the need for two additional categories of communication:

1. *Communication to "outsiders"* (usually customers) who have a right and a need to know. All too often the manufacturing companies neglect or avoid to inform their customers when shipping nonconforming products. The avoidance can be the result of bad experience, i.e., some customers will seize on such nonconformances to secure a price discount despite the fact that use of the product will not add to their costs. The neglect is more usually the failure even to face the question of what to communicate. A major factor here is the design of the forms used to record the decisions. With rare exceptions, these forms lack provisions which force those involved to make recommendations and decisions on (*a*) whether to inform the outsiders, and (*b*) what to communicate to them.
2. *Communication to insiders.* When nonconforming goods are shipped as fit for use, the reasons why are not always communicated to the inspectors and especially not to the production workers. The resulting vacuum of knowledge has been known to breed some bad practices. When the same type of nonconformance has been shipped several times, an inspector may conclude (in the absence of knowing why) that it is just a waste of time to report such nonconformances in the first place. Yet in some future case the special reasons (which were the basis of the decision to ship the nonconforming goods) may not be present. In like manner, a production worker may conclude that it is a waste of time to exert all that effort to avoid some nonconformance which will be shipped anyway. Such reactions by well-meaning employees can be minimized if the company faces squarely the question: What shall we communicate to the insiders?

15-3 INSPECTION PLANNING

Inspection planning is the activity of (1) designating the "stations" at which inspection should take place, and (2) providing those stations with the means for knowing what to do plus the facilities for doing it. For simple, routine quality characteristics, the planning is often done by the inspector. For complex products made in large multidepartment companies, the planning is usually done by specialists such as quality control engineers.

Locating the Inspection Stations

The basic tool for choosing the location of inspection stations is the flowchart (see, for example, Figure 11-1). The most usual locations are:

1. At receipt of goods from vendors, usually called "incoming inspection" or "vendor inspection."
2. Following the setup of a production process, to provide added assurance against producing a defective batch. In some cases this "setup approval" also becomes approval of the batch.
3. During the running of critical or costly operations, usually called "process inspection."
4. Prior to delivery of goods from one processing department to another, usually called "lot approval" or "toll-gate inspection."
5. Prior to shipping completed products to store or to customers, usually called "finished-goods inspection."
6. Before performing a costly, "irreversible" operation, e.g., pouring a melt of steel.
7. At natural "peepholes" in the process.

The inspection station is not necessarily a fixed zone such that the work comes to the inspector. In some cases the inspector goes to the work by patrolling a large area, performing inspections at numerous locations. The inspection station need not be located in or near the production area. Some inspection may be performed in the shipping area, at the vendor's plant, or on the customer's premises.

Choosing and Interpreting the Quality Characteristics

The planner prepares a list of which quality characteristics are to be checked at which inspection stations. As to some of these characteristics, the planner may find it necessary to provide information that supplements the specifications. Product specifications are prepared by comparatively few people, each generally aware of the needs of fitness for use. In contrast, these specifications must be used by numerous inspectors and operators, most of whom lack such awareness. The planner has a number of ways to help bridge this gap:

1. Provide inspection and test environments which simulate the conditions of use. This principle is widely used, for example, in testing electrical appliances. It is also extended to such applications as type of lighting used for inspecting textiles.
2. Provide supplementary information which goes beyond the specifications as prepared by the product designers and process engineers. Some of this information is available from published standards—company, industry, and national. Other information is specially prepared to meet the specific needs of the product under consideration. For example, in an optical goods factory, the generic term "beauty defects" was used to describe several conditions which differed widely as to their effect on fitness for use. A scratch on a lens surface in the focal plane of a microscope made the lens unfit for use. A scratch on the large lens of a pair of binoculars, although not serious functionally, was visible to the user and hence not acceptable. Two other species of scratches were neither adverse to fitness for use nor visible to the user, and hence unimportant. Through planning analysis these distinctions were clarified and woven into the procedures.
3. Help to train the inspectors and supervisors to understand the conditions of use and the "why" of the specification requirements.
4. Provide seriousness classification (see Section 15-4).

Detailed Inspection Planning

For each quality characteristic the planner determines the detailed work to be done. This determination covers such matters as:

1. The type of test to be made. This may require detailed description of test environment, test equipment, test procedure, and associated tolerances for accuracy.
2. The number of units to be tested (sample size).
3. The method of selecting the samples to be tested.
4. The type of measurement to be made (attribute, variable, other).
5. Conformance criteria for the units, being usually the specified product tolerance limits.

Beyond this detailed planning for the characteristics and units, there is further detailed planning applicable to the product, the process, and the data system:

6. Conformance criteria for the lot, consisting usually of the allowable number of nonconforming units in the sample.
7. Physical disposition to be made of the product—the conforming lots, the nonconforming lots, and the units tested.
8. Criteria for decisions on the process—should it run or stop?
9. Data to be recorded, forms to be used, reports to be prepared.

This detailed planning is usually embodied into a formal document which must be approved by the planner and the inspection supervisor. For a simple example, see Figure 11-3.

Supplemental Planning Information

For many types of product the inspectors are given responsibility beyond the rather narrow job of determining conformance to specification. They may have duties relating to customers' needs, to vendor relations, to process regulation, etc. In such cases the inspection planning will include providing the inspectors with the information needed to carry out such responsibilities. Examples of such information are:

1. The customer's order, which defines what is wanted, including the extent to which what is wanted is "special." This information is commonly provided to job shop inspectors.
2. Prior tests made on the same lot by vendors, production operators, etc. This information has application to the concept of audit of decisions described in Section 9-12 and Figure 9-4.
3. Information on quality of prior lots made by the same manufacturing source (vendor, operator, machine, process, etc.). Such information guides the choice of sampling tables and aids in interpreting the test data from the current lot.

Quality Control Manual

Many of the quality planning documents are designed for repetitive use. It is therefore common practice to design a quality control manual to provide an organized system for classifying, filing, and finding these repetitive use plans. For elaboration see Section 25-8.

15-4 SERIOUSNESS CLASSIFICATION

Quality characteristics are decidedly unequal in their effect on fitness for use. A relative few are "serious," i.e., of critical importance; many are of minor importance. Clearly, the more important the characteristics, the greater should be the attention they receive in such matters as extent of quality planning; precision of processes, tooling, and instruments; sizes of samples; strictness of criteria for conformance; etc. However, to make such discrimination requires that the relative importance of the characteristics be made known to the various decision makers involved: process engineers, quality planners, inspection supervisors, etc. To this end many companies utilize formal systems of seriousness classification. The resulting classification finds use not only in inspection and quality planning but also in specification writing, vendor relations, product audits, executive reports on quality, etc. This multiple use of seriousness classification dictates that the system be prepared by an interdepartmental committee, which then:

1. Decides how many classes or strata of seriousness to create (usually three or four).
2. Defines each class.
3. Classifies each characteristic into its proper class of seriousness.

Characteristics and Defects

There are actually two lists which need to be classified. One is the list of quality characteristics derived from the specifications. The other is the list of "defects," i.e., symptoms of nonconformance during manufacture and symptoms of field failure during use. There is a good deal of commonality between these two lists, but there are differences as well. (For example, the list of defects found on glass bottles has little resemblance to the list of characteristics.) In addition, the two lists do not behave alike. The design characteristic "diameter" gives rise to two defects—oversize and undersize. The *amount* by which the diameter is oversize may be decisive as to seriousness classification.

Normally, it is feasible to make one system of classification applicable to both lists. However, the uses to which the resulting classifications are put are sufficiently varied to make it convenient to publish the lists separately.

Definitions for the Classes

The pioneering system of definitions is that evolved in the Bell System during the 1920s. Most subsequent sets of definitions show the influence of this pioneering venture. Study of numerous such systems reveals an inner pattern which is a useful guide to any committee faced with applying the concept to their own company. Table 15-2 shows the nature of this inner pattern as applied to a company in the food industry. Table 15-3 shows the application of the classification concept by a manufacturer of automotive vehicles.

Classifying

This is a long and tedious but essential task. However, it yields some welcome by-products through discovering misconceptions and confusion among departments, thereby opening the way to clear up vagueness and misunderstandings. Then, when the final seriousness classification is applied to several different purposes, it is subjected to several new challenges, which provide still further clarification of vagueness.

A problem often encountered in practice is the reluctance of the designers to become involved in seriousness classification of characteristics. The designers may offer plausible reasons: all characteristics are critical; the tightness of

Table 15-2 Composite definitions for seriousness classification in food industry

Defect	Effect on consumer safety	Effect on usage	Consumer relations	Loss to company	Effect on conformance to government relations
Critical	Will surely cause personal injury or illness	Will render the product totally unfit for use	Will offend consumer's sensibilities due to odor, appearance, etc.	Will lose customers and will result in losses greater than value of product	Fails to conform to regulations for purity, toxicity, identification
Major A	Very unlikely to cause personal injury or illness	May render the product unfit for use and may cause rejection by the user	Will likely be noticed by consumer, and will likely reduce product salability	May lose customers and may result in losses greater than the value of the product. Will substantially reduce production yields	Fails to conform to regulations on weight, volume, or batch control
Major B	Will not cause injury or illness	Will make the product more difficult to use, e.g., removal from package, or will require improvisation by the user. Affects appearance, neatness	May be noticed by some consumers, and may be an annoyance if noticed	Unlikely to lose customers. May require product replacement. May result in loss equal to product value	Minor nonconformance to regulations on weight, volume, or batch control, e.g., completeness of documentation
Minor	Will not cause injury or illness	Will not affect useability of the product. May affect appearance, neatness	Unlikely to be noticed by consumers, and of little concern if noticed	Unlikely to result in loss	Conforms fully to regulations

Table 15-3 Seriousness classification of automotive defects

Class	Nature	Description	Examples
A	Critical to safety; essential to vehicle function	Defects which can endanger human life or can render the vehicle inoperative in an essential functional degree	Heat treatment of kingpins; pressure resistance of hydraulic brake hose
B	General function of vehicle; function of essential parts; appearance essential to the user	Nonsafety defects which might affect primary vehicle function; essential appearance characteristics	Noisy brakes; trunk lock will not open; body finish discolored
C	Functions of minor parts; appearance not essential to user	Defects which do not affect vehicle function or appearance essential to user. Defects neither A nor B	Rust on chassis; crooked identification decals on components

the tolerance is an index of seriousness, etc. Yet the real reasons may be unawareness of the benefits; other matters have higher departmental priority, etc. In such cases it may be worthwhile to demonstrate the benefits of classification by working out a small-scale example. In one company the program of classification of characteristics reduced the number of dimensions checked from 682 to 279, the effect being to reduce the inspection time from 215 min to 120 min.[1]

15-5 PRODUCT ACCEPTANCE

Of all the purposes of inspection (Table 15-1), the most ancient and the most extensively used is "product acceptance," i.e., determining whether "product" conforms to "standard," and thereby whether the product should be "accepted." All of these key words have more than one meaning, resulting in much confused communication.

Products and Standards

Product can mean a discrete unit, e.g., a pencil, a lamp, a refrigerator. For such discrete units the published quality standards are the requirements and tolerances set out in the design and test specifications published by the respective technical departments.

Product can also mean a collection of discrete units—a *lot*. The published standards for lot quality are usually contained in the inspection plans and sampling criteria published by the quality control department.

---

[1] *Quality Control Handbook,* 3rd ed., McGraw-Hill Book Company, New York, 1974, table 12-6 and associated discussion, p. 12-20.

Product can also exist in bulk—coils of wire, rolls of paper, tank cars of chemicals. For such cases the "unit" of product is a specimen while the lot is some or all of the bulk.

Table 15-4 shows the interrelation among these various types of product along with the nature of the respective standards.

In still more elaborate forms, "product" can mean a "system"—an automated factory, an airport control installation, a microwave communication network. For such cases the standard consists essentially of successful performance under field conditions. Accordingly, a performance test is conducted in the field as a prerequisite to acceptance by the customer. However, there are numerous prior tests on subsystems and even on the entire system. For example, some computer systems are assembled, tested, and "debugged" in special assembly factories. Then the systems are disassembled, shipped out to the site, reassembled, and tested under service conditions. The costs of running those special assembly factories run to many millions of dollars.

The inspection and test programs for these complex systems are necessarily quite elaborate, requiring a coordinated series of tests at successive levels of the product hierarchy—materials, components, units, subassemblies, assemblies, and subsystems. In addition, there are interface tests as well as special environmental tests for humidity, shock, vibration, etc. Preparation of such test programs obviously requires much knowledge about actual conditions of use as well as a clear understanding of the technology underlying the system design.

How Much Inspection?

The amount of inspection needed to decide the acceptability of a lot can vary all the way from no inspection to 100 percent inspection. The actual amount of inspection needed is governed mainly by the amount of prior knowledge available as to the quality and especially as to the *homogeneity* of the lot.

The presence or absence of this prior knowledge gives rise to several levels of amount of inspection:

1. *No inspection.* This is appropriate in cases where prior inspections on the same lot have already been made by qualified laboratories, e.g., in other divisions of the same company or in vendor companies. Prior inspections by qualified production operators are to the same effect.

2. *Small samples.* These can be adequate in cases where the process is inherently uniform and the order of production can be preserved. For example, in some punch press operations the stamping dies are made to a high degree of stability. As a result, the successive pieces stamped out by such dies exhibit a high degree of uniformity for certain dimensional characteristics. For such characteristics, if the first and last pieces are correct, the remaining pieces are also correct, even for lot sizes running to many thousands of pieces. In its generalized form, the press example is one of a high degree of process capability combined with "stratified" sampling—sampling based on knowledge of the order of production.

Table 15-4 Criteria for judging conformance of product in units and lots

Aspects of conformance	Product consists of discrete units		Product consists of bulk or a coalesced mass	
	Individual unit of product	Lot = collection of discrete units	Specimen from bulk	Lot = bulk or a coalesced mass
Usual name of subject matter of inspection:	Part, unit, component, assembly, product, etc.	Lot	Specimen	Lot, mass, bulk
Standard usually consists of:	Product specification, plus supplemental criteria in inspection plan	Sampling plan	Material specification	Sampling plan
Standard usually published by:	Product design department and inspection planning	QC department	Product design department	Product design or QC department
Standard usually expressed in terms of:	Natural units of measure	Percent defective	Natural units of measure	Percent conforming
Tolerance usually expressed as:	Maximum and minimum measurements	Allowable defects in sample	Maximum and minimum measurements	Maximum and minimum on averages; maximum on dispersion
Information on conformance usually derived from:	Measuring instruments	Sampling data plus prior knowledge of process (capability, order of manufacture, etc.)	Measuring instruments	Sampling data; inherent fluidity; prior knowledge of process
Criteria for judging conformance are:	Measurement versus tolerance	Actual defects versus allowable; evidence of process behavior	Measurement versus tolerance	Averages and dispersion versus tolerances; prior data

Small samples can also be used when the product is homogeneous due to its fluidity (gases, liquids) or due to prior mixing operations. This homogeneity need not be assumed—it can be verified by sampling. Even solid materials may be homogeneous due to *prior* fluidity. Once the fact of homogeneity has been established, the sampling needed is minimal.

3. *Large samples.* In the absence of prior knowledge, the information about lot quality must be derived solely from sampling, which means random sampling and hence relatively large samples. The actual sample sizes depend on two main variables: (*a*) the tolerable percent of defects, and (*b*) the risks that can be accepted. Once values have been assigned to these variables, the sample sizes can be determined scientifically in accordance with the laws of probability (see Chapter 16). However, the choice of defect levels and risks is largely based on empirical judgments.

Random sampling is clearly needed in cases where there is no ready access to prior knowledge, e.g., purchases from certain vendors. However, there remain many, many cases in which random sampling is used despite the availability of inputs, such as process capability, order of manufacture, fluidity, etc. A major obstacle is the lack of publications which show how to design sampling plans in ways which make use of these inputs. In the absence of such publications, the quality planners are faced with creating their own designs. This means added work amid the absence of protection derived from use of recognized, authoritative published materials.

4. *100 percent inspection.* This is used when the results of sampling show that the level of defects present is too high to go on to the users. In critical cases, added provisions may be needed to guard against inspector fallibility, e.g., automated inspection or redundant 200 percent inspection.

15-6 DISPOSITION OF NONCONFORMING PRODUCT

Once an inspector finds a lot of product to be nonconforming, he or she prepares a report to that effect. Copies of this report are sent to the various cognizant departments. This sets into motion a planned sequence of events. The lot is marked with a "Hold," and often is sent to a special hold area to reduce the risk of mixups. The schedulers look into the possibility of shortages and the need for replacement. An investigator is assigned to collect the type of information needed as inputs for the fitness-for-use decision as discussed in Section 15-3.

Decision Not to Ship

The investigation may conclude that the lot should not be shipped as is. In that event, the economics are studied to find the best disposition: sort, repair, downgrade, scrap, etc. There may be supplemental efforts of an accounting nature to charge the costs to the responsible source, especially where vendor responsibility is involved. There is also some degree of action to prevent a recurrence (see below).

Decision to Ship

This decision may come about in one of several ways:

1. *Waiver by the designer.* Such a waiver is a change in specification as to the lot in question and thereby puts the lot into a state of conformance.
2. *Waiver by the customer,* or by the Marketing Department on behalf of the customer. Such a waiver in effect supersedes the specification. (The waiver may have been "bought" by a change in warranty or by a discount in price.)
3. *Waiver by the Quality Control Department* under its delegation to make fitness-for-use decisions on noncritical matters. The criterion for "noncritical" may be based on prior seriousness classification of characteristics, on low value of product involved, or on still other bases. For minor categories of seriousness, the delegation may even be made to the quality control engineers or to inspection supervisors. However, as to major and critical defects, the delegation is typically to the Technical Manager, the Quality Control Manager, or to some team of managers.
4. *Waiver by a formal Material Review Board.* This board concept was originally evolved by the military buyers of defense products as a means of expediting decisions on nonconforming lots. Membership on the board includes the military representative plus the cognizant designer and the quality control specialist. A unanimous decision is required to ship nonconforming product. The board procedures provide for formal documentation of the facts and conclusions, thereby creating a data source of great potential value.
5. *Waiver by the upper managers.* This part of the procedure is restricted to cases of a critical nature involving risks to human safety, marketability of the product, or risk of loss of large sums of money. For such cases the stakes are too high to warrant decision making by a single department. Hence the managerial team takes over.

Corrective Action

Aside from the need for disposing of the nonconforming lot, there is a need to prevent a recurrence. This prevention process is of two types, depending on the origin of the nonconformance.

1. Some nonconformances originate in some isolated, sporadic change which took place in a well-behaved process. An example is a mixup in the materials used or an instrument out of calibration, or a human mistake in turning a valve too soon, etc. For such cases the local supervision is often able to identify what went wrong and to restore the process to its normal good behavior. Sometimes this troubleshooting may require the assistance of a staff specialist. In

any case, no changes of a fundamental nature are involved, since the manufacturing planning had already established an adequate process.

2. Other nonconformances are "repeaters." They arise over and over again, as evidenced from their recurring need for disposition by the Material Review Board or other such agency. Such recurrences point to a chronic condition which must be diagnosed and remedied if the problem is to be solved. The local supervision is seldom able to find the cause of these chronic nonconformances, mainly because the responsibility for diagnosis is vague. Lacking agreement on the cause, the problem goes on and on amid earnest debates about who or what is to blame—unrealistic design, incapable process, poor motivation, etc. The need is not for troubleshooting to restore normal good behavior, since normal behavior is bad. Instead, the need is to organize for an improvement project, as discussed in Chapter 5.

15-7 AUTOMATED INSPECTION

Automated inspection and testing are widely used to reduce inspection costs, reduce error rates, alleviate personnel shortages, shorten time of inspection, avoid inspector monotony, and for still other advantages. Applications of automation have been made successfully to mechanical gaging, electronic testing (for hugh volumes of components as well as for system circuitry), nondestructive tests of many kinds, chemical analyses, color discrimination, visual inspection (e.g., of large-scale integrated circuits), etc. In addition, automated testing is used extensively as a part of the scheduled maintenance programs for equipment in the field.

A company contemplating use of automated inspection first identifies those few tests which dominate the inspection budgets and use of personnel. The economics of automation are computed, and trials are made on some likely candidates for good return on investment. As experience is gained, the concept is extended further and further.

The wide adoption of automated testing proves the soundness of the concept and is a tribute to the resourcefulness which has been applied to the design of the test equipment. These designs, featuring modular construction, "master" test standards, and taped test programs, have attained high reliability, low setup time, and flexibility of application, not merely to existing products but to future products as well. Such designs have gone far to overcome the rigidity otherwise inherent in automated systems. The automated systems can outperform their human counterparts in productivity and freedom from error. However, they are not as adaptable as human inspectors, and it is sometimes necessary to modify the product design to make up for this difference. For example, certain surfaces readily grasped by human hands must be redesigned to greater precision so that they can be grasped by the equipment. The costs of such redesigns, of provision of multiple fixtures, etc., are a part of the return-on-investment equation.

A critical requirement for all automated test equipment is precision measurement; i.e., repeated measurements on the same unit of product should yield the "same" test results within some acceptable range of variation. This repeatability is inherent in the design of the equipment and can be quantified by the methods discussed in Section 16-6. In addition, it is essential that means be provided for keeping the equipment "accurate," i.e., in calibration with respect to standards for the units of measure involved. The methods for doing this are discussed in Section 16-6.

Still another aspect of automated test equipment is the problem of processing the data which are generated by the tests. Modern systems of electronic data processing make it possible for these test data to be entered directly from the test equipment to the computer without the need for intermediate documents. Such direct entry makes possible the prompt preparation of data summaries, conformance calculations, comparisons with prior lots, etc. In turn, it is feasible to program the computer to issue instructions to the test equipment with respect to frequency of test, disposition of units tested, alarm signals relative to improbable results, etc.

15-8 INSPECTORS: CAREERS; RECRUITMENT; TRAINING

The enormous growth in volume of inspection work has resulted in the appointment of numerous full-time inspectors. In the United States most of these inspectors are members of a large inspection hierarchy, which is in turn usually responsible to a central Quality Control Department of considerable stature in the company. One consequence of these developments is the emergence of potentially worthwhile careers for recruited inspectors. The existence of multiple grades of inspection work is one element of such careers. In addition, inspectors have the opportunity, through experience, training, and further education, to progress into technician or engineer categories, into supervisory posts (inspection or laboratory), into managerial posts in the quality control hierarchy, and into engineering work outside that hierarchy.

To convert these potential careers into realities requires first a general company policy and commitment to the career concept. In addition, it requires that the managers of the quality control hierarchy collaborate with the Personnel Department in making use of a wide array of skills and tools for recruitment, training, performance appraisal, etc.

Career Design and Job Design

A career is a recognized sequence of jobs designed to provide a logical, orderly progression for employee development and promotion. The existence of such a recognized sequence makes it easier to recruit and retain qualified inspectors. It also makes it easier to prepare programs for inspector training and development and to carry out promotions and transfers in a predictable, orderly manner.

One of the basic tools of personnel administration is the job description. It lists the job duties and responsibilities as well as setting out the needed qualifications of the employee. It is used to guide the recruitment, transfer, and promotion of inspectors. It is also used in job evaluation—establishing the grades, which in turn have a major influence on pay differentials and status. It is also used during appraisal of employee performance, and in still other ways.

Recruitment

The tools used for recruitment are the employment application, questionnaires, interviews, test batteries, and, of course, the job description. Test batteries can be helpful in identifying the presence or absence of specific skills needed on the job. (They must not be used for discrimination on any basis prohibited by law.) Some of these tests are quite useful for recruitment of inspectors.

Training

Training for inspectors has much in common with employee training in general. Use is made of on-the-job training, introductory courses, training manuals, audiovisual aids, etc. The content of inspector training is, of course, especially designed. It includes:

Knowledge of the materials, processes, and products and, if needed, of the basic underlying scientific disciplines.
Applicable measurement technology and, if needed, the underlying metrology.
Taking, recording, and analyzing data, including the associated mathematics and statistics.
Applicable company policy, organization, methods, and procedures; routines to be followed; documentation; etc.
Preparation of reports and other forms of feedback.
Safety regulations and practices.

A highly desirable addition is the opportunity to understand fitness for use—to see actual use of the product, to understand the "why" of the specifications, to see the processes, read customer reactions, etc.

15-9 INSPECTION COST PERFORMANCE

Inspection costs are a significant part of quality costs and have long been subject to conventional cost controls. These cost controls invariably take the form of establishing efficient methods, setting cost standards, measuring performance, and motivating all concerned to meet the standards.

Establishing Efficient Methods

The greatest potential source of inspection cost reduction is through reducing the need for inspection. This need arises mainly because there are too many defects in the product. Reducing the defect level involves "quality improvement," as discussed in Chapter 5. However, there are also ways of reducing inspection costs through use of the more conventional cost-reduction approaches.

The tools of quality control engineering can be useful for establishing efficient methods. Coordinated inspection planning helps to avoid duplication of inspection work. Sampling can be used to replace some 100 percent inspections (see Section 15-5). Automated testing can replace repetitive manual testing. Documentation can be simplified. The costs of perfectionism can be reduced through review of standards in their relation to fitness for use.

The tools of industrial engineering are available for analysis and improvement of inspection workplaces and methods. Work sampling can readily discover the extent to which inspectors are engaged in preparation work, conduct of actual inspection and test, paperwork, travel, waiting time, etc. In like manner, work sampling can discover the extent to which equipment is being utilized; i.e., are the observed equipment shortages real or are they due to variable work load scheduling? Classical methods study is readily applicable to improve workplace layout, eliminate waste motion, and reduce fatigue.

Much study has been devoted to the broad problem of designing processes, workplaces, instruments, etc., in ways which are compatible with the capabilities and limitations of human senses and muscles. These studies (which are variously called "human factors," "human engineering," "ergonomics," etc.) have application to planning of inspection work and design of the inspection workplace.[2]

Still another potential source of inspection cost reduction is to abolish the jobs of full-time inspectors and assign the work of inspection to be done by the production workers as a part of their job. Such a transfer is technologically feasible in some types of work, especially operations which are completely performed by one worker (rather than by a team) and in which the specified qualities are readily measurable at the end of the operation. Before such a transfer can be made, there must exist mutual confidence between managers and workers. In addition, the workers must be put into a state of self-control as far as quality is concerned. Once these criteria are met, training is conducted and examinations are given to determine which workers have become qualified to accept the responsibility of self-inspection. As such workers take on their new responsibilities, the jobs of full-time inspection are abolished but an audit (by the Quality Control Department) is established to assure that the workers make good product acceptance decisions.[3]

---

[2] See generally, *Quality Control Handbook,* 3rd ed., "Physical Facilities for Inspection," pp. 12-13 to 12-18; also "Inspection Cost Reduction," pp. 12-73 to 12-75. For some case examples, see Douglas H. Harris and Frederick B. Chaney, *Human Factors in Quality Assurance,* John Wiley & Sons, Inc., New York, 1969.

[3] For an extensive discussion, see "Product Acceptance by Operators," *Quality Control Handbook,* 3rd ed., pp. 11-19 to 11-22.

Establishing Cost Standards

Setting these cost standards involves a collaboration among the Quality Control, Industrial Engineering, and Accounting departments. In general, Quality Control determines how many tests need to be made, and of which type; the test equipment required; the consumable supplies needed; the support work necessary to assure that the results of test correctly reflect the actual condition of the products undergoing test. Industrial Engineering helps to provide methods which enable this essential work to be performed with optimal use of human and physical resources. In addition, Industrial Engineering uses tools such as time study and work sampling to establish standards of productivity —"how much is a day's work." Accounting then translates these work standards into cost standards through the company's budgetary process.

In this budgetary process *cost centers* are established for logical organization subdivisions, e.g., receiving inspection, final inspection, instrument laboratory. Account numbers are established to collect data on actual costs associated with these cost centers.

Establishing a budget for each cost center requires choice of an *activity index* which best reflects the extent to which plant activity will influence inspection costs. For example, in final inspection the most suitable index might relate inspection costs to volume of product, whereas in process inspection the relationship might be to the number of hours of production labor.

The cost standards established after all this procedure are mainly of two forms:

1. *Engineered standards.* These are based on converting the productivity standards into money. For example, in final test the standards for productivity are used to convert the number of units tested into equivalent standard hours. These hours are then converted into money by applying the appropriate salary and burden rates.
2. *Historical standards.* In the absence of engineered standards, practical managers look to see whether costs are rising or falling, and by how much. Here the activity index is used to make estimates, based on plant activity, of what should be the inspection costs. Such "variable budgets" come in several levels of sophistication, and the choice of these will depend on the amount at stake as well as on the effort needed to use the more refined budgetary designs.

Measuring Costs

Cost measurement is by conventional accounting tools. Inspectors are provided with account numbers for allocating their time and with logs for recording actual time spent, work performed, etc. These logs find their way to the accounting office, where they are "priced out." The resulting costs are then distributed to the appropriate accounts. Similarly, the forms for requisitioning supplies and services are so designed that copies bearing the account numbers go to the accounting office for pricing and processing. The data processing system then computes and publishes summaries of cost vs. budget. These reports go to the cognizant supervisors and managers, who then have the responsibility for reviewing the results and taking appropriate action.

15-10 INSPECTION ACCURACY PERFORMANCE

An important aspect of attainment of fitness for use is inspection accuracy. The inspection and test results should correctly reflect the conditions prevailing in the products and processes. Nonconformances should be discovered and brought to light. All concerned should be able to rely on inspection data as a valid basis for action.

Attainment of inspection accuracy depends in large part on the completeness of the inspection planning. In addition, it depends on the extent to which the plans are well executed. One of the elements of this execution is freedom from instrument error, which is discussed in Chapter 16. Another and major element is human error. Human inspectors typically find about 80 percent of the defects actually present in the product but miss the remaining 20 percent. This human error arises from multiple causes, of which three will be discussed.

Technique Errors

This generic term describes errors made *consistently* by some inspectors, because of a chronic deficiency, such as:

Lack of capacity: e.g., color blindness.
Lack of knowledge: e.g., education or training essential to the job.
Lack of "skill": i.e., lack of the knack possessed by others.

The consistent aspect of technique errors makes it possible to identify their presence by comparing the accuracy of various inspectors under comparable work conditions. A major form of this comparison is through submitting the same product to be inspected by multiple inspectors. The product submitted may be regular production or it may be a special "standard sample array" which has been carefully prepared beforehand. Some of the product units chosen for this array are in full conformity to standards. Others are nonconforming and represent a selected assortment of defect types and severities. When multiple inspectors go over the same array, the data disclose which errors are the result of vague standards, i.e., many inspectors make the same error; which errors are the result of shortcomings in specific individuals, i.e., only those individuals make many errors; which individuals are in difficulty only as to specific characteristics; etc.

Remedial action for technique errors is to supply what is missing—training, inspection aids, knowledge of the knack, etc. It is especially important to provide forthright answers to the inspector's question: "What should I do different from what I am doing now?"

In critical cases, e.g., involving human safety, the trend is to demand proof that the inspector does have the knowledge, training, and skills needed. Increasing use is made of certification programs involving formal training, examinations, certificates, licenses, and audits. Numerous standards for critical processes and products now require that only certified inspectors may perform the tests.

Inadvertent Errors

Inadvertent errors, like technique errors, are unintentional. However, inadvertent errors are not made consistently; they are made at random, both as to defect type and as to when they occur. (At the time of making an inadvertent error, the inspector is unaware that the error is being made.) Because inadvertent errors have their origin in human fallibility, the remedies involve either "foolproofing" against such fallibility, or use of nonhuman means, e.g., automation.

Inspection planners and supervisors have developed a wide array of methods for foolproofing inspection work as well as means for making it easier for the inspector to avoid errors. Some of these methods are similar to those employed in foolproofing the manufacturing process (see Section 11-3). In addition, there are applications of foolproofing which are special to inspection work. Templates may be used to make obvious those characteristics for which the inspector is responsible. Masks may be used to blot out those for which the inspector is not responsible. Comparison samples and overlays can be used to make it easier to judge conformance. Work can be organized so as to rotate inspectors among multiple inspection operations to minimize fatigue and loss of concentration.[4]

Some inadvertent errors are procedural in nature. In the absence of good foolproofing, it is quite possible to ship out products which have bypassed inspection inadvertently, or even products which inspectors have declared to be nonconforming. The product identification system must be thorough, with close control on inspection stamps and other forms of marking products as conforming. Responsibility should be individual and this should extend to packers and shippers as well as to inspectors.

Willful Errors

Willful errors are those made with an awareness that the error is being made and with the intention to keep it up. The broad causes of willful errors are quite varied and complex, and these causes are discussed in Section 6-5.

Willful inspection errors take on a variety of forms, each of which has its own remedy. The more important cases include:

[4] For more detail, see "Remedy for Inadvertent Inspector Errors," *Quality Control Handbook*, 3rd ed., pp. 12-54 to 12-56.

1. *Yielding to pressures* of production and other supervisors who outrank the inspector. The need is to imbue inspectors with the importance of factual reporting, and to shield inspectors from such pressures.
2. *Shortcuts* taken by the inspector to improve productivity, avoid disagreeable tasks, etc. The need is to discover such practices through audits, to remedy those job conditions which present the inspector with disagreeable alternatives, and to use disciplinary measures if that becomes necessary.
3. *Flinching,* which is the tendency of inspectors to falsify measurements which show products to be nonconforming by a small amount. In effect, the inspector first makes the conformance decision. Then he or she makes the fitness-for-use decision as to those units of product which are out of tolerance by an amount judged to be unimportant. The inspector, of course, has the clear responsibility to make the conformance decision but does not have the responsibility for making the fitness-for-use decision.

    Flinching can take place during inspection by variables, in which case the instrument readings are falsified. It can also take place during inspection by attributes, in which case the number of nonconforming units in the sample is falsified. Both forms of flinching can be detected by audits.

    Since flinching is by definition a form of false reporting, it is a serious matter. In its mildest forms, it confuses the jurisdiction over the decision making and chips away at the integrity of inspection reporting. In more severe forms and for critical products it can be a criminal offense which infects all who tolerate the practice.

    The constructive way of dealing with flinching is to stress the need for an atmosphere of respect for inspection reporting; to show by supervisory example that this policy has managerial support; to make clear the extent and the reason for the allocation of responsibility for decision making. This constructive approach must be combined with a managerial determination to deal firmly with inspectors who are unwilling to accept the concept of no compromise with falsification of readings. Such people are out of place on inspection jobs.
4. *Rounding off,* which is the discarding of some of the available accuracy of inspection measurement or reporting. A simple example is that of reading meters to the nearest scale division when it would be feasible to attain still greater precision by estimating the location of the needle between scale markings. In most cases this rounding off is harmless, and may even be a good way of avoiding preoccupation with needless detail. However, in some cases there is need for the attainable precision. For such cases it is necessary to specify "readings to be recorded to the nearest . . . ."

Measure of Inspector Accuracy

Some companies carry out regular evaluations of inspector accuracy, either as part of the overall evaluation of inspection performance or as an essential part of an incentive pay plan for inspectors. Either way, the plans employ a check inspector, who periodically reviews random samples of work previously inspected by the various inspectors. The check inspection findings are then summarized, weighted, and converted into some index of inspector performance.

Care must be taken to make such evaluations independent of "incoming quality," i.e., the level of defects in the products submitted to the inspectors in the first place. To illustrate, if all inspectors were equally accurate (e.g., all found 80 percent of the defects submitted to them to be found), then those inspectors lucky enough to be assigned to highly capable processes would have few defects coming to them and hence would miss fewer defects than would the unlucky inspectors. To make the accuracy of inspectors independent of incoming quality, it is necessary for the check inspector to review not only the products classified by the inspector as conforming but also the products classified as nonconforming. From the findings of the check inspection review plus those of the original inspection, the following formulas emerge:

$$\text{Accuracy of inspector} = \text{percent of defects correctly identified} = \frac{d - k}{d - k + b}$$

where d = defects reported by the inspector

k = number of defects reported by the inspector but determined by the check inspector not to be defects

$d - k$ = true defects found by the inspector

b = defects missed by the inspector, as determined by check inspection

$d - k + b$ = true defects originally in the product

Figure 15-1 illustrates how the percentage of accuracy is determined. The number of defects reported by the inspector, d, is 45. Of these, 5 were found by the check inspector to be good; i.e., $k = 5$. Hence $d - k$ is 40, the true defects found by the inspector. However, the inspector missed 10 defects; i.e., $b = 10$. Hence, the original number of defects, $d - k + b$, is 50, i.e., the 40 found by the inspector plus the 10 he missed. Hence

$$\text{Percentage of accuracy} = \frac{d - k}{d - k + b} = \frac{45 - 5}{45 - 5 + 10} = 80\%$$

In application of the plan, periodic check inspection is made of the inspector's work. Data on d, k, and b are accumulated over a period of months to summarize the inspector's accuracy, as, for example:

Job no.	Total pieces	d	b	k
3	1000	10	0	0
19	50	3	1	0
42	150	5	1	0
48	5000	10	4	0
⋮				
Total		200	30	0

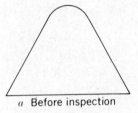

a Before inspection

$$\frac{d-k}{d-k+b} = \frac{45-5}{45-5+10} = 80$$

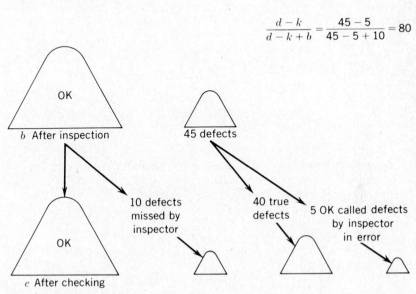

Figure 15-1 Process for determining accuracy of inspectors.

The totals give, for percent accuracy:

$$\frac{d}{d+b} = \frac{200}{230} = 87\%$$

PROBLEMS

15-1 Discuss the inspection of new homes with the appropriate municipal department. Determine the purpose of their inspection, the specification used, and how the inspection is conducted. Comment on this inspection from the viewpoint of the purchaser of a home.

15-2 Discuss the inspection of new roads with the appropriate municipal department. Determine the purpose of their inspection, the specification used, and how the inspection is conducted.

15-3 In one large company making consumer durable products, the Chief Inspector operated on the principle that disposition of nonconforming lots of components must be done in only three ways: (1) by scrapping them, (2) by repairing them to bring them into conformance, or (3) by securing a waiver from the design department. What she did not permit was a tryout to see if the components were usable despite the nonconformance. Her stated reason was that if she authorized such tryouts, the production people would devote their energies to tryouts rather than to making the components right in the first place. What do you think of this philosophy?

15-4 For any product acceptable to the instructor, prepare an inspection plan, including choice of inspection stations, definition of work to be performed at each station, criteria to be used, facilities to be supplied, and the records to be kept.

15-5 The following is quoted from the book *Why Not the Best?* by Jimmy Carter:

> Another improvement that occurred in the Transportation Department was the analysis of what engineers did in the supervision of highway contract fulfillment on construction of roads. We had engineers measuring and weighing all the ingredients that went into road plant mix, others who manned public scales to weigh the dump trucks full and empty as they carried the plant mix to the construction site, another supervising the dumping of asphalt mix on the road, the compaction of it with machines (they measured the thickness of it as it was done and then later certified that the job had been done properly). We changed all this to end-result inspection whereby all these men were replaced with one person who went along periodically as short sections of the highway were completed, made test borings, sent the sample to the laboratory where it was analyzed for content and thickness. Thereby, we not only saved tremendous personnel requirements, but let engineers again do what they were trained to do in supervising proper highway construction.

What do you think of the change introduced by (then) Governor Carter?

15-6 For any product or service acceptable to the instructor:

(*a*) Prepare a list of defects encountered during acceptance inspection and during use.

(*b*) Design a plan for seriousness classification of defects and apply the plan to the list in question.

15-7 Study the method used for dealing with nonconformance in any of the following processes: arrests for traffic violations, grievances under the collective bargaining agreement, protests over tax assessments, and any other process acceptable to the instructor. Report the plan in use, including the equivalents of inspector, designer, supervision, material review board, etc.

15-8 Certain plates stamped out in a stamping press include holes for which there are close tolerances for diameter and for distance between holes. In the discussion of how many pieces to gage for these dimensions, one proposal is to measure the first and the last piece for each lot and to accept the lot if both pieces conform to specification. A statistician objects to this proposal on the grounds that the sample is only two pieces and that if the lot were 50 percent defective, it could easily be accepted due to statistical variation. What is your opinion?

15-9 In some companies there are problems arising from pay differences between inspectors and production operators working on the same grade of work, i.e., evaluated as equal in grade by the same job evaluation plan. The difference in pay is due to the fact that the production workers have an opportunity to earn incentive pay through the piecework system, whereas the inspectors are paid only at the base rates. What would you do if you were the quality manager and faced this problem?

15-10 A large manufacturer of "minicomputers" is incurring high costs due to the need for assembling and testing the computers to discover and eliminate defects before the computers are installed in the clients' computer rooms. After this assembly, test, and repair, the computers are disassembled, shipped to the clients' facilities, reassembled, and checked out. How would you go about it to reduce the cost of preassembly and pretest?

15-11 Your company maintains a check on the accuracy of inspectors. It also carries out an outgoing product audit in which finished product is sampled and rated for quality under a plan of "demerits per unit." Figure 15-2 shows the charts of these two performance measures as prepared monthly for managerial review. Note that during the latest month, outgoing quality as measured in demerits per unit has gotten worse, while inspector accuracy has not changed. (All figures have been rechecked and found to be correct.) What might account for this seeming contradictory pair of reports?

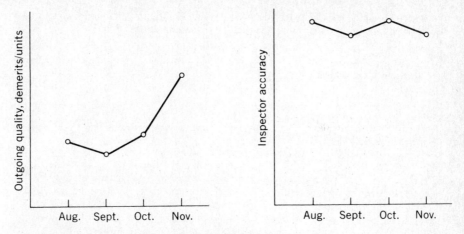

Figure 15-2 Results of product audit and check for inspector accuracy.

15-12 You are a quality manager engaged in a seminar with other quality managers to discuss common problems. A lively discussion has developed over some problems associated with pressures applied to quality managers. These pressures concern the shipment of nonconforming, unfit, or even unsafe products. In addition, the pressures concern the matter of the quality manager signing a test certificate or other document which puts him on record as having approved something when he was really against it.

Here are several of the problem categories identified by the group:

1. A lot of product has been made with a nonconformance to specification. All company managers (including the quality manager) are convinced that the nonconforming product is fit for use. They are not agreed on whether to tell the client about the nonconformance. The marketing manager is against informing the client on the ground that some clients use such information to wring a price concession out of the manufacturer.
2. A product lot contains a small percent of units which are clearly unfit for use. There is a debate on whether to sort the lot to remove the defective units or to ship the lot as is and pay any claims as they arise. The production manager (who wants to ship the product without sorting) contends the problem is purely economic and that the quality considerations are secondary.
3. A large electromechanical system has been made under a contract which includes a penalty clause for late delivery. The system has already met its test requirements and is being crated for shipment. At this point it is discovered that the test equipment used to test one of the subsystems was out of calibration at the time of making the test. Under the accepted practice in the industry, such a discovery throws suspicion on the quality of the subsystem and hence on the quality of the system. Unfortunately, the subsystem is not easily accessible. It is buried deep within the system so that it would involve a serious delay as well as a large expense to take the system apart, test the subsystem, and then put it all back together again. The manufacturing people take the position that the subsystem is OK despite the condition of the test equipment. They note that another subsystem, built by the same people using the same process, has just tested OK. They urge that the system be shipped based on this evidence of a reliable process and work force.
4. A product with a good safety record has resulted in a serious injury to a user. The injury involved a most unusual combination of unlikely events plus an obvious misuse by the user. The design manager defends the design on the record—the only known serious injury was associated with misuse.

What are your conclusions as to the position to be taken by the quality manager in the foregoing cases with respect to (*a*) shipping the product, and (*b*) signing the documents?

SUPPLEMENTARY READING

Subject	Reference
Conformance and fitness for use	*Quality Control Handbook*, 3rd ed. (QCH3), pp. 12-31 to 12-37
Inspection planning	QCH3, pp. 12-5 to 12-8 (in general). For case examples, study the various "industry" sections of QCH. Most of these devote space to inspection planning though sometimes under different names, e.g., control planning. Typical cases are inspection for automotive vehicles (pp. 42-23 to 42-27); for electronic components (pp. 38-13 to 38-16); in the food industry (pp. 31-12 to 31-14); in foundries (pp. 34-17 to 34-19).
Seriousness classification	QCH3, pp. 12-20 to 12-26 (in general). For case examples, see the the applications to automotive vehicles (sec. 42), food industry (sec. 31), graphic arts (sec. 40), household appliances (sec. 43).
Automated testing	Roy Knowles, *Automatic Testing: Systems and Application*, McGraw-Hill Book Company, New York, 1976
Inspectors: careers, recruitment, training	QCH3, pp. 17-2 to 17-22
Inspection cost performance	QCH3, pp. 12-70 to 12-80
Inspection accuracy performance	QCH3, pp. 12-51 to 12-63
Product acceptance	QCH3, pp. 12-26 to 12-31
Sensory evaluation	ASTM, "Basic Principles of Sensory Evaluation," STP 433, 1968. ASTM, "Manual on Sensory Testing Methods," STP 434, 1968
Inspection accuracy performance	QCH3, pp. 12-51 to 12-63; also D.H. Harris, and F.B. Chaney, *Human Factors in Quality Assurance*, John Wiley & Sons, Inc., New York, 1969. Good case material and discussion on coordinating human inspection with physical facilities.

EXAMPLES OF EXAMINATION QUESTIONS USED IN FORMER ASQC QUALITY ENGINEER CERTIFICATION EXAMINATIONS AS PUBLISHED IN *QUALITY PROGRESS* MAGAZINE

1 The inspection plan for a new product line may include: (*a*) detailed production schedule; (*b*) sampling procedures and techniques; (*c*) internal techniques for control and segregation of conforming or nonconforming product; (*d*) answers (*a*) and (*b*); (*e*) answers (*a*), (*b*), and (*c*).

2 Classification of defects is most essential as a prior step to a valid establishment of: (*a*) design characteristics to be inspected; (*b*) vendor specifications of critical parts; (*c*) process control points; (*d*) economical sampling inspection; (*e*) a product audit checklist.

3 When giving instructions to those who will perform a task, the communication process is completed: (*a*) when the worker goes to the work station to do the task; (*b*) when the person giving the instruction has finished talking; (*c*) when the worker acknowledges these instructions by describing how he or she will perform the task; (*d*) when the worker says that he or she understands the instructions.

4 The primary reason that nonconforming material should be identified and segregated is: (*a*) so that the cause of nonconformity can be determined; (*b*) to provide statistical information for the "zero defects" program; (*c*) so it cannot be used in production without proper authorization; (*d*) to obtain samples of poor workmanship for use in the company's training program; (*e*) so that responsibility can be determined and disciplinary action taken.

5 Sensory testing is used in a number of industries to evaluate their products. Which of the following is not a sensory test? (*a*) ferritic annial test; (*b*) triangle test; (*c*) duo–trio test; (*d*) ranking test; (*e*) paired-comparison test.

6 One of the major hazards in the material review board procedure is the tendency of the board to emphasize only the disposition function and to neglect the _____ function. (*a*) statistical analysis; (*b*) corrective action; (*c*) material evaluation; (*d*) tolerance review; (*e*) manufacturing methods.

7 A technique whereby various product features are graded and varying degrees of quality control applied is called: (*a*) zero defects; (*b*) quality engineering; (*c*) classification of characteristics; (*d*) feature grading; (*e*) nonsense—you cannot do it.

8 One method to control inspection costs even without a budget is by comparing _____ as a ratio to productive machine time to produce the product. (*a*) product cost; (*b*) company profit; (*c*) inspection hours; (*d*) scrap material.

9 In a visual inspection situation, one of the best ways to minimize deterioration of the quality level is to: (*a*) retrain the inspector frequently; (*b*) add variety to the task; (*c*) have a program of frequent eye exams; (*d*) have frequent breaks; (*e*) have a standard to compare against a part of the operation.

SIXTEEN

MEASUREMENT

16-1 INTRODUCTION

Measurement is as old as history. The ancient Egyptian unit of measure for length was the royal cubit, which was defined as the length of the forearm of the reigning pharaoh. From such an ancestry, the science of measurement (called *metrology*) was gradually evolved.

In the early days of inspection, correct measurements were recognized as important in determining the conformance of product to specifications. However, the recent emphasis on *prevention* concepts in the quality function has broadened the purposes of measurement. Measurements now provide information not only on individual units of product but also on lots, processes, and the measuring instruments themselves. In addition, tolerances have become smaller, requiring more precise measuring equipment. To maintain such precise equipment in good order requires "masters" with even higher precision. For example, gages that can measure in thousandths need to be periodically checked. This check requires other gages that can measure in ten thousandths or even millionths. This hierarchy of standards applies to many other types of measurement.

As explained later in the chapter, the effect of measurement error on product acceptance can also be important. For example, gasoline manufacturers must specify minimum octane and must have the ratings verified by state regulatory agencies. The measurement of octane has variability even when repeat tests are made. This measurement error has caused disputes with certain state agencies. Some states recognize the measurement error and allow for it in interpreting test results versus the specification. Other states do not. An attempt is currently being made to clarify the situation.

For these and other reasons, metrology has become an important part of a quality control program.

The quantification of product or process characteristics involves:

1. Definition of standardized units, called *units of measure,* which permit conversion of abstractions (e.g., length, mass) into a form capable of being quantified (e.g., meter, kilogram).
2. *Instruments* which are calibrated in terms of these standardized units of measure.
3. Use of these instruments to quantify or *measure* the extent to which the product or process possesses the characteristic under study. This process of quantification is called *measurement.*

16-2 UNITS OF MEASUREMENT

There are three systems of measurement: the English, the metric, and the Système International d'Unités (or SI). The units of measure are the language of measurement. A few examples of the units of measure under each of these systems is given in Table 16-1.

When the American colonies separated from England, the colonies retained the English system of measurement. At about the same time, the metric system was developed in France. The original metric system was primarily concerned with simple characteristics such as length, area, volume, and mass. As technology developed, there was a need to modify the original metric system. This modification was called the SI system.

The metric and SI systems are decimal-based, i.e., the units and their multiples are related to each other by factors of 10. The English system does not have this feature; i.e., a foot is 12 inches, a yard is 3 feet, etc. Most of the world now uses the metric system and is committed to the adoption of the full SI system. However, it was not until 1967 and 1975, respectively, that the United Kingdom and the United States decided to change to the SI system. In both

Table 16-1 Examples of units of measure for systems of measurement

Characteristic	English	Original metric	SI
Length	Foot	Meter	Meter
Time	Second	Second	Second
Force	Pound	Kilogram	Newton
Mass	Slug	Kilogram-second^2/meter	Kilogram

countries, the transition is occurring gradually. Both English and SI units are used in this book.

Table 16-2 lists the fundamental, supplemental, and derived units of the SI system.

Table 16-2 SI system units of measure

Characteristic	Unit of measure	Symbol	Formula
	Fundamental units		
Length	meter	m	
Mass	kilogram	kg	
Time	second	s	
Electric current	ampere	A	
Temperature	degree Kelvin	K	
Luminous intensity	candela	cd	
	Supplementary units		
Plane angle	radian	rad	
Solid angle	steradian	sr	
	Derived units		
Area	square meter	m^2	
Volume	cubic meter	m^3	
Frequency	hertz	Hz	(s^{-1})
Density	kilogram per cubic meter	kg/m^3	
Velocity	meter per second	m/s	
Angular velocity	radian per second	rad/s	
Acceleration	meter per second squared	m/s^2	
Angular acceleration	radian per second squared	rad/s^2	
Force	newton	N	$(kg \cdot m/s^2)$
Pressure	newton per sq meter	N/m^2	
Kinematic viscosity	sq meter per second	m^2/s	
Dynamic viscosity	newton-second per sq meter	$N \cdot s/m^2$	
Work, energy, quantity of heat	joule	J	$(N \cdot m)$
Power	watt	W	(J/s)
Electric charge	coulomb	C	$(A \cdot s)$
Voltage, potential difference, electromotive force	volt	V	(W/A)
Electric field strength	volt per meter	V/m	
Electric resistance	ohm	Ω	(V/A)
Electric capacitance	farad	F	$(A \cdot s/V)$
Magnetic flux	weber	Wb	$(V \cdot s)$
Inductance	henry	H	$(V \cdot s/A)$
Magnetic flux density	tesla	T	(Wb/m^2)
Magnetic field strength	ampere per meter	A/m	
Magnetomotive force	ampere	A	
Luminous flux	lumen	lm	$(cd \cdot sr)$
Luminance	candela per sq meter	cd/m^2	
Illumination	lux	lx	(lm/m^2)

16-3 STANDARDS AND TRACEABILITY

Any system of measurement must be based on fundamental units that are unchangeable. In ancient Egypt a "cubit" was a unit of measure and a black granite master cubit was maintained in the Pharoah's palace as a reference. The wooden cubits that were used for working purposes were required to be checked (i.e., calibrated) against the master cubit at the time of each new moon.[1] Today, a master international kilogram is maintained in France. In the SI system, most of the fundamental units are defined in terms of natural phenonema that are unchangeable. For example, the unit of measure for length is the meter. The meter is defined as the wavelength of a certain radiation of light. This recognized true value is called the *standard*.

Primary Reference Standards

In all industrialized countries there exists a national Bureau of Standards whose functions include construction and maintenance of "primary reference standards." These standards consist of copies of the International Kilogram plus measuring systems which are responsive to the definitions of the fundamental units and to the derived units of Table 16-2.

In addition, professional societies (e.g., American Society for Testing and Materials) have evolved standardized test methods for measuring many hundreds of quality characteristics not listed in Table 16-2. These standard test methods describe the test conditions, equipment, procedure, etc., to be followed. The various national Bureaus of Standards, as well as other laboratories, then develop primary reference standards which embody the units of measure corresponding to these standard test methods. In practice, it is not feasible for the National Bureau of Standards to calibrate and certify the accuracy of the enormous volume of test equipment in use in the shops and test laboratories. Instead, resort is had to a hierarchy of secondary standards and laboratories, together with a system of documented certification of accuracy.

Hierarchy of Standards

The primary reference standards are the apex of an entire hierarchy of reference standards (Figure 16-1). At the base of the hierarchy there stands the huge array of "test equipment," i.e., instruments used by laboratory technicians, workers, and inspectors to control processes and products. These instruments are calibrated against *working standards,* which are used solely to calibrate the laboratory and shop instruments. In turn, the working standards are related back to the primary reference standards through one or more interme-

---

[1] DeWayne Sharp, "Inching Toward the Metric System," *1976 ASQC Annual Technical Conference Transactions,* p. 382.

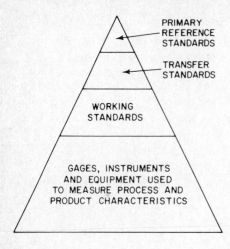

Figure 16-1 Hierarchy of standards.

diate secondary reference standards or *transfer standards*. Each of these levels in the hierarchy serves to "transfer" accuracy of measurement to the next-lower level in the hierarchy.

For example, a production operator uses a micrometer (a gage) to measure a length. This micrometer is periodically checked against a working standard, usually a gage block. The gage block in turn is periodically checked against a transfer standard, probably a master gage block. This master gage block is in turn checked against the primary reference standard. The process of comparing one standard against a higher-order standard of greater accuracy is called *calibration*. The ability to relate measurement results back to the primary reference standard is called *traceability* of the standard.

16-4 ERROR OF MEASUREMENT

Even when correctly used, a measuring instrument may not give a true reading of a characteristic. The difference between the true value and the measured value can be due to problems of:

1. *Accuracy.* The accuracy of an instrument is the extent to which the average of a long series of repeat measurements made by the instrument on a single unit of product differs from the true value. This difference is usually due to a systematic error in the measurement process. In this case, the instrument is said to be "out of calibration."
2. *Precision.* The precision of an instrument is the extent to which the instrument repeats its results when making repeat measurements on the same unit of product. The scatter of these measurements may be designated as σ_E, meaning standard deviation of measurement error. (The scat-

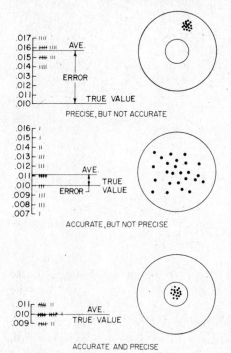

.017 ⎡ ////
.016 ⊢ ###### ////   AVE.
.015 ⊢ #### ///
.014 ⊢ ////
.013 ⊢   ERROR
.012 ⊢
.011 ⊢   TRUE VALUE
.010 ⎣

PRECISE, BUT NOT ACCURATE

.016 ⎡ /
.015 ⊢ /
.014 ⊢ //
.013 ⊢ ///
.012 ⊢ ///
.011 ⊢ ####   AVE.
.010 ⊢ ///   TRUE
.009 ⊢ /// ERROR⏌ VALUE
.008 ⊢ ///
.007 ⎣ /

ACCURATE, BUT NOT PRECISE

.011 ⎡ #### //   AVE.
.010 ⊢ #### #### / TRUE VALUE
.009 ⎣ #### //

ACCURATE AND PRECISE

Figure 16-2 Distinction between accuracy and precision.

ter is usually due to random error.) The lower the value of σ_E the more "precise" is the instrument (see Figure 16-2).

There is much confusion on terminology. Some literature uses the terms *accuracy* and *precision* interchangeably. The term *bias* is sometimes used to indicate systematic error. The confusion extends to instrument catalogs. Table 16-3 shows the statements on error of measurement as listed in three catalogs. The confusion is compounded because none of these catalogs defines the word "accuracy."

The American Society for Testing and Materials (ASTM) requires that, for all ASTM standard test methods, statements concerning sampling, accuracy, and precision must be included. A standard giving basic definitions has been prepared. These definitions have been included in the ASTM standards prepared for specific materials.[2]

ASTM recommends a variety of statements of accuracy and precision.

---

[2] See *ASTM Standards on Precision and Accuracy for Various Applications*, American Society for Testing and Materials, Philadelphia, 1977. The standard explaining the basic definitions is "E177-71 Use of the Terms Precision and Accuracy as Applied to Measurement of a Property of a Material."

Table 16-3 Comparison of catalog statements

Instrument	Manufacturer		
	A	B	C
Outside micrometer (0–1 in) (0–2.54 cm)	Accuracy 0.0001 in (0.000254 cm)	Accuracy is maintained at 0.00005 in (0.000127 cm)	No statement
Dial caliper	Accuracy to 0.001 in (0.00254 cm) per 6 in (15.24 cm)	Accuracy guaranteed within 0.001 in (0.00254 cm)	No statement
Electronic comparator	Repeatable accuracies to 0.000004 in (0.0000101 cm)	It repeats to within 0.000002 in (0.00000508 cm)	Total error is less than 1½% of full-scale reading

These are summarized in Table 16-4. The measures to be used in a given case depend on several factors:

1. The purpose of the statement on measurement error.
2. The relative magnitude of both the systematic error and the variability associated with the measure of precision.
3. Whether the values to be presented will remain fixed over different levels of material and different environmental conditions.

Any statement of accuracy and precision must be preceded by three conditions:

1. *Definition of the test method.* This includes the step-by-step procedure, equipment to be used, preparation of test specimens, test conditions, etc.
2. *Definition of the system of causes of variability,* such as material, analysts, apparatus, laboratories, days, etc. ASTM recommends that modifiers of

Table 16-4 Summary of ASTM indices of accuracy and precision

Accuracy	Precision
1. An estimate of the systematic error, possibly supplemented by upper and lower bounds.	1. Standard deviation, σ_E.
	2. Two sigma limits, $2\sigma_E$.
	3. Three sigma limits, $3\sigma_E$.
2. An amount for systematic error, dependent on the length of time since the last calibration of the equipment.	4. Difference two sigma limits. Less than 5% of all random pairs of measurements will differ by more than $2\sqrt{2}\sigma_E$.
3. A step-by-step procedure for applying successive corrections for different reasons.	5. Difference three sigma limits. Less than 1% of all random pairs of measurements will differ by more than $3\sqrt{2}\sigma_E$.
4. A calibration formula or graph.	

the word "precision" be used to clarify the scope of the precision measure. Examples of such modifiers are single-operator, single-analyst, single-laboratory-operator-material-day, and multilaboratory.

3. *Existence of a statistically controlled measurement process.* The measurement process must have stability in order for the statements on accuracy and precision to be valid. This stability can be verified by a control chart (see Section 12-6).

Examples of statements on accuracy and precision are the italicized statements below:

1. Repeat tests[3] are made by one operator on the flash point of a material. *For flash points below 220°F (104.4°C), the single operator standard deviation is 1.4°F (0.8°C). Therefore, results of two tests by the same operator on the same material should not differ from each other by more than 4°F (2.2°C). The value of 4°F (2.2°C) is the "difference two sigma limit,"* i.e., $2\sqrt{2}$ *(1.4), or 4°.*

2. Flash-point tests[4] on a material are made by different laboratories. *The multilaboratory standard deviation is 2.1°F (1.2°C) for flash points below 220°F (104.4°C) and 8.8°F (4.9°C) for flash points above 220°F (104.4°C). Therefore, results of two tests on the same material in two different laboratories should not differ from each other by more than 6°F (3.3°C) for flash points below 220°F (104.4°C) or by more than 25°F (13.9°C) for flash points above 220°F (104.4°C). The values of 6°F (3.3°C) and 25°F (13.9°C) are the "difference two sigma limits" calculated from* $2\sqrt{2}\sigma_E$.

3. An error-of-measurement study is made for a digital voltmeter using a 10.00-microvolt (μV) source as the standard value. Measurements taken at both 70°F (21.1°C) and 90°F (32.2°C) are shown in Table 16-5. The data can be summarized as follows:

	70°F	90°F
Average	9.98 μV	9.99 μV
Estimate of σ_E	0.0067 μV	0.0087 μV

The error of measurement can be summarized as follows:

	70°F	90°F
Accuracy	$9.98 - 10.00 = -0.02$	$9.99 - 10.00 = -0.01$
Precision	$\sigma_E = 0.0067$	$\sigma_E = 0.0087$

---

[3] Ibid., p. 6.
[4] Ibid.

Table 16-5 Data from error-of-measurement study on a digital voltmeter

70°F (21.11°C) data		90°F (32.22°C) data	
9.95	9.98	9.98	9.94
9.99	9.96	10.02	9.97
9.96	9.98	9.97	10.01
10.01	9.98	9.98	10.02
10.01	9.98	10.01	9.99

16-5 EFFECT OF MEASUREMENT ERROR ON ACCEPTANCE DECISIONS

The error of measurement can cause incorrect decisions on (1) individual units of product, and (2) lots submitted to sampling plans.

Two types of errors can occur in the classification of a product: (1) a nonconforming unit can be accepted (the consumer's risk), and (2) a conforming unit can be rejected (the producer's risk). Eagle[5] has investigated the effect of precision on each of these errors.

The probability of accepting a nonconforming unit as a function of measurement error (called test error, σ_{TE}, by Eagle) is shown in Figure 16-3. The abscissa expresses the test error as the standard deviation divided by the plus-or-minus value of the specification range (assumed equal to 2 standard deviations of the product).

For example, if the measurement error is one-half of the tolerance range, the probability is about 1.65 percent that a nonconforming unit will be read as conforming (due to the measurement error) and, therefore, will be accepted.

Figure 16-4 shows the percent of *conforming* units that will be *rejected* as a function of the measurement error. For example, if the measurement error is one-half of the plus-or-minus tolerance range, about 14 percent of the units that are really within specifications will be rejected because the measurement error will show these conforming units as being outside specification.

The test specification can be adjusted with respect to the performance specification (see Figures 16-3 and 16-4). Moving the test specification inside the performance specification reduces the probability of accepting a nonconforming product but increases the probability of rejecting a conforming product. The reverse occurs if the test specification is moved outside the performance specification. Both risks can be reduced by increasing the precision of the test, i.e., by reducing the value of σ_E.

McCaslin and Gruska[6] discuss measurement error for attributes gages. (This chapter covers variables gages.)

[5] A. R. Eagle, "A Method for Handling Errors in Testing and Measuring," *Industrial Quality Control*, March 1954, pp. 10–14.

[6] James A. McCaslin and Gregory F. Gruska, "Analysis of Attribute Gage Systems," *1976 ASQC Annual Technical Conference Transactions*, pp. 392–399.

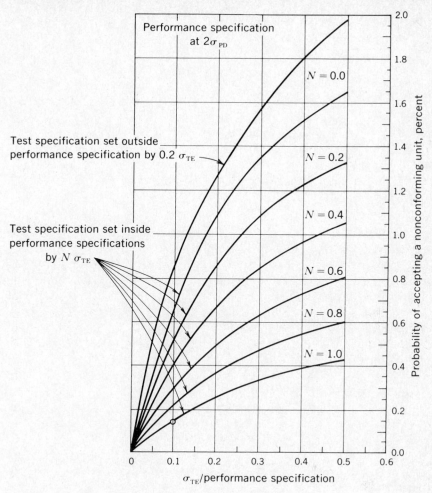

Figure 16-3 Probability of accepting a nonconforming unit. (From A. R. Eagle, "A Method for Handling Errors in Testing and Measuring," *Industrial Quality Control*, March 1954, pp. 10–14.)

Hoag, Foote, and Mount-Campbell[7] studied the effect of inspector errors on the type I (α) and type II (β) risks of sampling plans. For a single sampling plan and an 80 percent probability of the inspector detecting a defect, the real value of β is two to three times that specified, and the real value of α is about one-fourth to one-half of that specified.

Case, Bennett, and Schmidt[8] investigated the effect of inspection error on

[7] Laverne L. Hoag, Bobbie L. Foote, and Clark Mount-Campbell, "The Effect of Inspector Accuracy on Type I and Type II Errors of Common Sampling Techniques," *Journal of Quality Technology*, vol. 7, no. 4, October 1975, pp. 157–164.

[8] Kenneth E. Case, G. Kemble Bennett, and J. W. Schmidt, "The Effect of Inspection Error on Average Outgoing Quality," *Journal of Quality Technology*, vol. 7, no. 1, January 1975, pp. 1–12.

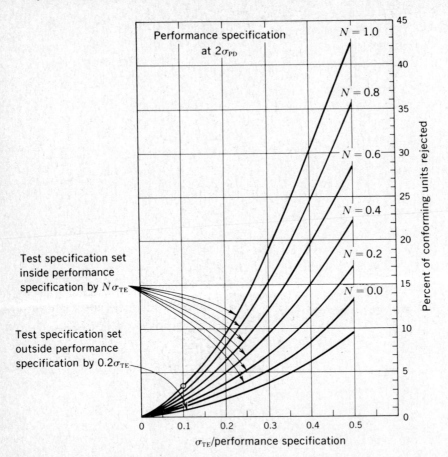

Figure 16-4 Probability of rejecting an acceptable unit. (From A. R. Eagle, "A Method for Handling Errors in Testing and Measuring," *Industrial Quality Control,* March 1954, pp. 10–14.)

the *average outgoing quality* (AOQ) of an attributes sampling procedure. They concluded that not only do the AOQ values change, but significant changes can occur in the shape of the AOQ curve. Case and Bennett[9] investigated the effect of both accuracy and precision on the overall costs associated with variables sampling plans.

All these investigations concluded that measurement error can be a serious problem. Greb[10] disagrees. He presents a contrasting view and discusses the conditions that must occur before the problem becomes serious.

[9] Kenneth E. Case and G. Kemble Bennett, "Measurement Error: The Economic Effect on Sampling Plan Design," *1976 ASQC Annual Technical Conference Transactions,* pp. 207–212.

[10] Donald J. Greb, "Does Bad Test Equipment Accept Bad Product?—A Quantitative Analysis," *1976 ASQC Annual Technical Conference Transactions,* pp. 389–391.

16-6 ANALYTICAL DETERMINATION OF ACCURACY AND PRECISION

The accuracy of measurement can be quantified by determining the difference between the true value of a characteristic and the average value of multiple measurements made on the characteristic. The question of "how many measurements" can be answered by confidence limit concepts (see Section 4-4). For example, suppose that σ_E is estimated as 2.0 and it is desired to estimate accuracy within 0.05 unit at the 95 percent confidence level. Then 62 repeat measurements should be taken on the same unit of product and the average of these calculated. The difference between the true value and the average of these repeat measurements is a measure of accuracy.

The basic procedure for determining the precision of a measuring process is to calculate the measurement variation that results if repeat measurements are made on one unit of product. The precision is calculated as a multiple of the standard deviation of these repeat measurements *about their own average*.

For both accuracy and precision the number of measurements taken should be large enough to evaluate the *stability* of the measurement process. Ideally, this is done by using an average and range control chart with a minimum of 100 total measurements divided into small subgroups (see Section 12-6). However, it is often not practical to obtain this many readings for an error-of-measurement study. As a rough test of stability, the individual measurements can be evaluated against $\pm 3\sigma_E$ limits about the average. This is illustrated in the following example.[11]

A micrometer was chosen at random from the half dozen available for use. Two operators were available and one was chosen by the toss of a coin. The operator made 20 measurements on a standard 1.000-in (2.540-cm) steel cube with the following results:

Average = 1.00403 in (2.55024 cm)
Standard deviation = 0.00024 in (0.00061 cm)

All observed values fell within ± 3 standard deviations of the average. The estimate of the systematic error is $1.00000 - 1.00403$, or -0.00403 (0.01024 cm). The single-operator-micrometer-day precision is ± 0.0005 in (0.0013 cm) (2 standard deviations), as defined in ASTM Recommended Practice E177.

16-7 COMPONENTS OF VARIATION

In drawing conclusions about measurement error, it is worthwhile to study the causes of variation of observed values. The relationship is

$$\sigma_{\text{observed}} = \sqrt{\sigma^2_{\text{cause } A} + \sigma^2_{\text{cause } B} + \cdots + \sigma^2_{\text{cause N}}}$$

[11] *ASTM Standards on Precision and Accuracy*, pp. 132–133.

The formula assumes that the causes act independently.

It is valuable to find the numerical values of the components of observed variation, because the knowledge may suggest where effort should be concentrated to reduce the variation in the product. A separation of the observed variation into the true product variation plus the other causes of variation may indicate important factors other than the manufacturing process. Thus, if the *measurement* error is found to be a large percentage of the total variation, this finding must be analyzed before proceeding with a quality improvement program. Finding the components (e.g., instrument, operator) of this error may help to reduce the measurement error, which in turn may completely eliminate a problem.

For example, information on the sources of variation in a digital voltmeter is presented in Table 16-6. This information is based on using 70°F (21.1°C) as a reference point. Thus the random and systematic error values for the temperature coefficient are for temperature deviations from 70°F (21.1°C). The values for random error are 3 standard deviation values. The expected voltmeter error at 70°F (21.1°C) is

$$E(70) = -5 \pm \sqrt{(3.0)^2 + (10.0)^2 + (10.0)^2 + (4.0)^2 + (2.0)^2 + (15.0)^2}$$
$$= -5 \pm 21 \ \mu V$$

The expected error at 90°F (32.22°C) is

$$E(90) = (90 - 70) + 0.5 - 5.0$$
$$\pm \sqrt{(3.0)^2 + (10.0)^2 + (0.7 \times 20)^2 + (10.0)^2 + (4.0)^2 + (2.0)^2 + (15.0)^2}$$
$$= 5.0 \pm 25.5 \ \mu V$$

Observations from an instrument used to measure a series of different units of product can be viewed as a composite of (1) the variation due to the measuring method, and (2) the variation in the product itself. This can be expressed as

$$\sigma_O = \sqrt{\sigma_P^2 + \sigma_E^2}$$

where $\sigma_O = \sigma$ of the observed data
$\sigma_P = \sigma$ of the product
$\sigma_E = \sigma$ of the measuring method

Solving for σ_P yields

$$\sigma_P = \sqrt{\sigma_O^2 - \sigma_E^2}$$

If σ_E is less than one-tenth σ_O, the effect upon σ_P will be less than 1 percent. A common rule of thumb requires that the instrument should be able to divide the tolerance into about 10 parts. As the effect is less than 1 percent, the rule of thumb seems uneconomically conservative for most applications.

For example, in the use of a certain new design of indicator gage, it was found that the σ_O was 0.0011 in (0.0028 cm). The shop questioned the validity of the gage. An experiment was conducted by having the gage check the same unit of product over and over again. The σ_E of these repeat readings was 0.0002 in (0.0005 cm). This includes the variation due to the instrument and the opera-

Table 16-6 Data on sources of variation in a digital voltmeter (microvolts)

Source	Random error	Systematic error
Nonlinearity	±3.0	—
Digitizer error	±10.0	—
Temperature coefficient/°F	±0.7	+0.5
Readability	±10.0	—
Reference Zener	±4.0	—
Standardization	±2.0	—
30-day stability	±15.0	−5.0

tor. Then

$$\sigma_P = \sqrt{(0.0011)^2 - (0.0002)^2} = 0.00108 \text{ in } (0.00274 \text{ cm})$$

This was convincing proof that the errors in the indicator did not materially exaggerate the variation in the product.

In another instance, involving the efficiency of an air-cooling mechanism, σ_O was 23 and σ_E was 16. Then

$$\sigma_P = \sqrt{(23)^2 - (16)^2} = 16.5$$

The measurement variation was almost as great as the product variation. Further study disclosed that the measurement variation was caused by several variables:

Variable	σ	σ^2
A	14	196
B	5	25
All other	7.2	52
Total		273

It became clear that real progress could be made only by improving variable A, and the engineers took steps accordingly.

Sometimes, a carefully designed experiment is necessary to develop quantitative estimates of the component causes of variation. This is particularly important in determining and analyzing the measurement process for several laboratories performing the same measurement ("interlaboratory tests").

16-8 REDUCING AND CONTROLLING ERRORS OF MEASUREMENT

Steps can be taken to reduce and control errors in both accuracy and precision. The systematic errors that contribute to inaccuracy can sometimes be handled by applying a numerical correction to the measured data. If an instrument has an accuracy of −0.001, then, on the average, it reads 0.001 too low. The data can be adjusted by adding 0.001 to each value of the data. Of course, it is preferable to adjust the instrument as part of a calibration program.

In a calibration program the measurements made by an instrument are compared to a reference standard of known accuracy. If the instrument is found to be out of calibration, an adjustment is made.

A calibration program can become complex. This is due to:

1. The large number of measuring instruments.
2. The need for periodic calibration of many instruments.
3. The need for many reference standards.
4. The increased technological complexity of new instruments.
5. The variety of types of instruments, i.e., mechanical, electronic, chemical, etc.

A potentially enormous volume of work on a calibration program can be reduced by using a calibration interval based on the amount of actual use of an instrument rather than simply a specified calendar time since the last calibration. Scott[12] reported that, in the first year of operation under the use concept, 10,000 fewer gages needed to be calibrated as compared to the previous system that used a calendar-time interval.

A calibration program should include provisions for periodic audits. These follow the general approach for quality audits (see Section 22-5). Schumacher[13] presents a thorough discussion of systematic measurement errors for standards and measurements.

Precision of measurement can be improved through:

1. *Discovery of the causes of variation and remedy of these causes.* A useful step is to resolve the observed values into components of variation (see Section 16-7). This can lead to the discovery of inadequate training, perishable reagents, lack of sufficient detail in procedures, and other such problems. This fundamental approach also points to other causes, for which the remedy is unknown or uneconomic, i.e., basic redesign of the test procedure. In such cases another approach is:

2. *Multiple measurements and statistical methodology to control the error of measurement.* The use of multiple measurements is based on the following relationship (see Section 4-3):

$$\sigma_{\bar{x}} = \frac{\sigma}{\sqrt{n}}$$

The formula states that to halve the error of measurement requires quadrupling (not doubling) the number of measurements.

---

[12] J. E. Scott, "Days Used Gage Program Drastically Reduces Wasted Calibration Time," *Quality*, February 1976, pp. 22–24.

[13] Rolf B. F. Schumacher, "Systematic Measurement Errors," *1978 ASQC Annual Technical Conference Transactions*, pp. 138–148.

As the number of tests grows larger and larger, a significant reduction in the error of measurement can only be achieved by taking a still *larger* number of additional tests. This raises a question concerning the cost of the additional tests versus the value of the slight improvement in overall accuracy. The alternative of reducing the causes of variation (by control charts or other techniques) must also be considered. Banker and Batayias[14] discuss a program for controlling the quality of laboratory measurements in a hospital. A computerized system is used to prepare control charts and other statistical information on a monthly basis for about 170 individual tests.

16-9 MEASUREMENT TECHNOLOGY

The early gages were designed to classify product as good or bad. Since then, the emphasis on defect prevention and on quality planning has demanded that the shop test equipment be able to perform additional functions, mainly:

1. *Indicating.* That is, the gages must show the "reading" along a scale of measurement. (The dial gage was the symbol of the indicating instrument until the advent of electronic readouts.) These readings become the feedback to operators for process control and to inspectors for product conformance decisions.
2. *Regulating.* In some applications it is economic to feed the measurements directly into the process so that the gage closes the loop to make the process self-regulating (see Section 11-8).
3. *Recording.* Increasingly, the burden of recording measurement data is being shifted from operators and inspectors to instruments especially designed to record data. These records are not merely a series of readings expressed in numbers. They include charts showing the data in time progression and related to tolerances or to control limits.
4. *Computing, summarizing, and reporting.* A further step is to feed the data into computers. Some of these computers are used to figure averages and standard deviations. Others summarize data and prepare reports for supervisory and managerial review.

These new and multiple functions have given rise to the name *quality information equipment,* to emphasize that the dominant role is to provide information.

Measurement technology, along with product technology and process technology, marches in the parade of increased complexity. This complexity applies not only to dimensional measurement but also to chemical, electrical, mechanical, and other characteristics. In this section the concept of a generalized measurement model will be presented, followed by an overview of techniques for dimensional measurement and nondestructive testing.

[14] Carol A. G. Banker and George E. Batayias, "Laboratory QC: Doctor, Is That Result Accurate?" *1978 ASQC Annual Technical Conference Transactions,* pp. 437–444.

Table 16-7 Generalized measurement system

Stage 1: Detector-transducer	Stage 2: Intermediate modifying	Stage 3: Terminating
Detects the input signal and transforms it	Prepares the information for stage 3	Provides the information in a usable form
Examples: contacting spindle, buoyant float, photoelectric cell, resistance	*Examples:* gearing, valving, lens, amplifying system	*Examples:* moving pointer and scale, digital meter, inked pen and chart

Most measurement systems fall within a general framework consisting of three stages. Beckwith and Buck[15] define these three stages as shown in Table 16-7. The examples in this table include mechanical, hydraulic-pneumatic, optical, and electrical applications. This three-stage model applies not only to dimensional measurement but also to most other forms, such as force, temperature, pressure, and mechanical, electrical, optical, and chemical characteristics.

Measurement systems fall in two categories: (1) direct, and (2) indirect or differential. In a *direct measurement,* the standard of measurement can be applied to the unit being measured and a reading obtained. The use of a graduated rule to measure a length is an example. *Indirect measurement* uses a transforming device along with connecting apparatus to convert the input to a useful form of output. An example of an indirect instrument is a dial indicator gage. In engineering work, most measurement is indirect.

Another classification of measurement is analog versus digital. In the analog mode, the measurement scale is continuous and the observations can take on an infinity of values in any given range. In the digital mode, the measurement scale is in discrete steps. Thus a clock with hands is an analog device but a clock that uses marked frames is a digital device.

One of the several major areas of measurement is dimensional measurement. A major phenomenon over the years has been a progression of complexity and precision. For example, the early days of measuring length used micrometers and calipers. A summary of some of these instruments is given in Table 16-8.[16]

Of increasing importance is *nondestructive testing* (NDT). This type of testing has two main applications: (1) detect flaws in materials and components, and (2) measure physical properties such as dimensions, hardness, conductivity, composition, magnetic and elastic constants, and other characteristics. Hayward[17] describes 70 specific NDT techniques, but these can be categorized into a small number of categories, as defined in Table 16-9.

[15] Adapted from T. G. Beckwith and N. Lewis Buck, *Mechanical Measurements,* 2nd ed., Addison-Wesley Publishing Company, Inc., Reading, Mass., 1969, pp. 12–13.

[16] For further information, see Daniel B. Dallas (ed.), *Tool and Manufacturing Engineers Handbook,* 3rd ed., McGraw-Hill Book Company, New York, 1976.

[17] Gordon P. Hayward, *Introduction to Nondestructive Testing,* American Society for Quality Control, Milwaukee, Wis., 1978.

Table 16-8 Summary of methods used in dimensional measurement

Measurement method	Approach
Direct measuring instruments (e.g., a micrometer or caliper)	The instrument provides a direct reading of the dimension.
Mechanical comparator (e.g., a dial indicator)	The instrument mechanically amplifies a small dimension so it can be observed on a measurement scale.
Electric or electronic comparators	The instrument electronically amplifies a small dimension.
Pneumatic (air) gages	The escape of air between air jets and the workpiece is compared with a master of known dimensional value.
Fluidics	Air flowing through tiny channels is used to gage, memorize, sort, switch, and actuate.
Contour projector and other forms of optical projection	The workpiece is placed in the path of a beam of light and in front of a magnifying lens system. This projects a silhouette of the object on to a screen. The silhouette is then compared to a chart gage having tolerance limits.
Interferometers and associated devices such as optical flats and autocollimators	A light source is applied to the workpiece and the instrument provides a measurement based on the interaction of light waves. A laser is sometimes used as a light source.
Coordinate measuring machines (CMM)	Measurements are taken on three mutually perpendicular axes. A CMM is often used as a layout machine before machining and for checking hole locations after machining. Computer control of the inspection and subsequent data analysis is also possible.

Table 16-9 Summary of nondestructive testing techniques

Technique	Approach
1. Mechanical-optical (e.g., liquid penetrant)	Test surface is covered with penetrating liquid that seeks surface cracks. Liquid in cracks bleeds out to stain powder coating applied to surface.
2. Penetrating radiation (e.g., X-radiography)	Penetrating radiation emitted by X-ray generator is imposed on test object. Radiation transmitted by test object is used to image or detect structures or flaws.
3. Electromagnetic-electronic (e.g., magnetic particle)	Test object is magnetized. Magnetic powder applied to surface accumulates over regions where a magnetic field emerges as a result of surface or subsurface flaws.
4. Sonic-ultrasonic (e.g., resonance ultrasonic)	Frequency is varied until probe introduces continuous and compressional ultrasonic waves into part at resonant frequencies for thickness gaging.
5. Thermal (e.g., contact thermometry)	Measurement of temperature and heat-flow variations through test object indicates thermal properties or anomalies.
6. Chemical-analytical (e.g., iron probe)	Specimen surface atoms are bombarded and ionized to determine chemical composition.
7. Image generation (e.g., fluoroscopy)	A fluorescent image is produced by X rays passing through a test object onto a fluorescent layer. An immediate and real-time image showing radiographic details appears on a screen.
8. Signal-image analysis (e.g., photographic extraction)	Photoreprocessing is used to enhance details in images. Photographs or radiographs are reproduced with modified density or contrast values to obtain a derivative image.

PROBLEMS

16-1 An instrument has been used to measure the length of a part. The result was 6.70052 cm. An error-of-measurement study was made on the instrument, with the following results:

Accuracy: +0.00254 cm (on the average, the instrument reads 0.00254 cm high)
Precision: 0.001016 cm (1 standard deviation)

Make a statement concerning the true value of the part just measured. State all assumptions needed.

16-2 The precision of a certain mechanical gage is indicated by a standard deviation (of individual repeat measurements) of 0.00254 cm. Investigate the effect on precision of making multiple measurements. Consider 2, 3, 4, 5, 10, 20, and 30 as multiples. Graph the results.

16-3 One ball bearing was measured by one inspector 13 times with each of two vernier micrometers. The results are shown below:

Measurement number	Model A	Model B
1	0.6557	0.6559
2	0.6556	0.6559
3	0.6556	0.6559
4	0.6555	0.6559
5	0.6556	0.6559
6	0.6557	0.6559
7	0.6556	0.6559
8	0.6558	0.6559
9	0.6557	0.6559
10	0.6557	0.6559
11	0.6556	0.6559
12	0.6557	0.6560
13	0.6557	0.6560

Suppose that the true diameter is 0.65600. Calculate measures of accuracy and precision for each micrometer. What restrictions must be placed on the applicability of the numbers you determined?
    Answer: A: accuracy $= -0.00035$, precision $= 1\sigma$ of 0.000075; B: accuracy $= -0.000085$, precision $= 1\sigma$ of 0.000036.

16-4 A large sample of product has been measured. The mean was 2.506 in and the standard deviation was 0.002 in. A separate error-of-measurement study yielded the following results:

Accuracy $= +0.001$ in
Precision $= 0.0005$ in (1 standard deviation)

The product has only a minimum tolerance limit. What should this limit be to take into account accuracy and precision and reject only 5 percent of the product?
    Answer: 2.502.

16-5 A sample of measurements shows a mean and standard deviation of 2.000 in and 0.004 in, respectively. These results are for the *observed* values. A separate error-of-measurement study indicates a precision of 0.002 in (1 standard deviation). There is no error in "accuracy." The dimension has a specification of 2.000 ± 0.006 in. What percent of the population has *true* dimensions outside the specification?

SUPPLEMENTARY READING

Section 13 of the *Quality Control Handbook*, 3rd ed., McGraw-Hill Book Company, New York, 1974, covers measurement, including measurement systems, measurement error, calibration, and measurement technology. Planning for quality information equipment is discussed on pp. 9-45 to 9-48. Application of nondestructive testing is discussed on pp. 37-7 to 37-8 (for mechanical components) and pp. 34-18 to 34-19 (for foundries). Pages 27-41 to 27-44 discuss techniques of planning interlaboratory tests.

A well-illustrated book on dimensional metrology is Ted Busch, *Fundamentals of Dimensional Metrology*, Delmar Publishers, Albany, N.Y., 1964. Another book on dimensional metrology is the *Handbook of Industrial Metrology*, prepared by the American Society of Tool and Manufacturing Engineers and published by Prentice-Hall, Inc., Englewood Cliffs, N.J., 1967.

A collection of papers on interlaboratory testing is contained in *Interlaboratory Testing Techniques*, American Society for Quality Control, Milwaukee, Wis., 1978.

EXAMPLES OF EXAMINATION QUESTIONS USED IN FORMER ASQC QUALITY ENGINEER CERTIFICATION EXAMINATIONS AS PUBLISHED IN *QUALITY PROGRESS* MAGAZINE

1 A variable measurement of a dimension should include: (*a*) an estimate of the accuracy of the measurement process; (*b*) a controlled measurement procedure; (*c*) a numerical value for the parameter being measured; (*d*) an estimate of the precision of the measurement process; (*e*) all of the above.

2 If not specifically required by the product drawing(s) or specification, a nondestructive test (NDT) may be required during production and/or during acceptance at the discretion of the quality engineer responsible for the inspection planning. This statement is: (*a*) false—because testing is limited to that specified by the design engineer; (*b*) true—because NDT is a form of inspection (with enhanced senses) not a functional test; (*c*) false—the quality engineer may impose NDT as he believes necessary but cannot delete it without design engineering permission; (*d*) true—because all acceptance testing and inspection requirements are up to quality engineering.

3 When specifying the "10:1 calibration principle," we are referring to what? (*a*) the ratio of operators to inspectors; (*b*) the ratio of quality engineers to metrology personnel; (*c*) the ratio of main-scale to vernier-scale calibration; (*d*) the ratio of calibration standard accuracy to calibrated instrument accuracy; (*e*) none of the above.

4 A qualification test is used to determine that design and selected production methods will yield a product that conforms to specification. An acceptance test is used to determine that a completed product conforms to design. On this basis, a destructive test can be used for: (*a*) qualification only; (*b*) qualification or acceptance; (*c*) acceptance only; (*d*) neither qualification nor acceptance.

5 Measuring and test equipment are calibrated to: (*a*) comply with federal regulations; (*b*) assure their precision; (*c*) determine and/or assure their accuracy; (*d*) check the validity of reference standards; (*e*) accomplish all of the above.

6 A basic requirement of most gage calibration system specifications is: (*a*) all inspection equipment must be calibrated with master gage blocks; (*b*) gages must be color-coded for identification; (*c*) equipment shall be labeled or coded to indicate date calibrated, by whom, and date due for next calibration; (*d*) gages must be identified with a tool number; (*e*) all of the above.

7 What four functions are necessary to have an acceptable calibration system covering measuring and test equipment in a written procedure? (*a*) calibration sources, calibration intervals, environmental conditions, and sensitivity required for use; (*b*) calibration sources, calibration intervals, humidity control, and utilization of published standards; (*c*) calibration sources, calibration intervals, environmental conditions under which equipment is calibrated, and controls for unsuitable equipment; (*d*) list of standards, identification report, certificate number, and recall records; (*e*) all of the above.

8 Quality information equipment: (*a*) is used only by the quality control function; (*b*) is used only for the purpose of accepting or rejecting product; (*c*) makes measurements of either products or processes and feeds the resulting data back for decision making; (*d*) includes automatic electronic instruments but not go/no go gages.

9 Calibration intervals should be adjusted when: (*a*) no defective product is reported as being erroneously accepted as a result of measurement errors; (*b*) few instruments are scrapped out during calibration; (*c*) the results of previous calibrations reflect few out-of-tolerance conditions during calibration; (*d*) a particular characteristic on a gage is consistently found out of tolerance.

10 A typical use for the optical comparator would be to measure: (*a*) surface finish; (*b*) contours; (*c*) depth of holes; (*d*) diameters of internal grooves; (*e*) all of the above.

ACCEPTANCE SAMPLING

17-1 THE CONCEPT OF ACCEPTANCE SAMPLING

Acceptance sampling is the process of evaluating a portion of the product in a lot for the purpose of accepting or rejecting the entire lot as either conforming or not conforming to a quality specification.

The main advantage of sampling is economy. Despite some added costs to design and administer the sampling plans, the lower costs of inspecting only part of the lot result in an overall cost reduction.

In addition to this main advantage, there are others:

1. The smaller inspection staff is less complex and less costly to administer.
2. There is less damage to the product; i.e., handling incidental to inspection is itself a source of defects.
3. The lot is disposed of in shorter (calendar) time so that scheduling and delivery are improved.
4. The problem of monotony and inspector error induced by 100 percent inspection is minimized.
5. Rejection (rather than sorting) of nonconforming lots tends to dramatize the quality deficiencies and to urge the organization to look for preventive measures.
6. Proper design of the sampling plan commonly requires study of the actual level of quality required by the user. The resulting knowledge is a useful input to the overall quality planning.

The disadvantages are sampling risks, administrative costs, and less information about the product than is provided by 100 percent inspection.

Acceptance sampling is used (1) when the cost of inspection is high in relation to the damage cost resulting from passing a defective, (2) when 100 percent inspection is monotonous and causing inspection errors, or (3) when the inspection is destructive. Acceptance sampling is most effective when it is preceded by a prevention program that achieves an acceptable level of quality of conformance.

There is need to emphasize what acceptance sampling does not do. It does not provide refined estimates of lot quality. (It does determine, with specified risks, an acceptance or rejection decision on each lot.) Also, acceptance sampling does not provide judgments on whether or not rejected product is fit for use. (It does give a decision on a lot with respect to the defined quality specification.)

17-2 ECONOMICS OF INSPECTION

There are three alternatives for evaluating lots:

1. No inspection at all.
2. Inspect a sample.
3. 100 percent inspection (or more).

An economic evaluation of these alternatives requires a comparison of *total* costs under each of the alternatives. Let

N = number of items in lot
n = number of items in sample
p = proportion defective in lot
A = damage cost incurred if a defective slips through inspection
I = inspection cost per item
P_a = probability that lot will be accepted by sampling plan

Consider the comparison of sampling inspection versus 100 percent inspection. Suppose it is assumed that no inspection errors occur and the cost to replace a defective found in inspection is borne by the producer or is small compared to the damage or inconvenience caused by a defective. The total costs are summarized in Table 17-1. These costs reflect both inspection costs and damage costs and recognize the probability of accepting or rejecting a lot under sampling inspection. The expressions can be equated to determine a break-even point. If the sample size is assumed to be small compared to the lot size, the break-even point, p_b, is

$$p_b = \frac{I}{A}$$

Table 17-1 Economic comparison of inspection alternatives

Alternative	Total cost
No inspection	NpA
Sampling	$nI + (N - n)pAP_a +$ $(N - n)(1 - P_a)I$
100% inspection	NI

If it is thought that the lot quality (p) is less than p_b, the total cost will be lowest with sampling inspection or no inspection. If p is greater than p_b, 100 percent inspection is best.

For example, a microcomputer device costs $0.50 per unit to inspect. A damage cost of $10.00 is incurred if a defective device is installed in the larger system. Therefore,

$$p_b = \frac{0.50}{10.00} = 0.05 = 5.0\%$$

If it is expected that the percent defective will be greater than 5 percent, then 100 percent inspection should be used. Otherwise, use sampling or no inspection.

The variability in quality from lot to lot is important. If past history shows that the quality level is much better than the break-even point and is stable from lot to lot, little if any inspection may be needed. If the level is much worse than the break-even point, and consistently so, it will usually be cheaper to use 100 percent inspection rather than sample. If the quality is at neither of these extremes, a detailed economic comparison of no inspection, sampling, and 100 percent inspection should be made. Sampling is usually best when the product is a mixture of high-quality lots and low-quality lots.

The high costs associated with component failures in complex electronic equipment coupled with the development of automatic testing equipment for components has resulted in the economic justification of 100 percent inspection for some electronic components. The cost of finding and correcting a defective can increase by a ratio of 10 for each major stage that the product moves from production to the customer; i.e., if it costs $1 at incoming inspection the cost increases to $10 at the printed circuit board stage, $100 at the system level, and $1000 in the field.[1] Such justification of 100 percent inspection is in contrast to the early days of statistical quality control when acceptance sampling was emphasized instead of 100 percent inspection.

Martin[2] discusses the break-even point in sampling for both nonde-

---

[1] "Wescom Inc.—A Study in Telecommunications Quality," *Quality*, August 1978, p. 30.

[2] Cyrus A. Martin, "The Cost Breakeven Point in Attribute Sampling," *Industrial Quality Control*, September 1964, pp. 137–144.

structive and destructive sampling. Dayton[3] includes the effect of inspection errors in 100 percent inspection.

17-3 SAMPLING RISKS: THE OPERATING CHARACTERISTIC CURVE

Neither sampling nor 100 percent inspection can guarantee that every defective item in a lot will be found. Sampling involves a risk that the sample will not adequately reflect the conditions in the lot; 100 percent inspection has the risk that monotony and other factors will result in inspectors missing some of the defectives (see Section 15-10). Both of these risks can be quantified.

Sampling risks are of two kinds:

1. Good lots can be rejected (the producer's risk). This risk corresponds to the α risk.
2. Bad lots can be accepted (the consumer's risk). This risk corresponds to the β risk.

The α and β risks are discussed in Section 4-7.

The *operating characteristics* (OC) *curve* for a sampling plan quantifies these risks. The OC curve for an attributes plan is a graph of the percent defective in a lot versus the probability that the sampling plan will accept a lot. As p is unknown, the probability must be stated for all possible values of p. It is assumed that an infinite number of lots are produced. Figure 17-1 shows an "ideal" OC curve where it is desired to accept all lots 1.5 percent defective or less and reject all lots having a quality level greater than 1.5 percent defective. All lots less than 1.5 percent defective have a probability of acceptance of 1.0 (certainty); all lots greater than 1.5 percent defective have a probability of acceptance of 0. Actually, however, no sampling plan exists that can discriminate perfectly; there always remains some risk that a "good" lot will be rejected or that a "bad" lot will be accepted. The best that can be achieved is to make the acceptance of good lots more likely than the acceptance of bad lots.

An acceptance sampling plan basically consists of a sample size (n) and an acceptance criterion (c). For example, a sample of 125 units is to be randomly selected from a lot. If 5 or less defectives are found, the lot is accepted. If 6 or more defectives are found, the lot is rejected.

The sample of 125 could, by the laws of chance, contain 0, 1, 2, 3, etc., even 125 defectives. It is this *sampling variation* that causes some good lots to be rejected and some bad lots to be accepted. The OC curve for $n = 125$ and $c = 5$ is curve A, Figure 17-2. (The other curves will be discussed later.) A 1.5 percent defective lot has about a 98 percent chance of being accepted. A much worse lot, say 6 percent defective, has a 23 percent chance of being accepted.

[3] Joseph D. Dayton, "Fine Tuning Inspection for Minimum Cost," *Quality,* November 1977, pp. 46–99.

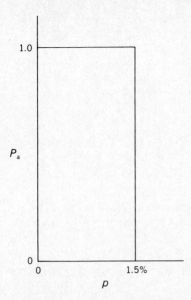

Figure 17-1 Ideal OC curve.

With the risks stated in quantitative form, a judgment can be made on the adequacy of the sampling plan.

The OC curve for a specific plan states *only* the chance that a lot having p percent defective will be accepted by the sampling plan. The OC curve does *not*:

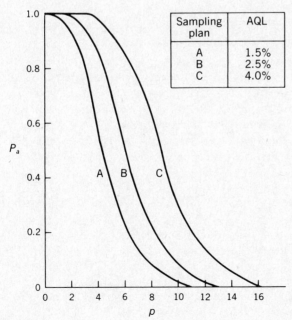

Sampling plan	AQL
A	1.5%
B	2.5%
C	4.0%

Figure 17-2 Operating characteristic curves.

1. Predict the quality of lots submitted for inspection. For example (Figure 17-2), it is incorrect to say that there is a 36 percent chance that the lot quality is 5 percent defective.
2. State a "confidence level" in connection with a specific percent defective.
3. Predict the final quality achieved after all inspections are completed.

These and other myths about the OC curve require a careful explanation of the concept to those using it.

17-4 CONSTRUCTING THE OPERATING CHARACTERISTIC CURVE

An OC curve can be developed by determining the probability of acceptance for several values of incoming quality, p. The probability of acceptance is the probability that the number of defectives in the sample is equal to or less than the acceptance number for the sampling plan. There are three distributions that can be used to find the probability of acceptance: the hypergeometric, binomial, and the Poisson distribution. When its assumptions can be met, the Poisson distribution is preferable because of the ease of calculation.

Grant[4] describes the use of the hypergeometric and binomial distributions.

The Poisson distribution yields a good approximation for acceptance sampling when the sample size is at least 16, the lot size is at least 10 times the sample size, and p is less than 0.1. The Poisson distribution function as applied to acceptance sampling is

$$P \begin{pmatrix} \text{exactly} \\ r \text{ defectives} \\ \text{in sample of } n \end{pmatrix} = \frac{e^{-np}(np)^r}{r!}$$

The equation can be solved using a calculator or by using Table C in the Appendix. This table gives the probability of r *or less* defectives in a sample of n from a lot having a fraction defective of p. To illustrate Table C, consider the sampling plan previously cited, i.e., $n = 125$ and $c = 5$. To find the probability of accepting a 4 percent defective lot, calculate np as $125(0.04) = 5.00$. Table C then gives the probability of 5 or fewer defectives as 0.616. Figure 17-2 (curve A) shows this as the value of P_a for 4 percent defective lot quality.

17-5 ANALYSIS OF SOME RULE-OF-THUMB SAMPLING PLANS

Rule-of-thumb sampling plans are frequently found to be inadequate when evaluated by an OC curve. The "10 percent sampling rule" is an example. For any lot size, a sample equal to 10 percent of the lot is selected. If there are no

[4] E. L. Grant, *Statistical Quality Control*, 4th ed., McGraw-Hill Book Company, New York, 1972, pp. 208–214.

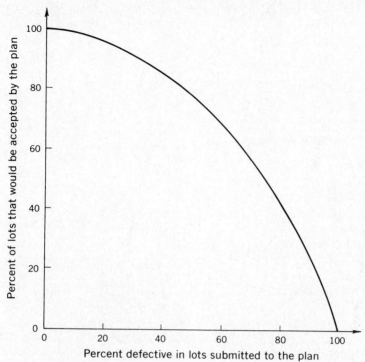

Figure 17-3 Operating characteristic curve for a rule-of-thumb sampling plan.

defectives found in the sample, the lot is accepted. If any defectives are found in the sample, the lot is rejected. It is usually presumed that with the sample always a constant percentage (10 percent) of the lot, the sampling risks will be constant. The 10 percent rule does *not* provide the same risks. This is demonstrated by Problem 17-16.

Another rule-of-thumb plan is an extreme one that might be proposed for a destructive test. The plan is this: Test one unit, and if it is acceptable, pass the entire lot. If it is defective, test a second unit. If the second unit is acceptable, pass the lot. If the second unit is also defective, reject the lot. Figure 17-3 shows the operating characteristic curve. Destructive testing necessitates small sample sizes but the operating characteristic curve shows that the sampling risks are so high for this plan that there is little protection against accepting bad quality. For example, if the lots submitted were about 70 percent defective, the probability of accepting such lots is 50 percent.

The point in showing the inadequacy of these rule-of-thumb plans is to emphasize that the intuitive approach can be so grossly in error as to seriously jeopardize the evaluation of a product. By deriving the operating characteristic curve the sampling risks become known. Even when these sampling risks are known, other considerations may dictate that a sampling plan be used which is

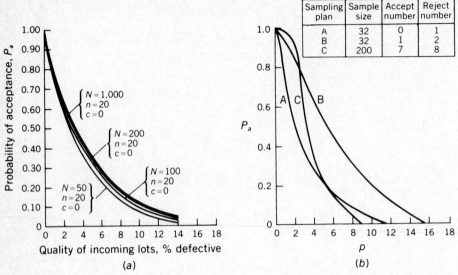

Figure 17-4 (*a*) Effect of changing lot size on OC curve. (*b*) Effect of increasing sample size and acceptance number on OC curve.

inadequate from a statistical point of view. However, it is important that the size of the risk be known before a final judgment is made. No sampling plan should be adopted without first seeing its OC curve.

17-6 EVALUATION OF PARAMETERS AFFECTING ACCEPTANCE SAMPLING PLANS

Sampling risks are affected by lot size, sample size, and the acceptance number (see Figure 17-4). In Figure 17-4*a* the lot size is changed but the sample size and acceptance number are held constant. Notice that the lot size has little effect on the probability of acceptance. If the lot size is moderately large (at least 10 times the sample size) and if the sample is selected randomly, the lot size has only a small effect on the probability of acceptance. It is tempting to conclude that lot size may be ignored in deriving a sampling plan. However, it is usually desired that larger lot sizes have a better operating characteristic curve in order to reduce the risk of error for costly amounts of product. The higher the amount at stake, the more precise should be the OC curve. Therefore, most sampling tables do show lot size as a parameter. (As the lot size increases, the absolute sample size increases but the ratio of sample size to lot size decreases.) The fact remains, however, that if all else is constant, the lot size has essentially no effect on the probability of acceptance.

The effect of other parameters is shown in Figure 17-4*b*:

1. When the acceptance number is zero, the OC curve is concave upward.

2. When the acceptance number is increased, the probability of acceptance, for low values of p, is increased.
3. Increasing the sample size and acceptance number together gives the closest approach to the ideal OC curve.

For safety-related products, there is a need for sampling plans with a zero acceptance number.[5] This is important for product liability implications and regulatory requirements. The effect of sample size can then be shown by the OC curve. This is illustrated in Problem 17-16.

17-7 QUALITY INDICES FOR ACCEPTANCE SAMPLING PLANS

Many of the published plans can be categorized in terms of one of several quality indices:

1. *Acceptable quality level (AQL)*. This is usually defined as the worst quality level that is still considered *satisfactory*. The units of quality level can be selected to meet the particular needs of a product. Thus, MIL-STD-105D[6] defines AQL as "the maximum percent defective (or the maximum number of defects per hundred units) that, for purposes of sampling inspection, can be considered satisfactory as a process average." If a unit of product can have a number of different defects of varying seriousness, then demerits can be assigned to each type of defect and product quality measured in terms of demerits. As an AQL is an *acceptable* level, the probability of acceptance for an AQL lot should be high (see Figure 17-5).
2. *Rejectable quality level (RQL)*. This is a definition of *unsatisfactory* quality. Different titles are sometimes used to denote an RQL; for example, in the Dodge–Romig plans, the term "lot tolerance percent defective (LTPD)" is used. As an RQL is an *unacceptable* level, the probability of acceptance for an RQL lot should be low (see Figure 17-5). In some tables, this probability is known as the consumer's risk, is designated as P_c, and has been standarized at 0.1. The consumer's risk is not the probability that the consumer will actually receive product at the RQL. The consumer will in fact *not* receive 1 lot in 10 at RQL fraction defective. What the consumer actually gets depends on actual quality in the lots *before* inspection, and on the probability of acceptance.
3. *Indifference quality level (IQL)*. This is a quality level somewhere between the AQL and RQL. It is frequently defined as the quality level having a probability of acceptance of 0.50 for a given sampling plan (see Figure 17-5).

---

[5] Edward G. Schilling, "A Lot Sensitive Sampling Plan for Compliance Testing and Acceptance Inspection," *Journal of Quality Technology*, vol. 10, no. 2, April 1978, pp. 47–51.

[6] "Sampling Procedures and Tables for Inspection by Attributes," MIL-STD-105D, now obtainable as ANSI Standard Z1.4, American National Standards Institute, 1430 Broadway, New York, N.Y. 10018.

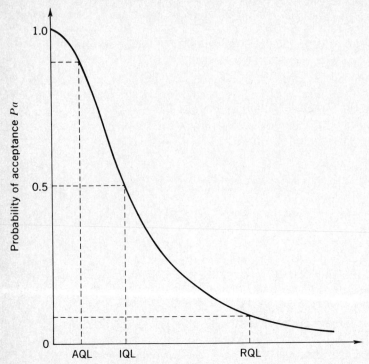

Figure 17-5 Quality indices for sampling plans.

4. *Average outgoing quality limit (AOQL).* A relationship exists between the fraction defective in the material before inspection (incoming quality p) and the fraction defective remaining after inspection (outgoing quality AOQ): $AOQ = pP_a$. When incoming quality is perfect, outgoing quality must also be perfect. However, when incoming quality is bad, outgoing quality will also be perfect (assuming no inspection errors) because the sampling plan will cause all lots to be rejected and detail inspected. Thus at either extreme—incoming quality excellent or terrible—the outgoing quality will tend to be good. Between these extremes is the point at which the percent of defectives in the outgoing material will reach its maximum. This point is the average outgoing quality limit (AOQL).[7]

These indices primarily apply when production occurs in a continuing series of lots. For isolated lots, the RQL concept is recommended. The indices were originally developed by statisticians to help describe the characteristics of sampling plans. Misinterpretations are common (particularly of the AQL) and are similar to those mentioned in Section 17-3. For example, a sampling plan based on AQL *will* accept some lots having a quality level worse than the AQL.

[7] For a sample calculation, see *Quality Control Handbook,* 3rd ed., p. 24-14; also fig. 24-8.

17-8 TYPES OF SAMPLING PLANS

Sampling plans are of two[8] types:

1. *Attributes plans.* A random sample is taken from the lot and each unit classified as acceptable or defective. The number defective is then compared with the allowable number stated in the plan, and a decision is made to accept or reject the lot. This chapter will illustrate attributes plans based on AQL, RQL, and AOQL.
2. *Variables plans.* A sample is taken and a *measurement* of a specified quality characteristic is made on each unit. These measurements are then summarized into a simple statistic (e.g., sample average) and the observed value compared with an allowable value defined in the plan. A decision is then made to accept or reject the lot. This chapter will describe an AQL variables plan.

A comparison of attributes and variables sampling is given in Table 17-2. The key advantage of a variables sampling plan is the additional information provided in each sample, which in turn results in smaller sample sizes as

---

[8] It is possible to combine an attributes and a variables plan into one. See *Quality Control Handbook*, 3rd ed., p. 25-13.

Table 17-2 Comparison of attributes and variables sampling plans

	Attributes	Variables
Type of inspection required for each item	Each item classified as defective or acceptable; go/no go type of gages may be used	Measurement must be taken on each item; higher skill level of inspection required
Size of sample		Saving of at least 30%* in sample size (if only one characteristic must be measured on each item and if single sampling is used)
Assumption of underlying distribution	None	Some distribution must be assumed (usually normal)
Number of characteristics that can be reviewed in one sample	Any number	A separate sampling plan is required for each characteristic to be reviewed
Type of information provided for use in correcting process	Number of defectives (if go/no go gages are used)	Valuable information on the process average and variation is available to indicate type of process correction required

*See A. H. Bowker and H. P. Goode, *Sampling Inspection by Variables*, McGraw-Hill Book Company, New York, 1952, pp. 32–33.

compared with an attributes plan having the same risks. However, if a product has several important quality characteristics, each must be evaluated against a separate variables acceptance criterion (e.g., obtain numerical values and calculate the average and standard deviation for each characteristic). In a corresponding attributes plan, the sample size required may be higher but the several characteristics could be treated as a group and evaluated against one set of acceptance criteria.

17-9 SINGLE SAMPLING, DOUBLE SAMPLING, AND MULTIPLE SAMPLING

Many published sampling tables give a choice among single, double, and multiple sampling. In single-sampling plans, a random sample of n items is drawn from the lot. If the number of defectives is less than or equal to the acceptance number (c), the lot is accepted. Otherwise, the lot is rejected. In double-sampling plans (Figure 17-6), a smaller initial sample is usually drawn, and a decision to accept or reject is reached on the basis of this smaller first sample, if the number of defectives is either quite large or quite small. A second sample is taken if the results of the first are not decisive. Since it is only necessary to draw and inspect the second sample in borderline cases, the average number of pieces inspected per lot is generally smaller with double sampling. In multiple-sampling plans, one or two or several still smaller samples are taken, usually continuing as needed, until a decision to accept or reject is obtained.[9] Thus, double- and multiple-sampling plans *may* mean less inspection but are more complicated to administer.

In general, it is possible to derive single-, double-, or multiple-sampling schemes with essentially identical operating characteristic curves.

17-10 CHARACTERISTICS OF A GOOD ACCEPTANCE PLAN

An acceptance sampling plan should have these characteristics:

1. The index (AQL, AOQL, etc.) used to define "quality" should reflect the needs of the consumer and producer and not be chosen primarily for statistical convenience.
2. The sampling risks should be known in quantitative terms (the OC curve). The producer should have adequate protection against the rejection of good lots; the consumer should be protected against the acceptance of bad lots.
3. The plan should minimize the *total* cost of inspection of all products. This

---

[9] If each small sample consists of one item, the plan is called an "item-by-item sequential sampling plan."

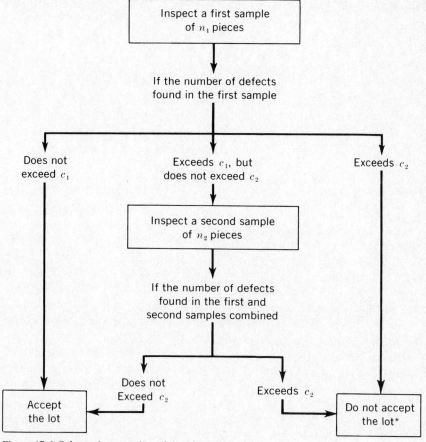

Figure 17-6 Schematic operation of double sampling.

requires careful evaluation of the pros and cons of attributes and variables plans, and single, double, and multiple sampling. It should also reflect product priorities, particularly from the fitness-for-use viewpoint.

4. The plan should make use of other knowledge, such as process capability, vendor data, and other information (see Section 17-20).
5. The plan should have built-in flexibility to reflect changes in lot sizes, quality of product submitted, and any other pertinent factors.
6. The measurements required by the plan should provide information useful in estimating individual lot quality and long-run quality.
7. The plan should be simple to explain and administer.

Fortunately, published tables are available which meet many of these characteristics. Figure 17-7 shows the sequence of steps in choosing a plan from

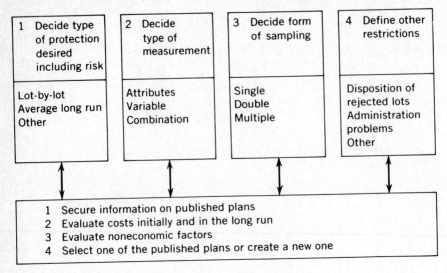

1 Decide type of protection desired including risk	2 Decide type of measurement	3 Decide form of sampling	4 Define other restrictions
Lot-by-lot Average long run Other	Attributes Variable Combination	Single Double Multiple	Disposition of rejected lots Administration problems Other

1 Secure information on published plans
2 Evaluate costs initially and in the long run
3 Evaluate noneconomic factors
4 Select one of the published plans or create a new one

Figure 17-7 Choosing a sampling plan from published tables.

published tables. The double arrows emphasize the need to balance desires against the properties of the published plans. Three basic plans will be discussed here. There are other published plans developed for specific applications, such as continuous production, bulk product, and reliability testing.[10] Under certain circumstances, control charts may be used as a basis for acceptance.[11] We now proceed to a discussion of three published plans.

17-11 MIL-STD-105D

MIL-STD-105D is an attributes sampling scheme. It was originally prepared for making lot decisions on military products but is now in general use for both military and civilian products.

The quality index in MIL-STD-105D is the acceptable quality level (AQL). The AQL is the maximum percent defective (or number of defects per 100 units) that is satisfactory as a process average. The probability of accepting material of AQL quality is always high, but not exactly the same for all plans. For lot quality just equal to the AQL, the "percent of lots expected to be accepted" ranges from about 88 to 99 percent. Defects are classified as "critical," "major," or "minor." The government may, at its option, specify separate AQLs for each class or it may use a further subdivision and specify an AQL for each individual kind of defect which a product may show. The choice may be made from 26 available AQL values ranging from 0.010 to 1000.0. (Values of

[10] See *Quality Control Handbook*, 3rd ed., secs. 24 and 25.
[11] Raymond Woods, "Effective, Economic Quality through the Use of Acceptance Control Charts," *Journal of Quality Technology*, vol. 8, no. 2, April 1976, pp. 81–85.

AQL of 10.0 or less may be interpreted as percent defective or defects per hundred units.)

The tables specify the relative amount of inspection to be used as "inspection level" I, II, or III; level II is regarded as normal. The concept of inspection level permits the user to balance the cost of inspection against the amount of protection required. The three levels involve inspection in amounts roughly in the ratio 0.4 to 1.0 to 1.6. (Four additional inspection levels are provided for situations requiring "small-sample inspection.")

A plan is chosen from the tables as follows:

1. The following information must be known:
   a. Acceptable quality level (AQL).
   b. Lot size.
   c. Type of sampling (single, double, or multiple).
   d. Inspection level (usually level II).
2. Knowing the lot size and inspection level, obtain a code letter from Table 17-3.
3. Knowing the code letter, AQL, and type of sampling, read the sampling plan from Table 17-4 (Table 17-4 is for single sampling; the standard also provides tables for double and multiple sampling).

For example, suppose that a purchasing agency has contracted for a 1.5 percent AQL. Suppose also that the parts are brought in lots of 1500 pieces. From the table of sample-size code letters (Table 17-3) it is found that letter K

Table 17-3 Sample-size code letters—MIL-STD-105D (ABC standard)

Lot or batch size	S-1	S-2	S-3	S-4	I	II	III
2–8	A	A	A	A	A	A	B
9–15	A	A	A	A	A	B	C
16–25	A	A	B	B	B	C	D
26–50	A	B	B	C	C	D	E
51–90	B	B	C	C	C	E	F
91–150	B	B	C	D	D	F	G
151–280	B	C	D	E	E	G	H
281–500	B	C	D	E	F	H	J
501–1200	C	C	E	F	G	J	K
1201–3200	C	D	E	G	H	K	L
3201–10,000	C	D	F	G	J	L	M
10,001–35,000	C	D	F	H	K	M	N
35,001–150,000	D	E	G	J	L	N	P
150,001–500,000	D	E	G	J	M	P	Q
500,001 and over	D	E	H	K	N	Q	R

Table 17-4 Master table for normal inspection (single sampling)—MIL-STD-105D (ABC standard)

Acceptable quality (each column given as Ac Re)

Sample-size code letter	Sample size	0.010	0.015	0.025	0.040	0.065	0.10	0.15	0.25	0.40	0.65	1.0	1.5
A	2	↓	↓	↓	↓	↓	↓	↓	↓	↓	↓	↓	↓
B	3	↓	↓	↓	↓	↓	↓	↓	↓	↓	↓	↓	↓
C	5	↓	↓	↓	↓	↓	↓	↓	↓	↓	↓	↓	↓
D	8	↓	↓	↓	↓	↓	↓	↓	↓	↓	↓	↓	↓
E	13	↓	↓	↓	↓	↓	↓	↓	↓	↓	↓	↓	↓
F	20	↓	↓	↓	↓	↓	↓	↓	↓	↓	↓	↓	0 1
G	32	↓	↓	↓	↓	↓	↓	↓	↓	↓	↓	0 1	1 2
H	50	↓	↓	↓	↓	↓	↓	↓	↓	↓	0 1	1 2	2 3
J	80	↓	↓	↓	↓	↓	↓	↓	↓	0 1	1 2	2 3	3 4
K	125	↓	↓	↓	↓	↓	↓	↓	0 1	1 2	2 3	3 4	5 6
L	200	↓	↓	↓	↓	↓	↓	0 1	1 2	2 3	3 4	5 6	7 8
M	315	↓	↓	↓	↓	↓	0 1	1 2	2 3	3 4	5 6	7 8	10 11
N	500	↓	↓	↓	↓	0 1	1 2	2 3	3 4	5 6	7 8	10 11	14 15
P	800	↓	↓	↓	0 1	1 2	2 3	3 4	5 6	7 8	10 11	14 15	21 22
Q	1250	↓	↓	0 1	1 2	2 3	3 4	5 6	7 8	10 11	14 15	21 22	↓
R	2000	↑	0 1	1 2	2 3	3 4	5 6	7 8	10 11	14 15	21 22	↑	↑

↓ = use first sampling plan below arrow. If sample size equals, or exceeds, lot or batch size, 00% inspection. do 100% inspection.

↑ = use first sampling plan above arrow.

Ac = acceptance number.

Re = rejection number.

plans are required for inspection level II. Table 17-4 states the sample size is 125. For AQL = 1.5, the acceptance number is given as 5 and the rejection number as 6. This means that the entire lot of 1500 articles may be accepted if five or fewer defective articles are found, but must be rejected if six or more are found.

Sampling risks are defined by the OC curve published in the standard. The curve for this plan is shown in Figure 17-2 as curve A.

The standard provides single, double, and multiple plans for each code letter (i.e., lot-size category). The plans for code letter K are shown in Table 17-5. Thus the three plans can be found under the AQL column of 1.5. For example, the double-sampling plan calls for a first sample of 80 units. If 2 or less defectives are found, the lot is accepted. If 5 or more defectives are found, the lot is rejected. If 3 or 4 defectives are found in the sample of 80, then a second sample of 80 is taken, giving a cumulative sample size of 160. If the total number of defectives in both samples is 6 or less, the lot is accepted; 7 or more defectives means lot rejection.

17-12 SWITCHING PROCEDURES IN MIL-STD-105D

MIL-STD-105D includes provision for tightened inspection if quality deteriorates. If two out of five consecutive lots are rejected on original inspection, a

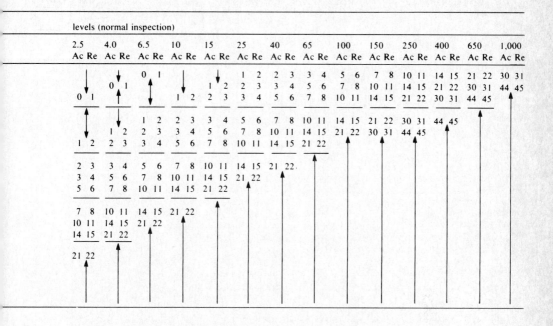

tightened inspection plan is imposed. The sample size is usually the same as normal, but the acceptance number is reduced. (The tightened plans do require larger sample sizes if the probability of acceptance for an AQL lot is less than 0.75.) For the example previously cited, the tightened plan can be read from Table 17-5 as a sample size of 125 and an acceptance number of 3.

MIL-STD-105D also provides for reduced inspection where the supplier's record has been good. When the process average is better than the AQL by 2σ or more, a reduced inspection plan may be used. A table of lower limits for the process average and rules governing normal and reduced inspection are provided in the standard. Under reduced sampling, the sample size is usually 40 percent of the normal sample size.

These switching rules apply when production is submitted in a continuing series of lots rather than isolated lots.

17-13 OTHER PROVISIONS OF MIL-STD-105D

The standard not only provides OC curves for most of the plans, but also average sample-size curves for double and multiple sampling. The latter curves show the average sample sizes expected as a function of the product quality submitted. Although the OC curves are roughly the same for single, double, and multiple sampling, the average sample-size curves vary considerably

Table 17-5 Sampling plan for sample-size code letter: K

Acceptable quality levels (normal inspection)

Type of sampling plan	Cumulative sample size	Less than 0.10 (Ac Re)	0.10 (Ac Re)	0.15 (Ac Re)	0.25 (Ac Re)	0.40 (Ac Re)	0.65 (Ac Re)	1.0 (Ac Re)	1.5 (Ac Re)	2.5 (Ac Re)	4.0 (Ac Re)	6.5 (Ac Re)	10 (Ac Re)	✗ (Ac Re)	✗ (Ac Re)	Higher than 10 (Ac Re)
Single	125	▽	0 1	Use letter L	Use letter L	1 2	2 3	3 4	5 6	7 8	10 11	14 15	21 22	✗	✗	△
Double	80	▽	*	Use letter M	Use letter M	0 2	0 3	1 4	2 5	3 7	5 9	7 11	9 14	11 16	...	△
Double	160					1 2	3 4	4 5	6 7	8 9	12 13	18 19	23 24	26 27		
Multiple	32	▽	*	Use letter J	Use letter J	# 2	# 2	# 3	# 4	0 4	0 5	0 6	1 7	1 8	2 9	△
Multiple	64					# 2	0 3	0 3	1 5	1 6	3 8	3 9	4 10	6 12	7 14	
Multiple	96					0 2	0 3	1 4	2 6	3 8	6 10	7 12	8 13	11 17	13 19	
Multiple	128					0 3	1 4	2 5	3 7	5 10	8 13	10 15	12 17	16 22	19 25	
Multiple	160					1 3	2 4	3 6	5 8	7 11	11 15	14 17	17 20	22 25	25 29	
Multiple	192					1 3	3 5	4 6	7 9	10 12	14 17	18 20	21 23	27 29	31 33	
Multiple	224					2 3	4 5	6 7	9 10	13 14	18 19	21 22	25 26	32 33	37 38	

Tightened inspection AQL labels (aligned with the same data columns):
Less than 0.15 | 0.15 | 0.25 | 0.40 | 0.65 | 1.0 | 1.5 | 2.5 | 4.0 | 6.5 | ✗ | ✗ | 4.0 | 6.5 | 10 | Higher than 10

Acceptable quality levels (tightened inspection)

△ = Use next preceding sample-size code letter for which acceptance and rejection numbers are available.
▽ = Use next subsequent sample-size code letter for which acceptance and rejection numbers are available.
Ac = Acceptance number
Re = Rejection number
* = Use single-sampling plan above (or alternatively use letter N).
# = Acceptance not permitted at this sample size.

because of the inherent differences among the three types of sampling. The standard also states the AOQL that would result if all rejected lots were screened for defectives.

The OC curves and AOQL values stated in the standard do *not* reflect the switching rules discussed previously. Schilling and Sheesley[12] have prepared tabulated values of OC curves, average sample number curves, average outgoing quality curves, and average total inspection curves under the switching rules. (The concept of average total inspection will be discussed later in the chapter.)

Finally, the flexibility of the AQL concept in MIL-STD-105D should be emphasized. AQL may be defined in terms of percent defective or defects per 100 units of product. A "defective" is a unit of product with 1 or more defects. Thus, if a product has 10 quality characteristics, any 1 defect on 1 unit will cause the unit to be classified as a defective if the AQL is defined in terms of percent defective. Instead, the AQL may be defined as number of defects per 100 units of product. For some products, it may be preferable to use defects per 100 units.

17-14 DODGE–ROMIG SAMPLING TABLES[13]

Dodge and Romig provide four sets of attributes plans emphasizing either lot-by-lot quality (LTPD) or long-run quality (AOQL):

Lot tolerance percent defective (LTPD): single sampling
double sampling
Average outgoing quality limit (AOQL): single sampling
double sampling

These plans differ from those in MIL-STD-105D in that they assume that all rejected lots are 100 percent inspected and the defectives replaced with acceptable items. Plans with this feature are called *rectifying inspection plans.* The tables provide protection against poor quality on either a lot-by-lot basis or average long-run quality. The LTPD plans assure that a lot having poor quality will have a low probability of acceptance, i.e., the probability of acceptance (or consumer's risk) is 0.10 for a lot with LTPD quality. The LTPD values range from 0.5 to 10.0 percent defective. The AOQL plans assure that, after all sampling and 100 percent inspection of rejected lots, the *average* quality over many lots will not exceed the AOQL. The AOQL values range from 0.1 to 10.0 percent. Each LTPD plan lists the corresponding AOQL and each AOQL plan lists the LTPD.

[12] E. G. Schilling and J. H. Sheesley, "The Performance of MIL-STD-105D under the Switching Rules, Part I: Evaluation and Part II: Tables," *Journal of Quality Technology,* vol. 10, no. 2, April 1978, pp. 76–83; vol. 10, no. 3, July 1978, pp. 104–124.

[13] H. F. Dodge and H. G. Romig, *Sampling Inspection Tables,* 2nd ed., John Wiley & Sons, Inc., New York, 1959.

Table 17-6 shows a Dodge–Romig table for single sampling on the lot tolerance basis. All the plans listed in this table have the same risk (0.10) of accepting submitted lots that contain exactly 5 percent of defective articles. For example, if the estimated process average percent defective is between 2.01 and 2.50 percent, the last column at the right gives the plans that will provide the minimum inspection per lot. However, the probability that a lot of quality p_t will be rejected is the same for all columns, so that an initial incorrect estimate of the process average would have little effect except to increase somewhat the total number of pieces inspected per lot. The selection of a plan thus requires only two items of information: the size of lot to be sampled and the prevailing average quality of the supplier for the product in question.

Process average is determined from past records, modified by any supplemental knowledge useful for predicting the expected quality level.

Table 17-7 shows a typical table of AOQL plans using double sampling. In contrast to the lot tolerance tables, this table gives plans which differ considerably as to lot tolerance but which have the same AOQL (1 percent). (The corresponding lot tolerances are, however, given.)

AOQL plans are appropriate only when all rejected lots are 100 percent inspected. The averaging of the perfect quality of the detailed lots with the poor quality of unsatisfactory lots occasionally accepted (owing to the unavoidable consumer's risk) determines the average outgoing quality and makes a limit possible. AOQL schemes are open to question where rejected lots are returned to an outside supplier, since there is no assurance that they will be 100 percent inspected and returned.

Sampling is uneconomical if the average quality submitted is not considerably better than the AOQL specified. For this reason the Dodge–Romig AOQL tables do not give any plans for process averages which exceed the AOQL. Similarly, lot tolerance plans are not given for process averages greater than one-half of the specified lot tolerance. Actually 100 percent inspection is often less expensive than sampling if 40 percent or more of submitted lots are rejected, since the expenses of administration of the sampling plan and of double handling of rejected lots are eliminated.

17-15 MINIMUM INSPECTION PER LOT

All Dodge–Romig plans are constructed to minimize the average total inspection (ATI) per lot for product of a given process average. This is an important feature of the Dodge–Romig plans and deserves further explanation.

Assume that a consumer establishes acceptance criteria as follows:

Lot tolerance fraction defective $p_t = 0.05$
Consumer's risk $P_c = 0.1$

A great many sampling plans meet these criteria; i.e., there are many combinations of sample size and acceptance number that would have an OC curve going through this point.

Table 17-6 Single-sampling table for lot tolerance percent defective (LTPD) = 5.0%*

Lot size	Process average 0 to 0.05%		AOQL %	Process average 0.06 to 0.50%		AOQL %	Process average 0.51 to 1.00%		AOQL %	Process average 1.01 to 1.50%		AOQL %	Process average 1.51 to 2.00%		AOQL %	Process average 2.01 to 2.50%		AOQL %
	n	c	%	n	c	%	n	c	%	n	c	%	n	c	%	n	c	%
1–30	All	0	0	All	0	0	All	0	0	All	0	0	All	0	0	All	0	0
31–50	30	0	0.49	30	0	0.49	30	0	0.49	30	0	0.49	30	0	0.49	30	0	0.49
51–100	37	0	0.63	37	0	0.63	37	0	0.63	37	0	0.63	37	0	0.63	37	0	0.63
101–200	40	0	0.74	40	0	0.74	40	0	0.74	40	0	0.74	40	0	0.74	40	0	0.74
201–300	43	0	0.74	43	0	0.74	70	1	0.92	70	1	0.92	95	2	0.99	95	2	0.99
301–400	44	0	0.74	44	0	0.74	70	1	0.99	100	2	1.0	120	3	1.1	145	4	1.1
401–500	45	0	0.75	75	1	0.95	100	2	1.1	100	2	1.1	125	3	1.2	150	4	1.2
501–600	45	0	0.76	75	1	0.98	100	2	1.1	125	3	1.2	150	4	1.3	175	5	1.3
601–800	45	0	0.77	75	1	1.0	100	2	1.2	130	3	1.2	175	5	1.4	200	6	1.4
801–1000	45	0	0.78	75	1	1.0	105	2	1.2	155	4	1.4	180	5	1.4	225	7	1.5
1001–2000	45	0	0.80	75	1	1.0	130	3	1.4	180	5	1.6	230	7	1.7	280	9	1.8
2001–3000	75	1	1.1	105	2	1.3	135	3	1.4	210	6	1.7	280	9	1.9	370	13	2.1
3001–4000	75	1	1.1	105	2	1.3	160	4	1.5	210	6	1.7	305	10	2.0	420	15	2.2
4001–5000	75	1	1.1	105	2	1.3	160	4	1.5	235	7	1.8	330	11	2.0	440	16	2.2
5001–7000	75	1	1.1	105	2	1.3	185	5	1.7	260	8	1.9	350	12	2.2	490	18	2.4
7001–10,000	75	1	1.1	105	2	1.3	185	5	1.7	260	8	1.9	380	13	2.2	535	20	2.5
10,001–20,000	75	1	1.1	135	3	1.4	210	6	1.8	285	9	2.0	425	15	2.3	610	23	2.6
20,001–50,000	75	1	1.1	135	3	1.4	235	7	1.9	305	10	2.1	470	17	2.4	700	27	2.7
50,001–100,000	75	1	1.1	160	4	1.6	235	7	1.9	355	12	2.2	515	19	2.5	770	30	2.8

*n = sample size; c = acceptance number.

AOQL = average outgoing quality limit.

"All" indicates that each piece in the lot is to be inspected.

Source: From H. F. Dodge and H. G. Romig, *Sampling Inspection Tables*, 2nd ed., John Wiley & Sons, Inc., New York, 1959.

427

Table 17-7 Double-sampling table for average outgoing quality limit (AOQL) = 1.0%*

Lot size	Process average 0 to 0.02%						Process average 0.03 to 0.20%						Process average 0.21 to 0.40%					
	Trial 1		Trial 2			p_t %	Trial 1		Trial 2			p_t %	Trial 1		Trial 2			p_t %
	n_1	c_1	n_2	$n_1 + n_2$	c_2		n_1	c_1	n_2	$n_1 + n_2$	c_2		n_1	c_1	n_2	$n_1 + n_2$	c_2	
1–25	All	0	—	—	—	—	All	0	—	—	—	—	All	0	—	—	—	—
26–50	22	0	—	—	—	7.7	22	0	—	—	—	7.7	22	0	—	—	—	7.7
51–100	33	0	17	50	1	6.9	33	0	17	50	1	6.9	33	0	17	50	1	6.9
101–200	43	0	22	65	1	5.8	43	0	22	65	1	5.8	43	0	22	65	1	5.8
201–300	47	0	28	75	1	5.5	47	0	28	75	1	5.5	47	0	28	75	1	5.5
301–400	49	0	31	80	1	5.4	49	0	31	80	1	5.4	55	0	60	115	2	4.8
401–500	50	0	30	80	1	5.4	50	0	30	80	1	5.4	55	0	65	120	2	4.7
501–600	50	0	30	80	1	5.4	50	0	30	80	1	5.4	60	0	65	125	2	4.6
601–800	50	0	35	85	1	5.3	60	0	70	130	2	4.5	60	0	70	130	2	4.5
801–1000	55	0	30	85	1	5.2	60	0	75	135	2	4.4	60	0	75	135	2	4.4
1001–2000	55	0	35	90	1	5.1	65	0	75	140	2	4.3	75	0	120	195	3	3.8
2001–3000	65	0	80	145	2	4.2	65	0	80	145	2	4.2	75	0	125	200	3	3.7
3001–4000	70	0	80	150	2	4.1	70	0	80	150	2	4.1	80	0	175	255	4	3.5
4001–5000	70	0	80	150	2	4.1	70	0	80	150	2	4.1	80	0	180	260	4	3.4
5001–7000	70	0	80	150	2	4.1	75	0	125	200	3	3.7	80	0	180	260	4	3.4
7001–10,000	70	0	80	150	2	4.1	80	0	125	205	3	3.6	85	0	180	265	4	3.3
10,001–20,000	70	0	80	150	2	4.1	80	0	130	210	3	3.6	90	0	230	320	5	3.2
20,001–50,000	75	0	80	155	2	4.0	80	0	135	215	3	3.6	95	0	300	395	6	2.9
50,001–100,000	75	0	80	155	2	4.0	85	0	180	265	4	3.3	170	1	380	550	8	2.6

*Trial 1: n_1 = first sample size; c_1 = acceptance number for first sample.
Trial 2: n_2 = second sample size; c_2 = acceptance number for first and second samples combined.
p_t = lot tolerance percent defective with a consumer's risk P_c of 0.10.
"All" indicates that each piece in the lot is to be inspected.
Source: From H. F. Dodge and H. G. Romig, *Sampling Inspection Tables*, 2nd ed., John Wiley & Sons, Inc., New York, 1959.

428

The total number of articles inspected is made up of two components: (1) the sample which is inspected for each lot, and (2) the remaining parts which must be inspected in those lots which fail to pass the sampling inspection.

For small acceptance numbers the total inspection is high because many lots need to be detailed. For large acceptance numbers the total is again high, this time because of the large size of samples. The minimum sum occurs at a point between these extremes. All Dodge–Romig plans meet the criterion of minimizing the average total inspection.[14]

17-16 ACCEPTANCE SAMPLING PLANS BY VARIABLES

In *attributes* sampling plans, each item inspected is classified as either defective or acceptable. The total number of defectives in the sample is then compared with the acceptance number and a decision made on the lot. In *variables* sampling plans, a *measurement* is taken and recorded for each item in the sample. An *index* (such as an average) is calculated from these measurements, compared with an "allowable" value, and a decision is made on the lot. The sample size and allowable value are a function of the desired sampling risks.[15] This chapter explains one published plan. (Section 10-5 explains another variables plan, known as the lot plot method.)

An example of a variables plan is MIL-STD-414, *Sampling Procedures and Tables for Inspection by Variables for Per Cent Defective.*[16] The format and terminology are similar to those of MIL-STD-105D; for example, the concepts of AQL, code letters, inspection levels, reduced and tightened inspection, and OC curves are all included.

MIL-STD-414 assumes a normal distribution and that information on variability is available or will be obtained in the sample. To provide flexibility in application, a number of alternative procedures are included. Only one of the procedures will be described here. A plan is selected as follows:

1. Select an acceptable quality level (AQL). Levels range from 0.04 to 15 percent.
2. Select a sample-size code letter based on the lot size and inspection level. Five inspection levels are provided. Level IV is considered normal and is used unless another level is specified. Table 17-8 is used to determine the sample-size code letter.
3. Select the sampling plan from a master table in section B, C, or D. Sections B and C contain plans for the case when the variability is unknown and is measured by the standard deviation or range, respectively. Section D provides the plans when the variability is known (in terms of standard

[14] For a sample calculation, see *Quality Control Handbook,* 3rd ed., pp. 24-16 to 24-17.
[15] See *Quality Control Handbook,* 3rd ed., sec. 25.
[16] Now available as ANSI Standard Z1.9.

Table 17-8 Sample-size code letters*

Lot size	I	II	III	IV	V
		Inspection level			
3–8	B	B	B	B	C
9–15	B	B	B	B	D
16–25	B	B	B	C	E
26–40	B	B	B	D	F
41–65	B	B	C	E	G
66–110	B	B	D	F	H
111–180	B	C	E	G	I
181–300	B	D	F	H	J
301–500	C	E	G	I	K
501–800	D	F	H	J	L
801–1300	E	G	I	K	L
1301–3200	F	H	J	L	M
3201–8000	G	I	L	M	N
8001–22,000	H	J	M	N	O
22,001–110,000	I	K	N	O	P
110,001–550,000	I	K	O	P	Q
550,001 and over	I	K	P	Q	Q

*Sample-size code letters given in body of table are applicable when the indicated inspection levels are to be used.

deviation). A plan from section B will be selected for the following problem.

Example[17] The maximum temperature of operation for a device is specified as 209°F (98.3°C). A lot of 40 is submitted for inspection. Inspection level IV with an AQL of 1 percent is to be used. The standard deviation is unknown. Assuming that operating temperature follows a normal distribution, what variables sampling plan should be used to inspect the lot?

One type of plan in section B requires that n measurements be taken, the average and standard deviation calculated, and an evaluation made of the number of standard deviations between the sample average and the specification limit. More specifically,

1. Compute the same average $\overline{X}$ and the estimate of the lot standard deviation s. Also compute $(U - \overline{X})/s$ for an upper specification limit U, or $(\overline{X} - L)/s$ for a lower specification limit L.
2. If the fraction computed in step 1 is equal to or greater than k, accept the lot; otherwise, reject the lot.

[17] Ibid.

Table 17-8 provides the code letter as D and Table 17-9 (Master Table B-1 in MIL-STD-414) provides the values of n and k as 5 and 1.53, respectively.

Now suppose that the measurements were 197°F (91.7°C), 188°F (86.7°C), 184°F (84.4°C), 205°F (96.1°C), and 201°F (93.9°C). This yields an $\overline{X}$ of 195°F (90.6°C) and an s of 8.81°F (−12.9°C). Then $(U − \overline{X})/s = (209 − 195)/8.81 = 1.59$. As 1.59 is greater than 1.53, the lot is accepted. The OC curve for the plan is included in the standard.

The reader is referred to the standard itself for other procedures and tables.[18]

17-17 SELECTION OF A NUMERICAL VALUE OF THE QUALITY INDEX

The problem of selecting a value of the quality index (e.g., AQL, AOQL, or lot tolerance percent defective) is one of balancing the cost of finding and correcting a defective against the loss incurred if a defective slips through in inspection procedure.

Enell[19] has suggested that the break-even point (see Section 17-2) be used in the selection of an AQL. The break-even point for inspection was defined as the cost to inspect one piece divided by the damage done by one defective. For the example cited, the break-even point was 5 percent defective.

As a 5 percent defective quality level is the break-even point between sorting and sampling, the appropriate sampling plan should provide for a lot to have a 50 percent probability of being sorted or sampled; i.e., the probability of acceptance for the plan should be 0.50 at a 5 percent defective quality level. The operating characteristic curves in a set of sampling tables such as MIL-STD-105D can now be examined to determine an AQL. For example, suppose that the device is inspected in lots of 3000 pieces. The operating characteristic curves for this case (code letter K) are shown in MIL-STD-105D and Figure 17-2. The plan closest to having a P_a of 0.50 for a 5 percent level is the plan for an AQL of 1.5 percent. Therefore, this is the plan to adopt.

Some plans (for example, MIL-STD-105D) include a classification of defects to help determine the numerical value of the AQL. Defects are first classified as critical, major, or minor, according to definitions provided in the standard. Different AQLs may be designated for groups of defects considered collectively, or for individual defects. Critical defects may have a 0 percent AQL while major defects might be assigned a low AQL, say 1 percent, and minor defects a higher AQL, say 4 percent. Some manufacturers of complex products specify quality in terms of number of defects per million parts.

---

[18] A summary is provided in *Quality Control Handbook,* 3rd ed., pp. 25-11 to 25-23.
[19] J. W. Enell, "What Sampling Plan Shall I Choose?" *Industrial Quality Control,* vol. 10, no. 6, May 1954, pp. 96–100.

Table 17-9 Master table for normal and tightened inspection for means based on variability unknown, standard deviation method*

Single specification limit, form 1

Acceptable quality levels (normal inspection)

Sample-size code letter	Sample size	0.04	0.065	0.10	0.15	0.25	0.40	0.65	1.00	1.50	2.50	4.00	6.50	10.00	15.00
		k	k	k	k	k	k	k	k	k	k	k	k	k	k
B	3	→	→	→	→	→	→	→	→	→	1.12	0.958	0.765	0.566	0.341
C	4	→	→	→	→	→	→	→	1.45	1.34	1.17	1.01	0.814	0.617	0.393
D	5	→	→	→	→	→	→	1.65	1.53	1.40	1.24	1.07	0.874	0.675	0.455
E	7	→	→	→	→	2.00	1.88	1.75	1.62	1.50	1.33	1.15	0.955	0.755	0.536
F	10	→	→	→	2.24	2.11	1.98	1.84	1.72	1.58	1.41	1.23	1.03	0.828	0.611
G	15	2.64	2.53	2.42	2.32	2.20	2.06	1.91	1.79	1.65	1.47	1.30	1.09	0.886	0.664
H	20	2.69	2.58	2.47	2.36	2.24	2.11	1.96	1.82	1.69	1.51	1.33	1.12	0.917	0.695
I	25	2.72	2.61	2.50	2.40	2.26	2.14	1.98	1.85	1.72	1.53	1.35	1.14	0.936	0.712
J	30	2.73	2.61	2.51	2.41	2.28	2.15	2.00	1.86	1.73	1.55	1.36	1.15	0.946	0.723
K	35	2.77	2.65	2.54	2.45	2.31	2.18	2.03	1.89	1.76	1.57	1.39	1.18	0.969	0.745
L	40	2.77	2.66	2.55	2.44	2.31	2.18	2.03	1.89	1.76	1.58	1.39	1.18	0.971	0.746
M	50	2.83	2.71	2.60	2.50	2.35	2.22	2.08	1.93	1.80	1.61	1.42	1.21	1.00	0.774
N	75	2.90	2.77	2.66	2.55	2.41	2.27	2.12	1.98	1.84	1.65	1.46	1.24	1.03	0.804
O	100	2.92	2.80	2.69	2.58	2.43	2.29	2.14	2.00	1.86	1.67	1.48	1.26	1.05	0.819
P	150	2.96	2.84	2.73	2.61	2.47	2.33	2.18	2.03	1.89	1.70	1.51	1.29	1.07	0.841
Q	200	2.97	2.85	2.73	2.62	2.47	2.33	2.18	2.04	1.89	1.70	1.51	1.29	1.07	0.845
		0.065	0.10	0.15	0.25	0.40	0.65	1.00	1.50	2.50	4.00	6.50	10.00	15.00	

Acceptable quality levels (tightened inspection)

*All AQL values are in percent defective.

↓ Use first sampling plan below arrow, that is, both sample size as well as k value. When sample size equals or exceeds lot size, every item in the lot must be inspected.

432

In practice, the quantification of the quality index is a matter of judgment based on the following factors:

1. Past performance on quality.
2. Effect of nonconforming product on later production steps.
3. Effect of nonconforming product on fitness for use.
4. Urgency of delivery requirements.
5. Cost to achieve the specified quality level.

17-18 FORMATION OF INSPECTION LOTS AND SELECTION OF SAMPLE

The importance of lot formation can be seen from an example.

Ten machines are producing the same product. Nine of these produce perfect product. The tenth machine produces 100 percent defectives. If lots consist of product from single machines, the defective product from the tenth machine will always be detected by sampling. If, however, the lots are formed by mixing up the work from all machines, it is inevitable that some defects will get through the sampling plan.

The fact that lot formation so strongly influences outgoing quality and inspection economics has led to some guidelines for lot formation.

1. Do not mix product from different sources (processes, production shifts, input materials, etc.), unless there is evidence that the lot-to-lot variation is small enough to be ignored.
2. Do not accumulate product over extensive periods of time (for lot formation).
3. Do make use of supplementary information (process capability, prior inspections, etc.) in lot formation. This information is especially useful when product is submitted in isolated lots or in small lots and may provide better knowledge on which to base an acceptance decision than the sampling data.
4. Do make lots as large as possible consistent with the factors listed above to take advantage of the fact that lot size has little effect on the OC curve (see Section 17-6). However, large lots may result in storage problems and production and delivery difficulties when a lot is rejected.

In acceptance sampling, the sample should be selected so that it is representative of the lot. This usually requires that it be a "random sample," i.e., chosen in a way that gives each possible sample in the lot an equal probability of being selected.[20]

---

[20] See *Quality Control Handbook,* 3rd ed., p. 24-7, for the use of random-number tables and other devices for selecting a random sample.

When the lots are known to come from different machines, production shifts, operators, etc., the product is actually multiple lots which have been arbitrarily combined. In such cases, the sampling is deliberately stratified; i.e., an attempt is made to draw the sample proportionately from each true lot. However, within each lot, randomness is still the appropriate basis for sampling.

Sampling Bias

Unless rigorous procedures are set up for sampling at random and/or by stratification, the sampling can deteriorate into a variety of biases which are detrimental to good decision making. The more usual biases consist of:

1. Sampling from the same location in all containers, racks, or bins.
2. Previewing the product and selecting only those units which appear to be defective (or nondefective).
3. Ignoring those portions of the lot which are inconvenient to sample.
4. Deciding on a pattern of stratification in the absence of knowledge of how the lot was made up.

The classical example is the legendary inspector who always took samples from the four corners and center of each tray and the legendary production operator who carefully filled these same spots with perfect product.

Because the structured sampling plans do assume randomness, and because some forms of sampling bias can significantly distort the product acceptance decisions, all concerned should be alert to plan the sampling to minimize these biases. Thereafter, the supervision and auditing should be alert to assure that the actual sampling conforms to these plans.

17-19 SAMPLING PROCEDURES BASED ON PRIOR QUALITY DATA

The plans discussed in this chapter make no assumption about the *distribution of percent defective* of lots submitted to the plan. This implies that all possible values of percent defective have an equal probability of occurrence. In practice, this is not true. As the plans provide protection against percent defectives that are unlikely to occur, the result is often excessive sample sizes.

Oliver and Springer[21] have developed tables, patterned after MIL-STD-105D, that incorporate data on the quality of previous lots into the sampling tables. The procedure is to calculate certain parameters from past lots and define the AQL, LTPD, producer's risk, and consumer's risk. The tables then provide sample size and acceptance criteria for single- and double-sampling plans. These are called *Bayesian sampling plans.*

[21] Larry R. Oliver and Melvin D. Springer, "A General Set of Bayesian Attribute Acceptance Plans," American Institute of Industrial Engineers, 1972 Technical Papers, pp. 443–455.

The steps are:

1. Collect quality data on previous lots of size N and sample size n. Calculate the fraction defective, p, in each sample.
2. Calculate the average fraction defective, $\bar{p}$, and the standard deviation of fraction defective, σ_p, using the basic formulas (see Section 3-5).
3. Define values for AQL, LTPD, and the corresponding producer's risk and consumer's risk.
4. Read the plan from the tables.

Example On a certain part, the percent defective (p) found in each lot (by 100 percent inspection or sampling) has been recorded. These p values were summarized by an average ($\bar{p}$) and standard deviation (σ_p):

$$\bar{p} = 1.80\% = 0.0180$$
$$\sigma_p = 0.99\% = 0.0099$$

It is assumed that the distribution of percent defective follows the beta distribution.[21] A sampling plan is desired to provide the following protection:

$$AQL = 1.5\% \text{ producer's risk} = 0.05$$
$$LTPD = 3.0\% \text{ consumer's risk} = 0.10$$

The *expected quality level* (EQL) is assumed equal to the past average, $\bar{p}$. The appropriate Bayesian single-sampling plan can be found in Table 17-10:

$$EQL/AQL = 0.018/0.015 = 1.2$$
$$LTPD/AQL = 0.03/0.015 = 2.0$$
$$\sigma/EQL = 0.0099/0.0180 = 0.55$$

The plan is $n = 59$ and $c = 3$. Select a random sample of 59 items. If 3 or less are defective, accept the lot. Otherwise, reject the lot. This plan has a 5 percent probability of rejecting a lot having AQL quality and a 10 percent probability of accepting a lot having LTPD quality.

A comparison of the Bayesian single-sample sizes in Table 17-10 with the single-sample sizes in MIL-STD-105D (Table 17-4) shows that the Bayesian approach usually requires much smaller sample sizes, particularly for low values of σ/EQL, i.e., small variation in lot percent defective.

In the Bayesian approach the derivation of a sampling plan requires an assumption of a probability distribution for incoming quality levels. If desired, the expected dollar loss due to accepting bad lots and rejecting good lots can be taken into account in deriving the sampling plan. (The incorporation of prior probabilities and losses into the conventional analysis is called *statistical decision theory*.)

The approach will be illustrated in terms of an example. Consider the following three sampling plans:

		Probability of incorrect decision on lot		
n	c	1%	4%	9%
50	1	0.0894	0.5995	0.0532
50	2	0.0138	0.3233	0.1605
50	3	0.0016	0.1391	0.3303

Table 17-10 Bayesian single-sampling plans with 0.05 producer's and 0.10 consumer's risks

	LTPD / AQL	$\dfrac{\sigma}{EQL}$, %	AQL, %												
			0.65		1.0		1.5		2.5		4.0		6.5		10	
			n	c	n	c	n	c	n	c	n	c	n	c	n	c
EQL/AQL = 0.8	2	25	13	12	13	12	13	12	13	12	13	12	13	12	13	12
		50	6	5	6	5	6	5	6	5	6	5	6	5	6	5
		75	4	3	4	3	4	3	4	3	4	3	4	3	4	3
	3	25	13	12	13	12	13	12	13	12	13	12	13	12	13	12
		50	6	5	6	5	6	5	6	5	6	5	6	5	6	5
		75	4	3	4	3	4	3	4	3	4	3	4	3	4	3
EQL/AQL = 1.0	2	25	8	7	8	7	8	7	8	7	8	7	8	7	8	7
		50	5	4	5	4	5	4	5	4	5	4	5	4	5	4
		60	5	3	5	3	5	3	5	3	5	3	5	3	5	3
		70	4	3	4	3	4	3	4	3	4	3	4	3	4	3
		74	3	2	3	2	3	2	3	2	3	2	3	2	3	2
		75	34	3	26	3	30	3	14	3	11	3	8	3	7	3
	3	25	8	7	8	7	8	7	8	7	8	7	8	7	8	7
		50	5	4	5	4	5	4	5	4	5	4	5	4	5	4
		75	3	2	3	2	3	2	3	2	3	2	3	2	3	2
EQL/AQL = 1.1	2	50	4	3	4	3	4	3	4	3	4	3	4	3	4	3
		60	4	3	4	3	4	3	4	3	4	3	4	3	4	3
		63	86	3	56	3	38	3	24	3	16	3	11	3	8	3
		70	134	3	88	3	59	3	35	3	23	3	15	3	10	3
		75	151	3	99	3	66	3	40	3	26	3	17	3	11	3
EQL/AQL = 1.2	2	25	5	4	5	4	5	4	5	4	5	4	5	4	5	4
		40	4	3	4	3	4	3	4	3	4	3	4	3	4	3
		45	4	3	4	3	4	3	4	3	4	3	4	3	4	3
		50	55	3	37	3	26	3	17	3	12	3	9	3	7	3
		55	134	3	87	3	59	3	36	3	23	3	15	3	10	3
		60	162	3	106	3	71	3	43	3	28	3	17	3	12	3
		75	196	3	128	3	86	3	52	3	33	3	21	3	14	3
	3	25	5	4	5	4	5	4	5	4	5	4	5	4	5	4
		50	4	3	4	3	4	3	4	3	4	3	4	3	4	3
		75	3	2	3	2	3	2	3	2	3	2	3	2	3	2

Table 17-11 Risk matrix

	State of nature		
	B_1	B_2	B_3'
Lot % defective	1	4	9
Probability of occurrence	0.40	0.35	0.25
Accept lot	0	0	200
Reject lot	150	100	0

Suppose that 5 percent defective is the dividing line between good and bad quality. Ideally, all lots less than 5 percent defective should be accepted; all lots greater than 5 percent should be rejected. The three plans listed above are submitted as reasonable attempts to approach the ideal. There are two errors that the plan can make: (1) rejecting lots having less than 5 percent defective, and (2) accepting lots having more than 5 percent defective. The likelihood of these errors can be read from the OC curves.

For simplicity in this example, it will be assumed that lot quality can only be 1 percent, 4 percent, or 9 percent with probabilities of occurrence of 0.40, 0.35, and 0.25, respectively. If a good lot is rejected by the sampling, an inconvenience cost of $150 is incurred. If a bad lot is accepted, the cost is $200. All of this is summarized in the loss matrix of Table 17-11.

The expected loss[22] can then be calculated as follows:

$$\text{E.L.} = \sum_{p=0}^{p=1.0} \left[\begin{pmatrix} \text{probability that} \\ \text{quality level} \\ \text{will occur} \end{pmatrix} \begin{pmatrix} \text{probability that} \\ \text{incorrect decision} \\ \text{will be made} \end{pmatrix} \begin{pmatrix} \text{dollar loss} \\ \text{due to incorrect} \\ \text{decision} \end{pmatrix} \right]$$

Thus the concept first considers the probability that a specific quality will be submitted and then, assuming that it is submitted, it considers the probability of making an incorrect decision. The product of these two probabilities is the chance that a specific quality will be submitted and an incorrect decision made. This is the only case that involves a dollar loss. Multiplying this probability by the loss gives the expected loss:

Plan 1 (n = 50, c = 1)

E.L. = 0.4(0.0894)150 + 0.35(0.5995)100 + 0.25(0.0532)200 = 29.01

Plan 2 (n = 50, c = 2)

E.L. = 0.4(0.0138)150 + 0.35(0.3233)100 + 0.25(0.1605)200 = 20.17

Plan 3 (n = 50, c = 3)

E.L. = 0.4(0.0016)150 + 0.35(0.1391)100 + 0.25(0.3303)200 = 21.48

---

[22] The expected loss is a special case of the expected-value concept. The expected value is the average value that will occur in the long run. Thus, the expected value in a toss of two dice is

$$2(1/36) + 3(2/36) + \cdots + 11(2/36) + 12(1/36) = 7.0$$

This indicates that plan 2 should be used. Stewart, Montgomery, and Heikes[23] discuss the application to double sampling.

The Bayesian and statistical decision theory approaches to acceptance sampling have been slow in developing due to controversy about the probabilities of occurrence. Some people believe that such probabilities can be set based on subjective opinions about quality levels. Others believe that the probabilities must be based on actual data. In the opinion of the authors, these probabilities must be based on actual data. However, in many cases such data are available, although not always in a convenient form. The challenge is to make use of all pertinent past data by developing ways to convert the data to probabilities of occurrence. If this is not done quantitatively, it *will* be done by default by practitioners, who must constantly use their past knowledge *intuitively* to arrive at compromise forms of action when sample sizes based on classical tables are larger than can be tolerated.

17-20 KNOWLEDGE BEYOND SAMPLING

Sampling data are only one of the sources of information on which to base decisions concerning the process. Other sources include:

1. *Data on process capability.* If we have learned that some aspects of the process are predictable (e.g., the standard deviation, the time-to-time drift in the average), this knowledge can be used to supplement the sampling data in making decisions on the process and on the product.
2. *Knowledge of a scientific or engineering character* pertinent to the process. For example, the inherent nature of a press operation is such that if the first piece and the last piece in a lot show perforated holes, it is inevitable that all the pieces in the lot will show the same perforated holes. In such a situation, a sample size of two pieces is adequate to make the decision provided that (*a*) the tools and the operation are of an "all-or-none" type, and (*b*) provision is made to preserve the order of manufacture.
3. *Sampling data from other sources,* e.g., vendors' test data, operators' measurements, automatic recording charts. Through the concept of audit of decisions (see Section 9-12) it is possible to validate these added sources of measurement, and then to use the data as an added input to decision making.

Procedures are not yet available to explicitly define how such knowledge should influence published sampling tables. Again, the practitioner is often forced to use such knowledge intuitively.

[23] R. Dennis Stewart, Douglas C. Montgomery, and Russel G. Heikes, "Choice of Double Sampling Plans Based on Prior Distributions and Costs," *Transactions of the American Institute of Industrial Engineers,* vol. 10, no. 1, March 1978, pp. 19–30.

PROBLEMS

17-1 A large gray iron foundry casts the base for precision grinders. These bases are produced at the rate of 18 per day and are 100 percent inspected at the foundry for flaws in the metal. The castings are then stored and subsequently shipped in lots of 300 to the grinder manufacturer. The grinder manufacturer has found these lots to be 10 percent defective. Upon receiving a lot the manufacturer inspects 12 of them and rejects the lot if 2 or more defectives are found. What is the chance that he will reject a given lot?

17-2 Verify the operating characteristic curve for a lot size of 200 in Figure 17-4a. Calculate at least three points by the Poisson method.

17-3 Using only the addition and multiplication rules for probability, verify the operating characteristic curve in Figure 17-3. Calculate at least three points.

17-4 The following double-sampling plan has been proposed for evaluating a lot of 50 pieces:

Sample	Sample size	Acceptance number	Rejection number
1	3	0	3
2	3	2	3

Using only the addition and multiplication rules for probability, calculate the probability of accepting a lot which is 10 percent defective.

Answer: 0.984.

17-5 Prepare the operating characteristic curves for a single-sampling plan with an acceptance number of zero. Use sample sizes of 2, 5, 10, and 20.

17-6 Table 17-6 provides an LTPD plan for a lot size of 800 and process average of 0.50 percent. The plan calls for a sample size of 75 and an acceptance number of 1. Prepare an operating characteristic curve by calculating at least three points. Also, calculate the average outgoing quality for each quality level.

17-7 A manufacturer wishes to sample a purchased component used in their assembly. They wish to reject lots that are 5 percent defective. The components are received in lots of 1000. From the past they know the supplier usually submits lots 2 percent defective or less. The vendor has agreed to 100 percent inspect all rejected lots. Find a sampling plan to meet these conditions.

17-8 A double-sampling plan is desired that will assure long-run average quality of 1% defective or better. All rejected lots will be 100% inspected. The lot size is expected to vary between 1200 and 1800. Past data show the supplier to average about 0.30% defective.

   (*a*) Define the sampling plan.

   (*b*) What percent defective in a lot would have a 10 percent chance of being accepted by this plan?

   (*c*) What is the probability that a lot which is 4 percent defective will be *rejected* on the *first* sample of the double-sampling procedure?

   Answer: (*b*) 3.8 percent. (*c*) 0.36.

17-9 You are quality manager for a company receiving large quantities of materials from a vendor in lots of 1000. The cost of inspecting the lots is $0.76/unit. The cost that is incurred if bad material is introduced into your product is $15.20/unit. A sampling plan of 75 with acceptance number equal to 2 has been submitted to you by one of your engineers. In the past, lots submitted by the vendor have averaged 3.4 percent defective.

   (*a*) Is a sampling plan economically justified?

   (*b*) Prepare an operating characteristic curve.

(c) If you want to only accept lots of 4 percent defective or better, what do you think of the sampling plan submitted by the engineer?

(d) Suppose that rejected lots are 100 percent inspected. If a vendor submits many 4 percent defective lots, what will be the average outgoing quality of these lots?

17-10 Refer to MIL-STD-105D with the following conditions:

Lot size $= 10,000$
Inspection level II
Acceptable quality level $= 4$ percent

(a) Find a single-sampling plan for normal inspection.

(b) Suppose that a lot is sampled and accepted. Someone makes the statement: "This means the lot has 4 percent or less defective." Comment on this statement. (Assume that the sample was randomly selected and no inspection errors were made.)

(c) Calculate the probability of accepting a 4 percent defective lot under normal inspection. *Answer:* (c) 0.98.

17-11 A manufacturer sells his product in large lots to a customer who uses a sampling plan at incoming inspection. The plan calls for a sample of 200 units and an acceptance number of 2. Rejected lots are returned to the manufacturer. If a lot is rejected and returned, the manufacturer has decided to gamble and send it right back to the customer without screening it (and without telling the customer it was a rejected lot). He hopes that another random sample will lead to an acceptance of the lot. What is the probability that a 2 percent defective lot will be accepted on either one or two submissions to the customer?
Answer: 0.42.

17-12 A customer is furnishing resistors to the government under MIL-STD-105D. Inspection level II has been specified with an AQL of 1.0 percent. Lot sizes vary from 900 to 1200.

(a) What single-sampling plan will be used?

(b) Calculate the quality (in terms of percent defective) that has an equal chance of being accepted or rejected.

(c) What is the chance that a 1 percent defective lot will be accepted?
Answer: (b) 3.4 percent. (c) 0.95.

17-13 Refer to problem 17-10. What sample size would be required by MIL-STD-414? (Assume inspection level IV, normal inspection, variability measured by the standard deviation, single specification limit, form 1.)
Answer: 75.

17-14 Refer to problem 17-12. What sample size would be required by MIL-STD-414? (Assume inspection level IV and Table 17-9 applies.)
Answer: 35.

17-15 For a specific part obtained from a supplier, past history is available on the percent defective of each lot. The data on percent defective have been summarized and show an average of 2.75 percent and a standard deviation of 1.74 percent. The lot percent defective follows a beta distribution. A sampling plan is desired that will meet the following risks:

AQL $= 2.5\%$ producer's risk $= 0.05$
LTPD $= 5.0\%$ consumer's risk $= 0.10$

Determine a sampling plan that meets these risks and makes use of the past history.

17-16 A rule-of-thumb sampling plan states that, for any lot size, the sample size should be 10 percent of the lot and the acceptance number should be zero. It is believed that this procedure will hold the sampling risks constant. Prepare the operating characteristic curves using this plan for lot sizes of 100, 200, and 1000. Calculate points for quality levels of 0, 2, 4, 6, 10, and 14 percent defective. Compare the three curves and draw conclusions about the sampling risks.

SUPPLEMENTARY READING

The *Quality Control Handbook,* 3rd ed., McGraw-Hill Book Company, New York, 1974, contains extensive material on acceptance sampling. The two basic references are:

Section 24, "Sampling by Attributes"
Section 25, "Sampling by Variables" (including sec. 25A, "Bulk Sampling")

In addition, the industry sections also contain material on acceptance sampling:

Paper industry: pp. 30-9 to 30-10
Food: pp. 31-18 to 31-21
Electronic components: pp. 38-7 to 38-8, 38-14 to 38-15
Support operations: p. 46-14

EXAMPLES OF EXAMINATION QUESTIONS USED IN FORMER ASQC QUALITY ENGINEER CERTIFICATION EXAMINATIONS AS PUBLISHED IN *QUALITY PROGRESS* MAGAZINE

1 In MIL-STD-105D, the AQL is always determined at what P on the OC curve? (*a*) 0.05; (*b*) 0.10; (*c*) 0.90; (*d*) 0.95; (*e*) none of the above.

2 The steeper the OC curve: (*a*) the less protection for both producer and consumer; (*b*) the more protection for both producer and consumer; (*c*) the lower the AQL; (*d*) the smaller the sample size.

3 For an operation requiring shipments from your vendor of small lots of fixed size, the sampling plan used for receiving inspection should have its OC curve developed using: (*a*) the Poisson distribution; (*b*) the hypergeometric distribution; (*c*) the binomial distribution; (*d*) the log normal distribution; (*e*) the Gaussian (normal) distribution.

4 Two quantities which uniquely determine a single-sampling attributes plan are: (*a*) AOQL and LTPD; (*b*) sample size and rejection number; (*c*) AQL and producer's risk; (*d*) LTPD and consumer's risk; (*e*) AQL and LTPD.

5 Selection of a sampling plan from the Dodge–Romig AOQL sampling tables: (*a*) requires an estimate of the AOQ; (*b*) requires an estimate of the process average; (*c*) requires sorting of rejected lots; (*d*) requires larger samples than MIL-STD-105D for equivalent quality assurance; (*e*) requires that we assume a consumer's risk of 0.05.

6 The AQL for a given sampling plan is 1.0 percent. This means that: (*a*) the producer takes a small risk of rejecting product which is 1.0 percent defective or better; (*b*) all accepted lots are 1.0 percent defective or better; (*c*) the average quality limit of the plan is 1.0 percent; (*d*) the average quality level of the plan is 1.0 percent; (*e*) all lots are 1.0 percent defective or better.

7 Prior to the use of any sampling plan, one must consider: (*a*) the consumer's and producer's risks must be specified; (*b*) the method of selecting samples must be specified; (*c*) the characteristics to be inspected must be specified; (*d*) the conditions must be specified (material accumulated in lots or inspected by continuous sampling); (*e*) all of the above.

8 The probability of accepting material produced at an acceptable quality level is defined as: (*a*) α; (*b*) β; (*c*) AQL; (*d*) $1 - \alpha$; (*e*) $1 - \beta$.

9 A large lot of parts is rejected by your customer and found to be 20 percent defective. What is the probability that the lot would have been accepted by the following sampling plan: sample size = 10; accept if no defectives; reject if one or more defectives? (*a*) 0.89; (*b*) 0.63; (*c*) 0.01; (*d*) 0.80; (*e*) 0.11.

10 Your major product cannot be fully inspected without destruction. You have been requested to plan the inspection program, including some product testing, in the most cost-effective manner. You most probably will recommend that samples selected for the product verification be based upon: (*a*) MIL-STD-105D, latest issue; attribute sampling; (*b*) MIL-STD-414, latest issue; variables sampling; (*c*) either answer 1 or 2 will meet your criteria; (*d*) neither answer 1 nor 2 will meet your criteria.

EIGHTEEN

CUSTOMER RELATIONS

18-1 CUSTOMERS, USERS, AND CONSUMERS

Customers are the source of income (sales) to manufacturing and service companies. As a consequence, much study has been devoted to customer relations, including the effect of quality on income. This study has been most extensive on the parameter "quality of design" or grade. More recently, increasing effort has been devoted to study of the effect, on income, of other parameters—quality of conformance, reliability, field service, etc. As to such parameters, quality affects not only the manufacturers' quality costs; it also affects the users' costs and satisfaction. In addition, the users' experiences (which they share among each other) also influence the ability of the manufacturers to sell their product.

Quality is defined as fitness for use, but there are multiple uses and multiple types of users. A company sells its products to a *customer*. The customer may be a manufacturer, in which case it will perform further processing on the product. That manufacturer is concerned with two kinds of fitness for use: fitness for its processing and fitness for *its* customers. For example, a chemicals company sells polymers to a plastics film processor. The processor is concerned with high productivity, low waste, etc., during processing. They are also concerned with the properties of the film, e.g., tensile strength, transparency, etc., since these properties are the concern of customers.

A customer may also be a merchant who buys in order to resell. The merchant is similarly concerned with two kinds of fitness for use: (1) fitness for ease of marketing, e.g., correct identity, protection during transport and storage, attractive display, ease of installation, etc., and (2) fitness for the use of the merchants' customers.

A *user* is one who receives the ultimate benefit of the product. The user

Table 18-1 Customer influences on quality

Aspects of the problem	Original equipment manufacturers (OEM)	Dealers and repair shops	Consumers
Makeup of the market	A few very large customers	Some large customers plus many smaller ones	Very many very small customers
Economic strength of any one customer	Very large, cannot be ignored	Modest or low	Negligible
Technological strength of customer	Very high; has engineers and laboratories	Low or nil	Nil; requires technical assistance
Political strength of customer	Modest or low	Low to nil	Variable, but can be very great collectively
Fitness for use is judged mainly by	Qualification testing	Absence of consumer complaints	Successful usage
Quality specifications dominated by	Customers	Manufacturer	Manufacturer
Use of incoming inspection	Extensive test for conformance to specification	Low or nil for dealers; in-use tests by repair shops	In-use test
Collection and analysis of failure data	Good to fair	Poor to nil	Poor to nil

may be an employee of a large organization, e.g., the machinist running a lathe, the stenographer operating a typewriter, the soldier firing a rifle. The user may also be a *consumer*, i.e., an individual who purchases for personal consumption or use, e.g., a student who buys a typewriter, or a hunter who buys a hunting gun.

This multiplicity of customers gives rise to a variety of influences, depending on whether the customer is economically powerful or not and on their technological sophistication. Table 18-1 summarizes the influences of various types of customers on various aspects of the quality problem.

18-2 USER VIEWS ON QUALITY

The user's views on quality can differ considerably from those held by the manufacturer. Some of the major differences are summarized in Table 18-2.

Products and Services

The user's concept is one of buying *services* even though the purchase contract is for a product. A purchased vehicle is bought to supply not only the service of transport but also other services as well: status, comfort, safety, appearance, etc.

Table 18-2 Contrasting views: users and manufacturers

Aspects of quality and cost	Principal views of the user	Principal views of the manufacturer
Subject matter of the sales contract	A service needed by the user	A product made by the manufacturer
Definition of quality	Fitness for use on arrival	Conformance to specification on test
Cost	Cost of usage, including: Original price Operation costs Maintenance Downtime Depreciation Loss on resale	Manufacturers' quality costs
Responsibility for keeping in service	Over the entire useful life	During the guarantee period
Spare parts	A necessary evil	A profitable business

Some manufacturers are well aware of this viewpoint of users and hence direct their sales propaganda accordingly. Propaganda for a dentifrice emphasizes clean teeth, better appearance, enhanced social life. Or the propaganda may emphasize the service performed, e.g., bolts and nuts become fasteners; aluminum siding becomes maintenance-free exteriors.

Definition of Quality

The user is concerned with product fitness for use at the time of receiving that product. Many manufacturers, while aware of this user's viewpoint, really put the emphasis on conformance to specification at the time of final test. This emphasis is mainly the result of the departmental structure and the resulting delegations of departmental responsibilities. The user is obviously not concerned with these departmental niceties.

Cost of Use

Some products are "consumed" soon after purchase, e.g., food, a bus ride, short-term rental of a facility. For such consumables, the price paid by the user correlates strongly with the user's cost of use. However, for long-life products there can be a considerable difference between purchase price and cost of use over the life of the product. The elements that contribute to this difference are listed in Table 18-2. We will return to this difference shortly in Section 18-9.

Value

Beyond these and other contrasts in views (Table 18-2) is the user's concept of *value*. This word is widely used in the marketplace to connote the relationship between the price paid for a product and the useful functions performed by that product. In competitive marketplaces, users try to make price comparisons together with comparisons of functions so as to secure the best value for their money.

In recent years manufacturers have undertaken to look more closely at this concept of value by employing a body of techniques called *value analysis* or, sometimes, "value engineering" (see Section 7-17).

Efforts to Reconcile Contrasting Views

A number of approaches are available for reconciling these contrasting views of users and manufacturers. Some approaches, e.g., market research, are carried out unilaterally. Others, such as standardization, are inherently multilateral in nature. Some approaches take place prior to negotiations in the marketplace. Others, e.g., contract negotiation, are a basic part of marketplace activity. Still others, e.g., field complaint analysis, take place after sale. Market research is one of the most rewarding approaches and is applicable to all stages of customer relations.

18-3 CONCEPT OF MARKET QUALITY

In market-based societies the interplay among sellers and buyers gives rise to an equilibrium for the various elements of purchase contracts—price, delivery schedule, warranty, etc. Quality is also one of these elements. The resulting competition in quality gives rise to an equilibrium for market quality.

In planned societies this equilibrium is often arrived at through standardization. Committees are formed, representing the various sectors of society which can make a useful contribution to preparation of the standards: government planning officials, research institutes, metrology laboratories, manufacturers, merchants, consumers, repair shops, technical societies, etc. The resulting standards become the basis for specifications, contracts, pricing, warranties, government regulation, etc.

In capitalistic societies the major force for arriving at this equilibrium of market quality is competition in the market. This is true even when quality standards have been established through voluntary cooperation. In that event, the competition becomes one of improving on the standard, so that market quality tends to improve progressively.

18-4 SOURCES OF MARKET QUALITY INFORMATION

A major source of market quality information is the quality alarm signals arising from field failure reports, customer complaints, claims, lawsuits, etc. These are insistent alarm signals and they are heeded by responding to each to set things in order. In some cases the problems are widespread, resulting in such serious consequences as extensive warranty charges, product recalls, or loss of customers.

Many companies maintain data systems and managerial reports which summarize and analyze the alarm signals to identify projects for improvement and to observe trends. The methods for making such analyses are discussed in Chapter 20. It will be seen there that most alarm signals are poor measures of quality—they are rather measures of expressed product dissatisfaction. A low level of alarm signals does not necessarily mean a high level of quality. Neither does the absence of product *dis*satisfaction mean that there is product *satisfaction*, since these two terms are not opposites. A product may be failure-free and yet not be salable because a competitor's design is superior, has a lower price, etc.

A second source of market quality information is the vast array of published data available relative to quality. Some of these data are internal to the company. Many are published external to the company. Examples are as follows:

Types of data	Sources
Field performance data	Customer service department
Trend of sales by model, customer, etc.	Internal sales analysis
Trends of competitor activities, dealer reactions, and other "field intelligence"	Reports of field sales force
Extent of field replacements due to failures in service	Sales of spare parts
Competitive quality ratings	Customers who buy from multiple sources
Independent quality ratings	Independent laboratories
Results of research on quality	Government departments, research institutions

It takes effort and some determination to find and process these data, but the result can be easier identification of opportunities for improvement.

These two major sources of market quality information, while necessary, are not sufficient. A good deal is missing, and this can be provided only through special studies of a market research nature.

18-5 MARKET RESEARCH IN QUALITY

In the broad sense "market research" is the activity of studying those aspects of quality which influence or are influenced by the forces in the marketplace. In that sense activities such as field complaint analysis or study of government research publications are a form of market research. In a narrower sense "market research" involves exploring the unknown and creating data where none existed before. These newly created data come from such approaches as developing a new test device to simulate fitness for use, study of competitors' products, and, especially, making tests and securing feedbacks involving customers, users, and consumers. In the discussion that follows, the term "market research" will be used in its narrower sense.

Purposes of Market Research in Quality

The broad purposes are mainly to:

Discover alarming situations for which existing alarm signals are silent.
Discover opportunities not disclosed by present information sources.
Test existing unsupported and even axiomatic beliefs.

More specifically, market research in quality looks for answers to some cardinal questions:

1. What is the relative importance of various product qualities as seen by the user? The answers provided by market research are typically different from the prior beliefs of the manufacturer. Sometimes the difference is dramatic.
2. For the more important qualities, how does our product compare with competitors' products, as seen by users?
3. What is the effect of these competing qualities (including ours) on users' costs, well-being, and other aspects of fitness for use?
4. What are users' problems about which they do not complain but which we might nevertheless be able to remedy?
5. What ideas do users have that we might be able to utilize for their benefit?

The Shaving System Case—A Consumer Product

The leading manufacturer of razors and razor blades was confronted by a new competing model which featured an ingenious improved blade-changing mechanism. When the competitor promoted the new model aggressively, the company marketing managers became apprehensive. They then succeeded in initiating a costly new product development to bring out a model that could match the competition. However, the top managers also authorized a field market research study to discover the reaction of consumers to the new development.

The planners of the research study identified the seven major quality characteristics of a shaving system. Next (through an intermediary market research company) they provided each of several hundred consumers with all three principal shaving systems then on the market. These users were asked to use each shaving system for a month and to report:

1. The ranking of the seven qualities in their order of importance to the user.
2. The ranking of the performance of each of the three systems for each of the seven qualities.

Table 18-3 shows the plan of the market research study.
The resulting data showed that, as seen by the users:

1. Ease of blade changing was the least important quality.
2. The competitor's new blade-changing mechanism had failed to create a user preference over competing forms of blade changing.

These findings denied the beliefs of the company marketing managers and came as a welcome surprise. They enabled the company to terminate the costly new product development then already in progress.

3. On one of the most critical qualities (product safety) the company's shaving system was inferior to both the competing systems. This came as an unwelcome surprise and stimulated the company to take steps to eliminate this weakness. Note that *this inferiority could not have been discovered from field complaints,* since no normal user would conduct such a comparative study on his or her own initiative. It was "an alarming situation for which our present alarm signals are silent."

The Heavy-Equipment Case—An Industrial Product

A company making industrial equipment decided to investigate its strengths and weaknesses in securing business and in meeting its clients' quality requirements. Because such equipment is sold through competitive bidding, the

Table 18-3 Market research study—the shaving system case

Qualities	Users' rankings			
	Gillette	Gem	Schick	Importance
1. Remove beard				
2. Safety				
3. Ease of cleaning				
4. Ease of blade changing				
5. ...				
6. ...				
7. ...				

Table 18-4 Market research study—the heavy-equipment case*

Parameter	Client response, %		
	Superior	Competitive	Inferior
Analysis of customer needs	46	32	22
Preparation of quality requirements and purchase order	63	19	18
Preparation of specifications and technical documentation	32	49	19
Quality of equipment	71	18	11
Quality and availability of spare parts	31	22	47
Quality of field repair service	41	32	27

*These numbers are fictitious. The actual numbers were significantly different and resulted in different conclusions.

bidding process itself was included in the study. Table 18-4 shows the plan of the study. Six important parameters were identified. The company's clients were then asked to rate the company's performance vs. competitors for the six parameters. Table 18-4 also shows the summarized data. These data bring out clearly the strengths and weaknesses.

Note in the foregoing that both "panels" were in a state of experience before being asked to give judgments. The clients who bought the industrial equipment already had much experience, and hence a simple questionnaire could provide useful answers. In the shaving system case, none of the panel members had experience in using all three systems. Hence it was decided to provide them with such experience before asking them for their judgments.

Discovering Opportunities

Market research in the field provides access to realities that cannot be discovered in the laboratory. The conditions of use can involve environments, loads, user training levels, misapplication, etc., all different from the conditions prevailing in the laboratory. The laboratory does provide a relatively prompt and inexpensive simulation which is most helpful for making many decisions. However, this simulation cannot fully disclose the needs of fitness for use under the actual conditions of use.

The field studies can provide not only access to the realities of the conditions of use; they can also provide access to the users themselves. Through access to the user, it becomes possible to understand those user problems that are not a matter of poor quality but for which the manufacturer may nevertheless be able to provide a solution. For example, most users prefer to avoid disagreeable, time-consuming chores. Our food processors have successfully transferred many such chores from the household kitchen to the factory (e.g., soluble coffee, precooked foods) and have incidentally greatly increased their sales.

Still other opportunities are disclosed by the ideas proposed and actions taken by users to solve their own problems. Some of these ideas and actions become useful inputs to the programs of the manufacturer.

Among the most useful inputs to a manufacturer are the quantified expressions of certain users' costs—those operating costs, downtimes, training costs, maintenance costs, etc., which the manufacturer might be able to reduce. Knowledge of the sums involved enables the manufacturer to estimate what the user would be willing to pay to secure the improvement. This is an obvious advantage in identifying opportunities. For example, an oil company offers a data processing service to clients. The company supplies forms for recording amount of fuel consumption, hours of use of equipment, equipment repairs, etc. The company then processes these forms to prepare tabulated summaries for the clients. In doing so, the company learns much about clients' economics, problems, etc.

Market Research Tools

These are limited only by the ingenuity of the researchers, but some tools have become so widely used that the approaches are tested and somewhat standardized. They include:

Interviews of users, by telephone or face to face.
Product samples sent to consumer panels. The product is "free" but the panel members have agreed to "pay" in data.
Test marketing on a limited scale before mass marketing.
Advisory panels of merchants.
Employee panels to serve as an early estimate of user reaction.

Such tools are applied using all facilities available: in-house laboratories for employee panel use; clinics for use by invited consumer panelists; manufacturing processes and field maintenance facilities of industrial customers, etc.

18-6 OPTIMIZING USERS' COSTS

Ideally, all segments of society should cooperate in ways that will make quality costs optimal for society as a whole. In practice, each of these segments of society is faced with competitive pressures which urge it to reduce its own quality costs to a minimum. These suboptimizations can and do result in raising costs for the economy as a whole. This problem has become widespread during the twentieth century largely owing to an explosive proliferation of complex long-life products. For such products (e.g., automobiles, television sets) the competition forces manufacturers, merchants, and repair shops each to optimize their respective quality costs. These suboptimizations are in many cases antagonistic to users' costs, notably those of small users.

While this is a widespread problem, there are many forces in the economy engaged in finding solutions. Obviously, organizations that have great economic and technological strength, e.g., large manufacturers, can defend themselves against some aspects of suboptimization. Smaller organizations, and especially consumers, are at a disadvantage and hence are largely limited to collective forms of solution. The principal approaches now taking place in the economy are discussed below.

Grades; Model Names; Product Labeling

Many users lack the facilities needed for judging the technological merits of modern products. These users (small industrial buyers, small merchants, and consumers) seldom have laboratories or access to technological expertise. As a result, they are unable to interpret technically worded specifications and standards, or to test products against specifications. For such users there have been evolved systems of nontechnical descriptions to assist them in purchasing to their needs.

Grades are differences in quality of design. For nontechnical users, grades are designated by simple words, phrases, or numbers. For example, a leading merchant uses three designations (good, better, best) to denote differences in quality of design for the same functional use. In some instances, e.g., automobiles, grade designations include model names to simplify user recognition.

The meanings of these grades and models are conveyed to users with varying degrees of effectiveness. Some product catalogs and brochures are quite descriptive as to the features of the respective models. In contrast, the meanings of grade designations, while well known to merchants, can be confusing and deceptive to consumers. A classic example is the grading of olives by size. The smallest is called "standard," there being no "small" olives.

Another system for consumer enlightenment is *product labeling*. Under this concept the manufacturer provides detailed information about ingredients used, instructions for use, cautions, etc., on the product label or other accompanying paper. Some of this product labeling is done at the initiative of the manufacturers; other such labeling is mandated by government authority. Both forms have their benefits and deficiencies. Manufacturers' labels tend to be limited to those features which can be understood by consumers. However, they also tend to weave in sales propaganda while playing down deficiencies. Government-mandated labeling tends to insist on much detail which is not understood or read by the great majority of consumers.

Warranty of Quality

Warranties are a form of assurance that products are fit for use or, failing this, that the user will receive some extent of compensation. In this sense the warranties constitute a system for reducing user costs of poor quality.

In most jurisdictions a seller, by the mere act of sale, makes two *implied* warranties:

1. A *general* warranty of "merchantability," i.e., fitness for the customary use of such products.
2. An added *special* warranty of fitness for the specific use to which the product will be put. This warranty is implied only if the seller knows what that specific use is.

Beyond the warranties (which are implied by law) there are added *express* warranties made by the seller or negotiated between the parties. For consumer products, most of such warranties are made unilaterally by the seller through oral representations about the product, display of samples, descriptions in catalogs, claims made in advertising, etc. In addition, there are specific statements of warranty published in documents which themselves are headed up by the word "Warranty." In the case of sales made to industrial companies, the warranties are sometimes specially negotiated, as are other aspects of the sales contract.

Traditionally, warranties as to quality were limited to replacement or repair of the product during the warranty period. With the proliferation of long-life products there has been an extension of warranties into parameters such as reliability, downtime, maintenance costs, etc. This extension is squarely in line with the need to optimize users' costs. This trend can be expected to continue.

In the case of warranties to consumers, the complications associated with long-life products has led to much confusion as to the meaning of the warranties, especially as to where the responsibility for action lies. This has given rise to national legislation which requires that warranties be clear, and which sets out some criteria for clarity.

Brand labeling is a special form of warranty associated with a specific product line sold under an identification or brand. This brand is traceable from the brand owner all the way to the ultimate user. Creating such a marketable brand normally involves establishing and adhering to sound quality controls so that the brand acquires a reputation for predictable quality. This reputation is combined with special warranties backed by the owner of the brand. The owner may be a manufacturer, merchant, industry association, producers' cooperative, etc.

Competition in the Marketplace

In market-based societies competition usually acts as a powerful system for reducing users' costs. Not only do consumers have an opportunity to carry out "shopping"; there are other and major forces in the marketplace which conduct shopping on a grand scale. Large merchants look for products that will avoid quality complaints and returns from their customers. Industrial buyers ask for competitive bids when making large purchases, and this competitive bidding increasingly includes quality. Contract negotiations are carried out with an eye on concessions that might be secured from competitors. These marketplace pressures have their impact on manufacturers, who look for ways to improve their quality performance so as to make it easier to meet competition. One of their tools for achieving such improvement is study of users' quality costs.

18-7 ANALYSIS OF USERS' COSTS

The foregoing approaches (to optimizing user quality costs) are broad in nature and apply to a great many transactions in the marketplace. These and other such approaches have aided the growth of commerce by:

Making buyer and seller relationships more orderly and predictable through standardization of marketing practice, e.g., use of grades and product labeling.
Providing remedies for earlier evils, e.g., private monopolies.
Creating new forms of assurance to both buyers and sellers, e.g., warranties and laws governing sales.

For the most part these approaches were evolved in centuries when products were comparatively simple as contrasted with the complex long-life products of the twentieth century. These modern products have greatly complicated the job of optimizing users' quality costs. To solve this problem requires first that the problem be understood. The present movement to quantify and analyze users' quality costs is an important step in this direction.

Because this new problem is still in the early stages of solution, various approaches or systems are in the process of evolution. Several of these are discussed below.

Warranty Charges

To a manufacturer, the most obvious user quality costs are those which the firm itself must make good under the warranty agreement. (Thereby these costs become a major part of "external failure" quality costs.) In addition, the manufacturer usually secures useful information on the nature of the field failures through service call reports and other documents which are the basis of the claims. To a considerable degree, these service calls are made by "captive" repair shops—either those of the manufacturer or the dealer. This use of captive repair shops greatly simplifies the data collection process. (The methods used for making the subsequent analyses are discussed in Chapter 20.)

Out-of-Warranty Charges

For modern long-life products, most user quality costs are *not* covered by the warranty. The typical warranty covers only about 10 percent of the useful life of the product, so that most product failures beyond the infant-mortality period take place out of warranty. In addition, some user costs such as downtime are not normally covered even during the warranty period.

In the early days of analyzing quality costs, manufacturers tended to limit their studies of external failures to those taking place during the warranty period. More recently there has been a trend to extend these studies to include the entire useful life of the product, since:

The out-of-warranty charges represent a real cost to the user and are becoming a factor in the users' decision of which products to buy.
For many of the out-of-warranty charges the remedy must come from the manufacturer through changes in designs, processes, etc.

Acquiring data on out-of-warranty charges is no simple matter. Now most of the maintenance is done by facilities other than captive repair shops, e.g., independent repair shops and user self-maintenance. These latter facilities are less useful as a source of helpful data, and it is also more difficult to secure access to such data as are generated. The more determined manufacturers are driven to "buy the data." They make arrangements with a representative sample of maintenance facilities to restructure the data system so that the data do meet the needs of the manufacturer. Then they buy the data, retaining an audit to assure that the data will be sufficiently valid to serve as a basis for sound decision making.

Warranty on Users' Costs

To a growing extent, the warranty concept is being extended to place predictable limits on users' costs. For example, a manufacturer of electrical generating equipment warrants to its industrial clients that the cost of power generated will be no higher than the cost of purchased power. If the cost is, in fact, greater than the cost of purchased power, the manufacturer agrees to pay the difference.

A variation on such warranty of user costs is the quality incentive contract described in Section 18-9.

These and similar contracts are imaginative approaches, and they add to the range of choice available for unifying the views of manufacturers and users. However, before such contracts are agreed to, it is necessary for the parties to set up the data systems and make the analyses needed to do their negotiating with knowledge of the facts.

Models for Analysis

As analysis of user costs has progressed, there have emerged some models that have made it easier to understand the forces involved. These same models also suggest directions for action. The major models involve (1) contracts based on amount of use, and (2) life-cycle costing which are discussed below. In addition, the models point to an extension of a long-standing form of collaboration known as application engineering.

Application Engineering

Application engineering is a form of technical assistance provided to users by manufacturers. The name is derived from the emphasis placed on helping users select that product which is best suited to their needs.

Selecting the most applicable product requires that the application engineer understand a good deal about the problems of the user, including economics. In this way the application engineering concept is one of the means available for optimizing user costs.

In practice, this form of technical assistance does not stop with sale of the product; it remains available to help the users if they encounter trouble during use. In providing this assistance during use, the application engineer is well placed to provide an added useful feedback to his or her own company.

(Companies that provide application engineering assistance are in effect selling both a product and a service, and their prices reflect this.)

18-8 CONTRACTS BASED ON AMOUNT OF USE

Contracts for services have long been based on payment per unit of use of the service. Charges for transportation, telephone service, central energy, etc., are all based on the amount of service used. Such contracts place on the service company all the costs of providing the service, i.e., manufacture, marketing, and maintenance. To illustrate, the Bell System carries out its various functions through wholly owned subsidiaries as follows:

Function	Carried out by
Research and development	Bell Telephone Laboratories
Manufacture	Western Electric Company
Marketing	Regional telephone companies
Maintenance	Regional telephone companies

This arrangement is generally in harmony with optimizing the costs of the users. For example, since the Bell System must pay the cost of field service calls, it tends to design and make the products in ways that will avoid service calls. In contrast, manufacturers of consumer goods are not normally required to pay the cost of field failures beyond the guarantee period, a fact which can lead to suboptimization that may be antagonistic to the users' costs.

The principle of contracts based on the amount of use is also being extended to purchase of products, in which case the "purchase" is really a purchase of use. Many fleets of automotive vehicles "buy" tires based on payment for distance traveled, i.e., based on use. Contracts for purchase of aircraft engines are virtually contracts based on hours of use.

The principle is also used for consumer products in the form of guaranteed minimum use. For example, if the automobile battery is under warranty for a year and fails after 9 months, it will be replaced at three-fourths of the price of a new battery.

The outlook is for a continuing extension of the concept of contracts based on use. The pace of this extension is limited by cultural resistance as well as by the details of application. It takes much ingenuity and extensive discussion among the parties to arrive at suitable contract terms. Nevertheless, there are powerful forces urging that quality costs be optimized for the economy as a whole. These forces, plus pressure by users to secure greater and greater "value," are bound in the years ahead to prevail over the present contract forms.

18-9 LIFE-CYCLE COSTING

The most complete model relative to user costs is the concept called *life-cycle costing.* (Other names are "cost of ownership," "mission cost," "cost effectiveness," "cost of use," etc.) The concept is applicable both to capital goods and to consumer goods. A model of the concept as applied to capital goods is shown in Table 18-5. The model shows the hypothetical user costs associated with competitive bids made by three companies, X, Y, and Z, to supply a piece of capital equipment. Study of the model gives rise to some serious questions:

1. Should the bidding be based on the original price of the equipment or should it be based on the life-cycle cost? The prevailing practice is to bid

Table 18-5 Life-cycle costing: capital goods ($000)

Elements of cost	Bidding company		
	X	Y	Z
Original price	42	60	47
Maintenance over life of product			
Labor	129	116	84
Spare parts	40	30	20
Paperwork	12	18	12
Operation costs (power, supplies)	235	225	245
Inventory management	60	45	30
Training	8	8	8
Downtime	80	100	70
Total life-cycle costs	606	602	516

Source: Adapted from *Business Week*, May 13, 1967.

on original price, but there is obviously much merit to bidding on life-cycle cost.

2. Would it be possible to redesign the equipment so that life-cycle costs could be reduced significantly? Often the answer is: "Yes, but there would be a (comparatively) small rise in original price." Some designers go further and state: "I already have such a design and I have proposed it to our marketing people. Their answer was 'Don't you dare. If you increase the original price I won't be able to sell it.'"

At present, use of the life-cycle cost concept is made in cases of widespread field failures which cause extensive claims and threaten the marketability of the product. Investigations are made, causes are discovered, and remedies are applied. All of this reduces the users' costs. In addition, the concept is used in specific cost-reduction projects, such as reducing cost of energy through equipment redesign. However, while the model is becoming widely known, it has not been widely adopted. There are two principal reasons:

1. The original price is known with precision but the follow-on costs are not yet known with precision.
2. There is a long-standing and deeply rooted practice of buying based on original price. The resulting cultural resistance is a serious obstacle to adoption of life-cycle costing.

One step in the direction of life-cycle costing has been the quality incentive contract as applied to maintenance costs. The parties agree on a base level of maintenance for the installed equipment. Then, by contract, any excess maintenance costs are shared by manufacturer and user, as are any savings in maintenance costs. This is clearly a step in the direction of unifying the interests of manufacturer and user.

Table 18-6 shows some actual life-cycle cost data for various consumer products. The same kinds of questions might be asked and the same kinds of

Table 18-6 Life-cycle costing: consumer products

Product	Original price	Operation plus maintenance	Total	Ratio, life-cycle cost to original price
Room air conditioner	$200	$465	$ 665	3.3
Dishwasher	245	372	617	2.5
Freezer	165	628	793	4.8
Range, electric	175	591	766	4.4
Range, gas	180	150	330	1.9
Refrigerator	230	561	791	3.5
TV (black and white)	200	305	505	2.5
TV (color)	560	526	1086	1.9
Washing machine	235	617	852	3.6

answers would be forthcoming. In addition, cultural resistance to buying on some basis other than original price is more severe among consumers than among industrial buyers.

18-10 MARKETING OF QUALITY

The "commercial" relationship between a company and its customers is carried out by the various arms of the Marketing Department. They disseminate advertising, submit bids, negotiate contract terms, fill orders, provide customer service, etc. Product quality plays a role in all these activities.

Marketing strategy is greatly aided by quality superiority. Marketers are well aware of this and are always urging designers and producers to come up with quality superiorities which can secure a better share of the market or higher prices. Marketers also devote much effort to propagandize those qualities for which their product is superior, in their advertising, sales promotion, and personal selling.

All other things being equal, a quality superiority can be converted into higher share of market or higher prices, *provided that the customer accepts the presence and usefulness of this quality superiority.* However, no manufacturer is able to attain quality superiority for all product features. Hence each competitor propagandizes those features for which its product is superior. The simple rules relating quality to share of market are as follows:

1. When a product has a clear quality superiority which a customer accepts (or can be induced to accept) as present and useful, then share of market is decided primarily by that quality superiority, all other things being equal.

It is common for industrial customers to seek out the quality differences in products supplied by competing vendors. Sometimes these differences are quantified through systems of quality rating (see Section 10-8). The resulting ratings are then used as inputs to the decisions of how to allocate the available business among the competing vendors.

Consumers also make product comparisons but lack the facilities to do this exhaustively. What often happens instead is that manufacturers make studies of competing products and single out the favorable aspects to be used in the marketing propaganda. For example, a manufacturer of sugar-coated chocolates identified a quality superiority—their product did not leave chocolate smudges on the hands, faces, or clothes of users. They dramatized this superiority in television advertisements by contrasting the appearance of children who had eaten their product with that of children who had eaten competitors' (uncoated) chocolate. Their share of the market rose dramatically.

2. When there is no quality superiority which the customer accepts as present and useful, share of market is decided primarily by superiority in the marketing skills of the competing marketers.

Significant quality differences are often translated into price differences. A common example is the price differential system widely used for product grade differences. In addition, there is wide use of price differentials to charge for added special features or options of the product. For example, in the steel industry, "commercial quality" sells at the base price. Any additional operations or tests requested by the customer are paid for as extras.

Absence of clear quality superiority (the usual situation) presents marketers with the difficult problem of making "distinctions without a difference." They resort to selective emphasis of those features for which they do have superiority. They make use of sensory appeals—styling, attractive packaging, etc. Their advertising makes emotional appeals. They exhibit the timeless bias of the seller by making exaggerated claims—"puffing." None of this is serious as applied to industrial buyers, since usually they have the means of cutting through the shrubbery and studying the product itself. However, consumers have a serious problem as far as complex products are concerned, since they cannot, by their own senses, distinguish the relative merits of competing products. We will look at this problem in Chapter 21.

18-11 ROLE OF THE QUALITY CONTROL DEPARTMENT

The growth of a central Quality Control Department has included a growth in activities related to customer relations. In many companies this department participates actively in matters such as:

Preparation of bid proposals.
Discussions with survey teams sent by prospective customers to conduct a vendor survey.
Test programs for qualification test samples to be submitted to prospective customers.
Material review boards to judge nonconforming products for fitness for use.
Design of data systems for field performance of the product.
Investigation of quality-oriented field complaints and field failures.
Analysis of field performance data.

In contrast, the Quality Control Department has played only a limited role in activities such as:

Market research studies of the sort discussed earlier in this chapter.
Evaluations of competitive products.
Study of user quality costs.
Evolution of contracts based on use or life-cycle costing.
Review of advertising for technical validity.

In areas such as this, quality managers have the potential for making useful contributions. In part, this potential arises from their general awareness of the nature of quality and quality problems. In addition, quality managers and their associates are among the best specialists in a company when it comes to structuring data systems, designing research programs, analyzing and interpreting data, etc., as applied to product quality.

The most promising area of future contribution is probably in market research. Here it is important to recognize a subtle distinction between (1) design of the market research plan, and (2) carrying out the details of the agreed-upon design. The latter can be assigned to any qualified investigator. However, the design of the plan starts by agreeing on: "What are the questions to which we need answers?" Such an agreement is properly the result of discussion among the various departments involved. In addition, such discussions will commonly establish the broad framework of the plan of study—those characteristics of the plan which satisfy the participants that they should be able to rely on the results of the study.

PROBLEMS

18-1 For any *consumer* product acceptable to the instructor, prepare a plan of market research aimed at:

1. Identification of the principal product qualities.
2. Ranking of these qualities in their order of importance to users.
3. Discovering relative performance of competing companies with respect to the principal product qualities.

18-2 For any *industrial* product acceptable to the instructor, prepare a plan of market research aimed at securing data similar to those set out in Problem 18-1.

18-3 For any industrial product acceptable to the instructor, prepare a plan of market research to secure data on:

1. The quality-related costs of the users.
2. The quality-related problems of users about which they do not complain but for which the manufacturers might have solutions.
3. The quality-related ideas of users which might be useful to manufacturers.

18-4 Walk through a food supermarket and identify some of the products for which there has been an extensive transfer of work from the household kitchen to food-processing factories. In addition, identify some further potentialities for such transfer. Report your findings, with special emphasis on the quality problems involved.

18-5 During World War II, Charles A. Lindbergh served as an advisor in the field of aviation. On one occasion he requested the War Department to arrange a conference with pilots who had seen combat in four-engine bombers. This was done, and Lindbergh's account of the meeting with three pilots appears in *The Wartime Journals of Charles A. Lindbergh* (Harcourt Brace Jovanovich, New York, 1970), pp. 617–620.

Lindbergh's questions ranged over a wide variety of topics: the telephone intercommunication system; four engines vs. two engines; amount and location of armor plate; effect of weather, etc. In turn, the pilots volunteered many comments. Lindbergh also recorded some incisive observations on how much confidence to place in pilots' reports, i.e., much depended on whether the pilot had used a device long enough to be accustomed to it. Read Lindbergh's account and, in the light of the concept of market research on quality, report your conclusions.

18-6 Study the methods used for advertising quality for any of the following categories of product or service: beverages; cigarettes; automobiles; household appliances; airline travel; moving picture entertainment; electronic components, e.g., resistors; and mechanical components, e.g., bearings. Report on the extent to which the advertising (1) identifies specific qualities; (2) quantifies the extent to which the product possesses these qualities; (3) engages in exaggeration or deceit; (4) appeals to various human traits, e.g., vanity, greed.

18-7 Study the possibilities of extending the concept of contracts based on the amount of use to any industrial product acceptable to the instructor. Report your findings.

18-8 Study the possibility of applying the concept of life-cycle costing to the sale of some consumer product acceptable to the instructor. Report your findings, including the need for contract provisions such as long-life maintenance contract, provision in the event of resale by the consumer, etc.

18-9 For any organization acceptable to the instructor, study the role of the quality control department with respect to customer relations. Report the activities in which the department does participate significantly. Report also your conclusions as to any need for widening or narrowing this participation.

18-10 You are participating in the preparation of a bid on a military optical system used for range finding. The military specification requires that the subsystems be interchangeable (so that in the event of damage, the failed subsystem can be unplugged and replaced with a spare). You know from experience that this is a wise provision in the specification. However, you are disturbed by the further requirement that the optical elements (lenses, prisms, etc.) within each subsystem should also be interchangeable. To your knowledge, this is a foolish requirement since the military has never had the very special repair and test facilities needed to reassemble optical elements in the field. To your knowledge, the military also lacks the means of testing for this interchangeability.

There is a procedure available for proposing a change in such unrealistic specifications, but you once went through this procedure and found it to be shockingly long and difficult. In addition, your company has had poor success in securing military business because of being underbid in price by competitors. You have for some time suspected that one reason for this lack of success is that your company does its bidding on the basis of meeting all specification requirements (sensible or not), whereas the competitors may be doing their bidding on the basis of meeting only those requirements which make sense.

You are now faced with making a recommendation on how to structure the bid with respect to the requirement for the unneeded interchangeability. What do you propose? Why? If you propose to bid on the basis of not meeting the "foolish" requirement, what do you propose to do in the event the military later finds out what has happened?

SUPPLEMENTARY READING

Subject	Reference
User views on quality	*Quality Control Handbook*, 3rd ed. QCH3, pp. 4-3 to 4-8
Concept of market quality	QCH3, pp. 4-8 to 4-16
Sources of market quality information	QCH3, pp. 14-2 to 14-6
Market research in quality	QCH3, pp. 14-6 to 14-12
Optimizing users' costs	QCH3, pp. 14-19 to 14-28
Contracts based on amount of use	QCH3, pp. 14-13 to 14-15
Life-cycle costing	QCH3, pp. 4-16 to 4-21

EXAMPLE OF EXAMINATION QUESTIONS USED IN FORMER ASQC QUALITY ENGINEER CERTIFICATION EXAMINATIONS AS PUBLISHED IN *QUALITY PROGRESS* MAGAZINE

1 The most important measure of outgoing quality needed by managers is product performance as viewed by: (*a*) the customer; (*b*) the final inspector; (*c*) production; (*d*) marketing.

NINETEEN

FIELD USE AND QUALITY

19-1 QUALITY PROBLEM AREAS DURING CUSTOMER USE

For long-life products, and to a degree for all products, the quality reputation of the manufacturer depends extensively on the quality of field performance—not just conformance to specification. Fitness for use is basic to satisfaction for the user, and this cannot be complete unless all field performance activities are well conducted.

The act of final product acceptance may be regarded as terminating the manufacture phase of the product. Following this act, and before customer use of the product, there take place a number of preuse phases: packing, shipping, receiving, storage. Finally, there are the usage phases: installation, checkout, operation, maintenance. Table 19-1 shows these phases,[1] categories affecting them, and the authors' opinion on significant problem areas.

The extent of field problems increases with product complexity. A summary of "problems" on two early missile programs is shown in Table 19-2. A "problem" here is not simply a failure or a nonconformance but a recurring condition that affects fitness for use in the form of lower reliability. Here, field aspects accounted for 23 percent and 10 percent, respectively, of all reliability problems. In the opinion of the authors, for long-life products of moderate to

---

[1] Based on the results of a task force of the Electronic Industries Association.

Table 19-1 Quality problem areas during customer use

	Activity phases						
Variables affecting phases	Ship	Receive	Store	Install	Align and checkout	Operate	Maintain
Personnel	*	*	*	*	*	*	*
Organization						*	*
Support equipment and tools						*	*
Major equipment	*	*	*	*	*	*	*
Information (procedures, specifications, etc.)				*	*	*	*
Materials and spares			*				*
Facilities/environment				*	*		*
Packaging design	*						

*Potentially significant problem areas.

high complexity, such field factors cause 20 to 30 percent of problems concerning fitness for use.

A major difference in factory control versus field performance control lies in the quality planning. During the last few decades, the concept of formal quality planning has taken a firm hold in manufacturing and quality control departments. Although some progress has been made, the quality planning for the operations of packaging, transport, storage, etc., has generally lagged in effectiveness. Quality planning and control for these operations must be placed on a basis of science and, to do so, greater formality will be required by enlarging the existing quality planning concepts to include quality planning for these additional operations. Staff quality specialists, in participation with materials management, transportation, etc., can develop a plan of control which is acceptable to all. The execution of this plan is then delegated to the regular departments

Table 19-2 Problems due to operational conditions

	Missile	
Cause	X	Y
Inadequate operating or maintenance procedures	6	13
Inadequate maintenance equipment	4	3
Product deterioration due to environment	3	1
Human error during maintenance	1	4
Inaccessibility to repair	1	—
Inadequate packaging	1	2
Defective spare parts	—	1
	16	24
Percent of all reliability problems due to operational conditions	23	10

(Materials Management, Transportation, etc.) and an independent audit conducted (see Section 22-3).

Quality planning for field activities should learn from the experience of formalizing quality planning in design and manufacturing activities. Those performing field activities (and design and manufacturing activities) that affect quality believe that their current activities are sufficient to make a quality product. If this is *not* the case, the new planning must explicitly show what these people are to do differently from what they are doing currently. Generalities are unacceptable.

19-2 PACKAGING, TRANSPORTATION, AND STORAGE

One major department store found that more customer complaints are caused by store activities in packaging and delivering the product than are caused by the original manufacturer. Several activities must be undertaken to minimize product degradation.

Integral Environmental Packaging

Integral environmental packaging refers to protecting the product from the environment, e.g., preserving metals from rusting, keeping moisture out of (or in) foods, shielding electronic products against electrical interference. The design of such integral environmental protection is properly a part of the original product design. As such, the protective aspects of the design should undergo the same design reviews, qualification testing, life testing, etc., as the product itself. In products such as drugs or precision electronics, the foregoing concepts are now commonplace.

Unitizing

Unitizing is the packaging of units of product in the smallest level of container.[2] The product may be packed only one to a container, e.g., a vacuum cleaner and its attachments. The product may also be packed many to a container, either in eggcrate fashion (e.g., a half-dozen electric lamps) or in bulk (e.g., 100 drug tablets in a bottle). During this unitizing, what is critical is to assure that:

The container marking corresponds to the product identity.
The quantity shown on the container corresponds to the quantity of product actually in the container.
The peripheral product (e.g., spare parts, mounting screws, maintenance supplies) are all there.

[2] This is sometimes called *packing*, to distinguish it from the original packaging, which provides environmental protection and identification of a single unit.

The product circulars, manuals of instruction, guarantee card, and other documents are all present.

The inspection stamps (evidencing conformance on test) are present.

The packaging materials are adequate to serve as a protective cocoon to shield the products against the hazards of further packaging, transport, and storage. There is often the need for specifying proper arrangement of packing materials (such as inserts) as a quality characteristic to be controlled just as with other characteristics. If possible, the packing assembly should be foolproofed to preclude any misassembly that would reduce the effectiveness of the protection.

Final Packaging

The unit packages are usually placed into larger containers for bulk shipment and added protection during transportation. These larger packages may consist of corrugated cartons, wooden cases, etc. Once again there is need to assure that the markings on the package correspond to the contents, that the quantities are correct, that the container design is adequate for protection, and that the shipping documents correspond with the goods.

Package Design

The most critical aspect of quality of packaging, transport, storage, etc., is the design of the packages. For integral environmental protection, this design is increasingly a function of product design itself and thereby is closely coupled with the needs of the product. For unitized packaging, especially for final packing, the practice varies widely. Often these activities are so divided among major departments that coordination is an intricate process.

For these divided responsibilities, especially for products that undergo numerous or critical handlings, it becomes important to look at handling and packaging from a systems viewpoint rather than from the viewpoint of numerous departments. The extent of handling during production, packaging, and transportation can be surprising. In one survey, handling costs were 22 percent of manufacturing costs and some estimates run as high as 60 to 80 percent.[3] A systems review for such cases can identify opportunities to improve the overall handling by methods such as:

1. Modifying vendor packaging. Some electronic components are blister-packaged in a way that allows testing without unpacking.
2. Starting unitized and other containerization at early operations or even the

---

[3] Harold T. Amrine, John A. Ritchey, and Oliver S. Hulley, *Manufacturing Organization and Management,* 3rd ed., Prentice-Hall, Inc., Englewood Cliffs, N.J., p. 161, 1975.

vendor's location. For example, the drug industry has evolved unitized packaging of dosages in which the identity of the dose (and even its own environment) are designed into the unit package and carry through to the patient.

3. Designing racks, trays, bins, tote boxes, etc., to provide optimal service to all companies and departments involved rather than to force added handling and repacking.

The systems concept is not limited to package design: it may need to be extended to adapt product and package to each other. One company[4] analyzed their cartons (products) and cases (packages) to determine the combined maximum compression resistance. This saved $50,000 annually in materials while increasing the compression resistance of the product/package system.

Transportation

Handling and transport introduce many perils to the product. Some of these are fully predictable: climatic temperature, humidity, vibration, shock (during automated handling). Others are the result of ignorance, carelessness, blunder, and even sabotage. For some of these perils the product is in greater danger from handling and transport than from usage.

Fiedler[5] recommends a seven-step program for protecting a product during transportation:

1. Define the packaging objectives.
2. Determine the method of shipment. Usually, about 80 percent of a manufacturer's products are handled by 20 percent of the available carriers and modes of shipment.
3. Determine the ability of the product to withstand the transportation hazards. Tests can be run which simulate shock, vibration, and other transport damage. The stresses are measured in terms of cycles per second, "g levels" of deceleration, pulse shapes, and still other quantified measures. The experience gained has found its way into specifications for packaging and vehicle loading.
4. Interpret the test data to compare the product's resistance to the simulated environment with the predicted environmental hazard level.
5. Decide on a course of action. This means deciding if a packaging material should be selected or some other course of action taken (e.g., modifying the product or changing the distribution method).
6. Select a packaging material.
7. Combine the package with the product and together subject them to final testing. This can be done by trial shipment or simulated laboratory testing.

[4] Robert M. Fiedler, "Portal to Portal Product Protection," *Quality*, May 1978, pp. 12–14.
[5] Ibid.

The packaging industry is now one of the largest industries in the United States. In some cases, packaging costs more than the product itself. The technology of packaging will become increasingly important to prevent product degradation during transportation and storage.

Storage

Immense quantities of raw materials, components, and finished products are constantly in storage, awaiting further processing, sale, or use. To minimize deterioration and degradation, various actions can be taken:

1. Establish the shelf life of the product based on laboratory and field data.
2. Establish standards to place limits on time in storage.
3. Date the product conspicuously to make it easy to identify the age of the product in stock.
4. Design the package and control the environment to minimize expected and unexpected degradation.

A common weakness in these programs is the failure to "date" the product conspicuously. Sometimes this failure is just due to poor technique; e.g., iron in open storage rusts away because the color of the rust preservative is not changed annually. However, some failure to date conspicuously is the result of marketing decisions; e.g., the dates are put on the back of the product or on the front in tiny print because the advertising has priority; there is a fear of dating the product in a way which enables the consumer to know if he is getting out-of-date product. These reasons, if ever valid, now have become obsolete. Conspicuous dating on outer cartons as well as on the unit package aids in traceability, stock rotation, and in establishing age of inventories.

Some products such as drugs may be made in batches that may be released only after tests are completed on a sample. When the batches are being held, special inventory procedures are needed to assure that unreleased product is not inadvertently sent to the customer.

Provision for Audit

The operations of packaging, transport, and storage are widely dispersed over multiple companies and departments. However, it is the manufacturer whose brand name is identified with the product that is inevitably regarded by the user as responsible for *any* failures, no matter how caused. In consequence, such manufacturers are faced with the need for auditing the extent to which practice in packaging, transport, and storage conforms to specifications.

The general approach to audit is explained in Chapter 22. Application of this general approach to the operations of packaging, transport, and storage runs into some special problems, especially with such transport and storage as are conducted by independent carriers and merchants.

19-3 INSTALLATION AND USE

Before the packaged product is put into use, it undergoes additional processing during distribution, assembly, installation and checkout, etc. These operations are quite as much a part of the progression of the product as design or manufacture, and they demand corresponding controls.

Processing during Distribution

The distribution process carries out such operations as breaking bulk, readjusting, adding reagents, touching up finishes, repackaging, etc. The planning of these operations should be a part of the overall product planning. The results of this planning should then be embodied in specifications to be used by the distribution organizations. Compliance with these specifications should then be audited independently.

In some cases it is found that the distribution process cannot be relied on to carry out these operations, e.g., international problems of language or culture, small retailers lacking in technological skills. For such cases the need is for a systems redesign which eliminates the necessity for technological skills or even for the operations. These problems can be at their worst when the operations are to be performed by the ultimate user.

On-site Installation by Specialists

This is the assembly setup which is conducted at the user's premises to put the product in a state of readiness to operate plus installation "in place" at the site. For some products the installation requires the services of specialists; for others users perform their own installation.

On-site installations may require:

1. *Special facilities to house the product* (plus its auxiliary equipment), including means for controlling the environment.
2. *Special tools and instruments.* All too often these are not as completely engineered as are the corresponding facilities in the factory because of the fact that many marketing and service departments have lagged behind the factories in use of formal quality planning and of quality specialists.
3. *Instructions for installing and checking out the product.* Written instructions for complex products are forever subject to omissions and mistakes because of sheer complexity. One of the failures in an early space shot was traced to the omission in checkout procedures of a certain adjustment on the product. The adjustment was not specified and hence not made. The launch was a complete failure. Such problems are not restricted to complex products.

Installation by User

For the consumer (the general public) the approach must be quite different from that for installation by specialists. Now the needs are:

1. Eliminate, as far as possible, the need for installation operations to be performed by the user.
2. For the needed operations, simplify and foolproof them through designing the product that way.
3. Prepare clear, illustrated step-by-step written instructions for the user. A review of various failures in user installation (and operation) soon discloses that the instructions had not been tested out on a panel of untrained users. No amount of analysis or logical reasoning by company specialists can fully anticipate user problems. All too often the instructions are tested out only on those who are already familiar with the product.

Example An expensive blackboard was purchased, installed, and used with ordinary chalk. However, the writing could not be completely erased even with great pressure on the eraser. Inquiry revealed that the board must first be rubbed with a thin coating of chalk and then erased before any writing is done. Without the coating (which is to be applied by the customer) the board will be ruined because the writing will not erase. There were no instructions about the need for coating. The board was damaged and required major repair.

Example A metal bookcase was shipped unassembled with detailed assembly instructions. The assembler was confused by the presence of a critical screw hole that was not mentioned in the instructions.

Use

Once the product has been made operable, use can begin provided that the user understands how to use the product. Here again, manufacturers have done a good deal to prepare an Operating Manual or Owner's Manual or other instruction for proper usage and maintenance. These manuals are quite rudimentary for simple products and grow to elaborate handbooks for complex products. Sometimes, extensive training programs are conducted by the manufacturer to assure that the user has trained personnel for operating and maintaining the product. Edy, Potter, and Page[6] describe the training activities conducted when a new jet airplane was first turned over to an airline. The training program was

---

[6] Paul Edy, Elaine Potter, and Bruce Page, *Destination Disaster*, Quadrangle Books (New York Times Book Company), New York, 1976, chap. 12.

abbreviated and may have been a factor in causing what was then the worst air crash in history.

While installation and usage by specialists (e.g., industrial equipment) tends to be professional, usage by consumers is characterized by much ignorance in several ways:

1. *Failure to use available information.* For example, a vacuum cleaner rotary brush encounters an obstruction and stops rotating. The Owner's Manual states clearly just what to do: remove the obstruction and reset the little red button. The user does not know this because he threw the Owner's Manual away when unpacking the cleaner, or because he kept the Owner's Manual but has no idea where it is or because it does not occur to him to refer to the Manual, or because it is simpler to arrange to have the unit serviced.
2. *Use under environments never contemplated.* For example, a householder finds her automobile door lock frozen on a subzero day. She uses a portable hair dryer to thaw out the lock, and the dryer fails. (It was not designed to be operated in subzero temperatures.)
3. *Application of stresses never contemplated.* For example, a manufacturer using glass bottles experiences much breakage at the beginning of the filling line. Investigation reveals that there is much more bottle-to-bottle contact than was originally anticipated. A simple increase in surface treatment thickness by the bottle manufacturer solves the problem.
4. *Failure to maintain.* Consumers are notoriously lax in following prescribed schedules for lubrication, cleaning, replacement of expendables, etc.

At the other end of the spectrum, users *improve* usage. Some consumers routinely tighten the screws of mechanical apparatus they buy. Others routinely resew the critical seams of the garments they purchase. Do-it-yourself enthusiasts may perform their own maintenance even during the guarantee period.

Often the interaction of the operator and the product is important. This can involve such factors as the anatomical dimensions of the operator; placement of push buttons and switches on products; physical loads imposed on the operator by the product; monotony and other psychological effects of the product operation; environmental effects produced by the product, such as noise and vibration; and workplace design, such as lighting, space, and other factors. Collectively, such matters are called "ergonomics" and need to be considered during the design phase of the product life cycle (see Section 7-16). However, even with such efforts human performance will still be less than perfect. Methodology has been developed to quantify human performance. Meister[7] discusses various methods.

The three principles of self-control that have previously been applied to

[7] David Meister, "Subjective Data in Human Reliability Estimated," *Proceedings, Annual Reliability and Maintainability Symposium,* 1978, pp. 380–384.

manufacturing (see Chapter 13) can also be applied to the product user. First, does the user know what he or she is supposed to do? This concerns the existence and adequacy of operating instructions, troubleshooting procedures, and preventive maintenance requirement. Second, does the user know what he or she is doing? This concerns the existence and adequacy of feedback signals from the product concerning performance (e.g., operating temperature) and early warning messages on impending trouble. Third, can the user take regulatory action? This concerns the user's ability to correct poor performance and have a convenient means of making the correction.

19-4 MAINTENANCE

One of the elements of fitness for use is availability. Availability is a function of reliability and maintainability (see Section 7-12). An adequate field maintenance program requires that product problems be correctly fixed and in a timely manner. For some consumer products, there are more complaints from customers on repair service than on the original product quality delivered. These complaints include both faulty repairs and long waits for the return of the product, resulting in lower availability of the product to the customer.

For simple products, a product malfunction can often be corrected by replacing the defective element. As products become more complex, the process of finding and correcting becomes more difficult. The usual steps are shown in Figure 19-1. These steps often require more resources than originally anticipated. Trained personnel, technical data, and test equipment must be planned far in advance to be completely ready when product enters the field. In addition, spare parts must be planned for in sufficient quantity and quality. A failure mode and effect analysis or a fault tree analysis (see Section 7-7) can be helpful in planning both preventive and corrective maintenance programs.

Developing an adequate field maintenance program becomes more difficult when the maintenance is performed by independent dealers. In one example, where dealers were having problems rebuilding heavy equipment, the original manufacturer concluded that the dealers would need to set up some of the elements of the quality control program used during original manufacture. The dealers' shops were viewed as an extension of the original manufacturing departments. This meant that the dealers had to be provided with technical assistance to set up such activities as inspection calibration, evaluation of potential suppliers, and incoming inspection of materials from suppliers.

19-5 CONFIGURATION MANAGEMENT

The complexity of some products can result in certain field problems that require the use of formal systems for controlling the "configuration" of the hardware itself. *Configuration* basically refers to the physical and functional characteristics of a product, including both hardware and software. Although

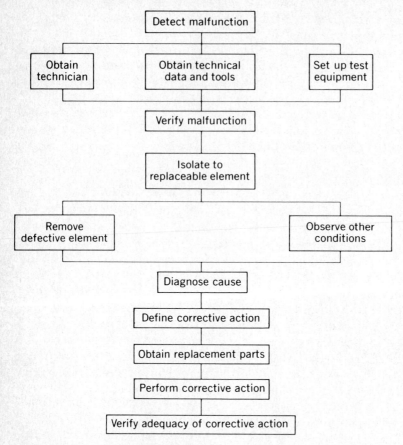

Figure 19-1 Steps in correcting a malfunction.

the problem is not unique to military products, certain conditions have resulted in an emphasis on complex military products.

Ideally, a complex product is thoroughly evaluated and changes are made during design and development so that the design released to production is "frozen." Of course, this is often not the case, and changes are made after production has started. Some recent military programs have gone even further by using the *concurrency principle* to reduce the time required to place new weapons in the field. This principle recognizes the possible need for further quality development after the initial units have been released to the field. Thus, design changes will be forthcoming and will require *effectivity decisions* (defining in which units of hardware the changes will be incorporated). If there are many changes and if most of them are to be made to units already in the field, the customer is confronted with a maze of questions:

1. Can and/or should all units in the field receive the change from an engineering point of view?

2. What are the maintenance problems involved in making the change in the field (personnel, facilities, time, etc.)?
3. How should changes in operating and maintenance instructions be made?
4. What should be done with spare parts that become obsolete by the change?
5. Will the change require any retraining of operator or other personnel?

The collection of activities needed to accomplish these changes for complex military products is called *configuration management*. A program usually has three elements:

1. *Configuration identification.* This is the process of defining and identifying every element of the product. A configuration established at a particular point in time is called a *baseline*. Configuration identification consists of three levels of baseline documents:
   a. The *functional baseline* defines the general requirements of an entire product.
   b. The *allocated baseline* defines the general requirements for a major item in the overall product.
   c. The *product baseline* defines the detailed requirements of an item. This baseline is used as a basis of reference from which all future changes are controlled.
   The baseline documents include drawings, specifications, test procedures, standards, and any other information which defines the physical and functional characteristics.
2. *Configuration control.* This is the process of managing the design change from the time of the original proposal for change through the approval or disapproval of the change. This involves the technical evaluation, costing, and determination of the specific serial numbers which will have the change incorporated (this is called the *effectivity* of the change). As the decisions affect many functions, a Configuration Control Board is often set up to review all proposed changes. The board may have representatives from engineering, quality control, field engineering, purchasing, manufacturing, and the customer. Usually, the chairman has the authority to make a decision on the change (the decision may be appealed through normal channels). The quality control representative may often be in the position of justifying the importance of a change to overcome the cost and schedule disadvantages that are often present.
3. *Configuration accounting.* This is the process of verifying that the changes are made in the hardware and software (at the proper points of effectivity) and documenting the changes. A formal accounting-type system is required because changes may continually be made. Every change to be made must be compatible with existing hardware from an engineering point of view. Thus the "configuration" of each unit of hardware must be recorded and reviewed in deciding which units will receive the change—again, a large but necessary paperwork system. A quality control department usually plays

the major role in verifying that the changes have been made and documentation completed.

Marguglio[8] presents a thorough discussion of the entire design change control process for complex products. McCarthy[9] explains how the principles of configuration management can be applied to computer software.

PROBLEMS

19-1 Visit any transportation service acceptable to the instructor involving loading, storage, crating, unloading, transport, etc. Some possible examples: a trucking terminal, a steamship pier, an air freight terminal, a commercial warehouse, the shipping area of a factory, the parcel room of the post office, and a rail freight yard. Study the processes in use and their likely effect on the qualities of the products undergoing these processes. Report your findings and conclusions.

19-2 Visit a manager who is exposed to problems of installation and operation of consumers' hardware, e.g., the buyer in the home appliance department of a department store or the service manager of a factory making home appliances. Secure information on major troubles encountered by users in installation and operation, and also on what steps are being taken to minimize these troubles. Report your findings and conclusions.

19-3 For some product approved by the instructor, study the operating and/or maintenance instructions. Report your findings and conclusions.

19-4 Select one of the field activities discussed in this chapter. Apply the concept of self-control (see Section 5-6) to evaluate whether the activity has been properly planned with respect to the effect on product quality. For each of the three criteria of self-control, list specific questions that can be asked to evaluate the planning.

19-5 Select a consumer product and make an ergonomics study to evaluate the adequacy of the design with respect to the operation of the product by a human being.

19-6 For any product acceptable to the instructor, prepare a plan of market research to secure data on the opinion of owners concerning the repairs made on the product by a dealer or manufacturer.

19-7 For any product acceptable to the instructor, list the misapplications and abuses of the product that occur during use.

19-8 For any product acceptable to the instructor, visit a repair facility and observe typical repairs made. Trace the steps taken and make a comparison to Figure 19-1.

SUPPLEMENTARY READING

Section 15 of the *Quality Control Handbook*, 3rd ed., McGraw-Hill Book Company, New York, 1974, covers field performance. Additional material applied to the automotive industry can be found on pp. 42-27 to 42-34 and material applied to household appliances on pp. 43-3, 43-4, 43-23, and 43-24. Pages 19-3 to 19-6 discuss configuration management.

The *Proceedings of the Annual Reliability and Maintainability Symposium* usually contain complete sessions on operational conditions, human reliability in product performance, and associated topics.

[8] B. W. Marguglio, "Quality Systems in the Nuclear Industry," chap. 16, *ASTM Special Technical Publication 616*, American Society for Testing and Materials, Philadelphia, 1977.

[9] Rita McCarthy, "Configuration Management and Software Reliability," *Transactions of the American Society for Quality Control*, 1975, pp. 49-55.

FIELD USE AND QUALITY— STATISTICAL AIDS

20-1 SIGNIFICANCE OF FIELD COMPLAINTS

Field complaints are a *poor* measure of product performance. Andreasen and Best[1] surveyed 28,574 consumer purchases in 26 product and 8 service categories. Complaints were first separated as to "price problems" and "nonprice problems." For the nonprice problems, the survey determined to what extent consumers took some type of complaint action. Over half of the consumers took *no* action when they were dissatisfied with the product or service.

Whether or not a complaint is made depends on several factors:

1. *The economic climate.* Complaints fall in a sellers' market and rise in a buyers' market, even for the same product.
2. *The age, affluence, technological skills, etc., of users.* Individuals react differently to defects—the same product generates complaints from some customers but not from others.
3. *The seriousness of the defect as seen by the user.* This is often influenced by the temperament of the user. For example, a missing toy in a cereal box is a serious problem to a child. In one company, complaint rates on cereals

[1] Alan R. Andreasen and Arthur Best, "Consumers Complain—Does Business Respond," *Harvard Business Review,* July/August 1977, pp. 93–101.

Table 20-1 Comparison of field and factory defects

Principal reasons for field returns	Percent of all field returns	Principal factory defects	Percent of all factory rejections
Product has odor	78	Dirt	46
Product crumbles	15	Discoloration	22
Product tears in use	6	Nicked	12
All other	1	All other	20

are about 1 per million packages compared to 4 per million packages for the premiums.

4. *Unit price of the product* (see Section 20-2).

Thus a low complaint rate is *not* proof of customer satisfaction. However, a high complaint rate is proof of dissatisfaction, and therefore the rate should be measured and watched closely.

Field Failures versus Factory Rejects

It is useful to compare periodically the list of principal field failures with the list of principal factory rejects. For example, in a company making rubber products, there was a drop in the sales of a major product type. The sales force blamed the drop on poor quality, whereupon the president ordered an improvement in quality. The factory complied by tightening up on quality standards, resulting in higher shop rejections (and higher costs) for dirt, discoloration, and other factory defects. Actually, the field problems were different (see Table 20-1): the factory "improvement" program was raising costs without solving the field problems.

20-2 EFFECT OF UNIT PRICE AND TIME ON COMPLAINTS

Complaint rates are strongly influenced by the unit price of the product.

For low unit prices of product, the complaint rate can greatly understate field difficulties; the complaint rate may need to be inflated from 20 to over 100 times to arrive at the actual defect rate.[2] For low-priced products the measure of outgoing quality must come from product audit. As low unit prices usually mean large-volume production, the cost of product audit will be relatively low, since the sample needed is only a small fraction of the total product. For high-priced products, the number of units is few, and the cost of product audit becomes prohibitive. However, the ratio of complaints to defects tends to approach unity, so the complaint rate tends to reflect product quality more closely, thereby minimizing the need for product audit (see Section 22-4).

[2] See *Quality Control Handbook*, 3rd ed., p. 15-16, for a breakdown by type of product.

The effect of time on complaint rates is influenced by the nature of the failure. A useful classification is:

1. *Infant-mortality failures,* i.e., misapplication, design weaknesses, factory blunders, shipping damage. These tend to show up early in service—usually within the stated or implied guarantee period.
2. *Accidents* arising from misuse in service, i.e., sporadic overloads, poor maintenance. Some of these take place within the guarantee period or the time span during which complaints are commonly entered.
3. *Wear-out,* i.e., failure in old age after giving acceptable service life. These seldom generate complaints.

To track these different types of problems, one consumer appliance manufacturer measures the service-call rate (number of complaints expressed as a percent of the units in the field) at the end of 30, 90, 180, and 365 days after delivery to the consumer. An automobile manufacturer tracks warranty charges per car after 3, 6, and 9 months of ownership by the consumer.

20-3 COMPLAINT INDICES

For field performance, the most widely used control subjects and units of measure are those shown in Table 20-2.

Usually, the manufacturer measures complaints only during the period that the manufacturer incurs charges on failures (i.e., the warranty period) while the user is concerned with the entire service life. Also, the user is concerned with various added costs caused by failures but which are not compensated by the

Table 20-2 Control subjects and units of measure for field performance

Control subject	Units of measure in use
Complaints	Total number of complaints
	Number of complaints per $1 million of sales
	Number of complaints per million units of product
	Value of material under complaint per $100 of sales for such products
Returns	Value of material returned per $100 of sales
Claims	Cost of claims paid
	Cost of claims per $1 million of sales
Failures	Mean time between failures (MTBF)
	Mean use between failures, e.g., cycles, miles
	Mean time between repair calls
	Failures per 1000 units under warranty
Maintainability	Mean time to repair (MTTR)
	Mean downtime
Service cost	Ratio of maintenance hours to operating hours
	Repair cost per unit under warranty
	Cost per service call

guarantees, e.g., downtime. Although these *user* aspects are difficult to measure, they do represent a critical source of information which can have an important effect on sales income (see Section 18-6).

The user costs associated with failures can be grouped into five categories:

R = repair cost
E = effectiveness loss (e.g., idle labor)
C = extra capacity required because of product downtime
D = damages caused by failure
I = lost income (e.g., profit)

If the categories applicable for a specific product are measured each year over the life (n) of the product and if i is the yearly interest rate, the total user failure cost (C_f) is

$$C_f = \sum_{j=1}^{n} \frac{1}{(1 + i)^j} (R_j + E_j + C_j + D_j + I_j)$$

This model collects all the costs associated with failures over the product life and takes into account the time value of money.[3]

20-4 OBTAINING CUSTOMER INFORMATION ON QUALITY

Ideally, the information system should report the number of failures (or other instances of trouble) experienced by the customers during or after the warranty period. In addition, the information must be in sufficient detail to determine failure *causes* from the symptoms reported. Finally, the information must show the effect of the failures on customer operations in terms of downtime, value of lost production, etc.

Such an ideal information system is rarely realized. Moreover, the difficulties of achieving these information system objectives for *all* units in the field often discourage companies from trying. One answer is to *sample* the units in the field. Usually, a small sample studied in depth will yield more useful results than processing inadequate failure reports for 100 percent of the units in the field.

The approach[4] at Buick Motor Division will serve as an example. Buick receives failure information from four sources:

1. Warranty reports.
2. Summary problem reports from each of the 27 zone managers throughout the country.
3. Individual product reports from dealer service people.
4. Special investigations.

[3] Frank M. Gryna, Jr., "Quality Costs: User vs. Manufacturer," *Quality Progress*, vol. 10, no. 6, June 1977, pp. 10–15.
[4] Personal communication to one of the authors.

A system was *additionally* imposed to obtain actual failed parts within a few days of the failure. The system covers a sample of only 37 dealers who sell a total of about 6 percent of the sales volume. The system provides for these dealers to send the failed parts (from all the cars they sell) to a central Buick location. With the part is included detailed usage information. These parts are then analyzed by a reliability engineer to determine the failure cause.

A large retailing organization[5] uses an early warning survey on new products. Pilot run and early production merchandise selected for the survey is identified with a special stock number. Stores are instructed to promote the sale of these units in a minimum time. During customer use, service calls are handled routinely except that additional follow-up is made to obtain sufficient detail on problems to permit analysis of the significance of the problems and the causes. This follow-up consists of customer visits by a service supervisor, and telephone plus mail surveys of customers using the products. The program includes checklists for use during customer contact.

Sometimes, it is beneficial to conduct a broader survey to determine the attitude of customers toward the products and services provided by a company. An example from a manufacturer of heavy equipment is shown in Table 18-4. This survey revealed serious problems not only with the hardware but also with the software and other services provided. The results were an important input for the redesign of the quality program so that it would include all functions affecting fitness for use.

20-5 PROCESSING AND RESOLUTION OF CUSTOMER COMPLAINTS

In small companies involved in few field complaints, there is little need for a systematic approach to complaint analysis. As the number of complaints increases, the need for a systematic approach also increases. However, in some companies, the lack of an organized approach has been a serious obstacle to sound customer relations.

Each quality complaint poses different problems requiring different programs of action:

1. Satisfying the complainant. This program is oriented to the complainant and hence is needed in virtually every case of complaint. This involves prompt restoration of service, adequate claim adjustment, and restoration of goodwill.
2. Preventing a recurrence of isolated complaints. It is common practice to bring isolated complaints to the attention of those who are suspected of having caused them and to ask them what they plan to do to prevent a recurrence.

[5] Sears, Roebuck and Co., *Early Warning Survey*, internal company document, Chicago, Illinois 60607.

3. Identifying those "vital few" serious complaints which demand that studies be made in depth to discover the basic causes and to remedy those causes. Usually, the decisive questions here are (a) whether the complaint is isolated or widespread, and (b) whether the complaint is on critical matters (e.g., safety, government regulations).
4. Analysis in depth to discover the basic causes of the complaint. This action is oriented to the product and is normally needed only in those vital few cases which are responsible for the bulk of the failures.
5. Further analysis to discover and apply remedies for the basic causes.

The approach for handling the vital few problems is shown in Figure 20-1. As the causes and remedies often involve many departments, a "corrective action group" is often formed with representatives from design, manufacturing,

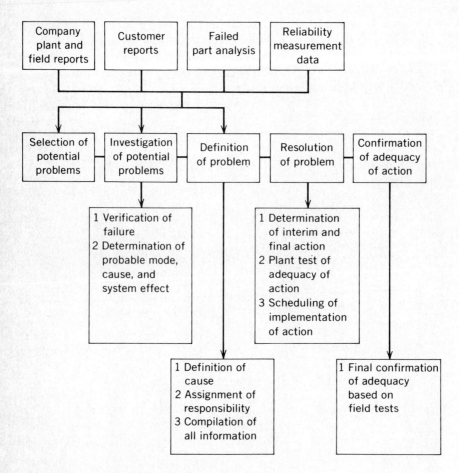

Figure 20-1 Corrective action system.

purchasing, quality control, and field service. The group jointly analyzes the data to select the vital few problems, conducts an initial investigation to prepare a thorough problem statement, and assigns responsibility for determining a remedy.

The group meets regularly to review all new complaints and to review progress on current problems. A problem agenda is sent out by the chairperson several days ahead of the meeting date. Minutes of the meetings, including a problem-status log, are formally recorded, and actions to be taken are documented and distributed to all concerned. This log summarizes each problem before the committee. It also shows the scheduled start and completion of activity, assigns responsibility, and lists action taken. It gives project management an indication of major problems and the status of corrective efforts. Additional effort may then be placed on troublesome areas as deemed necessary.

20-6 TECHNIQUES OF ANALYZING FIELD DATA

The analysis of field data can have several objectives, including problem identification, measurement of actual performance, and prediction of future performance. Among the techniques for problem identification are:

1. *Defect matrices.* An example of this form is a table in which the horizontal lines list the principal defect types and the vertical columns list the product types. The cognizant managers and specialists are able to recognize significance in the patterns which emerge, e.g., defects which are restricted to only certain product types or which affect all product types.
2. *Listing in order of importance.* This technique involves sorting and listing the basic data so that the resulting list shows the data items in their order of importance. Typically, the listing appears in such forms as:
   a. Failure rate by defect type.
   b. Unit repair cost by product type.
   c. Total repair cost by product type.
   d. Complaint rate by customer.
   Often these listings include columns for cumulative totals of all elements under study. A principal purpose of these listings is to permit focus on the "vital few."
3. *Cost analyses.* "External failures" is a standard category of "quality costs" (see Chapter 2). Most data systems provide for evaluating these costs using conventional subcategories, such as repair labor, parts and supplies, travel costs, etc. These cost analyses are useful to the quality control department in its role of using the quality cost figures to justify quality improvement programs.
4. *Spare-parts use.* Two methods of analysis are available:

a. The record of actual use on products as derived from the service reports. These records reflect the real consumption of these parts, but only if the service reports are accurate and complete.
b. The sale of spare parts to the distribution chain. This is also potentially unreliable, and to a greater degree, due to use of spare parts made by competitors' manufacturing sources and the fact that a sale to the distribution chain is not use—it is a transfer of inventory from one part of the chain to another.

Converting the basic data into usable form may require electronic data processing.[6]

In the measurement and prediction of field performance, several techniques are useful. One is the cumulative complaint analysis. This requires that the product be "dated" to show when it was made, sold, or installed.

The various dates are useful not only in disposing of complaints and claims for product of a slow-perishable character (candy, photographic film, etc.). They also can help in predicting the failure rate of various product designs.

Example Certain articles of women's clothing were tearing in service, and some were being returned. When the products made during one specific month were code dated, the cumulative returns reached 2 percent within 2 years after the date of manufacture. The resulting cumulative curve is shown on Figure 20-2. This 2 percent was regarded as tolerable. (At the unit price level of the product, it was likely that about 20 percent of the product was actually tearing in service.)

Meanwhile the research department evolved a new product which then went into full-scale production 14 months after the "specific month" noted above. The cumulative returns for the new product are also charted on Figure 20-2. Note that by use of a horizontal time scale based on "months following manufacture," the two curves both start at the origin and hence can readily be compared with each other. By such analysis the company could be informed *within the first few months* of the life of the new design that the new design had, as to the problem of tearing, made the situation worse rather than better.

The concept of analyzing data using the cumulative graphing approach has broad application.[7]

A technique for predicting future performance is the concept of *growth curves*. The concept assumes that the product involved is one that is undergoing continuous improvements in design and refinements in operating and maintenance procedure. Thus the product performance will improve ("grow") with time. An early application was for predicting future reliability based on tests

---

[6] See *Quality Control Handbook*, 3rd ed., sec. 20.
[7] See *Quality Control Handbook*, 3rd ed., pp. 15-17 to 15-20.

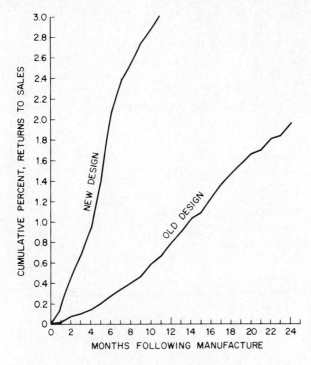

Figure 20-2 Comparison of cumulative return based on months since month of manufacture.

and early field data. One reliability growth model is that proposed by Duane.[8] He analyzed failure data for five different types of complex products. For these systems the observed cumulative failure rate versus cumulative operating hours fell close to a straight line when plotted on log-log paper (see Figure 20-3). For his data, the slope of the lines was about −0.5. The fact that the lines are parallel indicates uniformity in the rate of reliability improvement.

When the model has been proven to apply to a class of products, early field data can be plotted on log-log paper and a line drawn using the slope based on previous similar products. The extrapolation of the line then provides a prediction of future performance. This has several uses, including the monitoring of actual progress toward meeting some requirement.

The Duane model can be adapted for measures of use other than time. For example, a manufacturer of duplicating machines uses it to predict failure rates for new products by plotting failure rate versus cumulative number of copies run. Peacore[9] presents examples of the application of the Duane model. Jayachandran and Moore[10] describe a simulation study made to compare four growth models.

[8] J. T. Duane, "Learning Curve Approach to Reliability Monitoring," *IEEE Transactions on Aerospace*, vol. 2, no. 2, 1964, pp. 563–566.

[9] E. J. Peacore, "Reliability Developments—AWACS," *Proceedings, 1975 Annual Reliability and Maintainability Symposium*, January 1975, pp. 383–389.

[10] Toke Jayachandran and Louis R. Moore, "A Comparison of Reliability Growth Models," *IEEE Transactions on Reliability*, vol. R-25, no. 1, April 1976, pp. 49–51.

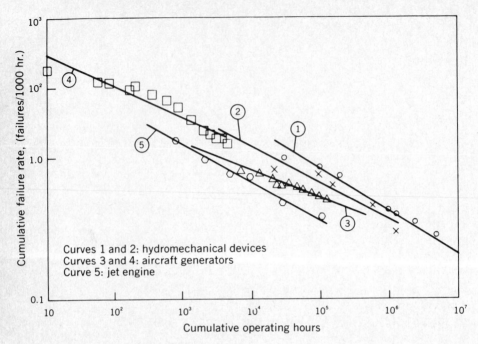

Figure 20-3 Example of reliability progress chart.

20-7 USE OF PROBABILITY PAPER FOR PREDICTING COMPLAINT LEVEL

Weibull probability paper (see Section 3-10) can be used to analyze early field data on warranty claims. Through such analysis it is possible to predict what will be the cumulative claims at the end of the warranty period.

Consider the repair information[11] on an electrical subassembly listed in Table 20-3. The cumulative repairs per 100 units is interpreted as a cumulative failure rate in percent. These data are summarized from a large number of warranty reports and thus the data can be plotted directly without using the median rank approach discussed in Chapter 3.

The Weibull plot is shown in Figure 20-4 (page 488). The 8 months of data have been plotted and a line drawn through the points. This line has been extended and it predicts the repair rate at the end of the 12-month warranty period to be 2.6 repairs per 100 units. Extrapolation of the line beyond the plotted points is valid only on the assumption that the failure pattern does not change.

Note that this Weibull paper includes a scale for estimating the Weibull slope or shape parameter (see Section 3-10). The slope can be found by drawing a line parallel to the line of best fit and through the point circled on the vertical scale. Here, the slope is read as 0.7. This defines the shape of the failure distribution and can aid in problem definition.

[11] "Reliability Methods, Module No. XII," Ford Motor Company, January 1972, pp. 11–13.

Table 20-3 Repair information on electrical subassembly

Time in service, months	Repairs per 100 units ($R/100$)	Cumulative $R/100$
1	0.49	0.49
2	0.32	0.81
3	0.24	1.05
4	0.24	1.29
5	0.21	1.50
6	0.19	1.69
7	0.19	1.88
8	0.23	2.11

For slopes < 1, the distribution is exponential and generally means that the failures are early failures due to manufacturing or assembly deficiencies.

For slopes > 1, the distribution is skewed or approximately normal and generally means that the failures are due to wear-out or fatigue, especially for higher slopes.

Extrapolation beyond the limits of actual data is always questionable. However, when extrapolated performance has been confirmed by actual performance on similar product lines, the approach may be justified. It should be stressed that decisions on the "vital few" warranty problems deserving major attention *must* and *will* be made by someone. Although the approach suggested here is not rigorous, it is a major step beyond intuitive decisions.

A special case of analysis involves the situation where the units in the field have been placed in service at different dates. Some of the units have failed at varying times and the remainder are in operation again with varying accumulated operating times. This type of data can be handled with "hazard plotting paper" for the Weibull or other distributions. King[12] describes the mechanics of analysis and the application to service and warranty problems. An associated problem involves changes in the size of a warranty population. This can occur due to changes in the quantity of product shipped and the number of items still under warranty. Some alternative methods for handling this situation are discussed by Handy, Lamberson, and Kapur.[13]

PROBLEMS

20-1 Propose one or more complaint indices for one of the following products: (1) any product acceptable to the instructor; (2) household refrigerators; (3) passenger automobiles; (4) corn processing by-products sold primarily to brewers of beer and pharmaceutical companies (for making medicine capsules); (5) the totality of products sold by a large department store; (6) jet engines for passenger planes.

[12] James R. King, *Probability Charts for Decision Making*, Industrial Press, Inc., New York, 1971, chap. 19.

[13] Rodney N. Handy, L. R. Lamberson, and K. C. Kapur, "Estimating Automotive Reliability," *1978 ASQC Annual Technical Conference Transactions*, pp. 44–52.

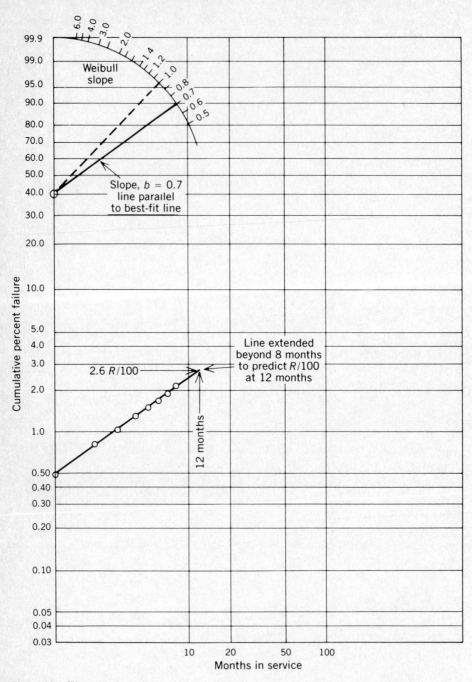

Figure 20-4 Warranty data plot.

20-2 Select a product which you or a friend owns and which has been tested and reported on in one of the consumer magazines.

(a) Comment on the adequacy of the tests made to evaluate competing brands.

(b) Compare the opinions of the user to the evaluation published in the magazine.

20-3 Visit a local manufacturer and report on the procedures used to process complaints and to summarize complaint information for executive action.

20-4 Warranty data on an ignition switch show that 0.15 percent have failed by 3000 miles, 0.25 percent by 6000 miles, and 0.40 percent by 12,000 miles. Predict the percent failure at 24,000 miles and at 50,000 miles. State the assumptions necessary.

Answer: 0.7 percent, 1.2 percent.

20-5 Past data on a certain type of windshield wiper motor indicate a Weibull slope of about 0.50. A goal of no more that 0.5 percent failures by 24,000 miles has been set. What percent failure observed at 6000 miles would indicate that the goal would probably not be met? State the assumptions necessary.

Answer: 0.22 percent.

20-6 Plants A and B are part of the same company and manufacture the identical product. The following data show the percent of returned product, by month, for each plant:

Month	A	B	Month	A	B
Jan.	0.4	0.2	July	0.5	0.2
Feb.	0.3	0.1	Aug.	0.2	0.1
Mar.	0.2	0.2	Sept.	0.3	0.2
Apr.	0.4	0.5	Oct.	0.3	0.2
May	0.3	0.3	Nov.	0.5	0.3
June	0.2	0.4	Dec.	0.4	0.1

Construct two plots, using ordinary graph paper. One plot should compare the two plants using noncumulative data. The other plot should use cumulative data. Comment on the two methods of plotting.

20-7 Data on returned product are summarized weekly for each of three products (A, B, and C). For each return, the primary reason for the return is noted: V for visual defects, E for poor electrical performance, and M for poor mechanical performance. Data are available for 3 weeks. For the first week, 26 units of product A were returned with a distribution of the reason as 5 V, 8 E, and 13 M. Product B had 8 units returned with 0 V, 3 E, and 5 M. Product C showed a tally of 34 units with 22 V, 10 E, and 2 M. For the second week, product A had 37 returns with 6 V, 11 E, and 20 M. Product B had 15 returns with 2 V, 9 E, and 4 M. Product C had 24 returns with 11 V, 8 E, and 5 M. Assuming that the data are representative of weekly returns, prepare a summary that indicates priorities for an improvement effort.

SUPPLEMENTARY READING

Quality Control Handbook, 3rd ed., McGraw-Hill Book Company, New York, 1974, pp. 15-7 to 15-20, 42-33, 42-34, and 43-22 to 43-24.

TWENTY-ONE

CONSUMER RELATIONS, PRODUCT SAFETY, AND LIABILITY

21-1 THE ORIGINS OF CONSUMERISM

The benefits of industrialization are accompanied by the risks of life behind the quality dikes. Protection against these risks requires awareness of their nature, along with the economic and technological resources needed to adopt protective measures. In general, large users of these benefits, i.e., large buyers of modern risk-bearing products and services, do have an awareness of the nature of the risks and do have good resources to take self-protective measures. In contrast, small users, especially consumers, are under significant handicaps. Their understanding of the risks is more limited, and their resources for self-protection are likewise more limited.

In the case of consumers (small buyers for self-use) the risks have grown to such an extent as to give rise to a new major force in the economy—a force known as *consumerism*. This force derives from sheer numbers—consumers exist in large numbers and most of them have votes, which is a great many votes. To organize these votes into some unified direction requires a commonality of unsolved problems along with leadership which offers to help solve those problems. Both of these elements had long been present in all economies, but they never had succeeded in attaining national attention until the 1960s.

During the 1960s the unsolved problems of consumers reached a crescendo while new flamboyant leadership emerged to attract national attention. This combination of events gave birth to the modern "consumer movement" and stimulated an extensive list of responsive reforms along with much new legislation to mandate reforms. The net effect has been to create a new major force in the economy in a manner similar to the emergence of industrial unionism during the 1930s. As yet, the form and direction of the leadership have not become clear, but there is little doubt that the trend which began during the 1960s is irreversible, i.e., it is most unlikely that the laws will be repealed.

To understand this consumerism movement, it is necessary to understand the unsolved problems which have stimulated the movement. Some of these problems are unrelated to product quality, e.g., product pricing in confusing terms. However, many of the problems are quality related. We will now examine several of the major categories of these problems along with the root causes and the emerging solutions.

21-2 PRODUCT KNOWLEDGE

Ideally, consumers should have knowledge about the quality of the product before they buy it. This ideal is actually approximated in the primitive village marketplace. Most of the products consist of natural materials or are made from natural materials. In such markets consumers have long familiarity with such products and can use their unaided senses to judge the essential qualities before buying the product.

As to products whose qualities cannot be judged by the unaided senses, consumers must use alternative sources of product knowledge. One of these alternatives is the information supplied by manufacturers and merchants. Historically, this information has been a mixture of fact and opinion garnished with more or less exaggeration or *puffing*.

In the village marketplace, puffing is not regarded as a form of misconduct since consumers can for the most part verify the quality by their unaided senses. Hence the courts tolerate such puffing under the doctrine *caveat emptor*—let the buyer beware. For modern products, the unaided senses of consumers are hopelessly inadequate to verify product quality, so that puffing becomes a form of *misrepresentation* which can and does mislead consumers in their efforts to evaluate competing products. There has been enough of such misrepresentation to make it a major consumer complaint.

Several approaches are in progress or under advocacy to abolish puffing and the associated misrepresentation:

1. *Industry restraints on puffing.* Some manufacturers and merchants are quite factual in their product information and they seem to thrive without the need for puffing.[1] Of those who do engage in puffing, some assert that they do it

---

[1] For an example of one company's efforts to face up to the problems of consumerism, see Esther Peterson, "Consumerism as a Retailer's Asset," *Harvard Business Review,* May/June 1974, pp. 91–101.

defensively, i.e., to avoid losing their business to others who do engage in puffing. Efforts to abolish the practice through voluntary industry codes or standards have not met with great success. It is difficult to get competitors to agree on standards which so directly affect income. It is even more difficult to secure enforcement of such voluntary standards.

2. *Government mandates.* There have long been laws to enable governments to stop deceitful business practices, one of which is misrepresentation of the product. Enforcement of these laws has been difficult in the shadowy area between traditional puffing (which has been permissible under *caveat emptor*) and outright misrepresentation. More recently, a new and useful doctrine has emerged—require the puffers to disclose the data behind their claims! The usual sequence of events is as follows:

   a. Manufacturer X publishes an advertisement making certain claims of superiority for their product.

   b. Manufacturer Y, a competitor, feels that these claims are false and are injuring them competitively. Hence Manufacturer Y complains to the regulatory authorities.

   c. The regulators request that Manufacturer X prove the validity of their claims by submitting their product data and market test data to the regulators.

   d. If Manufacturer X fails to prove such validity, the regulators order the firm to stop it. They also give the manufacturer unwelcome publicity by publishing the order.

   Beyond the mandates designed to stop misrepresentation, there are other mandates relating to positive disclosure. For some types of products it is required that manufacturers provide label information showing contents, ingredients, etc. This is widely done with respect to qualities affecting safety and health but is being extended to matters that affect consumer economics.

3. *Publication of manufacturers' test data.* There is some advocacy urging that manufacturers be required to make public their product test data as a source of consumer product knowledge. Manufacturers have traditionally resisted this idea on proprietary grounds, i.e., that such disclosure would enable competitors to obtain valuable data at no cost. There are also some objections on the grounds of possible misuse of the data by biased consumer advocates. This is no trivial objection, since some of the advocates are severely biased. In some other respects the resistance to disclosure is on shaky ground. For example, many perishable products carry date codes to show the expiration dates. However, some merchants and manufacturers resist "open dating," i.e., showing these expiration dates in a form that can be understood by consumers.

   In the case of the government restraints discussed above, the regulators have gotten around the contention of proprietary information. They agree to keep the data confidential and to use them only to judge whether the published product claims are valid.

4. *Independent product data sources.* (See below.)

21-3 INDEPENDENT LABORATORIES

Consumer needs for product information have given birth to consumer-oriented laboratories. The concept is that an "independent" laboratory can evaluate products and provide unbiased information to consumers. Such information can then be used by consumers for judging value in relation to price and thereby for making informed decisions as to which products to buy. These consumer-oriented laboratories have emerged in several forms.

Consumer-financed Laboratories

In this form the laboratory publishes test results and offers these to consumers in the form of subscription to the publications. The offer stresses how the consumer can save money by knowing the comparative test results of competing models.

In the United States a leading organization in this field is Consumers Union of United States Inc. It has about 2 million subscribers (out of about 70 million households). It buys up competitive models, tests them in its laboratory, publishes the results in its monthly journal, and issues an annual compendium summarizing the findings. Subscribers receive a mixture of objective data and subjective comment with respect to the following topics:

Quality of design. The reports compare design features for competitive models. These comparisons are tabulated and discussed in easy-to-understand lay language. For complex products, only a minority of quality characteristics are tested, but these are well chosen from the view of their impact on fitness for use. As to characteristics chosen, subjective ratings are made in several categories ranging from excellent to very poor.

Quality of conformance. The reports have negligible value as to this parameter, since the practice is to test only one unit from each model.

Availability. The single unit tested and the duration of the test are not enough to derive useful measures of mean time to failure, mean time to repair, etc.

Field service. The test laboratory is unable to quantify the quality of service rendered by manufacturers or merchants. In recent years questionnaires have been sent to subscribers to secure their experience with product failures and field service. The summarized returns are then published. However, the questionnaire method does not qualify as an objective evaluation of field service conditions. The consumer sample is secured from subscribers rather than from the general public. In addition, the data are derived from human memory and subjective appraisals rather than from controlled record keeping.

Prices. The reports present comparative prices for the competing models in a form which is most convenient for the user.

Recommendations. The reports also provide subjective commentary as to value, i.e., relation of price to quality. Usually, the bulk of the models are rated acceptable, with some rated lower or not acceptable. Occasionally, there is a "best buy" which is given prominence.

Despite the limitations in evaluating quality, the reports appear to have value to consumers, especially with respect to major purchases. However, the organization has had much difficulty with subscriber turnover and is forced to spend a shocking proportion of its budget in advertising to secure new subscribers to replace the dropouts.

Manufacturer-financed Laboratories

This type of laboratory derives its income from fees paid by manufacturers who need or want the "seal" of the laboratory in order to market their products.

Some of these seals (marks, labels, etc.) are mandated by law, e.g., export controls in some countries. Others are mandated by economic imperatives. For example, many fire insurance policies require that the electrical apparatus used bear approval of Underwriters' Laboratories, Inc. (UL). In consequence, manufacturers of electrical apparatus must secure UL approval to make it possible for their customers (e.g., electrical contractors) to use the products. Securing UL approval becomes an economic necessity, even though the manufacturers may be confident that their product poses no fire hazards.

Still other seals are not mandated by legal or economic imperatives. For example, some national standardization bodies (e.g., in Japan and France) offer use of their mark to manufacturers whose products, on test, meet the requirements of established standards for such products. Since such marks are not mandated, the manufacturers make their decisions on economic considerations—will the cost of the mark be repaid by a higher share of the market? To date, use of these voluntary marks is quite small in relation to the size of the consumer economy, e.g., 1 or 2 percent.

Government-financed Laboratories

These are widely used by governments in their role as regulators and as buyers. In addition, when governments buy consumer-type products, they tend to publish their findings for use by consumers.

In addition, some countries, e.g., in Europe, subsidize consumer-oriented agencies to carry out tests of competing consumer products and to publish the results for the information of consumers. Some of these agencies have their own laboratories; others subcontract the testing or acquire test data from consumer testing laboratories. Publication may be through journals to which consumers subscribe or through government bulletins and the press. In some countries, consumer product test results are discussed over the national television, with commentary by representatives from consumer groups, manufacturers, etc.

Conformance to Standard versus Fitness for Use

All national standardization bodies are active and highly influential with respect to industrial products, e.g., standardization with respect to metrology, material types, bulk sampling, material testing, etc. With respect to consumer products, the practice varies widely. Generally, the socialist countries and some developing countries make extensive use of national standardization for consumer products, whereas the industrialized market-based countries do not.

This variation in practice extends to the evaluation of products by independent laboratories. In all countries the manufacturer-financed laboratories and government-financed laboratories evaluate *industrial* products in terms of conformance to specification. However, with respect to *consumer* products, the independent laboratories are guided by the national policy with respect to standardization for consumer products. In those countries which do make wide use of national quality standards for consumer products, e.g., the socialist economies, the laboratories tend to emphasize conformance to those standards. In those countries which make little use of national standards for consumer products, e.g., the developed capitalistic economies, the independent laboratories emphasize fitness for use.

Objectivity of Laboratories

For consumers to rely on laboratory test results requires that the laboratories be "objective." In practice, it is quite difficult to attain full objectivity. The problem is not much one of assuring the honesty of the laboratory technicians. With rare exceptions, that can be taken for granted. The problem is rather in the design of the test programs, especially in the interpretation of the test results.

Some laboratory evaluations are suspect because the income of the laboratory is related to the results of the evaluation. For example, some manufacturer-financed laboratories offer to award their seal to products which meet their tests. However, the manufacturer must take advertising in the journal published by the laboratory, as well as paying the costs of the tests. The latter practice is natural enough (though even here some minimal safeguards are needed). The former practice is suspect because it tends to relate the laboratory income to the results of the test. In like manner, government-financed or -subsidized laboratories face the risk of political pressures when their findings conflict with the objectives of the political party or leaders then in power.

Consumer-financed laboratories exhibit biases of other sorts. These laboratories are normally part of a broader organization which is in the "business" of consumer advocacy, i.e., urging new legislation, filing lawsuits, carrying out propaganda, etc., all on behalf of consumers. Such organizations are quick to publicize failings of manufacturers and merchants while ignoring the contributory failings of consumers (see Section 21-10). The resulting bias becomes a way of life and is self-perpetuating. Only those with a known record of activism or sympathy for the consumerism movement are accepted as directors or managers in such organizations. Such self-perpetuating bias is an obvious threat to the objectivity of a laboratory manager. In addition, this bias tends to create self-sealing thought systems. For example, a consumer publication may be preparing an article on some subject for which its laboratory is unable to answer all questions (e.g., Is a certain drug dangerous? Is the oil shortage real?). To supply the answers, the publication must engage the services of an expert as an advisor. In such cases only those experts will be chosen whose views are known in advance to agree with the consumer-oriented philosophy of the employing publication.

21-4 CONSUMER PRODUCT FIELD FAILURES

Failures in the consumer product field take place in enormous numbers and give rise to much controversy, principally: Are today's products as good as their predecessors? Are today's manufacturers really interested in quality? Despite some seeming contradictions, the answer to both questions is an overwhelming "yes." Manufacturers have always been concerned with field failures because of the associated external failure costs and the related threat to their ability to sell the product. This concern has been evidenced by a continuing procession of product improvements aimed at increasing marketability and reducing field failure losses. (The need is not only to compete for the consumers' purchasing power; the need is also to avoid aggravating the merchant to such an extent that they drop the product line.)

Some of these quality improvements have been spectacular. Many synthetic materials greatly outperform natural materials. Automobile tires now have over 10 times the life of their early predecessors. Solid-state circuitry has greatly reduced the failure rates of electronic equipment, which once depended on the electron tube. Improved diagnostic tools and new drugs have contributed to a remarkable lengthening of the human life span. With the possible exception of handicrafts, there is virtually no product line in which today's products are inferior to yesterday's. Mainly they are much better.

The controversy arises mostly from three other phenomena. One is the "population explosion" of *products.* The growth in product population has been much greater than the decline in failure rates, so that the absolute number of failures is now higher than ever. For example, prior to 1946 there were no failures in television sets. That was the first year of manufacture—about 6000 were made. The failure rates were high. Even in 1954, eight years later, the failure rates during the first year were at a rate of about six per year. By 1972 the failure rate had declined to about one per year during the first year, but the number of sets in operation had reached about 113 million, of which 45 million were color sets.[2]

Second, there is evidence that consumer tolerance for esthetic defects has been tightening up so that blemishes, noises, etc., once tolerated, now attract attention and adverse reaction. Finally, new designs which are intended to make products more competitive are also a breeding ground for new quality failures. In due course these designs are "debugged," but meanwhile the failures tend to support some of the prevailing beliefs.

There is much evidence that consumers are tolerant of product failures provided there is redress when something of consequence is at stake. (When there is little at stake, the great majority of consumers do not take the time to complain.) However, the record on redress has been so poor as to become a major focal point for the advocates of reform (see below).

A special problem of consumer product field failures is that associated with dwelling house construction. For the great majority of consumers, the dwelling house is the largest investment made during their lifetime and also the one involving the largest loss if poorly constructed. Many states in the United States and a number of other countries have enacted legislation requiring the builder to post a bond to protect the home buyer for a period (one to several years) against latent defects.

21-5 REDRESS

Providing redress for consumer product failures requires minimally:

A policy of warranty which responds to the needs of consumers in the modern
world.
Communication to consumers, in unequivocal terms, of the steps to be taken by
them to secure redress.
Organization for prompt handling of consumer complaints, returns, claims, etc.
Repair facilities which offer prompt, skilled, and fairly priced field service.

It costs money to meet these requirements. Many manufacturers and merchants have paid this price. Many have not. In part, this difference contributes to the redress problem, since the companies who pay the price must be compensated either by way of a higher product price or by way of a service

[2] "The Productivity of Servicing Consumer Durable Products," Report No. CPA-74-4, Center for Policy Alternatives, Massachusetts Institute of Technology with The Charles Stark Draper Laboratory, Inc., pp. 37–40. RANN Document Center, National Science Foundation, Washington, D.C.

contract. The consumer who shops for low prices may thereby be deciding to gamble on not needing redress.

However, the bulk of the problem seems to have been a massive lag of the facilities for redress in relation to the needs. During the 1960s this lag brought about a widespread breakdown of customer service and redress. Warranties were vaguely worded as to what was guaranteed and also as to who would make good. Consumers were given lengthy runarounds between manufacturers and merchants and even among the numerous offices within large companies. Some companies established "hot lines," i.e., designated telephone numbers to be called collect in order to secure assistance.

Refereeing of debatable claims was and remains a difficult problem. Often there is a difference of opinion on the facts—what caused the failure. In these cases the need is for impartial and inexpensive ways to resolve the differences. Numerous experiments are being tried: special small claims courts, arbitration, use of the ombudsman concept, etc. As yet, none has emerged as a dominant solution.

Repair service is one of the worst problems in the redress complex. During the warranty period this service is usually provided by the manufacturer or the merchant, and such service has tended to be adequate. Beyond the warranty period the consumer makes wide use of independent repair shops, many of which have poor records as to promptness, competence, and especially basic honesty. There is probably need for new forms of nationally organized chain repair service shops to take over most of the work now done by these independent repair shops. Alternatively, it may be necessary for large manufacturers and merchants to organize matters in ways which take responsibility for repairs over the entire useful life of the product.

21-6 PRODUCT SAFETY

Until recently, most consumer products were familiar repetitions of products which had been grown or made for centuries. Many generations of use had identified most of the hazards, and this accumulated knowledge was transmitted to succeeding generations. Consumers could use their senses to identify many of the known dangers, e.g., poisonous plants, and could take protective action. Nevertheless, many injuries took place. Some were clearly related to dangers inherent in consumer products, e.g., food poisoning, cuts from knives, fires from kerosene lamps. Others were closely related to consumer carelessness and risk taking, e.g., falls down stairways, dangerous sports, alcohol.

During the twentieth century, new products presenting potential sources of injuries have been superimposed on these traditional (and continuing) sources: the automobile and other types of consumer vehicle; electrically driven household appliances, gardening equipment, hobby equipment, etc.; heating devices of many types; synthetic materials and chemicals of all sorts. Consumer use of these new products has resulted in still more injuries—a number about as large as those traceable to traditional sources, hence doubling the total. In addition, the injuries from these new sources seem to be of greater severity. Many deaths and serious injuries result from traffic accidents, high-speed machinery, combustible and explosive materials, carcinogenic (cancer-causing) materials, etc.

This rise in injuries has attracted the attention of numerous forces in the economy, and much has been done to improve the safety of consumer products. However, as in the case of product failures, although injury *rates* (per amount of usage) have been declining, the absolute number of injuries has been rising owing to the phenomenal rise in product population and product usage.

During the 1960s some earlier slow trends accelerated sharply and converged to bring about drastic changes, chiefly as follows:

1. The law courts had for years gradually weakened the defenses of industrial companies against lawsuits for injuries sustained from consumer products (see Section 21-7). During the 1960s these lawsuits accelerated, both in the number of suits and in the size of the awards to injured plaintiffs.
2. Consumer advocacy had for years moved at a relatively quiet, pedestrian pace. During the 1960s new, flamboyant leadership attracted national publicity, and generally accelerated the pace and force of this advocacy.
3. Legislators had long discussed the need for national laws to deal with consumer product safety. Except for laws with respect to food and drugs, little had transpired. During the 1960s numerous new national laws were enacted relative to consumer safety. Two of these were of the broadest significance: i.e., the National Traffic and Motor Vehicle Safety Act (1966), concerned with automotive vehicle safety; and the Consumer Product Safety Act, concerned with consumer products generally.

Traffic Safety

The most reliable measure of traffic safety rates is the fatality rate, since fatalities are usually well investigated and reported. Early in the century this rate was about 50 fatalities per 100 million miles of vehicle travel (about 30 fatalities per 100 million kilometers of vehicle travel). By the 1960s this rate had declined by about an order of magnitude. This decrease was the result of improvements in roads and vehicles, together with programs of driver licensing, training, etc.

The 1966 legislation involved two laws, one directed at the vehicle and the other at the motorist and the driving environment. However, the subsequent work of the National Highway Traffic Safety Administration (NHTSA) was directed overwhelmingly at the vehicle. NHTSA mandated numerous vehicle safety standards to serve three purposes:

1. To reduce accidents, e.g., vehicle collisions, vehicles running off the road, etc. Standards for this purpose were directed at brakes, tires, headlamps, etc.

2. To protect motorists from the effects of the "second crash." Standards for this purpose involved interior cushioning, passenger restraints, etc.
3. To provide information and documentation, e.g., manufacturers' records of compliance.

The subsequent decade witnessed a significant improvement in automotive traffic safety—a reduction of about one-third in the fatality rate. This reduction was traceable to the following components:

Component	Proportion of safety improvement contributed, %
Seat belts in use	33
Other mandated vehicle safety standards, e.g., padding for dashboards, locks for seat backs, etc.	11
Better highways	33
Reduction of speeds due to energy crisis	23
	100

The seat belts in use were spectacularly successful and relatively inexpensive, involving a cumulative cost of about $700 million. The other mandated safety standards (including seat belts not in use) contributed little to the improvement but were enormous in cost—about $9000 million cumulative. Collectively, these standards were not cost-effective.

Other countries have avoided such preoccupation with vehicle design and have looked to the driver as well. In most European countries enforcement of laws relating to drunken driving and excessive speeds is more strict than in the United States. Equally significant is the recent policy with respect to seat-belt usage.

Starting in 1970 the Australians mandated buckling of seat belts. The public accepted this and the result was a spectacular improvement both in seat-belt usage and in traffic safety. New Zealand and the countries of western Europe soon followed, with similar improvements. The indications are that these countries will overtake the Americans in attainment of safety improvements, and will do so without such huge expenditures.[3]

Consumer Product Safety

The second major law was the Consumer Product Safety Act of 1972. It was made applicable to a very wide spectrum of consumer products, but excluding products already involved in other legislation, e.g., motor vehicles, aircraft,

[3] Data and conclusions with respect to traffic safety are derived from J. M. Juran, "Automotive Safety Legislation—Ten Years Later," European Organization for Quality Control, 20th Annual Conference, Copenhagen, June 1976. Reprinted in *Quality*, October 1977, pp. 26–32; November 1977, pp. 54–60; December 1977, pp. 18–21.

food and drugs. The Act grants wide powers to a Consumer Product Safety Commission to establish data sources, conduct investigations, publicize findings, promulgate safety standards, test products for conformance, ban dangerous products, etc.

In its early years of operation the Commission tended to stress identification of concentrations of injuries which had their origin in consumer products.[4] These concentrations then became a major source of projects for action.

There is no recognized, broad-based measure of consumer product safety. There is, however, a data bank on safety in the home, maintained by the National Safety Council (425 N. Michigan Avenue, Chicago, Illinois 60611). The unit of measure is fatalities per 100,000 of population. This fatality rate has been in a steady decline over the last 40 years. There is no evidence of any change in this rate of decline in the four years (1972 to 1976) that followed the new consumer product safety legislation.[5]

Food and Drugs

Some accounts of early food and drug industry practice make dismal reading.[6] Food processing was done in many local plants with quality controls subject to the judgment of the local managers. Numerous patent medicines and nostrums were on sale, often harmless but in some cases based on alcohol or opiates. The prevailing concept was a carryover from the village marketplace—*caveat emptor.*

While most food companies were ethical and competent processors, the Pure Food and Drug Act of 1906 stimulated a good deal of activity for quality improvement, both at the industry level and the company level. Subsequent to 1906, still other laws were enacted relating to pesticides, food additives, color additives, packaging, labeling, etc. Standards have been established for grades of fruits, vegetables, poultry, meats and fishery products, as well as for identity, quality, and fill.

Similar legislative activity has taken place with respect to drugs and allied products, e.g., cosmetics, animal medicines, pesticides, etc. In one major respect the drug laws are far more restrictive, since no new drug may be marketed without prior approval by the Food and Drug Administration (FDA). In the drug industry many standards for products and assays are established by referencing the privately published major compendia, the *United States Pharmacopeia* and *National Formulary.*

While the laws conferred broad powers on the FDA, the early exercise of those powers was mainly directed to finished product quality. It was largely left

---

[4] The concentrations are discovered mainly through the National Electronic Injury Surveillance System (NEISS), a data bank which receives reports from a sampling of injuries.

[5] J. M. Juran, "Life Behind the Dikes of Quality Control," European Organization for Quality Control, 22nd Annual Conference, Dresden, June 1978.

[6] The original Pure Food and Drug Act (1906) was stimulated by the descriptions of conditions in the Chicago stockyards as narrated in Upton Sinclair's novel *The Jungle.*

to industry to establish the processes and quality controls needed to meet the standards. Generally, the companies responded well, and some developed highly sophisticated controls to meet and surpass the product standards. In addition, the companies, through the industry associations, established committees, industry research project conferences, publications, etc., to develop standards for various aspects of manufacturing and control practice.

More recently, the FDA promulgated standards of *good manufacturing practice* (GMP) based largely on the prior work of industry, and evolved in collaboration with industry committees. These standards go into a good deal of detail with respect to material controls, material storage, processing facilities, quality control procedures, laboratory controls, documentation, etc. The FDA has in addition conducted extensive inspections and audits to review industry adherence to GMP standards. In turn, these audits have stimulated more complete auditing practice within the companies.

21-7 PRODUCT LIABILITY

A major and growing consequence of unsafe products is lawsuits for personal injury. Such lawsuits were rare until the early twentieth century. Since then there has been a remarkable growth, one estimate[7] for the total liability claims throughout the United States being as follows:

Year	Number of claims
1963	50,000
1968	100,000+
1969	300,000+
1970	700,000+
1975 (projected)	1,600,000

This growth in number of claims has been accompanied by other trends[8] all adverse to the defendants, i.e., mainly the manufacturers. Judgments against defendants rose from 43 percent to 54 percent during the period 1965 to 1973. During the same period the size of the awards rose from an average of $11,644 to $79,940. Awards of over $1 million were unheard of early in the century but now are made regularly. The combined effect of all these trends has been to raise the cost of liability claims to proportions which have alarmed manufacturers, insurance companies, and other segments of society.

The reasons behind the trends are well known:

---

[7] Stanley J. Klein, "Product Liability in the 1980s," *Mechanical Engineering*, January 1974, pp. 10–13.

[8] Donald W. Segraves, "Product Liability Problems," *Quality Progress*, January 1977, pp. 16–18.

1. More and more manufactured products are in the hands of amateurs, thereby creating more opportunities for injury.
2. The traditional legal defenses of the defendants have been eroded. This erosion is the result of court decisions which have struck down the defense of "privity" and have shifted the burden of proof (as to negligence) from plaintiff to defendant.[9]
3. The new militancy of the consumer movement has tended to stimulate more aggressive consumer action generally.
4. The publicity given to large awards has also stimulated more lawsuits.

(In the countries of western Europe there are also some trends toward eroding the defenses of the defendants. However, there is no likelihood of lawsuits and claims rising to the alarming proportions prevailing in the United States, since the conduct of lawsuits is very different. In the United States it is quite legal to bring a "contingency suit," i.e., a lawsuit in which the plaintiff's lawyer receives no fee if the suit is unsuccessful but receives a healthy proportion of the award if the suit is successful. In Europe such suits are considered to be unethical and even illegal. Generally, in European practice the facts of the case and the size of the award are determined not by a lay jury but by judges, aided by technical experts. The awards generally do not include pain and suffering or punitive damages.)

Defensive Options

Until recent decades, manufacturers were readily able to absorb the cost of small claims and could insure themselves against the rare larger claims.

With the erosion of legal defenses and with the remarkable growth of claims and awards, the costs of insurance have risen broadly. This has become a severe problem, especially for companies in high-risk industries such as industrial machinery, industrial chemicals, pharmaceuticals, automotive parts, and medical devices. The problem is especially severe for small companies. In some specialties, insurance is now difficult to obtain and then only at high cost. In California many physicians (especially surgeons) went "on strike" to protest prohibitive insurance rates. Here and there manufacturers have abandoned product lines which were an undue source of liability claims, e.g., electric blankets. (This is also a form of going "on strike.") Alternatively, some manufacturers, as in pharmaceuticals, have delayed introduction of products. (Sale of "swine flu" vaccine was held up until the federal government provided insurance relief beyond that carried by the manufacturers.)

The alternative of legal relief is being widely studied. However, such relief

[9] See generally Michael Coccia, John W. Dondanville, and Thomas R. Nelson, *Product Liability: Trends and Implications*, American Management Association, New York, 1970. See also *Product Liability and Reliability*, Machinery and Allied Products Institute, 1967.

moves slowly since massive forces are involved. To quote the Interagency Task Force on Product Liability Briefing Report:[10]

> The law of product liability has become filled with uncertainties creating a lottery for both insurance rate makers and injured parties. A basic cause of this is the doctrinal conflict as to whether tort law should be a compensation system for persons injured by products or a means of apportioning responsibility based on fault.

In nonlegal language this raises the basic question: What should be the purpose of the law of injuries? Should the purpose be to find out who is at fault, and then to pay for the injury based on allocation of fault? Or, alternatively, should the purpose be to compensate the injured persons irrespective of fault? The latter concept is already on the lawbooks in some states in the form of "no-fault" insurance. In effect, the no-fault system avoids lawsuits by taxing all users of the products to pay for any injuries.

Meanwhile, the most intense action programs have been those of industrial companies directed at reducing the incidence of product-related injuries.

21-8 COMPANY PROGRAMS TO IMPROVE PRODUCT SAFETY

Company programs logically divide themselves according to the respective responsibilities of the major functions. These responsibilities have become well identified as a result of the numerous programs started and experience gained, especially since the 1960s.

Top management has the responsibility to promulgate the corporate policy with respect to product safety. The usual elements of this policy include:

A commitment to make and sell only safe products, and to adhere to published regulations, to support industry programs, etc.

Mandated formal design reviews and product reviews for safety.

Requirements that all company functions prepare formal plans setting out their roles in carrying out the corporate policy.

Broad guidelines for documentation, product identification, and traceability to assure product integrity and to assist in defense against lawsuits.

Guidelines for defense against claims, whether rigid or flexible.

Guidelines for evaluation of safety performance and publication of corporate reports on results attained.

Provision for audit to assure adherence to policy.[11]

Top management also has the responsibility for setting up such supplemental corporate organization structure as is needed to assist in carrying out the

---

[10] National Technical Information Service, 5285 Port Royal Road, Springfield, Virginia 22151.

[11] For a case example involving a program for an entire company, see Rayford P. Kytle, Jr., "Evaluating Product Liability Before Marketing," *Quality Progress*, February 1974, pp. 16–19.

policy on product safety. Usually this structure involves:

1. A product safety committee.
2. A corporate safety engineer[12] (or safety administrator).
3. Some degree of outside experts and observers.

The *product safety committee* typically carries out the following responsibilities:

Review and coordinate the programs which have been developed by the various company functions to set out their respective roles.
Coordinate the work associated with corporate projects such as development of a unit of measure to quantify safety, design of corporate reports to evaluate results and disseminate information, design of the system of audit needed to assure compliance.

The *safety engineer* carries out the detailed work of collection of information, analysis of data, and publication of reports. His responsibilities include:

Maintain liaison with the insurance company engineers and (sometimes) with government regulators.
Participate in investigation of injury cases.
Provide consulting assistance to various departments.
Conduct audits of adherence to safety policies.
Keep informed on developments in product safety programs outside the company and disseminate acquired information as appropriate.

Product design has the responsibility to:

Study injury data and use the findings as inputs to all designs.
Make product safety a formal design parameter.
Conform to government safety standards and industry safety codes.
Secure listings from test authorities, as needed.
Organize design and product reviews for safety, at appropriate stages of the product life cycle.
Review proposed material substitutions and cost reductions for their effect on product safety.
Adopt modern design techniques as appropriate: fault tree analysis; fail-safe concepts; in-house and field testing; Weibull and other modern test data analysis; designation of safety-oriented characteristics by a standard symbol on all specifications; coded identification of all safety-oriented compo-

[12] For a case example in which this role was played by the Systems Engineering Division, see Michael S. Heschel, "Hazards Reduction Improves Safety," *Industrial Engineering,* March 1974, pp. 8–11.

nents for use in traceability, reorders, and recalls; publication of product ratings.

Manufacturing has the responsibility to provide for control of safety-oriented characteristics throughout all stages of product progression: materials, processing, finished product, packing, storage, and shipping. Specific responsibilities include:

Provide foolproofing and automated testing as needed.
Provide for documentation and traceability.
Establish training programs and train personnel to meet qualification criteria for critical operations and tests.
Provide for motivation on product safety matters through explaining "why," through soliciting suggestions, etc.

Quality control has a varying range of responsibilities, depending on the nature of the product and the history of the company. The most usual responsibilities include:

Plan for inspection and test of safety-oriented characteristics.
Perform tests, analyze test data, and judge conformance.
Maintain calibration of test equipment.
Investigate nonconforming products and secure inputs to aid in disposition.
Participate in fitness-for-use decision. (The quality manager is typically secretary or chairman of the committee concerned with product recalls.)
Participate in analysis of injury cases, including tests on retention samples and review of product history.

Marketing has a wide array of important responsibilities relative to product liability:

Provide for labeling of dangerous products, including warnings, consequences, and remedies.
Provide packaging able to maintain the identity and the designed safety of the product.
Provide safety information to the marketing chain—distributors, dealers, installers, maintenance personnel—using manuals, exhibits, checklists, etc.
Provide manuals for users, explaining safe methods together with warnings of consequences of misuse.
Secure review of advertising from a technological and legal viewpoint.
Train the field sales force in contract provisions as well as in product safety aspects. (Any exaggerated claims of product safety, whether made by advertising or by the sales force, can be used against the company during lawsuits.)

Field service responsibilities include:

Assure that repairs, when made, leave the product in a safe condition.
Report near-injuries encountered as well as injuries.
Report observations on how the product is actually used. Some lawsuits hinge on the question of whether the product should be designed to provide not only for intended usage but also for actual usage (which includes some misuse).
Provide field service in a way which makes friends and thereby minimizes the likelihood of claims and lawsuits.

Responsibility for investigating injuries varies, but typically is divided among the insurance company, the legal department, and the appropriate technical departments. Irrespective of the allocation of responsibility, certain precautions should be taken:

Notify the insurance company promptly.
Assign only qualified experts to make the investigation.
Secure and retain the product unit asserted to have caused the injury.
Analyze the injury environment and product thoroughly to identify the precise failure mode.
Conduct laboratory tests with a view of reproducing the same failure mode. (If needed, secure verification from independent laboratories.)
Make use of modern analysis techniques: high-speed cameras, scanning electron microscope, etc.

21-9 CRIMINAL AND PERSONAL LIABILITY

Claims for damages are based on *civil liability*—compensation for losses due to personal injury or property damage. There is also *criminal liability,* which is based on an offense against the state. Criminal liability is an ancient doctrine and it has long been applied to problems of product safety. For example, one provision of the Code of Hammurabi stipulated that if a house collapsed and killed the occupant, the builder of that house should be put to death. Similarly, in medieval Europe, a baker who mistakenly mixed rat poison in with his flour was put to death when people died of eating poisoned bread.

The experience of centuries then evolved the *common law* and the subsequent criminal codes which established two grounds for imposing criminal liability in injury cases involving product safety:

1. The defendant had engaged in some sort of fraud—he or she was doing something wrong and knew it, or
2. The defendant was grossly negligent (as in the case of the baker).

What these two grounds have in common is that *the defendant was in direct personal control* and could have avoided the injury. A dishonest defendant received little sympathy. The baker made an honest mistake which had severe social consequences. He might well have received sympathy from some of the villagers. However, the decision was to inflict criminal punishment—the protection of society seemed to demand such punishment as an example to deter carelessness by others.

Until the growth of large organizations, the defendant in liability cases was typically an individual person, e.g., the artisan who made the product. The growth of modern industry has introduced some drastic changes never contemplated by the common law and the resulting criminal codes. Three of these changes have profoundly affected responsibility for product safety:

1. The emergence of the company, e.g., the corporation as a separate entity, has added a new major defendant to the list of targets in liability suits, both criminal and civil.
2. In large companies it is difficult to pinpoint personal responsibility—the responsibility for product safety is diffused among multiple departments and persons.
3. In working with new technologies, the consequences cannot be fully predicted from theoretical considerations or laboratory evaluations.

Diffusion of Responsibility

In large companies responsibility for overall results is widely diffused among the various functional departments as well as among the several layers of the hierarchy. This diffusion holds true with respect to product safety since various departments around the "spiral" contribute to fitness for use. As a result, individuals can be held responsible only for performing such actions and making such decisions as are set out in their assigned list of responsibilities, e.g., their written description. (The chief executive, however, is usually regarded as having responsibility for overall results.)

Despite diffusion of responsibility, it is still possible for individuals to be faced with personal liability. For example, if a designer miscalculates the stresses so that his or her design is unsafe and causes injuries, the designer might have difficulty defending himself or herself against criminal charges. So would an inspector who performed a test incorrectly and failed to detect a dangerous nonconformance. For such individuals the risk of criminal liability would be real. The risk of civil liability would normally be negligible, since the plaintiffs would have sued the company as well and would look for compensation from the richest guilty defendant. This would not be true as to self-employed specialists, e.g., surgeons, whose insurance would make them prime targets.

Until the 1960s it was rare for criminal charges to be brought against non-supervisory employees of manufacturing companies for reasons of product safety. The climate seems to have changed since that time under the advocacy of various consumer groups, government regulators, legislators, etc. Generally, however, the chief targets of these advocates are not the nonsupervisors but the managers and chief executives.

In addition, there have been some significant changes in the wording of the regulatory laws. Normally, they provide that ". . . any person who *knowingly* violates . . . shall be guilty . . . ." The significant change is in the deliberate omission of the word "knowingly."

In a precedent-setting case, a small company had violated the Federal Food, Drug and Cosmetic Act of 1938. The general manager was tried and convicted, despite lack of participation in the violation or even knowledge of the violation. The U.S. Supreme Court, by a five to four vote, upheld his conviction, explaining that the Act ". . . dispenses with the conventional requirement for criminal conduct—awareness of some wrongdoing. In the interest of the larger good it puts the burden of acting at hazard upon a person otherwise innocent but standing in a responsible relation to a public danger" (*United States* v. *Dotterweich*, 320 US 277).

In an extension of the Dotterweich case, the U.S. Supreme Court upheld the conviction of the president of a chain of 874 food stores, employing 36,000 employees. Here the president had been informed by the regulators of certain violations in the company's warehouses. He ordered the violations corrected and was assured that action would be taken, but in fact the corrective action had been only partial [*United States* v. *Park*, 421 US 658 (1975)].

It may well be that this feature of being criminally liable despite lack of knowledge of the violation will be repealed in future legislation. However, the very fact of its enactment is an indication of the climate which has prevailed.

Still another problem in criminal liability arises when an employee is urged by superiors or others who outrank him to take actions which he or she feels may result in unsafe product, e.g., a designer being urged by a superior to proceed with a design which the designer feels is questionable as to safety; a chief inspector being urged by the plant manager to accept a nonconforming lot which the chief inspector may feel has some possible safety hazards.[13]

In such situations the employee is faced with a conflict in responsibilities. There is a responsibility to the company. To fail to carry out the orders of the superior is insubordination and carries the risks of economic sanctions. However, the employee also has a responsibility to society to avoid actions which might endanger the citizenry. Hence to carry out the orders of the superior is to risk criminal prosecution.

To date industry has not fully taken steps to avoid putting employees into such impossible situations. The major needs are to:

[13] For a case example (engineers urged by their superiors to exaggerate a test report), see Kermit Vandiver, "Why Should My Conscience Bother Me?" This is Chapter One of *In the Name of Profit*, a collection of asserted misdeeds of corporations, Doubleday & Company, New York, 1972.

Establish clear guidelines which will explain to all concerned the need to avoid
   placing such pressures on individuals.
Designate some office at the corporate level to become an open door to receive complaints about such pressures.
Instruct all employees to the effect that they have a right and a duty to report
   such pressures to the "ombudsman" (the Swedish name for such an in-
   house recipient of complaints).

Unproved Technology

For centuries prior to the Industrial Revolution there prevailed long periods of
technological stability. Changes in designs, materials, processes, etc., came
slowly and by evolution rather than revolution. This pedestrian pace permitted
designs, once "debugged," to go on and on for decades with high predictability
as to performance, including product safety.

The revolution in technology plus the competitive marketplace has
changed this pattern of stability. Now changes come thick and fast: new materials, processes, products, test methods, etc. Each one of these innovations is
based on some new design concept and each undergoes some degree of evaluation before having its consequences go into the marketplace. These evaluations
are necessarily on some limited scale: engineering analysis, laboratory tests,
clinical tests, test marketing, etc. The subsequent full-scale production and use
sometimes disclose hazards not discovered during the more limited evaluations. In due course the hazards become known, revisions are made, and the
problems are eliminated. However, meanwhile injuries may have taken place,
with associated potential liability on the part of the companies or institutions involved. In addition, there are the potentialities of individual liability (civil or
criminal) for physicians, designers, quality managers, etc., despite their use of
the best techniques known. An instructive case is that of "retrolental
fibroplasia."

Prior to the 1940s there had been a high degree of brain damage in infants
born prematurely. A theory that this damage was caused by lack of oxygen
gained general acceptance by the early 1940s. In consequence, incubators were
built to permit keeping these infants in high concentrations of oxygen. This
resulted in a distinct reduction in the mortality rate. However, the oxygen treatment brought with it a new problem—a form of blindness through formation of a
fibrous tissue behind the lens of the eye (hence the name "retrolental
fibroplasia"). It then took several years for the medical profession to establish the
connection between the new disease and the use of oxygen. It took several
more years to discover that by restricting the oxygen levels it was possible to
retain the benefits of higher survival rates without subjecting the infants to
blindness. Nevertheless, liability cases have been brought by former premature
infants when they reached legal age two decades later. (The statute of limitations does not run against minors in such cases.) These cases were filed against

the physicians who had administered oxygen to them at the time they were premature infants. The physicians contended that they were using the best known techniques for saving the lives of such infants. Some of these cases have resulted in very large awards to the plaintiffs.

21-10 CONSUMER-CREATED QUALITY PROBLEMS

Consumers are an important source of consumer quality problems. For example, over a third of all service calls on household appliances have their origin in consumer misuse or neglect. Up to a point, it is easier to design foolproof products than to secure proper care by consumers. Beyond that point, further design becomes wasteful. In the case of consumer product safety, less than 25 percent of the injuries are preventable by product redesign.[14]

A good deal of damage to products is the result of consumer neglect. Consumer maintenance of products is notoriously poor and has led to extensive redesign to attain self-maintenance, e.g., self-lubricating bearings. Much neglect is the result of poor or confusing instructions provided by the manufacturer. However, many consumers discard the instruction books, lose them, fail to consult them, etc. Still other damage to products is through misuse. Machines are overloaded. So is electrical circuitry. Products are used in ways never intended by the design. For example, hair dryers are made to operate in refrigerators to do the defrosting, or are made to operate in freezing weather to thaw out a frozen automobile lock.

Consumers are a major direct source of some types of pollution. Beer cans and other refuse are left in parks, in rivers, in streets, etc., by consumers, not by manufacturers. In some countries the parks, rivers, and streets are free of such trash; in other countries, trash abounds. The difference is not in the contrasting actions of manufacturers but in the contrasting actions of consumers.

The most serious consumer-contributed quality problems are in the field of health. Consumers put themselves and others at risk by use of alcohol, tobacco, narcotics, etc. They overeat, neglect their teeth, delay visiting their doctors, are evasive about their symptoms, and fail to take their medication.[15]

The consumers' record on safety is no better, being at its worst in automotive traffic safety. The great majority of highway crashes are caused by drunken driving, excessive speed, vehicle maintenance neglect, etc. The resulting injuries could be reduced drastically by use of seat belts, but only 25 percent of American motorists use the belts. Consumers also engage extensively in dan-

---

[14] Private communication to J. M. Juran by a member of the Consumer Product Safety Commission.

[15] In one study it was found that of 180 outpatients, 77, or 43 percent, failed in one or more respects to comply with the prescribed medication program. Clifton J. Latiolais and Charles C. Berry, "Misuse of Prescription Medications by Outpatients," *Drug Intelligence and Clinical Pharmacy*, October 1969, pp. 270–277.

gerous sports, e.g., skiing. By failing to extinguish cigarettes and campfires, they burn up forests, hotels, and homes.

In matters of ordinary honesty, consumers are no different from other human beings. Consumers have certainly been subjected to much evasion and deceit by a segment of the business community. However, this is not just one-sided. Manufacturers and merchants put up with a good deal of similar evasion and deceit due to consumer misuse of the product, fraudulent claims, shoplifting, etc.

Despite the huge scale of these consumer contributions to poor quality, they receive little attention from reformers. Consumer advocates, fearful of antagonizing their clients, play down and even deny the existence of consumer failings. Government regulators and legislators, although not so outrageously biased, nevertheless are reluctant to insist on improved behavior by consumers (who are also voters). Hence a usual approach is to regard consumer failings as a fate rather than a problem, and to look elsewhere for problems, at lower political risk.[16] Even among manufacturers and merchants, there are many who are willing to endure a degree of abuse from consumers (who are also customers) during an era in which the business community is in a state of low public esteem.

21-11 POLICIES, GOALS, AND MEASURES

On the face of it everyone is "for" safety and health. All public pronouncements are to this effect. When people are killed or injured, the grief is genuine. Nevertheless, the practice differs widely from the pronouncements, as discussed in Section 21-10.

To date there is no agreed national policy on how to strike a balance between the urge to save human lives and the limitations of available resources. No one knows how to put a value on a human life or injury. If our resources were unlimited, we might well pay whatever was needed to approach perfection with respect to injuries. However, our resources are limited, and this forces the decision makers to confront the concept of striking a balance. The nature of this balance or "acceptable level of risk"[17] is open to debate, and some of the contesting views are far apart, since they proceed from widely different premises and responsibilities.

One approach actually in use is to find the *economic balance*. We do know how to estimate the economic effect of deaths and injuries. We also know how to estimate the costs of applying new safeguards. However, to date there has been only limited use of this concept of economic balance. Most of the people who urge the new safeguards have no responsibility for paying the costs. Most

---

[16] See Juran, "Automotive Safety Legislation—Ten Years Later."

[17] See in this connection, *Quality Control Handbook*, 3rd ed., "Acceptable Level of Risk," pp. 8-45, 8-46.

of those who resist the new safeguards have important vested interests in the costs.

In some areas of consumer safety we lack the essential facts on what is taking place, e.g., what are the injury rates, and are things getting better or worse? We lack such facts with respect to foods, drugs, and consumer product safety. In the absence of such fundamental information, no one can prove or disprove the usefulness of broad control programs. What we do have is information on specific concentrations of injury modes, together with which products are associated with such injury concentrations. Some of this information comes from industry analysis of injury reports. (Industry is also required, under most consumer safety legislation, to report injury cases to the regulators.) In addition, there is now a national data center (NEISS), which secures injury data (on a sampling basis) from hospitals and similar sources. These data, when processed, are useful for identifying projects for improvement.

National scoreboards on safety do exist with respect to traffic safety and factory safety.[18] These scoreboards are quite helpful in analyzing what has taken place over the years, as illustrated in Section 22-6. However, even with the existence of such scoreboards, the pressures of advocates who are supported by large numbers of voters can still prevail over the concept of economic balance. In the case of motor vehicles, the mandated safety standards, with a cumulative cost in excess of over $10,000 million, have not been cost-effective.[19] In addition, these costs were not the result of taxes directly levied by elected legislators. They were indirectly levied in the form of higher vehicle costs and thereby higher vehicle prices paid by the consumers whom they were intended to protect.

To date no method has been evolved to inform consumers convincingly of the extent to which they are paying for these regulatory programs and what they are getting in return. Neither has any method been evolved to make clear to consumers that they have a major influence on the cost of product liability in their capacity as jurors. The awards they vote are, in the last analysis, paid for by these same jurors in their capacity as consumers under a sort of lottery system.

Whether consumers could be stimulated to act on such information is open to doubt since there is no clear evidence that consumers regard product safety as a problem of major concern. If anything, the available information suggests that the problem has a low priority among consumers. A national opinion survey commissioned by Sentry Insurance Company found, among other things, that:

1. Consumer issues ranked in the middle range of public priorities, behind inflation, unemployment, and federal spending.

---

[18] The main data source is National Safety Council, 425 N. Michigan Avenue, Chicago, Illinois 60611.

[19] Juran, "Automotive Safety Legislation—Ten Years Later."

2. Only 1 percent (of 1510 consumers polled) thought product safety was the most important priority of the consumer movement.
3. Only 2 percent of those polled cited product safety as a reason for the growth of the consumer movement.[20]

However, product safety is regarded as a major problem by the insurance companies who have been confronted by the great rise in number and size of claims. Product safety is also stressed by consumer advocates who profess to speak for consumers. Product-related injuries receive considerable attention from the press and from legislators in specific instances. These are important forces in the economy and at present are the dominant forces.

PROBLEMS

21-1 The following are among the alternatives in use or under consideration for giving product information to consumers:

1. Evaluation of fitness for use by independent laboratories (consumer-financed or government-financed), together with judgments of value.
2. Establishment of product standards and evaluation of conformance to standard (by manufacturer-financed laboratories).
3. Mandated disclosure of test data by all manufacturers, with summaries and analyses prepared by independent laboratories.

Which of these (or which other method) would you choose in preference to the prevailing method of letting the consumer make his choice as best he can? Why?

21-2 Some industry associations, e.g., Association of Home Appliance Manufacturers (AHAM), have created an independent board to receive consumer complaints which have not been resolved to the satisfaction of the consumer. The board has the power to investigate, recommend, and publicize but not to enforce its recommendations. What do you think of this concept? Why?

21-3 Read the case of the airplane brake design referenced in footnote 13. Assuming that the facts are as asserted in that case, what action, if any, do you think an industrial company should take to avoid getting into such a situation?

21-4 It is common practice for company files to contain interdepartmental correspondence which includes the debates relative to the merits and deficiencies of alternative product designs, manufacturing plans, test methods, etc. In some lawsuits the plaintiff shows copies of such correspondence to the jury as evidence that the defendant company had been warned that the product as designed (made, tested, etc.) would be unsafe but that the company chose to ignore the warnings. What is your judgment as to the policy to be followed by the company in retaining such correspondence?

21-5 A salesperson is worried about the safety of a new product which the company is planning to market. He conveys his fears to his superior, who tells him to forget it. He goes up the line, to the district manager, the regional manager, and finally the corporate vice-president. The latter fires the salesperson on the grounds that he has made a nuisance of himself. In your judgment, were the salesperson's actions warranted? Was the vice-president's action warranted?

(See, in this connection, David W. Ewing, "What Business Thinks About Employee Rights," *Harvard Business Review*, September/October 1977, pages 81–94, especially p. 88.)

[20] *Quality Progress*, July 1977, p. 7.

SUPPLEMENTARY READING

Consumerism: *Quality Control Handbook,* 3rd ed. (QCH3), pp. 4-30 to 4-34.

Independent laboratories: QCH3, pp. 4-24 to 4-30.

Product safety: QCH3, pp. 8-44 to 8-56; also Willie Hammer, *Handbook of System and Product Safety,* Prentice-Hall, Inc., Englewood Cliffs, N.J., 1972.

Product liability: QCH3, pp. 14-28 to 14-32; also Irwin Gray et al., *Product Liability: A Management Response,* American Management Association, New York, 1975.

TWENTY-TWO

QUALITY ASSURANCE

22-1 THE NATURE OF ASSURANCE

The word *assurance* as used in this chapter has a meaning quite similar to the word "insurance." Both assurance and insurance involve a relatively small expenditure (of money or effort) for the purpose of securing some kind of protection against disasters. In the case of *insurance* this protection consists normally of payment of a large sum of money as compensation for the effects of the disaster. In the case of *assurance* the protection consists of information. This information serves one of two purposes:

1. To "assure" the recipient that all is well, e.g., the product is fit for use; the process is behaving normally; the procedures are being followed.
2. To provide the recipient with early warning that all is not well and that some disaster may be in the making. Through this early warning the recipient is placed in a position to take preventive action to avert a disaster.

In the village marketplace it is a simple matter to provide this quality assurance. The only persons concerned with product quality are the sellers and the buyers. The sellers are mostly either the farmers who grew the product or the artisans who fabricated it. Both of them have direct personal knowledge as a basis for their quality assurance. The buyers are mostly consumers buying for their own use. They assure themselves as to quality by using their senses to examine the product. They also derive added assurance from the reputation of the seller, about whom they also have personal knowledge.

With expansion of commerce and growth of technology, the list of those who require quality assurance has expanded far beyond the elementary list of maker-seller and buyer-user. The list now includes various managers of the manufacturing companies, purchasing agents, contracting officers, merchants, government regulators, insurance companies, consumer organizations, etc. In addition, the means of providing assurance has gone far beyond the rudimentary methods of using human senses in the village marketplace. These means now involve tests of all kinds, surveillance, documentation, warranties, etc. Table 22-1 shows the principal forms of information now used to provide quality assurance to various persons who have a need to know.

To provide such information on the scale demanded by industrial societies has required invention of forms of assurance which will:

1. Provide objective information, free from the biases of those who have some vested interest in the answers.
2. Avoid costly retesting and review.
3. Avoid extensive personal involvement by those who need the information.

Table 22-1 Forms of objective evidence used for quality assurance

| Persons requiring quality assurance | Natural products | Simple manufactured products | | Complex products |
		Short-lived	Long-lived	
Consumers	Direct sensory examination	Usage	Prior reputation of manufacturer; warranty	Prior reputation of manufacturer; warranty
Customers lacking technological capability	Direct sensory examination	Usage	Prior reputation of manufacturer; warranty	Prior reputation of manufacturer; warranty
Customers with technological capability	Direct sensory examination; test	Test; usage	Life test; usage data banks	Surveys; audits; test and usage data banks
Regulators	Direct sensory examination; test	Test	Life test; usage data	Surveys; audits; test and usage data
Managers of the manufacturing companies	Direct sensory examination; reports of complaints and returns	Executive reports of test results; usage, complaint, and returns data	Executive reports of tests; usage, complaints, returns; surveys, audits	Executive reports; surveys; audits

The two major forms of assurance which meet these criteria are (1) the summarized report (often called the executive report or management report), and (2) the quality audit.

Before we discuss these two major forms of assurance in detail, let us clear away the confusion which has arisen because the word "assurance" is used in multiple meanings. Some companies use the term "quality assurance" as the name for a department which has broad responsibilities in matters of quality, i.e., inspection, test, quality control engineering, reliability engineering, reports, audits, etc.

Another source of confusion has been the tendency in some companies to use the term "quality assurance" as synonymous with "quality control." In this book these terms are *not* regarded as synonymous. The distinction stated in ASQC Standard A3-1971 (also ANSI Z1.7 1971) is helpful:

> Broadly, quality control has to do with making quality what it should be, and quality assurance has to do with making sure quality is what it should be.

Because of the confusions noted above (and others), no one can know what the term "quality assurance" means in any one company without first finding out what are the activities represented by that term.

The concept of quality assurance has much in common with the concept of financial assurance. Over the centuries there has evolved a need for many people to have knowledge of the financial status of companies: money lenders, suppliers, insurance companies, shareholders, labor unions, tax collectors, etc. This knowledge is available in the financial statements published by the company. However, independent assurance is provided by the use of qualified independent auditors who make an examination and issue a certificate to the effect that:

1. The financial system of the company is such that, if followed, the reports will correctly reflect the financial condition of the company.
2. The system is being followed.

22-2 REPORTS ON QUALITY

For those engaged in managing or regulating large enterprises, the bulk of quality assurance is derived from multiple sources of operational information: laboratory tests, factory tests, field performance data, etc. This information is used in the first instance for operational controls, e.g., day-to-day regulation of factory processes and field performance. The same information, when summarized and converted into suitable form, becomes a major input to "executive reports"—a system of information which enables busy managers to become adequately informed as to quality performance and trends without becoming

Table 22-2 Operational quality controls versus executive quality controls

Aspect	Application to operational quality controls	Application to executive quality controls
Control subjects	Physical, chemical, specification requirements	Summarized performance for product lines, departments, etc.
Units of measure	Natural physical, chemical (ohms, kilograms, etc.)	Various: often in money
Sensing devices	Physical instruments, human senses	Summaries of data
Who collects the sensed information	Operators, inspectors, clerks, automated instruments	Various statistical departments
When is the sensing done	During current operations	Days, weeks, or months after current operations
Standards used for comparison	Specification limits for materials, process, product	History, competitors, plan
Who acts on the information	Servomechanisms, nonsupervisors, first-line supervisors	Managers
Action taken	Process regulation, repair, sorting	Motivation, change of plan, disciplinary action

heavily involved in day-to-day operations. Table 22-2 shows the interrelationship between operational and executive-type controls.

In many companies these summarized executive reports are supplemented by independent audit reports (Section 22-3). Such audits help to provide assurance that the report system correctly reflects what is actually going on with respect to quality.

The information needed by managers for executive control varies widely from company to company, depending on the nature of the product, the extent to which the control problems have been solved, etc. However, the *kinds* of information are quite similar despite these wide variations. Table 22-3 is a matrix which generalizes the executive report content.

Control Subjects

Executive control, like any other control, is based on the concept of the feedback loop as exemplified in Figure 11-4. Each feedback loop is built around a specific control subject. In the case of executive reports on quality, these control subjects exhibit a good deal of commonality. Virtually all companies have controls built around some of the control subjects of Table 22-3, and some companies make use of most of these control subjects.

Choice of control subjects is the most critical of all decisions involved in setting up executive controls. Omitting a vital control subject deprives the managers of vital information. Adding unneeded control subjects dilutes the attention given to the important matters.

A useful approach to choosing control subjects is to invite participation

Table 22-3 Matrix for executive reports on quality*

Control subject	Typical unit of measure	Usual departmental source of data	Typical standard	Typical format	Typical frequency
Negative customer reactions					
Complaints	Number of complaints per 1000 units; per $000 of sales	Field service	Historical	Narrative	M
Returns	Value of returns per $000 of sales	Accounting	Historical. market	Narrative	M
Service calls	Number of service calls per 1000 units under warranty; cost of service calls per 1000 units under warranty	Field service	Historical. market	Tabulation	Q
Guarantee charges	Dollars per 1000 units under warranty	Accounting	Historical. market	Tabulation	Q
Field performance					
Product reliability	Failure rate: mean time between failures	Field service	Engineered. historical. market	Charts	M
Spare-parts sales	Dollars of sales	Accounting	Historical	Tabulation	A
Product conformance on inspection. test	Defects per unit; process average for specific qualities	Inspection. test	Historical. engineered	Charts	M
Outgoing quality based on product audit	Demerits per unit	Quality assurance	Historical	Charts	M
Vendor quality performance	Dollars of cost per dollars of purchases	Accounting, quality control	Historical	Tabulation	Q

Subject	Unit of measure	Comparison basis		Form	Frequency*
Quality costs: appraisal, failure, prevention	Dollars per hour of direct labor; per dollar of direct labor, shop cost, processing costs, sales; per unit of product, equivalent product	Accounting, quality control	Historical, budget	Tabulation, charts	Q
Surveys; audits other than product audit	Various	Quality assurance	Plan	Narrative	S
Opportunities	Return on investment, other	Quality control	—	Narrative, tabulation, charts	Q
Customer relations on quality (other than alarm signals)	Various	Marketing, field service, quality control	—	Narrative	Q
Results of quality improvement programs	Dollars, return on investment	Quality control	Plan	Tabulation, narrative, charts	Q

*Frequency code: M = monthly.
Q = quarterly.
A = annual.
S = special.

from all key managers. Sometimes this is done on the initiative of the quality manager. He or she "makes the rounds," visiting each key manager in turn and securing their nominations for control subjects as well as their ideas on units of measure, standards, report frequency, etc. The quality manager then drafts up, publishes, and circulates an executive report package which is responsive to the consensus of the managers' views. After review and discussion, a final design is agreed on and this becomes the report package for the next several years.

Units of Measure

Executive reports are a summary of numerous inputs. Preparing such summaries requires creation of units of measure which summarize multiple performances, each measured in its own way. These summaries are usually prepared using one of the following forms:

1. *Arbitrary weighting.* A common method is the use of a system of demerits to assign weights to various types of defects to reflect their seriousness. The resulting demerits per unit of product is a common unit of measure applicable to a variety of products.

   Example A product audit system makes use of four classes of seriousness of defects. During one month the product auditors inspected 1200 finished units of product, with the following results:

Type of defect	Number found	Demerits per defect	Total demerits
Critical	1	100	100
Major	5	25	125
Minor A	21	5	105
Minor B	64	1	64
Total	91		394

   Although the 91 defects found represented many defect types and four classes of seriousness, the total demerits of 394 when divided by the 1200 units inspected gives a single number, i.e., 0.33 demerit per unit.

2. *Conversion into common measurement units.* A widely used example is the computation of cost of scrap, rework, etc., to provide a summary of the extent of quality failures. Here the numerous defect types are converted into a common unit of measure—money.
3. *Statistical indexes.* For example, in an improvement program it is common to establish departmental goals each of which is quantified by equating it to

"100 percent performance." Actual performance is then expressed in terms of percent of goal. This permits comparisons among departments despite wide variations in departmental technology.

Planning the Data System

Summarized reports are derived from numerous bits of data, each of which represents some action taken or decision made. To generate these bits of data requires a good deal of planning and coordination among numerous departments, including:

Designing a standard language for data recording and entry to the data processing system. This design includes establishing standardized terminology for describing defect types, failure modes, etc. In addition, the design requires assignment of code numbers to simplify data recording and entry as well as subsequent processing and summary.

Designing the data entry and processing methods. These are largely technological designs and are strongly influenced by the volume of data and the relative economics of alternative data processing methods.

Establishing coordinated timetables to provide the lead time needed to meet the final report deadlines.

Defining responsibilities of all departments and providing the associated training.

Providing checks against errors in reporting.

It takes a lot of tedious, unspectacular work to carry out such a program.

Measuring Performance

Acquiring data from the source departments involves solution of additional problems. Busy departments resist spending their time in record keeping, especially if the data provide no direct aid to meeting departmental goals. For example, an assembly department is forced into repair costs due to receipt of defective components from other departments. The assembly department will tend to resist keeping separate records of the repair time, saving the defective components, recording the defect types, etc.

A further problem is the sheer volume of data. Where the data acquisition is simple, e.g., direct entry from an automated instrument, this problem is solved by the modern computer. However, in other cases data acquisition is complex and costly. For example, a field service call can involve a great deal of data recording if there is to be a complete feedback for improving designs, processes, etc. For such cases the solution may lie in securing only a sample of the data. See in this connection Section 20-4.

Interpretation and Action

Interpretation of published information requires knowledge of the possible weaknesses in the data system. There are many ways in which seemingly valid data can lead to false conclusions. Here are some examples:

1. A new product model is put on the market. Many weeks go by during which the "service calls per thousand units under warranty" is a very low number. On the face of it, we have a highly reliable product. The real reason may be that the numerator (number of service calls) is out of time phase with the denominator (units under warranty) owing to the passing of time during packing, storage, shipping, unpacking, installation, etc.
2. When the validity of a report is questioned, the person who prepared the report may point to the large mass of computer data from which the figures were derived. However, it is easy to be fooled. Sheer volume does not by itself assure valid conclusions. Instead, it is the quality of the data which is decisive. A large volume of poor-quality data will still lead to poor conclusions. In contrast, even a sampling of high-quality data can lead to sound conclusions.
3. Sometimes a report contradicts what managers have learned from their own senses. "I don't care what the inventory report says. The bins are empty." What is significant here is that processed data are only the evidence of the deeds, not the deeds themselves. (In the inventory case the failure of the data to reflect the current facts could be due to any of several logical reasons.)
4. A report may fail to reflect the facts because the data sources have dried up. In some companies there is a prevailing "atmosphere of blame" with the result that anyone who prepares reports of deficiencies (scrap tickets, rework tickets, etc.) runs the risk of being blamed whether guilty or not. In such cases it is quite usual for people to stop making out the reports.

The availability of modern special-purpose computers is bound to improve the odds that the processed data reflect the facts. These computers are relatively simple to program, so that a specialized department such as Quality Control can do the programming without queuing up before the central computer room. In addition, these computers are often designed to avoid the keypunch bottleneck by use of other forms of data entry, e.g., optical recognition, voice recognition, etc.

The fact that the summarized reports show a need for action does not in itself assure that action will be taken. Some of this lack of action is traceable to laxity on the part of the managers. They should show by example that the reports are to be taken seriously, but sometimes they do not. When the managers thus fail to set a good example, the failure spreads to the subordinate levels as well.

Failure to take action may also be the result of differences in priorities between the managers and the editors of the reports.

Example 1 A report shows a rise in nonconformance to specification with respect to a certain quality characteristic. The manager takes no action because he or she believes fitness for use is protected.

Example 2 A report shows that present performance differs from the past by an amount that is statistically significant. (Such being the case, the cause is "findable" if we choose to look for it. If it were not statistically significant, there would be no point in looking for the cause, since we probably could not find it even if we tried.) However, the *economic* significance may be so small that the phenomenon is unable to secure any priority for action on the managers' list of problems.

Standards

Reports on performance have little meaning unless they are compared with standards to enable managers to judge whether action is needed or not. The more usual forms of standard are listed in Table 22-4, along with their bases and principal uses.

Format

The format used in presenting reports to managers depends largely on the personal preferences of the managers themselves. Most prefer reports in writing

Table 22-4 Types of standards used for executive reports

Type of standard	Standard is based on:	Managers use the report to answer the question:
Engineered	Studies made by engineers, e.g., material usage, labor hours	Are we attaining the results which the engineering studies showed were attainable?
Historical	Statistical computation of past performance	Are we getting better or worse?
Market	Market studies to discover performance of competitors	Where do we stand compared to our competitors?
Planned	Broad program of final results needed, and allocation to subprograms, e.g., reliability goals	Are we going to be able to attain the overall planned goal?

with supplemental oral briefings. There is also variation as to written reports. Managers with technological backgrounds prefer an array of charts which show trends and abnormalities at a glance.[1] Other managers tend to prefer narrative or tabular forms of reports. Most managers want reports to be summaries, with details available on request or attached as appendixes.

It is also useful to design reports in modular form to permit selective distribution to managers specifically interested. Such modular design permits a degree of flexibility in format as well.

Publication

Published reports should provide a degree of interpretation to assist managers in assimilating the significant facts in short order. Some of the more useful devices for such illumination include:

Listing of the vital few (not more than 10) quality problems which merit the personal attention of the upper management.
Progress reports on major programs under way.
High points of recent audits and surveys.
Major developments taking place inside and outside the company.
Previews of proposals which will be coming to upper management.
Identification of trends.

Opportunities

Most quality reports are designed to be used as alarm signals—to show the presence or absence of conformance to standard. It is a welcome plus if the report also deals with opportunities, i.e., identifying opportunities and reporting on progress in securing improvements. The most widespread use of this concept is in connection with quality cost studies. However, there is need to extend the idea to all other aspects of opportunities for improvement—field service, launching new designs, market research in quality, etc.

22-3 QUALITY AUDIT—THE CONCEPT

The *quality audit* is an independent evaluation of various aspects of quality performance for the purpose of providing information to those in need of assurance with respect to that performance. The most usual quality audits are made:

1. By companies to evaluate their own quality performance.
2. By buyers to evaluate the performance of their vendors.
3. By regulatory agencies to evaluate the performance of organizations which they are assigned to regulate.

[1] For examples, see *Quality Control Handbook*, 3rd ed., pp. 21-28 to 21-31.

Purposes of Audits

The usual purposes of quality audits are to provide independent assurance that:

Preparations for attaining quality are such that if followed the intended quality will in fact be attained.

Products are fit for use and safe for the user.

Laws and regulations are being followed.

There is conformance to specifications.

Written procedures are adequate and are being followed.

The data system is able to provide adequate information on quality to all concerned.

Corrective action is taken with respect to deficiencies.

Opportunities for improvement are identified.

Structuring the Audit Program

Audits are usually *structured,* i.e., they are designed to carry out agreed purposes and are conducted under agreed rules of conduct. To reach agreement on these rules and purposes requires collaboration among three essential participating groups:

The heads of the activities which are to be the subject of audit.

The heads of the auditing department(s).

The upper management which presides over both.

Unless such collective agreements are reached, there are risks that the audit program will fail. The usual failure modes are (1) an abrasive relationship between auditors and line managers, or (2) a failure of line managers to heed the audit reports.

Figure 22-1 depicts the typical flow of events through which audit programs are agreed on and audits are carried out. The resulting published statement of purposes, policies, and methods becomes the charter which legitimizes the audits and provides continuing guidelines for all concerned.

Policies to Be Observed during Auditing

In preparing the basic agreement on the program of auditing, it is quite helpful for the conferees to face and resolve certain policy questions which are common to many audits. These policy questions include:

Legitimacy The basic right to conduct audits is derived from the "charter" which has been approved by upper management, following participation by all concerned. Beyond this basic right, there are other questions of legitimacy— what shall be the subject matter for audit; should the auditor be accompanied during the tour; whom may the auditor interview; etc. The bulk of auditing practice provides for legitimacy—the auditor acts within the provisions of the

Figure 22-1 Steps in structuring an audit program.

	Audit department	Line department	Upper management
Discussion of purposes to be achieved by audits and general approach for conducting audits	×	×	×
Draft of policies, procedures, and other rules to be followed	×	×	
Final approval			×
Scheduling of audits	×	×	
Conduct of audits	×		
Verification of factual findings		×	
Publication of report with facts and recommendations	×		
Discussion of reports	×	×	×
Decisions on action to be taken		×	
Subsequent follow-up	×		

charter plus supplemental agreements reached after discussion with all concerned.

Scheduled versus unannounced Most auditing is done on a scheduled basis. "No surprises, no secrets." This enables all concerned to organize workloads, assign personnel, etc., in an orderly manner. It also minimizes the irritations which are inevitable when audits are unannounced. (There are, however, some situations, e.g., bank audits, where the need to avoid "cover up" may require surprise audits.)

Objectivity As far as possible, the auditor is expected to compare things as they are with some objective standard of what they should be. Where such standards are available, there is less need for the auditor to make a subjective judgment and thereby less opportunity for wide differences of opinion. However, provision should be made for challenge of the standard itself.

Verification of facts Auditors are universally expected to review with the line supervision the facts (outward symptoms) of any deficiencies discovered during the audit. The facts should be agreed on before the item enters a report going to higher management.

Discovery of causes In many companies the auditor is expected to investigate major deficiencies in an effort to determine the cause. This investigation then becomes the basis for the auditor's recommendation. In other companies the auditor is expected to leave such investigations to the line people; his or her recommendations will include proposals that such investigations be made.

Recommendations and remedies Auditors are invariably expected to make recommendations with a view of reducing deficiencies and improving performance. In contrast, auditors are commonly told to avoid becoming involved in designing remedies and making them effective. However, auditors are expected to follow up recommendations to assure that something specific is done; i.e., the recommendation is accepted or it is considered and rejected.

Human Relations

In theory the audit is a sort of instrument plugged into the operations to secure an independent source of information. Where it is a physical instrument, e.g., the propeller speed indicator on the bridge of a ship, there is no problem of clash of personalities. However, auditors are human beings and in practice their relationships with those whose work is audited can become quite prickly. Deficiencies turned up in the audit may be resented because of the implied criticism. Recommendations in the audit may be resented as an invasion of responsibilities. In the reverse direction, auditors may regard slow responses to requests for information as a form of grudging collaboration. These and other human relations problems are sufficiently important to warrant extensive discussion plus indoctrination of both auditing personnel and operations personnel with respect to:

The reasons behind the audits These reasons may have been well discussed during the basic formulation of the audit program. However, that discussion was held among the managers. There is also need to explain to the supervisors and nonsupervisors the "why" of the audits. (It is not enough to explain that upper management wants audits.) Obviously, all employees are also customers, consumers, and concerned citizens, so it is easy to point out the benefits they derive from audits conducted in other companies. In addition, it can be made clear that the managers, customers, regulators, etc., of this company likewise require added assurance.

Avoiding an atmosphere of blame A sure way to cause deterioration of human relations is to look for whom to blame rather than how to achieve improvement. Line managers as well as auditors can fall into this trap. An atmosphere of blame not only breeds resentment—it dries up the sources of information. The audit reports and recommendations should be problem-oriented rather than person-oriented.

Balance in reporting An audit which reports only deficiencies may be factual as far as it goes. Yet it will be resented because nothing is said about the far greater number of elements of performance which are well done. Some companies require the auditors to start their reports with "commendable observations." Others have evolved overall summaries or ratings which consider not only deficiencies but also the opportunities for deficiencies (see below).

Depersonalizing the report In many companies the auditor derives much influence from the fact that his or her reports are reviewed by upper management.

Auditing departments should be careful to avoid misusing this influence. The ideal is to depersonalize the reports and recommendations. The real basis of the recommendations should be the facts rather than the opinion of the auditor. Where there is room for a difference of opinion, the auditor has a right and a duty to give his or her opinion as an input to the decision-making process. However, any position of undue advocacy should be avoided, as this tends to reduce the auditor's credibility as an objective observer. (The ultimate responsibility for results rests on the line managers, not on the auditors.)

Competence of auditors To attain adequate levels of human relations as well as objective reporting requires that the auditors have the qualifications for both. Their basic education and experience should be sufficient to enable them to learn in short order the technological aspects of the operations they are to audit. Lacking this background, they will be unable to earn the respect of the operations personnel. In addition, they should receive special training in the human relations aspects of auditing as discussed above.

22-4 SUBJECT MATTER OF AUDITS

For simple products the range of audits is also simple and is dominated by product audits (see below). For complex products the audit is far more complex than mere product audit. In large companies even the division of the subject matter is a perplexing problem. For such large companies the programs of audit use one or more of the following approaches for dividing up the subject matter:

Organization units In large companies there are several layers of organization, each with specific assigned missions: corporate office; operating divisions; plants; etc. In such companies it is common to use multiple teams of quality auditors, each reviewing its specialized subject matter and reporting the results to its own "clientele."

Product lines Here the audits evaluate the quality aspects of specific product lines (e.g., printed circuit boards, hydraulic pumps) all the way from design through field performance.

Quality systems Here the audits are directed at the quality aspects of various segments of the overall systematic approach to quality.[2] A typical list of such systems would be:

General administration of the quality function.
Product development and design.

---

[2] For a case example, see Thomas G. Toeppner, "Implementing a Corporate Quality Assurance Activity in a Multi-Product Divisionalized Corporation," *1970 ASQC Annual Technical Conference Transactions*, pp. 1–13.

Vendor relations.
Manufacturing planning.
Process control.
Final product testing.
Field performance.

A system-oriented audit would review any such system over a whole range of products.

Specific procedures Audits may also be designed to single out specific procedures which have special significance to the quality mission: disposition of nonconforming products, documentation, instrument calibration, etc. (see Table 22-5).

Audit of Intentions and Preparations

These intentions consist of the familiar hierarchy of the tools by which managerial activities are carried out: policies, objectives, programs, plans, procedures, organization training, motivation, etc. Every one of these tools can be reviewed by auditors to judge their adequacy. For some (e.g., policies, objectives) it is difficult to find standards for comparison. As to such tools, the auditor's evaluation will be mainly subjective. For others there is available a good array of standards so that the auditor's evaluation will be more nearly objective. These standards are available from various sources such as:

Table 22-5 Systems audits

Scope or activity	Examples of specific tasks audited
Engineering documentation	Use of latest issue of specifications by operators; time required for design changes to reach shop
Job instructions	Existence and adequacy of written job instructions
Machines and tools	Use of specified machines and tools; adequacy of preventive maintenance
Calibration of measuring equipment	Existence of calibration procedures and degree to which calibration intervals are met
Production and inspection	Adequacy of certification program for critical skills; adequacy of training
Production facilities	General cleanliness and control of critical environmental conditions
Inspection instructions	Existence and adequacy of written instructions
Documentation of inspection results	Adequacy of detail; feedback and use by production personnel
Material status	Identification of inspection status and product configuration; segregation of defective product
Materials handling and storage	Procedures for handling critical materials; protection from damage during handling; control of in-process storage environments

Contracts with customers.

Customer and company quality specifications.

Regulatory specifications and handbooks.

National, industry, and company standards of all sorts.

The company manual on quality auditing.

Product Audits

The most widely used quality audit is an independent evaluation of "final" product quality to determine conformance to specification and fitness for use. This audit is performed by independent quality auditors who are responsible to a quality assurance department. The audit results are then made available to all cognizant managerial levels. The need for such audits is often questioned, especially since the audit is usually done right after the inspection and test department has finished its job. One contention is that the inspection and test results could provide a measure of the quality of the final product.

Actually, there is a good deal of logic for creating such product audits. In many cases the inspection and test department is subordinate to a manager who is also responsible for meeting other standards (schedules, costs, etc.). In addition, there is value in reviewing the performance of the entire quality control function, which includes inspection and test planning as well as the conduct of the tests themselves. Finally, the more critical the product, the greater is the need for some redundancy as a form of assurance.

Audit to evaluate fitness for use under actual conditions of use is both difficult and costly. Fortunately, for most quality characteristics identifiable by the user, it is feasible to conduct product audits on the basis of simulation in the laboratory. Hence for reasons of economy, most product auditing is done in the early stages of finished-product progression. The various alternatives for choice of stage of progression are shown in Table 22-6.

Table 22-6 Potential stages for product auditing

Stage at which product auditing is conducted	Pros and cons of using this stage
After acceptance by inspectors	Most economical, but does not reflect effect of packing, shipping, storage, or usage
After packing but before shipment to field	Requires unpacking and repacking, but evaluates effect of original packing
Upon receipt by dealers	Difficult to administer at such multiple locations, but reflects effect of shipping, storage
Upon receipt by users	Even more difficult to administer, but evaluates the added effects of dealer handling and storage plus effects of shipment to user and unpacking
Performance in service	The ideal, but also the most difficult to administer, owing to the number and variety of usages; can be simplified through sampling

For simple products it is feasible to buy a representative sample of finished goods on the open market. These samples are then checked for fitness for use and conformance to specification. In some companies such audits are conducted annually as part of the broad annual planning for the product line. Such audits may include a review of competitive product as well.

For complex consumer products, e.g., household appliances, it is feasible to secure product audit data at multiple stages of the product progression shown on Table 22-6. The most extensive product audit takes place immediately following factory inspection and test. Additional audit data are then secured from selected distributors and dealers under a special joint "open and test" audit. Similar arrangements are made to secure data from selected servicing dealers. In addition, use is made of the data from consumer "arrival cards." When properly arranged with due regard to time lags, all of these data sources can be charted in a way which shows trends as well as levels.[3]

A case example of product auditing is that of Collins Radio Company. (See the Wilson reference in Supplementary Reading.) Collins makes a wide variety of complex electronic systems for aerospace, military, and civilian applications, mainly of a communications character. Product auditing is done by a special product audit department. It has its own laboratory, located apart from the manufacturing area. It is staffed by qualified personnel and it reports to the quality assurance organization.

The samples selected for audit consist of completed electronic systems all boxed and ready to ship. As part of the audit, the boxes are opened up and the contents are checked for presence of the documents, accessories, operations manuals, etc., which will be expected by the user. Then the equipment is tested under simulated use conditions. Finally, the system is disassembled and the various units are inspected to specification and workmanship standards.

Errors found are brought to the attention of the appropriate departments. In addition, summarized reports are prepared and issued to show composited findings and trends. Errors are classified for seriousness, with a demerit number assigned to each class. Demerits per unit are computed and reported along with an index of overall quality. This index makes use of a factor of product complexity based on the "possible error count," which is a physical count of the number of potential assembly errors. For large equipments, this count can run as high as 25,000. The number of possible errors is also used as an equivalent to the number of units of product for some sampling purposes.

Audit of Vendor Practice

Audit of vendor practice is used primarily in connection with contracts for complex products. Such contracts necessarily involve purchase of vendor capabilities (e.g., design, manufacturing planning, etc.) to an extent such that the quality of the resulting product is determined mainly by the way in which the

[3] For a case example, see *Quality Control Handbook,* 3rd ed., pp. 41-2 to 41-6.

vendor exercises these capabilities. As a consequence, the buyer directs his or her attention to these capabilities at several stages of contracting:

1. *Preaward phase.* During this phase the purpose of the audit is to evaluate the various capabilities of the vendor and to judge what would be the performance if that vendor received the contract. In addition, the audit identifies weaknesses which the vendor may be asked to correct as a condition of securing the award. The preaward audit is directed mainly at:

    Quality policies, quality objectives, and organization structure.
    Control of design and manufacturing information.
    Subcontract relations, i.e., the quality activities of a vendor in relation to *its* vendors.
    Material control—identity, storage, transport, etc.
    Manufacture, i.e., manufacturing planning, process capability, process controls, etc.
    Inspection and test: facilities, planning, data system, instrument calibration.

2. *Contracting phase.* The contracting procedure includes agreement on broad quality programs. This is usually done by referencing specific published standards with additions or deletions. The resulting modified standards become the basis for the subsequent audits during the execution of the contract.

    During this phase the parties also agree on specific contract provisions for quality with respect to product specifications, manufacturing methods, process controls, test methods, test data, documentation, etc. In addition, they agree on the rules of conduct for the audits themselves.

3. *Execution phase.* During the performance of the contract, the audits emphasize adherence to policies, plans, procedure, etc. These audits are quite similar to those which are used for in-house reviews of execution vs. plan.

Audit of Execution versus Plans

A great deal of auditing time is devoted to examining how well the operations conform to plans, specifications, etc. Because operations involve huge numbers of actions and decisions, the audits of execution vs. plans must make skillful use of sampling. This sampling is multidimensional in character, involving multiple product lines, departmental functions, procedural subjects, etc. Some companies resort to formal matrices to design the sampling plans so as to secure coverage of significant variables at minimal auditing effort. (See the Purcell reference in the Supplementary Reading.)

Identifying Opportunities

An experienced and alert auditor is often able to discover opportunities for improvement as a by-product of his or her search for discrepancies. These opportunities may even be known to the operations personnel so that the auditor is only making a rediscovery. However, the line personnel may have been unable to act due to any of a variety of handicaps: preoccupation with day-to-day control, inability to communicate through the layers of the hierarchy, lack of diagnostic support, etc.

The auditor, through his or her relatively independent status, may be able to prevail over these handicaps. He or she is not preoccupied with day-to-day control. In addition, the auditor's reports go to multiple layers of the hierarchy and thereby have greater likelihood of reaching the ear of someone who has the power to act on the opportunity. For example, the auditor may find that the quality cost reports are seriously delayed owing to backlogs of work in the accounting department. His or her recommendation to computerize the reports may reach the person who can act, whereas the same proposal made by the operations personnel may never have reached that level.

22-5 CONDUCT OF AUDITS

Because audits serve as the basis for a good deal of managerial action, they tend to become surrounded with various rules of conduct to assure their objectivity and validity. In due course these rules of conduct are embodied in a company Quality Audit Manual. This manual sets out the guiding principles and procedures for the conduct of quality audits. Typical contents of such a manual include the following aspects of auditing:

Policies and purposes The manual describes the purposes that are to be served by audits and sets out the policies which are to guide all concerned.

Organization Normally, the auditing is assigned to a quality audit department which is responsible to a quality manager. There are also minority forms in which quality auditing is done by teams of managers or teams of supervisors, depending on the subject matter. In any case, the responsibility for audit must be made clear so that there are no doubts as to legitimacy.

Subject matter This is likewise identified and thereby legitimized. In addition, the manual sets out the principles to be followed in scheduling audits, conducting the sampling, and otherwise defining the subject matter to be chosen for audit. These principles then serve as a basis for working up each year the schedule of audits to be conducted.

Checklists It is common practice to provide auditors with guidelines which define the assigned subject matter and which help assure that the auditor will do a complete job within that assignment. In part these checklists are contained in the operating documents themselves: customers' orders, contracts, specifications, procedures, government regulations, etc. It is an invariable part of each auditor's job to become familiar with those provisions of such documents which bear on the assigned subject matter. Such provisions are automatically part of the auditor's checklist.

Additional checklists may be prepared based on the discussions during the evolution of the audit "charter." In addition, the experience gained during auditing identifies the more frequent weaknesses in the quality aspects of the operations. These weaknesses then enter the checklists as structured questions or as listed topics.

The structured questions may be broad, leaving much to the initiative and resourcefulness of the auditor:

Are the written procedures consistent with company quality policy?
Do the personnel understand the specifications and procedures?

An intermediate type of checklist identifies areas of subject matter which are to be checked, leaving it to the auditor to supply the detailed checklist. Typical examples of such areas of subject matter would be maintenance of machines and tools or control of engineering change orders.

In some companies the checklists go into great detail, requiring the auditor to check numerous items of operational performance (as well as recording the fact that such items were checked). For example, an auditor checking a test performed by an inspector would be required by the checklist to check the work of the inspector as to correctness of specification issue number used, list of characteristics checked, type of instruments employed, sample size, data entries, etc.

Reports of deficiencies The finding of a deficiency is surrounded with much formality. The auditor first discusses his or her finding with the supervisors directly involved to reach agreement on the facts. The discrepancy is then "written up," sometimes on a form designed specially for that purpose. Copies are sent to interested managers in advance of the summarized report of the broader audit. This same form sets in motion the train of corrective action.

Seriousness classification The basic definitions are agreed on along with lists of classifications for specific types of discrepancies which have already gone through the classification process. Demerits or weights, if used, are included.

The data system This includes the code number plan (to permit data processing), the methods of summarizing data, the kinds of indexes to be computed, and still other elements needed to convert the detailed findings into quantified summaries.

Report publication Agreement is reached on report format, responsibility for editing, lists of which managers are to receive what reports, etc. Design of the audit reports is often modular to permit selective distribution.

Corrective action This is also surrounded with formality. Operations managers are required to respond in writing as to what they plan to do with respect to discrepancies found or recommendations made. (Operations managers are not obligated to follow the recommendations. They may conclude not to follow them, in which case they state why not.) Aside from disposing of the specific instances turned up, this formality helps to assure that quality audits have a high priority of managerial attention.

22-6 SUMMARIZING AUDIT DATA

All audits involve review of numerous aspects of intended and actual performance. In these reviews most elements of performance are found to be adequate while some are found to be in a state of discrepancy. To report these findings requires two different levels of communication:

1. Report of each discrepancy to secure corrective action. These reports are made promptly to the responsible operating personnel, with copies to some of the managerial levels.
2. Report of the overall status of the subject matter under review. These reports are not yet standardized, but enough varieties have been on trial to identify some of the principal requirements of an overall report. To meet these requirements the report should:
    a. Evaluate overall quality performance in ways which provide answers to the major questions raised by upper managers, e.g., Is the product safe? Are we complying with legal requirements? Is the product fit for use? Is the product marketable? Is the performance of the department under review adequate?
    b. Provide evaluations of the status of the major subdivisions of the overall performance—the quality systems and subsystems, the divisions, the plants, the procedures, etc.
    c. Provide some estimate of the frequency of discrepancies in relation to the number of opportunities for discrepancies.
    d. Provide some estimate of the trend of this ratio (of discrepancies found to discrepancies possible) and of the effectiveness of programs to control the frequency of occurrence of discrepancies.
    e. Include a list of persons and areas visited, material reviewed, number of observations made, samples taken, etc. (Usually such detail goes into the foreward or the appendix. Either way it lends authority to the report.)
    f. Avoid antagonizing the operating managers and personnel by reports which though factual nevertheless seem to them to present a biased pic-

ture. The most common form of such objectionable bias is an audit report which shows nothing but discrepancies. The stated objection is that "Most of what we do is right, but you would never learn that from the report."

Seriousness Classification

Some of the audit programs make use of seriousness classification of discrepancies. This is quite common in the case of product audits, where defects found are classified in terms such as critical, major, minor, each with some "weight" in the form of demerits. These systems of seriousness classification are highly standardized.[4]

Some audit programs also apply seriousness classification to discrepancies found in planning, in procedures, in decision making, data recording, etc. The approach parallels that used for product audits. Definitions are established for such terms as serious, major, and minor; demerit values are assigned; total demerits are computed.

Units of Measure

In product audits the usual unit of measure is *demerits per unit of product*. The actual demerits per unit for the current month is often compared against past history to observe trends. Sometimes it is compared with competitors' product to judge our quality vs. market quality. A major value of a measure such as demerits per unit is that it compares discrepancies found with the opportunity for discrepancies. Such an index appeals to operating personnel as eminently fair.

For audits of plans, procedures, documentation, etc., it is likewise desirable to compare the discrepancies found against some estimate of the opportunities for discrepancies. Some companies provide for this by an actual count of the opportunities, e.g., the number of criteria or check points called out by the plans and procedures. Another form is to count the discrepancies *per audit* with a correction factor based on the length of time consumed by the audit. The obvious reason is that more time spent in auditing means more ground covered and more discrepancies found.

Summaries for Systems

In some companies the auditors undertake to summarize their findings into evaluations of the systems which collectively make up the overall quality program. In the A.O. Smith Corporation[5] example, evaluations are made of 30 activities grouped into seven quality subsystems, e.g., vendor quality, final product quality, etc. The audits evaluate each subsystem in terms of excellent,

---

[4] See *Quality Control Handbook,* 3rd ed., pp. 12-20 to 12-26.
[5] See the reference by Toeppner in the Supplementary Reading.

good, fair, poor, or unsatisfactory. The results are then published for each plant and each division. Still other evaluations include the quality cost system and the annual quality plan.

When audit results are summarized by divisions or plants, they tend to become part of the evaluation of the personal performance of the division general manager or the plant manager. If, in addition, these results are contrasted with each other in company-wide reports, there arises an implied competition. This steps up interest in the reports and also subjects them to closer scrutiny. In some companies the audit reports may be the basis for "certifying" the plant as to quality. (This is increasingly a practice used by government regulators.)

PROBLEMS

22-1 Visit a food supermarket and observe the extent to which shoppers make use of their senses in securing quality assurance of the raw and packaged food products they buy. Report your findings.

22-2 Visit a market which sells technological consumer products, e.g., radio sets, television sets, hi-fi equipment, and observe the extent to which shoppers make use of their senses in securing quality assurance of the products they buy. Report your findings.

22-3 Visit an apartment building and discuss with the superintendent the various means in use for obtaining early warning of various potential dangers, e.g., burglary, fire. Report your findings.

22-4 List the early warning devices in use in a dwelling house. Report your findings.

22-5 Study the instrument panels for as many of the following vehicles as are accessible to you: bicycle, motorcycle, automobile, bus, railway locomotive, truck, airplane, steamship. Prepare a table showing for each vehicle the instruments in use, the control subjects, the unit of measure, the source of the data, and the standard (if any) for performance.

22-6 For any industrial company to which you have access, list the executive reports on quality, showing the control subjects, units of measure, source of the data, standard of performance, format for presentation, and frequency of reporting.

22-7 For any company or institution acceptable to the instructor, design a system of executive reporting on quality, including (1) choice of control subjects; (2) units of measure; (3) form of standard to be used; (4) plan for securing facts on actual performance; (5) plan for comparing performance against standard; (6) format for a coordinated instrument panel.

22-8 You are a quality manager. You issue regular executive reports showing performance on matters of quality. You have observed that the line managers are generally not responsive when the reports show need for them to take action. Copies of these reports go to the upper management, who are also generally not responsive. What do you propose as a way out of such an impasse?

22-9 You are the quality manager. On one of the product lines, the report shows that power consumption has risen from the usual level of 35.5 watts to a level of 35.9 watts. This difference is, without a doubt, statistically significant. However, the line manager has taken no action to investigate the reason for the change on the grounds that (1) the product still conforms to the specification limit of maximum 36.4 watts, and (2) he must give priority to several other products in which there are failures to comply with specification. What action do you take?

22-10 Visit a nearby facility which is a part of a chain of such facilities, e.g., food market, restaurant, motel, gasoline station, etc. You will likely find that it is subject to periodic quality audits from some headquarters. Obtain a copy of the auditor's checklist, study it, and report on its contents with respect to the various aspects of quality audits discussed in this chapter.

22-11 For any manufacturing company to which you have access, secure a copy of the quality audit. Study it and report on its contents with respect to the various aspects of quality audits discussed in this chapter.

22-12 You are the quality manager for a company making clothes washing machines for household use. You have decided to create a product audit and to do the auditing at the following stages:

1. After factory inspection and test.
2. Upon receipt by dealers.
3. Upon installation in the users' premises.

Prepare a plan for conducting the audit at any one of these stages.

SUPPLEMENTARY READING

The nature of assurance

Juran, J. M. (ed.), *Quality Control Handbook,* McGraw-Hill Book Company, New York, 1974, 3rd ed., pp. 2-23, 2-24, 21-4 to 21-6.

Reports on quality

Juran, J. M. (ed.), *Quality Control Handbook,* 3rd ed., pp. 21-20 to 21-32.
Juran, J. M., *Managerial Breakthrough,* McGraw-Hill Book Company, New York, 1964.
   The second half of this book deals with the management control process. Specific chapters deal with: Control—A Panoramic View; Choosing the Control Subject; The Unit of Measure; The Standard; The Sensor; Mobilizing for Decision Making; Interpretation; Decisions on the Difference; Taking Action.

Quality audits

Handbook H50, "Evaluation of a Contractor's Quality Program."
Handbook H51, "Evaluation of a Contractor's Inspection System."
Handbook H52, "Evaluation of a Contractor's Calibration System."

   These three Department of Defense handbooks constitute the broad instructions which guide government inspectors in their evaluation of quality programs or systems established by contractors. In each case the evaluation is made relative to the associated government specification, as follows:

Evaluation handbook	Government specification*
H50	MIL-Q-9858A, Quality Program Requirements
H51	MIL-I-45208A, Inspection System Requirements
H52	MIL-C-45662A, Calibration System Requirements

   * Available from Government Printing Office, Washington, D.C.

Juran, J. M. (ed.), *Quality Control Handbook,* 3rd ed., pp. 21-6 to 21-20.
Mills, Charles A., "In-Plant Quality Audit," *Quality Progress,* October 1976, pp. 23–25. Includes an example of a checklist as applied to methods and procedures.
Purcell, Warren R., "Sampling Techniques in Quality Systems Audits," *Quality Progress,* October 1968, pp. 13–16. A basic paper on use of sampling in quality audits.
"Quality Audit—Development and Administration." This is a training course given by the Education and Training Institute of the American Society for Quality Control, Milwaukee, Wis. It also provides a collection of papers and literature on the subject.

Toeppner, Thomas G., "Implementing a Corporate Quality Assurance Activity in a Multi-Product, Divisionalized Corporation," *1970 ASQC Annual Technical Conference Transactions*, pp. 1-12. Includes a system of quantifying the results of audit in A. O. Smith Corporation.

Wilson, Myron F., "The Quality Your Customer Sees," *Journal of the Electronics Division, ASQC*, July 1967, pp. 3-16. The Collins Radio Company approach, with emphasis on fitness for use. Includes a system for quantifying the results of audit.

EXAMPLES OF EXAMINATION QUESTIONS USED IN FORMER ASQC QUALITY ENGINEER CERTIFICATION EXAMINATIONS AS PUBLISHED IN *QUALITY PROGRESS* MAGAZINE

1 Which of the following is not a legitimate audit function? (*a*) identify function responsible for primary control and corrective action; (*b*) provide no surprises; (*c*) provide data on worker performance to supervision for punitive action; (*d*) contribute to a reduction in quality cost; (*e*) none of the above.

2 In many programs, what is generally the weakest link in the quality auditing program? (*a*) lack of adequate audit checklists; (*b*) scheduling of audits (frequency); (*c*) audit reporting; (*d*) follow-up of corrective action implementation.

3 What item(s) should be included by management when establishing a quality audit function within their organization? (*a*) proper positioning of the audit function within the quality organization; (*b*) a planned audit approach, efficient and timely audit reporting, and a method for obtaining effective corrective action; (*c*) selection of capable audit personnel; (*d*) management objectivity toward the quality program audit concept; (*e*) all of the above.

4 Assurance bears the same relation to the quality function that _____ does to the accounting function. (*a*) vacation; (*b*) audit; (*c*) variable overhead; (*d*) control.

5 All quality information reports should be audited periodically to: (*a*) determine their continued validity; (*b*) reappraise the routing or copy list; (*c*) determine their current effectiveness; (*d*) all of the above; (*e*) none of the above.

6 Which of the following techniques would not be used in a quality audit? (*a*) select samples only from completed lots; (*b*) examine samples from viewpoint of critical customer; (*c*) audit only those items which have caused customer complaints; (*d*) use audit information in future design planning; (*e*) frequency of audit to depend on economic and quality requirements.

7 Which of the following quality system provisions is of the *least* concern when preparing an audit checklist for the upcoming branch operation quality system audit: (*a*) drawing and print control; (*b*) makeup of the MRB (material review board); (*c*) engineering design change control; (*d*) control of special processes; (*e*) calibration of test equipment.

8 You are requested by top management to establish an audit program of the quality systems in each branch plant of your firm. Which of the following schemes would you use in selecting the audit team to optimize continuity, direction, availability, and technology transfer? (*a*) full-time audit staff; (*b*) all-volunteer audit staff; (*c*) the boss's son and son-in-law; (*d*) hybrid audit staff [a proportion of answers (*a*) and (*b*)]; (*e*) any of the above will make an effective audit team.

9 An audit will be viewed as a constructive service to the function which is audited when it: (*a*) is conducted by nontechnical auditors; (*b*) proposes corrective action for each item uncovered; (*c*) furnishes enough detailed facts so the necessary action can be determined; (*d*) is general enough to permit managerial intervention.

10 Which of the following is not a responsibility of the auditor? (*a*) prepare a plan and checklist; (*b*) report results to those responsible; (*c*) investigate deficiencies for cause and define the corrective action that must be taken; (*d*) follow up to see if the corrective action was taken; (*e*) none of the above.

TWENTY-THREE

POLICIES AND OBJECTIVES

23-1 THE NEED FOR QUALITY POLICIES

A policy is a broad guide to action.[1] It is a statement of principles. A policy differs from a procedure, which details *how* some activity shall be accomplished. Thus a quality policy might state that quality costs will be measured. The corresponding procedure would describe how the costs are to be measured.

In small organizations where one person makes all of the key decisions there is no need to formalize and document policies. The principles can be deduced from the actions of this manager.

As organizations grow, more and more managers are engaged in making significant decisions. These decisions affect numerous people inside and out of the organization, including the managers themselves. Unless there is consistency in these decisions, there is no predictability; neither insiders nor outsiders know what to expect. An impersonal way of creating this predictability is to think through, write down, and publish the policies, which then become the basis for consistent conduct. For those working within an organization, policies provide guidelines for conduct. For those external to the organization, policies help to understand what to expect from the organization.

---

[1] The word "policy" is not standardized as to meaning. In many companies the organization charts and the procedures for control are assembled into a manual called the "policy manual" or "policy and procedures manual."

23-2 SUBJECT MATTER OF QUALITY POLICIES

The most common form of quality policy statement is a brief declaration such as the following:

> It is the policy of the company to provide products and services of a quality that meets the initial and continuing needs and expectations of customers in relation to the price paid and to the nature of competitive offerings, and in doing so, to be the leader in product quality reputation.

No one quarrels with such a statement. However, it is regarded by most managers as too vague to provide guides for conduct. (Hence the name "motherhood" policies; i.e., everyone is in favor of motherhood.) To be useful, quality policies should provide specific guides to action for specific, important matters.

For example, in vendor relations there is much debate on whether the buyer should provide technical assistance to vendors and whether there should be exchange visits between the buyers' and vendors' engineers to see the respective processes. In the Johnson & Johnson written policy on vendor relations, the following are included among the company's responsibilities to its vendors:

> 5. To place, whenever possible, the facilities of our research, development, and technical services at the disposal of our suppliers in order to help them with any problems they may encounter in supplying materials to our specifications and to aid them in developing better means for production and quality improvement.
> 6. To encourage exchange visiting by our suppliers' technical personnel and our technical personnel to observe our respective plant operations, thereby promoting a better understanding of mutual problems and objectives.[2]

Such published statements make clear, both to the company's managers and to the vendors' managers, the relationship to be established.

The subject matter of quality policies must be tailormade for each company. However, some matters are fundamental and should be considered by any company which is about to prepare written quality policy. These fundamental topics include:

What level of clientele constitutes the company's market? (This bears directly on choice of quality of design or grade.)

Is the company to strive for quality leadership, competitiveness, or adequacy?

Is the company selling standard products, or is it selling a service in which the product is one of the ingredients of sale? (This affects the emphasis on conformance to specifications versus fitness for use.)

Is the company to market its products on the basis of high reliability at higher initial price or lower reliability at lower initial price?

---

[2] Quoted through the courtesy of Johnson & Johnson, New Brunswick, N.J.

Should the effort be to optimize users' costs or manufacturers' costs?
Should the "abilities" (reliability, maintainability, etc.) be quantified?
Should the company rely for its controls on systems or on people?
Should quality planning be done by staff or line people?
Should the vendor be put on the team?
Should top management actively participate in quality planning and assurance, or should it delegate this to someone else?

As the company grows to an extent which involves it in multiple markets and products, it becomes evident that no one set of quality policies can fit all company activities. This problem is solved by creating several levels of quality policy, e.g., a corporate policy and divisional policies. The corporate policy applies companywide. It lists the subjects that are to be contained in the policies created by each division. Such subjects might include the preparation of a formal quality program, publishing of a quality manual that includes responsibilities, procedures, etc., and the provision for audit to determine the extent to which plans are adequate and are being followed. Policies can also be created for programmed activities such as reliability or for activities within functional departments.

23-3 EXAMPLES OF QUALITY POLICIES

Policies do *not* have to be vague. They can be specific enough to provide useful guidance. For example, the following corporate quality policies were prepared for discussion at a health products company:[3]

1. At both the corporate and plant levels, the Quality Control Department shall be independent of the Production function.
2. The company shall place a new product on the market only if its overall quality is superior to competition.
3. All tasks necessary to achieve superior quality shall be taken but each task shall be evaluated to assure that the investment has a tangible effect on quality.
4. Specific quality responsibilities for all company areas including top management shall be defined in writing.
5. Quality activities shall emphasize the prevention of quality problems rather than only detection and correction.
6. Quality and reliability shall be defined and measured in quantitative terms.
7. All quality parameters and tests shall reflect customer needs, usage conditions and regulatory requirements.
8. Total company costs associated with achieving quality objectives shall be periodically measured.
9. Technical assistance shall be provided to suppliers to improve their quality control programs.
10. Each quality task responsibility defined for a functional department shall have a written procedure describing how the task will be performed.

[3] Consulting practice of Frank M. Gryna, Jr.

11. The company shall propose to regulating agencies or other organizations any additions or changes to industry practice that will insure a minimum acceptable quality of products.
12. Each year, quality objectives shall be defined for corporate, division and plant activities and shall include both product objectives and objectives on tasks in the company quality program.
13. All levels of management shall have a defined quality motivation program for the employees in their department.

These policies were prepared to provide guidelines for (1) planning the overall quality program, and (2) defining the action to be taken in situations for which personnel had requested guidance.

After analyzing several years experience in reliability programs on different projects, an aerospace company evolved the following reliability policies:[4]

1. Reliability is an element of product performance distinct from capability. Capability is the ability of a product to perform a function. Reliability is the ability to perform the function *repeatedly* or when called upon to do so.
2. A reliability program must start in the proposal phase of a project and continue throughout design and development, production, test, field evaluation, and service use. This means that the program cannot be restricted to any one organizational unit, but must cover all units that affect the final field reliability.
3. Adequate funds must be provided for a reliability program and these must be determined during the proposal phase. This means that a complete reliability program must be developed in sufficient detail during the proposal effort to permit adequate costing.
4. The execution of a reliability program involves both technical tasks and a management task. The technical tasks consist of the efforts to design reliability into the product and maintain this reliability throughout production and field use of the product with minimum degradation. The management task consists of integrating all of the technical efforts, and controlling these efforts to assure that all necessary steps are being taken to achieve the required reliability.
5. Reliability *results* can only be achieved by actions taken by the line organization—the designer, the production man, the procurement man, etc. The reliability specialist provides guidance and assistance to the line personnel in executing their fundamental reliability tasks.
6. The program for each project must provide a written plan and must specify responsibility, procedures, and schedules.
7. The program must include controls which will detect and report to management all deviations between plans and actual performance.
8. The program must include suppliers as well as internal operations.
9. The overall integration and evaluation of the reliability program must be performed by an organization which is independent of those who are responsible for taking the detailed steps necessary to achieve the required reliability.

Once published, these policies were instrumental in gaining agreement on the reliability approach for new products.

Policies may also be needed within a functional department. For example,

[4] Frank M. Gryna, Jr., "Total Quality Control through Reliability," *1960 ASQC Annual Technical Conference Transactions*, pp. 295–301.

policies for use within a quality control department might include statements such as:

1. The amount of inspection of incoming parts and materials shall be based on criticality and a quantitative analysis of vendor history.
2. The evaluation of new products for release to production shall include an analysis of data for compliance to performance requirements and shall also include an evaluation of overall fitness for use including reliability, maintainability, and ease of user operation.
3. The evaluation of new products for compliance to performance requirements shall be made to defined numerical limits of performance.
4. Vendors shall be supplied with a written statement of all quality requirements before a contract is signed.
5. Burn-in testing is not a cost-effective method of eliminating failures and shall only be used on the first units of a new product type (or a major modification of an existing product) in order to get rapid knowledge of problems.

Note that these examples of policies state (1) a principle to be followed, or (2) *what* is to be done but not *how* it is to be done. The "how" is described in a procedure. Often it is best to have a *policy* instead of a procedure in order to provide needed flexibility for different situations.

23-4 FORMULATION OF QUALITY POLICIES

The concept of policies is accepted as beneficial by most personnel, but the complaint is often made that "management doesn't give us guidance in certain activities." Thus management is blamed for the lack of policies. In quality matters, as in other matters, management cannot be expected to recognize the need for and create the specifics of policies. The *process* of formulating policies requires that the key managers have the opportunity for participation but without the burden of performing the detailed staff work. One way to do this is to assign to a specialist the job of securing from the key managers:

1. Their nominations for what should be the subject matter contained in quality policies.
2. Their judgment as to what should be the direction of the company with respect to these subjects.

Through this method it is possible to discover the consensus among the key managers for the various subjects. A draft prepared in the light of this consensus then contains the basis for a meeting of the minds, even on abstract matters. This draft is prepared by the quality specialist for the review and approval of management.

The trend toward written quality policies has been accelerated by major forces. The forces include the dependence of consumers on a wider variety of products than in the past, liability matters, complex weapon systems, and government regulations. It is likely that this trend will continue.

Before a policy is published, it is well to face realistically the question: "Do we intend to adhere to this policy?" If there is doubt about this, the policy should not be published.

In the long run, insiders and outsiders alike draw their conclusions about company policy from the deeds. If, in addition, there is written policy and it conforms to the deeds, the written policy gains credibility. If, however, the written policy differs from the deeds, what is believed is the deeds. Not only does the written policy lose its credibility, but other pronouncements of the company become suspect as well. So important is the need for adherence to published policy that most companies establish audits to provide a feedback on how well the policies are being followed.

Finally, it should be recognized that policies are not cast in concrete and that provisions should be made for changes.

23-5 QUALITY OBJECTIVES

An objective is a statement of the desired result to be achieved within a specified time. Whereas *policies* provide broad guidelines on company affairs, *objectives* define specific goals. These goals then form the basis of detailed planning of activities. Objectives can be short range (say, 1 year) or long range (say, 5 years). The concept of *management by objectives* is widespread. Under this concept, managers participate in establishing objectives, which are then reduced to writing and become the basis of planning for results. Anderson describes the application of the MBO approach to quality.[5]

Objectives may be created for breakthrough or control. There are many reasons why companies create objectives for breakthrough:

1. They wish to attain or hold quality leadership.
2. They have identified some opportunities to improve income through superior fitness for use.
3. They are losing share of market through lack of competitiveness.
4. They have too many field troubles—failures, complaints, returns—and wish to reduce these as well as cutting the external costs resulting from guarantee charges, investigation expense, product discounts, etc.
5. They have identified some projects which offer internal cost-reduction opportunities, e.g., improvement of process yields or reduction of scrap, rework, inspection, or testing.
6. They have a poor image with customers, vendors, the public, or other groups of outsiders.

[5] Douglas N. Anderson, "Quality Motivation through Management by Objectives," *1971 ASQC Annual Technical Conference Transactions*, pp. 7–14.

7. There is internal dissension and the need to improve motivation and morale.

Objectives for breakthrough are not limited to "hardware" or to matters that can be counted, e.g., income, cost. Objectives for breakthrough can include projects such as a reliability training program for designers, a vendor rating plan, a complaint investigation manual, a reorganization of the quality control staff, or a new executive report on quality.

Some examples of corporate quality objectives prepared for a health products company for the coming year were:[6]

1. Quality costs for the company shall be reduced by _____ percent.
2. The material loss for the company shall not exceed _____.
3. The average leak rate for _____ product shall be reduced to _____.
4. The company shall have _____ Certified Quality Engineers.
5. Quality costs shall be determined for at least one product.
6. A specific in-process quality data analysis technique shall be developed and implemented for at least one product.
7. Numerical reliability and maintainability objectives shall be defined for at least one product.
8. A procedure that assures that all corporate product specifications are reviewed by the plants before plant production planning starts shall be implemented.
9. A procedure that assures that all specifications for suppliers are agreed to by the supplier before finalization of the purchasing contract shall be implemented.
10. A quality procedures manual shall be developed.
11. The President or Senior Vice President shall make at least _____ visits to customers to review product quality.

Note that these statements include a quantification either in terms of a product characteristic or a date (the end of the calendar year). These objectives cover both product characteristics and tasks in the overall company quality program. Quality objectives can also be created for individual departments.

Managers have many reasons for *avoiding* breakthrough. In such cases the objectives are to hold the status quo, i.e., maintain control at present levels. The more usual reasons for choosing control are that:

1. The managers believe that improvement is uneconomic; i.e., the cost of trying for breakthrough would not be recovered.
2. Present performance is competitive. Many managers regard "the market" as a sound standard since it embodies the breakthrough efforts of competitors.
3. There are few alarm signals—e.g., few complaints or internal flareups—to suggest the need for breakthrough.
4. There is need for breakthrough but it is not timely to undertake it because (a) there has been no agreement on the specific projects to be tackled or (b) the climate for quality breakthrough is unfavorable (e.g., too many other

[6] Consulting practice of Frank M. Gryna, Jr.

programs going; some key manager is not convinced; the breakthrough would require risky technological research).

The more usual objectives for control include holding the materials, processes, and products to specification; holding the field failures, complaints, returns, and other external performance measures to current levels; holding costs of inspection, test, scrap, rework, and other internal costs to current levels; holding the gains achieved by recent breakthrough projects.

23-6 FORMULATION OF QUALITY OBJECTIVES

In small organizations, the chief executive can determine what the quality needs are by personal observation and the executive can then set quality objectives accordingly. In large organizations this is not possible. For this situation one approach creates an interdepartmental mechanism to identify potential objectives, estimates their economic and other results, and determines their relative priorities.

Quality objectives can be identified from a variety of inputs, such as the following:

Pareto analysis (see Section 2-5) of repetitive external alarm signals (field failures, complaints, returns, etc.).

Pareto analysis of repetitive internal alarm signals (scrap, rework, sorting, 100 percent test, etc.).

Proposals from key insiders—managers, supervisors, professionals, union stewards.

Proposals from suggestion schemes.

Field study of users' needs, costs.

Data on performance of products versus competitors (from users and from laboratory tests).

Comments of key people outside the company (customers, vendors, journalists, critics).

Findings and comments of government regulators, independent laboratories, reformers.

Analysis of these inputs requires, as in formulating policies, a mechanism that gives the managers the opportunity for participation in setting objectives without the burden of performing the detailed staff work. Quality control engineers and other staff specialists are assigned the job of analyzing the available inputs and of creating any essential missing inputs. These analyses point to potential projects which are then proposed. The proposals are reviewed by managers at progressively higher organization levels. At each level there is summary and consolidation until the corporate level is reached. The foregoing process is similar to that used in preparing the annual financial budget.

23-7 THE ANNUAL QUALITY PROGRAM

In recent decades, the quality function has emerged as a major company function. So important a function now requires top-management leadership, but the leadership of the quality function has traditionally been delegated to middle managers. To give the leadership of the quality function to top management requires the creation of new management tools, and one of these is the annual quality program.

The annual quality program includes the policies, objectives, plans, and other elements of a broad approach for defining what needs to be done and how to do it.The annual quality program is similar to the annual financial budget, a device that enables top management to participate in the formation of financial policies, objectives, and plans and thereby to give leadership to the finance function. The budgeting process involves (1) a long-range program, (2) a broad estimate by top management of objectives for the next year, and (3) a coordinator to obtain departmental inputs, prepare the overall budget for management review, and report the results attained against budget.

The long-range program identifies challenges and opportunities for the future, outlines the broad responses needed, and establishes the quality goal for 5 to 10 years in the future. The program could include (but not be limited to) such matters as emphasizing fitness for use rather than conformance to specifications, optimizing user costs, and providing for top-management participation in quality planning.

The short-range program evaluates the present position with respect to quality, establishes the objectives for the coming year, and spells out the steps needed to reach those objectives. The short-range quality program includes objectives to increase sales (e.g., superior quality of design, superior availability) and objectives for reducing costs (e.g., reduced scrap, rework, and complaints).

A coordinator for the annual quality program would typically be the quality control department and would do the following:

Prepare a standard format for structuring the departmental programs.
Provide technical assistance to the departments during their programming.
Summarize the departmental programs for review by higher management.
Publish the final approved program.
Report results achieved against the objectives.

In this way the quality control department acts as the right hand of management for quality matters in a manner analogous to the role played by the finance department for financial matters.

The concept of the annual quality program is relatively new but provides the quality control department with the opportunity to provide leadership for a program that integrates all company efforts needed to achieve fitness for use.[7]

---

[7] For further elaboration see *Quality Control Handbook,* 3rd ed., pp. 6-14 to 6-19.

PROBLEMS

23-1 For an institution with which you are familiar, propose a list of five subjects for which quality policies are needed. For each subject, propose two alternative policies for consideration.

23-2 For an institution with which you are familiar, propose a list of five subjects for which quality objectives are needed. For each subject, propose one specific objective for consideration.

23-3 For a steel and wire manufacturer, provide an example of specific policies and objectives for each of the following subjects:

1. Quality costs.
2. Training in process control for production personnel.
3. Selection of suppliers.
4. In-process inspection.
5. Final inspection.

23-4 Many institutions have a general statement called a "quality policy." Often this is vague and states that the institution will supply the customer with "high-quality product." Obtain an example of such a statement and explain how it could be made more specific.

SUPPLEMENTARY READING

Quality Control Handbook, 3rd ed., McGraw-Hill Book Company, New York, 1974, sec. 3, covers quality policies and objectives. Additional material is presented in relation to quality leadership (pp. 4-15, 4-16), quality planning (pp. 6-1, 6-2, 6-7), vendor relations (pp. 10-4 to 10-6), market research (p. 14-7), computer organization (p. 20-37), and audits (pp. 21-6, 21-7).

TWENTY-FOUR

ORGANIZATION FOR QUALITY

24-1 QUALITY-RELATED TASKS

Attainment of quality requires the performance of many specialized quality-related tasks.[1] Contrary to widespread opinion, these tasks are *not* performed solely by a quality control department. Instead, many of these tasks are carried out as part of each of the numerous activities shown in the "spiral" (Figure 1-1) as well as among the coordinating activities. Table 24-1 gives some examples of these quality-related tasks.[2]

Some quality control tasks are sufficiently time-consuming to occupy the full time of employees, e.g., inspector, tester. Other such tasks are performed on a part-time basis by persons whose main job is doing something else, e.g., designer, production operator. One of the major problems in organizing for quality consists of:

Identifying the quality tasks which need to be performed.
Assigning clear responsibility for the performance of these tasks to specific departments.
Within specific departments, designing logical parcels of work to be assigned to individuals. These bundles of work are called "jobs."

---

[1] Another name for these quality-related tasks is "quality control work elements." See, in this connection, "The Basic Elements of Quality Control Engineering," American Society for Quality Control, 1961.

[2] For elaboration, see J. M. Juran (ed.), *Quality Control Handbook,* 3rd ed., McGraw-Hill Book Company, New York, 1974, pp. 7-2 to 7-4.

Table 24-1 Examples of quality control tasks

Activity shown on Figure 1-1, the "spiral"	Example of quality control task associated with that activity
Product development	Study customer needs for parameters of fitness for use
Product design	Conduct reliability analysis
Purchasing	Determine quality competence of prospective vendors
Manufacturing planning	Determine capability of processes to hold tolerances
Inspection and test	Prepare inspection manuals, systems, procedures
Field service	Respond to customer calls for service

There is a logic in how to organize, i.e., how to choose the department which is to perform specific quality tasks, and how to design jobs. This logic is based on considerations such as:

The extent to which the departments have been trained to perform the work.
The prior record of the departments in adapting to new assignments.
The general philosophy of the company in work assignment, e.g., use of staff personnel for planning.
The volume of work: greater volume leads to creation of more full-time jobs devoted to specialized tasks.

The variable nature of these considerations means that the job of organizing is never finished. Changes in volume of work, in growth of technology, etc., require corresponding changes in organization structure.

24-2 EVOLUTION OF THE INSPECTION DEPARTMENT

In earliest industrial history the productive unit was the artisan in the one-person shop. The artisan performed all tasks around the spiral, including the quality control tasks. (The exception was use of the product.)

With growth of industry, the shops grew to an extent such that the dominant productive unit was the multiartisan shop headed by a master. Now some of the quality control tasks grew and became so time-consuming that the master delegated their performance to an assistant. One of these tasks was that of examining the work in process to see whether the apprentices were learning to do their work correctly. Another such task was to examine the finished product to assure that it was fit for use before offering it for sale. The job of full-time shop inspector evolved in this way. So did the job of construction inspector (see Figure 24-1) though under a somewhat different chain of events. Prior to the Industrial Revolution, the chief form of recognition of quality-oriented tasks was through the full-time jobs of inspector and tester.

Note that the master of the shop was also the owner of the enterprise. As such, his or her income was dependent on product fitness for use. Under the

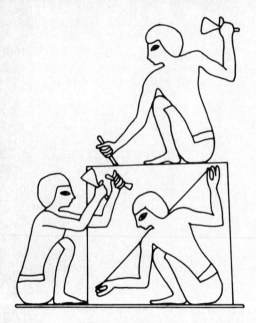

Figure 24-1 Ancient construction inspector.

circumstances, supervision of the shop inspector was done with an eye on the goals of the enterprise—to secure income by selling products which were fit for use.

Following the Industrial Revolution, the large factories became the dominant productive units. These large factories were organized into multiple production shops, e.g., foundry, machine shop, assembly. Each of these shops was supervised by a foreman (or similar title) and each had needs for product inspection. Usually, these needs were extensive enough to require full-time inspectors. In such cases the inspectors were made responsible to the shop foremen, as shown in the organization chart (Figure 24-2). This organization form was virtually a carryover from the forms prevailing before the Industrial Revolution.

The responsibilities of a foreman of a "captive shop" were obviously narrower than those of the proprietor of an independent shop. The latter had responsibility for general management, finance, and purchasing as well as for manufacture. However, in the early days of the factory system, the foreman's responsibilities for manufacture were quite broad, resembling those held now by a plant manager.

Over the decades that followed, the foreman's responsibilities were progressively narrowed, particularly with the rise of the Taylor system of "scientific management." This system involved a separation of planning from execution, and generally left the foreman with the narrow responsibility of executing plans and meeting goals prepared by the planners.[3]

[3] For elaboration, see *Quality Control Handbook,* 3rd ed., pp. 18-17, 18-18. See also J. M. Juran, "The Taylor System and Quality Control." This series of articles appeared in *Quality Progress* during the seven months May to December 1973.

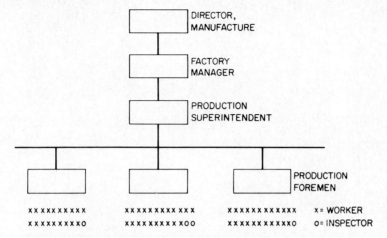

Figure 24-2 Organization for inspection, early factories.

The Taylor system placed great stress on productivity. In theory, the incentives for productivity provided for protection of quality. In practice, quality was jeopardized because the shop inspectors remained subordinate to foremen, whose first priority was to increase productivity. This weakness in organization was dramatized during World War I when much unfit product was delivered to the military customers. The response of many companies was to take the inspectors out of the production departments and to make them responsible to full-time inspection supervisors. In turn, these inspection supervisors were made responsible to the newly created office of chief inspector. The resulting organization chart for the early inspection departments is shown in Figure 24-3.

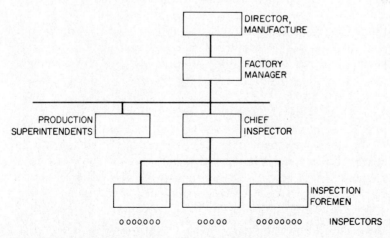

Figure 24-3 Creation of central inspection department.

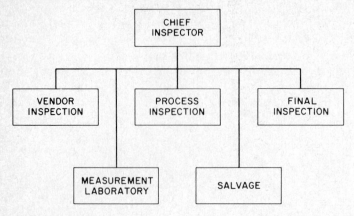

Figure 24-4 Early central inspection department, mechanical and electronic industries.

In the mechanical and electronic industries this early inspection department evolved further by adding new responsibilities such as disposition of non-conforming products (salvage) and, especially, the activities associated with product measurement: metrology; design of instruments, gages, and test equipment; maintenance of accuracy of measuring equipment; etc. Figure 24-4 shows an early form of such an inspection department.

The process industries tended to depart from this pattern by creating two types of inspection organization:

1. A laboratory for performing critical tests, e.g., product safety, structural integrity, functional fitness for use. This laboratory reported to the technical organization.
2. An inspection department for noncritical qualities, e.g., esthetic. This department reported to the manufacturing organization.

Figure 24-5 shows the typical organization form as evolved in the process industries.

As the chief inspectors solidified their organization status and as they gained experience, they began to become involved with other activities around the spiral. This movement accelerated during the 1940s, as discussed below.

24-3 EVOLUTION OF THE QUALITY CONTROL HIERARCHY

Prior to the 1940s there had been much discussion on evolving means for preventing defects from happening in the first place. Some chief inspectors had begun to take steps to establish data systems to provide a basis for prevention studies. Others had begun to become involved in quality planning, although much of this was in reality planning for inspection. These early steps toward prevention were accelerated during the 1940s by the quality problems asso-

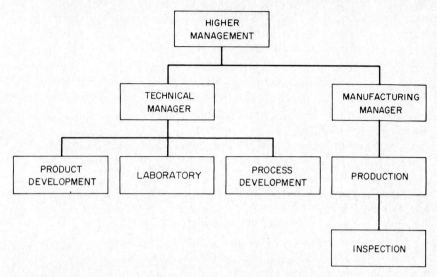

Figure 24-5 Early organization for inspection and test, process industries.

ciated with World War II and by the rise of the movement known as statistical quality control.

Effect of World War II

During World War II the manufacturing companies experienced great difficulties and delays in making defense products fit for use. The inability to deliver came dramatically to the attention of the upper managers. It became evident that whenever manufacturers undertook a drastic change in processes and products (such as was involved in the changeover to defense products) there was need for a systematic approach to quality planning and to defect prevention.

Following World War II there was a second major changeover, this time back to manufacture of civilian products. Again there were severe problems of making products fit for use. One result was a severe letdown in quality standards during the several years of shortages that followed the end of the war. What emerged was a new level of awareness by managers that attainment of quality demanded a level of planning and analysis much more extensive and formal than had ever been prior practice. It remained to find ways of organizing to perform this planning and analysis.

The Statistical Quality Control Movement

Prior to the 1940s various investigators in Europe and the United States had been looking into the possibility of applying statistical methodology to the problems of industrial quality control. The most extensive of these investigations were those carried out by Bell Telephone Laboratories, involving mainly (1) use of probability theory in sampling, and (2) use of significance theory in process control. During World War II these techniques were widely disseminated through courses conducted for industrial companies by the War Production Board. This same dissemination contributed to the formation of an American Society for Quality Control, to the establishment of a specialized literature, and to the beginnings of "professionalism" among the practitioners associated with the quality function.

Many of the attendees at the War Production Board courses attempted to apply the statistical techniques to their company's quality problems. Their enthusiasm and overenthusiasm resulted in so much uneconomic application that the movement suffered a setback. Nevertheless, the basic concept of a scientific approach to quality planning and analysis was sound and has endured. However, the specialists who later emerged to dominate the applications were mostly engineers rather than statisticians. As these engineers were appointed, it became necessary to choose a job title. What evolved as a consensus was the title "quality control engineer."

Quality Control Engineering and Quality Manager

It also became necessary to decide where on the organization chart to place quality control engineers. The dominant solution was to create a new department of Quality Control Engineering and to associate it with the Inspection Department by creating a new office—that of Quality Manager. The resulting form of organization as adopted in mechanical and electronic industries is shown on Figure 24-6.

The process industries also created departments of quality control engineering and offices of quality manager. However, they tended to assign these

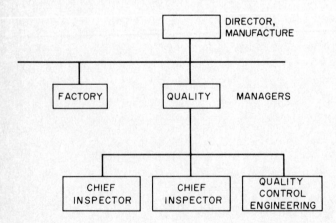

Figure 24-6 Organization for prevention, mechanical and electronic industries.

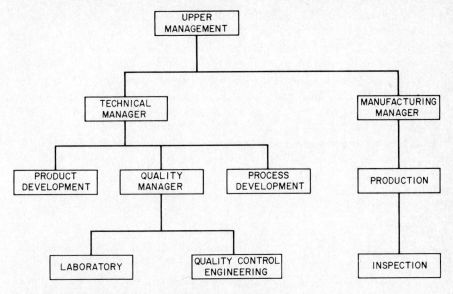

Figure 24-7 Organization for prevention, process industries.

new organizations to the technical side of the company, as exemplified in Figure 24-7.

Reliability Engineering

The 1950s marked a sharp acceleration of the previous trend to use of "complex systems," e.g., computers, advanced military systems, advanced aerospace systems, etc. As these systems went into use, they exhibited unacceptable field failure rates. Moreover, these field failures had their origin mainly in the original product development and design rather than in manufacturing errors.

To deal with this new major source of field failures there emerged a new specialty which came to be known as "reliability engineering." The specialists, who came to be known as "reliability engineers," offered to minimize the field failure rates by applying skills in design review, reliability quantification, environmental testing, structuring of reliability data systems, etc. Many companies accepted the offer and created the title of reliability engineer for the specialists. Some companies also created a new department of Reliability Engineering. (Other companies did not; instead, they placed the reliability engineers in the same department with the quality control engineers.)

The creation of the new specialty required also a decision as to where in the organization to locate it. There were various alternatives, and all were tried out.[4] Some reliability engineers are now to be found in the design engineering

---

[4] For elaboration, see *Quality Control Handbook*, 3rd ed., pp. 7-8, 7-9.

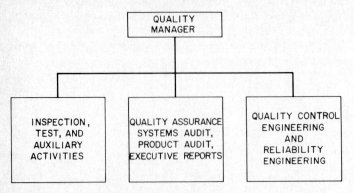

Figure 24-8 Organization form providing for reliability engineering and quality assurance.

departments carrying out activities such as qualification of components. However, most of them are found in the organization of the quality manager, the two most common forms being those in Figures 24-8 and 24-9. In the former, the reliability engineers share a common department with the quality control engineers, resulting in little change in the hierarchy.

In the form shown in Figure 24-9 there is a separate department of Reliability Engineering. There is also a separate department for Quality Assurance (see below). In addition, the head of the quality hierarchy is now a major manager who reports directly to the General Manager rather than to some intermediate manager. This organization form has become impressive in two ways:

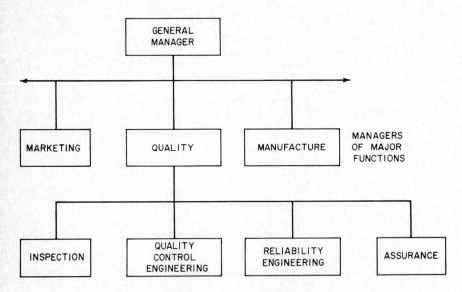

Figure 24-9 Organization of broad-based quality control department.

1. It has given unprecedented stature to the head of the quality control hierarchy.
2. It has become (during the mid-1970s) the majority organization form among the large manufacturing companies in the United States.

Quality Assurance

The 1960s witnessed an extensive growth of product safety legislation, liability suits, consumerism, and related phenomena. Collectively, these stimulated a growth in the use of forms of quality assurance, notably independent audits. The need for independence suggested that a separate quality assurance department be created, and this has become a widely used form.

Locating the quality assurance department in the hierarchy has involved use of the two organization forms shown in Figures 24-8 and 24-9. As noted, the latter is now the dominant form in large companies.

The Growing List of Activities

The emergence of the quality control hierarchy as a major company function is the historical result of adding more and more activities to the scope of the quality control department. Table 24-2 shows a list of these activities in their approximate chronological order. A study of the list makes clear that with each addition the quality manager has been exposed to more and more of the activities around the spiral. In addition, he has been exposed to other activities not shown on the "spiral" of Figure 1-1, e.g., industrial relations, finance, accounting, government regulation, etc.

Given such a broad list of activities, it is understandable why the stature of the job has risen—a broader pyramid means a higher apex. In addition, the list in Table 24-2 makes clear why the quality manager has increasingly become one of the logical means of coordinating all quality activities around the spiral.

24-4 THE QUALITY CONTROL ORGANIZATION IN PRACTICE

There is no "right" way to organize, i.e., there is no standard pattern of organization which fits all situations. Instead, consideration must be given to the benefits and detriments of the various alternatives. Since these benefits and detriments cannot be evaluated with precision, the final decision contains a degree of subjectivity. (It is probably more important for organization to be clear than to be "logical.")

The Single-Location Profit Center

A *profit center* is an autonomous business unit in which the general manager has command of those departments which determine the overall performance

Table 24-2 Activities assigned to quality control departments

Activity	Usual responsibility
Product inspection; final; process; vendor	Command
Measurement control	Command
Field complaint analysis	Analysis
Quality planning	Coordination
Inspection planning	Command
Statistical methodology	Consulting; analysis
Process control	Planning; assurance
Defect prevention programs	Planning; coordination
Analysis of causes of defects	Analysis; consulting
Vendor surveillance	Planning; assurance
Quality cost analysis	Planning; analysis
New product reviews; reliability; other abilities	Analysis; consulting
Motivational programs	Planning; coordination
Assurance	Planning; analysis
In process of evolution	
Quality policies and objectives	Coordination
Annual quality program	Analysis; coordination
Organization studies	Analysis; coordination
Customer viewpoint; consumerism; product liability	Analysis; coordination
Quality income studies	Analysis
Executive reports	Analysis; coordination
Inspection by operators	Analysis; audit
Government controls on quality	Coordination
Training for quality—all levels, functions	Planning; coordination

of that business unit, i.e., product design, manufacture, marketing, quality control, etc. This profit center may be an entire company or it may be an autonomous division of a large company. Where this profit center conducts all its affairs at one location, it is quite usual to organize for quality in the form shown in Figure 24-9. This form gives the quality manager command of the inspectors as well as the staff specialists. The need for such command is sometimes debatable. However, in the case of single-location profit centers, the continuing presence of the quality manager eliminates the frequent objection that day-to-day decision making will be delayed (owing to supervision by an absentee quality manager).

Coordination without Command

There are numerous situations in which quality-oriented tasks are performed by personnel who are not under the command of the quality control department. Production operators usually carry out process control; sometimes they perform product inspection as well. Full-time product inspectors sometimes report to production supervisors. Field failure data are collected and often processed by the field service department. Studies of competitors' quality may be conducted by the market research department. In these and other cases it is entirely feasible to secure adequate coordination without the need to impose command by the quality manager. This is accomplished by the effective and widely used formula shown in Table 24-3.

Under this formula there are two elements of coordination by the quality control department. The first is through participation in the design of the plan of how to attain quality—what tasks need to be performed, what are the criteria to be met. This plan is often drafted by specialists from the quality control department. However, it requires the approval of the line department before it becomes effective.

Once the plan is agreed upon, execution is delegated to the line department. This gives the line supervisor command of the personnel assigned to perform the day-to-day tasks needed to carry out the plan. Such command also enables the line supervisor to coordinate performance of the quality-oriented tasks with other tasks in the department. This coordination facilitates meeting the goals of productivity, schedule, etc., as well as quality.

The second element of coordination by the quality control department is the audit. This audit determines whether the execution is following the agreed plan. In addition, the findings of the audit are made available to the upper supervision to provide them with assurance that quality is being maintained (see Chapter 22).

Multiple Plant Organization

Many profit centers involve multiple plant locations, and sometimes these locations are widely scattered. For reasons of day-to-day control, each plant has a laboratory and an inspection force physically located at the plant site. The question then arises—Should the laboratory (and/or inspection force) report to the plant manager or to some divisional quality control department? There are two major organization responses:

1. The laboratories report to the division quality manager.
2. The laboratories report to the respective plant managers under an arrangement of "coordination without command," as shown in Table 24-3. Use of such an arrangement requires that the company define with precision what is included in the term "audit."

Table 24-3 Matrix for coordination without command

Activity	Responsibility for conducting this activity	
	Line department	Quality control
Prepare quality plan	×	×
Execute plan	×	
Audit to assure that execution follows plan		×

For example, a food-processing company established small processing plants in food-growing areas. Each plant was equipped with a laboratory for control of quality. These laboratories reported to the plant managers under the plan shown in Table 24-3. The audit included the following provisions:

1. Plant laboratory data were summarized weekly and sent to the central quality control office for review.
2. Duplicate samples were sent to the central office to be tested, using the concept of "audit of decisions."
3. Surveillance of plants and laboratories was maintained by the central office through periodic visits.
4. Disposition of nonconforming lots became a responsibility of the central quality control office. (Such lots constituted less than 2 percent of regular production.)

Under this arrangement the plant managers had complete day-to-day decision making relative to more than 98 percent of the production, which gave them effective control of day-to-day affairs. However, the plant managers were in no position to jeopardize fitness for use since they did not have the last word on disposition of nonconforming products.

Multidivisional Organization

Large companies are usually organized into autonomous divisions, each based on some product line, marketing channel, or other commonality. With rare exceptions, each of such autonomous divisions has its own quality control department, as shown in Figure 24-10.

Except in "conglomerate" companies, there exists some broad community

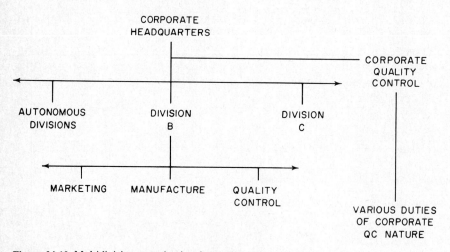

Figure 24-10 Multidivision organization for quality.

of interest among the divisions due to interdivisional sales, common technology, common brand name for marketing, etc. Such community of interest requires some form of coordination as to quality and other matters. With respect to quality, this coordination is supplied in a variety of ways:

1. Through an informal council of quality managers which, though lacking formal organization status, is nevertheless accepted by the quality managers and by upper management.
2. Through a formal council of quality managers such as has existed in IBM Corporation and the Dutch Philips Gloeilampenfabrieken. In such cases the duties of the council are defined and legitimized.
3. Through a corporate quality manager (see Figure 24-10 and discussion below).

Lacking any of these forms, there is no provision for coordination other than the contacts made as crises develop.

Multinational Organization

In some companies the divisions include foreign subsidiaries which derive autonomy from their status under local laws as well as from their status as profit centers. Nevertheless, these subsidiaries must maintain important ties to the parent company on matters of quality due to commonality in technology, markets, quality reputation, etc. The necessary coordination is usually provided by a parent company staff department organized as shown in Figure 24-11. This staff department carries out a variety of activities of a service, coordination, and assurance nature:

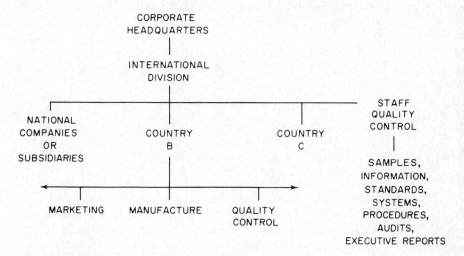

Figure 24-11 Multinational organization for quality.

Disseminating specifications and know-how as to materials, processes, and products.

Preparation of supplemental standards through use of international committees.

Filling requests for information and providing a degree of consulting service.

Checking product samples where the nature of the product permits easy shipment.

Receiving laboratory test reports and publishing comparative test results.

Auditing performance of subsidiaries through periodic visits.

Organizing periodic international conferences for discussion of mutual problems.

24-5 COORDINATION OF THE QUALITY FUNCTION

In tiny companies the owner coordinates all activities, including those related to attainment of quality. This coordination is done almost instinctively through the owner's personal participation in all essential activities.

As the company grows larger and larger, the work of attaining quality is divided among the various departments which collectively carry out the quality activities around the spiral. These departments, with the best of intentions, pursue departmental goals which can, and sometimes do, take precedence over attainment of quality. The quality activities become so numerous that the head of the company cannot possibly participate in all of them. Hence coordination by the head of the company disappears and some other form of coordination must be evolved.

(Personal coordination by the head of the company remains possible *provided* that there is created the quality equivalent of the annual financial budget and the periodic financial reports.)

The approach used for interdepartmental coordination takes two major forms:

1. Coordination for *control* is achieved primarily through employment of the feedback loop and through repetitive-use plans such as procedures and routines.
2. Coordination for *creating change* is achieved primarily through use of the project concept.

Coordination for Control

All control involves use of the feedback loop (Figure 11-4), which compares actual performance to standard and which sounds the alarm if the deficiency is too great. Much of the effort needed for coordination for control goes into setting up the numerous feedback loops and alarm systems for detecting quality deficiencies. These feedback loops take such forms as sampling to evaluate process and product quality, control charts, periodic check of calibration of measuring instruments, reports on quality, audits, etc.

Establishment of these feedback loops requires interdepartmental coordination. Usually, a committee or a staff department drafts up a proposal which is then reviewed by all concerned, amended, and approved. The approved version becomes a repetitive-use plan—a sort of impersonal coordinator. This succeeds because all have participated in creating the plan in the first place. Such plans are called "procedures," "routines," etc., and are very widely used in industry and elsewhere.

These procedures are deliberately designed to avoid burdening the managers and supervisors with the tasks of day-to-day control. Such tasks are delegated to nonsupervisors and automated devices, thereby freeing the time of the managers for matters which cannot be so delegated. However, when the alarms are sounded, the corrective action needed often requires participation by the supervisory hierarchy. This participation also requires some form of interdepartmental coordination.

Sometimes this coordination is on a crisis-by-crisis basis. Someone whose goals are threatened (e.g., a manager, a project engineer) takes the initiative to convene a meeting. Usually, such a meeting then sets in motion a train of events which ends up in corrective action.

Alternatively, the coordination may be through a standing committee. For example, in most companies there is a continuing procession of nonconforming lots of product. Each one of these requires a decision as to fitness for use plus associated actions, e.g., preventing a recurrence. In many companies there is a continuing committee (Material Review Board or similar name) to make these decisions and to take the associated actions.

Coordination for Creating Change

The enterprise is constantly engaged in creating beneficial change as well as preventing adverse change. These beneficial changes involve such matters as launching new product designs, or undertaking quality improvement programs. Creating these changes requires interdepartmental coordination. Several forms of such coordination are in use.

Procedures and routines Much of the work of "creating change" consists of processing small, similar changes. An example is the continuing introduction of new products into the product line, consisting of new colors, sizes, shapes, etc. Each such new product then must undergo an interdepartmental journey during which each department performs its special role, e.g., cost estimating, design, manufacture, test, etc. A common form of coordination is through written procedure. Usually, some staff specialist visits all departments to secure the respective managers' views as to their role in the sequence of events. Following these visits, the specialist drafts up an interdepartmental procedure which, if followed, would provide coordination while leaving it to each department to perform the departmental planning needed to process each such addition to the product line. This draft is reviewed, modified, and approved, after which it becomes a continuing impersonal coordinating device. This device is an effective, economic method for coordinating numerous, relatively simple changes.

The project manager concept For nonroutine, unusual programs of change, it is risky to use procedures and routines. Instead, the need is to design a special plan of coordination which fits the unique features of the unusual program and thereby improves its chances for success. One such special plan of coordination is the project manager form. Under this concept a project manager or project engineer is given the responsibility for coordination.

This project manager drafts a program of action consulting with the various departmental managers who will be involved in carrying out the project. Such a program shows:

The list of the tasks to be performed.
For each task, the names of the departments whose managers have agreed to collaborate in its performance.
For each task, which department has final authority for legitimizing the action taken.
The schedule showing time for commencing and for completing action.[5]

Following agreement on the program, the project manager remains in the picture to observe progress, expedite, sound the alarm in case of need, etc. The project manager's role may be limited to that of coordination, or it may extend to some degree of direct involvement, e.g., allocation of funds. In any case, the project manager concept can be of great value in coordinating critical programs provided that (1) the project manager is well qualified for such a role and (2) the line departments have genuinely accepted the concept.

Committees These are widely used to coordinate interdepartmental action on specific projects. Usually, such committees have legitimacy, i.e., they are appointed by the upper management under a written statement which defines responsibility and also authorizes the committee to hold meetings, request information, make recommendations, etc.

Choice of committee membership depends on the nature of the problem. A design review committee requires members who are able, from examination of design and test data, to provide early warning of high manufacturing costs, high field failure rates, or field maintenance troubles. Hence membership on such committees is commonly dominated by specialists in manufacturing planning, reliability engineering, and field service. In contrast, a committee which is to coordinate a broad quality improvement program would be dominated by line managers.

Many committees need a wide array of staff assistance—collection and

---

[5] For an example in graphic form, see *Quality Control Handbook*, 3rd ed., p. 6-2, fig. 6-5.

analysis of data, draft of minutes and reports, follow-up on recommendations, etc. In many companies this staff assistance is provided from staff departments, notably the quality control department. Section 5-5 discusses the respective responsibilities of committees and staff specialists.

In some companies, especially very small companies, the committees may be required to do their own staff work. This can be a serious handicap, since the time and skills needed for the staff work may be beyond the capacity of the committee members.

24-6 STAFF QUALITY ACTIVITIES

The words "line" and "staff" are loosely defined. Generally, *line activities* are those without which the enterprise cannot exist, e.g., marketing or manufacture. Generally, *staff activities* are those which, although not vital, are important to efficient operation. As applied to quality control, the staff activities are of several subspecies as shown in Table 24-4.

Life Cycle of Staff Activities

Staff activities may be centered around specific concepts, e.g., quality cost analysis, inspection planning. Alternatively, they may be centered around specific tools, e.g., quantification of reliability. A new staff activity is born when some advocate gets permission to try out a new concept or tool in his or her company.

If the tryout is successful, the results attained then attract attention and there arises a demand for extending the tryout into other areas to secure further benefits. The growing benefits then become the basis for company support in the form of legitimacy, funds, personnel, etc.

Table 24-4 Examples of staff quality activities

Staff department activities	Examples generally	Examples in quality control
Utility service for the line departments	Materials handling; plant maintenance; employee recruitment	Laboratory test services; instrument calibration
Coordination of departmental line activities which contribute to a common plan	Budget preparation; production scheduling	Quality planning; reliability planning
Advisory services to line departments	Legal services; technological expertise	Consulting in statistical methodology, metrology, reliability analysis
Control to see that operations conform to plans	Cost and expense reporting; internal audit	Executive reports; quality audits

As growth of the activity continues, experience is acquired through repetitive application in a variety of situations. This repetition tends to standardize the activity. The concept is duly spelled out in manuals of procedure. The tool is standardized in the form of charts, tables, computer programs, etc. Such standardization is evidence that the activity has matured to an extent which permits a transfer of the solved problems to the line departments.

For example, the preparation of sampling tables based on the laws of probability originally required that staff specialists evolve the conceptual approach to such sampling and then that they calculate the sampling tables. Next, the tables were tested out in a variety of applications, resulting in some modifications as well as much standardization. (Actually, various concepts were in competition, and some of them failed to survive the tests of practical application.) In due course the standardization became so extensive that in many companies the line personnel now apply the published sampling tables to their local needs based on rules set out in the published sampling procedures. In like manner, in some companies preparation of control charts is done by line personnel. Similarly, some designers have been trained to quantify reliability.

What these and similar trends have in common is a transfer to the line personnel of what was once a staff activity. Such transfers are generally beneficial because they enable the line people to apply the techniques without the need for intervention by someone else. In addition, these transfers keep the staff people working on unsolved problems rather than continuing to devote time to solved problems.

Staff Quality Control Departments

As noted in Section 24-3, the staff quality activities grew extensively starting during the 1940s. This growth resulted in creation of full-time staff quality specialists as well as separate departments to house them, principally departments of Quality Control Engineering, Reliability Engineering, and Quality Assurance. In turn, these specialists undertook to invent and apply the tools needed to carry out the staff activities associated with the list of Table 24-2.

Originally, the quality control engineers concentrated their attention on the problems of inspection and process control—problems which made use of statistical tools such as sampling tables and control charts. As they acquired experience, these engineers extended their activities into such areas as metrology, vendor relations, defect prevention, field complaint analysis, and quality cost analysis. These broader areas of application demanded that the engineers broaden their list of tools as well, and such has been the result. Collectively, the quality control engineers have done much to develop quality data systems, apply advanced statistical methodology (e.g., experimental design, evolutionary operation), introduce quality audit systems, define and standardize terminology, etc.

The reliability engineers emerged in response to a more specific need—the need to minimize field failures which had their origin in the original design.

These engineers evolved two sets of tools:

1. Technological tools for quantifying reliability (and maintainability) and for analyzing the product hierarchy so as to make reliability predictions. Some of the models needed to make the more complex analyses are quite intricate.
2. Managerial tools to assure application of the technological tools as well as to unify the company efforts toward attainment of high reliability. These managerial tools include such matters as:
   a. Broad policies and goals respecting reliability.
   b. Formal programs for performing reliability-oriented tasks.[6]
   c. Formal design reviews to examine designs and results of tests at various stages of product development.
   d. Systems of data collection and analysis to provide data banks and other information essential for reliability planning and analysis.

Use of formal departments for reliability engineering is largely restricted to those industries which are engaged in making complex systems and products involving numerous components and severe demands for continuity of performance. Industries whose products are less demanding nevertheless must carry out various reliability-oriented activities. However, they do so with less formality and at lower cost than would be the case with ultra-high-reliability products. While these latter industries often employ full-time reliability engineers, such engineers are fewer in number and are less likely to be housed in a separate department.

Competition among Staff Specialties

There is a good deal of overlap among the activities needed to attain quality, and this overlap extends to the job descriptions of the staff specialists. For example, attainment of product reliability requires a supply of reliable components. Since relations with vendors on quality matters are usually assigned to quality control engineers, there arises a potential jurisdictional question.

For some tasks it is easy to agree on whether to assign them to quality control engineers or to reliability engineers. For other tasks such agreement can be difficult or even hopeless. For still other tasks (as in the case of purchased components above) there must be a collaboration. In many cases the choice of assignment is not really important to the upper managers, since the skills of the two sets of specialists overlap. (It may seem very important to the specialists, since to them the size of their jurisdiction has a resemblance to property rights.) A useful rule in borderline cases is to make the responsibility clear for that case without deciding some broader principle of jurisdiction at the time. In due course, analysis of a series of such decisions may make the principle clear.

---

[6] For an extensive discussion, see *Quality Control Handbook*, 3rd ed., pp. 8-14 to 8-32. Figure 8-3 (p. 8-15) is an example of a time-phased reliability program.

There are also other specialties and specialists whose work can raise jurisdictional questions in relation to the quality specialists. For example, cost-reduction activities may be a part of the general job description of industrial engineers, operations research analysts, or value analysts. If one of these specialists undertakes a project to make cost reductions in the area of quality costs, there arises an obvious jurisdictional question. Here again the need is to make decisions on a case-by-case basis until a series of cases tends to bring out the principle involved. (Quite often the decisions of upper management in awarding projects are based not on the logic of organization principle but rather on the prior records of the competing departments for getting good results.)

Administration of the Staff Specialty

For the most part the staff specialists should stay out of day-to-day operations. Instead, they should work on those nonroutine problems which require solution but which require also a level of time and skills not normally possessed by the line supervisors. Such concentration on nonroutine problems, while proper, nevertheless makes it more difficult for the staff quality departments to secure their budgets and even to justify their existence. (Involvement in day-to-day operations gives the appearance of contributing to making and selling the product, and hence being useful or even essential.)

The usual solution to the budgetary problem is one of preparing an annual

Table 24-5 Approach to budgeting of staff quality activities

Quality staff activity	Examples of tasks	Method of budgeting
Analysis for quality improvement	Summarize available data; conduct Pareto analysis; test theories of causes of defects through study of process capabilities, defect concentration, etc.; conduct experiments to establish cause-and-effect relationships; test remedies to verify effectiveness.	Project-by-project justification based on estimating cost of study, value of remedy, return on investment, etc.
Quality planning	Analyze new or changed product or process; identify quality goals to be attained; identify the tasks to be performed to attain the goals; prepare proposals for accomplishing these tasks; secure line agreement to the resulting plans.	Past experience applied to anticipated volume of projects requiring planning.
Consulting	Conduct study of problems posed by "client"; prepare report and recommendations.	Past experience as to minor problems; case-by-case estimate as to major problems.
Auditing	As set out in Section 22-1	Past experience applied to proposed schedule.

budget which separates out the major staff activities and justifies each in a manner appropriate to that activity. Table 24-5 shows generally the approach used.

The manager of a staff quality department is well advised to review the budget estimates not only with his or her own superiors but with the line managers as well. He may not need their support during the affluent part of the economic cycle. However, when the economy declines, there is a general tightening of budgets and a disposition to question the continued existence of all activities which are not obviously linked to producing or selling products. At such times the line managers are often asked whether the staff quality departments have been helpful in improving operations. If these line managers have participated in review of the budgets (and thereby in helping to orient the staff efforts), the resulting activities are more likely to be of aid to the line managers.

Resistance to Change

Staff quality specialists are extensively involved in creating change and hence in dealing with resistance to change. See Section 5-7 for a discussion of this most important subject.

24-7 THE CORPORATE QUALITY STAFF

In multidivisional companies each autonomous division has its own divisional quality control department. Some of these companies have, in addition, a corporate staff department which is devoted to quality matters. This staff department is headed by a Corporate Quality Manager (or similar title) and appears on the organization chart in a manner similar to that shown in Figure 24-10.

The activities of the corporate quality staff vary from company to company but usually consist of a selection from those listed in Table 24-6. Some of these activities are mandated by top management, e.g., audit of divisional quality performance. However, most of the activities are undertaken only on invitation from, or agreement by, the divisional general managers.

The activities listed in Table 24-6 are often persuasive in creating a corporate staff department. Nevertheless, these departments have a mixed record of effectiveness and survival. In part, this record is due to the problems of finding a qualified corporate quality manager. Among other qualifications this manager requires:

1. An understanding of business matters sufficient to be attractive to the divisional general managers, each of whom regards himself or herself as managing a business.
2. An understanding of quality control matters sufficient to earn the respect of the divisional quality managers.
3. A personality which will simplify rather than complicate the organizational relationships.

Table 24-6 List of corporate quality staff activities

Assistance to corporate management
Develop corporate quality policies and objectives
Prepare and publish corporate reports on quality performance
Audit divisional quality performance
Audit divisional compliance to government regulations
Assistance to divisional management
Provide consulting service to divisional general managers
Provide assistance in startup of new divisions
Appraise performance of divisional quality managers
Participate in personnel actions involving divisional quality managers
Professional development
Keep informed on new developments which take place in the quality specialty generally
Disseminate this information to the divisions
Collaborate with selected divisions in trying out promising new concepts and tools
Prepare training programs, manuals, and courses
Conduct internal company conferences on matters of common interest
Publish internal newsletters, case histories, and other forms of exchange of experience
Coordination of corporate quality matters
Coordinate relations with standardization committees in government and industry associations
Coordinate relations with national standardization bodies
Coordinate relations with professional societies
Provide interdivisional coordination within the company

Such a specification is not easy to fill, and many corporate quality managers have been found wanting.

A further problem in survival of these departments is the lack of an agreed measure of effectiveness. (The measurable results appear in the performance reports of the divisions.) In consequence, top management looks to the division general managers for assistance in judging the effectiveness of the corporate quality staff. It follows that the divisions should participate in the process of defining the activities and setting the priorities of the corporate quality staff.

PROBLEMS

24-1 Conduct a research study and report on how any of the following institutions were organized for quality: (1) the Florentine Arte Della Lana (wool guild) of the twelfth, thirteenth, and fourteenth centuries; (2) Venetian shipbuilding in the fourteenth century; (3) construction of cathedrals in medieval Europe; (4) the Gobelin tapestry industry in the sixteenth and seventeenth centuries.

24-2 Study the plan of organization for quality for any of the following institutions and report your conclusions: (1) a hospital; (2) a university; (3) a chain supermarket; (4) a chain of motels; (5) a restaurant; (6) a manufacturing company.

24-3 For any organization acceptable to the instructor, make a list of the activities assigned to the

Quality Control Department. Compare your list with Table 24-2 and explain what might be the reasons for the difference between the two lists.

24-4 For any organization acceptable to the instructor, study the methods in use to attain (*a*) coordination for control; (*b*) coordination for change. Report your findings.

24-5 For any organization acceptable to the instructor, study the staff quality activities from the standpoint of their stage in the "life cycle" of staff activities. Report your findings.

24-6 You are the manager of a small plant manufacturing precision parts for customers who make various types of assembled units. You have three different processes (e.g., casting, stamping, and machine), each of which is supervised by a foreman. The foremen report to you through a general foreman. In each of these three departments are several inspectors, who report to the department foreman, to inspect the work of the department.

A year ago, you were impelled by the high incidence of customer complaints to institute a final inspection department, where all product now passes before shipment. This is headed up by a chief inspector, reporting to you. The institution of this department has successfully reduced the customer complaint problem, but the losses from scrap and rework are now prohibitive, since nothing much has been done to trace back and find the sources of the defects.

The chief inspector has studied modern quality control methods and believes she can accomplish some reductions. To do so, she urges that all the departmental inspectors now come under her jurisdiction and that she be allowed to allocate one particular person solely to the problem of searching out the causes of defects through capability analysis, control charts, etc.

The general foreman, on the other hand, argues that the main problem is the fact that final inspection is much too strict; he has to spend most of his time arguing with the chief inspector to convince him that certain defects are perfectly acceptable to the customer. He proposes that the chief inspector be brought under him so that decisions can be made more rapidly. If this is done, he would propose to leave the departmental inspectors as they are, but have the chief inspector train them in control-chart techniques. This, he believes, will be adequate to cope with the defect problem.

What are the advantages and disadvantages of each of these two plans? Which do you think has the greater prospect of success and why? As plant manager, what would be your decision?[7]

SUPPLEMENTARY READING

Subject	Reference
Quality-related tasks	*Quality Control Handbook*, 2nd ed. (QCH2), pp. 7-2 to 7-5
Evolution of the inspection department	QCH2, pp. 12-63 to 12-70
Evolution of the quality control hierarchy	QCH2, pp. 7-5 to 7-12
Quality control organization in practice	QCH2, pp. 7-12 to 7-15
Coordination of the quality function	QCH2, pp. 7-15 to 7-18; see also J. M. Juran, *Managerial Breakthrough*, McGraw-Hill Book Company, New York, 1964. Chapter 6, "The Steering Arm," generalizes coordination for creating change. Chapter 12, "Control—A Panoramic View," generalizes coordination for control.
Staff quality activities	QCH2, pp. 7-18 to 7-29
Corporate quality staff	QCH2, pp. 7-29, 7-30

[7] Course notes for Management Quality Control, U.S. Air Force School of Logistics, 1959.

EXAMPLES OF EXAMINATION QUESTIONS USED IN FORMER ASQC QUALITY ENGINEER CERTIFICATION EXAMINATIONS AS PUBLISHED IN *QUALITY PROGRESS* MAGAZINE

1 A fully developed position description for a quality engineer must contain clarification of: *(a)* responsibility; *(b)* accountability; *(c)* authority; *(d)* answers *(a)* and *(c)*; *(e)* answers *(a)*, *(b)*, and *(c)*.

2 When giving instructions to those who will perform a task, the communication process is completed: *(a)* when the worker goes to his work station to do the task; *(b)* when the person giving the instruction has finished talking; *(c)* when the worker acknowledges these instructions by describing how he or she will perform the task; *(d)* when the worker says that he or she understands the instructions.

TWENTY-FIVE

QUALITY INFORMATION SYSTEMS

25-1 DEFINITION AND SCOPE

A *quality information system* (QIS) is an organized method of collecting, storing, analyzing, and reporting information on quality to assist decision makers at all levels.

In the past, information on "quality" was concerned mainly with in-plant inspection data. However, products are now more complex, programs for controlling quality now span the spectrum of functional departments, and emphasis is now placed on fitness for use rather than conformance to specification. These changing conditions coupled with the advent of the computer have resulted in a broader viewpoint toward information on quality.

This broader viewpoint requires inputs from a variety of functional areas. It also recognizes that "information" not only consists of data but also other knowledge needed for decision making. Inputs for a quality information system include:

1. *Market research information on quality.* Examples are (a) customer opinions on the product and service being provided, and (b) results of customer experience that suggest opportunities for improving fitness for use.
2. *Product design test data.* Examples are development test data, data on parts and components under consideration from various suppliers, and data on the environment that the product may encounter.

3. *Information on design evaluation for quality.* Examples are minutes of design review meetings, reliability predictions, and failure mode and effect analyses.
4. *Information on purchased parts and materials.* Examples are receiving inspection data, data on tests conducted by a supplier, data on tests conducted by an independent laboratory on a procured item, vendor survey information, and vendor rating data.
5. *Process data.* These data cover the entire in-plant manufacturing inspection system from the beginning of manufacturing up to final inspection. Also included are process control data and process capability data.
6. *Final inspection data.* These data are the routine data at a final inspection.
7. *Field performance data.* Examples are MTBF and other data from a company proving ground, and warranty and complaint information obtained from the customer. It may also include configuration control data, defining exactly what hardware is included in each serial number of equipment sent to a customer.
8. *Results of audits.* This includes both product audits and systems audits.

Thus the scope of a quality information system may vary from a simple system covering in-process inspection data to a broad system covering all information applicable to the overall effectiveness of a product.

25-2 RELATION OF A QUALITY INFORMATION SYSTEM TO A MANAGEMENT INFORMATION SYSTEM

The concept of a *management information system* (MIS) has recently evolved. MIS attempts to provide all the information needs of management through one integrated system. The concept has several characteristics:

1. Information input and output are planned from an overall company viewpoint rather than separate departmental systems or handling each request for information on a case-by-case basis.
2. Information that ordinarily would be maintained in separate departments is consolidated to form what is called a *data base.*
3. There are several different uses for the same input data. (This justifies the integrated approach of a data base.)

MIS specialists believe that most information needs in a company should be provided for by one overall system.[1] When an organization does have an MIS, the system will impact on a quality information system. The impact can take various forms, as shown in Table 25-1. Such impact makes it imperative

[1] For a contrasting view of MIS, see John Dearden, "MIS Is a Mirage," *Harvard Business Review*, January/February 1972, pp. 90–99.

Table 25-1 Impact of MIS on QIS

Impact	Examples
1. The MIS data base provides product information that can be useful as bases for quality data.	1. Sales dollars, direct labor dollars, manufacturing cost, direct labor hours
2. Information on quality can be stored in the MIS and changes can be entered directly. The information can be drawn out as needed.	2. Information on quality costs, inspection and test data
3. Data analysis models can be incorporated in the MIS.	3. Pareto analyses, statistical analyses, trend analyses
4. Recently developed hardware and methods for data collection and transmission can be applied to quality information.	4. Special devices for data input, video display, computer graphics
5. Departments generating quality information can be required to submit it in the form required by the MIS data base.	5. Inspection and test data, reliability data, vendor survey data

that those designing a quality information system work closely with those who are responsible for the MIS.

25-3 PLANNING A COMPUTER-BASED QUALITY INFORMATION SYSTEM

A quality information system can use manual or computerized processing. This chapter emphasizes a computer-based system.[2]

The planning of a computer-based QIS can be complex. The road starts with the creation of a design specification for the system and preparation of a proposal indicating costs and time required. When the proposal is approved by management, the system is developed, tested, and implemented. Finally, provisions are made for review of system performance. Some of these steps will be discussed in this chapter.[3]

A system must be tailored to meet the needs of each individual company. However, the following principles are generally applicable:

1. Plan the system to receive information in almost any form imaginable. Although most of the information will be received on special forms, the sys-

---

[2] For a discussion of a manual system, see *Quality Control Handbook*, 3rd ed., pp. 19-6 to 19-29.

[3] Figure 25-1 and the discussion have been adapted from *Quality Control Handbook*, 3rd ed. Chapter 20 of the reference (prepared by J. E. Blum and R. S. Bingham, Jr.) provides further elaboration.

tem should make it possible to receive and process information by means of a telephone call, letters, or other media.

2. Provide flexibility for meeting new data needs. A cardinal example of this is the failure reporting form that must be revised periodically, because someone suddenly discovers a critical need for an additional item of information to be recorded.
3. Provide for eliminating collection of data no longer useful, and for eliminating reports no longer needed. This requires a periodic audit of the use (or lack of use) of the data and reports.
4. Issue reports that are readable, timely, and have sufficient useful detail on problem areas to facilitate investigations and corrective action.
5. Prepare summary reports covering long periods of time to highlight potential problem areas and show progress on known problems.
6. Keep track of the *cost* of collecting, processing, and reporting information and compare this cost to the *value* of the information.

An important tool in the planning stage is the flowchart. Flowcharts can be drawn at different levels of detail, to depict the steps in an information system. This facilitates analysis to assure that an efficient system will result.

To computerize the steps in an inefficient manual system is a mistake. This just mechanizes an inferior system. An example of the use of a flowchart to improve a system is shown in Figure 25-1. The flow sheet in Figure 25-1, part A, illustrates the information flow for one of several testing laboratories. Information associated with process type I was of substantial volume compared to that for other process types. In the laboratory, a tester, after completing the tests, marked an optical page reader sheet. At the end of the day, these sheets were collected from the various outlying divisions and sent to the data processing center, where the sheets were processed by the computer and daily detail and summary cards were punched.

The information for other processes was sent directly to the data processing center, where it was individually keypunched. The cards were sorted and collated. Following this, a computer analysis was performed to produce reports which were sent to the engineers and management on an exception basis.

This system had several disadvantages, including inaccuracies associated with extreme sensitivity of the optical page reader, poorly marked sheets, excessive time spent by testers filling out the page reader sheets, slow input of the page reader to the computer, and occasional delays in the transportation of the data to the data processing center. The system was redesigned to transmit the information after each test was completed through a badge and manual entry station via telephone lines to an off-line card punch located in the data processing center (see Figure 25-1, part B). This eliminated the trucking and the manual entry on the optical page reader sheet and allowed the operator to verify the accuracy of the data as entered. An edit program was built into the computer operations to test for "obvious errors." One of the controls on the input was an error listing sent to each Quality Control Department daily. From this, neces-

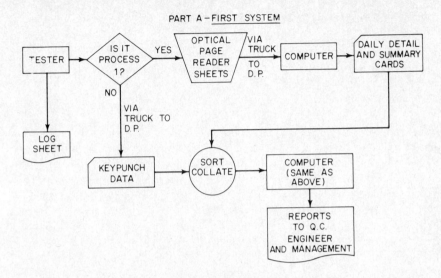

PART A—FIRST SYSTEM

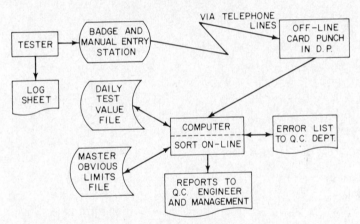

PART B—REVISED SYSTEM

Figure 25-1 Information flow—process review.

sary corrections were marked and returned to data processing. Errors were reduced by about 70 percent using the redesigned system.

With both systems, the data were obtained for process *review* purposes rather than for instantaneous process *control*. Another phase in the evolution of this quality information system provides direct entry to the computer system on-line (replacing the off-line card punch) with feedback to the test station and output either via cathode ray tube or on-line printer. The output calls for corrective action when points are out of control, when trends are seen, or when some unusual behavior (such as nonrandomness in the data) is detected.[4]

[4] See footnote 3.

25-4 ACQUISITION, STORAGE, AND RETRIEVAL

The principal subsystems of a computer system are shown in Figure 25-2.

The information must first be entered into the computer system in alphabetical or numerical form.

Several different methods and machines can be used including:

1. *Punched cards and punched paper tape.*
2. *Mark sense cards.* Data are entered on a card with an electrographic pencil. A machine then converts the markings into punched holes.
3. *Port-a-punch cards.* Data are entered by punching out the appropriate holes on a card. (This system is often used for tallying election votes.)
4. *Optical character recognition (OCR) devices.* The device reads either a mark (e.g., a filled-in area) or a clearly printed number or letter. An electrical pulse is then generated for entry into the computer system.
5. *Magnetic ink character recognition (MICR) devices.* The information is printed with a special magnetic ink. When this is passed through a magnetic field, the device generates pulses for entry into the computer system.
6. *Remote terminals.* A keyboard terminal is placed in a different location than the main computer. The keyboard is operated in the usual manner. As

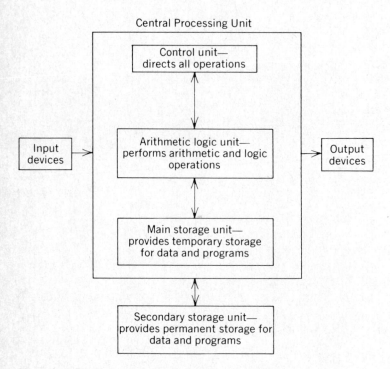

Figure 25-2 Principal subsystems of a computer system.

each key is depressed, pulses representing the data are sent to the computer.

7. *Voice data entry.* Information is transmitted directly to the computer by voice. Manual recording is eliminated.

Some of these methods may require changes in the forms used for recording the source information.

The importance of quality control of the source information cannot be overemphasized. (The acronym GIGO means "garbage in, garbage out.") Section 16-6 distinguishes between accuracy and precision of test data. In information systems, a distinction is sometimes made between these same terms. Accuracy usually refers to the degree that the information is correct, up to date, and complete. Precision usually applies to numerical data and refers to the number of digits included in the source data. In both cases, the coding techniques used to facilitate computer usage must be carefully chosen. This is necessary to assure that the final output can be generated in the form needed and in sufficient detail. Loup, Murphy, and Russell[5] describe the steps taken to control the quality of health information with respect to the coding, abstracting, processing, and reporting of information.

The heart of the computer is the central processing unit. The CPU consists of a storage unit, a control unit, and an arithmetic logic unit.

The storage unit within the CPU stores both the source information and the detailed instructions for analysis of the information and preparation of the output. This internal storage is called *memory.* There are also several means of external storage:

1. *Magnetic tape.* Information is stored on reels of magnetic tape. *Read/write heads* on the tape drive transfer the information onto the tape or read the information already recorded. Tape storage is a *sequential-aspect* medium; i.e., each item on the tape must be searched in sequence until the desired item is found. The other storage media listed below all have the property of *random access;* i.e., the read/write heads can move independently to any point.

2. *Magnetic disk.* Information is read or recorded in concentric circles on disks coated with a ferromagnetic substance.

3. *Magnetic drum.* Information is read or recorded on a revolving drum.

4. *Mass storage system.* The basic storage element is a strip of 3-in-wide tape. Up to 4720 of these tape strips, each holding 50 million characters, can be accessed through a single device in less than 3 s.

Often, information such as drawings, pictures, and signatures must be stored. This storage can make use of manual filing systems or photographic storage media such as microfilming.

---

[5] Roland J. Loup, Mary K. Murphy, and Cynthia L. Russell, "Quality Control in a Health Information System," *1978 ASQC Annual Technical Conference Transactions,* pp. 451–457.

25-5 PROCESSING OF DATA

The computer processes information in either one of two ways: batches or real time. In *batch processing,* the information is collected in groups (or "batches"), and each group is processed separately. In *real-time processing,* information is stored in the computer, is continuously updated, and is available for instant access by the user. An example of real-time processing is an airline reservation system.

To process the input data, the computer must receive a series of instructions directing it to perform a sequence of operations. These instructions are called a *program.*

Computer programming spans the spectrum of complexity, depending on the processing that is desired for the information. The following steps are usually required to create a program:

1. *Study the present system of information flow and the desired outputs for the future.* The present system should be thoroughly reviewed before proceeding with the development of a program. A system flowchart analysis is usually necessary (see Figure 25-1). In this step, thorough communication between the programmer and the user of the information is essential.
2. *Develop a programming plan.* The programmer develops an approach for the project. This approach can include deciding on input and output media, programming language, and the use of already prepared ("canned") programs.
3. *Detail the processing operations.* The programmer prepares detailed flowcharts describing all elements of input, processing, and output of information. These charts are drawn with special programming symbols and they become the basis of writing the actual program. The step includes provision for coding the input data to prepare the data for the computer.
4. *Write the program.* The program consists of a sequence of instructions written in a particular programming language and meeting the rules set up for that language. Examples of languages are FORTRAN (FORmula TRANslation system), COBOL (COmmon Business Oriented Language), and PL1 (Programming Language 1).
5. *Review the program for errors.* This "desk check" is necessary because of the difficulty of writing even a moderate-size program without making errors.
6. *Test the program on the computer and make corrections as required.*
7. *Document the program.* The documentation includes the flowcharts, listing of program steps, output format, and special instructions (if needed) for the operator of the computer.
8. *Evaluate the program.* This starts with the adequacy, to the user, of the output. The evaluation also includes the degree of documentation, the utilization of prepared programs, and the utilization of the full capability of the computer.

Table 25-2 Types of computer systems

Name of system	Cost*	Description
Maxicomputer	$300,000 and up	A general-purpose computer that is fast and can handle several tasks at the same time by time sharing
Minicomputer	$5000 to $100,000	A general-purpose computer but is slower and has less capacity than a maxicomputer
Microcomputer	$100 to $1200	Similar to a minicomputer but limited to a smaller number of functions
Programmable pocket calculator	$100 to $800	Limited to numerical calculations
Single-chip microcomputer	Under $15	Limited to a few specific functions on a small amount of data

*Cost as of 1978.

There are many computer programs available for use in quality control. These are primarily concerned with statistical techniques. The *Journal of Quality Technology*, published by the American Society for Quality Control, regularly runs a column providing the detailed programming steps for statistical techniques. Such programs can be used as is or incorporated as part of a larger program created to meet the needs of a specific user.

The expanded use of computers has been made possible by breakthroughs in computer hardware. For example, Berger[6] states that a *microprocessor* the size of a coin may have computing power equal to that of the largest computer existing in 1949 at a tiny fraction of the cost. Such breakthroughs have given rise to a variety of computer systems. These are described in Table 25-2.

Advances in computer hardware, both with respect to capability and price, offer an unlimited potential for quality information systems. If an organization does not wish to have its own computer, it can enter into a time-sharing arrangement on a computer owned by another organization. In this case, a remote terminal can be installed in the first organization. Information and the program is inputted through this terminal to the main computer housed in the other organization. Output is then received at the remote terminal. As an alternative to a remote terminal, the input can be prepared at one organization (in the form required by the computer) and then brought to the computer at the other organization.

25-6 OUTPUT OF INFORMATION

The media commonly used to provide output from a computer include:

1. *Line printer*. This directly provides a paper document giving the output. (When a document is provided, the output is called "hard copy.")

[6] Roger W. Berger, "Microcomputers and Software Quality Control," *1978 ASQC Annual Technical Conference Transactions*, p. 328.

2. *Punched cards and paper tape.* The results of the computer processing are converted into cards on tape. These can then be processed by a reader machine to produce a hard copy.
3. *Cathode ray tube (CRT).* The output is presented on a video display screen. The image is called "soft copy."
4. *Data plotters.* Several kinds of machines are available which present information in the form of graphs, pictures, maps, and even three-dimensional models. Shostack and Eddy[7] discuss the impact of computer graphics on decision making.
5. *Remote output terminals.* For small amounts of data, output can be directly obtained (in hard-copy form) at a remote terminal.
6. *Audio response unit.* This device presents the output in the form of prerecorded spoken words. This output can be relayed over a telephone.

The capability of the computer for analysis is virtually unlimited. Also, there are several different types of hardware for producing output. These two factors result in an unlimited volume of information provided in a variety of forms. However, the volume of information or the dramatic nature of the output (e.g., computer graphics or an audio response) does not mean that the information is useful for those receiving it. The reports to be generated should be carefully reviewed with users for both content and manner of presentation.

As an example of the processing and output of data, the following steps were taken for handling quality data from an assembly operation.

1. Assign code numbers for all possible defects. A "double coding" system minimizes the number of items in the defect code list and makes it easier to find code numbers which apply to particular defects found. In such a system, the first several digits identify the part involved (e.g., screws) and another set of digits identifies the trouble (e.g., loose).
2. Designate classes of defects such as major, minor, and incidental and assign demerit values, for example, 15, 5, and 1, respectively.
3. Record the assembly inspection results on a finished products analysis card. This card contains the product serial number and accompanies the unit as it proceeds to each inspection station. (Alternatively, the inspector could fill out a card for each defect noted.)
4. After the last inspection, keypunch the analysis cards and punch a card for each defect on the analysis card. (The first card contains a special punch in one column to provide a count of the total number of units inspected during the period.)
5. Accumulate the cards until the end of the period. The machine then sorts the detail cards, match-merges them with defect master cards, intersperse gang punches the class of defect and defect name, and groups them behind

---

[7] Kenneth Shostack and Charles Eddy, "Management by Computer Graphics," *Harvard Business Review,* November/December 1971, pp. 52–63.

the master unit-description cards. An accounting machine then prepares reports by defect number, by department responsible, and by inspector number.

a. The report by defect number contains product type, operation number, defect number, defect name, class of defect, trouble code, the total number of defects by class, the total units inspected, and the total defects found.

b. The report by department responsible contains similar information, except that it indicates the department responsible, rather than the operation number.

c. The report by inspector number contains the product type, operation number, inspector number, number of units inspected, and total number of defects by class.

6. Copies of the reports are distributed by the quality control engineer to the appropriate supervisors.

Data processing equipment also makes it possible to prepare from the same punched cards additional reports by operation number, by trouble code, and by class of defect. Reports of this nature pinpoint the specific defects and areas which need corrective action. A comparison from period to period indicates whether remedial action has been taken and points up the need for more intensive effort if the same defects appear on the reports repeatedly. Comparisons of sets of data should include a check on the statistical significance, particularly when small amounts of data are involved (see Section 4-7).

The report by defect number is used to prepare a demerit chart, which shows trends in product quality from period to period. Each point on the chart represents the average number of demerits per unit calculated by totaling the demerits and dividing by the total units inspected. For example, in December, 466 units were inspected, with these results:

Class	Demerit value		Number of defects		Demerits
I	15	×	594	=	8,910
II	5	×	3,817	=	19,085
III	1	×	1,718	=	1,718
					39,713

$$\text{Average number of demerits per unit} = \frac{39,713}{466} = 85.2$$

This report goes to the manager of quality control and to the works manager.

Another report which can be prepared is a list of the items appearing with the greatest frequency and of the items requiring corrective action most urgently. All the reports pinpoint specific defects, identify areas requiring action, and show the effects of remedial action.

Table 25-3 Summary of reports in an inspection information system

Name of summary	Description	Example
Part-operation accept/reject	Summarizes accept/reject information for each work area	In work area 5924, operation 85 on 40432 was highlighted as a poor performer; 46 inspections were made and 23 units were rejected
Part-operation listing	Summarizes fault categories for each part operation	For part operation 40432-85 there were 17 instances of "terminal solder missing" or 31% of the total faults for operation 85
Fault listing	Summarizes fault categories for each work area	For work area 5924, there were 52 instances of terminal solder missing or 28% of the total; of these 52, 6 were charged to operator 37157
Operator listing	Summarizes faults charged to each operator	Operator 37157 was charged with 24 faults, 6 of which were terminal-solder-missing
Monthly inspection report	This is a graphical and tabular summary of overall performance; it also lists the major problem areas; a separate page is prepared for each work area	For work area 5924, a graph of percent defective by month is plotted; for December, the major problem was on part operation 40432-85; 1693 units were inspected; 455 faults were found, of which 361 were due to operators; operator 37157 was a major contributor to defects, particularly missing and improper solder and wiring errors

Another example concerns the system designed by an electronics manufacturer for inspection data. The system had an objective of translating gross information into lower levels of detail so that engineers could isolate product faults. A summary of the output of this system is presented in Table 25-3. Note that Pareto analysis is used extensively in this system to help the engineers.

Some organizations use a "chart room" where a collection of graphs providing performance data on many activities is displayed and continuously updated. Leek and Riley[8] describe the application of this approach for quality information.

Where graphs are used extensively in reports, care should be taken to follow accepted graphing practices. The emphasis should be on clarity and ability to see trends. Scales that are complicated to read, such as special logarithmic scales, should be avoided for nontechnical users. Where performance scales do not start at zero, this should be clearly indicated. When available,

[8] Jay W. Leek and Fred H. Riley, "Product Quality Improvement Through Visibility," *1978 ASQC Annual Technical Conference Transactions*, pp. 229–236.

numerical objectives for performance should be included on graphs. Trends should be indicated by averages or moving averages. Time-series and forecasting techniques should be applied when appropriate.

25-7 CONTROLLING THE QUALITY OF COMPUTER SOFTWARE

Software is the collection of computer programs, procedures, and associated documentation necessary for the operation of a data processing system.

For many programs, it is virtually impossible to produce a program that is error-free. A complex program can contain several hundred thousand basic instructions.[9] Foster[10] states that software costs from $10 to $300 per instruction. Thus, when there are many instructions, there will be errors and the cost of software errors may be large. Barone and Harkness[11] describe a quality cost system used by one organization to measure software quality costs.

There is now general recognition of the seriousness of the software problem, and formal programs have been developed to attack the problem. The main elements of the program draw upon some of the techniques used in controlling the quality and reliability of physical products. Emphasis is on both the detection and prevention of errors. The elements usually include:

1. *Design review.* Several reviews are held. The purpose is to evaluate (*a*) the requirements for software, (*b*) the software design approach, and (*c*) the detailed design. Howley[12] states that about 60 percent of all software errors are introduced during the requirements definition and design phases.
2. *Documentation review.* The emphasis is on the plans and procedures that will be used to test the computer programs. Program packages are now available that test newly created computer programs.
3. *Validation of software tests.* This consists of reviewing the results of the tests to evaluate the software.
4. *Corrective action system.* This is similar to the system on physical products (see Section 20-5). It includes documentation of all software problems and the follow-up to assure resolution.
5. *Configuration management.* This is similar to the system used for physical products (see Section 19-5). The objective is to identify accurately different versions of the computer programs, prevent unauthorized modifications, and assure that approved modifications are executed.

[9] The development of special "higher-level" languages is drastically reducing the number of basic instructions required for each new program.

[10] Richard A. Foster, *Introduction to Software Quality Assurance*, privately published by Richard A. Foster, San Antonio, Texas, 1975.

[11] Robert E. Barone and Donald R. Harkness, "Innovations in Software Quality Management," *1973 ASQC Annual Technical Conference Transactions*, p. 155.

[12] Paul P. Howley, Jr., "Software Quality Assurance for Reliable Software," *Proceedings, Annual Reliability and Maintainability Symposium*, January 1978, p. 73.

The user of software may purchase it from a vendor. Both parties have a major role in the software quality effort. User input is particularly important during the requirements definition and design phases.

Coutinho[13] and Foster[14] describe the elements of a complete program.

25-8 QUALITY CONTROL MANUAL

A *quality control manual* is a document containing company policies and procedures affecting product quality. It serves as:

1. A reference for the policies and procedures as well as the reasons behind them. The manual provides proof that policies and procedures have been thought out and documents the reasoning to help those who must execute the plans.
2. A textbook for training. The widest training use is for the inspection and quality control personnel, but the training extends also to production supervisors, engineering personnel, and others.
3. A precedent for future decisions. The manual codifies past practice and agreements; e.g., quality standards can appear in the manual.
4. An aid to continuity of operations despite employee turnover. Without a manual, personnel changes can result in a change of practice, sometimes drastic. The manual helps to stabilize practice and to conduct operations based on "laws, not men."
5. A reference base against which current practice can be audited.

Some companies have required their vendors to prepare quality control manuals as an aid to vendor relations. The results have been mixed. In many cases, the vendor has benefited greatly from thinking through and documenting his procedures. In other cases, unnecessary formalization and documentation of practice has resulted in more expense than benefit from the manual. Blanket requirements that are arbitrarily made on all products and vendors are inviting unnecessary expense in the form of documentation that is used only to impress the organization that required it.

The manual usually contains procedures for the following areas:[15]

1. General
   a. Quality policies
   b. Organization charts and responsibility tables
   c. Definitions

---

[13] John De S. Coutinho, "Quality Assurance of Automated Data Processing Systems," Parts I and II, *Journal of Quality Technology,* vol. 4, no. 2, April 1972, pp. 93–101; vol. 4, no. 3, July 1972, pp. 145–155.

[14] Richard A. Foster, *Introduction to Software Quality Assurance,* privately published by Richard A. Foster, San Antonio, Texas, 1975.

[15] This is a revision of the list in *Quality Control Handbook,* 3rd ed., pp. 6-24 to 6-25. The reference includes examples of detailed subjects covered in each of these areas.

2. Managerial procedures
    a. Marketing
    b. New-product introduction
    c. Manufacturing quality planning
    d. Vendor quality control
    e. Inspection and test
    f. Measuring equipment
    g. Nonconforming material
    h. Postmanufacture
    i. Defect prevention
    j. Quality assurance
    k. Quality costs
    l. Usage and field service
    m. Quality motivation
    n. Personnel
    o. Statistical methodology
    p. Data systems

Although most quality control manuals include many of these areas, the selection of subjects and the development of procedures must be tailormade for each organization.

Supervisors are responsible for implementing procedures, but there are forces acting that often result in the need for independent audit of actual practice versus the manual. The supervisor does not have the time for organized follow-up on adherence to procedures and naturally relies on the personnel to follow procedures. Sometimes, conflicting pressures force the supervisor to knowingly deviate from approved procedures.

For these and other reasons, a periodic independent audit of practice versus the manual is often useful. The results of an audit are varied. Sometimes, the procedure is shown to be inadequate or even wrong. Sometimes, the procedure is fine but personnel are unable to execute it because of lack of knowledge, lack of adequate equipment, or other reasons. Sometimes, the procedure has been revised but the new edition has not yet been distributed. These audits are a part of the quality audit activity (see Section 22-3).

PROBLEMS

25-1 For any product or service acceptable to the instructor, propose a list of subjects for procedures in a quality control manual.

25-2 For any of the following, obtain the necessary information and draw up a flowchart for the data collection and analysis of: (1) an operation acceptable to the instructor; (2) final inspection results at a plant; (3) goods returned to a plant; (4) traffic fines; (5) complaints at a department store; (6) automobile accident insurance claims; (7) performance deficiencies by an athletic team; (8) loss of utility service to homes. Make recommendations or changes or additions.

25-3 For an institution with which you are familiar, evaluate the usefulness of at least two reports on product quality by speaking with those who receive the report. Set up a scale of frequency of use and obtain opinions on use and on shortcomings of the present report.

25-4 For the computer system in your organization, define the characteristics in terms of input devices, means of external storage, and output devices.

25-5 For an institution with which you are familiar, describe at least one area where manual processing of data could be justifiably replaced with automatic data processing using a computer.

25-6 Speak with people engaged in writing computer programs. Develop a list of common programming errors. For a sample of 10 programs, tally the frequency of occurrence for each type of programming error.

SUPPLEMENTARY READING

Section 20 in *Quality Control Handbook,* 3rd ed., McGraw-Hill Book Company, New York, 1974, is devoted to computers in quality control. Table 20-1 lists other sections of QCH that discuss the application of computers.

For an introduction to MIS, see Joel E. Ross, *Modern Management and Information Systems,* Reston Publishing Company, Reston, Va., 1976. For an introduction to computer systems, see Gerald A. Silver and Joan B. Silver, *Introduction to Systems Analysis,* Prentice-Hall, Inc., Englewood Cliffs, N.J., 1976.

A useful publication on the quality control aspects of computer software is given in the National Bureau of Standards Special Publication 500-11, *Computer Software Management: A Primer for Project Management and Quality Control,* U.S. Department of Commerce, Washington, D.C., 1977.

EXAMPLES OF EXAMINATION QUESTIONS USED IN FORMER ASQC QUALITY ENGINEER CERTIFICATION EXAMINATIONS AS PUBLISHED IN *QUALITY PROGRESS* MAGAZINE

1 In today's world, quality information documentation is called: (*a*) end-item narrative; (*b*) hardware; (*c*) data pack; (*d*) software; (*e*) warrantee.

2 The quality needs for historical information in the areas of specifications, performance reporting, complaint analysis, or run records would fall into which of the following computer application categories? (*a*) data accumulation; (*b*) data-reduction analysis and reporting; (*c*) real-time process control; (*d*) statistical analysis; (*e*) information retrieval.

3 In establishing a quality reporting and information feedback system, primary consideration must be given to: (*a*) number of inspection stations; (*b*) management approval; (*c*) timely feedback and corrective action; (*d*) historical preservation of data; (*e*) routing copy list.

4 All quality information reports should be audited periodically to: (*a*) determine their continued validity; (*b*) reappraise the routing or copy list; (*c*) determine their current effectiveness; (*d*) all of the above; (*e*) none of the above.

5 The basic steps in any data processing system using computers generally are arranged in which of the following orders? (*a*) data input, storage and retrieval, processing, and output; (*b*) collection, analysis, input, and output; (*c*) evaluation, keypunch, processing, and output; (*d*) recording, input, calculation, and output; (*e*) keypunch, FORTRAN programming, and output.

6 When planning a system for processing quality data or for keeping inspection and other quality records, the first step should be to: (*a*) depict the system in a flowchart; (*b*) hire a statistician; (*c*) investigate applicable data processing equipment; (*d*) determine the cost of operating the system; (*e*) start coding your input data.

7 The management team is establishing priorities to attack a serious quality problem. You are requested to establish a data collection system to direct this attack. You use which of these general management rules to support your recommendations as to the quantity of data required? (*a*) You have compared the incremental cost of additional data with the value of the information obtained and stopped when they are equal; (*b*) Your decision corresponds to the rules applicable to management decisions for other factors of production; (*c*) Your decision is based upon the relationship between value and cost; (*d*) All of the above.

8 Computer information processing can become available to any quality engineer through the use of: (*a*) a terminal and time-sharing agreement; (*b*) a batch-processing system in which data are brought to a central area for processing; (*c*) an in-house system with applicable software; (*d*) all of the above.

ANSWERS TO EXAMPLES OF EXAMINATION QUESTIONS USED IN FORMER ASQC QUALITY ENGINEER AND RELIABILITY ENGINEER CERTIFICATION EXAMINATIONS

(References: *Quality Progress*, February 1976, pp. 23–31; August 1978, p. 28.)

Chapter 1: **1**(c)   **2**(a)

Chapter 2: **1**(c)   **2**(d)   **3**(b)   **4**(c)   **5**(e)   **6**(e)   **7**(c)
           8(d)

Chapter 3: **1**(b)   **2**(b)   **3**(c)   **4**(b)   **5**(b)   **6**(e)   **7**(d)
           8(d)   **9**(d)

Chapter 4: **1**(a)   **2**(a)   **3**(d)   **4**(d)   **5**(b)   **6**(d)   **7**(c)

Chapter 6: **1**(e)   **2**(e)   **3**(d)   **4**(e)   **5**(a)

Chapter 7: **1**(e)   **2**(b)   **3**(b)   **4**(c)   **5**(b)   **6**(e)   **7**(c)
           8(d)   **9**(a)

Chapter 8: **1**(e)   **2**(b)   **3**(a)   **4**(d)   **5**(b)   **6**(c)   **7**(b)
           8(b)   **9**(d)

Chapter 9: **1**(e)   **2**(b)   **3**(a)   **4**(b)   **5**(a)   **6**(a)

Chapter 11: **1**(c)   **2**(a)   **3**(d)

Chapter 12: **1**(a)   **2**(a)   **3**(c)   **4**(a)

Chapter 14: **1**(b)   **2**(e)   **3**(d)   **4**(d)   **5**(c)   **6**(d)   **7**(b)
           8(d)   **9**(b)

Chapter 15: **1**(e)   **2**(d)   **3**(c)   **4**(c)   **5**(a)   **6**(b)   **7**(c)
           8(c)   **9**(e)

Chapter 16: **1**(c)   **2**(b)   **3**(d)   **4**(b)   **5**(c)   **6**(c)   **7**(c)
           8(c)   **9**(d)   **10**(b)

Chapter 17: **1**(*e*)   **2**(*b*)   **3**(*b*)   **4**(*b*)   **5**(*b*)   **6**(*a*)   **7**(*e*)
           8(*d*)   **9**(*e*)   **10**(*b*)

Chapter 18: **1**(*a*)

Chapter 22: **1**(*c*)   **2**(*d*)   **3**(*e*)   **4**(*b*)   **5**(*d*)   **6**(*c*)   **7**(*b*)
           8(*d*)   **9**(*c*)   **10**(*c*)

Chapter 24: **1**(*e*)   **2**(*c*)

Chapter 25: **1**(*d*)   **2**(*e*)   **3**(*c*)   **4**(*d*)   **5**(*a*)   **6**(*a*)   **7**(*a*)
           8(*d*)

APPENDIX

Table A Normal distribution*

Proportion of total area under the curve from $-\infty$ to $Z = \dfrac{X - \mu}{\sigma}$. To illustrate: when $Z = 2$. the probability is 0.9773 of obtaining a value equal to or less than X.

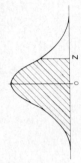

Z	0.09	0.08	0.07	0.06	0.05	0.04	0.03	0.02	0.01	0.00
−3.0	0.00100	0.00104	0.00107	0.00111	0.00114	0.00118	0.00122	0.00126	0.00131	0.00135
−2.9	0.0014	0.0014	0.0015	0.0015	0.0016	0.0016	0.0017	0.0017	0.0018	0.0019
−2.8	0.0019	0.0020	0.0021	0.0021	0.0022	0.0023	0.0023	0.0024	0.0025	0.0026
−2.7	0.0026	0.0027	0.0028	0.0029	0.0030	0.0031	0.0032	0.0033	0.0034	0.0035
−2.6	0.0036	0.0037	0.0038	0.0039	0.0040	0.0041	0.0043	0.0044	0.0045	0.0047
−2.5	0.0048	0.0049	0.0051	0.0052	0.0054	0.0055	0.0057	0.0059	0.0060	0.0062
−2.4	0.0064	0.0066	0.0068	0.0069	0.0071	0.0073	0.0075	0.0078	0.0080	0.0082
−2.3	0.0084	0.0087	0.0089	0.0091	0.0094	0.0096	0.0099	0.0102	0.0104	0.0107
−2.2	0.0110	0.0113	0.0116	0.0119	0.0122	0.0125	0.0129	0.0132	0.0136	0.0139
−2.1	0.0143	0.0146	0.0150	0.0154	0.0158	0.0162	0.0166	0.0170	0.0174	0.0179
−2.0	0.0183	0.0188	0.0192	0.0197	0.0202	0.0207	0.0212	0.0217	0.0222	0.0228
−1.9	0.0233	0.0239	0.0244	0.0250	0.0256	0.0262	0.0268	0.0274	0.0281	0.0287
−1.8	0.0294	0.0301	0.0307	0.0314	0.0322	0.0329	0.0336	0.0344	0.0351	0.0359
−1.7	0.0367	0.0375	0.0384	0.0392	0.0401	0.0409	0.0418	0.0427	0.0436	0.0446
−1.6	0.0455	0.0465	0.0475	0.0485	0.0495	0.0505	0.0516	0.0526	0.0537	0.0548
−1.5	0.0559	0.0571	0.0582	0.0594	0.0606	0.0618	0.0630	0.0643	0.0655	0.0668
−1.4	0.0681	0.0694	0.0708	0.0721	0.0735	0.0749	0.0764	0.0778	0.0793	0.0808
−1.3	0.0823	0.0838	0.0853	0.0869	0.0885	0.0901	0.0918	0.0934	0.0951	0.0968
−1.2	0.0985	0.1003	0.1020	0.1038	0.1057	0.1075	0.1093	0.1112	0.1131	0.1151
−1.1	0.1170	0.1190	0.1210	0.1230	0.1251	0.1271	0.1292	0.1314	0.1335	0.1357

Table A Normal distribution (*continued*)

Z	0.00	0.01	0.02	0.03	0.04	0.05	0.06	0.07	0.08	0.09
−1.0	0.1587	0.1562	0.1539	0.1515	0.1492	0.1469	0.1446	0.1423	0.1401	0.1379
−0.9	0.1841	0.1814	0.1788	0.1762	0.1736	0.1711	0.1685	0.1660	0.1635	0.1611
−0.8	0.2119	0.2090	0.2061	0.2033	0.2005	0.1977	0.1949	0.1922	0.1894	0.1867
−0.7	0.2420	0.2389	0.2358	0.2327	0.2297	0.2266	0.2236	0.2207	0.2177	0.2148
−0.6	0.2743	0.2709	0.2676	0.2643	0.2611	0.2578	0.2546	0.2514	0.2483	0.2451
−0.5	0.3085	0.3050	0.3015	0.2981	0.2946	0.2912	0.2877	0.2843	0.2810	0.2776
−0.4	0.3446	0.3409	0.3372	0.3336	0.3300	0.3264	0.3228	0.3192	0.3156	0.3121
−0.3	0.3821	0.3783	0.3745	0.3707	0.3669	0.3632	0.3594	0.3557	0.3520	0.3483
−0.2	0.4207	0.4168	0.4129	0.4090	0.4052	0.4013	0.3974	0.3936	0.3897	0.3859
−0.1	0.4602	0.4562	0.4522	0.4483	0.4443	0.4404	0.4364	0.4325	0.4286	0.4247
−0.0	0.5000	0.4960	0.4920	0.4880	0.4840	0.4801	0.4761	0.4721	0.4681	0.4641

Z	0.00	0.01	0.02	0.03	0.04	0.05	0.06	0.07	0.08	0.09
+0.0	0.5000	0.5040	0.5080	0.5120	0.5160	0.5199	0.5239	0.5279	0.5319	0.5359
+0.1	0.5398	0.5438	0.5478	0.5517	0.5557	0.5596	0.5636	0.5675	0.5714	0.5753
+0.2	0.5793	0.5832	0.5871	0.5910	0.5948	0.5987	0.6026	0.6064	0.6103	0.6141
+0.3	0.6179	0.6217	0.6255	0.6293	0.6331	0.6368	0.6406	0.6443	0.6480	0.6517
+0.4	0.6554	0.6591	0.6628	0.6664	0.6700	0.6736	0.6772	0.6808	0.6844	0.6879
+0.5	0.6915	0.6950	0.6985	0.7019	0.7054	0.7088	0.7123	0.7157	0.7190	0.7224
+0.6	0.7257	0.7291	0.7324	0.7357	0.7389	0.7422	0.7454	0.7486	0.7517	0.7549
+0.7	0.7580	0.7611	0.7642	0.7673	0.7704	0.7734	0.7764	0.7794	0.7823	0.7852
+0.8	0.7881	0.7910	0.7939	0.7967	0.7995	0.8023	0.8051	0.8079	0.8106	0.8133
+0.9	0.8159	0.8186	0.8212	0.8238	0.8264	0.8289	0.8315	0.8340	0.8365	0.8389
+1.0	0.8413	0.8438	0.8461	0.8485	0.8508	0.8531	0.8554	0.8577	0.8599	0.8621
+1.1	0.8643	0.8665	0.8686	0.8708	0.8729	0.8749	0.8770	0.8790	0.8810	0.8830
+1.2	0.8849	0.8869	0.8888	0.8907	0.8925	0.8944	0.8962	0.8980	0.8997	0.9015
+1.3	0.9032	0.9049	0.9066	0.9082	0.9099	0.9115	0.9131	0.9147	0.9162	0.9177
+1.4	0.9192	0.9207	0.9222	0.9236	0.9251	0.9265	0.9279	0.9292	0.9306	0.9319
+1.5	0.9332	0.9345	0.9357	0.9370	0.9382	0.9394	0.9406	0.9418	0.9429	0.9441

Table A Normal distribution (*continued*)

Z	0.00	0.01	0.02	0.03	0.04	0.05	0.06	0.07	0.08	0.09
+1.6	0.9452	0.9463	0.9474	0.9484	0.9495	0.9505	0.9515	0.9525	0.9535	0.9545
+1.7	0.9554	0.9564	0.9573	0.9582	0.9591	0.9599	0.9608	0.9616	0.9625	0.9633
+1.8	0.9641	0.9649	0.9656	0.9664	0.9671	0.9678	0.9686	0.9693	0.9699	0.9706
+1.9	0.9713	0.9719	0.9726	0.9732	0.9738	0.9744	0.9750	0.9756	0.9761	0.9767
+2.0	0.9773	0.9778	0.9783	0.9788	0.9793	0.9798	0.9803	0.9808	0.9812	0.9817
+2.1	0.9821	0.9826	0.9830	0.9834	0.9838	0.9842	0.9846	0.9850	0.9854	0.9857
+2.2	0.9861	0.9864	0.9868	0.9871	0.9875	0.9878	0.9881	0.9884	0.9887	0.9890
+2.3	0.9893	0.9896	0.9898	0.9901	0.9904	0.9906	0.9909	0.9911	0.9913	0.9916
+2.4	0.9918	0.9920	0.9922	0.9925	0.9927	0.9929	0.9931	0.9932	0.9934	0.9936
+2.5	0.9938	0.9940	0.9941	0.9943	0.9945	0.9946	0.9948	0.9949	0.9951	0.9952
+2.6	0.9953	0.9955	0.9956	0.9957	0.9959	0.9960	0.9961	0.9962	0.9963	0.9964
+2.7	0.9965	0.9966	0.9967	0.9968	0.9969	0.9970	0.9971	0.9972	0.9973	0.9974
+2.8	0.9974	0.9975	0.9976	0.9977	0.9977	0.9978	0.9979	0.9979	0.9980	0.9981
+2.9	0.9981	0.9982	0.9983	0.9983	0.9984	0.9984	0.9985	0.9985	0.9986	0.9986
+3.0	0.99865	0.99869	0.99874	0.99878	0.99882	0.99886	0.99889	0.99893	0.99896	0.99900

*Adapted with permission from Eugene L. Grant and Richard S. Leavenworth, *Statistical Quality Control*, 4th ed., McGraw-Hill Book Company, New York, 1972, pp. 642–643.

Table B Exponential distribution values of $e^{-X/\mu}$ for various values*

Fractional parts of the total area (1.000) under the exponential curve greater than X. To illustrate: if X/μ is 0.45, the probability of occurrence for a value greater than X is 0.6376.

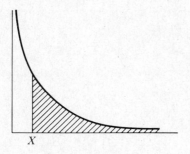

$\dfrac{X}{\mu}$	0.00	0.01	0.02	0.03	0.04	0.05	0.06	0.07	0.08	0.09
0.0	1.000	0.9900	0.9802	0.9704	0.9608	0.9512	0.9418	0.9324	0.9231	0.9139
0.1	0.9048	0.8958	0.8860	0.8781	0.8694	0.8607	0.8521	0.8437	0.8353	0.8270
0.2	0.8187	0.8106	0.8025	0.7945	0.7866	0.7788	0.7711	0.7634	0.7558	0.7483
0.3	0.7408	0.7334	0.7261	0.7189	0.7118	0.7047	0.6977	0.6907	0.6839	0.6771
0.4	0.6703	0.6637	0.6570	0.6505	0.6440	0.6376	0.6313	0.6250	0.6188	0.6126
0.5	0.6065	0.6005	0.5945	0.5886	0.5827	0.5769	0.5712	0.5655	0.5599	0.5543
0.6	0.5488	0.5434	0.5379	0.5326	0.5273	0.5220	0.5169	0.5117	0.5066	0.5016
0.7	0.4966	0.4916	0.4868	0.4819	0.4771	0.4724	0.4677	0.4630	0.4584	0.4538
0.8	0.4493	0.4449	0.4404	0.4360	0.4317	0.4274	0.4232	0.4190	0.4148	0.4107
0.9	0.4066	0.4025	0.3985	0.3946	0.3906	0.3867	0.3829	0.3791	0.3753	0.3716

$\dfrac{X}{\mu}$	0.0	0.1	0.2	0.3	0.4	0.5	0.6	0.7	0.8	0.9
1.0	0.3679	0.3329	0.3012	0.2725	0.2466	0.2231	0.2019	0.1827	0.1653	0.1496
2.0	0.1353	0.1225	0.1108	0.1003	0.0907	0.0821	0.0743	0.0672	0.0608	0.0550
3.0	0.0498	0.0450	0.0408	0.0369	0.0334	0.0302	0.0273	0.0247	0.0224	0.0202
4.0	0.0183	0.0166	0.0150	0.0130	0.0123	0.0111	0.0101	0.0091	0.0082	0.0074
5.0	0.0067	0.0061	0.0055	0.0050	0.0045	0.0041	0.0037	0.0033	0.0030	0.0027
6.0	0.0025	0.0022	0.0020	0.0018	0.0017	0.0015	0.0014	0.0012	0.0011	0.0010

*Adapted from S. M. Selby (ed.), *CRC Standard Mathematical Tables*, 17th ed., CRC Press, Cleveland, Ohio, 1969, pp. 201–207.

Table C Poisson distribution*

1,000 × probability of *r* or fewer occurrences of event that has average number of occurrences equal to *np*.

np \ r	0	1	2	3	4	5	6	7	8	9
0.02	980	1,000								
0.04	961	999	1,000							
0.06	942	998	1,000							
0.08	923	997	1,000							
0.10	905	995	1,000							
0.15	861	990	999	1,000						
0.20	819	982	999	1,000						
0.25	779	974	998	1,000						
0.30	741	963	996	1,000						
0.35	705	951	994	1,000						
0.40	670	938	992	999	1,000					
0.45	638	925	989	999	1,000					
0.50	607	910	986	998	1,000					
0.55	577	894	982	998	1,000					
0.60	549	878	977	997	1,000					
0.65	522	861	972	996	999	1,000				
0.70	497	844	966	994	999	1,000				
0.75	472	827	959	993	999	1,000				
0.80	449	809	953	991	999	1,000				
0.85	427	791	945	989	998	1,000				
0.90	407	772	937	987	998	1,000				
0.95	387	754	929	984	997	1,000				
1.00	368	736	920	981	996	999	1,000			
1.1	333	699	900	974	995	999	1,000			
1.2	301	663	879	966	992	998	1,000			
1.3	273	627	857	957	989	998	1,000			
1.4	247	592	833	946	986	997	999	1,000		
1.5	223	558	809	934	981	996	999	1,000		
1.6	202	525	783	921	976	994	999	1,000		
1.7	183	493	757	907	970	992	998	1,000		
1.8	165	463	731	891	964	990	997	999	1,000	
1.9	150	434	704	875	956	987	997	999	1,000	
2.0	135	406	677	857	947	983	995	999	1,000	

Table C Poisson distribution *(continued)*

np \ r	0	1	2	3	4	5	6	7	8	9
2.2	111	355	623	819	928	975	993	998	1,000	
2.4	091	308	570	779	904	964	988	997	999	1,000
2.6	074	267	518	736	877	951	983	995	999	1,000
2.8	061	231	469	692	848	935	976	992	998	999
3.0	050	199	423	647	815	916	966	988	996	999
3.2	041	171	380	603	781	895	955	983	994	998
3.4	033	147	340	558	744	871	942	977	992	997
3.6	027	126	303	515	706	844	927	969	988	996
3.8	022	107	269	473	668	816	909	960	984	994
4.0	018	092	238	433	629	785	889	949	979	992
4.2	015	078	210	395	590	753	867	936	972	989
4.4	012	066	185	359	551	720	844	921	964	985
4.6	010	056	163	326	513	686	818	905	955	980
4.8	008	048	143	294	476	651	791	887	944	975
5.0	007	040	125	265	440	616	762	867	932	968
5.2	006	034	109	238	406	581	732	845	918	960
5.4	005	029	095	213	373	546	702	822	903	951
5.6	004	024	082	191	342	512	670	797	886	941
5.8	003	021	072	170	313	478	638	771	867	929
6.0	002	017	062	151	285	446	606	744	847	916

np \ r	10	11	12	13	14	15	16
2.8	1,000						
3.0	1,000						
3.2	1,000						
3.4	999	1,000					
3.6	999	1,000					
3.8	998	999	1,000				
4.0	997	999	1,000				
4.2	996	999	1,000				
4.4	994	998	999	1,000			
4.6	992	997	999	1,000			
4.8	990	996	999	1,000			
5.0	986	995	998	999	1,000		
5.2	982	993	997	999	1,000		
5.4	977	990	996	999	1,000		
5.6	972	988	995	998	999	1,000	
5.8	965	984	993	997	999	1,000	
6.0	957	980	991	996	999	999	1,000

Table C Poisson distribution *(continued)*

np \ r	0	1	2	3	4	5	6	7	8	9
6.2	002	015	054	134	259	414	574	716	826	902
6.4	002	012	046	119	235	384	542	687	803	886
6.6	001	010	040	105	213	355	511	658	780	869
6.8	001	009	034	093	192	327	480	628	755	850
7.0	001	007	030	082	173	301	450	599	729	830
7.2	001	006	025	072	156	276	420	569	703	810
7.4	001	005	022	063	140	253	392	539	676	788
7.6	001	004	019	055	125	231	365	510	648	765
7.8	000	004	016	048	112	210	338	481	620	741
8.0	000	003	014	042	100	191	313	453	593	717
8.5	000	002	009	030	074	150	256	386	523	653
9.0	000	001	006	021	055	116	207	324	456	587
9.5	000	001	004	015	040	089	165	269	392	522
10.0	000	000	003	010	029	067	130	220	333	458

np \ r	10	11	12	13	14	15	16	17	18	19
6.2	949	975	989	995	998	999	1,000			
6.4	939	969	986	994	997	999	1,000			
6.6	927	963	982	992	997	999	999	1,000		
6.8	915	955	978	990	996	998	999	1,000		
7.0	901	947	973	987	994	998	999	1,000		
7.2	887	937	967	984	993	997	999	999	1,000	
7.4	871	926	961	980	991	996	998	999	1,000	
7.6	854	915	954	976	989	995	998	999	1,000	
7.8	835	902	945	971	986	993	997	999	1,000	
8.0	816	888	936	966	983	992	996	998	999	1,000
8.5	763	849	909	949	973	986	993	997	999	999
9.0	706	803	876	926	959	978	989	995	998	999
9.5	645	752	836	898	940	967	982	991	996	998
10.0	583	697	792	864	917	951	973	986	993	997

np \ r	20	21	22
8.5	1,000		
9.0	1,000		
9.5	999	1,000	
10.0	998	999	1,000

*Adapted with permission from E. L. Grant and Richard S. Leavenworth, *Statistical Quality Control*, 4th ed., McGraw-Hill Book Company, New York, 1972.

Table D Distribution of t*

Value of t corresponding to certain selected probabilities (i.e., tail areas under the curve). To illustrate: the probability is 0.975 that a sample with 20 degrees of freedom would have $t = +2.086$ or smaller.

DF	$t_{.60}$	$t_{.70}$	$t_{.80}$	$t_{.90}$	$t_{.95}$	$t_{.975}$	$t_{.99}$	$t_{.995}$
1	0.325	0.727	1.376	3.078	6.314	12.706	31.821	63.657
2	0.289	0.617	1.061	1.886	2.920	4.303	6.965	9.925
3	0.277	0.584	0.978	1.638	2.353	3.182	4.541	5.841
4	0.271	0.569	0.941	1.533	2.132	2.776	3.747	4.604
5	0.267	0.559	0.920	1.476	2.015	2.571	3.365	4.032
6	0.265	0.553	0.906	1.440	1.943	2.447	3.143	3.707
7	0.263	0.549	0.896	1.415	1.895	2.365	2.998	3.499
8	0.262	0.546	0.889	1.397	1.860	2.306	2.896	3.355
9	0.261	0.543	0.883	1.383	1.833	2.262	2.821	3.250
10	0.260	0.542	0.879	1.372	1.812	2.228	2.764	3.169
11	0.260	0.540	0.876	1.363	1.796	2.201	2.718	3.106
12	0.259	0.539	0.873	1.356	1.782	2.179	2.681	3.055
13	0.259	0.538	0.870	1.350	1.771	2.160	2.650	3.012
14	0.258	0.537	0.868	1.345	1.761	2.145	2.624	2.977
15	0.258	0.536	0.866	1.341	1.753	2.131	2.602	2.947
16	0.258	0.535	0.865	1.337	1.746	2.120	2.583	2.921
17	0.257	0.534	0.863	1.333	1.740	2.110	2.567	2.898
18	0.257	0.534	0.862	1.330	1.734	2.101	2.552	2.878
19	0.257	0.533	0.861	1.328	1.729	2.093	2.539	2.861
20	0.257	0.533	0.860	1.325	1.725	2.086	2.528	2.845
21	0.257	0.532	0.859	1.323	1.721	2.080	2.518	2.831
22	0.256	0.532	0.858	1.321	1.717	2.074	2.508	2.819
23	0.256	0.532	0.858	1.319	1.714	2.069	2.500	2.807
24	0.256	0.531	0.857	1.318	1.711	2.064	2.492	2.797
25	0.256	0.531	0.856	1.316	1.708	2.060	2.485	2.787
26	0.256	0.531	0.856	1.315	1.706	2.056	2.479	2.779
27	0.256	0.531	0.855	1.314	1.703	2.052	2.473	2.771
28	0.256	0.530	0.855	1.313	1.701	2.048	2.467	2.763
29	0.256	0.530	0.854	1.311	1.699	2.045	2.462	2.756
30	0.256	0.530	0.854	1.310	1.697	2.042	2.457	2.750
40	0.255	0.529	0.851	1.303	1.684	2.021	2.423	2.704
60	0.254	0.527	0.848	1.296	1.671	2.000	2.390	2.660
120	0.254	0.526	0.845	1.289	1.658	1.980	2.358	2.617
∞	0.253	0.524	0.842	1.282	1.645	1.960	2.326	2.576

*Adapted by permission from W. J. Dixon and F. J. Massey, Jr., *Introduction to Statistical Analysis*, 3rd ed., McGraw-Hill Book Company, New York, copyright © 1969. Entries originally from Table III of R. A. Fisher and F. Yates, *Statistical Tables*, Oliver & Boyd Ltd., London.

Table E Distribution of χ^2*

Values of χ^2 corresponding to certain selected probabilities (i.e., tail areas under the curve). To illustrate: the probability is 0.95 that a sample with 20 degrees of freedom, taken from a normal distribution, would have $\chi^2 = 31.41$ or smaller.

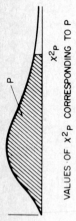

VALUES OF χ^2_P CORRESPONDING TO P

DF	$\chi^2_{.005}$	$\chi^2_{.01}$	$\chi^2_{.025}$	$\chi^2_{.05}$	$\chi^2_{.10}$	$\chi^2_{.90}$	$\chi^2_{.95}$	$\chi^2_{.975}$	$\chi^2_{.99}$	$\chi^2_{.995}$
1	0.000039	0.00016	0.00098	0.0039	0.0158	2.71	3.84	5.02	6.63	7.88
2	0.0100	0.0201	0.0506	0.1026	0.2107	4.61	5.99	7.38	9.21	10.60
3	0.0717	0.115	0.216	0.352	0.584	6.25	7.81	9.35	11.34	12.84
4	0.207	0.297	0.484	0.711	1.064	7.78	9.49	11.14	13.28	14.86
5	0.412	0.554	0.831	1.15	1.61	9.24	11.07	12.83	15.09	16.75
6	0.676	0.872	1.24	1.64	2.20	10.64	12.59	14.45	16.81	18.55
7	0.989	1.24	1.69	2.17	2.83	12.02	14.07	16.01	18.48	20.28
8	1.34	1.65	2.18	2.73	3.49	13.36	15.51	17.53	20.09	21.96
9	1.73	2.09	2.70	3.33	4.17	14.68	16.92	19.02	21.67	23.59
10	2.16	2.56	3.25	3.94	4.87	15.99	18.31	20.48	23.21	25.19
11	2.60	3.05	3.82	4.57	5.58	17.28	19.68	21.92	24.73	26.76
12	3.07	3.57	4.40	5.23	6.30	18.55	21.03	23.34	26.22	28.30
13	3.57	4.11	5.01	5.89	7.04	19.81	22.36	24.74	27.69	29.82
14	4.07	4.66	5.63	6.57	7.79	21.06	23.68	26.12	29.14	31.32
15	4.60	5.23	6.26	7.26	8.55	22.31	25.00	27.49	30.58	32.80
16	5.14	5.81	6.91	7.96	9.31	23.54	26.30	28.85	32.00	34.27
18	6.26	7.01	8.23	9.39	10.86	25.99	28.87	31.53	34.81	37.16
20	7.43	8.26	9.59	10.85	12.44	28.41	31.41	34.17	37.57	40.00
24	9.89	10.86	12.40	13.85	15.66	33.20	36.42	39.36	42.98	45.56
30	13.79	14.95	16.79	18.49	20.60	40.26	43.77	46.98	50.89	53.67
40	20.71	22.16	24.43	26.51	29.05	51.81	55.76	59.34	63.69	66.77
60	35.53	37.48	40.48	43.19	46.46	74.40	79.08	83.30	88.38	91.95
120	83.85	86.92	91.58	95.70	100.62	140.23	146.57	152.21	158.95	163.64

*Adapted with permission from W. J. Dixon and F. J. Massey, Jr., *Introduction to Statistical Analysis*, 3rd ed., McGraw-Hill Book Company, New York, copyright © 1969.

Table F **Ninety-five percent confidence belts for population proportion***

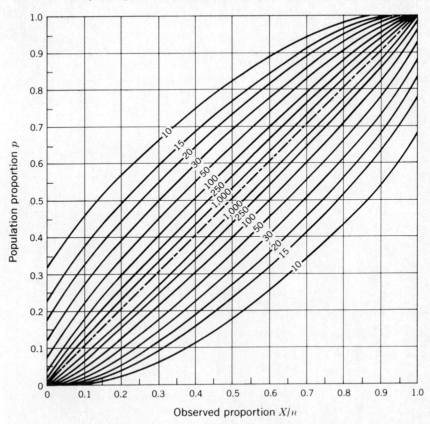

Observed proportion X/n

*From C. Eisenhart, M. W. Hastay, and W. A. Wallis, *Selected Techniques of Statistical Analysis—OSRD*, McGraw-Hill Book Company, New York, 1947.

Example In a sample of 10 items, 8 were defective ($x/n = 8/10$). The 95% confidence limits on the population proportion defective are read from the two curves (for $n = 10$) as 0.43 and 0.98.

Table G Distribution of F*†

Values of F corresponding to certain selected probabilities (i.e., tail areas under the curve). To illustrate: the probability is 0.05 that the ratio of two sample variances obtained with 20 and 10 degrees of freedom in numerator and denominator, respectively, would have $F = 2.77$ or larger. For a two-sided test, a lower limit is found by taking the reciprocal of the tabulated F value for the degrees of freedom in reverse. For the above example, with 10 and 20 degrees of freedom in numerator and denominator respectively, F is 2.35 and $1/F$ is 1/2.35, or 0.43. The probability is 0.10 that F is 0.43 or smaller or 2.77 or larger.

n_2 \ n_1	1	2	3	4	5	6	7	8	9
				$F_{.95}$	(n_1, n_2)				
1	161.4	199.5	215.7	224.6	230.2	234.0	236.8	238.9	240.5
2	18.51	19.00	19.16	19.25	19.30	19.33	19.35	19.37	19.38
3	10.13	9.55	9.28	9.12	9.01	8.94	8.89	8.85	8.81
4	7.71	6.94	6.59	6.39	6.26	6.16	6.09	6.04	6.00
5	6.61	5.79	5.41	5.19	5.05	4.95	4.88	4.82	4.77
6	5.99	5.14	4.76	4.53	4.39	4.28	4.21	4.15	4.10
7	5.59	4.74	4.35	4.12	3.97	3.87	3.79	3.73	3.68
8	5.32	4.46	4.07	3.84	3.69	3.58	3.50	3.44	3.39
9	5.12	4.26	3.86	3.63	3.48	3.37	3.29	3.23	3.18
10	4.96	4.10	3.71	3.48	3.33	3.22	3.14	3.07	3.02
11	4.84	3.98	3.59	3.36	3.20	3.09	3.01	2.95	2.90
12	4.75	3.89	3.49	3.26	3.11	3.00	2.91	2.85	2.80
13	4.67	3.81	3.41	3.18	3.03	2.92	2.83	2.77	2.71
14	4.60	3.74	3.34	3.11	2.96	2.85	2.76	2.70	2.65
15	4.54	3.68	3.29	3.06	2.90	2.79	2.71	2.64	2.59
16	4.49	3.63	3.24	3.01	2.85	2.74	2.66	2.59	2.54
17	4.45	3.59	3.20	2.96	2.81	2.70	2.61	2.55	2.49
18	4.41	3.55	3.16	2.93	2.77	2.66	2.58	2.51	2.46
19	4.38	3.52	3.13	2.90	2.74	2.63	2.54	2.48	2.42
20	4.35	3.49	3.10	2.87	2.71	2.60	2.51	2.45	2.39
21	4.32	3.47	3.07	2.84	2.68	2.57	2.49	2.42	2.37
22	4.30	3.44	3.05	2.82	2.66	2.55	2.46	2.40	2.34
23	4.28	3.42	3.03	2.80	2.64	2.53	2.44	2.37	2.32
24	4.26	3.40	3.01	2.78	2.62	2.51	2.42	2.36	2.30
25	4.24	3.39	2.99	2.76	2.60	2.49	2.40	2.34	2.28
26	4.23	3.37	2.98	2.74	2.59	2.47	2.39	2.32	2.27
27	4.21	3.35	2.96	2.73	2.57	2.46	2.37	2.31	2.25
28	4.20	3.34	2.95	2.71	2.56	2.45	2.36	2.29	2.24
29	4.18	3.33	2.93	2.70	2.55	2.43	2.35	2.28	2.22
30	4.17	3.32	2.92	2.69	2.53	2.42	2.33	2.27	2.21
40	4.08	3.23	2.84	2.61	2.45	2.34	2.25	2.18	2.12
60	4.00	3.15	2.76	2.53	2.37	2.25	2.17	2.10	2.04
120	3.92	3.07	2.68	2.45	2.29	2.17	2.09	2.02	1.96
∞	3.84	3.00	2.60	2.37	2.21	2.10	2.01	1.94	1.88

*n_1 = degrees of freedom for numerator; n_2 = degrees of freedom for denominator.

†Adapted with permission from E. S. Pearson and H. O. Hartley (eds.), *Biometrika Tables for Statisticians*, 2nd ed., vol. I, Cambridge University Press, New York, 1958.

10	12	15	20	24	30	40	60	120	∞
				$F_{.95}\,(n_1,\,n_2)$					
241.9	243.9	245.9	248.0	249.1	250.1	251.1	252.2	253.3	254.3
19.40	19.41	19.43	19.45	19.45	19.46	19.47	19.48	19.49	19.50
8.79	8.74	8.70	8.66	8.64	8.62	8.59	8.57	8.55	8.53
5.96	5.91	5.86	5.80	5.77	5.75	5.72	5.69	5.66	5.63
4.74	4.68	4.62	4.56.	4.53	4.50	4.46	4.43	4.40	4.36
4.06	4.00	3.94	3.87	3.84	3.81	3.77	3.74	3.70	3.67
3.64	3.57	3.51	3.44	3.41	3.38	3.34	3.30	3.27	3.23
3.35	3.28	3.22	3.15	3.12	3.08	3.04	3.01	2.97	2.93
3.14	3.07	3.01	2.94	2.90	2.86	2.83	2.79	2.75	2.71
2.98	2.91	2.85	2.77	2.74	2.70	2.66	2.62	2.58	2.54
2.85	2.79	2.72	2.65	2.61	2.57	2.53	2.49	2.45	2.40
2.75	2.69	2.62	2.54	2.51	2.47	2.43	2.38	2.34	2.30
2.67	2.60	2.53	2.46	2.42	2.38	2.34	2.30	2.25	2.21
2.60	2.53	2.46	2.39	2.35	2.31	2.27	2.22	2.18	2.13
2.54	2.48	2.40	2.33	2.29	2.25	2.20	2.16	2.11	2.07
2.49	2.42	2.35	2.28	2.24	2.19	2.15	2.11	2.06	2.01
2.45	2.38	2.31	2.23	2.19	2.15	2.10	2.06	2.01	1.96
2.41	2.34	2.27	2.19	2.15	2.11	2.06	2.02	1.97	1.92
2.38	2.31	2.23	2.16	2.11	2.07	2.03	1.98	1.93	1.88
2.35	2.28	2.20	2.12	2.08	2.04	1.99	1.95	1.90	1.84
2.32	2.25	2.18	2.10	2.05	2.01	1.96	1.92	1.87	1.81
2.30	2.23	2.15	2.07	2.03	1.98	1.94	1.89	1.84	1.78
2.27	2.20	2.13	2.05	2.01	1.96	1.91	1.86	1.81	1.76
2.25	2.18	2.11	2.03	1.98	1.94	1.89	1.84	1.79	1.73
2.24	2.16	2.09	2.01	1.96	1.92	1.87	1.82	1.77	1.71
2.22	2.15	2.07	1.99	1.95	1.90	1.85	1.80	1.75	1.69
2.20	2.13	2.06	1.97	1.93	1.88	1.84	1.79	1.73	1.67
2.19	2.12	2.04	1.96	1.91	1.87	1.82	1.77	1.71	1.65
2.18	2.10	2.03	1.94	1.90	1.85	1.81	1.75	1.70	1.64
2.16	2.09	2.01	1.93	1.89	1.84	1.79	1.74	1.68	1.62
2.08	2.00	1.92	1.84	1.79	1.74	1.69	1.64	1.58	1.51
1.99	1.92	1.84	1.75	1.70	1.65	1.59	1.53	1.47	1.39
1.91	1.83	1.75	1.66	1.61	1.55	1.50	1.43	1.35	1.25
1.83	1.75	1.67	1.57	1.52	1.46	1.39	1.32	1.22	1.00

Table H Limits for determining discrepancies between supplier's and consumer's attributes sampling inspections*

Number of defectives in supplier sample	Supplier sample size/ consumer sample size				
	1	2	3	5	8
0	3	2	2	1	1
1	5	3	3	2	2
2	7	4	3	3	2
3	9	5	4	3	2
4	11	6	5	3	3
5	12	7	5	4	3
6	14	8	6	4	3
7	15	9	6	5	3

*From Handbook H109, "Statistical Procedures for Determining Validity of Supplier's Attributes Inspection," Office of the Assistant Secretary of Defense, Washington, D.C., 1960.

Table I Factors for $\overline{X}$ and R control charts;*
factors for estimating s from R†

$\begin{cases} \text{Upper control limit for } \overline{X} = \text{UCL}_{\overline{x}} = \overline{\overline{X}} + A_2\overline{R} \\ \text{Lower control limit for } \overline{X} = \text{LCL}_{\overline{x}} = \overline{\overline{X}} - A_2\overline{R} \end{cases}$

$\begin{cases} \text{Upper control limit for } R = \text{UCL}_{\overline{R}} = D_4\overline{R} \\ \text{Lower control limit for } R = \text{LCL}_{\overline{R}} = D_3\overline{R} \end{cases}$

$s = \overline{R}/d_2$

Number of observations in sample	A_2	D_3	D_4	Factor for estimate from $\overline{R}$: $d_2 = \overline{R}/s$
2	1.880	0	3.268	1.128
3	1.023	0	2.574	1.693
4	0.729	0	2.282	2.059
5	0.577	0	2.114	2.326
6	0.483	0	2.004	2.534
7	0.419	0.076	1.924	2.704
8	0.373	0.136	1.864	2.847
9	0.337	0.184	1.816	2.970
10	0.308	0.223	1.777	3.078
11	0.285	0.256	1.744	3.173
12	0.266	0.284	1.717	3.258
13	0.249	0.308	1.692	3.336
14	0.235	0.329	1.671	3.407
15	0.223	0.348	1.652	3.472

*Factors reproduced from *1950 ASTM Manual on Quality Control of Materials* by permission of the American Society for Testing and Materials, Philadelphia. All factors in Table I are based on a normal distribution.

†Reproduced by permission from *ASTM Manual on Presentation of Data,* American Society for Testing and Materials, Philadelphia, 1945.

Table J Factors for finding target value*

$\dfrac{\delta}{\sigma}$	$\dfrac{g\sigma}{a-r}$	$\dfrac{\delta}{\sigma}$	$\dfrac{g\sigma}{a-r}$
4.00	0.00013	−0.10	0.86262
3.50	0.00087	−0.20	0.92942
3.00	0.00444	−0.30	0.99817
2.90	0.00596	−0.40	1.06876
2.80	0.00794	−0.50	1.14108
2.70	0.01046	−0.60	1.21503
2.60	0.01365	−0.70	1.29050
2.50	0.01764	−0.80	1.36740
2.40	0.02258	−0.90	1.44564
2.30	0.02863	−1.00	1.52514
2.20	0.03597	−1.10	1.60580
2.10	0.04478	−1.20	1.68755
2.00	0.05525	−1.30	1.77033
1.90	0.06756	−1.40	1.85406
1.80	0.08189	−1.50	1.93868
1.70	0.09844	−1.60	2.02413
1.60	0.11735	−1.70	2.11036
1.50	0.13879	−1.80	2.19732
1.40	0.16288	−1.90	2.28495
1.30	0.18973	−1.99	2.36437
1.20	0.21944		
1.10	0.25205		
1.00	0.28760		
0.90	0.32611		
0.80	0.36756		
0.70	0.41192		
0.60	0.45915		
0.50	0.50916		
0.40	0.56188		
0.30	0.61722		
0.20	0.67507		
0.10	0.73533		
0.0	0.79788		

*From William G. Hunter and C. P. Kartha, "Determining the Most Profitable Target Value for a Production Process," *Journal of Quality Technology,* October 1977, p. 180.

Table K Tolerance factors for normal distributions (two-sided)*

N	γ = 0.75					γ = 0.90					γ = 0.95					γ = 0.99				
P	0.75	0.90	0.95	0.99	0.999	0.75	0.90	0.95	0.99	0.999	0.75	0.90	0.95	0.99	0.999	0.75	0.90	0.95	0.99	0.999
2	4.498	6.301	7.414	9.531	11.920	11.407	15.978	18.800	24.167	30.227	22.858	32.019	37.674	48.430	60.573	114.363	160.193	188.491	242.300	303.054
3	2.501	3.538	4.187	5.431	6.844	4.132	5.847	6.919	8.974	11.309	5.922	8.380	9.916	12.861	16.208	13.378	18.930	22.401	29.055	36.616
4	2.035	2.892	3.431	4.471	5.657	2.932	4.166	4.943	6.440	8.149	3.779	5.369	6.370	8.299	10.502	6.614	9.398	11.150	14.527	18.383
5	1.825	2.599	3.088	4.033	5.117	2.454	3.494	4.152	5.423	6.879	3.002	4.275	5.079	6.634	8.415	4.643	6.612	7.855	10.260	13.015
6	1.704	2.429	2.889	3.779	4.802	2.196	3.131	3.723	4.870	6.188	2.604	3.712	4.414	5.775	7.337	3.743	5.337	6.345	8.301	10.548
7	1.624	2.318	2.757	3.611	4.593	2.034	2.902	3.452	4.521	5.750	2.361	3.369	4.007	5.248	6.676	3.233	4.613	5.488	7.187	9.142
8	1.568	2.238	2.663	3.491	4.444	1.921	2.743	3.264	4.278	5.446	2.197	3.136	3.732	4.891	6.226	2.905	4.147	4.936	6.468	8.234
9	1.525	2.178	2.593	3.400	4.330	1.839	2.626	3.125	4.098	5.220	2.078	2.967	3.532	4.631	5.899	2.677	3.822	4.550	5.966	7.600
10	1.492	2.131	2.537	3.328	4.241	1.775	2.535	3.018	3.959	5.046	1.987	2.839	3.379	4.433	5.649	2.508	3.582	4.265	5.594	7.129
11	1.465	2.093	2.493	3.271	4.169	1.724	2.463	2.933	3.849	4.906	1.916	2.737	3.259	4.277	5.452	2.378	3.397	4.045	5.308	6.766
12	1.443	2.062	2.456	3.223	4.110	1.683	2.404	2.863	3.758	4.792	1.858	2.655	3.162	4.150	5.291	2.274	3.250	3.870	5.079	6.477
13	1.425	2.036	2.424	3.183	4.059	1.648	2.355	2.805	3.682	4.697	1.810	2.587	3.081	4.044	5.158	2.190	3.130	3.727	4.893	6.240
14	1.409	2.013	2.398	3.148	4.016	1.619	2.314	2.756	3.618	4.615	1.770	2.529	3.012	3.955	5.045	2.120	3.029	3.608	4.737	6.043
15	1.395	1.994	2.375	3.118	3.979	1.594	2.278	2.713	3.562	4.545	1.735	2.480	2.954	3.878	4.949	2.060	2.945	3.507	4.605	5.876
16	1.383	1.977	2.355	3.092	3.946	1.572	2.246	2.676	3.514	4.484	1.705	2.437	2.903	3.812	4.865	2.009	2.872	3.421	4.492	5.732
17	1.372	1.962	2.337	3.069	3.917	1.552	2.219	2.643	3.471	4.430	1.679	2.400	2.858	3.754	4.791	1.965	2.808	3.345	4.393	5.607
18	1.363	1.948	2.321	3.048	3.891	1.535	2.194	2.614	3.433	4.382	1.655	2.366	2.819	3.702	4.725	1.926	2.753	3.279	4.307	5.497
19	1.355	1.936	2.307	3.030	3.867	1.520	2.172	2.588	3.399	4.339	1.635	2.337	2.784	3.656	4.667	1.891	2.703	3.221	4.230	5.399
20	1.347	1.925	2.294	3.013	3.846	1.506	2.152	2.564	3.368	4.300	1.616	2.310	2.752	3.615	4.614	1.860	2.659	3.168	4.161	5.312
21	1.340	1.915	2.282	2.998	3.827	1.493	2.135	2.543	3.340	4.264	1.599	2.286	2.723	3.577	4.567	1.833	2.620	3.121	4.100	5.234
22	1.334	1.906	2.271	2.984	3.809	1.482	2.118	2.524	3.315	4.232	1.584	2.264	2.697	3.543	4.523	1.808	2.584	3.078	4.044	5.163
23	1.328	1.898	2.261	2.971	3.793	1.471	2.103	2.506	3.292	4.203	1.570	2.244	2.673	3.512	4.484	1.785	2.551	3.040	3.993	5.098
24	1.322	1.891	2.252	2.950	3.778	1.462	2.089	2.480	3.270	4.176	1.557	2.225	2.651	3.483	4.447	1.764	2.522	3.004	3.947	5.039
25	1.317	1.883	2.244	2.948	3.764	1.453	2.077	2.474	3.251	4.151	1.545	2.208	2.631	3.457	4.413	1.745	2.494	2.972	3.904	4.985
26	1.313	1.877	2.236	2.938	3.751	1.444	2.065	2.460	3.232	4.127	1.534	2.193	2.612	3.432	4.382	1.727	2.460	2.941	3.865	4.935
27	1.309	1.871	2.229	2.929	3.740	1.437	2.054	2.447	3.215	4.106	1.523	2.178	2.595	3.409	4.353	1.711	2.446	2.914	3.828	4.888
30	1.297	1.855	2.210	2.904	3.708	1.417	2.025	2.413	3.170	4.049	1.497	2.140	2.549	3.350	4.278	1.668	2.385	2.841	3.733	4.768
35	1.283	1.834	2.185	2.871	3.667	1.390	1.988	2.368	3.112	3.974	1.462	2.090	2.490	3.272	4.179	1.613	2.306	2.748	3.611	4.611
40	1.271	1.818	2.166	2.846	3.635	1.370	1.959	2.334	3.066	3.917	1.435	2.052	2.445	3.213	4.104	1.571	2.247	2.677	3.518	4.493
100	1.218	1.742	2.075	2.727	3.484	1.275	1.822	2.172	2.854	3.646	1.311	1.874	2.233	2.934	3.748	1.383	1.977	2.355	3.096	3.954
500	1.177	1.683	2.006	2.636	3.368	1.201	1.717	2.046	2.689	3.434	1.215	1.737	2.070	2.721	3.475	1.243	1.777	2.117	2.783	3.555
1,000	1.169	1.671	1.992	2.617	3.344	1.185	1.695	2.019	2.654	3.390	1.195	1.709	2.036	2.676	3.418	1.214	1.736	2.068	2.718	3.472
∞	1.150	1.645	1.960	2.576	3.291	1.150	1.645	1.960	2.576	3.291	1.150	1.645	1.960	2.576	3.291	1.150	1.645	1.960	2.576	3.291

*From C. Eisenhart, M. W. Hastay, and W. A. Wallis, *Selected Techniques of Statistical Analysis*, McGraw-Hill Book Company, New York, 1947. Used by permission.

Table L Sample sizes and factors for constructing one- and two-sided tolerance limits*

		Normal distribution								Distribution-free			
		One-sided limits confidence level				Two-sided limits confidence level				Confidence level			
		0.90		0.95		0.90		0.95		0.90		0.95	
p	d	n	k	n	k	n	k	n	k	n	m	n	m
0.95	0.01	667	1.653	947	1.653	701	1.969	995	1.969	1361	68	1889	94
	0.02	159	1.679	226	1.679	169	1.998	239	1.995	343	17	471	23
	0.03	65	1.730	92	1.730	69	2.056	98	2.049	146	7	210	10
	0.04	30	1.834	43	1.834	33	2.175	46	2.159	84	4	111	5
	0.049	12	2.189	17	2.189	13	2.645	19	2.535	47	2	71	3
0.99	0.0050	251	2.373	356	2.373	266	2.625	376	2.623	1128	11	1562	15
	0.0060	163	2.398	231	2.398	173	2.653	245	2.649	819	8	1064	10
	0.0070	109	2.434	155	2.434	116	2.691	164	2.686	616	6	765	7
	0.0080	73	2.488	104	2.488	78	2.749	110	2.741	429	4	566	5
	0.0090	46	2.583	65	2.583	50	2.852	70	2.839	330	3	459	4
	0.0099	21	2.888	29	2.888	23	3.189	32	3.158	237	2	278	2
0.995	0.0025	342	2.620	485	2.620	362	2.853	513	2.851	2259	11	3128	15
	0.0030	222	2.644	314	2.644	234	2.878	331	2.875	1641	8	2132	10
	0.0035	148	2.678	209	2.678	156	2.915	221	2.910	1235	6	1533	7
	0.0040	98	2.728	139	2.728	104	2.968	147	2.961	860	4	1135	5
	0.0045	61	2.818	86	2.818	65	3.066	91	3.054	661	3	920	4
	0.0049	32	3.025	45	3.025	34	3.291	48	3.269	478	2	728	3

*From R. L. Kirkpatrick, "Sample Sizes to Set Tolerance Limits," *Journal of Quality Technology*, January 1977. pp. 6-12.

INDEX